Building Dynamic HTML GUIs

Building Dynamic HTML GUIs

Steven Champeon

David S. Fox

An imprint of IDG Books Worldwide, Inc.
An International Data Group Company

Foster City, CA ◆ Chicago, IL ◆ Indianapolis, IN ◆ New York, NY

Building Dynamic HTML GUIs

Published by
M&T Books
An imprint of IDG Books Worldwide, Inc.
An International Data Group Company
919 E. Hillsdale Blvd., Suite 400
Foster City, CA 94404
www.idgbooks.com (IDG Books Worldwide Web site)

Library of Congress Catalog Card Number: 98-75383

ISBN: 0-7645-3267-7

Printed in the United States of America

10 9 8 7 6 5 4 3 2 1

1B/QT/QU/ZZ/FC

Distributed in the United States by IDG Books Worldwide, Inc.

Distributed by CDG Books Canada Inc. for Canada; by Transworld Publishers Limited in the United Kingdom; by IDG Norge Books for Norway; by IDG Sweden Books for Sweden; by Woodslane Pty. Ltd. for Australia; by Woodslane (NZ) Ltd. for New Zealand; by TransQuest Publishers Pte Ltd. for Singapore, Malaysia, Thailand, Indonesia and Hong Kong; by ICG Muse, Inc. for Japan; by Norma Comunicaciones S.A. for Colombia; by Intersoft for South Africa; by Le Monde en Tique for France; by International Thomson Publishing for Germany, Austria and Switzerland; by Distribuidora Cuspide for Argentina; by Livraria Cultura for Brazil; by Ediciones ZETA S.C.R. Ltda. for Peru; by WS Computer Publishing Corporation, Inc., for the Philippines; by Contemporanea de Ediciones for Venezuela; by Express Computer Distributors for the Caribbean and West Indies; by Micronesia Media Distributor, Inc. for Micronesia; by Grupo Editorial Norma S.A. for Guatemala; by Chips Computadoras S.A. de C.V. for Mexico; by Editorial Norma de Panama S.A. for Panama; by American Bookshops for Finland. Authorized Sales Agent: Anthony Rudkin Associates for the Middle East and North Africa.

For general information on IDG Books Worldwide's books in the U.S., please call our Consumer Customer Service department at 800-762-2974. For reseller information, including discounts and premium sales, please call our Reseller Customer Service department at 800-434-3422.

For information on where to purchase IDG Books Worldwide's books outside the U.S., please contact our International Sales department at 317-596-5530 or fax 317-596-5692.

For consumer information on foreign language translations, please contact our Customer Service department at 800-434-3422, fax 317-596-5692, or e-mail rights@idgbooks.com.

For information on licensing foreign or domestic rights, please phone +1-650-655-3109.

For sales inquiries and special prices for bulk quantities, please contact our Sales department at 650-655-3200 or write to the address above.

For information on using IDG Books Worldwide's books in the classroom or for ordering examination copies, please contact our Educational Sales department at 800-434-2086 or fax 317-596-5499.

For press review copies, author interviews, or other publicity information, please contact our Public Relations department at 650-655-3000 or fax 650-655-3299.

For authorization to photocopy items for corporate, personal, or educational use, please contact Copyright Clearance Center, 222 Rosewood Drive, Danvers, MA 01923, or fax 978-750-4470.

is a registered trademark under exclusive license to IDG Books Worldwide, Inc., from International Data Group, Inc.

is a trademark of IDG Books Worldwide, Inc.

ABOUT IDG BOOKS WORLDWIDE

Welcome to the world of IDG Books Worldwide.

IDG Books Worldwide, Inc., is a subsidiary of International Data Group, the world's largest publisher of computer-related information and the leading global provider of information services on information technology. IDG was founded more than 30 years ago by Patrick J. McGovern and now employs more than 9,000 people worldwide. IDG publishes more than 290 computer publications in over 75 countries. More than 90 million people read one or more IDG publications each month.

Launched in 1990, IDG Books Worldwide is today the #1 publisher of best-selling computer books in the United States. We are proud to have received eight awards from the Computer Press Association in recognition of editorial excellence and three from Computer Currents' First Annual Readers' Choice Awards. Our best-selling ...For Dummies® series has more than 50 million copies in print with translations in 31 languages. IDG Books Worldwide, through a joint venture with IDG's Hi-Tech Beijing, became the first U.S. publisher to publish a computer book in the People's Republic of China. In record time, IDG Books Worldwide has become the first choice for millions of readers around the world who want to learn how to better manage their businesses.

Our mission is simple: Every one of our books is designed to bring extra value and skill-building instructions to the reader. Our books are written by experts who understand and care about our readers. The knowledge base of our editorial staff comes from years of experience in publishing, education, and journalism — experience we use to produce books to carry us into the new millennium. In short, we care about books, so we attract the best people. We devote special attention to details such as audience, interior design, use of icons, and illustrations. And because we use an efficient process of authoring, editing, and desktop publishing our books electronically, we can spend more time ensuring superior content and less time on the technicalities of making books.

You can count on our commitment to deliver high-quality books at competitive prices on topics you want to read about. At IDG Books Worldwide, we continue in the IDG tradition of delivering quality for more than 30 years. You'll find no better book on a subject than one from IDG Books Worldwide.

John Kilcullen
Chairman and CEO
IDG Books Worldwide, Inc.

Steven Berkowitz
President and Publisher
IDG Books Worldwide, Inc.

Eighth Annual Computer Press Awards ≥1992

Ninth Annual Computer Press Awards ≥1993

Tenth Annual Computer Press Awards ≥1994

Eleventh Annual Computer Press Awards ≥1995

IDG is the world's leading IT media, research and exposition company. Founded in 1964, IDG had 1997 revenues of $2.05 billion and has more than 9,000 employees worldwide. IDG offers the widest range of media options that reach IT buyers in 75 countries representing 95% of worldwide IT spending. IDG's diverse product and services portfolio spans six key areas including print publishing, online publishing, expositions and conferences, market research, education and training, and global marketing services. More than 90 million people read one or more of IDG's 290 magazines and newspapers, including IDG's leading global brands — Computerworld, PC World, Network World, Macworld and the Channel World family of publications. IDG Books Worldwide is one of the fastest-growing computer book publishers in the world, with more than 700 titles in 36 languages. The "...For Dummies®" series alone has more than 50 million copies in print. IDG offers online users the largest network of technology-specific Web sites around the world through IDG.net (http://www.idg.net), which comprises more than 225 targeted Web sites in 55 countries worldwide. International Data Corporation (IDC) is the world's largest provider of information technology data, analysis and consulting, with research centers in over 41 countries and more than 400 research analysts worldwide. IDG World Expo is a leading producer of more than 168 globally branded conferences and expositions in 35 countries including E3 (Electronic Entertainment Expo), Macworld Expo, ComNet, Windows World Expo, ICE (Internet Commerce Expo), Agenda, DEMO, and Spotlight. IDG's training subsidiary, ExecuTrain, is the world's largest computer training company, with more than 230 locations worldwide and 785 training courses. IDG Marketing Services helps industry-leading IT companies build international brand recognition by developing global integrated marketing programs via IDG's print, online and exposition products worldwide. Further information about the company can be found at www.idg.com. 1/24/99

Credits

ACQUISITIONS EDITOR
Ann Lush

DEVELOPMENT EDITORS
Luann Rouff
Matt Lusher
Denise Santoro

TECHNICAL EDITOR
Peter Merholz

COPY EDITORS
Nicole LeClerc
Ami Knox

PROJECT COORDINATOR
Susan Parini

BOOK DESIGNER
Kurt Krames

GRAPHICS AND PRODUCTION SPECIALISTS
Christopher Pimentel
Mark Yim

QUALITY CONTROL SPECIALISTS
Mick Arellano
Mark Schumann

PROOFREADING & INDEXING
York Production Services

About the Authors

Steven Champeon is a Senior Technical Consultant with hesketh.com/inc., specializing in medium- to large-scale custom corporate Web solutions. He has served as a technical editor for books published by IDG Books Worldwide, among others. He contributes frequently to online venues, including Stating the Obvious (http://www.theobvious.com), developer.com, and industry mailing lists. The offbeat observations nobody else will publish can be found at http://a.jaundicedeye.com.

He is a founding member of the Web Standards Project, and actively participates in and speaks at trade conferences. His reputation is built on a quick wit, a wry manner, and practical technical commentary. He lives and works in Raleigh, North Carolina.

David S. Fox is a New York-based novelist, screenwriter, and tech writer. He is the author of several books about Internet culture and technologies. When not scribbling, he spends his waking hours scrambling together Web-based multiplayer games. You can find him at http://www.actionworld.com/staff/dfox/.

To Heather, Mara, and Nokomis. —Steven Champeon
A Louisa, Por Todo. —David Fox

Preface

Welcome to *Building Dynamic HTML GUIs*. If you've been frustrated by the difficulty of developing dynamic client-side applications that work in the major browsers, if you are a designer who wants to make your interfaces more usable, or if you're just getting your feet wet with DHTML and are wondering what all the fuss is about, this is the book for you. Maybe you've bought a reference manual that shows you the details but doesn't help you assemble them into a big picture. Maybe you're a developer trying to figure out how to implement the interface a designer came up with; or maybe you're the designer, trying to find out what is possible without restricting yourself to a single platform and browser. By reading this book, you will learn everything you need in order to plan, design, test, and implement your DHTML application across browsers and platforms, and wind up with a more efficient interface to boot.

At the very least, you can fill your design or development toolbox with proven strategies for successful DHTML applications. It is our sincere hope that by reading and understanding the material in this book, you will spare yourself and your users countless frustrating hours. We know this because of the countless frustrating hours we put into making sure the modules and example application worked properly across browsers and on different platforms. In this book, we show you how to start on the right foot, with functionality and your interface, rather than starting deep in the bowels of browser-specific code and trying to port that code to a wider audience.

Why We Wrote This Book

It was a natural progression from mainframes and terminals through traditional, platform-bound client/server to platform-independent, client-side Web-based applications. The gap between server-based data management and user-centered interface design just keeps widening. DHTML enables you to make greater use of the Web than ever before, bringing to life truly interactive client-side interfaces beyond the point-and-click model of years past. However, vendor incompatibilities, introduced during the interminable browser wars, often prevent people from making the best use of DHTML.

We've seen many complaints from developers who started with browser-specific code only to realize that they would have to recode their entire component or application to meet new cross-browser requirements. Their anguished cries (and perhaps yours as well) convinced us to write this book. We've seen Web applications in general, and DHTML applications in particular, that could have benefited from a quick refresher course (or introductory survey) in the basics of interface theory. But as we looked around, we saw that:

- few people were talking about applying interface theory to the Web;
- if they were, they were talking about it in terms of traditional Web page layout, navigation, or site architecture rather than *application* interfaces;
- or they were making absurd claims that reflected a poor understanding of the sheer range of possibilities and existing categories into which Web sites and Web applications fall;
- or they were just *talking* about it and not actually *doing* it.

This book is our attempt to fix these oversights.

We've seen comfortable intranet environments with a single-browser standard turn into multiple-platform, multiple-browser environments as a result of mergers, acquisitions, and changes in management, catapulting happily complacent developers into new and often costly and frightening situations. How do you explain to a nontechnical executive that your Internet Explorer-specific application doesn't work in his or her favorite browser, Netscape Navigator (or vice versa)? Wouldn't it be better to start with a cross-browser application framework in the first place? Many developers simply don't have any guidance in how to do this well, and have no need to challenge vendors' claims that their products comply 100 percent with W3C standards. That is, until they actually put those claims to the test.

Larger Web application development projects often put their resources to poor use. Rather than encouraging their more highly skilled developers to work on reusable components and libraries that can then be plugged into rapid application development projects by less skilled coders, we see everyone straining to understand obfuscated, workaround-laden JavaScript code. Think of it as an archaeology of workarounds, often undocumented for reasons of "optimized download times" or as the result of insanely compressed development schedules. We can't blame the developer for having to deal with lousy code atop inconsistent implementations, but we can suggest ways they can make things better.

We dug deep into our experience designing interfaces for Web applications and developing both client-side and server-side solutions that deliver functionality to the widest audience possible. We applied strategies gleaned from the last 30 years of interface theory, software development, and systems architecture to create a library that hides the incompatibilities and makes it possible to build dynamic, client-side, cross-platform applications today. We then used that library to develop some useful modules that you can deploy in your own code without modification and without having to learn more than standard JavaScript, CSS, and HTML.

If you're interested in knowing more about the W3C DOM, XML, and other forthcoming standards, or you want to use action sheets, behaviors, and other platform-specific, nonstandard, proprietary extensions, this probably isn't the book for you. However, we suggest that you read it in addition to any of those other books. You won't regret it. We promise.

The bottom line is that we saw the potential for a powerful new breed of applications that solve real problems:

◆ Across browsers

◆ Across platforms

◆ Using rapid application development strategies

◆ Without separate development efforts

◆ Creating code that was clear, legible, and maintainable

◆ Making the best use of available development and design resources

◆ Resulting in usable interfaces that follow prevalent GUI conventions

So we wrote the book that shows you how.

What You Need to Know

We assume that you are familiar with JavaScript and programming in general, and that you know HTML and have dabbled with CSS at one point or another and understand how the three are related.

If this is the first time you've ever done any JavaScript programming at all, you may find the following IDG Books Worldwide books helpful:

◆ *Dynamic HTML*, by Shelley Powers, does a great job of introducing dynamic HTML for new users and even contains a few of the strategies we explore more fully in this book.

◆ *JavaScript Bible*, by Danny Goodman, is a comprehensive guide to JavaScript.

If you are unfamiliar with CSS, or need a refresher in how to mark up HTML files, these books (also from IDG Books Worldwide) might be helpful as well:

◆ *Creating Cool HTML 4 Web Pages*, by Dave Taylor, is a great introduction to HTML and covers the complete set of tags in HTML 4.0.

◆ *XML in Plain English*, by Sandra Eddy, provides a practical reference to XML, and discusses CSS in depth.

A list of useful resources is included in Appendix B, if you're looking for some light reading on some of the related topics we discuss in other sections of the book.

If you think you're ready for what lies ahead, here's a quick test. In order to develop DHTML applications, you will likely need to know the following:

◆ How to create new HTML, CSS, and JavaScript files and upload them to a Web server

◆ How to include JavaScript and CSS in HTML files, either as externally linked files or as embedded scripts and style sheets

◆ How to create new CSS style sheet definitions

◆ How to create new JavaScript functions and variables

◆ How to create new image files and upload them to a Web server

◆ How to choose colors from the 216-color "Web-safe" palette (though this isn't an absolute necessity)

◆ How to configure your browser for debugging purposes (so it always loads the latest version of a file from the server, for example)

◆ How to view source code from a Web site, either using your own editor or the browser's internal mechanisms (viewing the source for frames, for example)

◆ How a Web server works – at least a bit about the various HTTP request mechanisms, response codes, and their meaning

◆ How to differentiate between a network problem, a problem with your code, a problem with the browser you're using, an unrelated problem with another application on your computer, and an unrelated problem with a loss of electrical power to your computer. (It helps to be able to explain these differences to users when they submit bug reports against your applications, too. . . .)

Basically, you need to be comfortable with standard development practices, your environment, and the ways your environment may differ from others.

If most of these skill sets are ringing bells, you're probably fine. If your eyes glazed over after the first item, you may need to get one of the books listed in the previous section. If you have a few questions about the remaining skills, don't worry – we go into detail on how to do most of these things, even when it isn't the main point of each chapter. The bottom line is that you need to be able to follow along with the examples in the book, either by downloading the code from the Web site, or by typing in the examples and assembling the pieces yourself. We're not going to bore you with step-by-step instructions on how to start your browser, save a file out of your editor, and so on. We assume that you know enough to jump right in and get started.

What You Need to Have

In addition to the relevant skills listed above, you need the relevant hardware and software to do development. We don't assume that you are using source code control, although we highly recommend it. You can probably get by with the following:

◆ A computer

◆ A floppy disk drive

◆ A text editor

◆ Some sort of image creation software capable of saving GIF or JPEG files

◆ One of the major browsers that support JavaScript and DHTML, such as Microsoft Internet Explorer 4.0 or later and/or Netscape Navigator or Communicator 4.0 or later

Since pretty much everything we do in this book consists of manipulating text files, the development environment itself doesn't need to be all that robust. In fact, the example application in Part III was written on a variety of platforms, using a variety of different tools, and tested on them all. (For the curious, we'll post a colophon on the Web site.) If you really want to save yourself a lot of hassle, we recommend that you have at least:

◆ A Pentium or Macintosh PowerPC computer with 32MB RAM or more and sufficient disk space for development efforts, or a comparable UNIX box

◆ An editor capable of working with multiple files open that features JavaScript/HTML/CSS syntax highlighting, such as BBEdit, Emacs, or Allaire's HomeSite

◆ A network connection or modem dialup to the Internet or your intranet

◆ Both major browsers, and perhaps even multiple versions of each (where possible) for testing and debugging purposes

◆ Access to a Web server with cgi-bin access as well for implementation of back-end CGI scripts; alternately, if you are familiar with one of the various server APIs, it helps to use those instead for more arduous tasks

◆ A source code control system of some kind, such as RCS, CVS, or one of the Macintosh- or PC-based environments such as Visual SourceSafe

Now, armed with the necessary tools for your foray into the world of cross-platform dynamic HTML applications development, you should be ready to begin.

How to Use This Book

It is the solemn and deeply held belief of the authors that reading about code is about as useful as watching people exercise on television. You don't get any fitter unless you jump right in and get your hands dirty. Well, okay, so your hands don't get all that dirty using a keyboard, but you get the idea. This book should be used as an introduction to some of the most successful strategies used in interface theory and software development as applied to the realm of dynamic HTML rapid application development.

Conventions Used in This Book

Quite simply, we only use one typographical convention in the book. Inline references to code or markup, whether they are HTML, JavaScript, or CSS snippets, are shown in a monospace font. Code listings are set apart from paragraph text as follows:

```
function example(x) {
  var example_variable = 0;
  if(x) {
    example_variable = 1;
  } else {
    example_variable = -1;
  }
  return example_variable;
}
```

The programming style we use in the sample applications is simple, and looks a lot like the previous example. Code is indented two spaces in order to make the best use of the available space. The sample application code posted on the Web site, however, uses tabs, so you can display it at whatever tab settings you're comfortable with. We just find that two spaces is appropriate for JavaScript, because as a language its variables and document object references have a tendency to get rather long.

What the Icons Mean

Throughout the book, we've used icons in the left margin to call your attention to points that are particularly important.

We use Note icons to tell you that something is important — perhaps a concept that may help you master the task at hand or something fundamental for understanding subsequent material.

Tip icons indicate a more efficient way of doing something, or a technique that may not be obvious.

How This Book Is Organized

This book may be different from others you've read on the same or similar topics in that it splits the subject matter into three parts. Part I deals with interface theory, Part II introduces you to what we think is a helpful metaphor for thinking about dynamic HTML, and Part III is a discussion of our sample application and the dynamic HTML modules we used to create it.

Part I: The User Interface: History, Principles, and New Directions

In this part, we outline the history of interface theory, starting with a discussion of a few useful terms and approaches, and moving on to gradually more specific topics. We discuss the idea of an interface in Chapter 1, leading into a brief but fairly detailed overview of the various user interfaces in use over the years in Chapter 2. Chapter 3 is a discussion of several useful contexts and approaches for thinking about user interfaces and application development. In Chapter 4, we get right down to the heart of the matter, taking what we've covered in the previous chapters and applying it to the Web, including a discussion of those characteristics of the Web interface that owe their nature to more traditional interface design. We also ask if the Web has introduced new problems and ways of thinking about interaction that require Web application developers to take a new approach to interface design.

Part II: Dynamic HTML: An Overview

Part II consists of a complete overview of dynamic HTML, using a "noun-verb-adjective" metaphor to illustrate how HTML and JavaScript document objects may be manipulated using JavaScript functions and user-initiated actions, and how they may be given varying characteristics using color, font styles, and positioning. Chapter 5 jumps right in and talks about the "nouns" in our environment—JavaScript objects that reflect the structure of HTML (as well as XML) documents. The idea of a standard Document Object Model (DOM) is described in detail with examples. Chapter 6 makes the nouns active, showing how they may be acted upon by the "verbs" of JavaScript functions. These functions enable the user to access the application's functionality, and enable the developer to control the application's responses to user input. We discuss the history of client-side scripting in some detail, placing its present use in the context of both traditional interface design and application development while pointing the way to the future. Chapter 7 shows how simple "noun" and "verb" combinations are not very interesting without the use of "adjectives" (Cascading Style Sheets). We discuss the manner in which divorcing the *structure* of a document or application from its *presentation* makes for a much more flexible model, whether we're dealing with traditional SGML document archives, full of endless tables of military parts lists, or a multicolored dynamic HTML application with click-and-drag and free-form interface design. Chapter 8 rolls all of these concepts into a cohesive whole, leading the way toward modular component-based development, integrated subsystems, and finally, full-blown applications with all the interface features of traditional applications.

Part III: Examples of Good HCI with Dynamic HTML

The third and final section of the book deals directly with the issues raised by cross-browser and cross-platform applications development with dynamic HTML. We introduce this section in Chapter 9 with a full discussion of the cross-browser object wrapper library we use for the subsequent chapters. Included in the overview are oodles of helpful hints for designing your own object wrapper, dealing with browser- and platform-specific workarounds, and the importance of abstraction. The subsequent chapters present JavaScript modules that you can use in your own applications. Chapter 10 begins our sample application, "Executive Dynamic Poetry," which is a sort of blend between refrigerator magnet poetry and Buzzword Bingo. Chapter 11 dissects a multiple-page feedback form, showing how client-side applications can do anything the average CGI script forms processor can do. Chapter 12 deals with other kinds of feedback, from simple application status feedback to the user via a custom status message area, all the way through debugging information and an automated bug report form. Chapter 13 introduces the idea of user-configurable interfaces, using a full-featured color picker, cookies, and a generic Preferences module. Chapter 14 is where we add the traditional menu bar and menus to our application, giving it an appearance much like that of the average Macintosh application. Chapter 15 deals with online help, tool tips, and other integrated documentation mechanisms. The final chapter adds some unnecessary glitz to the application in order to demonstrate JavaScript timers and dynamic positioning. Every chapter contains source listings and a brief discussion of "Gotchas," or characteristics of the various browsers that you should look out for when coding your own applications.

Finally, there are appendixes containing references to other resources, tools, documentation of the `xplatform_wrapper` library, a bibliography, and a concise rundown of all the "Gotchas" we ran into while coding our sample application.

Getting More Information

There are dozens of high-quality resources for dynamic HTML on the Internet. Web sites, mailing lists, USENET newsgroups, discussion boards, and more provide a way for users of dynamic HTML to interact with each other, trade tips and tricks, ask desperate questions, and give informed answers. We encourage you to try out a few of these invaluable resources. You may find that you join the discussion as a novice and gradually become the one who answers most of the questions posed. It's been known to happen before.

However, due to the nature of the code in this book, which uses abstraction and modularity to hide the complexity of browser-specific implementation details from the application developer, you should probably direct any questions about its use to us. Most of the modules rely on the cross-browser object wrapper library, and subsequently they do not resemble the usual illegible "cruft" that populates most people's DHTML implementations. Anyone still in the "Dark Ages" of browser- and platform-specific development will only wonder what you're going on about, and will probably ignore you.

To that end (contacting us, not ignoring you), we have set up a Web site and mailing list for users of the object wrapper library and its associated modules. More information about the mailing list can be found, appropriately enough, on this Web site:

```
http://dhtml-guis.com
```

Giving Feedback

If you would like to contact Steven and/or David, e-mail us at the following addresses:

```
steve@dhtml-guis.com
david@dhtml-guis.com
```

In the event that this book becomes a bigger seller than *The Internet For Dummies*, we will probably be unable to respond to every message personally, as we will be deluged with e-mail. In the event that the book merely enjoys a modest success, we will continue to be workaday Web developers and our ability to respond personally to your e-mail will be similarly impaired. Please be patient with us. Post to the mailing list so everyone else can benefit from your question and any answers we or other members of the list may give.

Good luck, we hope you enjoy the book, and more important, we hope it changes your approach to the design, development, and maintenance of dynamic HTML applications.

Acknowledgments

As a first-time author, I find myself faced with a multitude of kind and supportive people to thank. Simon St.Laurent deserves mention for asking me to tech edit his *XML: A Primer*; without his help I would not have written this book at all. I would be quite delinquent if I didn't mention the members of the Project Cool dynamic HTML mailing list and the Webdesign-L list at hesketh.com, who have taught me more than I could describe here in a few words.

I would like to thank the friendly and courteous staff of Cup-A-Joe, the finest coffeehouse in Raleigh, North Carolina, for the late-night "Four Shot King Mocha," without which this book would never have been finished.

I would also like to thank the wonderful (and patient) folks at IDG Books Worldwide, including Ann Lush, Matt Lusher, Denise Santoro, Luann Rouff, Nicole LeClerc, and Susan Parini. They have been a true comfort to this first-time author, and I am grateful to them for their hard work and patience. Any errors in the book which [sic] survived the scrutiny of this dedicated group are mine and mine alone.

Thanks also to Peter Merholz, whose technical editing skills have ferretted out many a bug and strengthened many an argument. May he go on to write the definitive tome on interface theory. I am also grateful to my coauthor, David Fox, who rose to the occasion and wrote the middle section of the manuscript when time constraints made it impossible for me to do so. Jeff Veen gave freely of his time and insights into the future of Web interface design. Greg Knauss confirmed my belief that DHTML could help revolutionize the nature of the Web by saying "Wow" at just the right time. Shelley Powers and Danny Goodman and their fine books on DHTML influenced the design and implementation of the cross-browser wrapper library, and gave me the tools and examples I needed to take it to the next level. Jakob Nielsen took the time out of his busy schedule to clarify his stance on the importance of interface consistency, and for that I am in his debt.

I would also like to mention the cabal: you know who you are.

This book was written under the influence of Radiohead, Drive Like Jehu, Fugazi, Smoothieville smoothies (love that "P B and Hey!"), and the timeless jazz of John Coltrane. The Smashing Pumpkins, the fine guitar work of Richard Thompson, and pretty much everything by Tom Waits also contributed to the general air of madness under which the majority of the sample application was coded.

Above all, I am grateful to Heather and the staff of hesketh.com, who put up with my crawling into work in the early afternoon after many a long night of coding or writing. I told you I wouldn't be writing the book forever — it just seemed that way.

—Steven Champeon

Contents at a Glance

Contents

Part III: Examples of Good HCI with Dynamic HTML

Chapter 9   Implementing Effective User Interfaces with DHTML

Part I

The User Interface: History, Principles, and New Directions

CHAPTER 1:
What Is an Interface?

CHAPTER 2:
A Brief History of User Interface Design

CHAPTER 3:
Principles and Lessons Learned

CHAPTER 4:
Exploring New Directions for the Web

IN THIS PART:

What's an interface? In this section, we discuss interface theory both from the standpoint of traditional application-centric interface design and the new paradigms introduced by the Web. We cover the basics, including Donald Norman's thoughts about natural relationships between the elements of an interface and the "real world," Alan Cooper's provocative claim that idiom reigns supreme, and Brenda Laurel's ideas of computer programs as immersive environments. We then wrap up with an extensive discussion of the ways that the Web is changing the face (if you'll pardon the pun) of traditional application interface design.

Chapter 1

What Is an Interface?

IN THIS CHAPTER

♦ A quick, general overview of interface theory

♦ Why the best interfaces are invisible

♦ A few sometimes conflicting definitions of an interface and its elements

♦ Defining the term *interface*

The Interface: A General Overview

Few terms have been the subject of as much confusion as *interface*, especially when used in the context of computing. This confusion arises partly due to the nature of the word itself, which describes both the place where two disparate systems meet, and the manner in which they meet. There are graphical user interfaces, command-line interfaces, programming interfaces, hardware interfaces, and more. The term may even be used as a verb, meaning "to communicate." Before you sink into despair, however, upon realizing that the book you just paid hard cash for begins with the confession that its primary topic matter can be both noun and verb, let us say, "Don't panic!" This chapter discusses a variety of ways that leading theorists define the term *interface,* drawn from several different contexts. By the end of the chapter, you'll have a better understanding of interface theory, and amaze your friends and colleagues at cocktail parties with your in-depth knowledge of one of the computing world's most controversial topics. You'll also understand the working definition of interface used throughout the book.

In a very general sense, an interface is the point of contact or communication between two things. In common usage, the term *interface* refers to the useful surfaces of objects, such as the dial on a car radio, or the buttons on a telephone. More appropriately, it also refers to their organization, and, to some extent, their purpose. A radio dial isn't much by itself; it needs to be attached to a radio in order to function properly. A single telephone button – say, the button which is used to dial a "7" – is pretty useless without the telephone's circuitry behind it. If the buttons on the telephone were arranged in a different order, or if they weren't buttons at all, but rather a pressure-sensitive plastic bubble pad, the interface would have a drastically different look and feel. You'd be uncomfortable trying to dial your own phone number on a telephone whose numbers weren't labeled, or were arranged in a different order. You'd probably be able to call yourself if the arrangement of the numbers hadn't been changed, even if the labels were missing, but you'd be hard pressed (if you'll pardon the pun) to dial your phone number on a touch pad having a different arrangement of numbers and letters. To put it another way, you, by way of your experience with the telephone and other devices like it, bring part of the interface with you.

The Best Interfaces Are Invisible

An interface is best when it is invisible, when you never even think about it. When was the last time you had to think really hard before using your car's turn signal? Even when driving a new car, you can usually quickly figure out where everything is and how to use it. By contrast, everyone dreads the task of programming a VCR. This is because the interface must become — either by learning or through an appeal to previously learned or innate behavior — an extension of the task that it allows or enables. The car's turn signal seems natural to us in ways that arbitrarily labeled (or unlabeled) plastic buttons and LEDs do not. When the enabler gets in the way of the task, he can no longer concentrate on the task itself. The more technologically sophisticated our tools become, and the wider their audience and potential user base, the more important it is to provide simple ways to use them. Imagine having to concentrate every time you use a hammer, open a door, or add a new slide to an award-winning presentation. And yet, we regularly view and manipulate arbitrary multimedia data structures, organized via the principles of hypertext, and served by networked computers using a number of different protocols over widely varying electronic communications substrates. "Surfing the Web using a browser," the non-technical translation of the previous sentence, is just the latest in a long line of simplifications to what has become an incredibly complex environment.

We'd have to be out of our minds to think that human beings would have some innate, hardwired ability to understand how to use computers, which have been part of our society for less than sixty years. However, interface designers may take advantage of metaphors and what Donald Norman calls *natural mappings* — relationships drawn between existing and familiar capabilities and recollections. For example, spatial metaphors used to represent an object in space, or sound to represent degree or quantity. These metaphors, though, are limited in their scope, and tend to be too generic for extremely specific application. When natural mappings fail, providing an interface that is easily learned or on which we can all agree is one option worth considering. The challenges here are to leverage our previous experience with different things of the same type, and to reduce the unnecessary complexity of those things that have no meaningful correlate in our experience, or which stand in the way of comprehension and ease of use.

One of the most important questions an interface designer faces is how to balance a simple interface requiring complex learned behaviors against a more complex interface that maps more appropriately to the tasks at hand. A telephone is a simple tool, often having only 12 buttons, but the systems it provides access to, such as voice mail or Voice Response Units (VRUs), may be incredibly complex and packed to the gills with arbitrary functions. Some progress has been made toward standardizing typical functions, such as dialing an operator (dial "0") or accessing an outside line (dial "9" before the telephone number), but much work remains to be done. By contrast, many people use incredibly complex software programs every day, having learned their interfaces so well that they seem natural.

In this discussion and for the rest of the book, when we use the term *interface*, a human being is one of the two things that connects or communicates via the interface. To make this point explicit, we may use the more specific phrase *user interface*, which implies that there is a person – the *user* – on one side of the interface. On the other side of the interface may be a telephone, a keyboard, a monitor, or even a computer program's graphical representation of a telephone. Once we start to get into the details and implementation of dynamic HTML, the other side of the interface may be a set of HTML pages, some JavaScript, a Perl script running on a server somewhere, or even a database. We use the term *GUI*, or *graphical user interface*, to describe this sort of interface. The details don't matter that much; in fact, we cover some of the ways that user interfaces may soon be constructed using DHTML so that they may be used by the sight- or hearing-impaired, or even by users of the now-ubiquitous handheld portable organizers. The important thing to remember is that you form one part of the interface, with all your experiences, assumptions, and interactions, and the software forms another. Now let's dive right into the controversy surrounding the most appropriate metaphors for discussing the user interface, drawing on sources as disparate as theater, industrial design, software development, and even Web design.

A Few Definitions

People have been studying interface theory to one degree or another since the beginning of humankind's use of tools. Someone noticed, after a particularly frustrating experience with an ill-chipped piece of flint, perhaps, that some tools simply worked better than others. This insight has survived and thrived through the Industrial Age and into the Information Age, as our tools have become more complex, sophisticated, and abstract. We now have the ability, with powerful and inexpensive display technology, to invent whatever interface we can think of for whatever needs that we may have, drawing on as much or as little familiar territory as we wish. The advent and rapid popularity of networked computers has given us new spaces to explore – often without physical referent or convenient metaphors.

The overuse of the phrase "information superhighway," among others, to describe the Internet aptly demonstrates this paucity of helpful metaphors. The desktop publishing and office productivity revolutions have put enormous power into the hands of former novices, requiring that simple and easy-to-use interfaces be developed. Along with the desperate need for new ways of communicating with and effectively using our tools, the explosion in technology has also made it possible to explore new and heretofore inconceivable worlds – environments of our own making. And for every world, there must be an interface. Before we get too deep into discussions of the fanciful, however, we would do well to take a look at the work of one of the pioneers in the study of the design of everyday things.

Donald Norman: The Elements of Interface Design

Some things were just meant to be pressed. So why were they designed as though they should be pulled, turned, switched, slid, lifted, spun, waved, dropped, flicked, toggled, or even clapped at? Occasionally, inventive new ways of dealing with standard problems are developed, but for the most part elementary physics offers up pretty basic choices for dealing with things like doors and hammers. The problem, to paraphrase an old saying, is that if all you have is a button, the whole world looks as though it ought to be pushed. And if you really need your user to be able to pull, a button is a poor choice, indeed.

Donald Norman, in his book *The Design of Everyday Things*, outlines some of the more common problems with the design of industrial objects such as doors, cars, microwaves, telephones, radios, and VCRs. He also offers the conscientious designer a wealth of practical pointers and a theoretical framework for discussing and critiquing design from a usability standpoint. His insights have influenced other designers as well as people in widely divergent fields, including cognitive science, psychology, architecture, and organizational behavior.

Are the interfaces we design for our tools useful? How can we tell? Are our users to blame for mistakes commonly made while using our tools, due to laziness or simple human error, or are we to blame for building in inherent flaws, traps, and confusing features? Are there ways around these sorts of inherent unusability? What can we as designers do about this? Norman asks these questions and more.

STUDYING ERRORS, CONFUSION, AND THE ATTITUDES OF USERS AND DESIGNERS

Observation is the first step one takes in any scientific study. Therefore, Norman advises designers and others concerned about usability and the impact of bad design to pay close attention to the mistakes people repeatedly make when trying to use a tool for the first time. It is also important to take seriously those mistakes that more advanced users eventually build mechanisms around, effectively institutionalizing workarounds for design flaws. These sorts of flaws are obvious – if people are constantly walking right into the fancy new glass doors you just installed, odds are you need to compensate for their transparency. If an entire industry has been created to compensate for your omission of certain key components in your software's interface, perhaps it's time you added them. Are people always apologizing to you for making the same mistakes, such as pushing on the wrong side of a door handle, hanging up on you while trying to conference you in on another call, or taping an hour of static rather than the final episode of everyone's favorite long-running television show? Chances are there are flaws in the design of the tools they're using.

The attitude of a system's designer is bound to be different from that of the user encountering it for the first time, or someone who will use the tool day in, day out for years. Don't just ask yourself what the problems are, ask naïve users as well, or get skilled human factors engineers to come in and give the interface a spin. Don't just try to fix things after the fact, patching the existing interface as an after-thought. Incorporate proper design principles into the process of building your system and its interface to begin with. So what are some of these principles?

◆ Work with nature and previous experience.

◆ Work against nature where necessary to overcome weaknesses in design.

◆ Simplify, but don't oversimplify.

◆ Emphasize the key elements of your interface.

◆ Use constraints where possible to limit possible errors in interpretation.

◆ Design for error.

◆ Standardize if all else fails.

WORKING WITH NATURE, NOT AGAINST IT

Working with nature involves several concepts that are familiar to industrial designers, but may not be well known outside of that field or cognitive psychology classrooms. *Affordances, constraints, natural mappings, visibility, feedback,* and *direct manipulation* all describe characteristics of interfaces and interface design that leverage our natural understanding of objects in the world and their relationships to other objects. In general, building interfaces involves the creation of various objects or representations, interlocking parts or symbols, and their relationships. By maintaining a clear relationship between the objects and their representations, you encourage the user to forget about the differences between them and work directly with their representations. Through careful design of the relationships as a whole, you prevent errors from arising out of mistaken interpretation and false, if often creative, understandings of the relationships.

An *affordance* is an aspect of an object that reflects the ways in which it may be used. When we mentioned that some things were just meant to be pushed at the beginning of this section, we were talking about affordances. Choose your objects or representations carefully with respect to the way that they appear to be most useful. Be careful not to use a button for something that should be a dial, or a slider for something which might better be an on/off switch, and the confusion factor of your interfaces drops dramatically.

Fortunately, it is possible to draw some fairly good correspondences, as seen in Table 1-1, between objects having certain common affordances and the optional values those objects may be capable of representing. Some objects in the real world have no value, per se, but offer a clear and unmistakable affordance. One of Steven's favorite cartoons shows a man in a post office, with his foot up against the door, pulling the plate that reads "PULL" right off the door while another man looks on disgustedly from behind the counter.

TABLE 1-1 OBJECTS AND THEIR COMMON AFFORDANCES AND VALUES

Object	Affordance	Possible values
Dial or wheel	Turn	A range of discrete or continuous values
Button	Push	On/off, yes/no, any Boolean
Slider	Slide	A range of discrete or continuous values
Menu	Pull down, select	Any value or action signified by its items
Icon	Click	Any action signified by its owner
Switch	Switch	On/off, yes/no, any Boolean
Plate	Push	N/A
Bar	Push, drag	N/A
Handle or knob	Pull	N/A

Choose carefully when you design an interface using familiar objects with even more familiar affordances. In his design for the popular rant site Kvetch!, Derek Powazek chose an old-style radio metaphor, complete with dials. The idea behind the site is simple: You kvetch (complain) about various topics, using a handy forms interface, and the site feeds up a random complaint from the archives every few seconds. There are several topics, ranging from the ever-popular "love" and "money" to "politics" and "the Web." In order to access another topic, the user chooses a setting from the dial at top right, shown in Figure 1-1.

The use of a dial, which is usually grasped and turned in the physical world, to represent discrete choices fits right into the radio metaphor. However, the dial must be "turned" rather awkwardly using a mouse pointer. Is it the most appropriate interface element? Does it offer the most natural mapping of function to representation? In the final analysis, your user is the judge.

Constraints, unlike affordances, don't suggest an action or value, but inhibit possible actions so as to lead the user to the right conclusion or action. There are many different kinds of constraints, which Norman has classified into several categories:

◆ Physical: The constraint prevents some sort of physical action.

◆ Semantic: The constraint depends on knowledge of the situation, and can have only one meaningful resolution.

◆ Cultural: The constraint is not physical or semantic, but still depends on certain expected behavior, such as the fact that stoplights are to be obeyed or that signs are usually posted right-side up.

◆ **Logical:** The constraint is derived from a set of logical circumstances, such as there only being two choices; or natural mappings, such as associating a left arrow with movement to the left.

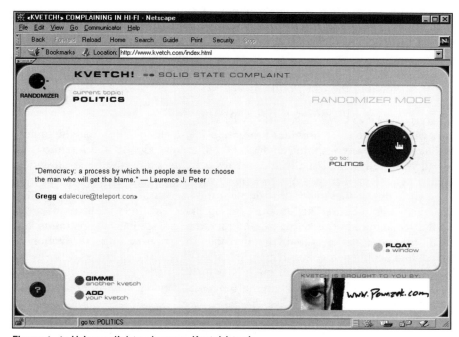

Figure 1-1: Using a dial to choose a Kvetch! topic

You can use many interesting combinations of affordances and constraints to create the right sort of environment or interface, directing the user towards desired actions and away from undesired actions. Of course, the effects of this balance can also backfire, so choose well!

Visibility, or *prominence*, is the degree to which elements in the interface are distinctly displayed or otherwise featured. Depending upon the application, it may be desirable to make some elements more obscure under certain conditions, and then display them prominently when they are needed. Kai's Power Tools, an application used for creating interesting and unique fractal shapes and other textures, uses this technique to great effect (as does Derek Powazek's Kvetch!). Visibility, despite the term's overwhelmingly visual connotations, may also refer to the use of sounds or even feelings to reflect certain conditions. The whistling of a kettle, which most of us take for granted, was actually designed into the product as a means of notifying cooks (presumably working in noisy kitchens) that the water inside was boiling away. Rumble strips on the street signify to the driver of a vehicle that they are not in their lane, or that they should slow down for a toll booth, yet in most cases are invisible grooves cut into the pavement.

The use of aural and tactile signals described previously is an example of *feedback*, yet another characteristic of well-designed interfaces. Every action and change of state in an interface should be signaled by some form of feedback. In many circumstances, an interface may also provide feedback that demands some sort of response from the user, such as a confirmation of an action before the action takes place, and then another instance of feedback when the action has been completed.

Direct manipulation is where you use objects in the world (or create them on a computer screen) to represent an object to be manipulated. Such representations enable the user to treat them as though they were real objects, and to manipulate them as they would in the real world.

WORKING AGAINST NATURE (IN A PINCH)

In many cases, an interface provides a situation in which an action may be undertaken that is potentially harmful, undesirable, or simply against the intentions of the designer of the system. Usually, but not always, this is a result of poor design or late changes to the system causing unintended conflicts with other parts of the system. You can address these instances through the use of *forcing functions*, which either prevent the undesired action from taking place, or direct the user toward a certain desired action. In this sense, forcing functions are similar to constraints, but the ideal forcing function should be invisible to the user until the action is attempted, and should sometimes remain invisible except for its effects. In general, forcing functions are better design choices than warnings, which the user might ignore. There are several forms of forcing functions, among them *interlocks*, *lockins*, and *lockouts*.

An *interlock* ensures that certain actions occur in a desired order and in no other manner. One example of an interlock is the switch controlling the light inside a refrigerator, which only turns on when the door is opened and turns itself off when the door is closed. Interlocks have many applications in industrial design, ranging from automobile ignitions that do not allow the engine to be started unless the vehicle's transmission is in park or neutral to phonographs that do not start spinning until the needle arm is swung out over the turntable.

A *lockin* simply keeps a state from changing or an action from stopping until the appropriate conditions are met. While the lockin is in effect, whatever it applies to remains in effect. In graphical user interface design, a commonly decried example of a lockin is the so-called *modal dialog box*, which prevents any other action from taking place until the dialog box is either canceled or approved. Most lockins in graphical interface design share in the bad reputation of the modal dialog box, and are generally avoided in favor of designs that do not force the user to respond immediately. Another good example of a lockin is found in older software installers, which used to require that all other running applications be shut down before the installation could take place. Many of these installers didn't allow the user to simply switch to the other applications, shut them down, and return to the installation. More recent installer programs are more forgiving in their attitude toward switching contexts, but as a result open up the user to potential damage to the system or other calamities if the warnings are not heeded.

A *lockout*, as one might expect, is a forcing function that prevents users from entering a place or state that might be dangerous to them in some way. The preceding example of a modern software installer might benefit from a lockout that simply refused to allow the program to run if there were any other programs running at the same time. This suggests that the error in design is not simply fixed by removing a lockin (the modal dialog box), but that the inclusion of a lockout earlier in the process would have prevented the problem from occurring altogether.

As a general rule, interface elements that provide affordances or other notifying or manipulating functions should be prominently displayed, while forcing functions should be invisible to the user. The controversy begins here, unfortunately, and there is little agreement among interface theorists as to the extent or degree to which the display of interface elements should be subdued or enhanced. Some argue that too much feedback and too many minor forcing functions dilute their effectiveness and irritate the user, and others argue that too subdued an interface is confusing to the average user. Still others take the position that interfaces should be flexible and configurable, enabling the user to determine the degree and type of warnings and feedback to which they are exposed. The way that human factors engineers and theorists carry on, you'd think they were economists.

GOOD USER-CENTERED DESIGN

The interface elements outlined previously provide a toolset from which to draw upon whether you are building an interface or designing an automobile. But how does a designer apply these elements? What kinds of approaches should you use when designing or implementing your interface?

As discussed previously, it is much better to work with nature and the user's experience rather than working around them, but there are many tools for both sets of circumstances. Here are a few rules of thumb to follow in the design of your interface:

- Simplification

- Prominence and appropriate placement

- Proper and well-considered use of constraints

- Design for error, rather than restrict the user after the fact as problems are discovered

When all else fails, you can always try for standardization. It is always possible to stop and try to reinvent the problem — you may find that the problem goes away when approached from a different angle with a different set of assumptions about the interface.

HOW DOES ALL THIS APPLY TO WEB USER INTERFACES?

Now that the basic elements and principles of Donald Norman's ideas have been covered, it's time to turn our attention to their application to the field of Web interface design. What can we learn from Norman's work, and how do we apply this knowledge to a better understanding of what a Web interface is, should be, and should not be?

First of all, although the specific problems relating to real-world objects as discussed by Norman do not apply to the Web, the same questions of affordances and constraints arise when dealing with their representations. The rule of thumb regarding designing for error, rather than around subsequent discoveries, applies to the design of any system, the Web being no exception. Designing for error simply means taking into account the fact that your users will make errors and expecting the most common errors. Well-designed applications build in appropriate responses and checks and balances against common errors, ensuring that if they occur the application responds with an explanatory message or warning before a potentially unwanted action takes place.

Paying attention to your users is key — especially as the cost of redesign for interfaces and underlying programming skyrockets, and the increasing complexity and enhanced possibilities for Web design continues to outstrip the available tools.

Much of this book deals with the issues surrounding the quest to bring Web interfaces up to speed with the last 20 years of software application interface design. One of the main characteristics of good Web design, whether in terms of pure graphic design and navigation, or in terms of more advanced applications, is that the interface is clean and uncluttered. This is in contrast to the urge followed by many amateur Web developers, whose insistence on flaming logos and other unnecessary cruft is legendary. Focus on the user, on delivering an unambiguous and direct interface and navigational model, and always listen to the feedback of naïve users. You may choose to educate the user where possible rather than redesign, but always remember that your intentions and clever ideas are for naught if the end user is confused, angered, or simply unable to make use of your final site or application design.

One quality of Norman's work is that it tends to focus on the careful production of artifacts (usually physical objects) that, for the most part, enter the world as designed and remain that way until they wear out, break, or are replaced by a newer version. As such, the importance of good design up front is highly emphasized. The same concerns are also applicable to traditional software application interface design, as applications are usually built, shrink-wrapped, and remain static throughout their useful lives. The Web, however, offers the developer myriad ways to continually improve upon his or her product based on feedback and the ever-changing requirements of the user and capabilities of the development environment.

Another characteristic of Norman's principles for design has to do with the relative simplicity of many of the components of a system. A telephone is a relatively simple product, although the systems that it becomes a part of may be needlessly complex. The emphasis on a fixed product, meant to be manipulated, assumes perhaps too static a set of requirements. The Web, by contrast, is always changing in terms of its content and interrelationships, and in terms of its capabilities.

One of the most important qualities of the Web and other new media applications and productions is their emphasis on drawing the user into a state of interaction never before possible. The psychology of the user of a Web application is, quite simply, different from that of the user of a volleyball, a door, a car, or other object from a world that assumes a simple and familiar sort of physics. We must take these concepts as defined and now apply them to the world of the *human-computer interface,*

The Flexibility of Web Site Interface Design — Myth or Reality?

Naysayers might claim that although Web sites may be more easily redesigned or tweaked than shrink-wrapped software or VCRs, it rarely happens, and, for the most part, they'd be right. Once an interface design or navigational scheme has been incorporated into a set of static pages, it often remains that way until the next complete overhaul or makeover. But more and more, template-driven publishing solutions such as Allaire's ColdFusion, Haht Software's HAHTSite, NetObjects' TeamFusion, Vignette's StoryServer, and numerous hand-rolled Perl and database solutions are taking a prominent place in the management of Web site publishing.

Automating the publishing process makes it easier to concentrate on nonautomated, oft-updated pages such as top-level home pages, but it also separates the variable content from more static navigational templates. This makes it possible to fine-tune the templates based on user feedback. It also makes it possible to enable users to define their own preferences as to the content itself, its presentation, frequency of updates, and more. I'd like to see a traditional software developer try that with a C++ application.

or *HCI*. This narrowing of scope from the entire world of human artifacts to the worlds inside and on the border between computers and humans may at first appear to be just that — a narrowing — but as you will see, there is no limit to the possibilities for products of the imagination. Brenda Laurel, whose ideas are discussed in the next section, talks about using the principles of drama for interface design. She takes these ideas to a new level of interaction and participation in the interface, rather than the relatively simple uses of stoves and doorknobs considered by Norman.

Brenda Laurel and Theater: UI as Stage

Brenda Laurel is perhaps most famous for her role as editor of the book *The Art of Human-Computer Interface Design,* sponsored by Apple Computer, Inc., which features the ideas and musings of many of the most important minds in the world of HCI. The stated purpose of the book was to take the notion of the interface as "a discrete and tangible thing that we can map, draw, design, and implement," and replace it with another based on "the cognitive and emotional aspects of the user's experience." After her work on cutting-edge interface design theory, she went on to write a book that went back to her roots in theater, to expound upon the use of theatrical direction and interaction in the user interfaces of tomorrow. To Laurel, the key to understanding the user interface is to move beyond our limited conceptions of it as a tool, and adopt a more dynamic, participation-oriented model. In such a model, the computer itself becomes a medium for artistic expression and empowerment of the user, rather than the technologists who created it. As most everyone who reads this book is likely to be one of those technologists, it makes sense for us to know and understand what she is saying.

Traditional interface design presumes a sharp distinction between the user and the system being used. Its elements tend to be task-oriented and objective, and aim for consistency and predictability rather than flexibility, openness, and immersion. The user is not expected to contribute substantially to the interface itself, but is rather seen as an almost passive observer until such a time as he is called to act, and only then in well-defined, anticipated ways. The emphasis is on the use of an overarching metaphor, such as the Macintosh desktop, to which all subcomponents are expected to conform. This approach has been widely criticized for its near-fascistic hold on the imagination of interface designers, whose contributions are always scrubbed free of personality, creativity, and other inconsistencies, in favor of the all-encompassing metaphor. This leads to some ludicrous situations, such as applications that have no text to cut or paste being required by user interface guidelines to provide an Edit menu that will never be used.

DIRECT MANIPULATION VERSUS DIRECT ENGAGEMENT

There are good reasons for this insistence on consistency, especially when viewed from the perspective of traditional interface design. When the basic assumption about the interface is that it enables the user to manipulate objects or representations of objects in order to accomplish a predefined goal or set of goals, consistency and the wise use of metaphor enables the user to more or less factor out the interface entirely, up to a point. That point, where direct manipulation of objects ends, and direct engagement between the user and his environment—virtual or otherwise—begins, is where Brenda Laurel takes us.

Direct manipulation is the replacement for earlier generations of command-line interfaces and even more indirect methods of communication with the computer, where the user issues instructions using an arcane, if powerful, syntax of sequential commands. The effects of such commands are only apparent if the programs they execute have any reason—usually defined by the program's creator—to provide feedback of any kind. In the world of direct manipulation, rather, every object represented by the computer is always visible to the user. The user is capable of affecting those objects via methods that appear physical in nature, are usually reversible, and are perceived as they occur. Moving beyond direct manipulation, then, requires that a new kind of environment be created in which the notions of manipulation, objects, and metaphor are replaced by the notions of actors, engagement, and environments.

Using the study of drama, a subject that necessarily involves the creation and staging of action as the main focus, Laurel turns traditional interface theory on its head. Rather than create objects to be manipulated through a mediating filter known as the interface, computers should create environments that enable the total immersion of the user as a participant. This notion of direct engagement with the task at hand as a means of moving beyond the simple world of representations of objects, which most modern interface design concerns itself with, provides interesting and illuminating insights into the nature of the human-computer interface. It directs us to rethink many of the assumptions, most of them steeped in the legacy of pre-graphical computers, that interface theory is founded upon.

Traditional interface theory presupposes the existence of mental models that the user forms in response to the representation of the objects on the screen, and their relationship to the unseen objects that presumably loom behind the interface. The computer is presumed to have certain preprogrammed assumptions about the behavior of the user that determine the realm of possibilities for action. In this scenario, the successful execution and completion of tasks is highly dependent on the user's mental model matching up to no small degree with that built into the system, and vice versa. The problem is that this collection of mental models is recursive, which is another way of saying that it never ends. Through their perceptions of the limitations of the interface as presented, users become aware of the system's assumptions about their behavior, and this awareness enhances their mental model. Frustration, anxiety, and anger result as users attempt to second-guess the system based on its behavior and response to the users' input. Eventually, users throw up their hands in despair, wondering why they can't simply do what they want, why they are crippled by an unresponsive and inflexible interface.

WHOLE ACTIONS WITH MULTIPLE AGENTS

Laurel's response to the problem of mental models and the archaism of metaphor-driven user interfaces is a shift in perspective from the creation of objects to be manipulated to the creation of theaters of engagement. In this scenario, the user goes into the experience as an active participant in and inhabitant of a new, more responsive environment. Rather than a one-on-one relationship between the user and interface, and a similar, but unseen, relationship between the interface and the system that lies beneath it, Laurel posits the computing experience as one that represents a "whole action with multiple agents" of which the user is only one. Moving from the metaphor of interface as a theater with an audience and actors, she recommends the inclusion of the user in the action itself.

Of course, the sort of environments that Laurel proposes are unlikely to be considered appropriate by developers of traditional office productivity applications — one has a difficult time imagining an immersive multiplayer spreadsheet tool, for example — but it is useful to remember that many such appropriate applications exist. Virtual reality, avatar-based chat, the manipulation and modeling of chemical data, flight simulators, and many other applications are becoming more and more commonplace. The designers of these systems are turning to new and different approaches for inspiration, and Laurel's ideas about action fit their purposes perfectly.

THE COMPUTER AS A MEDIUM, NOT A TOOL

Laurel's ideas are interesting, steeped in the language of the study of drama, but rather than go into them here, we should cut to the heart of the matter as it pertains to our present activity. Her critique of the interface stems from her perception of the limited power of metaphor, especially simple, object-driven, representational metaphor. She writes in *Computers As Theater,* "Interface metaphors have limited usefulness. What you gain now you may have to pay for later." By limiting the extent to which full, immersive environments may be created — as a tradeoff for the ease of use and consistency as compared to a command-line environment — the metaphor becomes a trap. In order to fully escape the overarching interface metaphor, whether it is of a desktop, a notepad, a virtual set of overlapping or tiled "windows," and so on, the user must leave the interface metaphor entirely.

Due to the stranglehold on your mental model held by the designers of the system and its applications, you must be willing to accept this mental model as your own in order to communicate with the system. If you mistakenly develop an alternate mental model, your ability to communicate and function within the interface is severely limited. This mistaken acquisition of a "false" mental model, as mentioned previously, is recursive. Unless you can correct it, you go on creating ever more elaborate models as variations on the theme, until finally your expectations of the computer are so out of whack that you abandon it in disgust. This is the situation Laurel wants to avoid.

Laurel's ideas are also important to Web designers and developers because the sites we create are rarely just applications, but are total environments built upon the extremely flexible foundations made possible by hypertext. The Webmaster or Web developer/designer is often required to provide full navigation and visual iconographies for the major areas of the site, providing a sense of "place" for visitors so they don't get lost in the maze of links and other situational factors in their interface. Laurel's approach of focusing on the actions that may be required by the user, rather than focusing on objects and their possible means of manipulation, is the shift in perspective that the Web designer needs in order to cope with this new medium. Her insistence that interactivity be the prime mover behind thinking about interface design is a breath of fresh air.

Alan Cooper and the Idiomatic Interface: The User's Mental Model

Alan Cooper is one of the most respected authorities on interface design currently working in the software industry. His classic book on the design of user interfaces, *About Face: The Essentials of User Interface Design,* describes many of the principles he developed while working on the interface design for Microsoft Visual Basic, which was itself hailed as a groundbreaking application from the standpoint of usability and power. His primary contribution to the study of interface design has to do with his pull-no-punches attitude toward traditional software interfaces, of which he is highly critical. In his view, the average user interface is tightly bound to the implementer's vision of the software, which rarely, if ever, has any direct bearing on the way the audience actually uses the software. The following section covers several of his concepts, focusing on the ideas of idiomatic interface design, the manifest model, goal-directed design, and what he calls *task coherence*. He sums up his approach in a simple directive: "Don't make the user look stupid."

IDIOM AND THE EFFECTIVE USER INTERFACE

Webster defines *idiom* as "An expression in the usage of a language that is peculiar to itself either grammatically (such as "no, it wasn't me") or in having a meaning that cannot be derived from the conjoined meanings of its elements." In the visual language of interfaces, this translates roughly into "an interface element whose use cannot be determined merely by looking at it in the context of the whole interface, but that may be learned quickly by the user." The insight here is that although there are enormous problems with the idea of metaphor, as discussed previously, there are ways of providing users with interfaces whose elements' use may be shown to them and that may be hard to forget once learned.

A Web browser's use of underlined words to represent hypertext links is a great example of an idiomatic user interface element. This is an unlikely association to expect a naïve user to make, but once shown how, it is difficult to forget. An unfortunate offshoot of the ease with which the "click on underlined things" idiom may be learned is that it relies on the user selecting the link. However, most traditional interfaces associate the double-click with an action, so the user sometimes learns the idiom incorrectly, or more accurately, applies one idiom to another environment. Once learned, the idea that you should double-click links is difficult to shake. It is, of course, unnecessary to double-click, but it rarely interrupts the action, so there is no real constraint to force the user to unlearn the incorrect behavior. During Steven's career as a Web consultant, this is one of the most common mistakes he's seen new users make.

In the end, the user decides which interface elements make sense and which do not, and to a large extent this is decided on the basis of what the user can remember when they need to. Cool, insanely efficient, cutting-edge technological advances will never achieve widespread popularity if they are too hard to remember how to use. Although metaphor can be useful for tying elements of an interface together, it is idiom that determines its success.

MODEL, MODEL, WHO'S GOT THE MODEL?

Cooper judges an interface not by its aesthetics, but by how effective its users become, how easily it is learned, and how coherent its elements are. Conflicts between the various affordances offered by the elements count against the effectiveness of the interface. This is because the interface is the only representation of the system that the user has. In using the system, the user develops what Cooper calls a *manifest model*, a sort of vague understanding of the system halfway between the interface and the actual underlying implementation it represents. The more coherent the elements of the interface, the more coherent the manifest model the user acquires. Interestingly, and perhaps most importantly, the manifest model does not have to map directly to the underlying system. In fact, it is best that it doesn't, because that sort of "implementation model" is exactly what Cooper decries and the average user dreads.

Cooper gives as an example the concept of files, which most of us know are collections of bytes on a disk somewhere that represent information of many types. Cooper takes this one step beyond our usual understanding, however, to point out that files not only exist on disk, but also in memory, as buffers. During editing, unless the user saves the buffer, differences accumulate between the version on disk and the one in memory. This problem is compounded by the fact that most interfaces, no matter how unsophisticated their users, assume that the user knows that disks are a storage device for persistent, session-independent storage of files. Many users don't even understand the difference between RAM, ROM, and fixed or removable media, so how can they be expected to understand the differences between a buffer and disk file?

The Macintosh provides an example of an interface element that started out life as an implementation model hack, quickly took on a helpful idiomatic usefulness, and over time became a problem component in an otherwise fairly coherent interface. The act of dragging a disk image to the trash can to eject the disk is problematic for several reasons. Thomas D. Erickson tells the story in the introduction to *The Art of Human Computer Interface Design*. With the original Macintosh, which lacked a hard disk, users had to frequently switch back and forth between floppies as they worked. In order to speed up the process of finding the right file on the right disk, the Mac kept a copy of the file list in memory, and a grayed-out disk image on the desktop. To eject a disk, the user chose the Eject command from a menu. To remove the unwanted grayed-out disk image, the user had to drag the image to the trash can. This cleared the file list from memory and uncluttered the desktop. A programmer, annoyed with the two-step procedure for a common activity, added a shortcut to the interface that enabled the user to drag the current disk image to the trash can, thereby both physically ejecting the disk and deleting the file list from memory. This controversial move violated the purity of the trash can metaphor, which assumed the users should treat the trash can as a place to discard and delete files. The new feature quickly caught on with users, demonstrating the power of idiomatic interface elements as well as the limitations of metaphor.

GOAL-ORIENTED INTERFACES AND TASK COHERENCE

Cooper makes another important point in *About Face*; namely, designing interfaces with tasks alone in mind goes against the fundamental purpose of software, which is to help users accomplish their goals effectively. Their goals may or may not have a direct relationship to the tasks that the software enables the user to perform, but software is often laden with patronizing or obscure error messages and confirmation dialog boxes that only serve to make the user feel stupid. The sad part is that this isn't necessarily the purpose of such interface elements, nor is it the programmer's intention.

Designing based on a program's intended functionality goes back to the "objects vs. actions" discussion earlier in this chapter. Rather than basing the interface on a piecemeal, one-to-one relationship between elements and the tasks they help the user to complete, or binding the elements to an overarching visual metaphor, goal-oriented design starts by defining the user's goals in general, and using them as a metric for whether or not to add features (tasks) later.

So how does an interface designer – or programmer working in tandem with a designer – proceed with building a useful and popular software application? The key lies in Cooper's idea of *task coherence,* which insists that the program remember the user's behavior and/or preferences in certain circumstances, from one session to the next, or from one performance of an action to the next. The idea is that if the program can remember the user's style or relative skill, it makes using the interface much less annoying. The eventual result is that users no longer feel like they are playing 20 questions with an amnesiac, but instead have a willing and helpful partner in the performance of what may be mundane, repetitive tasks.

MANIFEST MODELS AS APPLIED TO THE WEB

Showing a system to a new user is a great way to discover preconceptions and assumptions in your interface or in the design of a system. An example that illustrates this point is the idea of the Web as a network. Many Web applications are powered by databases and/or CGI scripts that by definition are not present on the client end of the system, but rather spew forth data that the client can understand and display. Often, these server-side systems deal with the data in an entirely different way than the client would understand. For instance, a server-side application might consist of a database, a set of templates, some code to process user preferences based on HTTP cookies, and an interface to the Web server daemon that processes user requests. All users see is that new and different stuff shows up on their computer monitor when they click *here* or *here.*

Cooper discusses the foolishness of disk-based file systems at great length in *About Face,* likening them to having refrigeration technology in every room of a house. Sure, they provide some benefits and are relatively economical, but there's really no need for the overreliance on disk technology. In fact, economics are the primary driving force behind disk-based storage, although privacy and independence from networking is also a major factor, which Cooper ignores. However, he raises a good point in that the implementation of disk storage and the file system have infiltrated every aspect of personal computing, largely to its detriment.

Many new users don't understand the idea of networks, and so the related items, such as modems, routing, addressing, the domain name system, backbones, packet filters and firewalls, and Web server software with database back ends don't make sense either. Drawing pictures doesn't even help, sometimes. So how can we expect the user to understand the delay caused by slow download times, Web server load, complex search strings requiring lengthy processing on the server, and so forth? The user wants to see immediate results, like switching a television channel. The user's favorite TV programs are delivered instantaneously, so why aren't Web pages? High-bandwidth networks are changing the perception that the Web is too slow, but they don't do much to educate anyone on the underlying model.

What the Web needs (and what it will soon have) is the capability to quickly deliver an application in its entirety to the client, and use the network for nothing but data transfer from the application to the server. With all but cache and persistent client-side cookies residing on the server end of the network, it would be possible to test out some of Cooper's ideas for replacing the file-centric model. It will be possible to get beyond a model many users have long taken for granted – despite its inherent clumsiness.

A Reasonable, If Lengthy, Compromise

By now you're probably wondering what all this has to do with dynamic HTML and the Web. You've probably entertained the idea of skipping ahead to the real meat of the book, the example chapters, or even perused the sample files on the Web site. Before we got too deep into the specifics of a new generation of interface-building tools, we wanted to be sure that you had a firm grasp of exactly what an interface *is*, a good idea of what it *can be*, and some cautionary tales about what it *shouldn't be*. We also wanted to be sure that you'd had a chance to think about the proper time for interface design – not at the end, as an afterthought to an almost finished system, but as an ongoing critique of the system itself, growing and evolving with the system during its initial development and through its full life cycle. So, without further ado, the working definition of the term *interface* that we'll be using throughout the rest of the book.

A *user interface* is the sum total of the emotional and cultural context in which users interact with a computer combined with their psychological, rational, and sensory experience of, reaction to, and interaction with the input and output devices that comprise it. It often arises out of many unstated assumptions on the part of the system's designers and programmers that determine its nature, but that remain unstated and must either be learned by or hidden from the user in the form of metaphor, messages and feedback, response time, or training.

Many interfaces are designed with the end goal of creating a consistent, objective environment for the completion of tasks. In many cases, however, an easily learned system designed around the key actions the user performs is more appropriate and more powerful. Simplicity in an interface is always a tradeoff between the complexity of the tasks and the procedures that the user needs to memorize.

Summary

◆ Interfaces are composed of many types of elements, ranging from the knobs and dials of a car radio to the menus, scrollbars, and buttons of a software application.

◆ Affordances, constraints, visibility, feedback, and direct manipulation all play an important role in the creation of an effective interface.

- Consistency, coherence, and well-defined metaphor may be useful, but should not prevent the use of easily learned and useful shortcuts.

- The user's goals, not the programmer's, should determine the interface.

- Pay attention to both new and experienced users and the ways they use (and abuse) your interface, and plan for error.

- Systems whose interfaces work with the user's preferences and style make the user feel smarter and more effective.

A well-designed interface takes into account the user's context, previous experience, and goals, compensating up front for the possibility that the user may make errors. It also realizes that making errors is a normal and productive part of the ongoing process of learning how to use the interface, and in the end makes the user more effective. Above all, a user interface should recede into the background, enabling the user to forget it is even there. In essence, we're trying to design interfaces that are invisible to the user.

Chapter 2

A Brief History of User Interface Design

IN THIS CHAPTER

- ◆ The archaic, but powerful, command-line interface

- ◆ Some characteristics of mainframe/terminal-based interfaces

- ◆ An introduction to the graphical user interface

- ◆ The confusing depths of hypertext

- ◆ The animated and challenging world of multimedia

- ◆ Interfaces for particular audiences

The Command-Line Interface

One of the earliest forms of human-computer interface (after the Hollerith punched card reader) was the *command-line,* or *shell-driven,* interface, introduced in the mid-sixties. With it, the user could attain new levels of productivity from the comfort of his or her own office. Gone were the days of having to know Boolean logic, electrical engineering, or arcane machine code. The useful and powerful shell allowed for completely new levels of abstraction, high-level programming, and direct access to the operating system's capabilities. One of the most popular command-line interfaces was (and still is) found in the UNIX operating system. From the early days of the Bourne Shell, or /bin/sh, to the current proliferation of enhanced shell environments such as bash (the GNU Project's Bourne-Again SHell), the Korn Shell, and Bill Joy's "C shell," the command-line interface has long been considered indispensable by adepts and a thing to be feared by novices. The popular DOS environment, early BASIC interpreters, and other operating systems had their heyday in the decades between the late sixties and early nineties, when the Apple Macintosh OS and its copycats (such as Microsoft Windows) made computing available to "the rest of us."

Steven learned BASIC on a Tandy TRS-80 Model III, using a BASIC command-line interpreter and cassette tape drive to type in and store lengthy BASIC programs. He used the computer for several months before anyone told him that

23

programs could be purchased on tape. Up to that point, he had relied on magazines and books such as David Ahl's *Creative Computing*, which contained printouts of tons of great BASIC programs mostly ported to BASIC by professional programmers who were personal computer hobbyists. He never did get a disk drive, as they were incredibly expensive, and, to his ten-year-old mind, kind of a waste. It was easy enough to type the programs in, after all. He'd had enough experience with cassette tapes going bad (usually due to the static caused by his cat sleeping on the tape drive) to know that paper printouts were far more permanent than electronic media.

You could say Steven was weaned on the command-line interface. It took him a long time to get used to these fancy new "gooey" things. . . .

An Overview of the Shell as Interface

It may seem odd in a book about building graphical user interfaces to spend any time at all on the text-based command-line interface. Yet, the command-line interface (CLI) is a powerful example of both the power and weakness of interfaces in general. UNIX serves as the environment for this discussion, because it's a CLI environment we're familiar with and it has a well-deserved reputation for being incredibly powerful as a result of its elegance and simplicity. On the other hand, UNIX has an equally well-deserved reputation among its detractors for being a cantankerous, inconsistent, hostile, and generally ill-designed patchwork of the whims and fancies of hundreds of different contributors who have not only extended the original simplicity and power of the interface, but increased its complexity a hundredfold. What better example to use for a discussion of Web interfaces?

Remember, an interface is just a way for the user to communicate with the system in a mediated fashion, as opposed to directly. The original UNIX environment expected the user (assumed to be a programmer) to be able to communicate directly with the system by way of a standard library of system calls in the C programming language, itself a giant step towards high-level usability. Previously, programmers had to learn the opcodes and assembly language for every CPU they wrote programs for.

The *shell* displays all of the fundamental characteristics of an interface. From some perspectives, it is even more direct than a graphical user interface, once you take into account that its designers had very different assumptions about its users. In addition, these assumptions were a reflection of the context that its users would bring to the environment. The shell:

- ◆ Is task-oriented
- ◆ Presents a consistent environment to the user
- ◆ Provides mediated manipulation of lower-level system objects
- ◆ Does not unnecessarily distract the user
- ◆ Provides a mechanism for status feedback
- ◆ Uses metaphor to hide unimportant details about the nature of the interface

We're not going to try to convince you that the shell is a panacea for the world's interface ills. However, it is important to be able to identify the common elements of any interface in order to learn how to recognize them in your own designs. In the next section, we point out a few of the characteristics mentioned above as they apply to the shell as an interface. By examining where the shell succeeds in providing an incredibly terse and powerful environment for programming and other tasks, and at where it fails by making that environment unnecessarily complex, you will learn valuable lessons about what to look for in your GUIs. More importantly, you can see past the visual nature of your interfaces to their actual worth in light of the principles of interface theory.

Some Fun UNIX Examples

UNIX is loved, hated, feared, and misunderstood. It's hard to have any experience with UNIX and the shell without coming to some appreciation of its power, and, at the same time, perhaps coming to a realization of its more glaring limitations. It has been said that technical support for GUIs would be so much easier if the tech support staff could just reach out and grab the mouse through the phone. This is due to the success of the GUI in making its users overlook essential details, which are often *too* detailed, when translating them into written or verbal instructions. It is common for advanced users of a system to assume that the novice is familiar with those things the more advanced take for granted as a part of the environment, such as the file system, horizontal scroll bars, or the use of keyboard shortcuts. In the UNIX shell environment, there is little fear of being distracted by an omnipresent menu bar, but the same tendency to overlook the obvious is found in any user of a well-implemented interface. Fortunately, because the shell is text-based, our examples are easy to cite. So let's look at a few UNIX programs and take them apart from the perspective of their interface.

It is important to understand how the shell works, however, before we get into the nitty-gritty details of its status as an interface. In the shell environment, the user is required to type the name of a command and its respective options into a command line, wait for it to execute, and then type another. The shell comes with three default handlers for input and output: STDIN, or STanDard INput; STDOUT, or STanDard OUTput; and STDERR, or STanDard ERRor. User input is received by way of STDIN, and the output from a program is sent to either STDOUT or STDERR. STDOUT may be redirected to another process, a file, or to the console, and STDERR is sent to the console unless otherwise directed. Therefore, a user may run a program and maintain tight control over where its input comes from, where its output goes, and how to receive any diagnostic, help, or error-related information. This commonly-touted (and fundamental) feature of the UNIX system enables all of its programs to receive input from other programs, send output to other programs or files, and still manage to provide feedback to the user's console.

Much of the UNIX toolbox, the set of common programs available on most all UNIX systems, has been programmed to leverage these input/output features. Programming takes on a linear quality, often making use of *pipelines*, or ordered progressions of programs whose output becomes the input for other programs. The event-driven quality of GUIs is notably absent, but it would be a mistake to say that the user relinquishes control over operation of the system just because they are deprived of menus, icons, and the mouse pointer. In a very real sense, the user is in total control, and has total responsibility for constructing correct strings of commands. Those concerned with ease of use have roundly criticized this unforgiving assumption on the part of UNIX's designers. However, the real problem with UNIX is that so many programmers have had a hand in creating the programs and defining their options, or *switches*, with few guiding principles or standards as to which switches should be consistent across programs. Switches have historically been one letter long, and are usually chosen for some mnemonic quality appropriate to the context in which they are used.

For example, most UNIX commands fail if not invoked properly, and print a usage statement to STDERR. This usage statement is sometimes automatically invoked if the user passes a -h switch to the program. Similarly, many programs recognize the -v switch as invoking the option that prints the program's version information. Unfortunately, some programs rely on a mnemonic that is best suited to the -h or -v switches, and so provide other ways to get the version or usage information. These conventions, rather than standards, are somewhat spottily implemented across the myriad versions of UNIX. Programmers have historically relied on manual pages, indispensable to the users of the system, as handy ways to provide explanations of each program's options and calling conventions. Much in the same way that personal information managers have relieved many an executive of the need to memorize telephone numbers, manual pages (or *man pages*, so-called because man is the command used to display them) relieve the user of the need to memorize widely disparate and arcane command-line switches.

Unfortunately, this means that some users spend as much time looking at the manual pages as they do actually working with the programs they purport to explain. As computers have gained a wider audience, the assumptions that could be made about their users have gradually been challenged, contested, and finally found wanting. Let's look at a few popular commands and deconstruct the rationale behind the sometimes baffling interface they present to the user.

FINDING STUFF WITH FIND

find is the UNIX command most commonly used to locate arbitrarily named files. Similar in purpose and design to the Windows 95 Find Files or Folders function, or the Macintosh Find command, find is a powerful and flexible tool. In addition to such tools as whereis, ls, locate, and which, used to find commands, manual pages, arbitrary files, and source code, the find command is a helpful and necessary navigational tool in an environment that assumes its users have a mental model of the file system in which they work at all times. When a file is "misplaced," or a user needs to know where some other file is kept, find is often the last bastion of hope after more specific tools have failed. So how is it used?

The `find` command takes several command-line options that may be combined in complex and powerful ways to print file listings, execute commands, and gather important information about modification times, ownership, size, and other characteristics. To the novice user, the manual page is no help, starting right out with a discussion of rules of operator precedence, arguments, expressions, special characters, assumed default settings, and return values. To the programmer, the manual page presents a wealth of useful information for combining the `find` command with others in order to perform complex tasks. But to the user who is just trying to find the report he or she mislaid before lunch, the default course of action is to ask a local guru to find the file for them. (We know — we're often called upon to do just that!)

On the Linux system Steven uses on a daily basis, the manual for `find` is over 11 pages long. The synopsis section at the top (shown in Figure 2-1), where one can usually rely on a terse listing of all acceptable command-line switches, says that `find` may be invoked as follows:

```
find [path...] [expression]
```

In order to figure out which command-line option is used to specify that the `find` operation should only print files of a certain type, the user is required to scroll down almost five pages. Then, there is another page of terse descriptions of the various arguments that may be given to the `-type` switch.

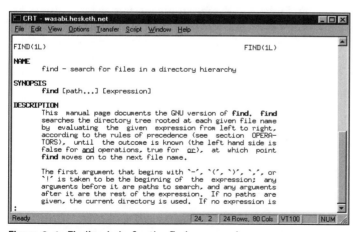

Figure 2-1: Finding help for the find command

By the time the user has studied up on the options, arguments, expressions, and various warnings about preventing possible misinterpretation of metacharacters by the shell itself, he or she may have forgotten the original task.

However, the skilled user can usually type a well-remembered and oft-used command in far less time than it takes Windows 95 to even start the Find Files or Folders application. Watching a skilled UNIX user in action is a fascinating exercise in patience, provided they are helping you and not simply amusing themselves. For some, the very act of calling up a manual page is enough to jar their memory, and to the untutored observer, a guru might well appear to be acting randomly, typing nonsensical streams of characters in an effort to confuse those who might be watching. What can be said about a command like the following?

```
find $HOME -type f -name '*~' -mtime 7 -exec /bin/rm -rf {} \;
```

Those readers familiar with UNIX — and the `find` command — might recognize this as a fairly typical system maintenance command that finds and removes all regular files with the extension '~' not modified in the last week from a user's home directory. Others may question specific portions of the command, such as the curly braces or backslashed semicolon, having never used the `-exec` switch before. Still others might recognize the environment variable `$HOME`, the regular expression denoting the pattern a filename must match, or even the `rm` command, which you may have used in other contexts to remove files. Users of the `vi` and `emacs` editors may recognize the tilde as a commonly used extension for backup files.

It is fairly clear, especially when the command is run and no visible output is produced, that this sort of interface asks a lot of the user. Not only is the user required to carry around a mental model of the environment, but he must also communicate his wishes exactly if he expects the shell to carry them out. Furthermore, with many commands, no visible or audible feedback reflects the success or failure of the action. From the standpoint of interface theory, particularly in respect to revisions made since the advent of GUIs, such an environment fails in several important respects:

- ◆ Status feedback ranges from poor to nonexistent.

- ◆ User error is not tolerated.

- ◆ Natural mappings are not employed.

- ◆ There is an overreliance on the accuracy of the user's mental model.

As a sometime UNIX trainer, Steven sees and hears a lot of complaints from first-time users, such as "How will I ever remember all this?" or "This is way too abstract for me — how do I know when I'm doing it right?" He usually has to reassure them that UNIX is not that bad despite initial appearances, and that its power and flexibility more than make up for the difficulty of learning it up front if they take the time to get into the proper mindset. Practice and devoted study, as well as the confidence that gradually comes after weeks and months of increased knowledge and continued success, can provide the user with the mental model and ability to deal with the abstract. This is, after all, how programmers generally think — in terms of the abstract problem domain in which their code must work. It's a shame, really, that novices tend to give powerful tools like the `find` command such a short shrift. It is hard to dispute, though, that many people don't have the time or the inclination to get up to speed on the total environment that the skillful use of such tools requires. In the next section, you will learn about the ways in which the consistency afforded one environment can become an overwhelming burden on another.

SED (LEANING TOOTHPICK SYNDROME)

`sed` was for a long time the standard editor used in pipelines and other situations that required output from a given program be processed for input into another program. The name `sed` itself stands for "Stream EDitor," and it was intended for precisely that. As opposed to editing a file in an editor, such as `vi`, `emacs`, or even Word, which results in a new file or a modified copy of an existing file, sometimes it's necessary to edit a stream of data that's on its way to another process. This type of editor is extremely useful when you have regular output (for example, from the `find` command) that you want to modify before sending to another program in a pipeline. Other tools, such as `tr`, `awk`, and `perl`, have also been used in similar circumstances. It is not unusual to see all four of these programs used in the same shell script for the simple reason that each has a concise syntax for dealing with certain kinds of problems.

`sed` is quite easy to use provided that the user knows a bit about regular expressions and the basic `STDIN/STDOUT` model employed by pipelines. Basically, you pipe some input into `sed`, providing a set of transformations to be performed on the input, and `sed` prints the results to the output, which may be a file, another process, or even the system console. Here's a typical `sed` command:

```
sed -e 's/laptop/notebook/g' catalog.html > newcatalog.html
```

The `-e` switch tells `sed` to execute the following argument as a command. The command itself, a simple substitution, replaces all occurrences of the string "laptop" with the string "notebook" in the file "catalog.html." If the first string occurs more than once on any given line, it is replaced each time. It then prints the results to `STDOUT`, where the shell redirects them into a new file named "newcatalog.html." What could be easier to understand? For that matter, what could be easier to type? This certainly saves time over editing each line in the file manually, especially if the product line contains hundreds or even thousands of items.

You can see from the relative ease with which the previous command was explained that `sed` can be employed with great success in simple cases (such as when the company decides, under legal pressure, that the term "laptop" is perhaps inappropriate for computers capable of generating enough heat to severely burn the unwary). However, there was nothing terribly complex about the previous command. Let's look at a case where `sed` might be used to solve a different problem. Suppose the file in question contains several HTML anchors, or links, whose contents are incorrect.

Building on the previous example, let's assume that the company has decided to change any URLs on their Web site that contain the strings "laptop" or "laptops," replacing them with the equivalent (and much less actionable) "notebook." We've already symbolically linked the old "laptops" directory to the newer "notebooks," and now it's just a question of finding all the old links and transforming them so they use the new form. With sed, this is straightforward. In fact, you could run the previous command on each file and come out with flying colors. Because "laptop" and "laptops" both contain the string "laptop," you can simply replace "laptop" with "notebook" and catch all occurrences – plural or otherwise. Voila!

Unfortunately, just as you're wrapping up for the day, your boss comes in and asks if your replace command renamed files, or just directories, that it found within URLs. Of course, you didn't consider that replacing "laptop.html" with "notebook.html" would cause a 404 File Not Found error for your users. Fortunately, you have backups, so you start over, using your existing command as a basis for the new one. This time, you look through a few more files to familiarize yourself with the possibilities. You notice, as you scan through the various files that were affected by your previous replacement, that you also changed the file that announced to your sales force that the word "laptop" should be replaced by the word "notebook," resulting in the phrase:

```
use the word "notebook" instead of "notebook".
```

This obviously will not do, so you decide to restrict your search pattern to /laptop/, figuring that this will only catch occurrences within URLs. Looking back to the command you used the last time you modify it appropriately:

```
sed -e 's//laptop///notebook//g' file.html > new.html
```

When you attempt to run the command, however, sed prints the following and exits:

```
sed: No previous regular expression
```

The problem here, of course, is that the forward slash (/) is used by sed to delimit the search and replace patterns. sed is confused because you haven't asked it to find anything – the search pattern is empty. Yet you're telling it to replace what it finds with the word "laptop." The extra garbage on the end of the command is also good reason for sed to complain and quit. Fortunately, sed provides a way for you to signify that any special character that would otherwise be given special meaning, such as the forward slash in the previous example, should instead be treated as the character itself. All you have to do is "escape" the special character (also known as a *metacharacter*, which suggests the big problem here) by preceding it with a backslash (\). Applying the necessary backslashes to the previous command results in this:

```
sed -e 's/\/laptop\///\/notebook\//g' file.html > new.html
```

Not too bad, but now instead of a quickly scanned search and replace operation, we have one in which the user is not only required to understand the operation itself, but must also bear in mind those characters that might otherwise give sed the screaming fantods. In time, given sufficiently complex operations to perform requiring the use of regular expressions to be carried out on data that contains several different possible metacharacters, the command becomes well-nigh unrecognizable. Worse, if you misplace one character, you need to debug your whole command. What was once a simple search and replace command has become a multiline nightmare, difficult to construct correctly and even more difficult to debug.

Now let's say that the next replacement we need to make involves single quote marks. Your site's esteemed marketing director never could quite learn the difference between the plural and possessive. As a result, you have a few hundred pages worth of unedited content, all of which refers to your "product's" when it should refer to your "products." Fortunately, you have a copy of sed.

Again, this should be simple. We just set up a loop that performs the following substitution on every file in the marketing directory, represented by the variable $file:

```
sed -e 's/product's/products/g' $file > ${file}-fixed.html
```

This simple command nets us:

```
Unmatched '.
```

In order for the command to work properly, we have to backslash the single quote, right?

```
sed -e 's/product\'s/products/g' $file > ${file}-fixed.html
Unmatched '.
```

Nope. Well, let's try putting double quotes around the search and replace operation:

```
sed -e "'s/product\'s/products/g'" $file > ${file}-fixed.html
sed: Unknown command
```

Nope. But wait — does this error, shown in Figure 2-2, mean that the shell doesn't know about sed, or that sed doesn't know how to deal with the single-quoted command we just passed to it?

We can try using double quotes instead of single quotes to the command being passed to sed and see if that works:

```
sed -e "s/product\'s/products/g" $file > ${file}-fixed.html
```

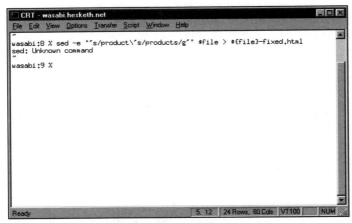

Figure 2-2: Is this the shell's error output, or sed's?

Yep, that works, in that sed no longer complains about not knowing the command, but now sed is looking for the literal string product\'s, which it's not going to find. Finally, we remove the backslash from the single quote and get the results we wanted in the first place. What were they again?

UNIX purists and adepts will immediately complain that this example is unfair, and that newer tools (such as perl) have become available that address the problems we demonstrate. The author of perl, the Practical Extraction and Report Language, variously describes the problem just discussed as "leaning toothpick syndrome," "punctuation overload," and "backslashitis," and provides several different methods of handling it. Please bear with us here; we're trying to prove a point about the importance of simple interface conventions, not beat up on UNIX tools. In fact, Steven used perl to solve a problem remarkably similar to the one discussed previously.

However, the fact remains that users are required to be aware of the problem they wish to solve, the syntactical conventions by which the solution might be expressed, and the syntactical conventions that interfere with the simple expression of the solution. At the same time, the user must hold a mental model of the changes that are likely to result. By requiring the user to implement workarounds for the very environment they are forced to work in, the shell severely limits ease of use. It also has a tendency to become a receptacle for exceptions to the rule rather than a clear, consistent, and coherent environment. In the next section, we spend some time talking about one particular exception to a common convention and discuss why the exception makes sense from a given standpoint, but more often results in frustration and error.

The previous sed example is just one instance of a serious flaw in the text-based command-line interface. Often referred to as "overloading an interface," it amounts to the use of a single symbol or object to represent many different possible meanings that differ according to context. Because this is one of the fundamental characteristics of text in any case, a text-based interface is bound to suffer from it. GUIs are not immune to this problem, however, despite the immense variety found in iconographic representations, as the need to quickly identify a function often limits the choice of icons to those more universally applicable. Studies have shown over and over again that icons (such as a mailbox to represent mail) are anchored quite soundly in the particular context in which they are created. Few, if any, universal icons exist, even within relatively homogeneous, technologically advanced societies. The problem is compounded when those accustomed to graphically-oriented interfaces try to step back into the world of the command line. They are used to certain types of interaction, direct manipulation, event-driven environments, and iconography instead of the slightly more abstract text- and command-based interface.

When you use a tool like sed as we did above, you are required to think on several levels at once, whether you know it or not. sed, like many other UNIX tools, is guilty of forcing the user to think one way when invoking the program itself, to think another way when telling the program specifically what to do, and, as if that weren't enough, to deal with the shell's vagaries as well. For example, you might first construct your general command without specifying which search and replace should occur, add the search and replace strings, and then perform a quick pass over the command to see if anything needs to be escaped to avoid problems with sed or the shell interpreting the search string as either a character with special meaning to sed, or with meaning to the shell. In the previous example, not only did we have to alter the way we were passing the command to sed, but we also had to alter it back after we decided on a different method of escaping metacharacters. In any case, you're probably wondering at this point what all this has to do with graphical user interfaces.

When designing a GUI, you are forced to make decisions based on the way the user is likely to interpret certain elements. By overloading the visual symbols used, you make the interface more difficult to use consistently, to say nothing of the manner in which the addition of alternate contexts complicates the programming required. The lessons to be learned here are simple:

- ◆ Don't overload your interface's elements.

- ◆ Don't require the user to remember what context they are in.

- ◆ Don't provide too many ways for the user to make mistakes.

- ◆ Do provide a simple and unobstructed method for the user to accomplish the task at hand.

When you design an interface, you establish certain conventions for representing the state of the application. Violate these conventions at your own peril, but the user is the one who suffers from an interface that is suddenly much more difficult to use consistently. In the next section, we discuss a common UNIX convention and the manner in which it is observed by one command and violated by another.

CHMOD/CHOWN/CP: A PROBLEMATIC CASE (-R VS. –R)

The concept of *recursion* plays an important role in the UNIX world, as it does within the world of programming in general. Simply put, recursion is a method for executing the same task on a series of objects until a certain condition is met. Usually (but not always), this also involves a program or function calling itself, and commonly refers to a task performed on all the files in a directory tree, including all of its subdirectories and their files. When you want to copy a directory tree and all of its files from one place to another, you use the UNIX command cp, short for "copy," using the recursive switch. The switch signifies that the command should be performed on not only those files in the current directory, but also on those of its subdirectories. Let's say you want to copy the directory tree found in dir/ to the directory /some/other/dir. You would use the following command:

```
cp -r dir/ /some/other/dir
```

The -r switch here means recursive. When the command is done executing, the entire directory tree found in the first directory has been copied to the second, creating it if necessary. This is wonderful, and exactly what we should expect. Like most early UNIX commands, everything is lowercase. Some UNIX instructors introduce their first class with a reminder that not only is UNIX case-sensitive, but that students from the DOS world should simply lowercase everything in UNIX. Later, the exceptions start to mount, but for introductory classes this is a handy rule of thumb.

Now, let's say that as part of the task of copying the files, you also want to change their ownership, effectively giving a copy of your files to another user to do with as they will. In the grand scheme of things, the set of commands required to perform this task might include not only the cp command with its -r switch, but also the chown command. chown is a simple command, taking as its arguments the user ID of the person who is to take ownership and the filename of the file to change. However, chown also has a recursive switch. So the user may assume that just as with cp, chown takes the -r switch. Surprise! It doesn't, as you can see in Figure 2-3.

```
chown -r schampeo /some/other/dir
chown: invalid option -- r
Try `chown --help' for more information.
```

We peek at the help message, using the switch suggested by the error message, only to find that chown instead uses the -R switch to signify recursion. Figuring out exactly why is an exercise best left up to the reader, although it may have something to do with the chmod command, discussed next. You see, the chmod command, used in UNIX to change the access permissions on files, has several switches and arguments. In UNIX, a file or directory may have read, write, and execute permissions assigned to the file's owner, group, or the rest of the world. Generally, these permissions may be represented either as octal numbers, which we won't get

into here, or as mnemonic clusters of letters such as those shown in the following
file listing:

```
-rwxrw-r--   1 schampeo hesketh         20 Aug  2 23:28 example
```

Figure 2-3: Getting help for the chown command

The first `rwx` represents the user's permissions, signifying that the owner may
read, write to, and execute the file. The second set represents the permissions held
by members of the user's group, meaning that the other members of the group `hesketh`
may read and write, but not execute, the file. Finally, everyone who is not part
of the `hesketh` group may read the file but not change or execute it. To change
these permissions, for instance, to forbid anyone outside of group `hesketh` from
reading the file at all, you would invoke the `chmod` command as follows:

```
chmod o-r example
```

This shorthand uses `o` to represent "other," the minus to represent the act of taking
away the particular form of access, and the `r` to represent the "read" access permissions.
(We won't go into whether it's a useful mnemonic, seeing as how Steven
always forgets and assumes that `o` represents "owner" instead of "other.") To make
it easier for the programmer to implement using the standard C library functions
for processing command-line switches, the useful function that enables the user to
change permissions recursively has been relegated to the `-R` command-line switch.
So, to take away others' right to read the files in the directory tree we just copied
above, we would invoke the following command:

```
chmod -R o-r /some/other/dir
```

In this case, the more common usage, that of `-r` representing "read" permissions, is the easier switch to type. The less common functionality is relegated to the realm of the uppercase. Because the `chown` and `chmod` commands perform similar functions — changing the ownership and access permissions associated with a file — whereas the `cp` command copies files to new locations in the file system, there are some interesting and valid reasons why such violations of convention are appropriate. From another perspective, one could ask whether the `-r` switch should even be called a convention. This begs the academic question and leaves the user struggling, however.

In recent years, UNIX system developers have begun to implement longer switches using full words rather than abbreviations to represent common functions. The POSIX standard specifies which words should be used to ensure commonality across all implementations. In the case we've been picking on, they have chosen `--recursive` to represent the user's will that the functionality be undertaken in a recursive manner, however appropriate. In fact, the Linux system Steven uses provides the `-R` switch to `cp` as an act of backwards adherence to convention, so it looks like things are starting to get easier to use. Of course, he's already learned the older syntax and used it incorrectly in so many circumstances he has practically burned them both into his psyche, so he always has to double-check before proceeding with the command.

The lessons to be learned here are twofold. The first lesson relates to the earlier warning about violating conventions and forcing the user to remember context in order to properly complete a task. The second lesson raises questions about how interfaces are learned. If a user learns how to accomplish a task one way, and then has difficulty applying exceptions to that knowledge in order to accomplish a related task, there is little you can do to reverse that damage. You can modify the interface to provide clearer methods of representing the task's context, but you do so at the risk of either irritating the accomplished user, or confusing the novice with more detail than they feel comfortable with. It is noteworthy that the `cp` command on Steven's system provides long switches for every short switch available. In our experience, very few introductory UNIX classes focus on the long switches, as they are not always available on every UNIX system. Therefore, it is likely that the only people using the longer switches are established programmers who are already extremely familiar with the functionality associated with each command, and who make a conscious decision to write verbose shell scripts. Of course, there are probably a few who got burned too many times by the `-r` vs `-R` problem, and who always type `--recursive`, but we bet they aren't the majority. To sum up this section:

◆ Don't expect your users to remember a zillion exceptions to a convention.

◆ Don't expect users to relearn an interface just because you find out later that it's broken and in need of a complete overhaul.

Some Benefits of CLIs

In the previous sections, we've shown in mind-bending detail how simple interfaces (such as the text-based command-line interface) may be subject to serious flaws by the very nature of their simplicity. Hopefully, we've also made it clear that part of the problem with UNIX has to do with the assumptions its designers made about its users. To a large extent, these problems weren't really problems until UNIX gained a large, nontechnical user base and those assumptions proved invalid. The CLI is powerful and flexible, especially for programmers and those for whom the assumptions that informed its design are still valid. For the sake of completeness, we recap some of these assumptions in this section. We also briefly summarize how – for those users about whom the assumptions are appropriate – the CLI provides a powerful, flexible, and often more direct model for interacting with the underlying system.

First, CLIs are powerful. It is possible to specify a command with a much greater level of detail, and with its own internal logic, using the command line. The text-based model provides almost infinite possibilities for creativity in as many different languages and environments as are possible. If the user doesn't like the quirks of a particular shell, they can choose another and still interact with the same underlying system. If the scripting language they know best doesn't support the sorts of tasks they are required to perform, they can learn one that does support those tasks.

The command-line interface is also extremely flexible. It is possible to combine the use of a shell with the use of other languages to invoke still other programs, using the output of one to serve as input for another, in an inherently customizable fashion. The UNIX philosophy of providing well-defined tools to perform specific tasks scales well when it comes to using the existing tools together to create new tools. It is a programmer's haven.

In a sense, as most skilled command-line users have found, using the keyboard alone to communicate with the underlying system can be much quicker than trying to switch back and forth between the mouse and the keyboard. It's more than just the physical aspects of using two different types of input devices, however. The switch from a visual, symbolic, metaphorical environment to a text-based, literal environment and back can be disorienting. For skilled users, fast typists, and programmers, the supposed ease of use offered by the graphical environment is a cumbersome burden and empty promise limited to the speed at which the user can manipulate menus, icons, and other single-action interface elements.

From the standpoint of interface design, the CLI represents a giant leap forward from the punched card days of yore. Careful study of the mistakes its designers made can be extremely fruitful for designers of future CLIs, not to mention GUI designers. A key benefit to CLIs in general, and UNIX and its ilk specifically, is the ability to connect to a server from anywhere using a client that supports the text-based interface. Because of its relative simplicity, it's possible to be logged into a server in San Francisco, California and have everything appear just as though it were running locally from your home in Raleigh, North Carolina.

It is possible, with special software, to use the network for the transmission of GUI sessions as well, as X Windows and Citrix's WinFrame have demonstrated with UNIX applications and Windows NT applications, respectively. And, of course, the Web is another example of how a remote server may transmit a GUI.

The implications of certain types of architectures, of which the UNIX command line is just one, are discussed later in this chapter and the rest of the book. For now, it is sufficient to realize that when you are logged into a remote system, every character you type is sent as is to the remote system. For all practical intents and purposes, the session is the same as it would be if you were logged in locally. The only difference is the manner in which traffic is transmitted between the user and the system—local keystrokes remain local, and remote keystrokes must be sent over the network between the systems. Mainframe systems, covered in the next section, offer another alternative for remote use and an interesting method of organizing their interfaces.

Mainframe Applications: Screens

The programmers and system designers who built the original mainframe systems were seldom motivated by the desire to provide a comfortable environment for programmers (as were the designers of UNIX), but rather by the necessity to provide usable, comprehensive, and monolithic *applications*. For the most part, mainframe applications then and now enable the user to manipulate data—to enter, update, view, or delete information in well-defined contexts. Usually, though not always, the business rules of an industry or corporation define these contexts.

One of the applications with which most of us are intimately familiar, but may have never seen, can be found at the airline ticket counter. How many times have you watched a ticket counter attendant tab through a million fields, staring intently at the screen before them, while you wait with a thousand-pound backpack on your back and a pet carrier in your hands? Now, due to the advent of the Web and the popularity of the Common Gateway Interface (CGI), anyone can see what the attendants behind the ticket counter have been seeing for years from the comfort of their own home or office. It's just that the screens are black type on white or gray backgrounds instead of neon yellow or green type on a black background, and they're visible from a browser. We can't show you screenshots from the terminals themselves. Fortunately, we can show you "Webified" versions of the same mainframe applications. So you'll just have to take our word for it that these Web-based applications are often little more than the characters that would be sent to the terminal, rearranged and returned to the browser instead.

The aptly named technique often employed by those who have to deal with mainframe, or *legacy* systems, when porting their interfaces to the Web is known as *screen-scraping*. Essentially, the mainframe sends a stream of characters to the terminal that the terminal interprets and uses to update the display. A screen-scraping application translates those characters into static displays capable of being sent back to the browser. Input is usually handled via forms, though advanced applications use techniques more appropriate than CGI for such tasks. The end result, however, is a Web-enabled series of screens, perhaps more suited to the mainframe environment than to the Web, especially in the age of advanced JavaScript and dynamic HTML.

The Computer Behind the Ticket Counter

The history of mainframes would not be complete without a discussion of the SABRE system, jointly developed by IBM and American Airlines to manage airline travel reservations and seating. At the time of its introduction, SABRE was the largest real-time corporate data processing system in existence, second only to those in use by the United States government. Over time, SABRE and its successors became the default means of obtaining ticket information, hotel and rental reservations, and other travel services. It was only natural that such a ubiquitous system should be ported to the Web.

There are actually many ways to connect to SABRE, but we'll focus on the screen-based implementation, easySABRE, which is much closer to the look and feel of the original terminal application, down to the screen. User input is given via a single HTML text input field, and there is a one-to-one relationship between the screens of the original interface and the Web version, with concessions for the inability to update the screen once it has been displayed on the client. When the user first enters the site, she is greeted with a screen that asks her to log in or choose one of several options, as shown in Figure 2-4.

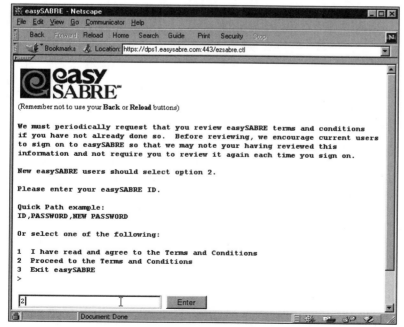

Figure 2-4: Emulating a mainframe interface via the Web

As the user progresses through the site, every option is marked — not with a hypertext link or other appropriate Web navigation, but with a numeric identifier that the user must type into the input field in order to proceed. The user is warned not to reload or attempt to use the Back button (see Figure 2-5, top left), thereby limiting the browser's interface severely, in addition to not making appropriate use of basic Web navigation. The screens are terse, 80 characters wide, and generally resemble what the average ticket clerk would see on their terminal.

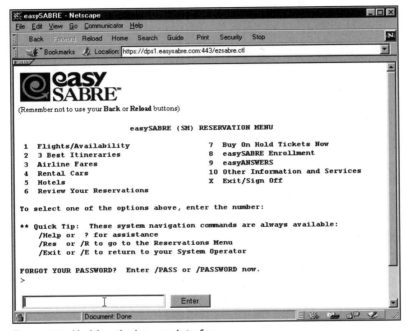

Figure 2-5: Limiting the browser interface

While its Web interface may not look like much, the easySABRE system is a technical marvel, and one of the oldest systems still operating in the world. Travelocity, another interface to SABRE, uses a more complex approach, requiring the user to enter a great deal of data all at once, and then accessing the back end system in order to determine what flights and other services are available. In addition, the Travelocity interface (shown in Figure 2-6) is geared towards the travel professional accustomed to booking flights in terms of "segments" rather than simply origin and destination cities.

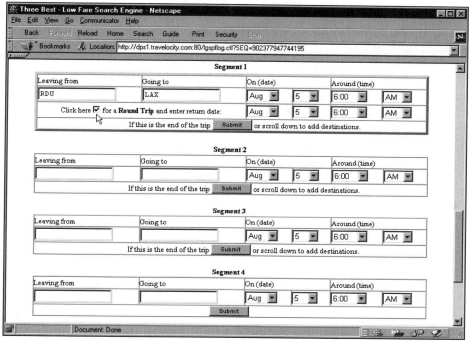

Figure 2-6: Travelocity's segment-based flight search interface

IBM's CallUp (and the "Webified" Version)

IBM's CallUp is another extensively used mainframe-based system that has been ported to the Web, although the Web interface does not allow for modification of most of the data it contains, likely due to security reasons. CallUp is a sort of employee directory and purchasing/procurement system interface that enables IBM employees to find other employees, order equipment, and perform other administrative duties via a terminal session. The searching functionality, in which one employee can find out phone and office numbers, organizational information, and so forth, has been ported to the Web, as shown in Figure 2-7.

The first thing one notices about the Web version of CallUp, shown in Figure 2-8, is that it is very simple, linear, and doesn't allow the user to edit most of their information or perform many of the functions available to the terminal-based user. This is typical of applications that have been ported, or *gatewayed,* to the Web, as the complex user input available to the terminal user is difficult to replicate from a basic Web interface.

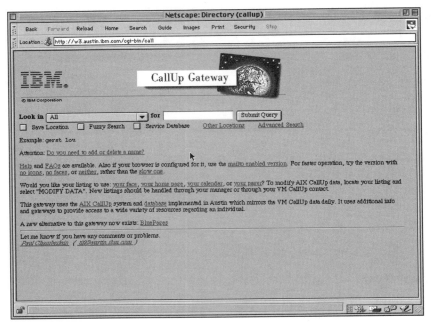

Figure 2-7: Using IBM's CallUp gateway

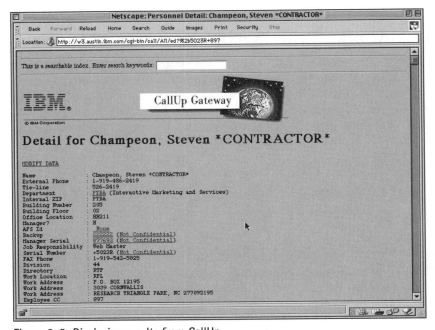

Figure 2-8: Displaying results from CallUp

When a developer modifies the code in an application so that it will run on a different platform, the resulting application is known as a *port*. When the developer simply provides a mechanism enabling users to access information from the application (running on its native system) to other systems, it is known as a *gateway*. Web browsers are often used to allow access to gatewayed information when it is not feasible to port the legacy application to every platform.

To summarize, screen-based systems are serial, fixed, and usually monolithic. They're hard to port and gateway to the Web. They generally exist in large corporate or government environments, and many early CGI applications took the screen model as their basic formula due to the difficulty of providing real-time interaction. In a sense, early CGI apps were even worse than mainframe/terminal apps, because they lacked the full input capabilities of terminals, but the power and cross-platform nature of CGI more than made up for it. Now it's time to try to correct some of those interface nightmares, if possible, using DHTML.

The Graphical User Interface

Studies into the feasibility of graphical user interfaces began in the early sixties, although what they termed graphical user interfaces then and what they are widely recognized as today are vastly different things. Ivan Sutherland is considered by many to be the father of the graphical user interface, beginning with a vector-based drawing program called Sketchpad, which he wrote for his dissertation in the computer science program at MIT in 1962. Using a light pen and a light-sensitive screen, the user could draw circles, lines, and points. Later experiments in GUI design were conducted by researchers at MIT, IBM, and quite notably by the Xerox Palo Alto Research Center, or Xerox PARC.

Xerox PARC and the Alto

While the rest of the world toiled to create better mainframe screen layouts, the researchers at Xerox PARC were developing a breakthrough technology based on a few simple ideas. Exploratory research into object-oriented languages had enabled the manipulation of onscreen bitmaps that graphically represented the user's environment in a new way. Instead of using text to interact with the system, the Alto, Xerox's attempt at a revolutionary personal computer system, used menus, icons, windows, and a mouse. The Alto was the first system to do so, though Xerox never marketed it. The Alto's successor, the Xerox Star, *was* marketed, but never sold very well. The most important thing about the Alto was not only that it served as a proof of concept, but that it also inspired the system programmers at Apple. Those programmers would eventually resolve several issues, such as overlapping windows and the click-and-drag problem that plagued the development of the Star.

Apple Lisa

The next step in the development of the graphical user interface was the Apple Lisa, inspired by the work done at Xerox PARC. First released in 1982, the Lisa featured floppy and hard disk drives, a mouse, and bitmapped graphics. Despite having a high price tag, and therefore limited commercial success (read: failure), the Lisa is important for being the first in a series of developments at Apple that led to the introduction of the Macintosh. In fact, many features present in the Lisa's operating system, such as limited multitasking, and desktop metaphor, such as stationery pads, were only later included in the Macintosh when they became affordable for Apple to implement.

Apple Macintosh

The Macintosh, as Apple's marketing efforts claimed, was "the computer that changed everything." Introduced during the 1984 Super Bowl, several months after the release of the IBM PC, the first Macintosh defined the graphical user interface for most consumers despite being underpowered and lacking software. All the elements that we find in today's modern GUIs were present in the original *desktop metaphor*, which consisted of a mocked up desktop that used icons to represent files, disks, and programs; menus that permitted the user to select tasks; windows to display the contents of open files and applications; and the mouse pointer to manipulate those objects. The Macintosh was a cheaper and more attractive presentation of many of the ideas present in the Lisa, but it sacrificed a great deal of the feature set in the process. Of course, the Macintosh proved immensely popular, eventually serving as the model for dozens of imitators – notably, Microsoft Windows.

Microsoft Windows, Windows 95

The story of the development of the original Microsoft Windows is awash in controversy over whether it was original and innovative, or merely a poor copy of the Macintosh. However, there can be no doubt that its success has changed the way people interact with their computers. Whereas the Macintosh has been remarkably popular with certain market segments (graphic artists and the desktop publishing industry, for example), Windows, by virtue of its being the first GUI for the widely used IBM PC, is the GUI that most people first used and that many continue to use. With the introduction of Windows 95 in 1995, Microsoft moved closer to a system that satisfied the needs of the novice user while remaining true to the goal of providing an improved GUI environment for business and personal software.

The X Window System

The traditionally text-driven command-line environment of UNIX systems was supplemented by the development of the X Window System at MIT. The idea was to provide a graphical user interface for UNIX and other systems based on the success of the Macintosh and Windows operating environments. One of X's essential differences was its separation of the application, or *client*, from the environment that displayed it, otherwise known as the *server*. X took this one step further, however, and also made it possible to choose different *window managers* that enabled the user to configure the look and feel of the overall GUI apart from the look and feel of individual applications.

 X uses the terms *client* and *server* in a confusing manner. We are now accustomed to thinking of the server as the remote computer and the client as the local computer. However, for X the server is running locally, enabling remote applications to display their interfaces to the user. When you hear people talk about *X servers*, they are really talking about the software that runs on the user's desktop.

The main significance of the split between client and server is that it is possible to run an application on a remote computer and display it locally, whether on a terminal or full-fledged workstation. Because the X protocols are platform-independent, it is possible, for example, for an application running on a UNIX server to display its interface on a Macintosh or Windows PC and for the user to interact with it as though it were running locally.

However, such interaction requires a lot of bandwidth, as the entire interface must be sent to the X server in order to be displayed. Every change in the application's display must be sent as well, and all user interaction sent back to the client. We examine in much greater detail the significance of networked applications and the client/server model in later chapters. Suffice it to say that the dream of a powerful, locally executed GUI application that leverages the network for data transfer is now within our grasp.

The graphical user interface has had a long and varied history, from the early vector-based days of Sketchpad to the development of the WIMP metaphor (Windows, Icons, Menus, and Pointers) through the introduction of the Macintosh and subsequent domination of the market by Microsoft Windows. The key elements of any GUI (and any hardware system that supports it) have been more or less decided. The mouse and mouse pointer, icons, windows, and keyboard interaction have been supplemented by other features and input/output devices, but the fundamental model is extremely pervasive. Perhaps this is because it is popular with users, or perhaps it reflects a certain lack of imagination on the part of most application interface designers. In any case, another extremely popular means of interacting with information, *hypertext*, involves some very different organizational concepts, which are described in the next section.

Hypertext and Hypermedia

One characteristic (and, indeed, a primary strength) of the WIMP environment is that it has a tendency to be extremely linear, direct, and simple. Objects on screen are intended to represent underlying system objects, or at very least, metaphorical wholes, complete and more or less self-contained. A file has an icon, fills a window, lives somewhere on disk, has a start and a finish, and rarely references other objects. There are notable cases where files do reference other objects, but such references are almost always intended to construct a single document out of its constituent parts, not allow the free-form tracing of its relationships, or the construction of objects consisting of little else besides those relationships. The term *hypertext,* coined by Theodor Holm Nelson during the early sixties, represents a system of information in which the resultant objects are not the goal, but rather the relationships between and the pathways through them. Nelson is widely recognized as both crackpot and genius for his seminal works on the theory of hypertext, but his ideas were foreshadowed by other thinkers and implemented by still others.

Vannevar Bush's Memex

Vannevar Bush, one of the leading scientific minds of his generation, was also a proponent of the popularization of science and technology. He believed that an educated public would benefit tremendously from, and demand the creation of, tools that would help them cope with what he saw as an increasing flow of information. This rising tide of information was due to the pervasive new media of his day, television and radio, but also to the increasing pace of scientific discovery and research. Bush, in his article for the July 1945 issue of *Atlantic Monthly,* "As We May Think," suggested that people needed a tool that would not only allow for the collation and organization of information, but that would also enable the user to build paths between bits of information, add annotations, and share those collections with others.

The article is interesting for this discussion because it is one of the first recorded treatments of associative connections between bits of information being as important or more important than the information itself; where technology, rather than a system of indexing, would enable people to access the information more naturally. In fact, Bush believed that his tool, called the *Memex,* would eventually replace the traditionally hierarchical methods of indexing and storage due to its closer accord with the way that people tend to remember and relate. Bush envisioned the device as a powerful microfilm viewer with extra capabilities for viewing several pieces of film at once based on the relationships between them. It would enable the user to construct even more sets of related information, annotating and storing such collections for later retrieval. Of course, his vision is much different than the disk- and removable-media world we now inhabit — or is it?

Ted Nelson's Xanadu

No one person has been more prolific from the standpoint of writing about hypertext than Theodor "Ted" Holm Nelson, the man who coined the term itself. His books tend to be flights of organizational fancy, being merely two-dimensional, serialized representations of the works he would produce if only his Xanadu software were in popular usage. Nelson originally envisioned Xanadu as a way to provide metered access to quotes from various literary works and appropriate compensation to the authors of those works, as well as a tool by which such authoring-by-quotation, or *transclusion*, as Nelson calls it, would be done. Xanadu became perhaps the longest-running vaporware project in computing history. However, his books, which talk about the principles around which Xanadu would be built as well as the general principles that govern any hypertext or hypermedia, are veritable gold mines of ideas, and served as the basis for many of the projects that followed.

HyperCard

Bill Atkinson's HyperCard was perhaps the most popular hypertext tool in history before the advent of the World Wide Web. By enabling the user to create hypertext and hypermedia collections known as *stacks* with simple, easy-to-use tools, HyperCard became the de facto method for distributing large collections of information (blending text, graphics, sound, and other, more traditional user interface elements such as buttons and scrollbars) as self-contained packages. Released in 1987, HyperCard gave Macintosh users and developers a way to share recipes, games, birdcalls, and all kinds of other information. Very active HyperCard communities are still around today. Many members of these communities consider other tools lacking in the unique combination of power, flexibility, and ease of use offered by HyperCard.

Gopher

Gopher will go down in history as a good idea that just didn't hit the mark. Designed to be a simple, but powerful, hierarchical text-based and menu-driven system for navigating through enormous quantities of information, Gopher was developed at the University of Minnesota in the late eighties. Its biggest weakness was that Gopher only enabled hierarchical navigation, as opposed to the free-form linking used by HTML and the Web.

Certainly, some of the better Gopher sites are more informative and better organized than many Web sites. However, Gopher's limited presentation and organizational options led users to abandon it in droves in favor of the more flexible linking model used by HTML. Over a 9600 baud modem connection, however, it's still pretty hard to beat.

The WWW/NCSA Mosaic

We probably don't need to explain too much about NCSA Mosaic and the World Wide Web to readers of this book. For the sake of completeness, though, it should be stated that the Web owes its phenomenal success and the Internet its astounding growth to one killer app from Illinois and its developers, Marc Andreessen and Eric Bina. NCSA, the National Center for Supercomputing Applications, was home to the development of Mosaic, a graphical browser for navigating the Internet. By including support for the various popular Internet protocols and services, such as ftp, Gopher, USENET, and the then almost nonexistent World Wide Web, Mosaic made it possible for nontechnical users to access the Internet in ways few people imagined. Mosaic was a major development in the usability of the Net, putting a GUI interface on what was previously a mostly command-line driven environment. For that reason alone, it would be worth consideration, but Mosaic also ushered in an age where everyone could become an interface designer just by making use of a few markup elements and graphics.

Unfortunately, Mosaic, and later Netscape Navigator, also introduced new interface and layout features (such as configurable background and link colors, frames, forms, and tables) that increased the complexity of interfaces beyond measure. Gone were the days of standard (if ill-chosen) link colors, the simple bulleted list, and the single-input query interface. Legions of amateur Web authors faced the task of choosing the appropriate interface elements for their applications, often with disastrous results. The debate over the proper use of the standard form elements, layout tricks, and color still rages on among usability experts, but on one thing they are unanimously agreed: Most Web design could stand to learn something about interface theory.

The hype that surrounded the advent of the Web made for a forgiving audience, who knew that a page may have been authored by someone no more skilled than themselves, but it also made for some seriously flawed and practically unusable interfaces. If you're reading this book, you have probably come to this realization on your own. Or perhaps you began your career in a different authoring environment with more powerful tools, and want to emulate the power and flexibility of that environment. Many Web designers started out in multimedia production using Director, Authorware, and other proprietary tools.

Multimedia

When most computer interaction took place via punched cards, if not through text entered into keyboards, *multimedia* simply meant the combination of two forms of media, such as text and images, or text and sound or video. For example, the Graphics Interchange Format developed by CompuServe, which provided a way to include multiple images and comments in a single file, is bare bones multimedia.

Over time, as authoring tools and display environments became more powerful and commonplace, multimedia has come to suggest interactive presentations, games, and educational software where the user often controls the pace and direction of a fully integrated production containing text, sound, video, and complex interfaces.

Interactive CD-ROM (Voyager, Microsoft Encarta)

Interactive CD-ROM production drove the popularization of multimedia to a large extent, promising entertainment and education to the growing number of people with home computers. Voyager, one of the drivers in the interactive CD-ROM market, produced magazines, cultural materials, documentaries, and educational aids. Voyager's products leveraged multimedia's capability to provide sound clips of famous musical works, pictures of far-off lands, and video of natural phenomena in concert with text descriptions and passages from travelogues, encyclopedia articles, and other information. The cost of producing CD-ROMs, combined with the hidden costs of licensing content, the limited capabilities of early hardware, and other factors eventually led to the disappearance of many of the original players in multimedia, leaving the field to the big corporate guns like Microsoft.

Microsoft's Encarta, an encyclopedia on CD-ROM, was an immensely popular multimedia application, demonstrating to the masses what could be done with the medium. It mattered not that much if the information presented was truncated to make room for the full-motion video. Users were captivated by the ability to watch a hummingbird feed while reading about ornithology, or see a mountain gorilla look contentedly out of their computer screen at them as they read the works of Jane Goodall.

Another attraction was the ability to follow cross-references simply by clicking on a link, which is hypertext at its diversionary best. Encarta eventually became a cornerstone of the Microsoft Network, oddly enough, pitching the high-capacity CD-ROM environment over the low-bandwidth Internet, while at the same time exploring newer storage technology such as DVD for update releases of the standalone product.

Interactive TV

The promise of high-bandwidth cable modems, programmable television sets, and HDTV led to a frenzy of activity around the idea of *interactive television* during the early nineties. Home users would be able to order on-demand videos, do their banking, buy stamps, and perform various other commerce- and entertainment-related tasks, all via an interactive TV interface.

Interactive TV is generally regarded as having been mostly hype, overshadowed by the Internet and too reliant on high-bandwidth connections such as cable modems, ADSL, and ISDN, but it may very well rise again with the eventual rollout of the necessary bandwidth. Oddly enough, interactive TV gave the Web a similarly hyped language, Sun Microsystems' Java, which started out life as a replacement for C and C++ for use in set-top boxes.

Kiosks

Another popular use for multimedia applications is the kiosk, like those found in shopping malls, sporting goods stores, and at other point-of-sale locations. Usually designed to be extremely simple and easy to use, kiosks often include touch screens, sound, and video. Some kiosks are limited to providing directions for confused or lost shoppers, but others are far more sophisticated and involve searchable databases for music, books, or movie catalogs, for example. Another popular use for kiosks is the interview, where a series of progressively more specific questions are posed and their answers gathered so as to direct the user to the information they require.

Other Currents

By no means does the foregoing list exhaust the possibilities for interface design, either in terms of functionality or target audience. Many other interfaces have been devised over the years in order to train or educate, demonstrate, and/or entertain. These special interfaces are often the result of very specific implementation goals. Many are not necessarily intended to provide the full functionality we are accustomed to as users of GUI-driven personal computers. However, some are notable in that they completely redefine the interface while running on a PC, and require the user to come to terms with them or not play at all.

Educational Interfaces

Educational software often provides a specialized sort of interface with its own unique challenges and assumptions about its audience. Because educational software is designed to teach through interaction, the underlying systems can become quite complex, not only dealing with regular interaction but also testing to see if user input is appropriate, and then responding with helpful hints or admonishing with warnings.

COMPUTER-BASED TRAINING (CBT)

Computer-based training programs are a special breed—a mix between demonstration and tracking of interaction. Because many CBT programs are meant to be used in a classroom setting or in self-paced individual training, they must be flexible enough to allow for both. Some focus on providing text-based instruction with screenshots (more or less like a book, only perhaps more portable), and others use detailed video and interactive forms to test your understanding of the material presented.

LOGO AND THE TURTLES

Logo, a dialect of LISP designed to help teach children the art of programming, was created at Bolt, Beranek and Newman during the late sixties. Wally Feurzeig, Paul Wexelblat, and Seymour Papert, the language's designers, built Logo with the aim of minimizing the arcana of programming syntax while giving instant feedback to the user. In its original implementation, the language interpreter controlled a small robot, nicknamed the "turtle" after its turtle-like shell. The user could control the turtle by running programs written in Logo, drawing multicolored lines on a piece of paper, or making the turtle rotate or travel in various directions. As time went on, it became cheaper to use graphics display terminals and abandon the use of the robot altogether, but the moniker stuck and much of Logo's terminology is stated in terms of the *turtle*, which is simply a drawing pointer. There is even a version of Logo that lets the user control their own LEGO robot, which they can build themselves.

An interesting facet to the Logo story is that rather than teaching facts or procedures, as is common in the computer-based training software mentioned above, Logo helps to teach children how to learn. The side effect, learning how to program, is less important than the problem solving, exploration, and empowerment that accompanies this sort of learning. Memorizing facts, figures, relationships, and so forth is tedious. Logo makes it possible for children and other users to explore relationships, coming up with their own approach to solving a problem or expressing a relationship. The sorts of discoveries made by the Logo researchers have wide-ranging implications for the design of interfaces in general, not just for educational software. Users, at any stage in their mental development, require interfaces that:

- Provide mechanisms that give the user immediate control of an object

- Provide simple commands and program structure without complex syntax

- Enable the user to identify with the object itself, rather than an abstraction

The definitions of *simple* and *complex* varies with the audience, as does the ability to handle abstractions, identify tasks with objects and representations of objects, and so forth, but the lessons of the turtle are universal.

Entertainment (from Pong to MYST and Quake)

When Steven was seven or eight, his father brought home a sleek silver box with detachable paddles and lots of wires coming out the back. He watched, interested, as his father plugged it in and wired it up to the television, and sat amazed as the TV screen lit up with a flying white dot and two little white lines that acted as paddles. They played their first few games of Pong. Of course, within a couple of years, the market for video games exploded, but he always remained more enamored of games like Asteroids, Star Castle, and Battlezone, whose simple vector graphics and no-frills interfaces would keep him enthralled for hours as he spent his lunch money in the arcade.

Games, by their nature, are intended to entertain. As a result, their interfaces generally need to make concessions to keep things simple: two buttons, a joystick or a paddle, and perhaps a foot pedal or steering wheel for racing games. Some games, to be sure, rank up with the Mayan Codex for complexity, but easy access to game functions is key. Interfaces designed to create the illusion of real-time interactivity, such as shoot-em-ups like Doom or Quake, need to be as simple as possible to use. Otherwise, the gamer gets tired of trying to remember how to pull out the tactical nuclear warhead launcher when menaced by aliens and goes off to play something else.

Still other games are designed to engage the user's intelligence, memory, and other less visceral capacities. One of the most popular games of recent years, MYST, uses puzzles and games in a fully rendered three-dimensional environment to draw the user into the story. As the user gets deeper into the game, more and more secrets are revealed, some of which apply to different levels of the game and help to solve the mystery. The interface itself is quite simple – all controlled by the mouse – but the world it reveals is incredibly complex. Music, sound effects, and stunning visuals are also vital for games aiming for the immersive effect, whether they are intellectual puzzles or multiplayer nuke-fests.

Summary

Interfaces come in all shapes, sizes, colors, and intentions. The audience, when you can accurately predict it, is the key to deciding how to construct the interface and what its goals should be. This chapter covered:

- ◆ The complexities that arise from simple interface elements

- ◆ How screens can be used to organize and manage access to functionality

- ◆ How organizational schemes appropriate for one environment or audience can be wildly inappropriate for others

- ◆ How the graphical user interface was born and developed over the past three decades

- ◆ How hypertext and multimedia promise more natural techniques for information management

- ◆ How interfaces for particular audiences compromise to fulfill their goals

Many different organizational systems and architectures underlie the interface and lend their own unique strengths and weaknesses to it. The designer must be careful to address the special challenges raised by the systems' underlying architectures in order to prevent inaccurate mental models from developing. The next chapter addresses this in more detail.

Chapter 3

Principles and Lessons Learned

IN THIS CHAPTER

- ◆ Interface types: task-oriented and goal-oriented

- ◆ The concepts of direct manipulation, modes, and context

- ◆ Keeping the user experience consistent

- ◆ Ways to express the user environment: metaphor and idiom

- ◆ More on mental models as they apply to the interface

- ◆ Building and scheduling for prototypes versus final implementations

- ◆ Usability testing as an eye-opener and confirmation of assumptions

HAVING DISCUSSED THE VARIOUS different types of applications and architectures you're likely to encounter in your work as an interface designer, it's time to pull back a bit and talk about the fundamental assumptions that fuel your design choices. Then, when you have a good grasp on some of the fundamentals, we'll dive back into the gory details of actually planning, building, testing, and reworking your interface.

Task-Oriented versus Goal-Oriented Interfaces

Designers must make some important decisions when planning an interface. In many cases, the requirements drive these decisions, but it helps to be aware of the overall picture. One commonly invoked distinction divides *task-oriented* interfaces from *goal-oriented* interfaces. A task-oriented interface tends to be fairly static, presenting elements for all the tasks the interface makes possible. A goal-oriented interface, on the other hand, develops and changes as the user proceeds toward the completion of a goal. We discuss some examples of each in the next couple of sections, and show you how to determine which type of interface you need to build.

Task-Oriented Interfaces

Office automation software, such as a word processor, text editor, or spreadsheet, is perhaps the most common task-oriented application. The choices presented to the user are fixed, and though they may vary by context (especially in feature-laden office suites), the tasks rarely change and do not vary in difficulty from one session to the next. If you want to check the spelling in the document you're working on today, you are able to do so in exactly the same way that you did yesterday. It doesn't matter how big the document is, how long you've been working on it, or how poorly (or well!) it is written.

So how do you know when you're dealing with a task-oriented interface? Ask yourself if the features of your application could be described independently, like different sections of a reference, a technical manual, or specification. If you can imagine your users skipping huge chunks of the manual to find out how to use one feature, neglecting the rest until such a time as those features are needed, odds are your application is mainly task-oriented.

To pose the same question another way, ask yourself if your application is linear. Do your users progress from one point to another, perhaps gaining points, solving puzzles, and interacting with the application in ways that change the environment, but not in ways that are easily reversed? If not, you might as well consider it task-oriented. Having no significant means of tracking progress or bringing about a fundamental evolution in the environment is a good indicator of task-orientation.

Of course, no application (or its corresponding interface) is completely one or the other. Games have preferences dialog boxes that may act as tiny task-oriented islands within oceans of goal-directed game-play. But lest you think that games are the only applications requiring goal-oriented interfaces, let's take a look at some other examples.

Goal-Oriented Interfaces

It may be obvious by now what characteristics qualify an interface as goal-oriented. If your application's interface or environment changes during the course of the user's interactions, or if the application itself is geared toward an end that may only be reached by way of a series of successfully completed events, it's clearly goal-oriented. Although games and other skill-based applications are obviously goal-oriented, many other types of applications feature these characteristics.

Recall the discussion of educational software in Chapter 2, "A Brief History of User Interface Design," in which the user builds on previous knowledge to accomplish newer, more challenging tasks. Or remember the example of demonstration software, which guides the user through a series of illustrative scenarios. Both of these types of software involve goals, although the tasks they present or illustrate may well be examples of task-oriented activity. Whereas a word processor doesn't increase in difficulty as we use it (at least we hope not), a demonstration version of the same software may include an interactive walkthrough where more and more difficult tasks are presented and their solutions discussed and dissected in order to show their workings.

This leads us to an interesting question: Is the Web task-oriented or goal-oriented? Some would have it one way, and others the opposite. The basic interface, after all, doesn't grow more difficult with use; hypertext links don't challenge the user with ever-increasing rewards for clicking the right link. Or do they? It is disingenuous to argue one way or the other. The Web presents simple tools that site designers and developers use to produce wildly divergent assemblages. There are instructional sites, personal productivity sites, reference sites, gaming sites, educational sites for children, Web-wide scavenger hunts, and much more. The Web's limits are defined by the imagination, not by restrictive categories such as those we have been discussing. With the tools provided us by dynamic HTML, we just extend the reach and functionality of either type of interface.

So when does a task-oriented interface become a goal-oriented interface, and vice versa? As we pointed out previously, although an application may have specifically goal-oriented intentions, it is possible to have completely task-oriented components. After all, at the level of the single interface element, it is rare to find one that evolves from representing a task to representing a goal. How do you design individual elements for one realm or the other? One way is to think in terms of the task an element represents, and in terms of its entire life cycle within the application. In other words, the importance of an interface element depends highly upon its context.

Direct Manipulation, Modes, Context, Consistency

A fundamental characteristic of the graphical user interface is its ability to represent its elements as though they were a part of the real world. Onscreen documents look like documents do in real life. Sliders, buttons, scrollbars, menus, and the mouse pointer all look like their real-life counterparts. But wait a minute. There are no scrollbars in real life, are there? No, but the basic metaphors of the desktop, or the icons representing files, programs, and the trash can (or recycle bin), all derive their representation from the nonvirtual world. The icons used in the Adobe Photoshop toolbar, shown in Figure 3-1, still portray tools that today's designers may never use, such as the cropping tool or airbrush. Why is this correspondence between the real world and the world of the system so important?

Crop tool →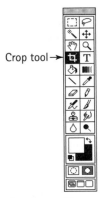

Figure 3–1: Has anyone using Photoshop today ever used a real crop tool?

The importance of metaphor in the graphical user interface environment follows from its primary intention: to enable the user to focus on the task or goal. The user should not need to remember the state of the system or translate her wishes into arcane commands, as we saw in the previous chapter with sed. The user should be able to click the mouse button with her finger and have that click correspond directly to an action on the screen, such as positioning the cursor in a document, opening a folder, or dragging a file to the trash can. This correspondence is known as *direct manipulation* and is the key to understanding everything else in the GUI world. In short, users should be able to act in ways that suggest or visually represent components of their corresponding real-life tasks. Want to throw that paper away? Drag the file's icon to the trash can. Some applications even extend the metaphor to apply to their own internal logic, such as Panic Software's Transit ftp tool, shown in Figure 3-2, where you can delete remote files by dragging them to a trash can icon within the application's main window.

In order to enable such a total identification of the real object and its virtual counterpart, you must follow several rules. Most of them are geared toward preventing dissonance between the user's experience of the real world and its digital doppelganger. A few are intended to make up for the fact that perfect identification is not possible, as well as to exercise the power of the computer beyond what is possible in the real world. After all, if working with computers presented a chaotic and random fantasyland where performing a task was no easier — and much more disturbing — than in real life, who would use computers?

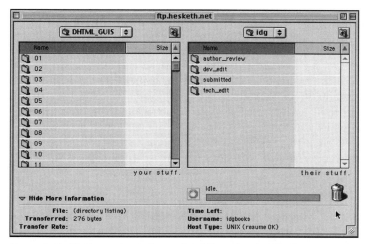

Figure 3-2: Making extended use of existing visual metaphors

Consistent Object Availability

Objects must be consistently and continuously visible, or available. Objects in real life do not fade or wink in and out of existence. Neither should our icons, buttons, and windows. This principle is stretched a bit, of course, when you consider the thousands of things that objects on the computer screen are capable of that real objects are not. As long as you follow the basic guideline of continuous presence, however, you may work around these other characteristics using other tools that might themselves represent actual objects. For instance, a tab might protrude slightly from the bottom of the menu bar of a word processor, enabling the user to hide the application's ruler with the click of a button. The same action might be performed equally well through the selection or deselection of a check box in a dialog box, but the more direct method is presented as well to help compensate for the slim chance of the ruler on a real typewriter disappearing. By way of analogy to the real world, an impossible real-world situation is allowed in the virtual environment of the word processor without disturbing the user's sense of the correctness of the interface.

This sense of everything being right with the interface allows for *transparency*, or the user's ability to concentrate on the task at hand without their mental model being challenged, treating the representation of the task on the screen as though it had a real existence. After extensive use, the user's conscious awareness of the interface fades due to its constant presence. Often, the metaphors and simplistic iconic representations must be pointed out to skilled users, who have long since assumed their reality in practical usage and forgotten their artificial nature.

When the task of providing objects for direct manipulation becomes a threat to the simplicity of the interface, compromises must be made. The use of text-based menu items to represent actions, for example, or status bars to inform the user of the state of the system, allows for *indirect manipulation*. Here, the user must perform some linguistic gymnastics and map the text label on a menu item to its corresponding action, rather than directly manipulating an object onscreen. Sometimes, it is simply impossible to provide a recognizable object, such as an icon, for a complex but common task. At times like this, a text-based menu item (such as the Empty Trash option) is more efficient than using an easily misunderstood iconic or objective representation (such as an icon of a sanitation engineer in an orange jumpsuit).

Speed and Feedback

All actions that the user can directly initiate should be able to be completed quickly. For actions that might take longer, or involve more complex background processes, the progress of the action should be represented to the user by a progress indicator, a status bar, or other feedback mechanism. This helps maintain the illusion of direct manipulation, even when the process is not in the user's hands. Often, this requirement of GUIs adds to system load and processing time, but maintaining the user's feeling of control over the situation is paramount and therefore justifies the extra time spent providing feedback. We discuss feedback mechanisms in more detail in Chapter 11, "The Hidden Feedback Form," and Chapter 12, "Other Kinds of Feedback."

Reversibility

Finally, to bring us around to where we started, any action undertaken by the user should be easily reversible by way of what is commonly called an Undo function. Any action not capable of being undone should provide a warning to the user alerting him to this fact. The problem with such notifications is that many common tasks are such that their reversibility is somewhat meaningless, and the user is merely burdened with constant reminders and requests for confirmation. Such instances are perhaps best served by forcing functions, discussed in greater detail in Chapter 1, "What Is an Interface?" By making it difficult for a user to initiate this sort of task accidentally, you reduce the need for a warning or confirmation.

The reason behind the requirement for ease of reversibility is that computers enable us to perform unnatural tasks that have no counterpart in real life. Examples include scrolling through a document, flipping through multiple open windows, activating pull-down menus, and even manipulating the cursor or mouse pointer. Because many of these tasks involve using the mouse or keyboard, they are not only prone to mistaken input, but also involve natural manipulation with potentially unintended consequences. Selecting and dragging and dropping text in a text editor or word processor is a good example. The process of selection is somewhat natural, and commonly performed. However, it is then possible (and highly likely) that the user will drag and drop the selected region into a section of the document where she did not intend for it to go. Such mistakes are side effects of the ease of use of the interface, and the user must be able to undo them easily with visible results or other notification.

The careful use of context is a commonly used mechanism for limiting the complexity of an interface. Out of a retinue of thousands of tasks, only a few are appropriate at any given moment in time. Goal-oriented interfaces arrange these tasks according to the current stage in the total course of the application, while task-oriented interfaces limit the user's access to actions in other ways. Some early attempts at providing a limiting context were simply reflections of the designers' and programmers' mental models, or of limitations in the software itself. Over time, interface theory has denounced a few of these limiting mechanisms. One, the modal dialog box, has become almost incontestable evidence of poor design, both from a programming standpoint and from the standpoint of the interface designer.

Why Are Modal Dialog Boxes Evil?

First, let's talk about what a modal dialog box *is*. A modal dialog box is a window that denies the user access to any other system functionality until it has either been recognized and dealt with (as in the case of a necessary or recommended action), or canceled, often terminating the action that spawned the dialog box in the first place. Modal dialog boxes are used for:

◆ Presenting status or error information (often called a *message box*)

◆ Asking the user for input or confirmation (often called a *prompt*)

The problem with true modal dialog boxes is that they interrupt the program flow as well as the user's flow. Nothing can proceed until the dialog box is acknowledged, as in the case of an error message, or until further information has been gathered, as in the case of confirmation dialog boxes, which often contain messages of their own notifying the user of a need to deal with an unexpected condition.

In some cases, such as unexpected errors, the modal dialog box is fine and the interface designer and user should recognize it as a helpful part of the application. However, it is too common that the modal dialog box, as in the sample shown in Figure 3-3, simply represents a poor information-gathering process that might be worked around, or pre-empted, by the gathering of appropriate input in the first place. Also, if the process that keeps presenting confirmation dialog boxes is expected to do so repeatedly, it should give the user a way to override it. This input should enable the user to confirm all file deletions within a given directory, for example, or allow the application to close all of its windows after one request for confirmation, rather than asking the same question before closing each window.

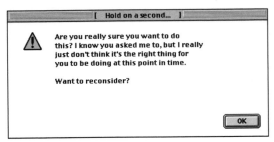

Figure 3-3: Modal dialog boxes can be used to do
some really annoying things

The modal dialog box problem represents a recurring theme in user interface design: the issue of appropriate abstraction and applying a single user input to a collection of similar tasks. By grouping similar tasks and building an application that demonstrates a capability to deal with such groupings, you make the use of your interface much less tedious. Another issue that usually comes up is how much redundancy the interface designer should provide.

Redundancy: How Many Different Ways Can the User Do the Same Thing?

Many people have input in deciding what features a given application should have. The programmer, project manager, marketing and sales departments, and even executive management all contribute to the definition of an application's feature set. It is up to the interface designer, however, to determine the best ways to expose those features to the user. We've discussed the relationship between objects, such as icons, which represent a simple task, and the more indirect text-based menu items, which may or may not map one-to-one to that simple task. When objects and menu items do map to the same function, the designer runs the risk of confusing the user, especially if both elements are present to the user at the same time.

In addition to those elements subject to direct manipulation even if their object involves a certain degree of indirect manipulation (such as selecting a text menu item by directly manipulating the pull-down menu), there is the question of keyboard shortcuts, macros, and other controlling input. It is not uncommon for an application to feature one or more of the following ways to initiate the same action:

◆ A metaphorical or iconic representation of an object, manipulatable by the mouse

◆ An icon on a toolbar

◆ A text label on (hopefully) a different toolbar

◆ A menu item

- ◆ A keyboard shortcut (also known as an *accelerator*)

- ◆ A response to a dialog box

- ◆ A side effect of another action

As you can see, this is quite a list, including extremely different methods of performing the same action. So how do you know when to provide one or more of these methods? The best answer, and the one that should be put into practice whenever possible, is that *you don't know*. Whenever you can, you should provide interfaces that are configurable by users themselves, giving them control over their interface. We delve further into this topic in Chapter 13, "User-Configurable Interfaces." For now, we should discuss the flip side of redundancy, often referred to as *overloading*.

Overloading: How Many Ways Can the User Do Different Things but Appear to Be Doing the Same Thing?

A prominent and controversial issue that always comes up when dealing with graphical interfaces is that of when, and how, to overload an interface element. *Overloading* refers to the practice of allowing the same interface element to represent different tasks depending upon the context it is invoked in. Because of the nature of graphical interfaces, the vocabulary of simple icons is extremely limited. The indirect method, that of providing text menu items, extends the reach of the interface to include the whole of written language. However, due to space considerations, such menu items and text labels on toolbar elements tend to be short and obscure. So how does the designer deal with a limited iconographic library and an obscure text vocabulary?

One answer is to use tricks such as intermittent *tool tips* or *help balloons,* activated if the mouse pointer lingers too long over a given element. The tool tip can deliver more information in a smaller space than the label can, but it is also subject to space limitations. The help balloon or file can often deliver too much information, and requires a more active intervention on the part of the user to initiate such verbose assistance. In any case, neither of these options addresses the fundamental problem of knowing when and why a given element's function changes. They merely provide a means by which the user can check the state of the element and perhaps learn about the function currently associated with it.

There are many ways in which an element can be considered overloaded. Depending on the element, overloading may be related to any of the following characteristics of the element:

- ◆ Its icon or text label

- ◆ Its placement or orientation

- ◆ Its state (for example, grayed-out menu items)

- Its color
- Its font
- Its size

The cursor or mouse pointer is a common victim of overloading. Due to overreliance upon the pointer for direct manipulation of objects, the pointer is often used as the following:

- A status indicator (the animated hourglass or watch icon)
- A positioning tool for selecting the object of the next mouse click
- A tool for dragging and dropping objects, text, or other elements (such as the thumb on a scrollbar, or buttons on a configurable toolbar)

The context in which the mouse pointer is overloaded is usually obvious, either by use of different pointer icons (also known as *cursors*) or other, separate status indicators. For the Web, and specifically for dynamic HTML or Java applications, the application may not be allowed to modify the mouse pointer. This restriction, often the result of a demand for stringent security (and possibly overridden by signed documents or other authentication mechanisms), puts a heavy burden on the casual developer not to associate too many functions with a single element. This has the unfortunate effect of shifting the load (or overload, as the case may be) to other less prominent elements.

 Cascading Style Sheets level 2 gives the developer ways to alter the appearance of the mouse pointer, or cursor, depending on the state of the application. At the time of this writing, however, the only browser to implement this mechanism properly is Microsoft Internet Explorer 4.0. With luck, the new versions of Netscape Navigator and Internet Explorer will both support this handy feature, making it available to the developer of cross-browser DHTML applications.

So how do you avoid confusing users? The answer is not clear. You can try the approaches outlined above (tool tips, help balloons, and other status identifiers), or you can simply limit the functionality of your interface. Serious interface designers don't accept either of these approaches, though. In some cases, as mentioned, it is possible to gain access to the functionality specifically forbidden to you, as with signed scripts or applets. Education is an important factor, but it is unfortunately out of your hands beyond the small efforts you may undertake with tool tips, help balloons, and so forth.

One tactic for avoiding confusion involves grouping your interface's elements (and their functionality) such that the context clearly determines the intended use of a given set. Even this is unsatisfactory, though. Emacs, the famous programming text editor, enables developers to create new editing modes, many of which use new menus and menu items, or modify the mode line (a sort of status bar) to reflect their presence. A great many of these modes also override the Tab or Enter keys, and modify their usual functions to control automatic indentation or commenting, to interpret LISP code in a buffer, or even – go figure – to insert a tab or enter character into the buffer itself. For example, when editing a Perl script in Emacs, a common mode uses the Tab key for the following functions, invoked depending on the situation:

- Indenting the current line of code

- Commenting out the current line of code

- Inserting a comment at the end of the line of code

- Removing a comment from the current line of code

Oddly, perhaps, there is no way to insert a tab character by itself when in `perl-mode` in Emacs. The Tab key is completely overloaded to the point of having replaced its default action, the insertion of a tab character, by a number of different functions. Fortunately, there isn't much use for tab characters in Perl scripts, other than those automatically inserted for the purpose of indenting code.

Let's take a step back from the specifics of particular interface elements and discuss some strategies that begin with the entire interface, treating it as an integrated whole.

Metaphor and Idiom, Mental Models

One extremely common and successful approach to top-down planning and integration of interface elements involves treating each element as an extension of a basic metaphor. This approach enables the individual elements to borrow from the strength of the overarching metaphor, reducing the need for each element to stand alone – something that is difficult in most circumstances, anyway, due to the extremely varied range of associations that people have with visual representations.

A popular work on the study of language, *Metaphors We Live By*, by George Lakoff and Mark Johnson, discusses metaphors as figures of speech that relate directly to our physical experience of our environment. These metaphors act as a base for embellishments on central themes. Starting with the idea of "more is up," derived from human beings' experience with piles of things, the authors demonstrate the manner that such basic ideas, or "root metaphors," influence other linguistic constructions.

MORE IS UP; LESS IS DOWN

The number of books printed each year keeps going *up*. His draft number is *high*. My income *rose* last year. The amount of artistic activity in this state has gone *down* in the past year. The number of errors he has made is incredibly *low*. His income *fell* last year. He is *under*age. If you're too hot, turn the heat *down*.

Physical basis: if you add more of a substance or of physical objects to a container or pile, the level goes up.

Lakoff, George, and Johnson, Mark. *Metaphors We Live By*. Chicago: Chicago University Press, 1979.

The use of metaphor in visual interfaces follows a similar model, making certain allowances for the differences between spoken or written language and visual representations. The interface designer starts with a basic metaphor, and then extends it with carefully chosen interface elements that play off users' associations with the basic metaphor.

This can have comical or confusing results, however, as the assumptions that go into making a leap from the base metaphor are often subjective and unlikely to translate across cultural boundaries. One solution to such confusion is to depend on *idiom*, or interface constructions that do not rely exclusively upon the metaphor, but are simple to learn, understand, and remember. Rather than assuming that a desk always has a telephone on it, and therefore that a telephone icon on the desktop will be universally recognized, for example, the interface designer might provide an element that diverges from the user's experience but whose appearance is unlikely to be mistaken for anything else. Such design strategies take the approach that something that is unusual but easily learned is better than something that is familiar but easily misconstrued.

Most interfaces balance the use of a basic metaphor with idiomatic elements in order to provide the most efficient use of the strengths of both approaches. In the following sections, we examine several examples of both approaches, discussing where they succeed and where they fail in order to help you decide when to use what approach in designing your interface.

The Macintosh Desktop Metaphor

The Macintosh desktop metaphor is perhaps one of the most famous interface metaphors in history. By treating the entire user experience as an extension of the familiar desktop, the Mac provides a context for understanding individual elements of the interface as visual representations of objects found in the user's everyday environment. A document may be represented as a window when it is being edited, as an icon when it is being moved from one folder to another, or even by its name in a list of other documents in the folder. The idea behind the desktop metaphor is to map representations of familiar objects to the user's existing understanding of those objects in the real world. The representation of a given object may even take different forms depending upon the context in which the user is manipulating it. This metaphor, while extremely powerful, can become somewhat restrictive due to its simplicity.

The desktop metaphor works very well when you are dealing with things usually found on someone's physical desktop, such as documents or folders. However, computers and electronic documents have supplanted physical desktops, paper documents, and file cabinets. This evolution of the user experience creates some interesting problems. For example, paper documents have some very restrictive characteristics, including many that electronic documents were intended to overcome. You cannot edit them without creating a new document, for example. However, you may make comments in the margins, or if the document is double-spaced, you may suggest and note changes between the lines.

Another problem with the desktop metaphor involves the use of nested folders, which rarely occur in real life. When was the last time you put a report in a folder, put that folder in another folder, and so on until you had filed away all of your documents in one huge and overstuffed folder? The point is that we interact with paper documents in very different ways than we interact with their electronic counterparts. As a result, any computer interface metaphor must carefully balance the need to recreate the real world with the need to extend or restrict due to the freedom and flexibility computers provide.

WIMP: Windows, Icons, Menus, and Pointers

While the intuitive mapping of a paper document to a document-like onscreen representation may seem like a no-brainer, millions of things in the computerized office have no real-life analogy. Some of these objects were created to compensate for the unique constraints imposed by the computer, others to deliberately limit the complexity resulting from the computer's enormous flexibility and power.

The comprehensive metaphor composed of windows, icons, menus, and the mouse pointer developed at Xerox PARC during the seventies is usually referred to as the WIMP interface. The Macintosh desktop metaphor uses WIMP extensively, and its interface is often billed as intuitive and easy to learn and use. However, it comes as a surprise to many that its main components do not correspond to objects in the world outside the computer. Think about it. When was the last time you saw a glass window containing a document, a list of options presented on a window shade, or scrollbars on your newspaper? Yet it is likely that you use these conventions every day, paying no regard to their complete lack of direct correspondence to anything in your environment. Weird, isn't it?

WINDOWS

Windows were created as a way to maximize the screen real estate available to the user for the display and manipulation of documents and other data. Originally, windows did not overlap, but were often tiled or shown one at a time to the exclusion of other open documents. Once certain technical hurdles were overcome, and a sufficiently powerful drawing package was created, the window as we know it today — overlapping and adjustable — was more or less ready for the mainstream. Other characteristics of windows include the following:

◆ A title or other means of identification

◆ The ability to resize and position the window

◆ The ability to close or hide the window

Many windows act as the main interface container for an application, and therefore contain menu bars and menus, status areas, and possibly other, subordinate windows. If you take the loose definition of a window, which often amounts to little more than a rectangular, bitmapped area of the screen, many of the following interface elements we've discussed fall into the window class:

◆ Application windows

◆ Document windows

◆ Alert boxes or status messages

◆ Dialog boxes, modal or otherwise

Taken from a certain perspective, you can even consider the desktop as nothing more than a peculiar sort of window. That would be stretching it a bit, though. For that matter, it is evident that icons occupy rectangular areas of the screen as well, but are not windows. Suffice it to say that a window is characterized by its capability to act as a container for documents and/or as a base for other interface elements, such as buttons, scrollbars, and so on.

ICONS

The idea of using a smaller iconic representation for a computer file or application is new, but humankind has created and used icons since before recorded history. So why is it so hard to create icons whose meaning the user immediately grasps? Well, for starters, icons are extremely complex little bits of culture. An icon designer must consider not only an icon's meaning or representation, but also the limitations on size, shape, color, and eventual display and rendering, as well as its relationship to other icons in whose close proximity it is likely to come. One icon of a group of related icons — for example, those representing all of the document types a given application can create — must reflect similarity within the group, but also differentiate itself from the others. Some factors that influence the usability of a given icon include the following:

◆ Familiarity to the user

◆ Clarity of its depiction or representation of its object

◆ Simplicity of design

◆ Relationship to other icons of the same type or used by the same application

◆ Appropriateness of the sign used to represent the object

◆ Context and history of the icon

Many icons try to do too much visually, or simply try to map themselves to inappropriate objects. Nouns and simple actions are more easily represented by way of an icon than are complex sequences of behavior or collections of attributes. Others assume too much about the user's environment or experience, and therefore fail to convey an accurate message. Still others are excellent icons, but are used in an inappropriate context with regard to the rest of the application's interface. Remember that icons primarily provide a way for the user to directly manipulate an object or initiate an action, and are supposed to do so in a small amount of screen real estate. When an icon is not appropriate, a more text-based approach may be required, such as that often used by menus.

MENUS

Menus are extremely simplistic but effective visual mechanisms for providing the user with a reminder of all actions and settings available to them at a glance. They also maximize screen real estate (this is becoming a theme, here. . .), and make it possible for the designer to organize the application's functionality in accordance with the user's expectations, or with the task at hand. This approach is highly preferable to merely reflecting the organization of and relationships between the application's subsystems. The menu structure should only present available actions, using mechanisms (such as graying out a menu item) to hide or otherwise signal that a menu item is not available. Some menu systems allow for *nesting*, or hierarchy, which greatly increases the flexibility available to the designer, but may also make the interface more difficult to learn and use if operated improperly.

There has been much research in recent years exploring the effectiveness of different organization techniques. Perhaps foremost among the issues uncovered is that of how many levels a hierarchical menu should contain, commonly referred to as the "depth versus breadth" matter. The key seems to be maintaining a balance between the time required to accomplish an objective within the menu system and the complexity of the list of available options. A menu with lots of top-level options (breadth) can make it difficult for the user to pick the action out from all the choices, or lessen the clarity of an item's description. Menus with lots of nesting (depth) increase the time required to find an action despite reducing crowding on the main menu, and contribute to a higher likelihood of error.

You can employ many organizational techniques across the extensive range of possible uses of menus. Because a menu item may represent any option, whether it is an action, a setting, or a choice of objects on which to operate, the guidelines governing their arrangement may vary widely. A list of font options, for example, might be best arranged alphabetically. A list of font sizes, on the other hand, might be best arranged numerically. Items representing actions should be grouped together according to their commonality or their relationship to other actions affecting similar objects. Whatever manner of organization you choose should be consistently applied across the whole application, and should also follow system guidelines. If the system your application runs on always uses alphabetical ordering for settings, such as font names, you should use that method as well in your application.

Your choice of menu and item wording should be simple, usually in terms of the action it calls, and should use keywords and verb-object constructions as well as parallel constructions for similar types of tasks. You should word each action in such a way as to maximize the distinction between one action and another — uniqueness is very important for menu and item naming. If your system enables the association of keyboard accelerators with menus and menu items, these accelerators should use mnemonics easily remembered by the user, such as Ctrl+S for the Save function. The whole point of accelerators is to avoid having to browse through menu items with the mouse pointer, looking for the appropriate action.

Although it is preferable in most cases to assign keyboard accelerators that bear some relationship to the name of the action they perform, there may be good reasons to name them differently. For example, the Macintosh uses ⌘ -Z for Undo, ⌘ -X for Cut, ⌘ -C for Copy, and ⌘ -V for Paste, because they are found in consecutive order along the bottom of the QWERTY keyboard. This is a good example of idiom applied wisely. Even though ⌘ -P might have been a better choice for Paste, human factors were taken into account and idiom relied upon to overcome any dissonance caused by the unlikely pairing of "v" with "paste." This solution also avoids internationalization issues, where the mnemonics may no longer make sense.

POINTERS

Perhaps the single most important qualifying characteristic of visual interfaces is that they enable the user to interact with the system using the mouse or other pointing device, rather than a keyboard. The mouse pointer enables the user to directly manipulate objects on the screen, rather than having to use a text-based command language. In the majority of GUI environments, the developer to chooses different mouse pointer icons to represent different states and contexts to the user.

In essence, the pointer replaces many of the traditional mechanisms by which the application communicates its current state to the user. In a command-line environment, the program might print status messages to the console, informing the user that the program is running, or waiting for input. In a GUI environment, the pointer takes the form of an hourglass or watch to represent the fact that the application is busy doing something. In more advanced applications that enable even more complex manipulation of the objects onscreen, the pointer might take the form of an eye dropper to signify that the user should click to select a color, or a hand to signify that the pointer is currently positioned over a link.

Why WIMP Is So Prevalent

The WIMP metaphor has become incredibly prevalent in the past 15 years for a number of reasons. It solves many of the problems facing the interface designer, including:

◆ Limited screen real estate

◆ Interface consistency

◆ Natural mapping and direct manipulation (the physical mouse corresponds to the onscreen pointer)

The use of a mouse pointer to provide direct manipulation of objects within an interface with limited screen real estate leverages interface consistency and ease of use. It is an incredibly powerful mechanism for the application developer. Windows that may overlap and move into the background fit well with the way people work, switching from one task to another almost constantly during the course of a workday. Icons provide excellent and immediate recognition of the documents and programs they represent far more effectively, for example, than file extensions or the long, overwhelmingly informative file naming conventions found in VMS. Finally, menus provide a way to remind the user of the possible actions that she may take at any point in time, rather than forcing the memorization of obscure command languages.

Your kids will never know how easy they have it today, surfing the Web with a simple point-and-click interface. When we first got on the Internet, before the Web existed, we had to use a terminal application to read e-mail, and downloading files was a complicated matter. We used a text-based menu-driven system to select a protocol by which the computer we were connected to would download the file to its local file system. We then needed to select another protocol (such as Zmodem) to download the file from the host computer to the local machine. The file usually had a name like "device:directory[filename.txt];version," where every part of the filename represented some characteristic of the file as it was stored on the host computer. It was, to say the least, non-intuitive.

Why WIMP Isn't the End-All-Be-All

Despite its popularity, the WIMP metaphor is not the final word on graphical user interface design. The contexts in which it is applied have their weaknesses, such as those related to the Macintosh desktop metaphor, and it is quickly becoming recognized that WIMP has practical limits. As applications become more complex, the simplicity, clarity, and directness of WIMP are challenged by the sheer variety of tasks required of it.

When an application has a few dozen commands and supports only a few major operations, or when users are not enabled to customize their environment to any great extent, WIMP is extremely useful. It is only when the number of operations supported by a given application reaches into the hundreds, or when the number of file types balloons into the thousands, that the icon space, menu organization, and so forth become extremely crowded. What made WIMP so attractive in the first place is now making it difficult to sustain. In a sense, this is not a problem with WIMP so much as it is an indicator of its success. A major application, such as a word processor, adds toolbars to provide quick iconic access to popular or common functionality, and makes it more difficult to provide icons that readily distinguish between functions. Similarly, menu space becomes crowded, requiring the application to hide certain functionality — either beneath a set of hierarchical menus, or by hiding and showing menus based on the application's state. Many settings are moved out into dialog boxes of their own, with some approaching the original complexity of the application itself a few revisions back.

Iconography has limited effectiveness cross-culturally, as people's experiences are broad and cultural differences enormous. Even if the application's icon designer is familiar with the iconography of the target culture, he or she still faces the same issues — overloading, differentiation, and appropriateness — only now with enhanced pressures placed by internationalization of an interface. This pressure in turn forces system design decisions to be made in a more modular fashion to enable the further separation of underlying systems from the interface itself. To be fair, these challenges are not only faced by the WIMP metaphor; any interface relying on iconography for a majority of its presentation is particularly susceptible.

One school of thought holds that a major weakness of the WIMP metaphor is that it was intended as a vehicle for the creation, not the consumption, of documents. Many of the actions that users feel comfortable with during the creation of a document, such as scrolling, become more difficult when reading a document someone else has created. Part of the reason for the problem involves a lack of context. When users create a document, they are familiar with its contents, and therefore have no problem scrolling to different pages. When they read a document someone else has created, however, context and familiarity are lacking. This problem is especially acute in Web design, where pages often include design elements that do not suggest, or that suggest poorly, that there is more to the document than is visible on the screen at any given time.

SOME SOLUTIONS

One of the strengths of the WIMP metaphor is how easily it is extended to deal with challenges as they arise. We've already mentioned toolbars, which are basically just icons arranged in an order similar to that of the menus that provide another mode of access to the functionality. Tool tips, increasingly complex scrolling mechanisms (such as Page Up buttons inside scrollbars), and retractable pop-up menus help to overcome some of the weaknesses involved in the use of icons, large documents inside windows, and screen real estate and overcrowded menus, respectively. Each enhancement to the basic metaphor represents another challenge to simplicity and ease of use, even as they combat the complexity of other parts of the interface.

One other solution to menu overpopulation involves contextual menus that rely on a keyboard-mouse combination, a multiple-button mouse, or simply a click-and-hold to reveal menus particular to the context in which the user clicked the mouse.

Keyboard shortcuts may be overloaded in specific contexts, such as a dialog box, as long as the actions they perform are clearly marked or intuitive (for example, using the Tab key to move the focus from one interface element to another). This reduces the risk of running out of key space, but requires the migration of application functionality to dialog boxes, perhaps launched by menu items, itself another solution to menu overcrowding.

OTHER APPROACHES

Beyond the simple combination of menus, icons, and windows used solely for application or document containment, myriad variations and extensions to the base metaphor may be made without compromising its essence. Examples include the use of dialog boxes for everything from confirmation of an action to complete mini-applications designed to manage entire application subsystems, such as print setup, styles management, or annotation handling.

Other interface enhancements are beyond the scope of the original WIMP metaphor, but coexist peacefully with it. One example is the venerable *tab widget*, which enables the designer to group related interface elements, save screen real estate, and generally work around the limitations or hassles of having to launch multiple dialog boxes for somewhat related functions, such as managing user preferences. Another example is the *tree widget*, found in the Windows file manager, which enables the user to navigate a hierarchy such as a file system without revealing the entire thing at once, or restricting the visibility of all other parts of the hierarchy. Many enhancements have been made to the original scrollbar, adding numerous overloaded functionalities to the basic thumb-and-arrow arrangement. Some examples include the following:

◆ Page Up and Page Down buttons.

◆ Double arrows (one of each direction at each end, so the user doesn't have to mouse all the way to the top to scroll up or vice versa).

◆ Thumbs whose length is modified to reflect the length of the document. This last enhancement can be problematic for large documents, as the thumb gets very small, indeed.

The WIMP metaphor has lasted several decades and shows little sign of slowing down. Despite its weaknesses, the core model has survived many attempts to suggest alternatives, seeming to enable a customization that overcomes many of the weaknesses inherent in the model itself. In addition, no strong contenders have shown themselves — at least within the core space WIMP has carved out for itself. As new environments arise, however, and the mental models they require prove more challenging to the basic metaphor, it is likely that WIMP will be discarded in favor of more appropriate models. For the purposes of building dynamic HTML applications, the WIMP model is more than appropriate, enabling as it does for interface consistency and a well-understood and easily learned basis for basic interface functionality. Clearly, some of the fundamental interface assumptions need to be rethought in order to grapple with the new era of networked computing. The file/folder/disk model is one metaphor whose assumptions are coming under fire, as shown in the next section.

Where Does This File Exist?

The whole idea of files on disk representing files on a desk is stretched past its breaking point, especially in a networked environment. Alan Cooper reviews the problem with the file metaphor and its repercussions for interface design in his book *About Face: The Essentials of User Interface Design*. The problem, as Cooper sees it, is that for most end-user applications there is nothing to inform the user that their file exists both on disk and in memory, or whether the "file" being edited bears a one-to-one relationship with the "document" the user thinks he is editing. When the user closes an application such as a word processor, they are prompted to choose whether to save their file. In Cooper's view, this represents a problem for the interface designer, especially when the application presents the file as a document, but treats the document as a file in a file system.

The problem only gets worse when we move from the local environment of a standalone computer to the global environment of networked computers, especially the Web. Due to the existing mechanisms for dealing with security, it is possible with dynamic HTML applications for users to modify their environment extensively but not be able to save the state of their environment to the local file system. Cookies and other mechanisms, such as server-side storage of form data, may be leveraged to ensure that no data is lost at the end of a session, but the appropriate notification mechanisms must also be deployed to reassure users that their information is saved. How do we confront the problem of data storage and notification in a transparently networked environment when many users have a hard enough time telling the difference between a file in memory (or a *buffer*) and a file on disk? This says nothing of the potential for such files to be combined in multifile documents, for that matter. The answers are not clear.

One approach worth considering involves the use of forcing functions, as discussed in Chapter 1, "What Is an Interface?" When a user closes a window, ending a browser session, an event handler may be defined that prompts the user to save or discard changes. This is unsatisfactory, especially because this irritating prompt is one of the things that Cooper decries in his book. It may make sense to go ahead and save the environment as well as is possible without prompting users, and prompt them when they resume the application the next time as to whether they want to continue where they left off, or start fresh. None of these solutions is terribly exciting, though, and in cases like this, there may be no satisfactory answer.

The relatively low level of granularity achieved by the client/server relationship (as opposed to the application/file system relationship) enables the developer to avoid certain issues related to what Cooper calls *positional retrieval*. As contrasted to *identity retrieval*, which involves having the user remember the name of the document or other collection of information, and *associative retrieval*, which enables the user to search for the document based on certain of its qualities, positional retrieval is perhaps the more difficult of the three. Positional retrieval requires the user to remember not only what she is looking for (its name or qualities), but also how it stands in relation to the peculiarities of the storage mechanism. Reducing the perceived complexity of the storage environment is helpful, but perhaps not the only answer.

Situations such as these call for extensive planning, design, and user testing to ferret out the developer's assumptions made inherent in the system. One mechanism for testing these new situations and your responses to them involves prototyping.

Prototyping

What the heck is prototyping and why should you care? *Prototyping* is the construction of an application for the purposes of testing the assumptions that went into its design, before entering the full development process. Prototypes are built so that errors and mistaken assumptions may be searched out and fixed before much development time is wasted building something that doesn't meet the needs of the user. This topic and the topic discussed in the next section, usability, go hand in hand. Prototypes are not always constructed solely for the purpose of testing usability, but also to test performance, try out new technologies as bases for further development, and experiment with new interface ideas and underlying subsystems. However, it is with the former that software prototypes are usually most concerned.

The Importance of Prototyping

Prototyping can save costly development time and redesign efforts before they occur by exposing the user to some or all of the original design team's ideas. By enabling a user to interact with a partially completed system or interface, it is sometimes possible to generate entirely new ideas that the developer or interface designer didn't consider during the initial design process. Perhaps the most important aspect of the prototyping phase results from giving the user a real interface with which to test out the original requirements – usually given as bulleted lists of features and functionality, rather than as full-blown interface ideas. Often the translation between requirements in written documentation and the actual interface reveals gaping holes in the requirements themselves, as the user realizes that what was specified does not completely cover the full functionality required of a system or application. Another aspect of prototyping with real interfaces is that many users cannot properly conceptualize or communicate their needs unless they get a chance to interact with a working model. For this reason alone, prototypes are an absolute necessity for large systems or those that are costly to develop and/or implement.

The Many Different Kinds of Prototypes

Prototypes come in all shapes, sizes, and colors. Some prototypes are developed in a language other than that used for the final application. Still other prototypes are merely provided as examples of the final look and feel for purposes of testing the arrangement of interface elements before any actual development is done at all. In building Web sites, the ease with which a single page or small collection of pages may be built in order to demonstrate a given layout far outstrips the effort that goes into the final site-wide implementation.

LIMITED FUNCTIONALITY PROTOTYPING

Many interface prototypes are developed using the same technology used in the final product, but without actually hooking in the code that the interface will drive. This is done in order to test a given GUI toolkit, for example, or to make a particular interface experiment available for user testing.

LOOK AND FEEL PROTOTYPES

It is common for developers working in environments where the final product is a compiled C or C++ application to use a different technology for prototyping. Often, developers make this decision based on the relative ease of use of various interface design tools. When Steven worked in the Emerging Technologies department of a software company, he used Microsoft Visual Basic (VB) to develop prototypes for applications that were to be deployed across platforms, and used C++ libraries that were cryptic and difficult to use and lacked interactive drag-and-drop interface design tools. The VB environment made it easy to create functional prototypes to show to his clients without having to provide the fully developed C++ version, saving time and making incremental updates based on user feedback possible within relatively short time frames. As DHTML has become more stable, Steven uses it instead of VB and other tools for prototyping the interfaces for applications that will eventually be completely server-driven.

The Meaning of Prototyping in Rapid Application Development

The software industry has historically faced constant challenges placed by ever-shortening time frames for development. In the sixties, for example, sometimes the development of a single application could take several years. Nowadays, a software company that can't turn out a new version of its software in a few months is challenged by another that can. In response to such pressures, various methodologies have arisen, mostly aimed at reducing the complexity of software design and the project management process. One such methodology is *rapid application development*. It involves compressing time frames for virtually every phase of the development life cycle. One area in which it actually calls for lengthening the process is interface design and prototyping. If a solid design can be arrived at before the actual coding starts, much of the iterative process of refining the coded interface (due to user feedback, changing requirements, and the like) can be reduced to a one-time implementation. When compressing your development timeline is your only hope of beating your competitor to market, reducing the commonly iterative phases of development is one of the few areas where you can cut development time.

GUI DESIGN PROTOTYPES

As mentioned above, sometimes the line is blurry between functional prototypes on the one hand, and simple layout and design examples on the other. It is common for Web designers to provide sample layouts for Web sites as static images that they later implement using actual HTML. The effort saved by this practice increases with the complexity of the user interfaces that clients demand. Three years ago, it was reasonable to claim that a Web site could function as its own prototype, because the effort that went into revising it to suit user feedback was minimal. As things become increasingly complex, and the differences between the various versions of the browsers widen, this is no longer the case.

ARCHITECTURE DESIGN PROTOTYPES

One key point to note when discussing prototyping in a Web environment is that the relationships between the various interfaces comprising an application are often more important than the individual interface elements themselves. As sites get larger, and their functionality becomes more complex, these relationships and the interface elements required to navigate them become paramount. Sites, unlike applications, also have a tendency to grow, rather than remaining static over the lifetime of a single version. The interface, color scheme, branding, and so on may remain constant, but the actual content of the documents changes with great rapidity. Traditional application developers never had to deal with these issues, as their job was to develop and distribute systems whose relationships did not change at all between versions.

Architectural prototypes, or prototypes designed to test the higher-level relationshipsbetween areas of a site or functionally distinct interfaces, are extremely important. Many interface designers, who cut their teeth on such traditional applications, tend to be too rigid in their definitions of how a Web site interface should function. They forget that the Web site is in a constant state of evolution and flux, and as such requires new rules for planning, execution, and maintenance.

The "Plan to Throw One Away" Model

A classic work on software development, Fred Brooks' *The Mythical Man-Month: Essays on Software Engineering*, declares that project managers should plan to "throw one away," using the justification that if you don't plan for such a possibility, you will probably end up having to later in the process anyway. There are many reasons why you end up throwing your first cut in the garbage. The main reason is that software development is often directed toward entirely new products, whose use was not foreseen, and whose requirements differ substantially from the applications that preceded them. Another reason has to do with the experience of the average programmer. Even good programmers learn as they code, and they often find better ways to implement something the second time they approach a problem. The promise underlying the threatening pronouncement suggests that it is actually better to have a programmer design something twice or even three times, and its quality improves in an iterative fashion.

MAKE MISTAKES EARLY, BEFORE THINGS ARE CAST IN STONE

The complexity of a system has a tendency to inflate the cost of its production. To borrow an analogy from the construction of mechanical goods, if the pieces on the basis of which a factory is retooled are incorrectly designed, then the entire factory must be retooled as well, resulting in enormous losses of time and resources. Applications and the interfaces that provide the face they present to the user are interdependent to an enormous degree. By providing some or all of the elements of an interface in prototypical form, you can analyze the interdependencies and rework them before you design the systems they relate to.

PROGRAMMERS LEARN FROM IMPLEMENTING THE SYSTEM ITSELF

Another facet of software development that becomes blatantly obvious after a few tries is that programmers are a strange bunch. Not only do they spend their entire lives in front of whiteboards, cathode ray tubes, and pizza counters, but they also have an annoying habit of never letting go of a problem until they've thought it through at least five or six times. The lucky ones get paid to do this, of course, but it is common for many to simply pursue a programming problem even after the application that brought it into their heads has been shipped, the company folded, and the stock options redeemed for Monopoly money. Therefore, it is best if the project manager in charge of exploiting these energies does so within the time frame allotted for the development of a single application. Legion are the tales of those who forced a programmer to tackle a problem, implement it, and move on, only to find that the programmer was still working late nights on the same problem long after his legitimate involvement in the project was over. The moral: Throw one away, and let the same programmer develop the second or third version during the course of the same project.

Naturally, there are some problems with the throw one away approach. First, it's only worth something if the same programmer or team of programmers that produced the first implementation is kept around for the next attempt. Barring that, it is vital that the original developers keep good documentation of the process and any pitfalls or shortcomings encountered along the way. Second, time may not always allow the development of complete applications merely to throw them away. In this case, it is up to the project manager to ensure that the application is broken up into small, manageable subsystems, each of which may be ranked in order of difficulty or importance to the final product. There are several schools of thought on how to approach this decomposition of subsystems. One school suggests that subsystems that promise to be the most difficult to implement should be tackled first. That way, the remaining pieces may be assembled quickly on the basis of how the more difficult problems were solved. One problem with this approach is that many applications are developed relatively independently of their interfaces as a result. As we have seen above, it is better to design the interface and subsystems in tandem to ensure that the user interface isn't tacked on as an afterthought. Another school suggests that the easy pieces be tackled up front, and that the more difficult components may be easier to implement when hooks to the rest of the application are already finished. The risk here is that the more difficult pieces either never get finished or require reworking of the already completed components, sending the whole project into churn. You have to rely on your instincts and knowledge of the nature of your application to decide what approach best suits your application. In any case, the user is the ultimate judge of whether you have succeeded.

Usability

Usability testing is a way of uncovering and articulating unspoken design assumptions about the interface. By exposing the application to the actual end user while it is still in development (through the use of prototypes), developers get to find out how wide a gap exists between their assumptions and the way the system will actually be used. There are many well-documented approaches to usability, but they all stress the importance of the following:

◆ Non-interference with the user while they use the system

◆ Careful record keeping and observation

◆ Summaries and analyses of common behaviors as well as unique deviance from expected behavior

◆ Asking the user to explain their thought processes as they use the system

Through the use of such tactics, assumptions that the developer makes while implementing the system or that the designer makes while building the interface are uncovered. Often, the user also makes assumptions about the interface known to those who are taking notes on the user's progress. It is revealing just how often these assumptions differ, and a lesson well worth learning for user and developer or designer alike. The user is crippled by a lack of knowledge about the system, and the developer is equally at a disadvantage by knowing so much about the system.

One key to understanding the way that an interface will eventually be used involves watching the user as they try to construct a mental model of the system based on the interface alone. Slight flaws in the interface can balloon into incredible mistaken assumptions on the user's part, as they apply their experience with other software and operating system environments to your interface.

Many usability testing methods attempt to provide heuristics by which an interface may be measured against others for its usability. One popular method is to assign the same tasks, such as finding a particular piece of information, to a group of users and keep track of how many of the tasks each user successfully completes. This is beneficial in that it provides a basis for understanding the usability of a system across several different types of users, but it has drawbacks. For example, many systems — especially Web interfaces — are not designed solely around the idea of information retrieval. Navigation, interaction, and branding also enter into the design of most sites. Some sites, for that matter, do not present the user with any real information, but are intended solely for entertainment, or building brand identity. It all comes down to using your best judgment and understanding the nature of your application.

Cultural experience is also a major determinant in how the user's mental models are constructed, and should be taken into account when revising the interface based on such feedback. When the time comes to implement the interface again, whether for the next revision or as a last-minute update based on user feedback, it is vital to keep in mind the potential for changes to the interface to radically change the relationships between the elements of your interface. These relationships can alter the mental models formed by users as they interact with your system. Schedule user testing of some sort after every major change to your application. Your application will be better for it, and your users more productive, too.

Summary

In this chapter, you learned the following about the principles of interface development:

- ◆ There are two major types of interfaces: task-oriented and goal-oriented.
- ◆ Direct manipulation is a key to providing a transparent interface.

◆ Keeping the user experience consistent is important in reducing the time required for the user to learn and gain competency in using your application.

◆ You have numerous ways to construct the user environment, including the use of overarching metaphors and the well-planned use of interface idioms.

◆ The user develops mental models of your system based on the interface alone.

◆ Scheduling for prototypes and throwaway implementations can make the difference between a good interface and a great one.

◆ Usability testing can function as an eye-opener and reveal characteristics of your application that reflect developers' assumptions.

The next chapter discusses ways that these principles of interface development may be applied to the Web as a new environment, and when they should be obeyed and when they need to be revised to suit the unique needs of this new environment.

Chapter 4

Exploring New Directions for the Web

IN THIS CHAPTER

- ◆ Following interface design conventions
- ◆ Does the Web have a standard set of interface elements?
- ◆ Navigation as interface
- ◆ Making your site accessible

A NUMBER OF USABILITY EXPERTS have been calling recently for the adoption of a standard Web interface. In other words, these experts suggest that every site on the Web should work the same, look the same, and follow the same rules. What would it mean to have every site on the Web adopt a single interface standard? Why would anyone make such a demand? Who are they speaking for? What can we do to help widen the playing field while establishing interface conventions that won't confuse users?

Does the Web call for a new kind of interface? Or does it call for many new kinds? What are they, and how are they related to and where do they diverge from conventional interface ideas? What are the unique demands placed on Web interface designers, and what are some of the technologies and solutions they propose?

Lots of questions confront the interface designer on the new frontier. The real question is whether the answers are available now, or if they need to be discovered every day by everyone involved.

Defining Conventional Web Interfaces

The Web began as a text-only medium — a powerful, hypertextual alternative to Gopher, the hierarchical alternative to ftp. The only interface elements developers had to worry about were links, and whatever their current OS offered by way of conventions. The Web was just one application on your desktop. Nowadays, it is becoming clear that the Web is not just one application among many, but is the platform for a future generation of Web-based applications.

So, which interface elements are native to the Web, and which have been devised? Is there any way to categorize these elements and establish or document conventions for their proper use, or is it too early to tell? In any case, we think there is a lot of work that needs to be done in order to encourage certain "best practices" – both clever and obvious solutions to common interface problems.

Early, Web-Native Interface Conventions

The line between interface and simple onscreen document formatting was a lot less clear in the early days of the Web. There were no images, forms, client-side scripts, applets, plug-ins, or other such clutter to stand in the way of a good, solid, several pages long bulleted list. But does a bulleted list count as an interface? It did in the early days, when the bulleted list was the default format for reeling off a bunch of links to other pages or sites. When Netscape introduced their earliest integrated newsreader, the interface consisted of – yep, you guessed it – bulleted lists, containing links to USENET postings. Of course, this was all in the context of a larger environment, the browser itself, which had the usual interface fare: buttons, menus, text fields, and so on. When you don't have many interface elements to choose from, you must either overload existing elements, or strike off in new directions and invent more. Both of these things happened.

Let's look at some early interface conventions and discuss their impact on the subsequent evolution of the browser as it went from being an application that could display simple documents to an application delivery platform in its own right.

BLUE/RED/PURPLE LINKS? YUCK.

Mosaic, the first graphical browser, established some unfortunate interface conventions. The only thing Mosaic had to do was display formatted documents using the font faces and sizes chosen by the user, though some platforms provided more flexibility than others in this regard. However, the most important feature of the interface, the hyperlink, was more or less etched in stone.

Links were underlined in bright blue if they hadn't been followed, and in red or purple once they had been visited. This was done so that users could see where they had been, and determine what links had not yet been followed. On some systems, the link itself turned red while the user clicked on it. On the Macintosh, users had complete control over their interface. They could choose link colors and decide whether or not links should be underlined, as you can see in Figure 4-1 and Figure 4-2. Still, the author of the document didn't have any control at all over how these things were displayed, so thousands of early users of the Web learned to associate underlined blue text with the hyperlink.

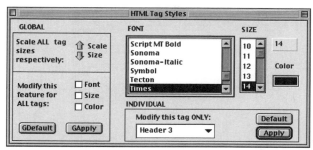

Figure 4-1: Tag styles could be changed using the MacMosaic 1.03 Styles dialog box

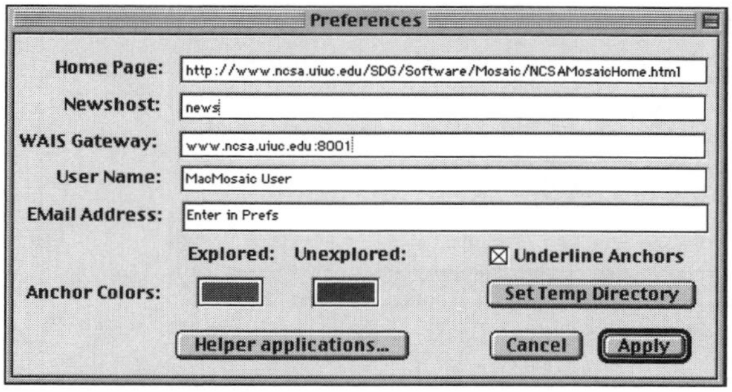

Figure 4-2: The MacMosaic 1.03 Preferences dialog box, demonstrating anchor colors

Looking back, it seems like a safe bet on the part of the original Mosaic developers. The default document background was either gray or white, the text defaulted to black, and that didn't leave many primary colors to choose from. It has since been pointed out that the opposite choice might have been just as good or better. Cool colors tend to recede into the background, whereas hot colors jump into the foreground. Using red for a followed link went against years of research into color theory and our reactions to the use of color. Others argue that it is more a matter of intensity rather than hue, and that the blue used as the link color is actually brighter than the red used for a followed link. No matter – the choice was made, and a convention was established almost overnight. Figure 4-3 shows Steven's current home page in MacMosaic, complete with big blue borders around the hyperlinked images. (You'll have to trust us when we say they're blue.)

Figure 4-3: Steven's home page in MacMosaic 1.03

When Netscape Navigator 1.0 was released, Web page authors were able to specify their own choices of link color, visited link color, background, and more. (We won't discuss the use of goofy psychedelic background graphics here, on the assumption that you already know better than to obscure the legibility of your pages.) Suddenly, the opportunity to break an established convention was at hand. People went wild, specifying any and all colors with reckless abandon, much as they had with fonts when the Macintosh introduced desktop publishing a decade before. With the advent of the <FONT> element in Navigator 2.0, colored text wasn't just for links anymore.

Even so, usability experts recommend that Web page authors stick with the tried and true blue link, saying that the convention was already established. Does this make sense? If a convention was established and then broken years before the majority of users joined the Web, does the convention still hold? At this stage in the game, where recent additions to the HTML/CSS/JavaScript mix make it possible to specify hover colors for links in Internet Explorer, it seems questionable. At best, it's a convention that is on its way out.

You should adhere to the following Web interface rules, in any case:

◆ If you're going to change your link colors, avoid using blue for anything but links.

◆ If you're not going to use blue, then at least be consistent in your use of link colors.

◆ If you're going to specify font colors for text other than links, don't use blue at all for that text.

◆ If you specify link colors, use different colors for new and followed links.

◆ Don't force underlining on any text, link or not.

The bottom line here is that although the convention may be broken in the sense that authors are no longer expected to follow it, it is still active in the minds of many and you should avoid confusing your users. You may not like the idea of underlined blue links, but forcing regular nonlinked paragraph text to a nice, underlined blue is a great way to seriously undermine the usability of your interface. Deviate from previously established convention at your own risk, but to apply the form of that convention to other things is to invite serious cognitive dissonance on the part of your users.

Make sure your interface uses an internally consistent color scheme, and that it doesn't require users to relearn a new interface with every site they visit. Above all, don't expect them to abandon their previous understanding of an established interface by applying its conventions to other, unrelated things.

IMAGES AS NAVIGATION

The introduction of the *inline image*, an image file displayed within the text of the current document, changed the Web in ways that are now hard to imagine. (Does anyone even remember when Mosaic launched a helper application just to view JPEG files?) Suddenly, the text-only landscape was splashed with color. Bulleted lists had tiny colored balls to set them off, instead of the usual solid black dots. The time required to download a page increased exponentially, but people didn't seem to care much. The tradeoffs were worth it.

Next on the list of improvements was the image map. An image could not only represent a single destination, but it could also be subdivided into sections, each with its own link. Some early applications of this were amazing. The Xerox PARC Map Viewer, with its click-and-zoom interface, dazzled everyone. You just picked a zoom factor using a radio button, and then clicked wherever you wanted the next map to be centered. It was a far cry from the text-driven interfaces of years past.

One of the first problems faced by designers was the fact that linked images were wrapped by a 2- or 3-pixel-wide blue border. Some designers rebelled, refusing to link to images at all. Still others, such as the HotWired site designers, realized that it was better not to fight, and instead embraced the blue and incorporated it into their designs. One of the first HotWired home pages (otherwise known as *front doors*) featured an image map that contained its own blue background, shown in Figure 4-4. The point was to force the link border to blend in with the rest of the image so it was no longer noticed. (Again, you'll just have to trust us when we say that the background is blue.)

Figure 4-4: HotWired's designers embrace the blue image border

Next in the line of conventions to take a beating was that of the flat page. In 1994, the drop shadow was all the rage. It seemed that everywhere you turned there was some artificially enhanced three-dimensional effect. Between beveled edges on navigational buttons and drop shadows behind graphical text, such as the contrived example in Figure 4-5, things were popping out at you and breaking free of the flat plane (not to mention the dreaded `<BLINK>` tag). You can date many sites with a remarkable degree of accuracy based on the extent to which they use drop shadows and beveled buttons.

So do these relatively simplistic characteristics shared by many of the first Web sites constitute bona fide interface conventions? Let's think about it. When you see underlined blue text, do you assume it might be a link? When you see a beveled button, perhaps with multiple text labels, do you move the mouse over it to see if you can tell whether clicking on the graphic in different spots takes you to different destinations? More importantly, do your users? How does the inclusion of form elements change this basic set of assumptions?

Figure 4-5: Drop shadows and beveled edge buttons

A FINE SELECTION OF STANDARD FORM ELEMENTS

Form elements are interface elements. How have they been employed beyond their traditional uses? Can we even say that just because early forms (especially those with more than one element) required a Submit button in order to function properly, that this, too, constitutes a convention? Or would it be wiser to stay the course we've been taking so far in this section, warning against trying to override existing conventional usage while encouraging nontraditional uses for form elements? Let's look at the original usage of various form elements, and then discuss some innovative ways that these elements have been extended to solve new interface problems.

With the introduction of JavaScript came the ability to control form elements with amazing flexibility. With a few lines of code, one could create a clock, a scrolling marquee, and even ASCII art animations in <TEXTAREA> fields. Like most early uses of new technology, these had a certain "cool factor" that was influenced primarily by their novelty. If you had a certain Photoshop plug-in, you could quickly create buttons with beveled edges. If you knew about the LOWSRC attribute for the <IMG> element, you could dazzle your friends with an ugly, dithered, but quickly downloaded image with a high-color version following quickly on its heels. If you could hack HTML and knew how to copy and paste, you could add collapsing menus to your frameset, or incorporate an annoying scrolling status bar message. Few people actually used these enhancements effectively, but it didn't matter. The simple fact was that you could, and if you did it first, everyone would be ripping off your code and markup. It was geek heaven.

Of course, it was a total nightmare for users, who had to deal with problems galore trying to navigate through the jungle of flashing, scrolling, sliding, and animated cruft. Not all of these new enhancements were strictly fluff, though. Some were serious attempts to provide solutions to pressing interface problems.

One such use involves the <TEXTAREA> element, shown in Figure 4-6, marked up so that it contains a license agreement or other important but incredibly long document. The use of the form elements to present both interface options (Accept or Decline) at once, while still enabling the user to read the entire document inside the <TEXTAREA>, is an excellent example of innovation.

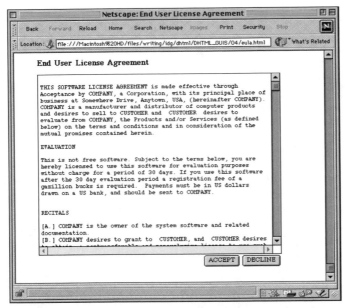

Figure 4-6: An innovative use of the TEXTAREA as interface element

Another use of form elements, albeit slightly more suspect, involves form buttons as navigation. Each button on the form in Figure 4-7 represents an alternate navigation option. The buttons are required in order for form data to be propagated correctly through the tool suite, but it calls into question how far a given element can be overridden. What was once used to submit a form and to return it to its original state now becomes the bearer of arbitrary meaning.

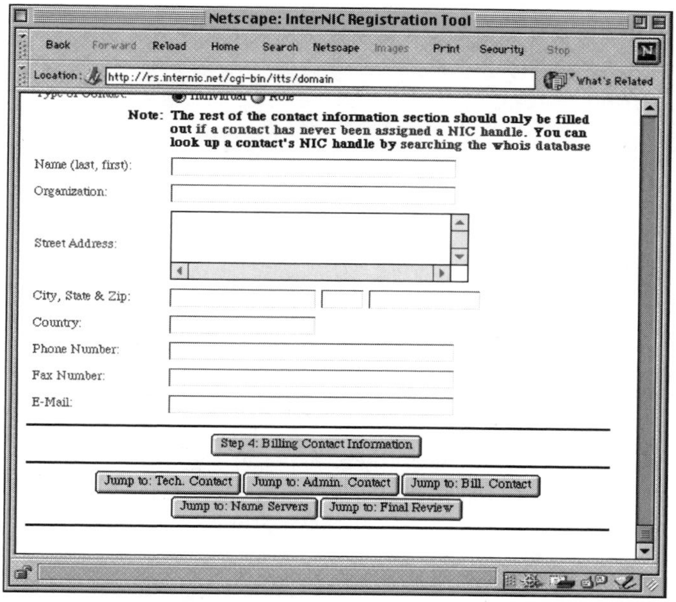

Figure 4–7: Form buttons as navigation

Another great example of a way that the power of JavaScript has extended traditional form elements involves the ubiquitous *quick navigation* option lists, where each option refers to a URL. When the user selects a given option, shown in Figure 4-8, they are immediately taken to the URL corresponding to that option.

The easier it is to implement hacks like these, the more widespread they become. This popularity may show either that the hack is helpful for the user, or that the Web designer found it an easy way to solve a navigation problem that would otherwise require careful planning of information architecture. Regardless, it extends the traditional use of forms to new levels, and therefore represents a worthy topic of discussion.

It is even possible to construct whole interfaces out of nothing but option lists. One of the authors of this book recently worked on a project where the user was repeatedly asked to choose from a set of options, each representing a category or feature of the company's hardware, software, and services. The user might find herself selecting Hardware, then Server Hardware, then High-End Database Server Hardware, and so on, until she was redirected to a Web site with more information about the only suitable product in the company's line given her choices. Oddly enough, this option list interface was eventually rolled into another online application that used radio buttons instead of option lists to represent the choices.

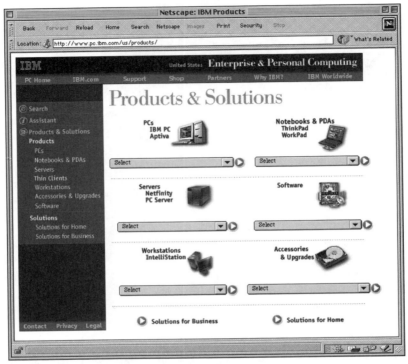

Figure 4-8: Using option lists as navigational aids

SCROLLBARS – VERTICAL AND HORIZONTAL

Users don't like to scroll, or so programmers are told. Yet, some Web designers are making extensive use of scrollbars to create innovative and unusual designs. One example of a horizontally scrolling site uses a dungeon metaphor in keeping with the overall medieval theme of the site. Users are invited to click on the entrance to the dungeon, whereupon they are guided through a series of tunnels, each displaying a piece from the designer's portfolio. Figure 4-9 shows this innovative portfolio.

Emulating Existing Interface Conventions

A common interface design practice online, especially in the early days of tables and transparent GIF images, was to simply design your front door out of the interface elements most familiar to the designer or the expected audience. How to do this? Why, use whatever default interface elements happen to be on your system, of course. There are some problems with this, the most important one being the cross-platform nature of the Web. If you're a Windows 3.1 user who's only seen a

Macintosh in a consumer electronics superstore, an emulated Macintosh interface isn't going to mean much to you. Many sites also use other interface elements, such as icons, to represent navigational opportunities. Let's look at a few and decide if they make sense.

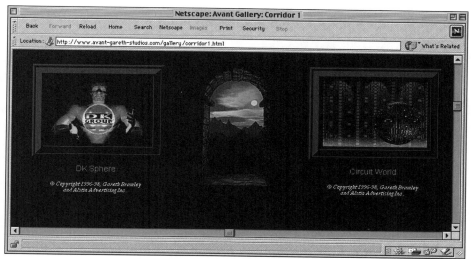

Figure 4-9: Gareth Bramley's portfolio uses horizontal scrolling and a dungeon metaphor

USING WINDOW STYLES, ICONS, AND OTHER VISUAL CUES

Many sites geared toward users of a particular platform or operating system use the icons and window styling of that platform to induce a comfort level and immediate association in the minds of their visitors. This can be useful in the short term as it avoids having to teach the user a new interface metaphor. In the long run, though, it may cause problems as the user tries to make the interface perform exactly as he is used to, resulting in frustration when familiar elements don't deliver the expected functionality. Another issue is that such design requires extensive use of graphics in order to produce the desired effects.

When Steven was designing his first Macintosh-based Web site for a private intranet, he stuck with the tried and true Macintosh desktop metaphor and used familiar icons that linked to the appropriate information. He soon realized, however, that the state-of-the-art technology at the time didn't allow for much flexibility in how he structured his site, shown in Figure 4-10. Eventually, the desktop became a giant image map, slow to load and display, and difficult to modify. His only defense is that at least he learned his lesson early.

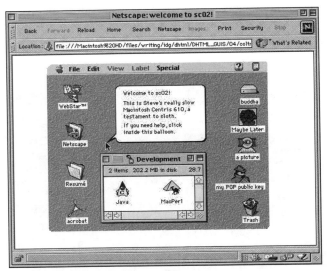

Figure 4-10: Steven's first Mac-based Web site

Another site that uses a Macintosh interface and dynamic HTML to provide a familiar environment is the Panic Software site. It doesn't try to emulate the entire interface, but restricts itself to a Mac OS 8 window and several icons, as shown in Figure 4-11. They also use a DHTML representation of Stickies, a software application included with the Macintosh operating system distribution, as a way to provide news and other pertinent and oft-updated information.

This site works because it uses the Mac OS interface in clever and consistent ways. Most of the interface behavior the user expects to find is implemented, including the window shade effect, active go-away boxes that close open windows, and the ability to click-and-drag on the window's title bar to reposition the window. The company designs Macintosh software, so they assume the audience is familiar with the Macintosh interface.

One irritating (but relatively effective) tactic involving a sort of trompe l'oeil effect is the use of familiar interface elements in banner advertising. The last couple of years have seen a marked increase in banner advertisements that resemble Windows 95 windows, alert dialog boxes, progress bars, and the like. One particularly obnoxious banner shows a window whose contents are suggestively obscured. Steven had to catch himself from trying to drag the window open further, resulting in an unintended click-through as the banner was linked to another site.

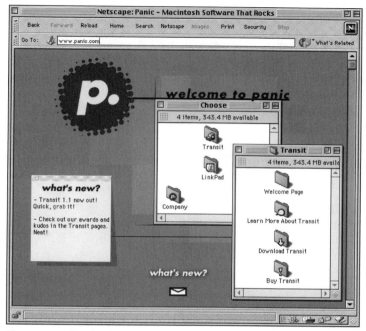

Figure 4-11: The Panic Software site, demonstrating an emulated Mac interface

SOME MORE TRADITIONAL INTERFACE ELEMENTS IN USE ON THE WEB

Another popular interface construct being used these days as dynamic HTML becomes more acceptable, *click and drag* involves the use of dynamically positioned elements on the screen. The user can click to select and then drag the elements around and position them as he likes, resulting in a more flexible interface. The biggest problem with this technique is the question of how to inform the user that he can do it in the first place.

In early demonstrations of our sample application that employed this technique, the users we showed it to had to be told that they could in fact click and drag the words around on the page. Once they realized what the interface was capable of, they quickly adapted, but overcoming the technological limitations of previous generations of browsers is often easier than overcoming an ingrained sense of those limitations in the users themselves.

An interface tactic made popular by Netscape's Netcenter and HotWired's Webmonkey sites, among others, the layer-based collapsing hierarchical menu is a good example of how dynamic HTML can add incredible functionality and at the same time annoy the user to no end. When Netscape rolled out its first dynamic HTML menu, shown in Figure 4-12, it took far too long to download and usually interrupted users as they were trying to do something else. Netscape eventually scrapped it in favor of the Yahoo! portal metaphor.

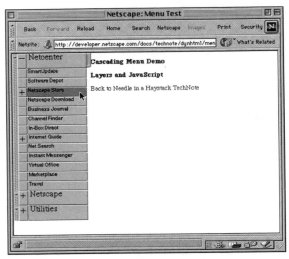

Figure 4-12: The Netscape dynamic HTML menu demo

Webmonkey, however, continues to use their menu, shown in Figure 4-13, which is a stripped-down version of the same idea. The nature of each site's audience is one factor that contributed greatly to the failure of the former and the continued use of the latter. Netscape's home page remains the default home page for tens of millions of users who may be simply unaware that they can actually change the setting in their browser. Webmonkey, on the other hand, caters to an extremely savvy and technically proficient set – the early adopters and Web developers who enjoy testing the cutting edge.

We've covered quite a range of interface ideas, from the early link color choices to near-complete emulation of existing operating system interfaces using DHTML and layers. Many of the conventions we've discussed are merely suggested rather than absolutely binding, but they should be respected in any case due to the possibility of confusing their adherents. The traditional form elements have been adapted to new uses, especially with the advent of client-side scripting, and visual metaphors such as beveled buttons are still extremely popular. Overall, most of these interface ideas stay within the bounds of what is provided by HTML and simple JavaScripts, or attempt to emulate existing interfaces from other environments.

Figure 4-13: The Webmonkey dynamic HTML menu system

So what happens when designers and programmers abandon the traditional interfaces altogether? Through the use of plug-in technologies such as Flash and Shockwave, or QuickTime VR, new media comes full circle from its early days in the development of multimedia CD-ROMs. Java, a complete programming language and environment, provides endless opportunity to develop new interfaces and establish conventions of its own. Let's take a look at some of the ways that this is happening.

Pushing the Envelope, Just a Bit

New, Web-based technologies are making it possible to get completely arbitrary with interface design, which is no longer bound to form elements and links. For the most part, designers and programmers cooperate to provide usable interfaces that are not too far afield of tradition. But some applications are really pushing the envelope, due either to an experimental attitude on the part of the designers and programmers or to the demands imposed by completely new environments.

BROWSER PLUG-INS

So far, we have restricted our discussion to what you can do with HTML and JavaScript using traditional interface elements in innovative ways. However, the Web contains far more than simple HTML. With the introduction of the Netscape browser plug-in architecture, as well as Sun Microsystems' HotJava browser and Java programming language, suddenly interfaces could be as complex or as nontraditional as you could make them. Still other environments came into being to address deficiencies in text-driven hypermedia.

VRML   Mark Pesce created the Virtual Reality Modeling Language (VRML) in order to bring a three-dimensional space to the Web. Using simple shape and texture definitions, entire worlds were brought to life that contained their own sense of place. You were suddenly able to navigate not only from page to page as before, but literally sail through a representation of three-dimensional space containing planets and trees and walls and houses. As you might imagine, this required new interfaces, new tools, and a new understanding of what it meant to be in cyberspace.

The earliest VRML browsers and browser plug-ins enabled the user to move about within the 3D representation by manipulating the mouse. Moving the mouse forward moved the user forward in space. Moving the mouse to the left or right rotated the user's viewpoint around a vertical axis, and then pulled the user back. In another of the modes provided, the user could adjust their elevation on the z plane, or manipulate a wire-frame representation of a globe to maneuver within the space. Various VRML browsers and plug-ins provided a wide range of different tools for exploration. A more recent VRML browser plug-in, shown in Figure 4-14, displays a virtual office Steven built a few years ago.

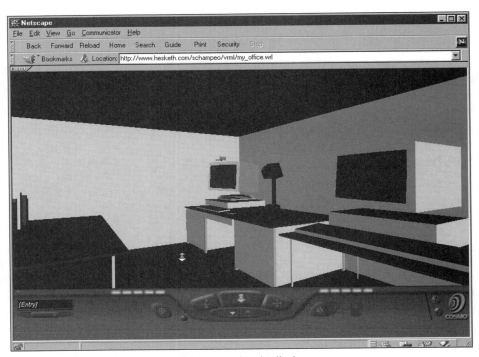

Figure 4-14: An example of a VRML browser plug-in display

Obviously, the introduction of entirely new modes of representation required the introduction of new interface mechanisms. But what of the context shifts required when an existing interface builder is ported to run within Web browsers?

TCL/TK   John Osterhout created the Tool Command Language (TCL) to provide a generic mechanism for controlling applications via a powerful scripting language. The idea was to reduce the number of one-off scripting languages developed to support scriptable applications. Just one example of this sort of interaction between an application and an embedded scripting language involves the use of TCL to define and drive menu systems and major modes for a text editor. Tk is an extension to TCL that provides a way to build visual interfaces and script their behavior using TCL.

As with nearly everything else on the planet, TCL has been ported to run within Web browsers as a plug-in. As a result, it is possible to create Tk-based interfaces within the browser window and then control them using TCL scripts. There are even efforts underway to integrate TCL and Java. The end result is yet another kind of programmable interface with its own display characteristics.

JAVA AND THE AWT, SWING, AND OTHERS
Java is a complete programming language designed for use in set-top boxes, but quickly repurposed to run inside Web browsers. Java applets can create their own interfaces using the Abstract Windowing Toolkit (AWT), as well as more recent interface widget sets such as Swing. Programmers often use Java to provide powerful menu systems, image map-based navigation systems, and even complete, self-contained applications. One of the winners of the first Java applet contest created an entire terminal emulator that could be used to log into a remote computer — all from within the context of a Web browser window.

Due to the way that Java was implemented across platforms, using hooks into the target system's windowing toolkits, a Java applet using the AWT could use the Windows widgets on Windows machines, the Macintosh interface on Macintosh systems, and Motif on UNIX. Alternately, Java supplies its own interface look and feel with extension widget toolkits. All of this variety adds up to a pressing need to establish new interface conventions as well as to observe existing conventions on the target platforms. When the target platform is a Web browser, things become more complicated, obviously, due to the browser's cross-platform nature.

A popular use for Java within the context of regular Web sites is the creation of menu systems for navigation that provide functionality far beyond that provided by HTML, especially in earlier browsers, which support Java but not dynamic HTML. Of course, menus come in all shapes, colors, and sizes, and have widely divergent feature sets. One popular Java-based menu system, shown in Figure 4-15, allows for extreme configuration flexibility by using images and other mechanisms to define the look and feel of the interface.

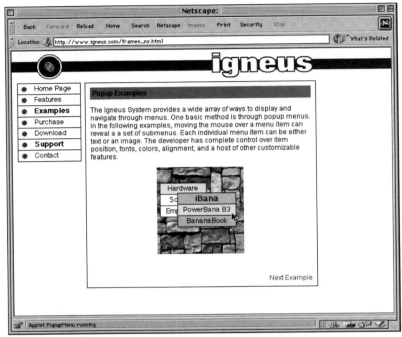

Figure 4-15: An example of a Java menu system from Igneus

SHOCKWAVE AND FLASH

Shockwave and Flash are popular non-HTML multimedia formats for the delivery of vector graphics, animations, sound, and other dynamic content. Shockwave is in fact a form of multimedia created from Director movies that provides full programmability, event-driven interaction, and interface creation. Flash is used for vector graphics and sound, and expands the capabilities of online multimedia in a highly optimized fashion. Using these technologies, it is possible to create entire multimedia applications with arbitrary interfaces and run them in most Web browsers.

As may be evident even from this cursory review of a few of the many technologies available, the art of online interface design runs the gamut. From the earliest days of the Web to the present day and beyond, it seems nearly impossible to establish a set of binding interface conventions. There are, of course, conventions that any interface designer or programmer should be aware of, but equally inviting are the possibilities for redefining them or introducing new mechanisms.

It would be simple if the Web were simply a collection of sites containing bulleted lists of links to corporate policies or annual reports. Anyone venturing onto the Web today, however, eventually realizes that there is a lot more going on. The Web is a hotbed of creative envelope pushing, and a crucible from which new conventions and perhaps even new attitudes toward the interface itself may emerge. The drive toward reductionist, functional, portal sites only highlights the way in which other sites have left the user struggling to understand these new interface paradigms.

Moving Beyond Conventional Interfaces

Now that you've learned about some of the more conventional Web interface ideas, what else can you do? The sky is the limit, it would seem. So where do you start? Does it make sense to try to limit the interface when so much is still being defined? What interface elements needed for everyday applications are missing from the Web? How can you use dynamic HTML to provide some of those missing pieces? Where is it inappropriate to apply dynamic HTML?

Perhaps more importantly for our purposes here, what kinds of environments will demand custom interface elements, and will we be able to meet those demands with dynamic HTML?

Unconventional Interface Elements

Many applications have special requirements. It is in the nature of an application to have some sort of distinguishing characteristic or unique requirement that makes it necessary to create something new in order to meet the needs of the app.

We've talked about some of the familiar contexts in which standard HTML interface elements are useful. In other cases, we've discussed how you can extend these standard elements to provide innovative new functionality using scripting and creative layout. However, we've barely scratched the surface. The interface elements described in the following sections are used in a multitude of contexts that are not provided at all by the base set of HTML form elements.

SLIDER BARS

Slider bars, or *sliders,* are a common interface element that enables the user to select a value among a range. Although often used for the selection of arbitrary values, they may also be used to represent discrete choices where each value is also represented by a color or other distinguishing characteristic relative to which the slider is positioned. For a limited range of values, option lists could be used, but it is often considered useful to display the entire range of values and enable users to see the effects of their choice as they slide the element along the range.

In our sample application, we use sliders to provide the user with an opportunity to set each of the red, green, and blue values for a Web-safe color. Figure 4-16 shows this custom color picker. The user can then apply the newly defined color to any of the exposed preferences settings, such as the color of the playing field.

COLOR PICKERS

Sliders are often used in *color pickers* to represent the value of a color or component of a combination of colors. There are many other factors involved, including a fixed number of colors to choose from, or a series of related characteristics such as hue, saturation, and value. There are also playful uses, such as the Macintosh crayon color picker, shown in Figure 4-17, which enables the user to choose colors from a visual representation of colored crayons.

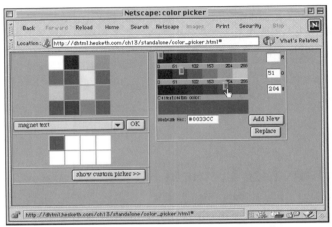

Figure 4-16: The custom color picker, demonstrating the use of slider bars

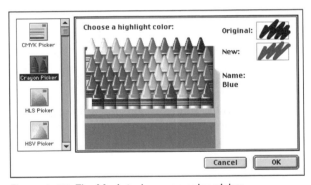

Figure 4-17: The Macintosh crayon color picker

DIALS

The dial is another interface element found in many contexts involving a choice between either discrete or continuous values. Dials are usually circular in nature, with marks representing gradations or other choices. Derek Powazek's Kvetch! site, shown in Figure 4-18, uses a dial to represent the choice between several topics about which the site's users can kvetch, or complain.

Figure 4-18: Kvetch.com's dial as topic selector

FREE-FORM INTERFACE ELEMENTS

At the other end of the spectrum of interface elements we find anything ranging from deliberate attempts to mislead users or get them to question their assumptions about the interface and their interaction with it, to elements simply provided to meet unique requirements. Some interfaces include helpful (if ultimately annoying) animated paperclips or talking cats. Still others, like the popular Neko and Xeyes programs, are intended to amuse or aid the user in search of their cursor. Neko features an animated kitten that chases the cursor, represented as a tiny mouse, all around the user's screen. Some users find these kinds of elements, some of which should be considered applications in their own right, useful or entertaining. Xeyes, for example, displays a pair of eyes on the user's menu bar or other area of the screen that follow the cursor around, making it easier for the user to keep track of it.

An entire class of free-form interfaces has formed around applications designed to enable the user to manage notes and other information in ways intended to mirror the way that he or she thinks. These information managers, such as the Brain from Natrificial, LLC, use various mechanisms to enable users to display the relationships between their jottings and manipulate them accordingly. These applications are obviously operating under a different set of assumptions about the best way to manage information, and therefore require new and innovative interfaces.

Why This Is Both Challenge and Opportunity

The increasing power of personal- and workstation-class computers is enabling a revolution in the way that applications are designed, both from the standpoint of the interface itself and from the architectural perspective. Once standard assumptions about our operating environments are no longer valid, or have been expanded to include networking, hypertext, multimedia, and other powerful tools and technologies.

The problem with this expansion and revision of assumptions is that the interfaces we use every day were founded upon certain assumptions, and our applications were written to work within them. The new assumptions require a radical inquiry into the validity of our interfaces and the design of our applications. Even something as simple as networked file sharing becomes unrecognizable or challenges both the user and the designer when taken to the next level.

Users are challenged because they are now tasked with working within new environments, even as their interfaces are built on increasingly outdated assumptions.

Designers are challenged with discovering new interface ideas that more accurately reflect the new environments, while at the same time maintaining some continuity with the comfortable interfaces of today and yesterday.

AN OPPORTUNITY TO DISCARD OUTDATED METAPHORS

One of the benefits of this revision of and inquiry into the assumptions underlying our interfaces is that it provides us with an opportunity to discard metaphors that no longer suit our purposes. Interface theorists are starting to agree that metaphors, especially those of a visual nature, are less useful now than they used to be, and may even present obstacles to learning where they once provided stepping-stones. Of what use is a traditional desktop metaphor for a generation that has always had a computer?

Perhaps more importantly, what use is a file and folder organizational metaphor in the age of increasingly networked, database-driven applications? Specialized, task-oriented applications seem increasingly restrictive as groupware and integrated office suites become commonplace. The need for software broken into components is on the rise, as chunks of data and other information must be displayed in multiple formats and to many different audiences. It is safe to say that the revolution in the underlying technologies will take shape as an evolution in interface design. What shape will our interfaces take, though? Will they be able to reflect the new realities accurately, or will they continue to stand in the way of progress?

WIMP: RIP?   The WIMP interface doesn't show any signs of going away just yet, though there are certainly applications that don't fit into its constraints. Specialized tweaks and new methods will likely continue to supplant the model as appropriate to meet the demands of new problems. As we've seen, floating palettes and toolbars have extended the icon, and merged the menu with a more persistently visible model.

The pointer has been extended to support things like styluses and pressure-sensitive tablets, and cursors have become very dynamic indeed, including animations and context-sensitivity. As mentioned earlier in the discussion of VRML, there is a lot of potential for alternate pointing devices and use of the third dimension that hasn't been tapped yet.

Windows themselves haven't changed much, although they provide for more user-configurability, as Windows 95, the UNIX X window manager Enlightenment, and the popular Macintosh control panel Kaleidoscope have shown. Other interface elements, such as scrollbars, continue to evolve with innovative ideas like having double arrows at each end to reduce the mouse movement required to scroll a document.

The WIMP model will be around for a long time, we suspect. As long as there are applications that deal with the same constraints that WIMP was designed to overcome, WIMP will continue to provide solutions. WIMP is also remarkably resilient, and coexists peacefully with extensions that handle the things that it doesn't. Future revisions will happen at the level of abstraction directly above that addressed by WIMP, and will change the mental models WIMP implements without necessarily modifying the core interface ideas themselves.

IS THE DESKTOP/FILE SYSTEM MODEL STILL RELEVANT?   The real question is if existing interfaces accurately reflect a file system model. If so, are they too tightly bound to the ideas of disk, file, and folder? Can they be extended to support the Web? If not, then what *is* the best model to use?

A good place to start is by asking what the fundamental unit of data in your system is. The answers may surprise you, especially if you are used to dealing with files. Remember that the file is just a storage mechanism — a way of collecting all of the data relevant to a particular situation into one place. Folders are just abstractions that help the user deal with lots of different files by organizing them into collections according to a scheme. Subsequently, it is just as possible to use a different scheme, a different level of abstraction, or a different mental model.

On the Web, we are already becoming used to looking for information in terms of the URL, remote server, or subsite, or by keyword lookup at a search engine or directory. This is in sharp contrast to opening a file from a folder on a local hard drive, although the model is similar.

It all comes down to a matter of the reliability of the storage medium, and your corresponding comfort level with the medium. When hard drives were new, expensive, and not always reliable, floppies were still used for backup and data transfer. When network connectivity was unreliable, people kept local versions of files on their local hard disk and copied them to the network for sharing purposes. The more reliable new technologies become, the more comfortable users are with the idea of using them to store their data. As users become more comfortable, they simplify their metaphors, or the metaphors are simplified for them without their noticing.

As metaphors shift, the technology that underlies them often shifts as well, sometimes without even requiring a corresponding modification to the metaphor itself. A file from the early Macintosh system bears little resemblance to a file used on it today. Today's files use more resources, different formats, and are part of a much more complex system. They are stored on different file systems, accessed by way of different drivers, and so forth. Yet, we still think that the icon on the desktop refers to "a file." The same is true of HTML files, which use an extended protocol (HTTP/1.1) and are served by much more complex server software (such as Apache), and perhaps even generated on the fly to suit the user's conditions and requirements at the time (using CGI, PHP, ASP, or client-side scripts). They are still called "Web pages," though, reflecting the static terminology of books and paper.

With the rise of full-blown applications, the facade of simplicity will shift (if it is not discarded altogether), and will be replaced by a more suitable means of describing the different classes of Web content. A URL that launches a complete, client-side, mortgage preapproval and loan management application is a far cry from a page containing a bulleted list. The user may not be able to bookmark it, for example, or if they do, the existing bookmark scheme may not include support for appropriate session variables and so forth.

The idea and implementation of enabling the user to save data from a dynamic HTML application may be incredibly similar in process, interface, and metaphor to that experienced by the non-networked desktop user. However, its implementation may use CGI or a server module to retrieve data from the application, perhaps preprocess it on the client end, and finally store it as a field in a database rather than as bits on a local disk drive. The end result is the same – the data is stored – but this raises the questions, "How is the data to be retrieved?" and "How does the user refer to the data?"

WHAT WILL REPLACE THE FILE?   Many people have voiced ideas as to what kind of model will replace the file/folder/disk storage metaphor. Most have agreed that the network will be the fundamental driver in changing people's perceptions of how their data is created, stored, and retrieved, but nobody can say with certainty what language we will use to describe its components.

The key characteristic of the file, at least for this discussion, is its name, or label. We create files, give them names, and save them within a hierarchical system formed of folders. Each folder has a label as well. The label or label chain is used to retrieve the file at a later time. Users are accustomed to this system because they have used it for decades. But as we hinted at earlier, there are other mechanisms already being used for retrieval, such as URLs, keywords at search engines, and so forth. Users are already quite comfortable with the idea of retrieving information using nontraditional means.

The next step is to determine how network data storage will evolve. Retrieval is the easy part, as anyone can be informed of the appropriate label, or reference, to the data in question. That label may then itself be stored, passed around, or what have you. Storage involves more complicated demands on users, particularly if they are expected to assign the label. The mechanisms required must be simple, reliable, and easily taught; if complexity is inherent in them, that complexity must be hidden from the user just as it is within the existing system.

Alan Cooper, in his book *About Face: The Essentials of User Interface Design*, raises some extremely interesting questions for the future of data storage metaphors, some of which are very relevant to the future of dynamic HTML applications. He begins with distinctions between files in memory and files on disk. Why do applications ask users if they want to save files they have opened and modified? Why don't applications assume users want to save everything they do, and then ask if they want to treat a particular set of changes — a point on the revision timeline — as a separate document?

He then proceeds to question revisions and their granularity. What counts as a complete revision? At what point do we want to create a new document and break with the revision chain, and when do we merely want the application to remember — and label — the document's state? Cooper uses the terms *snapshot* and *milestone* to refer to these different, but related, document concepts. A *snapshot* is a copy of a document stored separately from the document. Changes made to the first document are not reflected in the snapshot. A *milestone*, however, is merely a labeled point along the document's revision chain. By providing new terminology that replaces the outdated but entrenched terms and accurately reflects the way we use the file system model, Cooper frees us from the tyranny of convention.

According to Cooper's view, that the user knows so much about the technology underlying the file system metaphor suggests a serious problem for two reasons. First, users are unlikely to knowingly give up the environment they're familiar and comfortable with even when their mental model of the system no longer corresponds to the reality. Second, the fact that the users know so much about the underlying model is indicative of the lack of faith they had in it in the early days. All too often, users learn more about the underlying implementation out of fear for the security of their data. The hidden metaphor behind the implementation is insufficient to convince them of the implementation's soundness.

To summarize, the key to comprehending the next generation storage and retrieval model is understanding the ways that people actually use the current system, and providing them with new terminology and software that hides the gory implementation details from them. As with anything new, the user may reject the new model out of hand, clinging to existing (and familiar) models, even if they are horribly flawed. Faith in the reliability and stability of the new system is a prerequisite for adoption, as is the clear evidence of the benefits of such a system.

The Web used a different system, the URL, to refer to its resources. People adopted it because there was no other way to use the Web. Over time, as they used the Web more, people realized that they wanted better ways to track, store, and manage their resources, and they developed new ways to do so. Bookmark managers, Internet shortcuts, and so forth all hide the complexity of URLs to some extent. Eventually, the URL, too, will fade into the background, just as it is no longer necessary for the user to know anything about disk blocks and sectors, or inodes (the low-level mechanism UNIX uses to manage files on a disk).

THE MANY CHALLENGES

Usability engineers are jumpy folks. Why? Because they are often called in to figure out why seemingly rational interfaces fail. The following sections describe some of the ways that existing interface metaphors fail, and new, groundbreaking interfaces completely baffle the user. The issues affect everyone from the programmer and interface designer to the user, including those users obliquely affected by differences between multiple applications.

USERS UNFAMILIAR WITH NEW INTERFACES   The first (and often most visible) challenge to the introduction of a new interface model is user acceptance. Most users don't like change. They may be ten times as productive, their frustration levels may go down, and they may be able to use the new system more comfortably than any other they have ever used. . . eventually. It takes time, and during that time users judge your interface on its resemblance to the one it is intended to replace. The very features that introduce the most change may be the features that cause the most frustration among users.

Always remember that your users have likely invested a great deal of time and effort into becoming accustomed to the old environment. Where possible, try to leverage the existing interface and gradually move the user to the new methods and models. Many applications feature compatibility modes for the applications they are designed to compete with or replace. By emulating the environment of the existing tool, you win the trust of the user. Over time, you are able to introduce new and innovative features that extend the existing application rather than abruptly replace it.

INTERFACE DESIGNERS UNFAMILIAR WITH PROCESS   When an interface is in flux, the designer is required, just as the user is, to straddle the boundary between the new and the old, respecting both. When the designer is unfamiliar with the process that an interface must enable, or when terminology used to express it changes, confusion and poor design are likely results. Designers are subject to the same inertia that affects users. They like to work within a consistent arena with well-defined rules just as much as users do.

Because they are often called upon to manage the transition from one process and implementation to a newer process with different assumptions, designers must be careful to balance the two. They must also determine the appropriate time to roll out new and innovative features based on the user's response to those features. Sometimes it is best to wait and provide subtle shifts in the interface without making clean breaks with the past.

PROGRAMMERS ASKED TO BREAK NEW GROUND   Programmers are not immune from the issues faced by users and designers, either. When given the choice between an implementation that is proven to work and one that attempts to break new ground at the risk of not working right for the first few iterations, many programmers prefer the proven solution.

The criteria may be different from that faced by the user but the end result is the same. Fear of change and the instability introduced by change can lead to a less daring or less efficient implementation.

UNINTENDED CONSEQUENCES OF THE NOVEL   Some of the classic software development stories tell of new applications designed to mirror existing processes that sometimes introduce changes in the process itself, requiring updates that more accurately reflect the new process. This iterative cycle can be incredibly frustrating, as the programmers begin to suspect that the requirements were not clearly defined in the first place, and the users suspect that the application is only going to introduce new inefficiencies to make up for those that it eliminates.

Unfortunately, this is a fact of life in the world of software development. The best way to combat the syndrome is to ask probing questions directed at documenting the process as it exists, but that also ask if there might be a more appropriate way to do things.

Moving Beyond Tradition

The new era of networked, cross-platform applications will combine lessons learned from the past 30 years of interface theory with new problems that result from exposure to new environments and their assumptions. Mental models will be constructed and quickly found wanting, and will be replaced by newer, better, more appropriate models, or the interfaces of the past will prove capable of riding out the storm. It is unlikely that there will be no change at all in the way that users interact with their applications.

The task at hand involves accurately understanding the manner in which our current assumptions and implementations reflect the actual needs of the user. In addition, there is a definite need to forecast the way that such needs will evolve, given new situations. Our interfaces need to reflect these new ways of working and thinking.

The Importance of Navigation

One of the most commonly cited differences between so-called traditional software and the interfaces used by new media (or multimedia) applications is the latter's need for navigation. Why is navigation so important? Is it really that crucial for Web applications to be concerned with strategies usually associated with Web sites? Are we just placing a new moniker on an old interface problem? How does the introduction of a need for navigation affect the manner in which interfaces are defined?

A Recap of Traditional Goal-/ Task-Oriented Interfaces

Goal-oriented interfaces are serial, proceeding toward a defined conclusion. Task-oriented interfaces display a tendency to revolve around single movements, where the user chooses a task, performs it, and is done. They are iterative in nature, based on repetitive performance. No interface is truly one way or the other — aspects of both are often combined. For example, an interface might provide access to tasks in order to enable completion of a goal.

The key characteristic of traditional interfaces, however, is their static nature. Applications are designed, implemented, and then released. Interfaces are static, designed primarily with the functionality of the application in mind. Evolution usually only occurs discretely as major revisions to the software are released. By contrast, Web sites are highly dynamic, changing to reflect new requirements and deliver new content. Navigation is the crux between the static nature of a design and the dynamically changing character of the site's interface. By providing a relatively static, high-level infrastructure by which the user can maneuver around in and between sections of a site, navigation provides constant updates to the individual components of the site itself, and must also adapt to reflect entirely new components.

How does the addition of navigability affect the design of applications? Are you tasked with making dynamic HTML applications whose interface is as static as those of traditional applications, or do you need to provide for the sort of evolution that a navigational structure enables in content-oriented Web sites?

Is Navigation a Goal or a Task?

This is not an easy question to answer. It's probably not the best way to think about it, anyway. Individual acts of navigation are tasks performed, sometimes on the way to accomplishing a goal, but not necessarily. Technically, a navigation scheme is a static, high-level abstraction placed atop a dynamic set of content that enables users to find what they are looking for. Much has been made of the relationships between the rules of traditional interface design and those governing the design of a solid navigation scheme.

For the most part, navigation occupies a higher position in the hierarchy of abstractions than do the tasks represented by given interface elements. But to a certain extent, a menu system and a navigational scheme are remarkably similar in scope and design. They both offer the user a direct means of access; navigation gives access to content, and a menu system gives access to functionality. Menu systems, such as those used in traditional interfaces, may even be used to enable the user to navigate around a site. They both use clustering; menu items are grouped together under menus, and navigation has major and subordinate characteristics.

Mental Models of Navigation and Structure

Users form both immediate and gradual mental models of systems as they are used. The primary challenge for designers wishing to integrate navigation into an interface is to encourage the acquisition of accurate models by the user. In the case of traditional interfaces, the intent of the design is to reflect accurately the aggregate functionality available to the user. In navigational schemes, the intent of the design is to aggregate the content available to the user. When we integrate functionality into a site as well, we must provide navigation that accurately reflects this crossing of the border between content and functionality.

Applications whose functionality is spread across several modules, each of which may be accessed separately, must use navigational strategies to inform users that they are about to enter the application at a certain point. Here the lines begin to blur between content and functionality. Users must be given a navigational scheme that encourages them to build the appropriate mental models of the entire system, from both content-oriented and functional standpoints. So how is navigation commonly organized for content-oriented sites, and how does this need to adapt to functionality-oriented sites? Let's start with hierarchy, which is perhaps truest reflection of the way that content is actually stored on a site.

HIERARCHY

Web sites that consist primarily of static content, perhaps in the form of Web pages stored in directory trees, are fundamentally hierarchical in nature. Navigation may choose to either reflect this hierarchy or distract the user away from it. In smaller sites, the closer the navigation reflects the hierarchy, the more accurate the mental model acquired by the user. But what of larger sites, or sites where content changes rapidly?

CLUSTERS

A common approach to larger sites involves clustering related forms of content and providing high-level navigation to those areas, with sub-navigation that lets the user drill down further into the actual content. The mental model acquired in this case is still fairly hierarchical, although the larger the site, the more opportunities exist to introduce non-hierarchical, or hypertextual, connections between content in one area and content in another. Too many cross-links and the user gets lost, having had their mental model stretched out of whack by the sheer number of nodes.

THE SHELL NAVIGATION/INTERFACE MODEL

One solution to the problem of the acquisition of inaccurate mental models in large or constantly updated sites is the so-called *shell* model. This approach, common to news sites and others oriented toward quick drill-down by the user, involves reproducing all or most of the navigation on every page. Users don't need to develop a mental model of the system because their options are always available, much as menus and menu items are in traditional applications. The downside to this model is that such navigational redundancy often results in a cluttered interface, with row after row of links down one side of the page, or across the top or bottom navigation bar. The perceptive reader will notice that the shell model attempts to address the same problems as the traditional menu model does, but isn't as successful from the standpoint of maximizing screen real estate. Perhaps DHTML solutions will be able to help future implementations of the shell model?

NAVIGATING TO FUNCTIONALITY

The primary challenge faced by designers building navigational schemes that must take functionality into account is the difficulty in distinguishing between links to content and links to functionality. One approach involves exposing the functionality on the same interface as the links to content, as with search form inputs or newsletter subscription forms, but this is only feasible for rather limited functions of an interface.

When the application in question is large or complex, the designers of the system must consider either the possibility of breaking its functionality into smaller components, each of which may be navigated to, or providing a well-labeled mechanism that launches the entire application.

Granularity

The question remains: How does the designer encourage the formation of appropriate mental models? Fortunately, several levels of granularity are available to the designer, similar to the way that tasks and menu items are matched up in traditional interface design. The designer must break the system down into its components, providing navigation to each component as appropriate to the nature of the system in question. These components come in several forms.

PAGES, FRAMES, AND WINDOWS

The most obvious level of granularity available to the designer of navigational schemes is the individual page. Because all links are made to pages, the question becomes one of determining the ways in which the various pages may be created to aggregate certain specific content areas or functionality. Framesets may be used to reflect the natural divisions between parts of a site, such as navigation versus content. New windows may be spawned, each containing the final object of navigation, or even containing further navigational options.

SITES AND SUBSITES

The *subsite* is also useful as an organizational technique for large sites or sites that contain several different kinds of content areas. The key to successful subsite design is to provide cues to the user that they have entered a whole new area of the site that differs substantially from the others. These cues may take the form of different color or layout schemes, or they may use different headers to help distinguish between the different areas. Individual subsites may contain their own internal navigation, as well as navigation back to the high levels of the site, or within areas on the same level.

Navigation Is an Environment

Put bluntly, navigation provides a sort of environment in which the user is either made to feel comfortable, in control, and grounded, or uneasy, helpless, and lost. The navigational environment must coexist with the actual content of the site without becoming confusing to the user.

IT JUST HAPPENS TO BE STREWN ABOUT OUR INTERFACE

Much as menu systems provide access to major functionality within an application, navigation provides access to the major content areas within a site. The interesting thing about navigation, especially in very large sites, is that it is slippery, defined with respect to the site currently being visited. The trick is to distinguish between internal navigation for the current area and any higher-level navigation that provides access to the other areas.

Often, this distinction is maintained by keeping high-level navigation in a different area of the screen from internal navigation. Depending upon the nature and complexity of the site in question, this may mean that the major navigation occupies the top of the screen, perhaps directly beneath a header, while the internal navigation is interspersed throughout the content, or placed on a sidebar or in the page footer.

In summary, navigation performs the same or similar functions within a content-driven interface as menu systems and other interface elements perform within a functionality-driven application. Navigation maps forms of access to content just as menu items map forms of access to available functionality. When navigation within a hybrid site consisting of both content and application functionality must deal with providing access to both, great care must be taken to ensure that the user is not confused as to where the navigation will lead them.

Reaching the Rest of Us

One characteristic of interface design that we haven't covered yet is *accessibility*. For some, the word refers to the practice of ensuring that users with disabilities aren't denied access to the basic functionality available to other users. Another aspect of the term reflects the provision of alternative and redundant methods of performing tasks; providing keyboard shortcuts for mechanisms commonly performed using a mouse, for example. The most commonly used of these mechanisms, the ALT attribute to the IMG element, simply enable users who surf without their browser set to automatically download and display images to have access to navigation and other content.

Any interface designer must be aware of the accessibility mechanisms available to them for use in their designs, as well as the nature of their audience. For applications, they must be creative and understand that direct support for an accessibility mechanism (such as long image descriptions, defined in HTML 4) doesn't necessarily rule out an alternate method of providing such access. In any case, it is important for anyone building Web sites to know about and understand the issue.

Accessibility as a Metric for the Success of an Interface Design

One of the oft-touted benefits of the Windows interface is the extent to which it provides keyboard accessibility to most, if not all, of its interface elements. Users can reasonably expect to be able to keep their hands on the keyboard without having to resort to the mouse at all for most purposes. The Macintosh, on the other hand, emphasizes the use of the mouse, which influences the design of its applications. UNIX users are naturally more accustomed to using the keyboard, although an increasing number of applications are available for the various GUI window managers with varying mouse/keyboard accessibility.

Dynamic HTML is currently still very reliant on the mouse, due to its uneven support for keyboard event handling across platforms. Common keys, such as the arrows and function keys, do not work well across platforms and in most cases are not supported at all. This places a serious handicap on the designer of DHTML applications, as commonly expected features such as tab order, support for the Macintosh ⌘ key, and other platform-specific keyboard capabilities are simply unavailable. Modifier keys are still limited to Shift, Ctrl, and Alt, and designers must also ensure that their shortcuts do not conflict with pre-existing shortcuts in the browser or underlying OS.

One area of accessibility for which dynamic HTML may prove to be quite useful is that of user configurability. Interfaces that enable users to choose their colors, font sizes, and so forth are much friendlier than those that don't.

Accessibility and redundancy of access mechanisms are metrics by which we can measure the overall success of a traditional interface. Unfortunately, DHTML applications will remain subpar until more support for these mechanisms is added.

Efforts Under Way to Promote Accessibility

There are many efforts under way to promote widespread accessibility, most notably the World Wide Web Consortium's Web Accessibility Initiative. The WAI was set up in response to a recognition that much of the Web lies off limits or presents severe limitations to people with disabilities or with unique requirements, such as those browsing via palmtop computers, those surfing without image downloading enabled, or the blind accessing the Web using text-to-speech readers.

Because of the complexity of the issue and the increasing use of WYSIWYG authoring tools, the WAI presents a set of guidelines for both authors and developers of Web authoring software. Each guideline is presented along with a priority for its implementation, recommended alternate means of implementing each guideline, and other suggestions.

 The W3C's Web Accessibility Initiative has released the first working draft of its guidelines. You can find more information at the following URL:

`http://www.w3.org/WAI/`

"But It Isn't Feasible for Us to Implement Accessible Interfaces. . . ."

As with any situation involving the need to make your application or interface more complex, adding accessibility often incurs additional costs of development and maintenance. Your first reaction may be that such costs make it infeasible to add support for such mechanisms. However, it is important to realize that many states are requiring that public information, such as that provided by state governments or other public agencies, be accessible to everyone. Be sure to find out more about what is required in your area before you shrug off accessibility as a "nice-to-have" feature – it may be an inescapable requirement.

Summary

Phew! After that whirlwind tour of some of the most important developments in the history of the user interface and how they can be expected to continue evolving in the new medium of the Web, you're probably eager to get to the heart of DHTML. Before we do that, though, let's recap some of the conventions and other ideas we covered in this chapter:

◆ The convention of underlined blue text representing a link is no longer universal, but in nonlinked text, the use of underlines and blue text should be avoided.

◆ Using images and the image map for navigation must be supplemented with text links or alternate text labels to guarantee accessibility.

◆ Many of the conventions established during the Web's heyday are now seen as passé, evidence of the age of a site, or poor taste on the part of the designer.

◆ Form elements have appropriate default uses, but are often used in surprisingly innovative ways to provide new solutions to pressing interface problems.

- Many sites try to emulate existing OS conventions, some more successfully or more appropriately than others, depending on the audience and purpose.

- Browser plug-ins, embedded multimedia, and applets are changing the face of the Web, but are still not universal or are too slow to make part of the default navigation scheme for your site.

- Despite the profusion of available interface elements, many are still lacking and need to be implemented in dynamic HTML.

- Many interface metaphors will evolve and be replaced, while others will be flexible enough to adapt to the Web.

- Navigation changes the idea of what constitutes an interface and presents unique challenges to the traditional developer.

- Making your interface accessible is a primary goal and often a requirement, but limited support in dynamic HTML is an obstacle and a challenge.

The Web has introduced a number of interface conventions, made significant use of existing conventions, and changed the way that people think about ease of use, especially with regard to electronic information systems. Many of the conventions touted as being carved in stone are actually not very well recognized, but should be respected if possible. Many other conventions are being determined as the days pass, but the majority of Web sites and Web-based applications remain hard to use and inaccessible to many. The designers and programmers who build the next generation of tools, both for the end user and for authors, must take these issues into account.

Part II

IN THIS PART:

Confused about what exactly dynamic HTML is? No need to fear — we present the technologies that comprise DHTML using an easy-to-grasp noun-verb-adjective metaphor. Each of the requisite technologies is presented: HTML and the Document Object Model, JavaScript, and Cascading Style Sheets. By mapping nouns to document objects, verbs to JavaScript functions, and adjectives to Cascading Style Sheets, we show you how to build sentences and paragraphs (components) so that you can write stories (applications) of your own.

Chapter 5

The Document Object Model: Nouns

IN THIS CHAPTER

◆ What dynamic HTML is and isn't

◆ Musing about a standard API for Web Documents

◆ Why we need a Document Object Model (DOM)

◆ How the DOM organizes documents

◆ What the HTML DOM specification looks like

◆ Other document models

What Does Dynamic Really Mean?

The word *dynamic* indicates flow, energy, and intelligence — everything about life itself that human beings cherish. Dynamism is the ability to keep moving, to cleverly read the environment and alter it at any time to better fit in, and to morph from situation to situation like a shrewd chameleon.

Before dynamic HTML, Web pages were just that — flat *pages,* similar to a magazine ad or a newspaper article. You could read them and you could click a link to go to another page. But that's all, folks.

Then Web servers caught the dynamic bug, making it possible to customize pages (depending on various conditions) before they were passed along. If you viewed a page of stock market quotes, for instance, new values popped up in your HTML depending on when you grabbed it.

But dynamic HTML goes further. Dynamic HTML pages can change even after they've been loaded. This is no small thing. What this means is that yesterday's Web page is today's free-flowing networked software application.

With dynamic HTML, graphics can slide across the screen, and over and under one another. Forms can modify and check themselves depending on the information typed into them. New pages can be constructed entirely from scratch based on where a user clicks or drags without having to waste time contacting a Web server.

As dynamic HTML matures, the sky becomes the only limit. Dynamic HTML breaks all boundaries and enables endless opportunities for a full interface design, helping people to perform more advanced tasks than ever, do them better, and glide through the whole ordeal faster.

Dynamic HTML Isn't a Language

Dynamic HTML is not a computer language. It isn't a technology or a brand. Nobody owns it and no one company or person created it. Not Netscape, not the World Wide Web Consortium, not even Big Daddy Microsoft. Dynamic HTML is just a concept that defines how Web pages (the core of which are always HTML) can be altered, adjusted, and otherwise manipulated on the fly. Dynamic HTML is composed of many technologies. The purpose of this part of the book is to introduce you to these technologies. They include the Document Object Model (DOM), JavaScript client-side scripting, Cascading Style Sheets (CSS), and more. Today's dynamic HTML naturally relies on the Hypertext Markup Language, because HTML is the basis of pretty much every modern Web page. However, as we discuss later in the chapter, the future of the Web will also make heavy use of the Extensible Markup Language (XML). As new technologies overtake these old ones, dynamic HTML, being the dynamic creature it is, will be able to keep up.

Dynamic HTML Works Like a Language, Though

So what *is* dynamic HTML? In its most basic incarnation, dynamic HTML is just a Web page laid out with Cascading Style Sheets (CSS) and then controlled using a client-side scripting language such as JavaScript.

The tricky part is getting it all to work with various versions of Netscape Navigator, Internet Explorer, other browsers, multiple client-side scripting languages, and other markup and layout languages. And then to take that and get it to work on every computer platform known to humankind.

The Language of Language

Language is perhaps the best example of dynamism. As soon as a thick dictionary comes off the weary presses, it is out of date. New slang is invented, new uses are concocted, or a new accent or dialect crops up. Yet despite its inherent wiliness, we humans use language as our primary means of communication. In fact, it is precisely the dynamism of language that makes it so useful. If you can't say what you want with the vocabulary and grammar at hand, you can invent something new. Sure, it makes for confusion at times, but it also makes for limitless potential.

At the heart of any language is its structure: nouns, verbs, adjectives, and adverbs. Languages around the world differ in the order that these structures are used. Sometimes an adjective follows a noun, sometimes it precedes it, and sometimes the two mesh to form a brand-new word. However, almost every language juggles these building blocks of objects, actions, and descriptions.

Nouns Are Objects

Without nouns where would we be? Heck, the word we itself wouldn't be around if there weren't nouns. Nouns are objects, and objects are the building blocks of the world. Everything you contact with your senses is a noun. "People, places, and things," is the rule of thumb they teach in elementary school. Nouns are the first words most children learn to speak (for example, "Ma-ma" and "Da-da"). This is because nouns don't require any special leap of logic; there's nothing abstract about a noun. Nouns are convenient labels that you can stick on things you want to talk about. Nouns just are.

Look at a Web page. What do you see? There are buttons, images, text, and tables. These are all objects. If you peek behind the scenes at the HTML source code, you also see very clear objects: the *tags*. `<P>` and `<TABLE>` and `<FORM>` are all objects. Each of these element objects may also have several attributes, and these attributes are objects in and of themselves. The Web browser uses these objects to assemble every Web page that you see.

XML documents, too, break down into a nice collection of objects. An XML parser goes through an XML document and figures out what the objects are and how they relate. A browser can then handle these objects appropriately.

Because objects are so tangible, they are a good place for us to start our journey into our dynamic system at hand, dynamic HTML.

Creating Standard Nouns for Web Documents

The problem with nouns is that they're just symbols. Nouns themselves are meaningless unless you are speaking the right language. If you hand a Golden Delicious apple to an infant, a Frenchman, an apple expert from Washington, and a woman from Bombay, they each see, hold, and touch the same apple. They each think, "Ah, an apple" in their own way. But they each use widely different nouns to describe the apple.

The Puzzling World of HTML Objects

Web pages are like bowls of fruit containing some apples, some oranges, and a bunch of bananas. A text layout effect in Internet Explorer and one in Netscape Navigator may look similar, but the HTML code behind the effects may differ widely. Similar-seeming still lifes, then, may actually be made up of slightly different combinations of fruit. Web designers struggle every day to make pages that look the same in Internet Explorer and Netscape Navigator, often resorting to sneaky tricks and out-and-out hacks.

Even if two browsers work with the same HTML code, the way that Internet Explorer 4.0 interacts with the code is very, very different from the way Netscape

Navigator 4.0 does. They both break down the HTML page into objects, but the manner in which they arrange and render these objects varies a great deal. If you want to speak to these browsers and have them manipulate objects in custom ways, you are often left with confusion. So given the same apple within the same bowl of fruit, Navigator calls the apple by one name and Internet Explorer calls it by another.

For instance, Internet Explorer 5.0 represents everything in a very flat way. Suppose you have a layering of three objects. If you want to access the deepest object's *left* property (its location on the page), you might access the apple object as follows:

```
document.all.apple
```

If you wanted to grab the same apple in Navigator 4.5, you might need to go through nested layers:

```
document.layers['apple']
```

Without a standard way of talking about objects, it is impossible to create and maintain a library of techniques that can be used between all brands and versions of browsers.

What is needed, then, is a way to compare apples to apples and oranges to oranges.

Beyond HTML: XML and Markup Documents

As long as we're talking about the standard nouns, we might as well mention XML. The Extensible Markup Language (XML) is a generalized language that enables the insertion of full-fledged data structures into Web pages, and much, much more.

XML enables developers to describe any type of document with any elements or attributes they desire. This turns XML into a metalanguage. All the legal HTML tags, for example, can be described using XML, with a few minor modifications.

It is important to grasp the difference between XML and HTML. HTML is a hardwired markup language; it is very useful for accomplishing a set goal, but you cannot extend it beyond its goal. XML, on the other hand, is all about extension. It lets authors define their own tag and attribute names. For instance, if a circus wanted to publish documents about their operations, they could use XML to invent special tags like <CLOWN>, <LION>, <ELEPHANT>, and <ANIMAL>. Parts of the document tagged with these special tags could then be displayed or parsed in some special way, such as that shown in Listing 5-1.

Listing 5-1: An example of an XML snippet

```
<ANIMAL>
  <LION>Simba</LION>
  <ELEPHANT>Dumbo</ELEPHANT>
</ANIMAL>
```

The circus could place this information in a database, print it out as a report, or manipulate it in any other way they find useful.

An XML document can also contain a description of these tags and how they relate to one another (known as a *Document Type Definition,* or *DTD,* which is discussed later in this chapter) so that applications can flip through a given XML file and determine whether or not it follows its own rules for how it is created.

In addition, HTML documents are by and large flat, beginning with the <HTML> tag and ending with the </HTML> tag. XML documents can have nested structures that are arbitrarily deep, depending on how the document type has been defined. This provides a much richer way to store data. This book, for instance, could be marked up as an XML document. A smart browser could then read in the document and, if set up to do so, show only the chapter headings. Click on any chapter heading and its subheadings automatically expand out. Click again and you get a list of all the sub-subheadings. Click enough times and eventually you have the text itself.

Both HTML and XML are derived from the Standard Generalized Markup Language (SGML). SGML is a very complicated and feature-rich way of creating document types. XML is a pared-down version of SGML that only contains the most commonly used pieces. XML is sometimes referred to whimsically as "SGML-Lite."

Despite their differences, though, both XML and HTML create *markup documents*. These markups only describe data; they don't explicitly define the way it should be presented. Arranging data through markup enables Web browsers (or other applications) to parse in the necessary information and then output the results appropriately. This easy-to-learn document structure made authoring Web pages quite simple and is part of the reason why the Web took off so fast. Right now, you can enjoy most Web pages on dozens of different browsers on numerous operating systems.

Parsed markup documents are also the source of all our headaches, and the reason why the same Web page looks so frustratingly different from browser to browser. Because markup languages such as HTML generally separate the document's structure from its presentation, the browser must have a way of providing and applying the rules for presenting the document. In today's browsers, these rules are hardwired. This means that a slight difference between the hardwired rules from one browser to the next can result in unalterable display discrepancies that the document author must deal with any way they can.

The Importance of an XML Document Model

XML needs a standard way of representing itself. Even more so than HTML, XML documents are often parsed and dynamically constructed on the fly. It is imperative for developers to have a way to look through an XML document and assign each object a certain style. The results of this parsing may be a visual flowchart, a database table, or it may even break down into a standard Web page with pretty pictures. Or, as is the beauty of dynamic HTML, the document can have a menu at the top that lets a user view all of the above, depending on his or her preference.

In order to have true interaction with XML, many different applications must be able to read XML in and parse XML out. Unless these applications agree on a way to break down the messiness of XML into the same objects, the world will be full of inconsistencies, bugs, glitches, and mistakes.

Having XML without a standard document model would be like giving a message written in English to a translator who then transcribed it into Spanish and handed it to a different translator who scripted it back to English. The gist of the original message would probably be there, but important details and nuances would likely be missing.

Creating an API

An *application program interface* (API) is a fancy term for a very beautiful and simple concept: using an agreed-upon set of names and formats for the variables and methods that can and should be used in a computer program. These variables and methods expose the rough and tumble underlying functionality in tightly controlled, orderly ways. By only giving specific access through a few doorways, a distinction is made between a low-level software programmer and an application programmer. An API can remain the same from an application programmer's point of view, even as the underlying software internals are tweaked or even radically revised.

For example, suppose somebody created an API for elevators. The API would likely have the following *properties*, or pieces of information that could be accessed or set:

- `floorAt` — An integer (whole number) property that keeps track of the floor the elevator is currently at.

- `movingUp` — A Boolean (true or false) property that indicates if the elevator is currently moving up. If this is false, the elevator must be moving down.

The API would also have a bunch of *methods*, or actions that could be performed. These might include the following:

- `DownPressed(f)` — A method that lets the elevator know that the down button was pressed for floor *f*. The elevator should be smart enough to keep a list of these presses so that it can stop at appropriate floors.

- `UpPressed(f)` — A method that lets the elevator know that the up button was pressed for floor *f*.

- `Stop()` — A method that immediately stops the elevator in case of a fire.

- `AlarmPressed()` — A method that automatically stops the elevator and sounds an alarm when the alarm button is pressed.

Every elevator could do something slightly different with the information passed back and forth. Some elevators may have an indicator light to show whether the car is rising or descending, or to show the current floor. The API may be extended so that banks of elevators could communicate smartly with one another, and multiple elevators could pick up the most passengers in efficient ways without stopping redundantly at the same floor.

In essence, though, the API works the same for all elevators. When an elevator reaches a new floor, the `floorAt` property is adjusted. When the elevator changes direction, it alters `movingUp` appropriately.

Elevators around the world could use this API. This standard would enable elevator installers to create customized software to control many brands of elevators, so that every elevator would be easier to install, configure, test, and repair. An API would enable two different software companies to come up with two different elevator solutions. Anyone who wanted to install an elevator could pick the software package that interfaced perfectly with the elevator.

Method Acting

Methods are the parts of an API that actually do the dirty work. Methods generally take some information in as parameters, perform some sort of action, and can optionally spit some information back out. They may also be used to force an action to take place on an object without any parameters or arguments at all.

Let's look at a simple method called `multiply`. The `multiply` method takes in two integer number parameters, a and b, and tosses back a third integer that is the product of a and b. The API might look like this:

```
integer multiply(integer a, integer b)
```

If you decide to implement this API, all you have to do is be sure you have a method somewhere in your application called `multiply` that takes in two integers as parameters. How you do the multiplication is up to you. If you want, you can add a b times. Or you can call a low-level multiplication function on your CPU. Either way, anybody who uses your API should be able to call the `multiply` method.

It should then return the same, proper result. For example:

```
a = multiply(2,3)
```

The value of a should be six.

What We Want: A Web Browser API

Many software engineers around the world are busy drinking lots of Coke and hacking away at Web browsers as we speak. We don't want to make their life harder by telling them how to write their programs. All we ask is that they implement an *open* API. In other words, they should make sure their programs can handle a list of important programming procedures and properties. We don't care how they do it, we just want them to do it and use standard names for things. This way, a programmer can write an application that uses the same methods and properties regardless of the platform, and the browser can implement these methods and properties however it likes. The programmer no longer has to test for the platform and browser and supply appropriate workarounds. Everybody is happy.

To sum it up, what we're looking for is a consistent nomenclature for parsed documents. We need to find a noun for every possible object in our Web page that the world can agree upon.

When one country successfully invades another, the victor's language is invariably taught in schools. People who were used to one language are forced to redefine their world in a strange tongue. The reason for this is that an old culture is difficult to hold on to without its associated language. One language means a more homogenous culture—a group that can easily communicate. The downside, of course, is that as language becomes standard, rich and unique cultures are lost.

Much like ethnic or political groups, various browser companies want to keep their own cultures—their own way of speaking about the world and representing objects. The Web is at an early enough stage, however, where no unique cultures need to be drastically ransacked to achieve the goal of total communication. Most parties seem to agree that diverse world cultures are fascinating, but diverse Web cultures make for confusion and difficulty. Most major software companies and players are working together, more or less, to come up with an API that works for everybody. The result of this is the World Wide Web Consortium's Document Object Model (DOM) working group.

Structural Isomorphism

A key feature of DOM is *structural isomorphism.* This fancy phrase simply means that no matter how a document winds up being presented, it eventually breaks down into the same model. In other words, if Netscape Navigator, Internet Explorer, and Browser X show us a Web page, it may look a bit different from program to program. But if these browsers share a DOM, they take this Web document and break it down into the same hierarchy of objects for developers to control and use. This also ensures that all documents support the same programmatic methods. This guarantees that interacting with the Web page using a language such as JavaScript is the same from browser to browser. It's as simple as that. (Was that simple?)

Once the DOM is accepted (spoken) by every browser across the land, it will form the basis of a truly dynamic HTML. Having one standard language, of course, means that special features are sometimes lacking. Not to worry, though, you can always count on future versions of Netscape Navigator and Internet Explorer to come up with proprietary technologies to supplement the standards. Of course, it is these once-proprietary technologies that form the basis for many of the standards themselves. All we really care about at this point is finding a common denominator so we don't have to write versions of our applications specialized to individual platforms and browsers.

The Birth of the Document Object Model

The Document Object Model working group was originally formed to come up with a standard way for a programming language to access the components of Web pages. Experts from Microsoft and Netscape alike came together to try to agree upon a fair and logical way of talking about Web objects.

However, there's more to the world than HTML and Web pages. Vendors who work with SGML and XML also wanted to get in on the action. There are plenty of SGML/XML documents out there. And because SGML is much, much older than HTML, there have already been many attempts to come up with a consistent nomenclature for it. The most notable SGML object model is SGML Groves. The World Wide Web Consortium DOM working group judiciously decided to use this standard as its basis.

Level 0

The first crack at a DOM was to document what already existed. The preeminent browsers of that time (mid-1997) were Netscape Navigator 3.0 and Microsoft Internet Explorer 3.0. These browsers gave developers a little bit of client-side control of the Web document.

Both browsers had a pretty nice implementation of JavaScript that let programmers access some objects. For instance, you could easily grab basic information about the Web browser itself such as the name of the browser, its version number, and the URL that it was currently browsing.

This early version of JavaScript enabled you to deal directly with forms (including the fields in each form), various frames, embedded plug-ins, links, and, eventually, images. This enabled some neat things:

◆ **Form validation** — You could perform an instant check if you wanted to limit an input field to digits between zero and nine. If somebody typed in an illegal value, you could pop up an alert box and let him or her know.

◆ **Link Rollovers** — You could roll over a hyperlink and some text in the status bar at the bottom of the browser would give you more detailed information about the place you were about to visit.

◆ **Frame Tricks** — You could click on one link and change two different frames at once. (Neato!)

◆ **Image Rollovers** — You could roll your mouse over an image and, voila, it changed to another image.

◆ **Plug-in Detection** — You could tell if the user had installed a certain plug-in. If the user hadn't installed the plug-in, you could direct him where to download it.

There were many inconsistencies between browsers, however. Internet Explorer, for example, didn't have any way of letting you access or dynamically change images. Explorer also had something called JScript, which was kind of like JavaScript, but not quite. It was just different enough to be confusing. To make matters even worse, Explorer let programmers use a variant of Visual Basic, called VBScript, to access document objects. Clearly, something had to be done to fight back against the balkanization of the Web.

The level 0 DOM, then, is a way of consistently accessing objects that works with the 3.0 versions of browsers.

Level 1

The working group then set about the thankless task of creating an official Document Object Model that could immediately be used by future versions of Navigator, Explorer, and other browser vendors. They knew that they'd never be able to capture everything there is to know about a document into a single specification, so they divided their tasks into level 1 and level 2.

The current version of the DOM is level 1. The abstract of the level 1 specification states the following:

"The Document Object Model provides a standard set of objects for representing HTML and XML documents, a standard model of how these objects can be combined, and a standard interface for accessing and manipulating them. . . The goal of the DOM specification is to define a programmatic interface for XML and HTML."

Let's analyze what this all means:

◆ *"Standard set of objects"* — *Objects* refers to the names of properties or pieces of the document that can be accessed or set. In other words, all the elements and their attributes that compose a document. The DOM should specify anything that the user agent (the Web browser or parsing application) knows about and uses. If there are any unknown elements or attributes, such as those invented by XML, these too are made into generalized objects.

◆ *"A standard model"* — This is all about syntax. We want to know how objects fit together. What elements in a document have what attributes? And what types of data can these attributes contain? What elements can contain other elements, and when? A text input field, for instance, must always be part of a form. A definition list item must be part of a definition list. In other words, what are the exact relationships and collaborations among all the objects?

◆ *"Standard interface"* — This refers to a way for a scripting language to programmatically create, modify, and otherwise access the objects. We are also talking about the API itself — the methods that can be called to perform common tasks with these objects, and the properties of each object that may be set by way of a script.

Level 1 was intended to be as backwardly compatible as possible with level 0.

So what's missing in level 1? Perhaps the easiest way to answer that question is to look at what's planned for level 2.

Level 2

Level 2 of the Document Object Model, which has not come out at the time of this writing, will go a step further:

◆ Events such as mouse clicks, keyboard hits, and window switches will be standardized so that they too can become cross-platform and cross-language.

◆ Rich queries will be handled. This will enable a standard way to search for very specific information within the text or data in a document.

◆ A common set of nouns will be defined to enable access to the properties of Cascading Style Sheets (CSS). Eventually, XML style sheets (XSL) will also be handled.

◆ A way of ensuring that a given document is validated by a Document Type Definition (DTD) will be included. In other words, a document will clearly state what markup language it is written in and include the DTD. The DTD describes the capabilities of the document type, including nesting rules for elements, each element's attributes and their supported values, and so forth. Documents with a DTD will then be validated to ensure that they follow the rules set in the DTD.

Level 3 and Beyond

Future levels of the DOM specification are expected to go beyond the world of the document and strike all the way to the operating system. Eventually, there may be some standard way for an application to interface with the windowed world where the document exists. For instance, there will be a common way to open another application, or to throw up various modal dialog boxes to give messages to a user.

A security model will also be crafted. This will define how secure a document is, whether it can access a user's hard disk, write to memory, modify files, and so on.

Finally, there will be some standard way of safely accessing threads, enabling several programs or routines to run at once.

In total, a level 3 DOM promises to lay the groundwork for full-fledged software applications.

Document Object Model Requirements

As you can see, the DOM is quite a useful notion. While there's a certain elegance to all this standardization and specialization, it is not essential for a developer or interface designer to know every inch of the DOM by heart.

The key, then, to using the DOM is knowing what types of objects are available, and which methods should be called to access, change, insert, or delete these objects and their properties. In other words, you should know how the DOM specification is organized so that you can use it as a quick reference tool.

Level 1's General Requirements

Level 1 of the DOM is broken down into two parts: DOM Core and DOM HTML. The core cleanly and thoroughly lays out the rules. It explains how a document should be broken down, how its objects should be organized, and how these objects are related to one another.

Some methods and properties in the core DOM are characterized as follows:

◆ Fundamental — These are methods that must exist in your document's structure as specified if you plan to create an API for this DOM.

◆ Extended — These are objects and methods that must exist in any XML application.

The HTML-specific version of the DOM exists for several reasons. Foremost, the DOM intends to be compatible with older versions of Web browsers, and thus makes sure to include any major methods found in Netscape Navigator and Internet Explorer. Further, the DOM working group wanted to make sure there was an object structure that was easy for HTML scripters to understand and use, as they are the main audience.

DOCUMENT METAINFORMATION

Other than knowing what is inside a document, it is often important to know a few things about the document itself. The DOM handles this metainformation, including:

◆ The source location of the document file

◆ The date the document was created

◆ Any cookies that the document uses (Cookies are explained in general terms in the next chapter, and used in Chapter 13.)

XML "DOCUMENTS"?!

Because XML can store any amount of information in very layered ways, it's not really accurate to call an XML file a document. Depending on the application, a user may not want to read through all the information contained in an XML file. Rather, they just use it to look up specific chunks of information. XML files are often more like collections of data than neat, crisp pages. However, when all of this data is finally handled, what comes out the other end is clearly a document, albeit a customized, reduced one. One way to think of XML is as a platform- and application-neutral mechanism for transferring the contents of databases or more restricted queries against a database. There are many other applications for XML, however.

So for clarity's sake, let us refer to a document as any HTML or XML structure. As such, we can still have a Document Object Model for XML, it just needs to be a lot broader and more generalized than our HTML DOM. This is because XML documents may contain arbitrary elements and attributes, as opposed to the limited set defined by the HTML DTDs.

Future Requirements

Level 1 of the DOM does not cover all the objects necessary for fully interactive and full-featured Web applications. However, work is underway to provide for other important object models. An overview of some of these models follows.

STYLE SHEET OBJECT MODEL

A separate Style Sheet Object Model is very important for the future of dynamic HTML. A Style Sheet Object Model gives developers a standard way of changing and accessing the style of the document, specifying exactly where objects are placed and what they look like. This opens up the visual world of fonts, colors, background, and layout boxes. These graphical elements are the face of interface design.

The first Style Sheet Object Model focuses on the widely used Cascading Style Sheets (CSS) technology. The model enables a developer to change the selectors, rules, and properties of style sheets. Because style sheets are often derived from one another, a standard way of linking, importing and using alternative style sheets has been developed.

In addition, the Style Sheet Object Model covers any style classes, elements, selectors, and inline styles (styles defined directly in HTML). Because Cascading

Style Sheets are well-defined and widely used, it shouldn't be long before an official Style Sheet Object Model is fully drafted and accepted.

We delve heavily into styles and how they work as the adjectives and adverbs of dynamic HTML in Chapter 7, "Cascading Style Sheets: Adjectives and Adverbs."

EVENT OBJECT MODEL

If style sheets are the face of an interface, events are its nerves, its interactivity. And what is an *interface* if not an interactive face?

An Event Object Model is a way of capturing events – things that either the user or the system triggers – and then performing some action at that time. This model must work on any operating system or computer platform. An event model is like a patient ear, just waiting to hear a particular command. When you speak this command, the model kicks into action and does whatever you tell it to do. Everything a user can do can be tied to an event: moving the mouse, pressing the mouse button, releasing the mouse button, pressing a key, opening a window, accessing another window, running out of memory, closing the program. Everything. Time itself is also an event. Waiting for a given amount of time to pass, or waiting for a particular time is an important part of the event model.

You can also program objects themselves to trigger events. For instance, if a user changes some attribute of Object A, it can be made smart enough to change Object B and Object C. This can cause a chain reaction that makes it possible to alter the way every aspect of the document's presentation with the click of one button.

A good event model system enables all these events to be caught and used, and thus provides truly interactive documents. More importantly, as we discuss in later chapters, the standard event model will make it so that programmers no longer have to include workarounds for the various platforms based on which events are supported.

Other requirements of an Event Object Model include the ability to:

◆ **Override default behaviors** – For instance, when a user clicks the Close box in the upper corner of a window, the window generally closes. A document should be able to capture this window closure and perform some other action. Perhaps it pops up a dialog box asking, "Are you *sure* you want to quit?"

◆ **Bubble through the structural hierarchy of the document** – For instance, if a user clicks on an object that is nested within another object, it should pass the click event up to its parent.

ERROR REPORTING OBJECT MODEL

Whenever there is a legal way to do things, there is, by extension, an illegal way. While programming all these objects and manipulating them, tons of exceptional circumstances arise and out-and-out mistakes are naturally made.

Future DOMs will go into great detail about ways to track and report these errors. When something bad happens it will throw an *exception,* a special object in and of itself indicating what went wrong. Exceptions can be caught and analyzed and mistakes can often be ignored or recovered from.

SECURITY OBJECT MODEL

Anybody who uses or develops for the Web must always think of privacy and security. DOM level 1 uses the *sandbox* model of security, meaning that it operates in its own little world and may not exit that world. A script implementing level 1 DOM cannot write to a user's hard disk, access the operating system, or even load information from anywhere other than its home network domain.

Future security requirements include the following:

- ◆ The ability to safely have multiple *threads* operating on the same object. Threads are two-program processes running at the same time. Whenever you multitask, your various applications each run within their own process, and each application may involve further subprocesses, each running within their own thread.

- ◆ The ability to lock an object that is currently being modified so that another thread does not modify it at the same time.

- ◆ The ability to always keep a consistent copy of the current document in memory. This means that a document can be copied or accessed at any point in time, even if it is currently being changed.

- ◆ The inability for scripts on one Web page to access objects on another page, or within another frame, when this isn't desired.

- ◆ The ability for Web applications to work across firewalls and not compromise firewall security.

- ◆ The ability to make certain high-risk objects secure so that they cannot be accessed, or can only be accessed by somebody with the proper password or credentials.

Eventually, this full-security API will be fully implemented. You may find that several of its features are already implemented, albeit in proprietary fashion, by the current crop of browsers.

USER AGENT IDENTIFICATION OBJECTS

Every document needs to know a few things about the application (or *user agent*) it lives in. Currently the DOM provides a way to find out the brand of the agent (Navigator, Internet Explorer, and so on) as well as its version number.

Eventually the DOM should provide a way to find out which MIME types the user agent supports, the plug-ins that are installed, and other browser-specific details.

THE DOCUMENT TYPE DEFINITION (DTD) OBJECT

The major difference between the core DOM and the HTML application is that the HTML DOM is able to rely on the presence of a predefined Document Type Definition (DTD) for HTML and thus deal effectively with any HTML tag that exists.

A DTD is a rigid, complete overview of every element and attribute supported by a given type of document. A good DTD completely explains every possible aspect of a given document type. The HTML DTD, for instance, lists the name of every element, where it may be placed, and what attributes it may contain.

Think of a DTD as a perfect grammar handbook that also happens to contain every word available in the language. Theoretically, if there were a DTD for the English language, a person could use it to construct a perfectly legal sentence. Any sentence that didn't fit within the DTD would not be valid.

XML itself has no one Document Type Definition. This is because XML is not a type of document, but more of a formal metalanguage – a way to define document types. XML, in essence, is a way of creating custom DTDs. Various applications such as browsers, search engines, and databases can then read this DTD and know how to arrange the objects in a given XML document, and if the document is legal.

Level 1 of the HTML DOM relies on the transitional and frameset DTDs for HTML 4.0. The level 1 DOM does not cover Cascading Style Sheets or an HTML event model. You can find the HTML 4.0 transitional DTD at `http://www.w3.org/TR/REC-html40/loose.dtd`. The frameset DTD is at `http://www.w3.org/TR/REC-html40/frameset.dtd`.

Future versions of the DOM will also provide a method to test whether or not the current document is valid, given a DTD.

Organizing the Document

The DOM is the taxonomy of a Web document. This is similar to the way the diverse animal kingdom is broken down. Linnaeus came up with the original biological taxonomy system that zoologists use today, and its hierarchical style makes it easy to classify any living creature.

Animals are broken down into kingdom, phylum, class, and so on, all the way down to species. The DOM attempts to order all the objects in a document in a similar fashion, for easy access and control.

Human beings, for instance, have the following taxonomy:

`Animalia.Chordata.Mammalia.Primates.Hominidae.`*`Homo.sapiens`*

(We arbitrarily used periods to separate each level.)

Each level tells us something about ourselves and our relationship to other species in that level. For instance, the fact that we're in the Primate order tells us that we share many characteristics of other primates such as chimpanzees and baboons (some of us more than others). Being in the Chordata phylum tells us that humans have a backbone and spinal cord.

By the way, we lied when we said we picked periods arbitrarily. The DOM also uses periods to separate the levels of a document's objects and subobjects.

A DOM's-Eye View of a Typical Document

The DOM arranges all the objects in a sort of tree known as the *tree structure model*.

The main root of every document is the `document` object. The branches of the `document` object are the components of your document. You can access the document object in JavaScript by simply using:

```
document
```

Most likely, the object you want to know about or change is part of `document`. The object contains any HTML snippet used on a Web page. This includes the anchored hyperlinks and their properties, images, forms, each `<P>` paragraph, and the rows and columns of tables.

All in the Family

DOM turns your Web page into a close-knit little family unit. Each major family has its *parents*, and these parents have *children* under their control. For instance, to access all the headers of a document, you would use the following:

```
document.head
```

`document` is the parent object and `head` is the child. Another example is:

```
document.body
```

This corresponds to the HTML `<BODY>` element. In this case, `body` is `document`'s child. Therefore, `body` and `head` are *siblings*, which means they have some things in common, like any naturally born brother and sister.

Note that many of these families are quite prolific. Most parents have dozens of children, and most of these children have children of their own. Even great-grand-children are not rare.

For instance, all the forms in an HTML document are stored in a `forms` object. This `forms` object is a child of the `document` object. Therefore, if you had a form named "myform" with an input field named "myinput," the taxonomy of the field would have the following structure:

```
document.myform.myinput
```

In other words, we start at the document root and branch up, finally getting the object we want.

If a child cannot or does not have any other children, it is known as a *leaf*. This is because you can think of the document as a tree. The trunk splits off into several main branches, each of which has many smaller branches. At the end of it, though, is the lonely leaf. Nothing branches off a leaf. Technically, however, each leaf may have properties, such as style information or other values; it just doesn't contain any more element objects.

Consider the simple HTML document shown in Listing 5-2.

Listing 5-2: A very simple HTML page

```
<HTML>
<HEAD>
<TITLE>Sample</TITLE>
</HEAD>
<BODY>
<H1>Hello!</h1>
<IMG SRC="hi.gif" ALT="Hi there!">
<P>Welcome.</P>
<P>I am happy.</P>
</BODY>
</HTML>
```

The DOM would represent its structure as a tree, as shown in Figure 5-1.

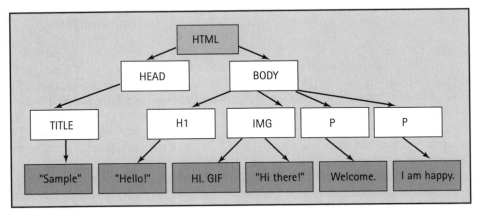

Figure 5-1: The structure of the objects within a simple HTML page. The uppermost node is the root. The nodes at the bottom are leafs. Notice that the IMG object has two children, an SRC (HI.GIF) as well as an ALT ("Hi there!"), to correspond with the two attributes in the tag.

The relationship for an XML document is similar, as shown in Listing 5-3 and illustrated in Figure 5-2.

Listing 5-3: A very simple XML bit

```
<ANIMAL>
  <NAME>
   <LATIN>Martes martes</LATIN>
   <COMMON>Pine Marten</COMMON>
  </NAME>
  <HABITAT>
   <ECOSYSTEM>Deciduous Forest</ECOSYSTEM>
   <ECOSYSTEM>Coniferous Forest</ECOSYSTEM>
  </HABITAT>
</ANIMAL>
```

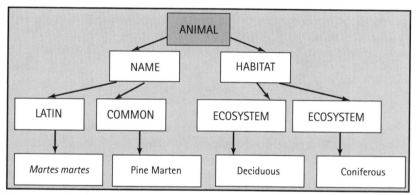

Figure 5-2: The structure of the objects within a simple XML document

What's in a Name?

Suppose you want to access a particular object within a vast tree. What's the best way to do so? The answer depends on who is doing the accessing. Every object can be reached in various ways. Parents can easily access their children, siblings can easily access each other, and objects in different families can just call one another by name.

If you are an HTML pundit, you know that most items can be named using the NAME attribute. For instance, an image can be named as follows:

```
<IMG SRC="hell.gif" NAME="hell">
```

Let's explore some of the ways that you could access and use this object.

MOVING DOWN THE TREE

You can reach most anything in the document by starting with the `document` object and traversing down each level, separating each level by a period, swinging like a monkey up the branches of your document's tree. So to access the hell image, you could use the following:

```
document.hell
```

If you wanted to access a particular property of the hell image, such as its source URL, you would go a step further:

```
document.hell.src
```

Notice that the DOM uses the same nomenclature as the HTML tag itself. This makes things very easy to remember and deal with. If you know HTML, you pretty much know the objects in the HTML DOM.

If you wanted to modify hell's source on the fly using JavaScript, you would call:

```
document.hell.src = "heaven.gif";
```

Anybody looking at the Web page would see the image change. This is how those nifty rollover images you've probably seen around are created. JavaScript waits for the mouse to roll over an image and then changes the image's `src`.

See how easy it is? You updated hell to heaven with one simple command.

Remember the `myinput` input field from the previous section? It probably looks something like this in HTML:

```
<HTML>
<HEAD><TITLE>A simple field</TITLE></HEAD>
<BODY>
<FORM NAME="myform">
<INPUT NAME="myinput">
</FORM>
</BODY>
</HTML>
```

So, if you wanted to find out what the value of the input field was set to, you could access the following:

```
document.forms.myform.myinput.value
```

In addition, you could easily set the value to anything you want at any time by having JavaScript perform:

```
document.forms.myform.myinput.value = "anything you want";
```

ACCESSING AN OBJECT NUMERICALLY

It's important to know where every object in a document lies in the greater scheme of things. Suppose you're interested in a hyperlink anchor. Where is this anchor located, relatively speaking? How many anchors came before it and how many are after it?

Every object of the same type in a document, as such, is put in an array depending on the order in which that object appears. An *array* is essentially a numbered list that is accessed using the square brackets. For instance, if you have ten images in a document, the first image is known as:

```
document.images[0]
```

We start with zero because in the language of computer bits and bytes the first number is always zero. The sixth image that appears on the page would then be:

```
document.images[5]
```

When using arrays, you have to be careful not to access an element that is not in the array. For example, if you access the tenth element and the array is only nine elements long, you are in for some big errors.

ACCESSING AN OBJECT DIRECTLY

You might have noticed how long and unwieldy some object representations are. This is why the DOM also enables you to reach the image by name, without having to weave through all the layers of objects:

```
document.images['hell']
```

The Internet Explorer DOM even lets you access the object's name without any annoying taxonomy at all, so you could simply use the JavaScript command:

```
hell.src = "heaven.gif"
```

You will also eventually learn how a specific image can be accessed using its ID or by a special class type. For instance:

```
<IMG SRC="hell.gif" NAME="hell" ID="HellPic23">
```

The image could just as easily be accessed using:

```
HellPic23.src = "heaven.gif"
```

Nondocument Information

The Document Object Model also goes beyond the document at hand to give you access to information about the outside world — for example, the Web browser (user agent), parts of the operating system, and more.

◆ **Web browser information** — You can find out the type of browser being used by the end user. This basic, obvious, and important piece of information is held in the `navigator` object. The URL of the current Web page, another important thing that you need to know, is held in the `location` object. The DOM may also be aware of what MIME types are handled, what plug-ins are installed, and so on.

◆ **System information** — You can capture and use basic system resources such as the date and time. Most of these system objects can't be changed, but they can be harnessed to, say, change a Web page automatically over time.

◆ **Window information** — You can find out how many browser windows are open, where they're located, and how big they are. This is done with the `window` object. The `window` object also contains the `frames` object, which has information about the size and content of any frames.

The Guts of the DOM

Let's quickly go over exactly how the DOM is structured, without delving into too much detail about specific properties or methods. Understanding the classes of objects and how they relate to one another helps you read through the DOM specification, if you are interested in doing so.

The DOM Structure Model

The main object in the DOM is the `Node`. *Nodes* are simply containers that hold anything at all — integers, text, or entire collections of other nodes. Nodes always hold a list of their children and their parents so that they can be linked together, defining their space in the document tree. A `NodeList` interface holds an ordered collection of sequentially numbered nodes, and a `NamedNodeMap` holds an unordered collection of nodes.

The DOM's core nodes are divided into the following major types:

◆ `Document` — This is the root of the document's tree. If you want to access any information about the document itself, it's in here. You can create a new `Element` node by calling the `createElement` method and passing it a character string called `tagName`.

◆ Element — Any element, such as HTML or XML markup, is part of the element family. Elements consist of a tagName and a list of attributes. If an XML element has any nested elements, these branch off as child elements. Any properties of the element branch off as an Attr object. A specific attribute can be accessed using the following method:

getAttribute(name)

A specific attribute can be set using the following method:

setAttribute(name,value)

The getAttributes method returns an ordered list of all attributes.

◆ Attr — Attributes are always children of elements and come in many shapes and sizes. Attributes always have a *value* that may be Text (a string) or an EntityReference.

◆ Comment — This node has no children. It contains all the comments in a given document.

◆ CharacterData — This node holds a text string or other character data. Its attributes include data (the actual data); and length (how many characters long the data is). It has methods that enable you to access a substring of the data; to append more characters onto the data; or to insert, replace, or delete characters within the data list.

◆ Text — This node has no children. It holds the textual value of an element or attribute. It derives from CharacterData.

◆ CDATASection — This node has no children. It contains *escape blocks* — a special way of holding nonstandard text or other special characters that you would normally think of as markup. For instance, the less-than bracket (<) is used to create tags. Thus, if your document actually contains a less-than bracket, it needs to have a special representation.

◆ DocumentFragment — This is lightweight subset of Document. It provides a handy way of grabbing a branch of the document tree and moving it around or splicing it onto another document.

Other major nodes in the core DOM exist to provide full handling of XML. These nodes include the following:

◆ DocumentType — This node cannot have children. It simply holds the DTD for a given document, with all its legal entities and notations. The DocumentType for an HTML document is null.

◆ Notation — This node holds a DTD notation. In other words, it contains the format from which other nodes can be created. DOM level 1 doesn't contain a method for these nodes to be modified. As such, these nodes can merely be accessed, not set.

◆ Entity — This node enables you to access an entity definition in a XML document. These entities may be accessed before or after they have been completely parsed out. An entity node has no parent.

◆ EntityReference — This node is part of an entity and points to the data or structures that the entity holds.

◆ ProcessingInstruction — This node has no children. It holds an XML processing instruction, which is a special command that must be given at any point to the XML processor.

 Web developers should rarely have to deal with the core DOM nodes, methods, or attributes. For instance, you hardly ever see a DocumentFragment being set in JavaScript. These core nodes are of interest only insofar as how the DOM is set up. Once major browsers fully support the official DOM, however, the nitty-gritty specifics become much more important.

The HTML DOM Structure Model

All the HTML-specific nodes are stored in a node type called HTMLCollection. Every HTML node can be referenced by its *name* (a string) or its *index* (a long integer).

THE HTMLDOCUMENT INTERFACE

A special HTMLDocument node is at the root of it all. It contains every element in the document. It also contains the following properties:

◆ title — The title of the page.

◆ referrer — The Web page the user just came from.

◆ fileSize — The size of the HTML document.

◆ fileCreatedDate — The date the HTML file was created.

◆ fileModifiedDate — The date the file was modified.

◆ fileUpdatedDate — The date the file was last updated.

◆ domain — The network domain that the document resides in.

◆ URL — The URL of the current document.

◆ body — An HTMLCollection of all the elements in the document's body.

◆ images — All of the images in the page.

◆ applets — All of the applets in the page.

◆ links — All of the links in the page, including a collection of all <AREA> tags.

◆ forms — A collection of all of the forms.

◆ anchors — All of the named anchors in the page.

◆ cookie — Any cookies the page stores.

The document also contains the following methods:

◆ open() — Opens a new window containing a copy of the document.

◆ close() — Closes the current document window.

◆ write(in wstring text) — Writes out some specific text that can contain any other HTML tags. For instance:

```
document.write("<IMG SRC='heaven.gif'>");
```

◆ writeln(in wstring text) — Writes out a line of text and ends it, for good measure, with a carriage return.

◆ getElementById(in wstring elementId) — Returns any element based on its unique ID.

◆ getElementsByName(in wstring elementName) — Returns a NodeList of all the elements that have this name.

THE IDL DEFINITION

Every property and method discussed above is represented in the DOM specification using the Interface Definition Language (IDL). The IDL was created by a standards body known as the Object Management Group (OMG), and is commonly used by programmers to describe API interfaces in a manner independent of the actual programming language. The IDL itself is only important insofar as it provides a consistent way to explain each DOM object and its interface. In other words, here is yet another language of nouns, verbs, and adjectives to describe our document object nouns.

For instance, the IDL definition of the HTMLDocument node is:

```
IDL Definition
interface HTMLDocument : Document {
         attribute  DOMString         title;
readonly attribute  DOMString         referrer;
readonly attribute  DOMString         domain;
readonly attribute  DOMString         URL;
         attribute  HTMLElement       body;
readonly attribute  HTMLCollection    images;
readonly attribute  HTMLCollection    applets;
readonly attribute  HTMLCollection    links;
```

```
readonly attribute   HTMLCollection        forms;
readonly attribute   HTMLCollection        anchors;
         attribute   DOMString             cookie;
void                 open();
void                 close();
void                 write(in DOMString text);
void                 writeln(in DOMString text);
Element              getElementById(in DOMString elementId);
NodeList             getElementsByName(in DOMString elementName);
};
```

Once you learn how to read an IDL definition, you know everything there is to know about a given interface.

The above IDL looks at the HTMLDocument interface. Note that in this use of the word, "interface" doesn't mean user navigation or GUI, but rather the framework in which every object exists and can be referenced. This is a common programming concept.

We see that HTMLDocument *extends* from the core Document interface. This means it shares all of Document's attributes and methods but then goes a few steps beyond. Anything you can do to a Document you can do to an HTMLDocument — it is a specialized type of Document node.

HTMLDocument contains a bunch of attributes, some of which can be written to and some of which are readonly and thus cannot be modified. It then has five methods. Some of these methods take in no input (open() and close()). Other methods take in a DOMString, a character string represented by a phrase in quotes such as:

```
"mystring"
```

Most of these methods return nothing, or void. One returns an Element node, and one returns an entire NodeList.

The HTMLElement Interface

Every HTML element falls under this interface. Every element has its own id (unique identifier), title (advisory title), lang (language code), dir (direction in which the text or tables are to be printed), and className (the class attribute) that can be set or accessed.

This basic information is enough for simple HTML tags that have no attributes, such as the <HEAD> heading, the <B> bold and other font tags, <SUB> subscripts and other special tags, <STRONG> and other phrase tags, <DT> definition terms and other list tags, and so on.

Most HTML elements, however, have their own unique interfaces to handle their own special attributes. Following are some of the major elements and their breakdown.

THE BODY

The HTMLBodyElement contains information that normally goes in the <BODY> tag. Its attributes include the following:

- ◆ background – A URL of the background image to be tiled behind the Web page.

- ◆ bgColor – The color of the background for pages that have no background image.

- ◆ text – The default color of text in this document.

- ◆ link – The color of linked text that has not yet been clicked.

- ◆ aLink – The color of active links (links that have been clicked down upon, but not released yet).

- ◆ vLink – The color of links that have already been visited.

HYPERLINK ANCHORS

HTML documents usually have hyperlink anchors that enable users to click to another page. The interface that contains these links is called HTMLAnchorElement. Some of its major attributes are:

- ◆ href – The URL to link to.

- ◆ name – The name of the anchor for mid-document jumps.

- ◆ target – The frame that the linked document should open in.

The anchor object also has two methods: blur() to remove the keyboard focus from the link; and focus(), to gain the focus. A link that has focus can be followed when a user presses Enter. As another example, a form element may be given the focus during validation if the user has left a required field blank.

IMAGES

Images may be created or accessed by calling HTMLImageElement. The properties of images correspond exactly to the <IMG> tag:

- ◆ src – The source filename containing the image.

- ◆ lowSrc – A file containing a low resolution copy of the image.

- ◆ name – The name of the image.

- ◆ align – How the image should be aligned vertically or horizontally relative to neighboring elements.

- ◆ alt – Alternate text for browsers that do not display images, or for browsers that print a message when the mouse rolls over the image.

◆ `border` — The width of the border around the image.

◆ `height` — The height in pixels in which the image should be drawn.

◆ `width` — The width in pixels of the image.

◆ `hspace` — Horizontal blank margin space to the right and left of the image.

◆ `vspace` — Vertical blank margin space above and below the image.

◆ `longDesc` — A URL that points to a long description of the image.

◆ `isMap` — The image is a server-side image map.

◆ `useMap` — The image is part of a client-side image map.

FORMS

The `HTMLFormElement` is an element in itself, and is also a collection of other elements, the fields of the form. Its properties include `method` and `action`, or how the form is submitted and via which protocol. Its methods are `submit()` and `reset()`.

STYLES

The `HTMLStyleElement` interface holds very basic style information that could easily tie into a future Style Sheet Object Model. The Boolean attribute `disabled` can be set to enable or disable the given style sheet. The `media` property is a string that defines the target media. And the `type` property holds the name of the style sheet language being used.

More detailed information about styles can be found in Chapter 7, "Cascading Style Sheets: Adjectives and Adverbs."

The Current State of Affairs

Both Netscape Navigator 4.5 and Internet Explorer 5.0 — the latest browsers as of this writing — claim in their press releases to support dynamic HTML features. Indeed, both browsers contain some aspects of the official Document Object Model, as well as custom object models of their own.

Navigator enables access to many aspects of an HTML page but does not fully support the official World Wide Web Consortium DOM recommendation. Version 5.0 promises to support all standards fully. Until then, Navigator's biggest deviation from the DOM standard is something called the `<LAYER>` element. Layers enable you to stack one object on top of another. This can create groovy effects such as dropshadows or captions that overlay photographs. A developer can also access any layer using JavaScript and change some of its properties, such as its color or visibility. The width and height of windows is also now easy to access using JavaScript. A cleverly written JavaScript, in fact, can completely reshape the look and content of a page each time it is loaded or over a period of milliseconds.

Microsoft, meanwhile, takes the idea of controlling objects and really runs with it. They have implemented a majority of the earliest version of Cascading Style Sheets, which are a way of laying things out explicitly. Internet Explorer 4.0 and later, in essence, give free access to all the objects on a Web page. Navigator 5.0 should provide similar access. Netscape has recently released its new layout engine for the 5.0 generation, code-named Gecko, which also claims full support for Cascading Style Sheets and the DOM. So the future looks bright – or brighter, at least – for cross-platform dynamic HTML applications. There are still a few bugs and inconsistencies in both browsers, but they're heading in the right direction.

The bottom line is that each browser uses different DOMs, which negates the whole point of a DOM to begin with. Both browsers speak with roughly the same nouns, but Internet Explorer has a bigger vocabulary. Both Navigator and Internet Explorer have specialized nomenclature, which further complicates things. If you write a script specifically for Navigator, odds are it flubs in Explorer, and vice versa.

The third part of this book talks about ways to combat this problem today and in the future.

Summary

- ◆ Dynamic HTML can be thought of as a language with its own nouns, verbs, and adjectives.

- ◆ The objects in a document – the elements, the attributes of the elements, and the text and graphics – are the nouns.

- ◆ The official Document Object Model provides for a standard way of representing and accessing these objects so that scripts across applications, across platforms, and across the world can deal with objects.

- ◆ Objects in the DOM are laid out hierarchically and accessed in various ways, depending on the browser.

- ◆ Today's browsers manifest slightly different Document Object Models.

The next chapter shows you a way to actually do something with all these objects. It covers the "verbs" of dynamic HTML: client-side scripting with JavaScript.

Chapter 6

Client–Side Scripting: Verbs

IN THIS CHAPTER

- ◆ How scripts breathe life into document objects

- ◆ What clients are

- ◆ Why client-server networking works

- ◆ Advantages of client-server interfaces

- ◆ How clients communicate with servers

- ◆ Server-side scripts

- ◆ A comparison of popular client-side scripts

- ◆ Why JavaScript is the scripting language we use in this book

- ◆ Some basic JavaScript examples

- ◆ Unleashing the true power of client-side scripting

DOCUMENTS AREN'T DYNAMIC until their objects are able to move around, update their contents on the fly, or otherwise change their appearance. These changes must be made using some sort of program. In this chapter, you will learn various ways to control Web pages programmatically, and why client-side scripts put the *dynamic* in dynamic HTML.

I Want Some Action!

Treating documents as collections of related objects helps us to reduce complex elements and attributes to manageable chunks and their properties. Now that you have all these nifty objects, you don't just want to stare at them — you want to play with them. You want to change their attributes, add them or delete them, search them, color them, do the hokey-pokey and move them all around.

A language with only nouns is a still life; it's not really a language at all. Verbs are what make a language zing, jump, leap, run, exist, or hide. Nouns, in fact, are only interesting when we assign actions to them, command them, or talk about all the things they've accomplished. The first thing a baby usually does is point to a person or object and say its name: "Ma-ma." The second major linguistic step a baby takes is to ask for something — to personalize nouns and make them useful. To say, "I *want* Ma-ma."

Verbs add the dynamic to dynamic HTML. The key to verbs is a handy little technology called *client-side scripting*. Scripts are written in a computer language that enables objects to be manipulated in extremely useful ways. They give you the ability to craft fully functional Web page interfaces.

The Client

In the beginning of computing history, there was a lack of communication. Dumb machines could provide the user with access to data but that was about it. And then programmers created *clients* — machines that could not only display data from remote computers but also do a lot of things on their own, such as processing the data. Programmers looked at this technology and saw that it was good. But not good enough. . . .

It's instructive and downright interesting to review how the network topology known as *client-server* came about, and what its powerful implications for interface design are.

Dumb Terminals and Weary Mainframes

The earliest networks consisted of super-powerful computers called *mainframes* sending data to lots of little, brainless *terminals*. These terminals were no more than monitors and keyboards that enabled a remote user to patch into some of the mainframe's power. The first terminals, in fact, were basically electronic typewriters, and didn't even have screens, just a roll of paper. Eventually, cathode ray tubes were hooked up to provide simple text displays.

Mainframes indeed are powerful. These suckers often take up entire rooms and can support thousands of possible users at once, who can each type in requests for information. The mainframe then processes all these requests and sends back thousands of different responses.

In essence, this system is like having one computer brain with a whole bunch of different keyboards attached. Everything depends on the mainframe. The mainframe is Atlas, holding the weight of the entire network on its hunched silicon shoulders.

PROS

Having centralized power gives the mainframe all the control, which has some distinct advantages. You can keep important data absolutely safe as long as you never send it out to a nonsecure terminal. In addition, if the database or software changes at all, terminals do not have to be updated because they contain no smarts at all. They are just glorified keyboards.

CONS

The terminal-mainframe system is about as slow as a network can be. Every key that a user types on a terminal is sent to the mainframe the moment it is pressed. This makes for constant traffic, and means that the mainframe has to piece together a heck of a lot of information.

There is also no way for the same terminal to access different mainframes. If you have an IBM terminal and you want to access a database on a Unisys machine, you need a new terminal with a special wire running directly to the new mainframe. In other words, networks are closed and proprietary.

WHAT DUMB TERMINALS LOOK LIKE

Interface-wise, this system is raw and unwieldy. Access to original mainframes is completely command line. The mainframe sends you a request similar to the following:

```
Please enter your password:
```

Then you type it in. Often, to save network traffic, requests aren't even worded as friendly as all that. You just see a response – maybe a period – when the mainframe has finished processing the command key you just typed.

Basically, there is little interface to speak of.

Terminals Hit the Road

Eventually, modems were invented and became widely used. This enabled terminals to access mainframes remotely, even across the world. Soon it became clear that it would be extremely useful to widen the scope of networks and enable the same terminal to access several mainframes.

Terminal emulation software was developed so that various mainframes could communicate with the same terminal. Terminal emulation makes one terminal pretend to be another mainframe brand's terminal type. This enables a dumb terminal to accept data from many different types of mainframes.

This is pretty useful. A travel agent with offices across the country can use terminal emulation on one machine to access several large databases of flight costs and timetables, even if the various databases are stored on mainframes that use different *protocols*, or ways of communicating. The big drawback to all this is that phone lines via modems are much slower than a direct mainframe connection. If you thought networking was slow before, it just got even slower.

WHAT TERMINAL EMULATION LOOKS LIKE

Terminal emulation software was expanded to enable smarter text-based screens to be sent and returned. You can type a letter anywhere on your terminal screen using cursor movement keys, and the letter as well as its position is sent to the mainframe.

In other words, a mainframe returns data and places that data anywhere on your screen it wants. This provides common interface elements such as menus at the top of the screen, and status bars at the bottom of the screen.

ARPANET: The Internet Is Born

In the late sixties, the Department of Defense used lots and lots of really long wires to directly connect major mainframes all over the country. They called this network ARPANET, named after the Advanced Research Projects Agency. The idea was connect networks redundantly. That way, that if an atomic attack smashed one node out of commission, another workable route could very well be found.

This spurred a growth of new technologies. Terminal emulation got smarter and prettier, resembling the screens we know today. The File Transfer Protocol (FTP) was invented as a way to send files from one computer to another, in a vendor-neutral manner. The Simple Mail Transfer Protocol (SMTP) enabled e-mail to be sent back and forth as well.

Meanwhile, though, a true revolution was underway as client-server networks became popular.

The Terminal Gets Smarter

Soon cheap and reliable personal microcomputers were developed. These computers were fully autonomous and self-sufficient. They had their own memory and could even store a limited amount of information on tape.

As microcomputers became cheaper and more powerful, it made sense to replace dumb terminals with smart PCs. After all, many tasks in a typical university, government, or corporate office environment don't require a mainframe at all, such as word processing a memo, writing simple programs, or playing a game of Space Invaders. Microcomputers can handle these tasks like a charm.

Various terminal emulators were written for microcomputers, enabling them to access mainframes the way a dumb terminal could. As far as networking capability, however, this made microcomputers no different from their predecessors, the dumb terminals.

Eventually, though, people figured out ways to hook these microcomputers together. This was the birth of the local area network. E-mail could now be sent back and forth; information could be shared; and if the network was fast enough, two-player Pong was even a possibility.

Early Client–Server Networking

Concurrent with the evolution of the microcomputer was the development of a new network architecture known as *client-server*. This meant that a microcomputer network was divided into machines called *clients* and *servers*. Many clients would be served by one server. Servers are often more powerful than clients and handle any tasks or resources that a bunch of computers around the network need to share.

For example, a *print server* takes the print requests from dozens of clients, queues them up, and prints them out in a fair order on any available printers. A *mail server* takes in tons of different e-mail messages, figures out where each message needs to be routed, and then zips the message off. It also stores any incoming mail. *Database servers* enable many clients to view or change a database simultaneously. Similarly, servers can be set up to enable clients to load up a powerful application, such as a word processor, saving lots of space on the their hard drives.

 The same machine can act as a client and a server. For instance, a computer that is used as the print server might also be used just like any other machine on the network. The only drawback to somebody working on such a machine is that when print requests come in, their machine might slow down while handling the printing tasks.

The computing power had moved to the masses. Instead of having one centralized mainframe do all the work and have all the control, the centralized resources were only used when needed. Even the name *client-server* implies that the power is now in the hands of clients, or individual machines. The server is only a slave that, dutiful as a liveried butler, gives clients the services they need to function.

In addition to client machines, any piece of software that accesses a server is also called a client. Likewise, the software application that handles client requests is called a server. Every Web browser is a type of client, and the software that delivers up Web sites is a Web server.

PROS

Client-server systems have many advantages over the terminal-mainframe architecture. For one, client-server systems greatly reduce network traffic. A good server only sends the bare minimum amount of information a client needs to function, and only when the client asks for it. Most of the processing is now done on the client.

A mainframe must constantly keep its connection to a terminal open, keeping an ear out for any data the terminal might send. A server, on the other hand, can just hang around idle and perform other tasks until it receives a request from a client. It then opens a connection, performs the request, and closes the connection as soon as possible.

Another big plus is the distribution of tasks. Suppose a user wants to print a document, send an e-mail, and access a networked database all at once. A dumb terminal has to send each request, one at a time, to the mainframe, and the mainframe has to handle each wildly different task in turn. In the client-server world, however, these three tasks can be sent to three different servers — a print server, a mail server, and a database server — each of which is carefully set up to specialize in the task at hand. This distribution is very cost-effective too, because servers are very cheap compared to mainframes. New servers can always be added to offset tasks as demand for network services increases.

The biggest difference between terminal-mainframe and client-server systems is where all the computing actually happens. The client performs most of the moment to moment work in client-server systems. For instance, in a common multiplayer chess game, the client paints the chessboard, plays any sounds, and figures out which moves are valid. The server only acts as a go-between with the client sending in any moves it makes and receiving any moves that the opponent makes.

Another big difference, which we discuss in great detail soon, is where data is stored. Dumb terminals have no storage capabilities at all. Client computers, however, can store anything they want, and can keep messages, data, or documents local. This means that you can switch a client off, turn it on again the next day, and it will still be at the same place, with the same data, as the day before. A server does not need to send everything over again from scratch.

Keep some of these advantages in mind as we move on to discuss the way the Web works.

CONS

Client-server topologies have some of the same problems as mainframe-terminal systems. If many people try to access a server at once, the server may grind to a halt. Strides have been made to combat this problem, including smarter distribution of resources and three-tier topologies (a server's server, enabling two servers to act together to handle one service).

On the other side of the coin, if only a few people use a server to communicate, it is a bit of a waste. Why send information through a middleman when it's faster to send it directly to the computer you want to reach? To address this, a topology known as *peer-to-peer* was invented, enabling many clients to communicate in a ring, among themselves. Each client acts as a server, and when the time comes, transmits information to the next client down the line.

For a large network like the Internet, however, the client-server model provides a nice balance of power and speed.

WHAT CLIENT SCREENS LOOK LIKE

Client-server architecture has many implications for interface design. No longer is the mainframe taxed trying to format and arrange informative screens. The window dressing is thrown out the server's window. Instead, all interface design is done on the client. This even enables two clients to receive the same data from a server and have two completely different graphical user interfaces.

In other words, as far as interface design is concerned, the sky (or the client's memory and computing power) is the only limit.

The Web as a Client-Server System

The World Wide Web of the late nineties is based on Web servers sending requested information to Web clients known as *browsers*. This information is sent using a special protocol known as the Hypertext Transfer Protocol (HTTP), hence all those "http://" Web addresses.

HTTP alone does not take full advantage of its client-server status. In a way, HTTP makes Web browsers act much like dumb terminal emulators. Web servers send all the Web page information, and the only thing a user can do is click a link and send a request for a new page. If the user needs to refresh some information, the server must send the entire Web page anew.

How HTTP Works

Whenever you type in or click a URL, your Web client opens up a connection with the server and requests the information you asked for. An HTTP *request* includes all sorts of information. Suppose you are on the Web page http://www.example.com/main.html, and you click to go to http://www.info.org/goodstuff/. The request looks a bit like this:

```
GET /goodstuff/ HTTP/1.0
User-Agent: Mozilla/4.0 (compatible; MSIE 4.01; Windows NT)
Accept: text/html; */*
Referer: http://www.example.com/main.html
Host: www.info.org
```

This request contains the brand of Web browser you are using and other important information, such as the type of data to accept and where on the server the desired data resides.

Mozilla was the development code name for the first Netscape Navigator project. Some versions of Internet Explorer also refer to themselves as Mozilla in the User-Agent header so that early browser-sniffing servers don't ignore their requests. In addition, many independent programmers are now hacking away trying to improve the open Navigator source code in an attempt to come up with a new, power-packed Mozilla browser. Check out http://www.mozilla.org/ for more information.

The Web server analyzes this request. It then sends back a nifty little packet of information to the Web client known as the *response header*. If the page or resource doesn't exist, the server sends back an error message such as:

```
HTTP/1.0 404 Not Found
```

Web server administrators customize this error response so that it sends a prettier page that explains what went wrong, or even pops up a search form to help the user find the page they were actually looking for:

```
The Web server cannot find the file or script you asked for. Please
check the URL to ensure that the path is correct.
Please contact the server's administrator if this problem persists.
```

If all goes well, however, the server sends back the Web page, preceded by a response header that looks something like this:

```
HTTP/1.0 200 OK
Date: Mon, 02 Nov 1998 13:21:03 GMT
Server: Apache/1.2.6
Content-type: text/html
```

The header is always followed by a blank line and the *message body*. In this case, the message body is the HTML of the requested page.

The Web server then closes the connection.

HTTP 1.1

HTTP version 1.1 is very similar to HTTP 1.0, except that it enables buffered packets and *keep-alive* connections. What this comes down to is that a client can request several things within the same TCP connection. HTTP 1.0 worked like a really inefficient airline attendant. Suppose you wanted honey-roasted peanuts and a martini. First, you'd need to wave your hand wildly to get the attendant's attention. Then you could ask for a martini. The attendant would go to the kitchen and bring one back for you. You would then need to grunt and groan to get the attendant's attention again if you wanted to ask for some peanuts. HTTP 1.1 enables you to ask the attendant for a martini, receive it, and then ask immediately for some honey-roasted peanuts.

Keep alive means all of this give-and-take can happen during the same TCP connection, which avoids lots of network overhead.

What HTTP Lacks

As you can see, HTTP is very simple and straightforward. Client asks, client receives. This has some drawbacks, however. HTTP is *stateless* — it doesn't keep any information about the client around from one session to another. Once a server is done sending its stuff, it closes its doors, and its mind, for good. Until the next request, anyway. But by then it will have forgotten that it ever served you before.

The statelessness of HTTP means the server doesn't have to waste space and memory keeping things around. Instead, the client must send any and all applicable information along with each request.

What is lacking is the concise, back-and-forth free flow of information that typical client-server applications demand. An application should be able to keep all sorts of valuable variables around and use them whenever they are desired.

There are ways to combat this statelessness, such as the use of cookies or long URLs with tracking information tacked on to the end of them. We discuss these technologies a bit later in this chapter, and in detail in Chapter 8, "Tying Things Together: Sentences and Paragraphs." In the end, though, the most efficient Web applications avoid the server altogether as much as they can and keep their own state. The way to achieve this is with client-side scripting.

From Read-Only to Read-Write

A key element to any software application is being able to keep important pieces of information around for further use. What good is a word processor if it doesn't enable you to store a copy of the document you are working on? Furthermore, if an application asks a user for his or her setting preferences or password, these details should be stored somewhere where they can be retrieved quickly and usefully. The capability of information to hang around and be readily available when needed is known as *persistence*.

Taken a step further, the key element of any client-server software application is the capability to read and write to the server at any point – to upload only the most necessary packets of data and to receive a quick response. This achieves the client-server ideal and lets the process work the way it is supposed to, with the client performing all the tasks it can and using the network to handle the communication. The server is responsible for long-term data storage or providing shared access to data.

HTML documents themselves have no direct way of reading from or writing to a client's hard drive. In part, this is for safety's sake. Not being able to access the hard drive means that viruses, harmful Trojan horse programs, and other unsolicited data can't and won't be passed down. This also means that information about the user can't be easily kept around.

HTML by itself also has no capability to explicitly read and write from the server. Pages can only use forms that spark the Web browser into calling special programs on the server known as *CGI scripts,* which have a whole host of limitations. We discuss these scripts in the next section.

Shifting Power to the Client

Having Web servers send each new Web page, one after the other, is akin to the old days of computing when mainframes would send a bunch of characters to dumb terminals to be recreated into quasi-interesting screens.

This screen-at-a-time paradigm works as a short-term solution, but it is very limiting if completely extensible applications are desired. First, it takes a great deal of time to keep sending new pages down the data line. Second, the look of such a system is hardly seamless. A server sending out one page at a time appears more like a clunky flip book than a contiguous software application.

Giving clients the ability to craft a Web page at any moment gives developers control over the precise look and feel of the interface. Developers can then create interfaces that enable the user to have a lot more control over their environment. With dynamic HTML, developers can design applications in which users do things like drag and drop taskbars wherever they like them. Or developers can create an application that enables users to set options dictating the look and feel of their computing experience.

The Web Page as a Living, Breathing Creature

Standard HTML pages are rather flat. The HTML markup is read in by the browser and then parsed — broken down into its sections, such as headings, images, or paragraphs. The Web browser then *renders,* or paints, the page. At that point, the Web browser relaxes, having no more work to do. Sure, it needs to scroll the page up or down a bit, but other than that it has nothing to process until the user clicks a new link and a new Web page is loaded.

Modern dynamic HTML browsers act more like complete operating systems. They must always be on their toes, alert for events. Commands may be sent at any time based on anything the user does, such as roll the mouse or hit a key. These commands can cause the browser to create and perhaps display some new HTML dynamically.

A dynamic browser provides true interactivity with the user. Any aspect or part of a Web page can change drastically based on nearly anything the user does without a whole new Web page having to be loaded. This makes users feel less like they are browsing from page to page and more like they are immersed in an environment that responds to their needs.

This, in essence, provides the entire application in one package, rather than in discrete parts.

The Ideal: Letting Clients Be Clients and Servers Be Servers

To sum it up, the client-server ideal is to use the client for all interactivity and to use the server only for data transfer. Compare that to standard HTML where most custom Web applications are created on the server and then shipped, one page at a time, all the way to the client, which acts as nothing more than a glorified window. How antiquated!

As an example, let's look at an online store that sells nuts. The shopping experience should go as follows:

1. The user sees a list of the nuts that are available.

2. The user clicks on a nut type (say, hazelnuts) to learn more about it.

3. The user clicks a Purchase Now button. A form comes up asking for shipping address and credit card information.

4. The credit card information is processed. A receipt is returned letting the user know when his or her nuts will arrive.

Table 6-1 compares each of the preceding four steps using the "Old Way" (flat HTML) and the "Ideal Way" (dynamic HTML):

TABLE 6-1 USING THE SERVER FOR ALL TASKS VERSUS USING THE SERVER FOR DATA TRANSFER ONLY

Step	THE OLD WAY	THE IDEAL WAY
1	The server keeps a list of the latest nut inventory and uses this to craft a special Web page. It then sends this along to the client.	One large Web page is sent to the user, once. This is cached, if possible. The next time the user visits the nut store, all the latest changes are sent up at once.
2	The client sends a request to the server, asking for the hazelnut screen. An entirely new Web page is sent, and the screen is totally redrawn. It may be generated dynamically, pulling information from a database.	The user already knows the latest price of hazelnuts, because he or she received this in Step 1. A quick panel slides in with a beautiful picture of the nuts and all relevant information.
3	A query is sent to the secure server asking once again for the price of hazelnuts, and the appropriate form is crafted. The order form is served up.	The screen wipes cleanly, and a cool dialog box appears with the necessary fields. If the user has shopped the store before, lots of fields are already filled in. These may be saved on the client side and no call to the server is necessary.
4	The credit card information is sent to secure server. The server sends back a simple response indicating success and a receipt is printed. The user is then returned to the main selection screen.	The credit card information is sent to the the secure server. A new Web page is cranked out containing the receipt. If the user wants to shop again, he or she must begin at Step 1.

The big difference, then, is between *data transfer* and *application transfer*. Standard HTML sends an entirely new application or application subset at every step of the process, lugging forth lots of big messages over the network in order to shake hands and stay in sync. But if the server sends most of its data during the application boot up and stores this information on the client, the server rarely needs to be queried.

Accessing a server is generally the slowest part of any application, and reducing this as much as possible can shave time and bandwidth off a Web application.

Another thing to note is that due to this front-heavy data transfer model, a dynamic HTML Web application is no longer as dependent on the network to survive. With original HTML, if the network stopped working, or became very sluggish, every step of the process either would fail completely or be slogged down, making the user cringe with impatience. With dynamic HTML, if the network goes awry, the client holds all the cards and can either make its best guess, displaying the latest information it has, or can wait gracefully until the connection is reestablished. In the meantime, the user can continue to interact with the application.

Getting the Client to Talk to the Server

There have been many leaps in technology that enable Web clients to communicate with Web servers in more useful ways. Let's quickly review some of the core methods that enable Web servers to deal with Web clients.

CGI Scripts

Almost all Web servers include the Common Gateway Interface, or CGI. This is a special way of having the Web browser contact a customized program, called a *CGI script,* right on the Web server. The Common Gateway Interface enables a Web server to pass data submitted by a form by way of a standard protocol into the script program. It passes this data either as *environmental variables* – data stored by the operating system – or as standard input. The script then analyzes or uses this information, and prints out its own custom HTTP server response.

Typical uses of CGI scripts include the following:

◆ Creating Web pages that contain changeable information (for example, stock quotes, daily news, and so on). Instead of calling up a Web page, the user calls up a CGI script directly and a custom Web page is crafted based on current data.

◆ Changing images, such as page counters. The data that CGI scripts return is usually an HTML Web page, but it can be in any format, including an image. Instead of inserting a standard GIF or JPEG image in a Web page, then, developers could call to a CGI script. A custom image could then be grated together and served up fresh and tasty.

◆ Analyzing and storing form data in a database. A user types his name, credit card number, and billing address in a form. This is relayed to the server and stored in a big database. The script also verifies the credit card number and returns a page to the user, telling him of any problems, or if everything checked out okay.

CGI programs can be written in nearly any language that the Web server platform supports. Common languages are C, C++, Perl, Java, AppleScript, or Visual Basic.

HOW CGI WORKS

CGI scripts are typically called in one of two ways:

◆ As URLs — Using the GET method, any résources that need to be passed onto the script are stuck after the URL in an anchor. A question mark indicates the beginning of the parameters, and the ampersand delineates various parameters from one another. For instance:

```
http://www.example.com/cgi-bin/myprogram.cgi?param1=value1&
param2=value2
```

◆ From forms — In this case, the input fields in the form are passed along to the script using either the GET or POST methods. POST delivers form data directly to the CGI script using the standard input.

Many specialized characters such as spaces or question marks cannot be sent to CGI scripts explicitly. These characters are replaced by a percentage sign followed by the hexadecimal value representing the character's ASCII value. You can find encoding values at http://www.w3.org/Addressing/rfc1738.txt.

The script then parses these input fields and returns an HTML page or other resource, building it from scratch, including the response header, a blank line, and the content, as shown in Listing 6-1.

Listing 6-1: A common CGI script response

```
# Tell the browser that we are outputting html.
print "Content-Type: text/html\r\n";
print "\r\n";
print "<HTML>\r\n"
print "<HEAD><TITLE>Sample</TITLE></HEAD>\r\n";
print "<BODY>\r\n";
print "A response generated from a <I>cgi script</I>\r\n\r\n";
print "</BODY>\r\n\r\n";
print "</HTML>\r\n\r\n";
```

Other content types include *text/plain*, *image/gif*, or *image/jpg*. In essence, you can create and send along any document type. You can even send a document type that does not exist. However, this confuses the Web client. When a Web browser receives an unsupported document type, it generally asks the user if he wants to download the file to disk.

WHY CGI IS GREAT (PROS)

The gateway interface opens a whole new world of Web interaction. No longer is a Web server just a way to deliver prewritten pages. Now servers can send along dynamic information that is assembled based on the time, the current data in a database, or information that the user has submitted.

The interface for programming CGI scripts is also quite easy to follow. Special libraries have been written in C, Java, and Perl, among other languages, to make the process of parsing input and formatting response output even easier.

WHY CGI ISN'T SO GREAT (CONS)

Anybody who has ever filled out a form on the Web knows how excruciatingly long it can take the form to be submitted after pressing the Submit button. Let's look at a simple CGI script that takes in a user's name and returns a Web page welcoming the user by name. The process is as follows:

1. An HTML page with a form asks for a user's name.

2. The user types in her name and hits the Submit button.

3. The client opens a connection with the server and waits. . . .

4. The data is posted to a CGI script on the Web server. More waiting. . . .

5. The script creates a brand-new HTML page from scratch and sends it. More waiting. . . .

6. The client finally receives the new page, loses the old page, and closes the connection.

Other problems with CGI include memory and performance issues. Whenever a CGI script is run, a new process is spawned. This is important in case two users in various corners of the world access the same script at the same moment. That way, User B can access a script even if User A is already using it.

This is a great idea in theory until three or four or ten thousand users try to access the same CGI script. Suddenly the Web server screeches to a halt, slowing down everybody's response time, causing them to wait longer and longer periods of time for their results.

Yet another problem is compile time. Most CGI scripts are written in Perl because it is so easy to learn and convenient to use. However, every time a Perl script is run, it needs to fire up a session of the Perl interpreter, which takes up even more memory than the script itself. This problem can by bypassed, however, by using a compiled language such as C or C++.

The biggest problem with CGI is that it does not live up to the client-server ideal. The server side is still handling the major processing work, and then shipping it all the way across the network to the dumb client.

Extending the Server: Custom APIs

Many Web servers have a built-in API, with lots of methods and variables that enable a script to directly control any aspect of the server. This enables the server to handle requests and responses directly in any way a developer desires. Rather than using inefficient CGI mechanisms, these extensions enable developers to literally build their code right into the server itself.

There are as many custom server APIs as there are servers. Netscape uses the appropriately named Netscape Server API (NSAPI), and Microsoft's IIS exposes functionality via their ISAPI. The popular Apache server was designed with a modular architecture that enables developers to extend the server's capabilities, while leaving it to handle the boring stuff like requests, logging, and security. A popular use of the Apache module interface is to include a persistent Perl process, making the execution of CGI scripts written in Perl much more efficient.

PROS

Extensions provide a great deal of power over the server. As with CGI, a developer can peek at or work with any aspect of the request-response process. A developer can even use the API to script special authentication elements or to make up a special format for URLs. Special logs with customized information can be kept and stored in unique ways. Almost anything that a developer could do with CGI is achievable with extensions. In addition, extensions can do things that CGI cannot, such as acting as a proxy server or having processes share the same memory.

Server extensions are also pretty fast. There's little run-time overhead because no separate process is initiated. Instead of the server taking the time and resources to pass off form information to a separate CGI script, for example, it handles the data itself as part of its usual workings. Embedding the functionality right in the server is highly efficient.

CONS

Programs written as extensions generally stay in memory as long as the server is running. If you have lots of extensions, they take up lots of memory.

Also, because server extensions are persistent, they have to have all sorts of error-catching mechanisms in order to recover from bad cases. If a file is opened and not closed, it remains open until the entire server is reset. A bad CGI script may crash and thus fail to return the proper Web page. A bad extension, on the other hand, could crash the Web server and bring down an entire Web site. This makes development of extensions a time-consuming task involving lots of testing and debugging.

Though there have been some major improvements, extensions share most of the same problems as CGI scripts. There's still a relatively long connect time for the client to access, and they still put all the onus of computing on the server.

Java Servlets

Sun Microsystems' Servlet API plugs Java programs into Web servers, providing a full range of server-side programming goodies. Like server extensions, servlet classes are loaded along with the Web server and remain in memory for fast access.

You can find more information about servlets at `http://jserv.java-soft.com/products/java-server/servlets/index.html`.

PROS

Java is well liked for its ease of use and its ability to "write once, run anywhere." In other words, the same Java classes can work on a variety of platforms and environments. There are many good graphical environments in which to develop Java applications, such as Microsoft Visual J++ and Symantec Visual Café.

Java, being a Net-enabled language, is essentially written from the ground up to work well over the Internet. Its objects are very easy to plug into one another and swap, making servlets easy to administer.

Java also has a very tight security model.

CONS

The Java Virtual Machine (JVM) must always sit in memory as a separate process. This can eat up resources and often needs a dedicated machine of its own. The JVM compiles Java classes on the fly, making them extensible.

Java is also a young language and still has bugs that need to be worked out. Many of the objects that come standard with other languages, such as interface widgets and other such libraries, are still being developed for Java. Debugging Java is also difficult due to its run-time compilation, as it is sometimes unclear whether a bug is occurring within the Java code itself, or within the current virtual machine.

And, yet again, servlets still force the server to do all the dirty work.

Server-Side Includes

Most modern Web servers support Server-Side Includes (SSI). These includes are generally simple tokens that can be set directly within the HTML of a Web page. When the server sends such a page, it scans for any SSI tokens and may change the contents of the Web page at that point.

For instance, a Web page can be smart enough to look at the time of day and send a page with a sun as its background image if it's morning and a moon as the background if it's night. A more complex usage is to look up some information in a database, such as a field that describes a product the user is interested in, and put this information directly into a Web page.

SSI is transparent to users because they never see actual tokens, just the modified final HTML page that the server sends. These pages usually have the .shtm, .shtml, or .sht extension, depending on the server, but that is the only indication to the user that he is viewing a SSI document.

SSI tokens are placed inside HTML comments and look like this:

```
<!--#tag variables-->
```

 You can get a full specification of the SSI format at `http://hoohoo.ncsa.uiuc.edu/docs/tutorials/includes.html`.

The Apache Web server uses something called XSSI (eXtended Server-Side Includes) that has a few tokens that go beyond the standard NCSA includes. You can find more details on XSSI at `http://www.apache.org/docs/mod/mod_include.html`.

PROS

Because SSI works as part of the Web server, it acts like a CGI script or server include in that it is guaranteed to deliver the same HTML page to any client. That means a page can be formatted to work equally well with a text browser such as Lynx or the latest version of Netscape Navigator.

In addition, SSI launches no new process, and thus costs the server nearly no extra memory.

CONS

SSI can handle only simple tasks, and is not as full-featured as CGI methods, which can essentially perform any function the programmer can think of.

SSI also has a few security risks, as the Exec token can run any program on the server, including ones that can crash it. You can disable the Exec token, but a lot of otherwise useful functionality is lost.

If a server is taxed with lots of hits of the same page, the extra time it takes to parse through every HTML document that it sends can add up. There are ways to cache pages once they have been parsed, but these are not widely used.

Like CGI and extensions, SSI is dynamic only on the server. Once it is served up to the client, it is as flat and stale as any other Web page.

Active Server Pages (ASP)

Microsoft went a step beyond SSI with the invention of Active Server Pages (ASP). An HTML Active Server Page has some special tags that look like this:

```
<% ASP Commands %>
```

As with the DOM discussed in the last chapter, each ASP command has properties that can be read or set, as well as methods that take in some variables or objects and sometimes spit something else out. In fact, ASP takes advantage of two important object models: COM (Component Object Model) and DCOM (Distributed Component Object Model).

For instance, you could use the ASP Write(String) method to print out a line of text by using the code in Listing 6-2.

Listing 6-2: A dumb ASP page

```
<HTML>
<HEAD>
<TITLE>Example 1</TITLE>
</HEAD>
<BODY >
<% Response.Write("I just printed this using ASP.")  %>
</BODY>
</HTML>
```

 You can find more information about ASP at http://www.microsoft.com/workshop/server/asp/ASPover.asp.

PROS

ASP is as extensible and full featured as CGI scripts while at the same time relying on the server to parse and compile the final document. ASP has native support for both VBScript and Jscript, and thus is very easy to learn and use. You can also plug in toolboxes that let you write ASP pages with Perl or Java.

The IIS4 Web server has some very useful objects that you can control with ASP, making it very, very easy to access ODBC databases or send e-mail.

ASP runs as a service and can take full advantage of multithreaded operating systems. The other big plus is that you can develop ASP in a visual environment such as Visual C++. These environments commonly have tools such as wizards and debuggers that make writing ASP pages quite simple.

CONS

ASP is very nice and useful if you happen to be using a server that supports the technology. However, there's still a big processing hit when many clients try to grab the same ASP page at once.

In addition, the server is still doing all the page creation and updating work. Something drastically different is needed.

Java Applets

Java applets are powerful little programs that are inserted smack into HTML pages as follows:

```
<APPLET CODE=myapplet.class WIDTH=300 HEIGHT=200>
<PARAM NAME="myparameter" VALUE="myvalue">
</APPLET>
```

PROS

Java applets have most of same advantages as servlets. Because Java is an entire language in itself, it has the ability to draw graphics, play sounds, or handle complex processing tasks. You can achieve all sorts of dynamic effects using an applet: pull-down menus, drag and drop, icons, and so forth.

The cross-platform capabilities of Java enable a developer to create one applet and have it work in any Java-enabled Web browser. *Signed applets* let users grant a Java applet full rights to their systems. This enables applets to stroll out of the sandbox model of security and perform nearly any major task, such as writing to the hard drive, accessing any Web server, or painting to video memory.

Theoretically, a Java client can be written to achieve the ideal client-server data transfers you desire. Java applets are compiled and processed completely on the client. As such, Java is a true client-side solution.

CONS

The cross-platform abilities of Java aren't quite there yet. Different browsers support different versions of the Java run time. This means that the same applet does not work equally well in all browsers. In fact, complicated applets sometimes crash the browser.

Another drawback to applets is that they really take the user away from the Web browser, interface-wise. The applet must completely take over a rectangle within the screen. The speed and ease of HTML are lost, and the Web page becomes nothing more than a container for a wonderful Java applet. In addition, Java is often overkill. Java performs visual tasks that the browser already "knows" how to do. It's like strapping a rocket engine onto a bicycle to make the bike go faster.

Compared to a typical dynamic HTML page, a Java applet that performs the same functions generally has a much larger file size. Once an applet is downloaded, there is also a very lengthy initialization process. Nor is Java the type of technology that average developers can use. It is a much more intense programming language that often relies on advanced techniques such as double buffering, sockets, thread synchronization, and exception handling.

 JavaScript or other client-side scripts can, however, interact with public Java variables and methods, giving developers and users the best of both worlds.

ActiveX Controls

ActiveX controls are very similar, in practice, to Java applets. An ActiveX control only needs to be downloaded once. At that point, it is stored in a secure place on the client's hard drive. ActiveX controls can be embedded into Web pages using code similar to the following:

```
<OBJECT ID="MyObject" WIDTH=90 HEIGHT=50 CLASSID="CLSID:D7053240-
CE69-11CD-A777-00DD01143C57">
<PARAM NAME="myparameter" VALUE="myvalue">
</OBJECT>
```

PROS

These controls are based on well-known Microsoft programming widgets, and interact seamlessly with Windows and other Microsoft applications. There are tons of ready-made ActiveX objects, code, and programming wizards out there to help you easily create the effect or application you desire.

ActiveX is another true client-side solution. Good objects can be written so that servers are only queried when the object explicitly needs something from it.

Because you do not need to download the controls repeatedly, ActiveX bridges the gap between client application and the Web browser, providing fast, full-featured, and extensible programs.

CONS

Only Windows versions of Internet Explorer handle ActiveX objects well, though there is a plug-in for Netscape Navigator. In other words, ActiveX is not a cross-platform technology.

Also, ActiveX objects are usually signed by a particular company. A user sees this signature and can choose to install the component or not. Once a certificate is accepted, however, an object has full reign over a user's system. Many users do not wish to take chances with this security risk and therefore reject ActiveX components.

As with Java, ActiveX controls are very large and often use redundant functionality.

Plug-In Applications

Any application at all can be placed inside a special framework, enabling it to be plugged in to Netscape Navigator or Internet Explorer. This is generally done using the <EMBED> tag.

PROS

The application looks and acts any way the software engineers and interface designers desire. It can interact with any specially designed server in any way it deems necessary.

CONS

Plug-ins vary in how they work from browser to browser. A custom version of a plug-in must generally be written for every operating system and browser. In addition, installing a plug-in is not seamless. A user must explicitly choose to install the application, run a setup program, possibly shut down their browser or their entire computer, and then restart it all and return to the original Web page. Most Web users just move on.

In addition, there is little relationship between a Web browser and a plug-in application. The browser may pass media files along to the plug-in, but that's about it. The browser generally acts as a sort of bed upon which the application rests.

Client-Side Scripting to the Rescue

Finally, we come to *client-side scripting*. Scripts are sets of easy commands that can be placed directly in the HTML of a page. A typical script is added as shown in Listing 6-3.

Listing 6-3: A typical JavaScript

```
<script language="JavaScript">
<!-- // This comment tag makes the following script invisible
    // to older browsers.
// Functions look like this:
function launch(input)
{
    // The input is handled.
    output = input;
    return output;
}
// -->
</script>
<noscript>
```

```
Information here is printed out to browsers that <B>do not
support</B> the scripting language.
</noscript>
```

The script is usually placed in the head of an HTML document, though pieces of script can be found sprinkled anywhere throughout the document.

There are many different client-side scripting languages. The main thing to remember about a client-side script is that it exists completely in the world of the client.

Scripts are read in by browsers along with the rest of the HTML code. As it comes across a script, the browser follows the code to a T. Some pieces of script are triggered by events, which means they sit around until a mouse is rolled or clicked, or a certain amount of time has passed. At that point the script runs. When you roll your mouse over an image, it might call a function to switch the image, giving you some quick and easy feedback.

For example, the following script detects mouse rollovers in links and then changes the `src` attribute of an associated image. `heaven.gif` changes to `hell.gif` and then back again when the mouse moves away:

```
<a href="#"
  onMouseOver="document.myImage.src='hell.gif'"
  onMouseOut="document.myImage.src='heaven.gif'">
<img src="heaven.gif" name="myImage" width=100 height=50 border=0>
</a>
```

This is a typical, but very basic use of client-side scripting.

The particular magic of client scripts is that they are interpreted on the fly. This makes them quite different from other client-empowered solutions such Java or ActiveX, which are precompiled.

COMPILED LANGUAGES VS. INTERPRETED LANGUAGES

C, C++, Pascal, and other such languages are *compiled languages*. This means all the code is run once through a *compiler*. The compiler crunches all the routines into binary code — the ones and zeros that trigger commands and calculations within the computer's processor. Compiled languages generally output EXE or other such executable files. A compiled application cannot easily be viewed, modified, or passed between systems. This is why software that works on a Macintosh cannot work on a PC.

Java programs are compiled into something called *bytecode*. These bytecode classes are then passed through a special *run-time interpreter* that follows the byte commands. This makes Java a lot easier to use from platform to platform. However, by and large, it is as immutable as any other compiled language.

TCL, Perl, the UNIX shells, JavaScript, VBScript, and many other server-side scripts are *interpreted languages*. This means that their functions and routines must run through an interpreter any time they are executed. Of course, this takes quite a bit of extra time; a routine must be interpreted into binary code and then executed.

The big advantage is that interpreted scripts are very easy to change and distribute. A script can even be used to create a brand-new script on the fly. As long as a given operating system has an interpreter, the same piece of script works just fine on it.

Client-side scripts, in essence, use the best of both worlds. They use the browser's compiled libraries for all processor-intensive tasks such as graphics rendering, multimedia, and network messages. The interpreted script passes in values to compiled methods. This provides speed as well as extensibility.

PROS

The biggest plus with client-side scripting languages is that they plug right into documents. This is the perfect place to interact directly with the document objects discussed in the last chapter. By snagging hold of HTML elements and pieces, you can change anything and everything about the state of the document at will.

Client-side scripts use the browser to perform most intensive tasks, such as graphics and network connections. This enables a novice programmer to work with the script and achieve highly impressive results while shedding little sweat. Most common scripts can easily be copied and pasted.

Relying on the browser's power can also make for compact scripts. A bone-simple Java applet that creates a button that animates when the mouse clicks it would need to be a few dozen lines of code. A similar client-side script could perform the animation in about two lines, hardly putting a dent in the size of the HTML document. We should note, however, that the size of file changes drastically from application to application. In many cases, Java applets can be far more compact than a full-featured JavaScript application.

Also, because no code needs to be compiled, client-side scripts are easy to maintain. Standard applications must go through a lengthy recompiling and retesting process.

CONS

Few client-side script development environments have wizards or debuggers, making complicated applications a bit difficult to work with.

Because the client does all the compilation on the fly, client-side scripts are a bit slower than precompiled code. However, this is offset by the fact that the code usually just hooks into the browser's native routines, which are extremely fast and optimized.

Client-side scripts cannot generally perform any functions that the browser itself does not handle or perform. As browsers become more like operating systems, however, with a very wide selection of graphical, math, and network methods, this becomes less of a limitation.

The biggest disadvantage is compatibility between browsers. Server-side solutions deliver the same HTML code to every browser in the world. Client-side script only works for the browser it was written for. This disregards any old or nonstandard browsers.

In addition, the way Netscape Navigator and Internet Explorer handle client-side scripts differs, making scripts written for one browser worthless on the other. Not to worry, though, Part III of this book, "Examples of Good HCI with Dynamic HTML," uncovers ways to achieve the same results in different browsers. Making wrappers that enable scripts to work anywhere is one of the main themes of this book.

More Scripts Than You Can Shake a Stick At

The benefits of client-side scripting were recognized early on. Back before Internet Explorer really existed, the second version of Netscape Navigator included some rudimentary scripting abilities. Since then, the development of scripts has had its ups and downs, its pros and cons.

Many languages have been used as client-side scripts. What are the differences between them? Which one is best?

Nature Abhors a Standard

Every developer has her favorite scripting language. Oftentimes, a developer uses a language for many years for a job and becomes a virtuoso in it. Other times a developer particularly admires the philosophy of architecture behind a certain language. This is why you can still find some people who like word processing using the keyboard-only vi editor (an environment that has no menus at all). It takes forever to learn, but once you know it, it's faster than anything else.

More so, browser companies want to control the client-side scripts. Having authority over a powerful scripting language is equivalent to owning all the verbs in a language. Because client scripts run only on the client, whoever owns the language owns control of that client. As such, Netscape, Microsoft, and others have held hard and fast to various languages of choice.

On the server side, developers can use any script that, in the end, produces valid HTML. They can even write their own language if desired. But because client-side scripts are closely tied to HTML (through the DOM) and parsed in by browsers they must be somewhat standardized. If you write a script that a browser cannot interpret, in a worst-case scenario, your dud code could crash the browser and come up with tons of bugs. The best-case scenario is that any of the nifty features you have scripted into the page could not work at all.

As such, forging a client-side script that everyone can use was and still is highly necessary. While browsers don't agree to the letter about which scripting languages to support, JavaScript has emerged as a de facto standard. You can handle most dynamic HTML functionality with JavaScript.

It was a long, hard path even to get this far. Netscape fired the first shot in the scripting-standard wars.

Netscape: LiveScript and JavaScript

Netscape invented a language that was released in their Navigator 2.0 beta: LiveScript. This set of routines was patterned after Java, and resembled the syntax of Java expressions and the way the flow of the program was controlled.

LiveScript supported the basic primitive types of numbers, Booleans, and strings. It very smartly dealt with and converted between these types. There was no need to declare each variable. For instance, look at the following sequence:

```
a = 134;
b = "mystring" + a
```

This would automatically make b into a string containing `mystring134`. There is no need to declare that b is a string. LiveScript figured it out based on the context.

LiveScript also supported basic functions that could take in variables and output the same primitive types: numbers, Booleans, and strings. The capability to get and set properties was the keystone of LiveScript. It made many properties of the current HTML document available, such as:

◆ **The content of forms** – This enabled an embedded LiveScript to check a phone number field in an order form, for example, to be sure the number was in the proper format. If the phone number was typed in wrong, a message could immediately pop up explaining the proper format.

◆ **Page navigation** – Whenever a page was opened or closed, or a link was clicked, LiveScript could catch this and perform many functions such as printing out a message or playing a sound effect.

LIVECONNECT

One of LiveScript's most useful capabilities was to access objects within the Netscape Navigator page. This technology was known as LiveConnect. For instance, you could pause, rewind, or stop embedded videos. You could play audio files at will. And you could call Java methods, enabling LiveScript functions to control the behavior of applets.

JAVASCRIPT

Netscape soon changed LiveScript's name to JavaScript, due to its strong similarities to Java, as well as for marketing reasons. The Java language was very highly hyped at the time, so the name JavaScript had some strategic marketing value behind it as well. Netscape also made the standard open, hoping that Microsoft and other browser makers would insert JavaScript abilities into their browsers and thus ensure its widespread use and survival.

In the early days of JavaScript, there was no real Document Object Model. The properties that JavaScript exposed were useful, but limited. Many of the properties seemed arbitrarily picked. For instance, you could play around with forms but not with images.

Microsoft: JScript and VBScript

Microsoft joined the client-side script wars with its 3.0 version of Internet Explorer. It had a language that was based on JavaScript called JScript. Its primary focus, however, was something called VBScript.

VBSCRIPT

This client-side language was a subset of Visual Basic, a programming language that had a lot of support due to its ease of use and its visual programming interface. VBScript simplified this already simplified language. One of its most interesting features was the capability to add special controls to Web pages such as scroll bar areas, buttons, or pull-down menus.

VBScript, however, was heavily geared toward Windows platforms only. It was not supported at all by Netscape Navigator, which was the most frequently used browser of that time. This made pages scripted with VBScript nearly worthless to most people.

VBScript has since become cross-platform and, though it only works on Internet Explorer, it is sometimes used in small pieces to achieve results that JavaScript cannot.

JSCRIPT

Microsoft bit the bullet and also included a version of JavaScript called JScript. It had the same syntax and flow of JavaScript. Unfortunately, it provided access to properties that Netscape's JavaScript did not support. It also had a few syntax discrepancies with JavaScript that caused some well-written Netscape Navigator scripts to cause bugs on Internet Explorer and vice versa.

PerlScript

Another scripting language that halfheartedly tried to join the wars was PerlScript. This language is based on Perl, a popular language that combines some of the easiest features of C and the UNIX shell and is widely used to create CGI scripts.

There are commercial PerlScript packages available that plug into Web servers. However, neither Microsoft nor Netscape explicitly support PerlScript. This makes it a useful plug-in for servers, but entirely useless as a widespread client-side script.

Standards

Noticing the vast advantages of client-side scripts but aghast at the differences between Netscape and Microsoft's implementation of these scripts, developers across the world clamored for some sort of standard.

In late 1996, it was decided that a standards body should manage the task of documenting JavaScript and opening its functionality up to the world, so that other vendors could provide compatible implementations. The task fell onto the shoulders of the European Computer Manufacturers Association, or ECMA.

ECMASCRIPT

EMCAScript is strongly based on JavaScript. It is an object-oriented programming language that, as the specification states, is for "performing computations and manipulating computational objects within a host environment." In essence, ECMAScript is the open version of JavaScript, based on JavaScript version 1.1.

This definition strikes upon the most noteworthy aspect of client-side scripting: the ability to use it as a way to play with the objects within a Web document. In other words, we have finally found the verbs to use with our dynamic HTML nouns.

The language consists of *properties*. Properties can be thought of as collections that can contain any or all of the following:

- ◆ **Primitive values** — Strings, numbers, or Booleans.

- ◆ **Other properties** — This enables properties to have children, and gives order and hierarchy to a large collection of properties.

- ◆ **Methods** — Functions that can return either properties or primitive values.

ECMAScript also has all of the goodies that you would expect in a useful language:

- ◆ **Global objects** — Objects that can be accessed from any script in the document, enabling information to be shared.

- ◆ **Array objects** — Numbered lists of objects.

- ◆ **Math objects** — The capability to perform important calculations, such as finding the square root of a number.

- ◆ **The capability to access browser objects** — This provides a framework for controlling windows, dialog boxes, text area, menus, anchors, frames, history lists, and cookies, and a way of inputting and outputting data.

And the Winner Is . . . JavaScript

The latest versions of Microsoft Internet Explorer and Netscape Communicator by and large support a version of JavaScript that fulfills the ECMAScript specifications. This makes JavaScript cross-platform and cross-browser. As such, the latest ECMAScript-compatible versions of JavaScript are the clear winners of the script wars. JavaScript has some unique advantages:

- ◆ JavaScript is tried and true. It is also an open standard. Any software vendor can use JavaScript without having to purchase a license. Many

Web developers are already very familiar with its syntax and its quirks. It has proven itself by performing well with style sheets, Java applets, plug-ins, and other dynamic HTML components.

♦ JavaScript has many of the object-oriented advantages of Java. JavaScript is simpler than Java, though, because it is essentially only interested in document objects and therefore does not need libraries full of graphics routines, GUI control widgets, input/output, or network calls.

♦ Most importantly, the latest JavaScript versions interact completely with most HTML code, providing complete access to most every element in the document.

NOT QUITE PERFECT

Despite being a standard, JavaScript still can only act upon the DOM presented to it. Because Internet Explorer and Netscape Navigator still use slightly different document models, the API to hook into these models cannot be quite standardized.

As such, the JavaScript that performs a legal action in Navigator sometimes does nothing or causes errors in Internet Explorer. The purpose of Part III, especially Chapter 9, "Implementing Effective User Interfaces with DHTML," is to introduce cross-browser JavaScript *object wrappers*. These wrappers provide a way to take any object in either browser and have JavaScript work with it without having to write your application once for each browser, or litter your application level code with tests for the current browser vendor and version.

Early JavaScript Tricks

A bit later on in this book, we explore complex ways to make JavaScript interact with the Document Object Model and Cascading Style Sheets. In the meantime, though, it might be useful to take a quick tour through some of JavaScript's earliest uses. Studying this code is an instructive way to bone up on the important features of JavaScript.

DIALOG BOXES

JavaScript can be used to pop up alarm or confirmation boxes, which are very handy methods of getting information to users and/or obtaining input.

The following code puts up a button that, when pressed, creates a simple alarm box that says: "Alarm!" When the user clicks OK, the box disappears:

```
<form>
<input type="button" value="Click For Alarm"
onClick="alert('Alarm!')">
</form>
```

MESSAGES IN THE STATUS BAR

Another common use of JavaScript is to give users a bit of information when they roll over a link, helping them decide if they want to click it. Figure 6-1 illustrates rolling a mouse over a link and displaying a message in the status bar. The code to achieve this is a bit messy, but fits on one line:

```
<a href="newpage.htm" onMouseOver="window.status='This will take you
to a new page!'; return true;" onMouseOut="window.status='';">An
Amazing New Page!</a>
```

This captures the `onMouseOver` and `onMouseOut` events.

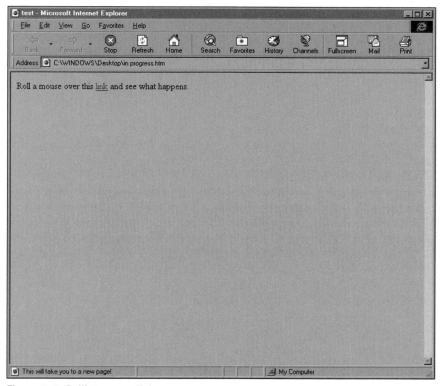

Figure 6-1: Rolling over a link

SCROLLING

Early JavaScript also had the capability to wait for a certain period of time. This provided cool timed effects. For instance, scrolling status marquees could be dropped into any page.

Text is written to the status bar, as in the preceding example. The timer then pauses for a second or so. The text is then redrawn, shifted over one character to the right. Repeated enough times, it looks like the text is scrolling.

Timeouts can be set as follows:

```
setTimeout("alert('Time is up!')", 3000);
```

We discuss timers in detail in Chapter 16, "Timers and Other Fun Stuff."

RELOCATING

JavaScript is also a very useful way to go to a new Web page without having to click a link. This is accomplished by changing the `href` property of the `location` object. The following creates a button that takes users to the Netscape home page:

```
<form>
<input type=button value="Netscape"
onClick="location.href='http://www.netscape.com'; ">
</form>
```

VALIDATING FORM INPUT

One of the most timesaving capabilities of JavaScript is the analysis of input forms right on the client. No time-wasting server queries are necessary. For instance, you can easily validate a field in a form to check to see if a vaguely valid MasterCard number was typed in. In this case, "valid" is a very, very basic check. All you validate is that the length is 16 characters long and that the first two numbers are between 51 and 55. The code to do all this is in Listing 6-4.

Listing 6-4: Checking credit card data right on the client

```
<html>
<head>
<script language="JavaScript">
<!-- // Hide code from older browsers
function testit(form) {
  ccnumber = form.mynum.value;
  if((ccnumber.length == 16) &&
    ((ccnumber.substring(0,2) >= "51") &&
    (ccnumber.substring(0,2) <= 55))) {
      alert("Valid Credit Card!");
  } else {
      alert("Illegal Credit Card, You Crook!");
  }
```

```
}
// -->
</script>
</head>
<body>
<form name="myform">
Enter a valid Mastercard number:
<input name="mynum">
<input type="button" value="Test It" onClick="testit(this.form)">
</form>
</body>
</html>
```

OPENING A WINDOW

Another cool JavaScript feature is the capability to open a new document in a custom-sized window. For instance, to pop up a new window that contains the new-page.htm document in size 400 × 300, with no menu bar, status bar, or tool bar:

```
open("newpage.htm", "displayWindow",
"width=400,height=300,status=no,toolbar=no,menubar=no");
```

DEALING WITH MULTIPLE FRAMES

You can also use JavaScript to change two or more frames at once. This is very useful for multiframe sites where one click of a button updates any or all of the panes. A function to open two separate URLs in two frames is:

```
function twoframes(url1, url2) {
  parent.frame1.location.href = url1;
  parent.frame2.location.href = url2;
}
```

CALCULATING DATA

JavaScript often acts as a substitute for CGI scripts by handling the data in a form and coming up with a response. For instance, you can perform simple product calculations in the script in Listing 6-5.

Listing 6-5: Multiplying two entries in a form

```
<html>
<head>
<script language="JavaScript">
<!-- // Hide code from older browsers
  function multiply() {

    x = document.myform.num1.value;
    y = document.myform.num2.value;
```

```
    a = x * y;
    alert(x+" times "+y+" equals "+a);
  }
// -->
</script>
</head>
<body>
<form name="myform">
First Number : <input name="num1"><BR>
Second Number: <input name="num2"><BR>
<input type="button" value="Multiply"
 onClick="multiply()">
</form>
</body>
</html>
```

BROWSER DETECTION

JavaScript can easily detect what brand and version of browser the user is currently using. It can use this information to launch an appropriate Web page, custom-tailored for the browser type.

The code to do it can be found in Listing 6-6.

Listing 6-6: Figuring out what browser you're running on

```
<script language="JavaScript">
<!--// hide from older browsers
// Loads a new Web page
function launch(thepage) {  document.location.href = thepage + ".html";
}

// Detects the type of browser being used
if (navigator.appName.indexOf("Netscape") != -1) {  // Using Netscape
  launch("nspage");
}
else if (navigator.appName.indexOf("Microsoft Internet Explorer") != -1)
{  // Using Internet Explorer
  launch("iepage");
} else {
  // Using Neither
  launch("blandpage");
}
//-->
</script>
```

ON-THE-FLY DOCUMENTS

A more advanced use of JavaScript is to craft custom HTML pages based on user input. This can be done by spitting out a sequence of `document.writeln()` methods containing the new HTML markup.

The code shown in Listing 6-9 opens up a new window and creates a custom document within it.

Listing 6-9: Creating a custom document

```
<script language="JavaScript">
<!--// hide code from older browsers
function NewDoc() {
  newWin = open("", "displayWindow",
    "width=500,height=400,status=yes,toolbar=yes,menubar=yes");
  // Open the document for writing
  newWin.document.open();
  // Create the document
  newWin.document.write("<html><head>");
  newWin.document.write("<title>Custom Doc</title>");
  newWin.document.write("</head>");
  newWin.document.write("<body>");
  newWin.document.write("<h1>This is a custom, brand-spanking new
  document.</h1>");
  newWin.document.write("It was created on the fly!<P>");
  newWin.document.write("Pretty <B>cool</B>, eh?");
  newWin.document.write("</body></html>");
  // close the document
  myWin.document.close();
}
// -->
</script>
```

AND MORE . . .

Early JavaScript has even been used to create advanced widgets and tools. For example, the retractable-expandable menu shown in Figure 6-2 was made entirely using JavaScript. You can find more information and the complete script to achieve this at `http://www.geocities.com/Paris/LeftBank/2178/ftexample.html`.

When a plus sign is clicked, submenus pop out. When a minus sign is clicked, submenus are retracted, cleaning up the structure.

As we go on to create dynamic applications in Part III of this book, you shall soon see that handy tools like this are only the beginning.

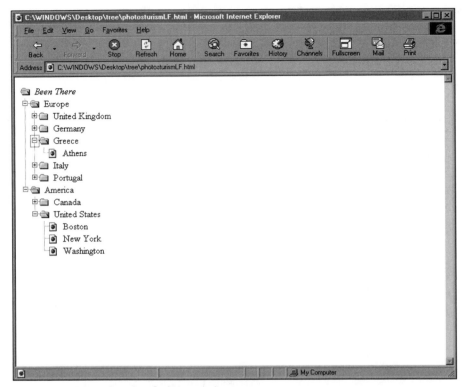

Figure 6-2: A complete JavaScript menu bar system

Nouns Come Alive

JavaScript sounds very useful, doesn't it? But it's the way JavaScript works behind the scenes that gives it its true power. The JavaScript language is a tricky beast. It seems very simple on its surface, but what it really does is unleash all the browser's power. By giving developers access to any Web page object, the nouns of dynamic HTML truly come alive.

Object-Oriented Programming

The biggest distinction between programming languages is their architecture – the approach a programmer must take to create the application he or she wants. Older languages such as C are *procedural*. That is, the programmer creates methods (procedures or functions) that perform routine tasks. The program then cycles through and calls these functions as often as necessary. Data is stored in containers that can hold any type of data. The methods can pass references back and forth to these containers of data.

With the onset of C++ and Java, however, *modular* or *object-oriented programming* became much more popular. Objects are special structures that contain not only data, but also any of the methods that can act upon that data. This gives each object all sorts of intelligence about where it fits in with the rest of the world, enabling several independent modules to be linked together cleanly in one program. A method within an object can be designed to take any other object as input, or spit out any object as a return value. Modules can also be derived, or *subclassed* from other objects, sharing all of their functions and data and then creating more and more specialized objects.

If you recall from the last chapter, this is exactly how the Document Object Model works. JavaScript is object oriented and thus ties in perfectly with the DOM and Web pages themselves. For instance, the image element is a special type of object that is extended from the generic element object, which in turn is *descended* from the document object. An image object can be passed into a JavaScript method that changes one of its properties, such as its source file.

Because JavaScript has no strong *type checking,* it is valid to write code that does this:

```
function changeSrc(theimage,newsrc) {   theimage.src = newsrc;
}
```

The above method works under the assumption that theimage is an image object and newsrc is a string. If illegal values are inputted, JavaScript returns an error.

 JavaScript lacks Java's strong type checking. The above method in Java would need to state explicitly the type being sent to the method, as follows:

```
public void changeSrc(Image theimage,String newsrc) {
   theimage.src = newsrc;
}
```

A MORE LENIENT FORM OF JAVA
In addition, JavaScript enables objects to be easily created without having to explicitly define them, as in Java but with less explicit casting. You can begin working with an image simply by assigning it to a variable:

```
myimage = document.images.theimage;
```

In Java, you would need to define a new object:

```
myimage = new Image(document.images.theimage);
```

This simple distinction makes writing quick and dirty programs in JavaScript much easier than in Java. The downside, however, is that without explicitly stating what every type of object is, JavaScript often makes some wrong assumptions and requires extra debugging.

Harnessing Events

Without events there are no verbs. Your brain reacts to events, making you behave the way you do. For example, if you touch something hot, your hand jerks away. If you smell something foul, you make a sour face. In order for your body to do something active, it generally needs something external to trigger it.

Dynamic HTML, like any living body, lives and reacts through events. Events within each object trigger scripted functions the way input to a brain triggers behavior.

Events themselves are nouns—part of the Document Object Model and part of specific objects. They are things that happen. Not every object supports every event. For instance, only elements such as input boxes and link anchors that can actually get the user's focus (generally indicated by a blinking cursor in the box) can trigger an onFocus event.

MORE THAN CLICKS

Clicking on a hyperlink was the Web's prototypical event—click and jump to another page. The full document model supports a heck of a lot more than clicks, though. Every time a user changes anything about or around a document, the event model knows about it. Whenever a user moves the mouse, for instance, the coordinates of the new position are fired off to JavaScript. The event model also knows if the mouse button is down at any point. In this way, objects can be dragged and dropped.

In many cases, a JavaScript function hasn't been written to catch an object's event. In this case, nothing special happens, and the object just acts the way it normally acts by default. Hyperlinks clicked go to the link's URL, text boxes clicked gain focus and enable the user to type in them. If a developer so desires, she can capture any event and do with it what she will. Dynamic HTML enables developers to create a wacky page that overrides the normal functions. Clicking on a link could change the color of the next paragraph. Clicking inside a text box could open a new window.

Events are discussed in more detail in Chapter 9, "Implementing Effective User Interfaces with DHTML."

JavaScript handles more than mouse clicks. All of the following types of events can be captured and used in the latest versions of JavaScript:

◆ The page is opened, closed, loaded, or unloaded.

◆ The mouse is clicked, double-clicked, released, or moved.

◆ Any object is dragged and then enters, leaves, or is dropped into a target area.

- The mouse cursor enters or exits the space of an object.

- An error occurs.

- Help is requested about the object.

- The state of any object changes.

- A field gains or loses blur or focus, or the text in a field changes.

- Any key is pressed or released.

- The window is resized, minimized, or scrolled.

- The document is printed.

- An image download is aborted.

- A cut, copy, paste, select, or deselect occurs.

- Data from an applet or other provider is about to be sent, has been sent, or changes.

 Some of the above actions are currently only supported by Internet Explorer 5.0, and thus are not dealt with in this book.

Saving State

The capability to track information between Web pages is essential. For example, if a user enters his name in a form on Page A, it is common courtesy to have his name already filled in on another input form on Page B.

One way to reserve state is to keep it on a server. If you type in your name on Page A, it is uploaded to a server database. When you visit page B, the server uses CGI or an include or ASP to craft the new form page from scratch, automatically inserting your name in the input field.

However, you should be keenly interested in avoiding unnecessary data transfers between the client and the server as much as possible. Such transfers can be disruptive to the page's state, and when your entire application is resident in the current page, having it just disappear just so a server can acknowledge receipt of a small chunk of data is counterproductive and counterintuitive.

One way to avoid having the page refresh after every data transfer is to split the Web page into frames. The top frame can have global JavaScript variables that keep any useful information. The bottom frame can then change and access the variables from the top frame when needed.

A cleaner method involves the use of cookies. Cookies enable Web pages to keep any data desired, turning a stream of unrelated pages into a linked, full-featured application. JavaScript has the ability to set and read simple cookies. If you type in your name on a form in Page A, JavaScript could then capture the text-changed event and store a cookie that looks something like the following:

```
"name"= "Jane Doe"
```

A link is then clicked, bringing you to Page B. When the page first loads, some JavaScript reads in this *name* cookie and inserts your name into the proper field on the form.

The server can also set and retrieve cookies, making them an important tool for data transfer. We discuss how to use cookies in Chapter 8, "Tying Things Together: Sentences and Paragraphs." Specific examples of cookie use can be found in Chapter 13, "User-Configurable Interfaces."

In the preceding example, of course, we could cut down on server data transfer even further by never loading Page B at all. Instead, some JavaScript code in Page A could be triggered to create and display a new Page B on the fly. In such a case, your name wouldn't need to be stored in a separate frame or cookie — it could remain in a global JavaScript variable.

Looking for Action?

So let's review. JavaScript gives us full programmatic power over the objects in our document without having to rely on servers. In full, JavaScript gives us the following types of actions:

- The events model enables JavaScript to catch nearly any action that a user performs and handle it, changing the objects on the page in any way desired based on the event.

- Common programming structures such as for loops and while loops enable methods to be repeatedly called, and enable any aspect of any object to move or change over time.

- Variables enable objects within a page to be stored, created, manipulated, and passed around.

- Arrays enable lists of objects to be created and passed around.

- The `Math` object adds the ability to perform important calculations such as finding the square root of a number. Routines such as the trigonometric sine function (`Math.sin`) can come in handy when it comes time to do things like animate objects in curved paths around the screen.

◆ The `Date` object gives programmers access to the current date and time.

◆ Special methods enable developers to pop up dialog alert boxes, create common input and output widgets, and link these to any object on the page.

All these actions, taken together, provide you with a rich vocabulary of verbs that you can use to control nouns. The Document Object Model breaks up a document into a nice tree of components. Client-side scripting ties directly into this tree and provides the pathway to access these components and push them around.

So if you take a simple HTML page, as shown in Figure 6-3, it can be broken down through the JavaScript in Listing 6-10.

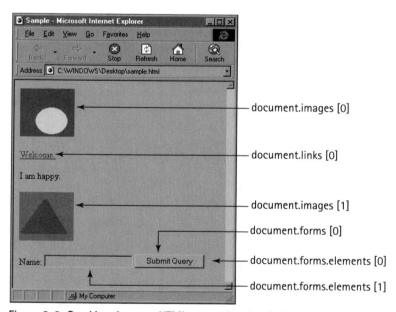

Figure 6-3: Breaking down an HTML page using JavaScript

Listing 6-10: A very simple HTML page put through the JavaScript paces

```
<HTML>
<HEAD>
<TITLE>Sample</TITLE>
</HEAD>
<BODY>
<IMG SRC="hi.gif">
<P><A HREF="welcome.htm">Welcome.</A></P>
<P>I am happy.</P>
```

```
<IMG SRC="bye.gif">
<FORM>
Name: <INPUT>
<INPUT TYPE=SUBMIT>
</FORM>
</BODY>
</HTML>
```

The JavaScript representation of every major object is as follows:

```
                        document
                            |
images[0]  links[0] images[1]  forms[0]
                            |
        elements[0] elements[1]
```

You could access the submit button of the form by using:

```
document.forms[0].elements[1]
```

Summary

You now understand the power of JavaScript, as well as some of its limitations. Specifically, on the upside, JavaScript is tied directly to document objects and provides a programmatic way to control them. On the downside, JavaScript implementations differ from browser to browser, creating a lot of confusion.

We also covered the following:

◆ Originally, Web pages were static and relied on the server to distribute them.

◆ This rigidity put too much pressure on servers and had several drawbacks, especially in the way that Web application interfaces were limited.

◆ Data transfer of nondynamic HTML pages is relatively inefficient.

◆ Client-side scripting provides an elegant solution, enabling documents to be completely controlled on the client's end.

◆ JavaScript has emerged as the preeminent client-side scripting language.

◆ JavaScript functions act as the verbs to the Document Object Model's nouns.

Now that we've covered verbs and nouns, we have a fully functional language. But a certain something is still missing; applications still lack color, flavor, size, and shape. In a word (or two), we are missing adjectives and adverbs.

The next chapter shows you ways to describe objects, and use verbs to modify these descriptions. This helps round out dynamic HTML into a working language.

Chapter 7

Cascading Style Sheets: Adjectives and Adverbs

IN THIS CHAPTER

- ◆ What styles are

- ◆ Why styles are separated from HTML

- ◆ Various style languages

- ◆ How style sheets work

- ◆ Cascading Style Sheets (CSS)

- ◆ Style sheets with positioning: CSS-P

- ◆ The eXtensible Style Language (XSL)

- ◆ Using style sheets with HTML

- ◆ Using style sheets with JavaScript

A World without Style Is a Bleak, Bleak World

Just as a handful of verbs and nouns alone does not a very effective or interesting language make, a handful of objects does not a document make.

HTML is great for quickly distributing documents across the Internet. However, despite some innovation in page design, HTML documents are, by and large, full of text and graphics but empty of style. This is as it should be, because HTML is all about the formatting of a document, not its flighty design details.

What do we mean by style? Surely a Paris supermodel and a Texas cowboy would define style differently. The question would have Picasso and Van Gogh up all night arguing, not to mention a Mac designer and a UNIX programmer. But in the world of the Web, style is simply defined as the way elements on the page actually *look*. This includes font family, font size, color, position, spacing between lines, margin width, borders, and other typographical elements that print designers and everyday word processor users have for so long taken for granted.

In other words, Cascading Style Sheets provide the adjectives and adverbs to go with the nouns of the Document Object Model and the verbs of JavaScript.

The Way It Was

Take a look at Figure 7-1. A pretty simple document, right? For the longest time this combination of colors, fonts, sizes, precise positions, and overlapping layers was impossible to achieve on the Web, short of inserting a huge graphic designed in a different program such as Adobe Illustrator. Developers only had simple descriptor tags to work with such as <H1> for headings, which would usually appear a little bolder and bigger; <I> for italics, which would usually appear in a slanted font; and <B> for bold, which would usually result in a heavier font. (Usually. . . .)

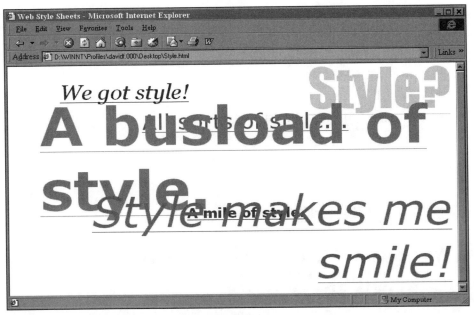

Figure 7-1: A bunch of colorful phrases, overlapping

Browsers are hard-coded for how headings, paragraphs, and bold text are supposed to look. Browsers read in HTML files and render out pages based on these default styles. If you don't like the way paragraphs are spaced, tough luck. For instance, if you don't want paragraphs to have a line between them, but just a small indentation, there's no way to achieve this short of tricky HTML that uses a nonbreaking space at the beginning of each section. Designers often get around the browser's built-in style prejudices by hacking together strange Web pages using <BR> breaks instead of paragraphs, or weird invisible spacer GIFs to achieve margins. Messy stuff.

The addition of tables — precisely sized rows and columns of text or graphics — enabled developers to somewhat space out text the way they liked it. Tables are still a royal pain in the neck, complete with their own oddities. Half of the time tables don't work quite the way they are supposed to, and act one way on Internet Explorer, another on Netscape Navigator, and yet another on the Macintosh versions of the browsers.

Then Netscape introduced the <FONT> tag. This new HTML element enabled developers to specify the size or color of a piece of text:

```
<FONT SIZE="3" COLOR="red">Some Text</FONT>
```

However, neither tables nor new elements are enough – they're too little too late. This makes for a cluttered and nonintuitive way to design. HTML developers have to become con artists, specialists in cheating HTML to achieve layouts that aren't supposed to be possible. Even after stretching HTML to its limits, designers still pull their hair in frustration, unable to get quite the look they desire.

Some purists argue that styles are unnecessary, and are, in fact, just flourishes that artsy-fartsy designers insist on that have no bearing on the real meat of a Web page. Of course, these purists often think that graphics in general are overkill, as are background colors and even headings. What purists are forgetting, however, is that the user experience — or interface — is dependent upon the precise layout and look of elements.

In a sense, though, these purists are right. It's no oversight that HTML has almost no style to it. HTML was built from the ground up to be a *structural* markup language. That means it only defines how a document is supposed to split up into elements in very general terms, and enables every browser to interpret those elements.

The Way It Is

Then along came style sheets. Style sheets enable designers to specify the exact font, spacing, and location of every element easily. Any HTML *container*, an element that has both an opening and closing tag, such as <B> </B>, can be explicitly defined. Designers can also craft and apply special classes of styles to any element. Style sheets even enable elements to be layered on top of each other, bringing Web pages into the third dimension – or at least the second-and-a-half dimension. This enables designers to create things like drop shadows, captions that overlap images, and anything else they can think of.

Web designers finally have the same control over the look of their pages as desktop publishing designers. Not only is this a more intuitive way for designers to work, but it also saves on download time. Instead of using tons of weird tags to try to define a Web page's look, the browser is smart enough to read in styles and apply them beautifully.

Another huge advantage with style sheets is the ability to apply a style en masse to elements throughout an entire Web site with one simple style file. For example, the <H1> heading holder can be defined as red, 15-point, bold Courier text justified to the right against a white background bar. The code to achieve this looks something like Listing 7-1.

Listing 7-1: Customizing the look of a level one heading

```
H1 {
  color: red;
  background: white;
  font: bold 15pt "courier,monospace";
  text-align: right;
  padding: 0.2em 10em 0.2em 1em;
  }
```

The designer could then use this style over an entire Web site. If the style file changes, every level one heading on the entire Web site changes, just like that. No need to go through and recode tables, headings, or <FONT> tags.

 Another huge advantage of style sheets is that documents written in common desktop publishing and word processing formats can be easily converted to HTML and look exactly (or very, very close to) the way they were designed.

The Elements of Style

How did styles come about? Long before HTML and the Web, there were many standards bandied about with the intention of making documents easy and fast to distribute, publish, and print. There were plenty of document formats already floating around. Most of these formats were connected to a specific computer platform or even a special piece of hardware, such as a printer. A group of researchers at IBM created GML, the Generalized Markup Language, in order to provide a device-independent format for document structure. As they worked with GML, they realized that the world could really use a good, standard, structural markup language. Specifically, they wanted to provide a way to itemize the rules that defined a document type and described its structure. This set of rules became the Standard Generalized Markup Language, or SGML.

SGML was revolutionary for the way that it separated a document's *structure* from its *presentation*. A document could now be defined in terms of the elements that fit together to form its structure. The appropriate processing rules for its presentation could be defined later. HTML itself is an application of the rules of SGML, though like any rebellious youth it has certainly diverged a bit from its strict, structure-oriented parentage.

What follows is a brief description of ways that people have tried to provide flexible and powerful methods to specify the presentation of structural documents. This brief, historical tour of the last 20 years of document styles gives HTML and style sheets some larger context. Let's begin with some of the nonstructural options available, so we can better understand the reasoning behind using HTML in the first place.

Page Description Languages

If you want to preserve a document's look, why not just use an exact listing of graphic layouts, positions, and fonts to delineate a document precisely? This is the idea behind *page description languages*; they describe exactly what is where on the page.

Common page description languages are Rich Text Format (RTF), Portable Document Format (PDF), and PostScript. These formats are often used to share documents between word processors and vector layout programs such as Quark or Illustrator. These formats are also widely used to send documents directly to laser printers and create exact copies. At first glance, page description seems like an ideal way to publish documents across the Web.

The biggest problem with page description languages, however, is that they are all style and no structure. The generality that HTML provides is lost. With or without styles, HTML is a generalized description of the document's content, not a snapshot description of the way the ink on the paper appears. This enables HTML documents to work on any browser or operating system. It even enables HTML to be easily translated into Braille, to be spoken by a computerized voice over a telephone, or to be formatted for the tiny screen of a PalmPilot or pager. Heck, HTML could even be used to write smoke messages across the sky.

Description language documents consist of dozens of explicit coordinates for each line or dot on the page. In some cases, they contain precise mathematical formulae that describe the objects' curves, positions, and relationships. The description language barks out, "Make my page look exactly like this or else!" HTML, on the other hand, consists of markup that essentially says, "This is how my page is organized. Please make it look as nice as you can. Thanks ever so much."

The key point to remember here is that in the real world of the Web, different platforms and operating systems support different font families, window sizes, and aspect ratios. This makes it impossible to ever capture the exact look of a document's layout and have it be the same from machine to machine. Unlike page description languages, style sheets sit atop HTML and retain most of a document's original look, but never all of it. In the majority of cases, this is enough.

DTD and FOSI

So how does HTML work, again? HTML has a hardwired set of tags that result in the browser displaying a document's elements with a hardwired set of styles. In other words, HTML publishers have no control over semantic or typographic aspects of a Web page. Each browser determines on its own how a given tag looks when its text is eventually rendered.

HTML is so rigid because its parent language, SGML, does not define any style information. Universal SGML browsers read in a document and figure out its structural definition. How the document ends up looking depends on how the SGML browser is set up to display it.

The rules for an SGML document's elements are stored in a Document Type Definition (DTD) file. A DTD file is basically a listing of element types, the possible structure of the document using the elements, and the attributes of each element.

What if you want to define an SGML document's style? The typographic look and feel for each element and attribute in the DTD may be stored in a Formatting Output Specification Instances (FOSI) file. This lists the precise font family, font style, font size, justification, and so on. A FOSI is just another specialized SGML document, created from tags and attributes. The document is parsed using the same mechanisms that are used to parse other SGML document types. The SGML processing application simply grabs the definitions from the FOSI document and uses them to set whatever internal display settings are needed to properly display or print the document that originally referenced the FOSI. Our current understanding of style sheets comes from early experiments with FOSI and other such style specifications.

To sum up the differences between the original HTML specification and SGML:

◆ HTML has a fixed DTD and inflexible formatting rules. Authors had little or no control over the look and feel of an HTML document or the structural elements and attributes that made up the document.

◆ SGML may be used to define sets of structural tags, giving it the power to create languages like HTML. It can associate styles with these structural documents using a FOSI or other similar methods.

Many document publishers desired a markup language that had a predefined and clean set of tags, like HTML, but with the capability to customize styles, too. This would provide a format that could be read in and parsed quickly, and looked the way that publishers wanted. One result was the Hypertext Delivery Language (HDL). Clearly defined styles are included within every HDL document.

DSSSL: A Full Style Sheet Language

Those interested in a standard for styles looked keenly back at SGML, the fountainhead of HTML. The FOSI standard for style sheets, lacking some degree of programmability and support from vendors, soon gave way to a new style standard given the lengthy name of *Document Style Semantics and Specification Language*, or *DSSSL*.

DSSSL acts as a sister language to SGML. SGML describes the logical structure of documents: what contains what, what follows what, what elements come together to make up the crux of the document. DSSSL describes how these elements should be presented, or processed. A DSSSL definition maps out each markup tag from a document onto the process that the tag's contents should go through when being displayed.

For example, a DSSSL definition could state that any elements named `pretty` should always be outputted as a heading element presented in 20-point Arial font, centered in the page, and colored orange.

DSSSL can even map the markup from one DTD into another DTD. This makes it very useful for translation. Special DSSSL definitions enable the same document to be outputted on a computer screen, in Microsoft Word, in Braille, in smoke in the sky, or in any other way that can be defined.

DSSSL is a very broad and ongoing standard, and can act as all of the following:

- ◆ **A style language** — Describing what each element on a page looks like as far as color, font, size, spacing, and position.

- ◆ **A flow object language** — Defining how all the document's page breaks, paragraphs, headings, and artwork are laid out. All HTML elements, for example, are essentially *flow objects*, or special tags that determine how a document should be structured.

- ◆ **A transformation language** — Translating a document into another SGML language by changing tags and their attributes.

- ◆ **A document model** — Describing the relationship of every object on the page by putting it into a document tree.

- ◆ **A query language** — Searching quickly for items within a document using various filters.

DSSSL-Lite: For Electronic Use Only

DSSSL was one huge mother. Because many of its elements had no place in World Wide Web publishing, a subset called DSSSL-Lite was created to provide a common style sheet language for the Web. DSSSL-Lite is, in essence, the same idea as FOSI. The only difference is that FOSI was designed as a way to describe how an SGML document could be printed out on paper. Because the physical print world must deal with a much higher resolution and many typographic possibilities, FOSI supports numerous very specific and tedious style details. For example, the print world is concerned with leaving extra margin space for loose-leaf pages, printing a document on both sides of the page, and printing flyers four to a page. The computer world has no such concerns.

DSSSL-Lite, then, is limited to the electronic display of SGML documents. DSSSL-Lite as an initiative for specifying online document styles is dead, but many of the ideas live on.

CSS, CSS-P, and XSL: The Latest Standards

Eventually, DSSSL-Lite evolved into simpler standards that worked hand in hand with the current HTML technology. First came Cascading Style Sheets (CSS). This language enabled developers to create specific color, font, and spacing styles for any HTML element. The next stage was Cascading Style Sheets with Positioning (CSS-P), which enabled rich layout of HTML elements.

 CSS-P was not officially a W3C Recommendation, but rather an immediate working draft intended to enable implementation of certain of the features of CSS level 2 in the Netscape and Microsoft browsers.

The latest standard is the *eXtensible Style Language (XSL)* — a way of adding styles and flair to XML documents. XSL is also a full transformation language with support for flow objects, queries, and more.

Cascading Style Sheets Basics

The World Wide Web Consortium came out with the level 1 Cascading Style Sheets standard in the middle of 1996. When Internet Explorer 3.0 arrived on the scene with CSS support, many designers were so happy they nearly wept. There were so many good, good things about style sheets.

For one, no longer were designers restricted to having Web browsers dictate how each element type looked. Designers had so much power it was almost dizzying. If a designer wanted to, she could make level one main headings (<H1>) really, really tiny, and level three subheadings (<H3>) take over the entire page. Why not?

Also, Web pages could finally look really cool without one having to cut blocks of stylized text out of design software and paste them into Web pages as heavy GIF graphics.

The State of the Style

Unfortunately, Explorer 3.0 support for CSS was scant at best. The style sheets were also fraught with bugs and weird inconsistencies. To make matters worse, Navigator still didn't support any of this. This meant that designing CSS Web pages would leave more than half of your viewers looking at a bland, ill-designed page.

Then Netscape Navigator 4.0 came out with CSS support, along with a few proprietary elements such as <LAYER> to enable positioning. Naturally, these diverging paths for styles were not similar enough to each other, and made cross-browser style design a total headache. There were also new sets of bugs to worry about. And lots of people were still using older browsers that had no CSS support.

At the time of this writing (the dawning of 1999), the development notes of the 5.0 versions of the major browsers claim that they support the full Cascading Style Sheets spec, as well as CSS positioning. If these implementations become official, many big name sites will finally begin to use style sheets with gusto.

Units of Measure

In order for styles to work, they must use an agreed-upon syntax — an understood unit of measure. In the world of the Web, several units make sense, depending on whether you're talking to a print designer, a graphic designer, or a programmer. For Cascading Style Sheets level 1, the units we care about are length and color.

LENGTH

In the world of style sheets, size does matter. Length is used to talk about the size of fonts, the size of borders, the position of boxes, and so on. Size can be expressed using a wide variety of units.

For documents that look good across diverse browsers and display types, relative measurements are often used. A relative unit explains an element's size relative to another length, usually the length of the window or the font size currently being used by the element. These units include the following:

- ◆ em — Ems, or the size of the letter *m* in the font being used by the element. This is equal to the type size. A 12-point typeface would have an em size of 12 points. An em is sometimes called a mutton.

- ◆ ex — The x-height is the height of the letter *x* in the current font. This is equal to current font height.

- ◆ % — This handy unit is the percentage of an absolute size. Instead of giving an exact location, for example, you can specify where an object should be relative to its margin. Or, instead of giving the exact value of a line height, you can express it as a percentage of the current font size. Percentage measurements only make sense with certain styles that are generally based on more absolute values. A font family name, for instance, cannot be expressed as a percentage.

- ◆ Special keyword values can also be used to define styles. Every style property has its own keywords. For example, a set of stored absolute font sizes can be expressed using any of these keywords: xx-small, x-small, small, medium, large, x-large, or xx-large. In addition, the relative keywords larger and smaller can further hone a font based on its absolute size. Combined, these keywords provide a handy way of defining elements relative to one another.

There are also a number of absolute measurements for specific placement and sizes:

◆ px — This is short for *pixels*. A pixel is the smallest point of light on a computer screen. If your screen has a resolution of 1,024 × 768, you can imagine a grid 1,024 pixels wide and 768 pixels high. Pixels make up any text or image that appears on your screen. Depending on your graphics card and monitor settings, a pixel can range from two colors (black and white) to millions of them (providing realistic photo quality). Pixels are useful for very precise layouts.

◆ pt — Points. This is a typographic term. 72 points equal an inch.

◆ pc — Picas. This is another typesetting term. 12 points equal one pica.

◆ in — Inches. This is a handy real-world measurement. An inch equals 2.54 centimeters.

◆ cm — Centimeters.

◆ mm — Millimeters, for times when you have to go small.

All sizes are positive by default, but you can place a minus sign before the measurement to indicate negative values.

COLOR

Color can be expressed in one of two ways: keywords or RGB values.

Just typing in the desired color as a keyword is the quickest and easiest way of giving elements color. It also makes style sheets much easier to read. You can find legal color keywords in Table 7-1.

TABLE 7-1 VALID CSS COLORS

aqua	gray	navy	silver	blue	lime	purple	white
black	green	olive	teal	fuchsia	maroon	red	yellow

If you desire a more specific color, it can be expressed as a *red-green-blue triple*, or RGB. Any color on a computer can be defined as a mixture of red shades, green shades, and blue shades on a scale of 0 to 255. For example, black is the lack of all color, and has the RGB value of (0,0,0). White is all colors pumped to the max at (255,255,255). Yellow is (255,255,0).

Colors are usually expressed using the tag rgb with the three values separated by commas within parentheses. For instance, yellow is:

```
rgb(255,255,0)
```

In addition, you can use percentages instead of integer values. For example, a perfect, flat gray can be defined as half red, half green, and half blue:

```
rgb(50%,50%,50%)
```

Color can be expressed as a hexadecimal value, in which case it must begin with the tag #. For example, chartreuse is:

```
#7FFF00
```

CSS Level 1

The first level of the Cascading Style Sheets specification supports five major types of style properties:

- ◆ Fonts
- ◆ Colors
- ◆ Text
- ◆ Boxes
- ◆ Classification

Before we delve into these specific properties, let's cover exactly how a style property is defined.

The CSS Format

The general format of a style rule is the name of the element to modify, called the *selector,* followed by curly brackets surrounding a *declaration* that contains the style's property, a colon, and that property's value. For instance, to set all <H3> headings to red you would use:

```
H3 { color: red }
```

H3 is the selector, color is the property, and red is the color's value.
We cover how to implement styles within HTML in the next section.

 Comments can be placed in CSS style sheets by surrounding the commentary in C-like comment tags /* and */. For example:

```
H3 { color: red } /* This is a comment here. */
```

GROUPING

CSS enables you to group selectors or declarations quite easily. If a particular style applies to several elements, just separate each selector by a comma. For instance:

```
H1, H2, H3 { color: red }
```

If you want to play around with several properties of one selector, just separate each with a semicolon:

```
H3 {
   color: red;
   font-family: sans-serif;
}
```

CHILDREN AND PARENTS

Most HTML elements are contained within other elements. Any element that exists within the context of another is called a *child.* In the following example, the first level heading is the parent and the bold text in the middle is its child:

```
<H1>This is a heading with some <B>bold</B> text in it.</H1>
```

A child with no defined styles always takes on, or *inherits,* the styles of its parent. If it has special styles these may, in some cases, be based on the parent's styles. Often times a child's style has a percentage or a relative keyword that is based on some attribute of its parent.

All HTML elements within the main body of the document are children of the `<BODY>` tag, which is the default parent for most elements you will deal with. Exceptions to this are any elements that appear in the document header, which are children of the `<HEAD>` tag.

If you want to set up a style for a specific parent-child combination, you can do so by listing the parent followed by the child *without* a comma. Suppose you don't really want to affect bold text in general. If you just want all bold text that appears in level one headings to be blue, simply use the following style:

```
H1 B { color: blue }
```

Don't get confused by the difference between grouped selectors (separated by commas) and contextual selectors (no commas). The first is a shorthand way of saying, "These style definitions apply to all of these elements," and the second says, "These styles only apply to these elements nested inside these elements."

Fonts

Fonts are the lodestone of design. The font chosen for a piece of text often says more than the text itself. Fonts can be sloppy, edgy, formal, effeminate, outspoken, obnoxious, or timid. In other words, fonts are all the adjectives that enable us to express ourselves.

FONT FAMILY

The main attribute of a font is the family it falls in. Designers can use any font desired. If the font exists on the user's system, a given element appears in that font.

In addition to defined fonts, CSS defines five general font families that can be used as an alternative in case a specific font can't be found. These families are:

- ◆ serif — Fonts with modest flourishes or serifs at the tips of the main strokes of letters.

- ◆ sans-serif — Fonts without flags on the letters.

- ◆ cursive — Scripted fonts.

- ◆ fantasy — Stylized fonts.

- ◆ monospace — Fonts in which every letter has the same width, like those of a typewriter. Such a font is useful for strict formatting within columns.

A list of as many font families as desired can be used, separated by commas. If the first font family does not exist, the second is tried, and so on.

A font-family property usually has a general font as its last attribute — a catchall in case nothing else is available. For instance, the following style tries Times New Roman, then New Century Schoolbook, and finally just uses the default serif font:

```
H3 { font-family: "times new roman", "new century schoolbook", serif }
```

FONT STYLE

The style of the font is set here. The choices are normal, italic, or oblique. Italics are a script-like twist to a font family that makes it nearly cursive. Oblique fonts are slanted to the right, and are essentially the same as italics in most computerized implementations. To make all level three headings italic, use the following style:

```
H3 { font-style: italic }
```

FONT VARIANT

The only values of this property are normal (the default) and small-caps. The latter is used for situations where some text should be written entirely in a capital font, with the actual capitals being a bit more pronounced than the lowercase letters. For instance:

A SMALL CAP FONT

To make all bold text into small caps, you would use the following:

```
B { font-variant: small-caps }
```

FONT WEIGHT

This property determines how heavy, or **bold,** a font is. The property can take a value from 100 to 900, where 100 is a very faint font and 900 is a very pronounced font.

There are also four set keywords: normal (a value of 400), bold (700), bolder, and lighter. The bolder and lighter keywords are relative to the current value of the font weight. For instance, look at the following:

```
H1 { font-weight: bold }
STRONG { font-weight: bolder }
```

In this example, the first level heading is bold. If a <STRONG> element is placed within a heading, its text is bolder than bold — in other words, a value of 800.

FONT SIZE

This basic property is used to set the exact size of a font. You can specify any point size using any of the valid measurement units. In addition, two relative keywords, smaller and larger, make the text about 150 percent smaller or larger. For example, this level one heading has an absolute font size of 24 points:

```
H1 { font-size: bold }
```

The bold tag, meanwhile, can be given a relative value:

```
B { font-size: larger }
```

No matter where a bold piece of text is placed, then, it is larger than its surrounding text.

ALL FONT PROPERTIES

All font properties can be set with one property called `font`, as well. The format is as follows:

```
<font-style> <font-variant> <font-weight> <font-size>/<line-height>
<font-family>
```

All of these values are optional, except for `font-size` and `font-family`. To make a generally small, but bold and oblique font you could use the following:

```
P { font: bold oblique small serif }
```

Or, to specifically define a 14-point Arial font:

```
P { font: 14pt Arial, sans-serif }
```

Colors and Backgrounds

The hue of a piece of text, as well as the background it is placed against, goes miles and miles toward achieving design goals. White on black is stolid and plain, while orange on purple polka dots is intense and gross.

There are several properties for setting color and background in CSS level 1.

COLOR

The foreground color of any element can be set using the `color` property. Any RGB or keyword color can be plugged in.

For example, to set all level three headings to fuchsia you would simply use:

```
H3 { color: fuchsia }
```

BACKGROUND COLOR

Similar to color, you can easily set the background color of any element:

```
H3 { background-color: fuchsia }
```

BACKGROUND IMAGE

The source filename of any image can also be placed behind any element. This provides very unique and stylized effects. This is done by handing in a URL:

```
H3 { background-image: URL(http://www.example.com/paper.gif)}
```

BACKGROUND POSITION

Every element is placed within a rectangular *bounding box*, not including its padding, border, or margin. The `background-position` property specifies where the upper-left corner of a background image, if it exists, should be drawn relative to the element's own upper-left corner. You need to specify an *x* coordinate (the horizontal position) and a *y* coordinate (the vertical position). Each value can be expressed as a relative percentage or keyword: `top`, `center`, or `bottom` for the *x* coordinate; and `left`, `center`, or `right` for the *y* coordinate. You can also use an explicit and absolute measurement.

To drop a background image in the top left corner of the box, you could use any of the following:

```
H3 { background-position: 0% 0% }
H3 { background-position: top left }
H3 { background-position: left top }
```

Values can be combined as well. To drop a background image halfway across the element and one inch down you could use:

```
H3 { background-position: 50% 1in }
```

BACKGROUND REPEAT

When a background image is used, it can either be tiled repeatedly across the width and/or height of the element or just pasted in its given position. The position, by the way, is set by the `background-position` property.

Legal keyword values for `background-repeat` are `repeat`, `repeat-x` (horizontal tiling), `repeat-y` (vertical tiling), or `no-repeat`.

So, to have the image of paper tile itself vertically for all level three headings you could use:

```
H3 {
background-image: URL(http://www.example.com/paper.gif);
      background-repeat: repeat-y;
}
```

BACKGROUND ATTACHMENT

Depending on the effect you wish to achieve, you might want the background of an element to remain glued to the back of the browser window or to scroll when the page is scrolled.

Use the `scroll` keyword to have background images scroll, which is their default behavior. If you want them locked in place like a sort of watermark, use `fixed`. This is especially useful when defining the background of the entire page, that is, the `<BODY>` element. For example:

```
BODY {
    background-image: URL(paper.gif);
    background-repeat: repeat;
    background-attachment: fixed;
}
```

ALL BACKGROUND PROPERTIES

As with font, you can set all background properties with one catchall `background` property. The format is:

```
<background-color> <background-image> <background-repeat>
<background-attachment> <background-position>
```

You can set any or none of the properties. So if you wanted an image with polka dots placed behind every paragraph, tiling down vertically, and starting from the upper-middle of the element's area, you could use:

```
P { background: purple url(polka.gif) repeat-y fixed top center }
```

Text

In addition to font that describes each letter, it's important for designers to know how text is spaced out and aligned relative to other elements, helping to define lines and paragraphs. These text properties provide the adjectives that customize the intricacies of the text.

WORD SPACING

How much space should there be between words? This is indicated as follows, using any measurement unit:

```
P { word-spacing: 0.5em }
```

Note that negative values are legit, though they might make for cramped text.

LETTER SPACING

This indicates how much space should lie between each letter in an element. For example, to have bold text spaced to one-tenth of an em:

```
B { letter-spacing: 0.1em }
```

TEXT DECORATION

This property enables you to underline, overline, strikethrough, or blink a given piece of text. Just use one or a few of the keywords: none, `underline`, `overline`, `line-through`, or `blink`. To make all the level two headings underlined you would use:

```
H2 { text-decoration: underline }
```

VERTICAL ALIGN

The `vertical-align` property enables you to specify how an element lines up with its parent element. Legal keywords are:

- `sub` — The element becomes a subscript to the parent.

- `super` — The element becomes a superscript to the parent.

- `baseline` — The *baseline,* which is the line that the character is drawn upon, aligns with the bottom line of the parent. Note that with some fonts, letters like p and q have tails that dangle below the baseline.

- `middle` — The midpoint of the element (half of its vertical height) lines up with the middle of the parent element.

- `text-top` — The element's top lines up with the top of the parent element's font.

- `text-bottom` — The element's bottom lines up with the bottom of the parent's font.

- `top` — The top of the element aligns with the tallest element on the current line, whether it is the parent element or not.

- `bottom` — The bottom of the element lines up with the lowest element on the current line.

Alternatively, you can specify a percentage value instead of an alignment keyword. This raises the baseline of the element a certain percentage of the current element's line height over the baseline of the parent. Negative percentage values are allowed as well, enabling the element to drop below its baseline.

TEXT TRANSFORM

This nifty property can transform the text into all uppercase, all lowercase, or simply capitalize the first letter of every word. The keywords are `uppercase`, `lowercase`, and `capitalize`, respectively.

For example, to make all paragraphs capitalize their first letters:

```
P { text-transform: capitalize }
```

TEXT ALIGN

This sets up the horizontal alignment of text. Possible values are, naturally, `left`, `right`, `center`, and `justify`. To center all of the text in a document, you could use:

```
BODY { text-align: center }
```

TEXT INDENT

This property enables you to set the indent of the first line of text in a given element. For example, to indent all paragraphs a generous inch and a half, you would use:

```
P { text-indent: 1.5in }
```

LINE HEIGHT

This property enables you to set the distance between adjacent lines of text. This can be designated as a unit of length or as a percentage of the current text height. To plop the equivalent of two lines between each line of text, you could use:

```
P { line-height: 200% }
```

Boxes

In the world of the level 1 CSS, every element is trapped inside a box. Surrounding each box is invisible padding, a border, and an invisible margin. Figure 7-2 illustrates this.

Figure 7-2: All content is placed within bounding boxes

The box properties enable you to set the size and border of the boxes that bound the content of every element.

Setting the size of boxes is especially useful for images, enabling you to scale or expand images on the fly. The size of the bounding box for text is generally not played around with much. If a given text element doesn't fit within its box, it is generally scrollable.

WIDTH AND HEIGHT

The width and height properties set the size of the box itself. These are set to auto by default, snapping the box to the actual size of the image, or the logical size in which to place the text. The width and height can also be explicitly set using any of the valid units of length.

The size settings can also be expressed as a percentage of the parent element's size. To set a 200 × 500 pixel box for all images, you would use:

```
IMG {
  width: 200px;
  height: 500px;
}
```

FLOATING AND CLEARING

Every element's box can also be set to float on a certain side of the page. Valid settings are `left`, `right`, and `none`. If an element is set to float on the left, for instance, its box is located on the left side of the parent element, and text within the box of the parent element wraps on the right side of the floating child element. This makes for a nice-looking way to wrap text around an image.

The `float` property is generally only used on images:

```
IMG {  float: left; }
```

In addition, the `clear` property enables any element that exits adjacent to floating element to avoid being wrapped. An element can be cleared to the `left`, `right`, or `both`. A cleared element does not flank floaters. For example, if one image is set to float left and it happens to overlap with an element that is cleared to the left, the cleared element appears below the left-floating image:

```
H1 { clear: left }
```

MARGINS

The margin is the outermost perimeter of any element. A margin, when set, provides the specified amount of blank space between the current element and any adjacent elements. This enables pages to be defined as either cramped or very carefully spaced out.

Every margin property takes in a valid unit length or can be expressed as a percentage of the parent's width. Negative values are allowed.

The margin properties include the following:

- ◆ `margin-left`
- ◆ `margin-right`
- ◆ `margin-top`
- ◆ `margin-bottom`

In addition, the `margin` property itself can contain values that apply to all four margins. For example, to be sure all images have half an inch of space around them:

```
IMG { margin: 0.5in }
```

You can specify all four margin sizes in top, right, bottom, and left order, respectively:

```
IMG { margin: 1.5% 0.25in 1% 0.8cm }
```

PADDING

Padding is very similar to margins in format. The padding indicates the space between an element and its border. Like margins, padding has the properties:

- ◆ `padding-left`
- ◆ `padding-right`
- ◆ `padding-top`
- ◆ `padding-bottom`

There is also a `padding` property that acts exactly like `margin`.

BORDERS

The whole reason to have padding and margins is that there's something we want to stick in between: borders. A border can greatly enhance an image or block of text, making it leap out from the page.

The border width properties can either be given an explicit length, or set to `thin`, `medium`, or `thick`. The properties can be set for any side of the border:

- ◆ `border-left-width`
- ◆ `border-right-width`
- ◆ `border-top-width`
- ◆ `border-bottom-width`

The generic `border-width` property can be used to set all of the borders at once. For example, to adjust the top, right, bottom, and left borders, respectively:

```
IMG { border-width: 10px thick thin thin }
```

If only one value is included, then all four widths are set to that value.

The border can have up to four styles, one style for each side. Possible values are:

- `none` – No border. This is the default.

- `dotted` – Lines made up of tiny perforated dots.

- `dashed` – Dashed lines, like a cut out coupon.

- `solid` – A thick, unbroken border.

- `double` – A double line, with a space between the two lines.

- `groove` – A 3D etched groove.

- `ridge` – Like a groove, except it sticks out instead of being recessed.

- `inset` – A 3D effect based on the border's colors, making it look pressed within the page.

- `outset` – A 3D effect making the contents stand out from the page like a button.

To set the top and bottom of a border to solid, and the left and right of a border to ridged, you would use:

```
IMG { border-style: solid ridge }
```

Once you've decided on the type of border to use, you can set its color with the `border-color` property:

```
IMG { border-color: blue }
```

There are also a few shorthand methods for setting the width, style, and color of each of the border's sides:

- `border-left`

- `border-right`

- `border-top`

- `border-bottom`

For example, if you wanted all level one headings to have a thin, ridged blue line above them, you could use:

```
H1 { border-top: thin ridge blue }
```

If your border has the same attributes on all four sides, these can be set at once using the `border` property. For example:

```
P { border: thick dotted green }
```

This surrounds all paragraphs with a thick, dotted green border.

Classification

A few style properties don't set the physical styles of elements so much as group them into certain categories that define how they are laid out on the screen or page. The `display` property indicates how elements are displayed on the page. It can take one of four keywords: `block`, `inline`, `list-item`, or `none`.

The *block* type is the standard format for most text elements, positioning the element in one bounding box or block relative to other boxes. A `list-item` is like a block, but indented — like a standard `<LI>` HTML list item in an ordered `<OL>` or unordered bullet list `<UL>`. An `inline` display draws the box on the same line as the previous element. And `none` makes the element invisible.

Another property is `white-space`, which defines how white spaces, tabs, carriage returns and linefeeds are handled. Possible values are `normal`, `pre`, and `nowrap`. A standard HTML page, for example, has a `normal` handling, where tons of spaces in a paragraph are condensed into only one space. The `pre` setting makes every space count, having white spaces count as any other character. The `nowrap` setting makes space count, and furthermore does not wrap the line when it has reached the end until a `<BR>` break is called.

LISTS AND THEIR STYLES

Numbered or bulleted list elements (or any element that has been set to the `list-item` display, for that matter) may choose to modify the `list-style-type` property. This can take keywords for various types of bullets: `disc`, `circle`, `square`; or for various types of numbered lists: `decimal` (numbered), `lower-roman` (lowercase Roman numerals), `upper-roman` (uppercase Roman numerals), `lower-alpha` (lowercase letters), `upper-alpha` (uppercase letters); as well as `none`.

List elements can also be handed in the URL for a custom image. This image is then used as the bullet. For example:

```
UL { list-style-image: url(mybullet.gif) }
```

The `list-style-position` element can take either `inside` or `outside`, and indicates how a list is indented relative to its list marker. Setting a list position to `inside` causes the second line of a bulleted list to begin right beneath the bullet. To illustrate:

```
* This is the first line.
This is the second line.
```

The position, type, and image of a list can be set all at once using the shorthand `list-style` property. For example, to make a list that uses uppercase Roman numbers on its inside:

```
UL { list-style: upper-roman inside }
```

Positioning: CSS-P

So far we've got the adjectives to cover how things *look,* but what about where things *are?*

CSS-Positioning (or CSS-P, for those in the know) enables you to separate the elements of a Web document into an ordered collection of boxes. Anything at all can be positioned – a given type of HTML element, a specific paragraph, images, or other media types.

CSS-P enables you to not only position these boxes anywhere you want, but also gives you the ability to layer the boxes on top of each other, bringing Web pages (in a manner) into a limited third dimension. When text or graphics fill these boxes, they can either be cropped or wrapped around – you make the call.

Netscape originally implemented positioning by introducing the LAYER element, a special container that could be laid out on the Web page in a specific location. The official CSS spec took layers a great stride further in enabling *any* HTML element to be positioned.

The chief properties of CSS-P enable you to:

◆ Position the box

◆ Clip the box

◆ Make the box visible and invisible

◆ Layer boxes

Positioning the Box

Position any CSS box using the `left` and `top` properties. These properties do just what they suggest: set the number of pixels, or inches, or any other legal unit the upper-left corner of the box is offset from the left and the top.

Negative values are often used to kick an element higher or to the right.

As with standard style sheets, you can use the `width` and `height` properties to set the size of the box. However, CSS-P adds the capability to set the size of boxes as a percentage of the parent element. For example, to make an image that has no parent elements take up half the screen:

```
IMG {
  width: 50%;
  height: 50%;
}
```

ABSOLUTE AND RELATIVE POSITIONING

There are two ways to position boxes: *absolutely* or *relatively*. You can decide how to lay out each box using the position property. It takes either the absolute or (you guessed it) relative keyword.

A relatively placed box is shifted from the point where it would have naturally wound up, had there been no positioning. This is the default setting for HTML elements.

Absolute boxes, on the other hand, are positioned from the upper-left corner of their parent element. If the box has no parent, it is positioned based on the upper-left corner of the Web page itself.

If you wanted a piece of text to be dropped 33 pixels over from the left of the page and 85 pixels from the top, you would use code similar to the following:

```
H3 {
  position: absolute;
  left: 33px;
  top: 85px;
}
```

Or, you could achieve a sort of superscript effect by having bold text positioned a few pixels higher than where it would normally appear:

```
B {
  position: relative;
  top: -15px;
}
```

Overflow

Now that you're bounding everything in boxes, what happens when you run out of room? What if you drop a huge screen-sized image in a 50 × 50 box? Or what about the entire text of *Crime and Punishment* in an area the size of a postage stamp?

This concern is handled using the overflow property. The keyword values are:

◆ clip — If the contents overflow, they are discarded. Images are cropped, and text is cut short. Most browsers behave this way unless they are told otherwise.

◆ scroll — A vertical or horizontal scroll bar (or both) is created, enabling the user to see everything that exists. This often looks clunky, but ensures that no content is lost.

◆ none — The box boundaries are ignored and content overflows if necessary.

Visibility and Invisibility

The content of a box can be made visible using the visibility property. The values are visible and hidden. This is a very powerful command enabling you to preload up to dozens of graphical elements and then show only the relevant ones to the current task.

For example, you could turn off all images by using:

```
IMG { visibility: hidden; }
```

Netscape Navigator supports the slightly different keywords show and hide. These differences are covered in detail in Part III of this book.

Thinking In Two-and-a-Half Dimensions

One of the neatest things about CSS-P boxes is how they can be layered atop each other. This means elements are not only placed *near* where you want them to go, but *exactly* where you want them to go, even if something else is already there.

 By default, all bounding boxes are transparent. But the content of each box (as of CSS level 1) is opaque unless it is an image such as GIF with special transparent pixels.

Because elements can overlap, there needs to be a system to determine which elements are up front and which are layered in back and possibly hidden entirely. The z-index is just the property we need. This corresponds to the line moving into the page and out of the page, along the *z* axis of a graph. An element with a higher z-index appears atop one with a lower z-index. There is no order of magnitude; compared to a z-value of 1, a z-value of 2 and 1,000 are equivalent. The z-value may also be negative.

An element's z-index is always relative to its parent. If an image within an area has a high z-value, it lies at the top of that area. However, if the area itself has a low z-value, the area may be layered beneath other sibling or parent elements.

You can exploit this layering system to achieve great effects, such as animations in which little cartoon characters walk in front of and behind each other, or text captions that overlay photographs.

In the following example, any elements using `styleA` lie beneath `styleB`:

```
.styleA { z-index: 1 }
.styleB { z-index: 4 }
```

By default, layering is achieved automatically in HTML based on a first come, first served basis. The first elements on a page are placed at the bottom of the layer stack and later elements, if overlapping, are atop.

Positioning Problems

When it comes to positioning, there are a few rules of thumb to keep in mind. It's amazingly useful to be able to place elements at the precise pixel you desire, but recall that browser windows can be resized at any time. People work with widely varying resolutions. Ideally a page should look good whether it is being viewed on the latest Pentium II with a 20-inch monitor; on a handheld Newton; on WebTV; or on an old 386 with a 300 baud modem and a black-and-white monitor all held together with duct tape.

Absolutely positioned elements, even those with their overflow property set to `scroll`, draw scroll bars at the outer edges of the box. This means that bars may appear beyond the bounds of what some users can see. This can make your content impossible to get at.

CSS Level 2

The level 2 specification of Cascading Style Sheets goes several steps further than level 1, enabling even more control over the positioning and look of documents. The idea is to have enough styles so that documents can be formatted for any medium including Web pages via telephone (aural style sheets); pagers; projection systems for big presentations and slide shows; handheld devices; Braille readers; and more. In order to deal with all of these media types, new properties that handle things like the rate of speech will be introduced.

Level 2 also pays more attention to page media – that is, how HTML files are actually printed out on pages. For instance, the location of page breaks can be cleanly specified.

The most important element of level 2 is the capability to position fixed elements anywhere on the page within rectangular boundaries. These element containers can be layered on top of each other, and be visible or invisible. This special positioning also includes settings to indicate how text or graphics that overflow from their set box sizes should be handled. All of this has been separated into a standard known as CSS-P, which was defined in the previous section. The 4.0 versions of the major browsers already handle some form of CSS-P.

In addition, the level 2 specification contains the following:

◆ The ability to use more colors and fonts. For instance, fonts that aren't currently on the user's system can be downloaded from any library on the Web, so the user can see what the designer sees.

◆ More useful property keywords. For example, a font's size can easily be scaled to match the average size of that system's icons.

◆ The ability to change some colors or text when a mouse hovers over an element, resulting in things like context-sensitive tool tips.

◆ The ability to internationalize documents. Bidirectional text can be implemented for languages that are read right-to-left, such as Hebrew. Quotation marks and list numbers can be made to point in the proper direction. All others styles can be customized based on the current language being used to browse.

◆ Greatly enhanced counters and numbering.

◆ The ability to create, align, and lay out tables.

◆ The ability to blow up a document or parts within a document through magnification. This enables the same page to be seen at a size comfortable to the user. This could also be used to create tons of zoom-in and zoom-out effects.

◆ The ability to create dynamic outlines with automatic numbering. This enables effects such as a structured table of contents that can automatically update itself based on a document's contents.

◆ The ability to precisely space elements from their baselines with better vertical alignment.

◆ The ability to achieve graphically intensive effects on the fly with text drop shadows and other cool filters.

◆ The ability to define user interface details such as cursors, so that the cursor changes as it encounters different elements. Rolling over an element that can be handled, for instance, might show a special hand or crosshairs icon, as mused about in Chapter 3, "Principles and Lessons Learned." Cursors and tool tips can guide users through applications with unprecedented ease.

◆ The ability to set styles based on context, and set attributes with search patterns. For example, to set the color of "all paragraphs followed by an image element."

The level 2 specification can be found at:

`http://www.w3.org/TR/REC-CSS2/.`

All of these enhancements have fantastic implications for dynamic HTML and interface design.

Level 3 and Beyond

The Cascading Style Sheet working group is currently putting together a level 3 specification that includes anything that didn't fit in level 2. It also deals with even more advanced style properties such as headers, footers, and pagination.

Level 3 will also likely have methods for laying out text within complicated columns by setting widths, the gutter control, column rules, and more.

Another great addition will be access to operating system environmental variables. This will enable developers to know a user's windows colors, icon schemes, desktop patterns, and the size of various windows, and help them to customize detailed interfaces that flow well with the user's current preferences.

eXtensible Style Language (XSL)

As useful as Cascading Style Sheets are, they are still tied strongly to HTML and the orderly way that HTML is parsed and rendered. As applications become widespread, however, the ability to lay out the same information in a number of very different ways will become important. This is a perfect job for XML, and the reason why XML is often touted as the "future language of the Web."

The eXtensible Style Language, or XSL, is a language based strongly on DSSSL written for and in XML. XSL is to XML, more or less, as CSS is to HTML. It follows the XML object model, making it easy to manipulate using JavaScript.

They key difference between XSL and CSS is that XSL is a *transformation language.* In other words, its properties not only define what elements should look like and where they should be placed, but also how they should be translated and structured within another document. An XSL processor reads in a source document's *source tree,* searches it based on a set of matching criteria, rearranges it using special templates, and assembles a brand-new document or *result tree.* What this amounts to is taking a document marked up using one Document Type Definition and producing a brand-spanking-new document marked up using a completely different DTD. This gives XSL the capability to out-and-out covert any XML document into legal HTML with built-in CSS or any other style out there.

For example, an XSL sheet can be written to search through a huge book and come back with a dynamic table of contents created automatically based on the level one and level two headings. It could even come back with highly specific information, such as the first paragraph of every odd chapter. When linked to JavaScript, this could all be done on the fly with the press of a button.

Searching the Document

A number of special characters and formats enable XSL to search a document quickly for certain criteria. The main XSL element is `template`, which creates a template that alters the source tree. The result tree is always squeezed within these templates, giving them defined styles.

A common search directive for `template` is `match`. Matching is a process that scales through the source tree and returns a certain element, attribute, content, collection of elements, or type of tag. These matches can get pretty advanced. You can search for an element at any level in the source tree, or a tag that has another tag as its context. XSL can match based on child or parent elements, or based on the position of the element in the document. You can even create an XSL command, for example, that grabs only the first occurrence of a particular element and does something nifty with its content. You can use wildcards to search for tags that start or end a certain way. You can also search based on the depth of a tag in the XML document tree.

IT'S ALL ABOUT CONTEXT

As your XSL file parses through a source tree, it keeps track of where in the tree it is currently searching. The node it is currently searching is the *context*. If you are at the root of the source tree and you search for all elements of type X, then all the X elements in the entire tree will be returned. However, if your context is within in a certain branch, then only child X elements are dealt with.

DUELING RULES

If a given element matches more than one template, the more specific match is used. For example, if you search for a NAME element by itself and a NAME element that is within a MAMMAL element, the second template is used. The way it works is intuitive. In essence, the more detailed a rule is, the more specific it is deemed to be.

The criteria that determines the specificity of a rule is based on things such as the number of wildcards, the priority level of the template, the importance level of the rule, and the number of ID and CLASS attributes being searched for in the pattern.

PATTERN MATCHING

To find nodes within the current context, you use a bunch of special characters. Let's go through some quick examples of XSL pattern matching. Seeing how it all works is a painless way to quickly pick up the main XSL concepts.

For example, to grab the root level of the source XML document, you use a slash:

```
<xsl:template match="/">
```

One of the most useful XSL patterns is the asterisk, or wildcard. This is a short-hand way of grabbing any element at all. So to snag all the elements that exist within any MAMMAL element, use:

```
<xsl:template match="//mammal/*">
```

Once you've snagged the elements you want, you can start searching for elements that contain various attributes.

 You can use parentheses to group various patterns together.

In addition, you can use brackets to create filters that weed out various aspects of the XML elements. You can fill brackets with a number, and ask for a specific element that is placed within the document. To find the third MAMMAL element in a document, for instance:

```
<xsl:template match="mammal[3]">
```

You can also filter out an element based on its child elements.

In addition, you can use the and, or, and not Boolean keywords to further modify the match. This lets you get really advanced with your search criteria. To find all ANIMAL elements that contain either a child HABITAT or an ENVIRONMENT element:

```
<xsl:template match="mammal[habitat $or$ environment]">
```

If you think this is getting complicated, you ain't seen nothing yet. The at sign (@) is used to dig out an attribute. Let's say you have an XML element that looks something like this:

```
<MAMMAL SIZE="tremendous">
```

You can find any MAMMAL tag that has the SIZE attribute at all by using:

```
<xsl:template match="/mammal[@size]">
```

In addition, you can find the specific tremendous mammal element by using XSL code like this:

```
<xsl:template match="/mammal[@size = 'tremendous']">
```

You can also search for the specific value of a tag. To find the first NAME element within a MAMMAL element that contains Pine Marten:

```
<xsl:template match="mammal[name = 'Pine Marten']">
```

The any and all keywords are very useful for grabbing values. Keywords such as less than (lt) and greater than (gt) enable you to perform binary comparisons. For instance, you might want to find an element that has a numerical value of greater than 700, or a text value higher in the alphabet than X.

Processing the Document

Once desired elements or attributes are matched, the XSL processor creates a result tree full of nodes. The contents of these nodes can be outputted or transformed in a wide variety of ways. For example, you can do something for each occurrence of a certain tag or word within the tag's contents.

The basic XSL elements you can write sheets with include:

- ◆ xsl:stylesheet — This is the first element of any style sheet. It contains all the templates that should be applied to the source tree to create the result tree.

- ◆ xsl:template — This element contains the template that takes in nodes that meet a certain match criteria and then uses these nodes to spit out the given elements, attributes, directives, text, or other values.

- ◆ xsl:value-of — This element copies the value of the source node into the final document. If the node is a tree of many nodes, then this returns all of the text in the current element's subtree.

- ◆ xsl:attribute-set — This element enables you to create an attribute that contains a certain style. This attribute can then be used with xsl:use at any point as part of a template.

There are also a number of XSL elements that enable you to pick and choose from, or loop through, collections of nodes. These conditional elements make XSL into a low-key but quite adept programming language.

- ◆ xsl:for-each — A very common element that loops through a node list of multiple elements, enabling you to perform actions with each one.

◆ `xsl:choose` — This combines with the `xsl:when` and `xsl:otherwise` elements to perform several actions on one group of elements, based on various conditions. This is similar to the `switch-case` operations in Java and C. For example:

```
<xsl:choose>
 <xsl:when match="*[size = 1]">
  <H1>
 <xsl:when match="*[size = 2]">
  <H2>
 <xsl:otherwise>
  <H3>
</xsl:choose>
```

◆ `xsl:if` — This element checks for a certain condition.

The second beta of Internet Explorer 5.0 supports an even more enhanced version of XSL.

FLOW OBJECTS

XSL does not output an HTML document; rather, it outputs a result tree that can, if desired, be outputted as an HTML document. In order for an XSL style sheet to be easy to write and read, the specification supports all HTML 4.0 tags and CSS properties as *flow objects*. These are special tags that format the resulting tree's content in special ways. In essence, you're using XSL to create an HTML document out of XML.

Though flow objects look a whole lot like their HTML and CSS counterparts, there are some slight differences between them. Legal XSL is a lot stricter than HTML. For one, all flow objects must be uppercase. Flow objects must also have closing tags for all open tags. If you are using a standalone tag such as `<IMG>` or `<HR>`, you must indicate this with a trailing slash:

```
<HR/>
```

Whenever an end tag is optional in HTML, it should always be used in XSL templates. For example:

```
<P>This is my paragraph.</P>
```

Any attribute values must always be in quotes. You should assign values to attributes that normally do not have values, even if they are fake. Here are two examples of nonvalid XML code:

```
<INPUT CHECKED>
<INPUT VALUE=myvalue>
```

These can be fixed as follows:

```
<INPUT CHECKED="true">
<INPUT VALUE="myvalue">
```

Likewise, all CSS properties can be applied by tacking on a STYLE attribute to any HTML flow object. They may also be used directly as attributes themselves. For example:

```
<P STYLE="color: red; font-style: italic;">
```

 CSS properties must be in lowercase.

In addition to the standard CSS styles, the XSL specification includes a more advanced set of flow objects based on the DSSSL style sheet language. These advanced style properties help process a document for print, other languages, and more. Because these are not applicable to Web applications, most browsers do not support these objects.

As the specification evolves, styles that have no place in the world of the Web will likely be weeded out.

PUTTING IT ALL TOGETHER

Let's go through some examples of how these elements are used.

 As of this writing, only the Internet Explorer 5.0 beta 2 supports XSL. The format of IE XSL differs slightly from the World Wide Web Consortium specification. The Internet Explorer usage of xsl:process is called xsl:apply-templates. It is used in the same way — either with a select attribute or with a trailing slash:

```
<xsl:apply-templates/>
```

For example, we can have XSL look for any ANIMAL element and sandwich its full contents within a standard HTML paragraph tag, as shown in Listing 7-2.

Listing 7-2: Wrapping all ANIMAL elements in paragraph tags in legal XSL

```
<?xml version="1.0"?>
<xsl:stylesheet xmlns:xsl="http://www.w3.org/TR/WD-xsl">
```

```
<xsl:template match="//animal">
 <P>
  <xsl:process-children/>
 </P>
</xsl:template>
</xsl:stylesheet>
```

Note that every XSL style sheet must be a legal XML document, and must start and end with the xsl:stylesheet element.

A MORE DETAILED EXAMPLE

Let's look at a full example of XSL in action. First, take a base XML source file containing all of the information you want to deal with. You can find this source in Listing 7-4.

Listing 7-4: A simple XML file

```
<?xml version="1.0"?>
<animals>
  <mammals>
    <name>Pine Marten</name>
    <latin_name>Martes martes</latin_name>
    <description>
       <fur>dark brown</fur>
       <tail>long, fluffy</tail>
    </description >
    <ecology>
     <place>Scottish Highlands</place>
     <place>Grampian</place>
     <place>Southern Scotland</place>
    </ecology>
  </mammals>
</animals>
```

You could now write the XSL template in Listing 7-5 to go through the document, and search for every "animals/mammals" element. It could then output the contents of the "name" element as a level one heading. Then it should loop through the remaining contents and list all the ecology items in an ordered list. Sounds complicated, but this is actually a very simplified example of what XSL is capable of.

Carefully study the XSL code in Listing 7-5.

Listing 7-5: The XSL file to process the XML in Listing 7-4

```
<?xml version="1.0"?>
 <xsl:stylesheet xmlns:xsl="http://www.w3.org/TR/WD-xsl">
   <xsl:template match = "/">
```

```
<xsl:for-each select ="animals/mammals">
   <H1 style="font-weight: bold; color: red">
     <xsl:process select = "name"/></TD>
   </H1>
   <OL style="font-weight: italic; color: green">
     <xsl:for-each select = "ecology/item">
        <LI><xsl:process-children/>
     </xsl:for-each>
   </OL>
</xsl:for-each>
</xsl:template>
</xsl:stylesheet>
```

The code in Listing 7-5 goes through the above XML and outputs a target document that looks like Listing 7-6.

Listing 7-6: The result tree. Looks a lot like HTML, doesn't it?

```
<H1 style="font-weight: bold; color: red">Pine Marten</H1>
<OL style="font-weight: italic; color: green">
<LI>Scottish Highlands
<LI>Grampian
<LI>Southern Scotland
</OL>
```

When put through a Web browser, you get a lovely page with a red, bold heading and green, italicized list items.

Now imagine using this on a vast database of, say, all the animals in the world and you're really talking turkey. And buffalo. And wombat. And sheep. . . .

It's easy to see XSL's power. A different template could have created wildly different results based on the same source document. XSL is also particularly adept at applying CSS styles to tags, making it highly effective as a full style sheet language for XML.

The Best of All Worlds: DSSSL and HTML with CSS

If you're a DSSSL geek or CSS weenie, you might notice how similar many XSL concepts are to the languages you know and love. Indeed, XSL is based entirely on DSSSL. Whereas DSSSL used the LISP-derived language Scheme, XSL uses a more tag-oriented syntax, but the transformations are expressed in similar ways. In other words, it uses DSSSL semantics of a tree of flow objects without the highly complicated DSSSL syntax. As the specifications for XSL and DSSSL evolve, many efforts will be made to converge the two technologies so that XSL comes out as a valid subset of DSSSL.

XSL also uses key concepts and terminology from Cascading Style Sheets. It supports all CSS functionality, enabling you to present your result tree using any valid CSS property. This makes XSL completely compatible with HTML with CSS.

Where XSL Is At

Believe it or not, we've only scratched the surface of all the XSL elements and patterns. Currently, Microsoft's Internet Explorer 5.0 beta 2 does a thorough job handling XSL. Netscape also claims that it will implement the latest XSL specification as soon as it can get around to it. The specification is still being debated and worked on, however, so the names of elements and methods are completely up for grabs. The power of XSL is unmistakable, and within a few years XSL may likely be the engine running the most complex Web applications.

Using the Adjectives and Adverbs

Actually adding style rules to HTML pages is quite straightforward. A style rule can be applied to any legal HTML element, any class of elements, or any specific part of the document.

Declaring the Style

We already have covered how to use a standard HTML element as a selector. Just plunk down the name of the tag and follow it with the declaration:

```
H1 { color: red }
```

Easy as pie!

But what if your application — like most Web pages — has a uniform color and style scheme that applies to most HTML tags. It seems a bit redundant to declare the same style over and over again. Or what if you want to base styles on things that have nothing to do with HTML tags, such as whether you are dealing with the first element on the page.

Luckily, CSS and HTML 4.0 have teamed up to bring you the CLASS and ID attributes.

DOING IT WITH CLASS

Putting an element in a certain class is like adding it to a special list of elements. You can then look at or modify this special all at once. Any tag at all can be classed. Following are some examples:

```
<IMG SRC="hello.gif" CLASS="naughty">
<A HREF="test.html" CLASS="polkdadotted">
<P CLASS="interesting">
```

On the style side of things, you can set up a class by picking any convenient name and preceding it with a period. For example:

```
.interesting { color: blue }
```

You can also customize classes for a specific HTML element. This lets you use two or more styles with one element, based on its class. This is done by having an HTML selector followed by a period and then the name of the class. For example:

```
H3.interesting { color: blue }
```

Document-wide and global styles are often performed on classes rather than specific elements. For example, the following code creates two styles: "interesting" and "boring." These are then applied to various elements, as shown in Listing 7-7.

Listing 7-7: Applying a class of styles to an element

```
<HTML>
<HEAD>
<TITLE>A Classy Example</TITLE>
 <STYLE TYPE="text/css">
 .interesting { color: red }
 .boring      { color: blue }
 </STYLE>
</HEAD>
<BODY>
 <H1 CLASS=interesting>My This Is Neat</H1>
 <P CLASS=boring>Yawn, this is tiresome.</P>
</BODY>
</HTML>
```

GETTING ID'D

Every HTML element can also have a unique ID, indicated by the ID attribute. This is similar to HTML's NAME attribute, but can apply to any element at all. This ID is sometimes generated by a special HTML editor to ensure its uniqueness. If you craft your own IDs, pay careful attention to be sure each is unique.

For instance, a paragraph's ID might look like:

```
<P ID=k2338a>
```

You can give any ID a custom style by preceding the ID with the pound sign. This enables specific elements to have specific styles. For instance, the previous paragraph – and only that paragraph – could be colored red by using the following declaration:

```
#k2338a { color: red }
```

Applying the Style

The key is to know where you want the styles to be applied:

- **Locally** — Inlined styles enable any and every element on a Web page to have its own look. The style is placed right in the tag.

- **Document-Wide** — Various *classes* of styles can be set up and customized. These can have any name you want, such as "important" and "greenish." Any HTML element can then be placed within a class and immediately take on that style.

- **Globally Linked** — One style sheet of various classes can be created to apply throughout an entire Web site. This enables designers to create universal templates without having to painstakingly edit every single Web page. If the entire look and feel of the site needs to change drastically, then only the style sheet needs to be altered. The new look cascades throughout the site.

 Although the official CSS spec states that styles can be applied to any HTML tag, Netscape Navigator 4.0 only supports style positioning for body containers. In other words, styles only work properly for major block elements such as `<SPAN>` and `<DIV>`. Any elements that need be positioned, then, should be placed inside a `DIV` area to ensure cross-browser compatibility. Part III of this book covers ways to deal with this incompatibility in great detail.

LOCALLY

Changing a common HTML element so that it appears exactly the way you like is an easy task. Styles can be inserted right within the HTML tag using the `STYLE` attribute.

For example, the code in Listing 7-8 prints a standard, boring heading and then prints out a cool, customized heading.

Listing 7-8: Creating an inline style

```
<H1>This Is A Boring Heading</H1>
<H1 STYLE='color: pink; background: black; font-size: 20pt; line-
height: 15pt; font-weight: bold; font-family: Arial,Sans-Serif;
text-align=right;'>
This Is An Awesome Heading!</H1>
```

Notice that all the style properties are surrounded by single quotes, as some of the values require standard double quotes.

The Web page that would result from the above code appears in Figure 7-3.

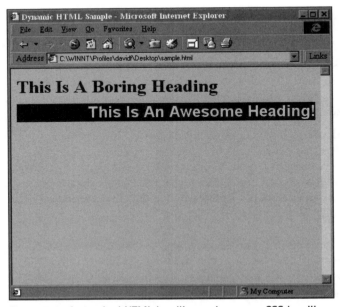

Figure 7-3: A standard HTML headline and a snazzy CSS headline

DOCUMENT-WIDE

Styles become even more useful when you apply one template for an entire Web page. This lets you throw together a few snippets of code that drastically changes everything at once.

Document-wide styles should be placed in the `<HEAD>` area of a Web page, between special `<STYLE>` tags, given a type of "text/css":

```
<STYLE TYPE="TEXT/CSS">
```

These are not only generally more useful than inlined styles, they are also infinitely easier to read. For example, Listing 7-9 achieves a very customized set of headings and paragraphs.

Listing 7-9: Creating styles throughout a document

```
<HTML>
<HEAD>
<TITLE>Some Styles</TITLE>
<STYLE TYPE="TEXT/CSS">
<!--
```

```
H1 {
  color: blue;
  background: white;
  font-size: 15pt;
  font-style: italic;
  font-family: "Courier,Monospace";
  text-align: right;
}

H2 {
  color: pink;
  background: black;
  font-size: 10pt;
  font-weight: bold;
  font-style: italic;
  font-family: "Courier,Monospace";
  text-align: right;
}

P {
  color: red;
  font: 12pt "Arial,Helvetica,sans-serif";
  text-align: justify;
}
-->
</STYLE>
</HEAD>
<BODY>
<H1>This is a Level One Heading</H1>
<P>And this is a standard paragraph. Notice how it is justified,
like the text in a book. I'll keep rambling here for a while so you
can see this effect in action. Pretty nifty stuff, eh?</P>
<H2>A Level Two Heading</H2>
<P>More standard paragraph stuff.</P>
</BODY>
</HTML>
```

Notice that the styles are surrounded by HTML comments. This ensures that this style text is not seen and rendered by browsers that do not support CSS.

You can see the results of the above code in Figure 7-4.

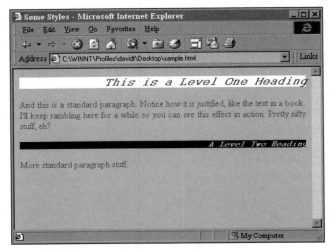

Figure 7-4: A styled HTML document

GLOBALLY LINKED

The next step is to create styles that automatically work throughout any entire Web site. These global styles are achieved by linking style sheets to HTML documents.

First, you need to create a separate style sheet file, which usually has the `.css` extension. The `.css` file looks exactly like a document-wide style sheet, except for the fact that it has no body, as shown in Listing 7-10.

Listing 7-10: A global style sheet that can be linked in

```
<HTML>
<STYLE TYPE="TEXT/CSS">
<!--
BODY {font: 10pt "Arial,sans-serif"};

H1 {
  color: blue;
  background: white;
  font-size: 15pt;
  font-style: italic;
  font-family: "Courier,Monospace";
  text-align: right;
}

H2 {
  color: pink;
  background: black;
  font-size: 10pt;
```

```
   font-weight: bold;
   font-style: italic;
   font-family: "Courier,Monospace";
   text-align: right;
}

P {
   color: red;
   font: 12pt "Arial,Helvetica,sans-serif";
   text-align: justify;
}
-->
</STYLE>
</HEAD>
<BODY>
</BODY>
</HTML>
```

Suppose you saved the style sheet in Listing 7-10 as a file named `mystyles.css`. You could then apply the style sheet to any Web page by creating a link:

```
<HEAD>
<LINK REL=stylesheet HREF="mystyles.css" TYPE="text/css">
</HEAD>
```

You could link this sheet to thousands or millions of documents. If you wanted to change the style of all level three headings, for instance, you would only need to modify the lone `.css` file.

WORKING IN HARMONY: CASCADING

Many levels of style sheets can cascade together. If a style for a particular class or element is defined twice, the more local definition always wins out. A local style sheet takes precedence over document-wide styles, and document-wide styles squash globally linked styles.

How to Use Styles from JavaScript

Now that we've used the adjective and adverbs of styles to electrify our documents, we can capture the styles with JavaScript and dynamically turn hot to cold, huge to tiny, left to right, or make any other stylistic change. Fonts can grow before your eyes. Images can dance across the screen. Borders can flip around. Text can divorce itself from its original font families. Background colors can change so fast you feel like you fell back into the sixties. Accessing style finally unlocks the full power of your document, giving you full control over every aspect of an application.

The Document Object Model lets you access any of these styles using basic scripting techniques. The key lies in the `style` object.

For example, if you have an object with an `id` of "id23," you can modify its color using:

```
id23.style.color  = red;
```

If you wanted to change the color of a class named "awesome," you could use:

```
awesome.style.color = red;
```

 Naturally, Netscape Navigator 4.0 and Internet Explorer 4.0 have different implementations of accessing styles via JavaScript, due to their differing DOMs. To achieve the above color change in Netscape JavaScript you would have to use:

```
document.layers.['awesome'].color = red;
```

And in IE you would need to use something similar to:

```
document.awesome.style.color = red;
```

Part III of this book deals with techniques to work around these annoying differences. For the remainder of this chapter, however, we only deal with Explorer's object model, as it does a much better job of following the official specification.

An Example: Dynamically Changing Positioning

Listing 7-11 shows an example of how to change an element's position every time it is clicked.

Listing 7-11: The box graphic jumps to the left when it is clicked

```
<HTML>
<HEAD>
<TITLE>An animating box</TITLE>
<STYLE type="text/css">
<!--
#mybox {
    position:absolute;
    left: 100px;
    top: 100px;
    width: 50px;
    height: 50px;
```

```
}
-->
</STYLE>
<SCRIPT language="JavaScript">
<!--
  function moveme()
  {
    mybox.style.left = 0;
  }
// -->
</SCRIPT>
</HEAD>
<BODY>
<IMG ID="mybox" SRC="box.gif" onClick="moveme()">
</BODY>
```

When the page is first loaded, the box appears positioned 100 pixels over. When the image is clicked, the `moveme()` function is called. This sets the left of the box to 0. The box jumps over to the window's left border.

This is a simplistic example of an advanced concept — adjectives can be given life with the verbs of JavaScript.

Using XSL from HTML

An XSL style sheet can be linked from an XML by using:

```
<?xml-stylesheet href="mysheet.xsl" type="text/xsl" ?>
```

Internet Explorer 5.0 beta 2 includes the ability to embed XML and XSL using the `<XSL>` tag. Any XML can be embedded smack within an HTML document using the `<XML>` tag:

```
<XML ID="myxml">
  <animal>
    <name>Pine Marten</name>
  </animal>
</XML>
```

You can also call up a separate `.xml` file using the `SRC` attribute:

```
<XML ID="myxml" SRC="customer.xml"></XML>
```

Likewise, you can call an XSL file:

```
<XML ID="myxml" SRC="coolstyles.xsl"></XML>
```

Additionally, XSL elements can be used within any HTML block. A `DIV` element is a good place to store things. Thus, a typical XSL file would have this format:

```
<DIV xmlns:xsl="http://www.w3.org/TR/WD-xsl">
<xsl:for-each select="animal">
  <H1>
   <xsl:value-of select="name"/>
  </H1>
</xsl:for-each>
</DIV>
```

Summary

♦ Styles are a way of separating the look and layout of a document from its content and structure. Separating styles is important because they often differ based on where a document is being distributed, whereas the structure of the document never changes.

♦ Cascading Style Sheets evolved as a way to add font, color, text, spacing, and border styles to HTML.

♦ CSS-P added the ability to position and layer the elements in a document.

♦ The eXtensible Style Language adds styles to XML. In this case, "styles" is used is the broadest sense, making XSL a full transformation language capable of taking XML elements in and outputting nearly any valid document in return.

♦ CSS is used inlined, within the document, or globally within HTML.

♦ Styles can be applied to entire types of tags, common classes, or unique ID'd elements.

♦ Styles and XSL fit snugly into the Document Object Model, enabling styles to be modified easily using JavaScript.

Styles are the adjectives and adverbs that round out the language of Web applications. JavaScript verbs use these style adjectives to change the look or position of any element noun.

The next chapter deals with tying everything together — nouns, verbs, adjectives, and adverbs — and crafting complete sentences and paragraphs. The end result is a rich application that lives right on your Web page.

Chapter 8

Tying Things Together: Sentences and Paragraphs

THIS CHAPTER SHOWS YOU how to piece together the nouns, verbs, and adjectives of the last three chapters to achieve interface goals and create sentences and paragraphs – that is, full-fledged components and Web applications.

Destination: Applications

What exactly is a computer application? We've been bandying the term about for a while now. When we say we want to use dynamic HTML to build full applications, what do we really mean?

An application does just what its name implies: it *applies* technology to perform a specific function. A word processing application helps you compose words. A spreadsheet arranges and crunches numbers. A paint application makes it simple for you to lay out colorful pixels and make pretty pictures. A game lets you fire a nail gun at saliva-dripping aliens.

Are standard HTML Web pages considered applications? If not, what would one of these newfangled Web applications look like?

The Look and Feel of Traditional HTML

The language of HTML launched a revolution. A few years ago only true geeks could tell you what HTML meant, much less how to use it. These days, many elementary school students know it by heart. Millions of people have worked with it, at least on some base level, to craft personal Web pages. Even the most codephobic graphic designer must have some knowledge of HTML if she hopes to design for the Web.

A Web browser itself is clearly an application – a program that delivers content from faraway networks and formats it all nice and pretty for you. But can typical Web *pages* be considered applications? Most of them are just documents in the same way as a word processor's text documents and a spreadsheet's worksheets.

Currently, there are only a few application-like pages out there: sites that help you shop, search, learn, or play. Let's face it, the level that most Web applications hover at is pretty shallow. It's all about clicking, filling in forms, waiting for a new page, and more clicking.

Web pages are generally passive and external to you. You read them and move on.

THE INTERFACE OF WEB PAGES

Standard Web pages are simple. This is their downfall as well as their greatest asset. You don't have to learn much to surf the Web. Roll your cursor over a phrase or picture that interests you. If the cursor turns into a hand, you can click there to find out more. Repeat ad nauseam.

Most of a Web page's interface, though, depends on the Web browser. Moving forward and backward, scrolling, and opening new windows are all things that the Netscape Navigator and Microsoft Internet Explorer menus and toolbars handle. Ignoring that, let's look at the Web page itself. What types of feedback do Web sites have to communicate with the user? What sophisticated ways are there for sites to be navigated?

USER FEEDBACK

For the most part, Web pages are all about pointing and clicking. The more advanced Web pages have a bit more interactivity. They enable you to use forms that contain input fields, selection menus, pull-down menus, check boxes, radio buttons, and text areas. These widgets are standard and easy to understand. They accept input from a user, send the information to a Web server, and then bring up a new page based on that input.

The most application-like sites such as bookstores and online banking services have pages and pages of these input boxes. A user clicks through the pages and accomplishes some goals, perhaps ordering books or paying bills. The process is generally slow, involving lots of waiting for new pages to stream down.

NAVIGATION

Many ideas have cropped up for how to navigate sites. In the end, though, it always comes back to some sort of menu bar to go to major sections and some sort of site map to see an overview of all the pages.

It always comes down to this fact: HTML pages are just that — pages. And while the design of the pages can mimic more traditional applications, there's still a seam between each major section of the site that involves a hit to a Web server. Even if common navigation elements stay the same, the screen must change and be refreshed with each new page. This flicker, this pause, breaks up the user's experience. This gives HTML sites a vastly different psychological feel than traditional applications.

You may be wholly immersed in the content of a page for a limited period of time. But as soon as you click for some new information, your browser logo animates and chugs along and you become aware that you are viewing a Web page in a Web browser. You become aware, on some level, that there are layers and layers of servers, routers, and wires separating you from the data on the page.

Some sites use frames to navigate between sections. Frames are nice because they don't need to be refreshed. A menu bar can stay intact at the top of a page while the bottom area changes drastically. Frames achieve a better level of immersion, making sites a lot more like traditional applications. However, frames are limited. They may not appear anywhere on the screen, and there's no way to perform special effects such as changing a frame on the fly or having a user drag the menu to a more convenient spot on the screen. Frames are more empowering to the user, but also very limiting compared to the limitless interface components of traditional applications.

The Look and Feel of Traditional Applications

The applications on your hard drive are very different from Web pages. A typical application is huge, taking up megabytes of space. You generally use an application with the hope of coming up with something solid such as a spreadsheet detailing your company's outstanding profit model; a three-dimensional animation of the Death Star exploding; a database full of recipes; or the Great American Novel. Some applications, such as video games, leave you with a feeling of euphoria and a high score to brag about. And educational applications try hard to teach you things, leaving you with a little more knowledge than you had coming in.

If a traditional application needs to access a remote machine to grab or submit some information, it generally tries to do it as unobtrusively as possible. When traditional applications do reach out through networks, they try to only send little bits of information. The graphics, text, programming methods, libraries, and other elements that make up the application are usually stored right on your computer's memory or hard drive where you can access them quickly.

All of this combines to make traditional applications active rather than passive. They are the canvasses you paint upon, and the worlds you are submerged in. They often have tons of options and preferences, enabling you to tailor your experience based on your needs or tastes.

THE INTERFACE

Whether you are using a UNIX, Macintosh, or PC platform, most applications take place in a windowed environment, giving users a very similar experience. All of the action takes place in a frame that can be maximized, minimized, closed, resized, and moved about by clicking or dragging on various elements on the window's top title bar.

Within the window itself there are usually menu items at the top of the screen that enable you to select from a hierarchy of commands. These windows often have the same general layout from application to application: a File menu, an Edit menu, a few more generalized menus, and finally a Help menu on the far right.

The most frequently used commands are usually represented as a toolbar of buttons. With one click of an icon, your document is printed, or a new document is opened. And most applications have a status bar on the bottom telling you important information about the current state of affairs: What task is being performed? What page are you on? What file is being downloaded?

Advanced applications let you customize your menus, toolbars, and everything else. Sometimes you do this using a special dialog box. Other times you just slide or drag interface elements where you want them.

The world outside of the application is also windowed, and shares many of the same interface elements. The windowed environment has become a standard way of launching and flipping between programs. Multitasking happens when you have several windows open at once and click between them. Most modern applications can even communicate directly with each other, enabling you to drag a spreadsheet from one window and drop it into a report you're creating with your word processor.

Many larger applications even have a windowed document interface of their own. These windows within windows enable you to have several documents open at once, side by side or layered on top of each other, so that you can switch between them and share data.

USER FEEDBACK

There are only so many doorways through which a user can talk to his machine, including the keyboard, a mouse, and maybe a joystick. Mouse clicks and drags, keyboard hits, window closes, and joystick presses are handled fully by traditional applications.

Tool tips may pop up when your mouse rests over a button, letting you know where that button leads. Many of today's applications even respond to context clicks—clicking the right mouse button or holding down the button for an extended period of time. This lets a user access the most important commands relevant to a particular task.

In other words, every square pixel of screen real estate is wired to accept and make use of your input. There are very few elements of an application's interface that don't respond in some precise way to a mouse click or other input.

NAVIGATION

The word *navigation* often doesn't even apply to traditional applications. In a word processor, for instance, you may move from composing a document to performing a spelling check on it but it's generally just a dialog box that pops up within the same window. You never feel separated from the document you are working on. Any commands you perform from changing the print settings to adjusting the font family all take place within the same window. You never really leave until you close the document or close the application.

Other applications, such as educational CD-ROMs, often have main menus and subareas that have vastly different looks and feels. But navigating from one area to another is usually immediate. Well-designed titles don't squash the previous interface so much as move it about or change some of its elements. For example, imagine you are playing around with a CD-ROM that tells you about Einstein's life. There's a tab on the side that lists every major section on the CD-ROM: His Life, His Theories, and His Thoughts. You click the tab that takes you to the His Theories section. The background now fades away and changes into an image of equations and star maps. A new menu that lets you browse through various aspects of the theory of relativity slides in from the top. But the main navigation tab on the side stays intact. You never feel lost.

When you first load up a traditional application, it may take some time to get used to the interface and understand all it can do for you. A good interface nudges you away from mistakes and helps you realize its full potential. Once you've made that initial investment of attaching yourself to the interface and learning what it can do for you, it never leaves you behind in the dust.

The Look and Feel of Web Applications

A Web application is a program that works like a traditional application but that is tied in directly to the Web. That means a Web application, though initially residing on a Web server, uses the power of your client computer to achieve its goals. Complete Web applications are delivered to clients in one package, and after that point the program only talks to the server when it absolutely needs to.

Web applications exist in a strange netherworld between client and server. The idea of local files and directory systems becomes almost irrelevant. True, the application may be stored on the client in a *cache* and, true, some persistent data may be stored on the client using cookies. But that's it. The application generally doesn't deal with your hard drive beyond that because of the security risk, not to mention the inefficiency. The application's real birthplace is the server. Its temporary home, though, is your client machine.

 Because a Web application resides on the server, it's easy for the developer to constantly update the application with any new features or bug fixes.

The goal for Web applications is to create an interface that appeals to and works for the masses like HTML, and yet helps the user achieve complicated tasks intuitively, just like the best traditional applications.

This begs the following questions: Why not just use standard software applications that make use of Internet technologies? What's so special about having applications run smack inside of Web browsers?

There are two answers. The first has to do with you, the readers of this book—developers and interface designers.

By making tools available that enable developers of all levels to compile their own network-aware applications, the power and potential of the Web will rise meteorically. Only hardcore software engineers can create standalone Internet applications. But modern Web browsers act as more than just windows that can display pretty documents. By putting the power to design applications in the hands of actual designers you've got a tremendous revolution on your hands.

The second answer also has to do with you as a user who wants to harness computer applications to make work and life easier. The Web, by nature, is delivered cross-platform. Almost everybody who is connected to the Internet has and uses a Web browser. If a good application could be made to work in any Web browser, on a UNIX machine, a Mac, a Windows box, or even handheld devices and over the telephone, then that application can literally serve the world. What this means is that documents and ideas could be shared and distributed among an unprecedented mass audience. The entire world could plug into what is essentially the same application. It's only a matter of waiting for this killer app to be designed.

A NEW INTERFACE

Web applications have their own features, problems, and implications built into them from the start. There are more questions than answers, at this point. For example, where are Web applications stored after they are initially downloaded? How much data from a Web application should reside on the server and how much on the client? Which browsers should the Web application work within? But the biggest unanswered question is: What does a Web application look like?

For starters, most Web applications stand on the shoulders of giants that succeeded before them. Standard HTML form widgets such as input areas, check boxes, pull-down menus and the like will be the first interface elements to be used because they are already built into HTML. After that, common interface items such as menu bars, status bars, toolbars, tool tips, expandable and collapsible trees, tabbed options boxes, and others will likely be implemented because almost every computer-savvy user knows what these metaphors mean.

Because Web applications are a hybrid of traditional HTML pages and traditional applications, they need to borrow from the best of both worlds. They don't exist on your hard drive, and yet they do exist on your computer. What implications does this have?

Web applications should work on any browser, any screen size, and possibly even on handheld devices, electronic Braille readers, and telephones. Obviously, this means some *major* overhauls in interfaces. At the very least, interfaces will have to be extremely flexible.

Another big change is that applications will soon enter the multiuser realm. Just as multiplayer games have had to undergo new designs to work for several people at once, so will Web applications. Imagine being able to drag a document from one window that represents an open document on one computer, and drop it into another window that represents a document on a computer halfway around the world.

Some of the interface principles discussed in Part I need to be rethought a great deal. This chapter reviews the technology behind many of those principles in light of the new face of Web applications.

Creating the Web Application

For starters, let's figure out how we can use the Document Object Model, Cascading Style Sheets, JavaScript, and other core technologies to achieve one of these Web applications.

The recipe for success is quite simple, in theory at least:

- **Start with some** *things*. These things can be any interface item that exists or that you create. Buttons, menus, boxes, pieces of text, icons, arrows, tabs. The sky of your imagination is the limit. These are the nouns of the Document Object Model.

- **Harness the things with programming.** Do stuff to them or make them react to your input. This uses the verbs of JavaScript.

- **Position and style the things.** Modify the way they look, where they're located, or even whether they should be visible. This uses the adjectives and adverbs of Cascading Style Sheets.

- **Keep the state.** Save any preferences or data you'll need to use the next time you run the application.

- **Communicate.** If necessary, access a server and send it information or commands. And, of course, enable the server to send data to you.

Step 1: Start with Some Things

Every creator must make something out of nothing. Artists square off against a blank canvas (or screen). Writers tap their quills against a virginal white page (or screen). Accountants stare wistfully into an empty ledger (or screen) full of zeros. The Web application developer begins with an empty Web browser.

The first step for any creator is to jump into it and start creating some *things*. These things may be edited, changed, or completely deleted later. But what happens later is almost irrelevant. The key is to create as few or as many things as you think you need to achieve your goals. Only then can you start playing with these things and seeing what works and what doesn't, slowly making the magic happen.

The Data Isn't Important, at First

At first glance, data seems like the heart of any application. Word processors have documents. Games have levels and high scores. A bookstore has information about millions of books. Data is the information that your application uses in order to function.

When designing an application, you might be tempted to start with the data. After all, what is a bookstore without books? If you're building a bookstore shopping application you eventually need a list of all the relevant data: the titles, prices, facts, reviews, book cover images, and so on. Maybe this data already exists on a database on some server somewhere, maybe not.

The thing is, the data isn't an important first step. The important thing is to have a good framework in which to store and read the data. A good bookstore application doesn't just have a mode for user shopping, it also has a special password-protected mode for administrators to add their own data. It's possible, in fact, to create a fantastic bookstore shopping application that has no data whatsoever. Data just involves the time of adding in records.

Worrying about data before having an application is like buying a truckload of books before you have scouted out the location for a bookstore and installed some shelving. Word processor applications create documents. Likewise, a bookstore application should have the capability to create titles to shop for. These new book titles can always be typed in by hand or imported from another format, and the database can be built up over time.

The Importance of Interface Elements

The real keys to Web applications are the user interface elements. The interface, as you recall, is anything and everything a user might see on the screen. And when it comes down to it, what else is there?

The interface elements you first design are likely to be very graphical. Even elements like menus that appear to be text and buttons are often created using some sort of graphics, giving them a specific look and feel. Whenever you can get away with using text, however, you should. Text is rendered much faster and takes up much less memory than graphics, which means the application downloads faster and doesn't hog the client's resources.

What you put in the interface is, of course, up to you. Speaking very generally, there are three types of elements you should include:

◆ Elements such as toolbar buttons or menu items that accept input and trigger various commands

◆ Elements such as status bars, readouts, or other icons that indicate a certain state of affairs

◆ Design elements that affect the look or feel of the application

BUILT-IN ELEMENTS

Most modern browsers have several interface widgets built in, as required by the HTML 4.0 specification. For example, if you want your application to have a check box, a text area, or a pull-down menu, you don't need to design it yourself from scratch. Netscape Navigator, Internet Explorer, and even text browsers like Lynx have these elements included in their engine, and enable you to access them easily.

Actually, dynamic HTML enables you to override a browser's standard interface elements. For example, you can make scroll bars that look like train tracks or check boxes that look as if they were drawn with a crayon.

There is a distinct advantage, however, to using the built-in components. They are fast, easy to program, and require no extra graphics to download.

STANDARD INTERFACE COMPONENTS

As dynamic HTML has become more widespread, many individual developers and companies have created standard interface components. *Components* are reusable elements that can easily be dropped into any application and controlled and communicated with. For example, several tab components out there enable you to create a dialog box with tabs at its top and various options and settings beneath each tab. All you need to do is specify the details.

Having big libraries of common components allows for *rapid application development*, or *RAD*. Instead of designing each interface item from scratch, you can spend your time designing the interface as a whole using these common elements.

Later on in this chapter, we discuss ways to turn elements into components using scriptlets, action sheets, and DHTML behaviors.

UNIQUE ELEMENTS

No matter how many tried-and-true components you string together, if you want your application to be unique it needs unique interface elements. Unique elements are especially necessary for design elements such as a background and styles that give your application the specific look you desire.

Dynamic HTML gives you much control over the coloring and border style of any section of the screen. Using styles instead of bulky graphics is a cheap and quick way to add lots of personal character to your application.

The Application Skeleton: The Markup

Once you know which elements your application requires, you must put them into a document. This is the perfect time for a *markup document* — a file that specifies the elements in the page and how they relate to one another. What better (or other) markup language to use than HTML?

And so you haven't divorced yourself from old-fashioned HTML at all. Rather, you use the base organizational capabilities of HTML to put together the framework for your application.

 More advanced applications might need to go beyond the standard tags of HTML and use their own custom tags. Having custom tags also makes it easier for developers to remember which elements do what. For example, a menu component could be created that enables you to encapsulate it as something like:

```
<MENU CHOICES="Open, Save, Print"></MENU>
```

The latest 5.0 versions of the major browsers purportedly support XML documents, embedded right within an HTML base.

A Sample: Creating Some Things

Suppose we want a very, very simple application. For example, suppose you want a message such as, "I'm not here now!" to appear on the screen when a user leaves his or her machine. Let's call the application "Out To Lunch."

The way it should work is as follows:

♦ A text area prompts a user for his or her message. By default it has the following message: "I'm out to lunch, go away!"

♦ When the user presses a button that says, "Go Out To Lunch," the button should change and say, "Come Back From Lunch." In addition, the out to lunch message should scroll in big red letters across the bottom of the screen, from right to left.

♦ When the user returns from lunch, he presses the Come Back From Lunch button. The button should now say Go Out To Lunch again. The scrolling out to lunch text should disappear.

Kind of a dumb application, but useful for illustrating how Web applications are built. The interface elements you need are:

♦ An input area

♦ A Go Out To Lunch / Come Back From Lunch button

♦ A bar separating the input section of the application from the scrolling section

♦ An area to scroll some text

The simple HTML document in Listing 8-1 has all of these elements, laid out the way we want them. If we were to put this application framework in a Web browser, it would look similar to Figure 8-1.

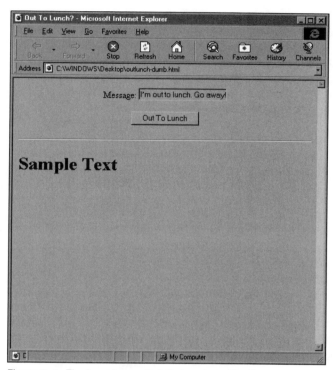

Figure 8-1: The bare-bones Out To Lunch application

Listing 8-1: Markup for the Out To Lunch application

```
<HTML>
<HEAD>
<TITLE>Out To Lunch?</TITLE>
</HEAD>
<BODY>
<CENTER>
<FORM>
Message: <INPUT ID="lunchmessage" VALUE="I'm out to lunch. Go
away!">
<P>
<INPUT TYPE="button" ID="lunchbutton" VALUE="Go Out To Lunch">
</FORM>
```

```
</CENTER>
<HR>
<!-- This is the area in which we will scroll our text. -->
<H1 ID=scroll> </H1>
</BODY>
</HTML>
```

The DOM Is Your Friend

Remember the Document Object Model? The main point of the DOM is to be able to programmatically access the objects in a Web page. The whole idea of putting these Web application elements into a markup document is to expose them to JavaScript so that they can be harnessed. And that's where the fun really begins.

Step 2: Harness Those Elements!

An interface by itself is hardly an application, just as a person's face is not a person. An interface is all flash, no substance. What makes applications really useful is their interactivity – their capability to accept some type of input from a user and use that input to cross digital oceans and move binary mountains.

The Out To Lunch example, by itself, is nothing more than a somewhat ugly Web page. See Figure 8-1? You get about as much interactivity out of the actual Web page as you do out of the figure. Fill in the form and nothing happens. Click the button, nada.

What you need to do is harness the elements, change them, use them, and abuse them. The way to do this is, of course, with client-side scripting. In this case, let's use our old favorite, JavaScript.

What to Do? What to Do?

What is JavaScript capable of, exactly? Using the DOM's tree it has access to any of the elements in a document, any of the attributes of that element, and any of the text that the element surrounds.

Combining everything, JavaScript gives you access to *objects*, their *properties*, special *methods*, *collections*, and *events*.

You can find a full reference of all valid JavaScript objects on Microsoft and Netscape's Web sites. Appendix B at the back of this book lists additional resources.

Objects

In the language of JavaScript, as well as in the language of the DOM, each element is known as an *object*. An HTML element and a JavaScript object are basically the same thing. For the sake of this discussion, however, we'll refer to an *element* as a markup tag within the HTML while an *object* is that same component as a JavaScript variable that can be passed around and manipulated.

In addition to every HTML tag, some of the major objects are:

◆ document – The root document that contains all tags.

◆ navigator – Returns information about the Web browser such as its brand and version.

◆ style – Returns access to the style properties of the current object. If the style was set as a global or linked style then it can be accessed using the currentStyle property. Note that only Internet Explorer currently supports this object.

◆ screen – Information about the current screen such as its available width, height, and pixel color depth.

Properties

The attributes of an HTML element are accessible to JavaScript as properties. You can read, add, or change any of these properties.

For example, a simple check box is not so simple. Naturally, a check box has its *value*. The value property is a simple state; either true if the box is checked, or false if the box is not checked. In addition, an HTML 4.0 check box has all of the following properties that can be changed or used:

◆ name – A descriptive name.

◆ checked – The check box is initially checked.

◆ disabled – The check box is not valid given the current state of affairs.

◆ size – The size of the check box.

◆ tabindex – The check box's position in tabbing order.

◆ accesskey – The key to access the check box.

◆ alt – A short description.

◆ usemap – A client-side image map should be used.

Note that Netscape Navigator 4.0 only supports `name` and `checked`, whereas Internet Explorer 4.0 supports all of the above except for `usemap` and `alt`.

In addition to these checkbox-specific properties, a check box also has all the style and position properties of *any* HTML element.

This means that at any point, JavaScript can be used to turn a check box on or off, disable or enable it, change its `alt` description, modify its tab index, and much more. JavaScript can also insert a fresh check box on the fly, or get rid of a check box that's already there.

That's a lot of properties. And that's just for a measly check box. Basically, every HTML element's attributes are legal JavaScript properties. In Internet Explorer 4.0, all the CSS styles are properties as well. Depending on the browser version being used, you may have up to 400 possible properties to play with.

With all of these possibilities, the big question every application has to ask itself is what to do, and when.

THE CONTENTS

The contents of an element — the text and markup that appears sandwiched between two markup tags — is yet another property that you can play around with.

In Internet Explorer 4.0, the `innerText` property is used to grab the actual text between any two container elements. For example, given the markup:

```
<P ID="cool">I am just so cool.</P>
```

The inner text, "I am just so cool" can be obtained using:

```
cool.innerText
```

The text can even be changed on the fly:

```
cool.innerText = "Change me, baby!";
```

Methods

JavaScript methods enable you to perform almost any operation that a user or the Web browser itself can perform. You can use methods to scroll a page, select a specific input item in a form, fill that in, remove elements from a page, add elements, and more.

Other special methods include:

♦ `alert(message)` — Creates a pop-up modal dialog box. The box contains the text in *message*. When the user hits OK, the box disappears.

♦ `writeln(message)` — Outputs text to the document at the current location, as if it had been part of the original HTML.

- `click()` — Simulates a mouse click on any element. Similar methods exist for most events. This method exists in Internet Explorer 4.0, but not Netscape Navigator 4.0.

- `createElement (tagname)` — An element is created and can then be added to any point in the document model. Similarly, an `insertAdjacentElement(sWhere,oElement)` method enables you to drop a new element immediately before or after any existing element. Also, a `createStyleSheet()` method enables you to create new style sheets for the current document. These methods are also only currently found in IE 4.0.

Collections

In addition to specific objects, JavaScript provides access to certain collections of objects including:

- `all` — Every object on the page. This object is specific to Internet Explorer 4.0.

- `anchors` — All the hypertext anchors within the current page.

- `links` — The links within the current page.

- `forms` — All the forms within the current page.

- `frames` — The frames that make up the current page.

- `images` — The images within the page.

- `applets` — All the Java applets on the page.

- `scripts` — The script blocks within the page. (Not supported in Navigator 4.0.)

- `styleSheets` — The style sheets used in the page. (Not supported in Navigator 4.0.)

- `embeds` — All the objects embedded into the current page.

- `plugins` — Any plug-ins that are in the page.

- `attributes` — All the attributes of the current object. (Not supported in Navigator 4.0.)

- `elements` — All the elements within the current object. (Not supported in Navigator 4.0.)

- `bookmarks` — All the bookmarks that have been saved. (Not supported in Navigator 4.0.)

- `cells` — All the cells of a table. (Not supported in Navigator 4.0.)

◆ `rows` — All the rows of a table. (Not supported in Navigator 4.0.)

◆ `children` — All the objects that descend from the current object. (Not supported in Navigator 4.0.)

The collections provide quick access to specific elements. They also make it easy to do things like make an entire element and its child elements disappear from the screen in a flash.

Events

Our good friend the check box can react to the following events:

◆ `onfocus` — The check box has the focus. That is, the user has tabbed to this element and is currently deciding whether to check the box or not.

◆ `onblur` — The check box has just lost the focus it had. It is blurred (out of focus).

◆ `onchange` — The value of the check box has just been changed.

In addition to these check box-specific events, the check box can handle document-wide events, such as a window being resized. In Internet Explorer 5.0 beta 2 there are even more advanced events to handle. The check box, for instance, can react when something has been dragged onto it or when the page has been printed.

Putting It All Together

Though there are millions of combinations of commands and methods and possibilities when it comes to harnessing elements, there are really only two major categories of things you want to do, when it comes down to it:

◆ Manipulating elements

◆ Letting elements react

MANIPULATING ELEMENTS

This seems obvious, as the reason to have elements around is to do stuff to them. In the world of the DOM, you can do nearly anything to any element on the fly that you could have done initially though creating a markup document.

You can get really complex. For example, you can have one element trigger another element when it is triggered, which then triggers a change in a third element. One click of a button can set your entire application abuzz with activity.

Typical things that are done to elements include moving them, deleting them, changing their appearance, changing their content, or animating them. When you build your own element item you must also think about the things that should be done to it in order to get it to behave the way you desire.

LETTING ELEMENTS REACT

Only a user can really tell an application how to behave. The application exists for the sake of the user, and it's the things the user does with her mouse, keyboard, or other input device that really matter.

As such, every object reacts to user events. Some objects have default reactions, and other objects tend to goodheartedly ignore things that are done to them. In either case, you can harness any element and tell it exactly what to do when it receives an event.

Because every object often has dozens of events associated with it, even the simplest application is faced with an ungodly number of choices as far as how to react. It's great knowing that you can have elements react to nearly anything. But what exactly is worth reacting to? And what should be done?

OR BOTH!

Many elements act as both input items and indicators. The most obvious example is a radio button or other type of sticky button. Radio buttons enable a user to select one, and only one, option from a list of choices. When a user clicks a radio button, whichever button had previously been pressed becomes unpressed. And the button that was just pressed remains inset, indicating that its item is the current selection — that its radio station is currently playing.

Oftentimes an indicator is also a button. For example, the Netscape Navigator or Internet Explorer logos in the upper-right corner of Web browsers animate when the browser is fetching information from the Internet. The logos can also be clicked to jump to Netscape or Microsoft's home page, respectively.

In the Out To Lunch application, the Go Out To Lunch button acts a sort of indicator as well as a button. It says "Go Out To Lunch" when you have not yet gone to lunch and "Come Back From Lunch" until you return. This is not, however, a very good interface design. The button might be mistaken for the current status. Ideally, some other indicator should exist, or the entire Go Out To Lunch text input area should slide away or disappear entirely when not in use.

The Feedback Loop

In practice, every application works as a give-and-take feedback loop. Some elements react to things that the user does and this triggers other elements to change. Flowcharts are special diagrams that can help design and draw connections between these feedback loops. Most applications require some user input in order to determine the next step to take.

Almost every application works this way. It waits for events and then reacts to those events. A word processor may seem like child's play — hit a letter and it appears on the screen. What you're actually doing, however, is a complicated ballet between your keyboard and your monitor. A word processor document on your computer screen is *not* the document itself. It is just another interface item that shows you the content of your document, which is actually stored somewhere in the computer's memory. Stated another way, the word processor page is nothing more than a text panel that serves to remind the user of the letters he or she already typed.

So if we take a behind-the-scenes look at a word processor, what's *really* going on? The user hits a key. The word processor then realizes a key was hit and stores this key. It then changes the document in memory by inserting a new letter at the current cursor position. Depending on a number of factors and settings, the entire contents of the document might shift over to make room for that letter, or that letter might automatically trigger a word wrap, bringing the current word to the next line. In any case, the page interface element on screen is updated to reflect the new status of the document. That's a really long way to go from keyboard hit to display.

Another important thing to note is that an event might not be a user event at all. Take a simple, passive application that paints an analog clock. Assume that all it does is show the time; you can't set the time or do anything else fancy, such as trigger alarms. The passage of each second is considered an event. And each of these events triggers the second hand interface element to be drawn at a slightly different angle, giving it the illusion of movement around a circle.

The user inadvertently performs other events. These include error conditions, such as running out of memory or trying to access a file that doesn't exist.

Making Out To Lunch React

Harnessing elements in an application means focusing on two aspects: how the elements behave, and how the user's behavior should affect the elements (events). Let's try to take care of both the behaviors and the events for the Out To Lunch application.

 The JavaScript throughout the rest of this chapter only works on Internet Explorer 4.0 or greater. There are ways of performing similar behaviors in Netscape Navigator 4.0, but these are a little more unseemly and don't really fall in line with the official DOM. Further differences between Navigator and IE, and how to combat those differences, are discussed in great detail in the third part of this book.

BEHAVIORS
Let's look closely at the Out To Lunch application. Which elements do we want to change?

◆ The Go Out To Lunch button should change to Come Back From Lunch and then back again.

◆ The sample message at the bottom of the screen should change to the input message when the user hits the Go Out To Lunch button.

- The sample message should also scroll when the user is out to lunch. Other times, the space should be empty.

The first item is easy enough. You can change the label of a button by setting its value property. You already have set the ID of the button to lunchbutton. This makes the button easy to grab.

You can initially change the button by using the code:

```
document.all.lunchbutton.value = "Come Back From Lunch";
```

And you can change the button back using:

```
document.all.lunchbutton.value = "Go Out To Lunch";
```

Cool!

Now what about the second behavior — changing the message at the bottom of the screen? This, too, is a snap using JavaScript. You've made an empty level one heading that has an ID of scroll. You can change the value of the heading's text by altering the innerText property. For example, to make the heading say "Some New Text" you would use:

```
document.all.scroll.innerText = "Some New Text";
```

In this case, you want to plunk down the message that the user typed in the input field. That message can be grabbed by snagging the input field's value property. Because the input field has an ID of lunchmessage, its full value is:

```
document.all.lunchmessage.value
```

So to change the heading at the bottom of the document into whatever has been typed in the input box you would use:

```
document.all.scroll.innerText = document.all.lunchmessage.value;
```

Now what about the third item — making the heading scroll across the screen? How could you do this? You could append a space before the message every few seconds and make the message grow and appear to move across the screen. But that would look kind of goofy. Wouldn't it be nicer to continuously and smoothly scroll the message, a few pixels at a time?

Um . . . it doesn't look like nice scrolling will be easy, given what you've got so far. Scrolling consists of precise positioning, and right now you're letting the Web browser position your objects wherever it pleases. Let's come back to scrolling, namely in the section titled "A Stylish Out To Lunch," a bit later in this chapter.

EVENTS

Now, in order to achieve the results you want, what events do you care about catching? There are only two events that we can think of:

◆ Hitting the Go Out To Lunch button. This sets the whole application into action.

◆ Hitting the Come Back From Lunch button. This stops the mechanism.

Because the Go Out To Lunch and Come Back From Lunch buttons are actually the same button – just with a different value – you can achieve everything you need to using the simple onClick event inserted into the button element.

Let's harness the click and call a JavaScript function called clicked(), which you will create:

```
<INPUT TYPE="button" ID="lunchbutton" VALUE="Go Out To Lunch"
onClick="clicked()">
```

The full code to handle all of the events and behaviors is shown in Listing 8-2.

The Out To Lunch application now has some basic behaviors going on with it. If you click the button you see the new message snap into place at the bottom of the screen, and the button's caption is Come Back From Lunch. If you click the button again the message will disappear and the button's caption changes back to Go Out To Lunch.

You're almost there. But something is missing.

Listing 8-2: The basic scripts for the Out To Lunch application

```
<HTML>
<HEAD>
<TITLE>Out To Lunch?</TITLE>
<SCRIPT LANGUAGE='JavaScript'>
 function clicked()
 {
    var lb = document.all.lunchbutton;
    if (lb.value == "Go Out To Lunch")
    {
      lb.value = "Come Back From Lunch";
      document.all.scroll.innerText =
document.all.lunchmessage.value;
      scroll(true);
    }
    else
    {
      lb.value = "Go Out To Lunch";
      document.all.scroll.innerText = "";
```

```
        scroll(false);
    }
 }
</SCRIPT>
</HEAD>
<BODY>
<CENTER>
<FORM>
Message: <INPUT ID="lunchmessage" VALUE="I'm out to lunch. Go
away!">
<P>
<INPUT TYPE="button" ID="lunchbutton" VALUE="Go Out To Lunch"
onClick="clicked()">
</FORM>
</CENTER>
<HR>
<!-- This is the area in which we will scroll our text. -->
<H1 ID=scroll> </H1>
</BODY>
</HTML>
```

This is starting to look like an application. But you've still got a few problems. For one, you wanted the text at the bottom of the screen to scroll. And you're not sure how to do this by adjusting the standard properties of your elements using JavaScript.

You also wanted the text at the bottom to be a large, red font. You could have used the <FONT> tag along with the color attribute, but perhaps there's a better way to go. . . .

Step 3: Positioning and Styling Elements

The key to adding the finishing touches to an application is styles. Cascading Style Sheets not only enable you to lay out the elements exactly where you initially want them to appear, but also enable full access to any positioning or style property. This means that elements can now zing around the screen, fly beneath and above each other, change font and color at the drop of a hat, and generally make your application come alive.

Initial Styles

Setting the initial style of an application is useful just for making it look good. By specifying the colors, sizes, fonts, and position of all the text on a page, you can work with very precise elements.

After all, a bottom status bar is a misnomer unless it is truly smack at the bottom of the application, beneath everything else. And if your application has a lot of buttons or toolbars you want to be sure that these are located in proper areas, giving your user enough space to perform other application tasks.

Hiding Elements

One of the best places to place your elements is off the screen entirely. No, we're not pulling your leg. Oftentimes, you want interface elements that only appear at certain times. For example, you might have an entire pop-up menu that should only pop up when the right mouse button is clicked. Or you might have a fancy dialog box that should only appear when there's been an error. It's often a good idea to create any of these elements up front and drop them in your document, but then hide them offscreen until they are needed.

Alternatively, or additionally, elements can be hidden by changing their visibility. The only problem with merely making an element invisible is that it still takes up space on the screen, which is sometimes not desired.

On Internet Explorer 4.0, visibility can be altered using:

```
theelement.style.visibility = "hidden";
```

Using Styles to Talk to Older Browsers

Yet another reason to hide things is to handle browsers that don't support style sheets. For example, you could make a "hidden" class that essentially colors text the same color as the background:

```
<STYLE TYPE='text/css'>
.hidden {
  display: none;
  color: white;
}
</STYLE>
```

You could then use this hidden class of text to print out instructions or apologies for those users unfortunate enough to be using older browsers:

```
<P CLASS=hidden>This page needs style sheets to look good!</P>
```

You might be wondering what the value is in hiding items at all. Why not just create these items at the time they're needed, and dispose of them when they're not useful anymore? Using the DOM, after all, it *is* possible to add and remove elements from the document at any point in time.

On-the-fly additions and deletions, however, are not very efficient. Instead of taking a few moments to generate a new pop-up menu while the user is in the thick of things, it usually makes more sense to spend the time while the application is booting up and crunching out the necessary elements. This way, as soon as the user hits the right mouse button, the pop-up menu snaps into place. Furthermore, 4.0 browsers don't support DOM additions and deletions yet.

A Stylish Out To Lunch

You can now go through your Out To Lunch applications using styles to achieve the results you originally wanted. First off, you can set the heading at the bottom of the page — the one with the ID of `scroll` — completely offscreen. Pick an outrageous value and push it a negative 5,000 units off where it would normally reside on the left of the page:

```
<STYLE TYPE='text/css'>
  #scroll {
     position: relative;
     left: -5000;
     color: red;
  }
</STYLE>
```

You can now construct a `scroll()` function that accepts a parameter indicating whether scrolling should be on — either `true` or `false`. Let's assume you want the scrolling to start from the right side of the page and then inch its way across to the left side. Once the left side is reached, you want to snap the text back to the right and continue this until the user returns from lunch.

To turn scrolling on, the first thing you would do is set the heading all the way to the right side of the page. In fact, set it so far over that it's still hidden, right past the Web browser's right border. But it doesn't stay there for long. To move it, just set the scroll text style's `pixelLeft` property to the document body's `offsetWidth`:

```
document.all.scroll.style.pixelLeft = document.body.offsetWidth;
```

You can then call the `scroll()` function. There are four possible states you must handle:

 ◆ **Turn scrolling on.** What you should do is set the scroll text to the right of the page using the current `offsetWidth`. Then call `scroll(true)`.

- ◆ **Scrolling has been turned on.** Whenever `scroll(true)` is called it adjusts the scrolling text ten pixels to the left. When the text reaches the left side of the screen (its `pixelLeft` value is 0), snap the text back to the right of the page using the `offsetWidth`. Then set a timer and tell the timer to call the `scroll(true)` function again after 50 milliseconds has elapsed. This creates a nice, smooth scroll.

- ◆ **Turn scrolling off.** To do this, just set the text back at its offscreen position of -5000 and get the heck out.

- ◆ **Scrolling has just been turned off.** In this case, do a check to see if the text is located at -5000. If so, you know that scrolling has been turned off and you should just quit. You should perform this extra check during the `scroll` function just in case the timer calls the `scroll(true)` function a few moments after you've turned scrolling off.

Listing 8-3 puts it all together then. When the application is loaded into a Web browser it works just how you envisioned it. Type in some text, hit the Go Out To Lunch button and — voila! — your message scrolls beautifully across the bottom in a lovely red font. See Figure 8-2 for an example, though naturally you don't get the full effect, being that the text is a different shade of gray and is unmoving.

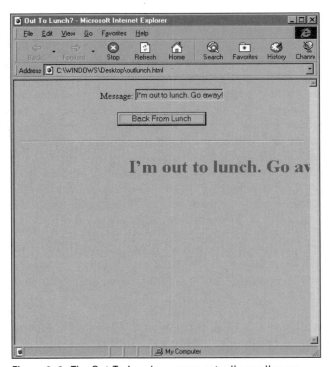

Figure 8-2: The Out To Lunch message actually scrolls now

Listing 8-3: The full Out To Lunch application, using styles

```
<HTML>
<HEAD>
<TITLE>Out To Lunch?</TITLE>
<STYLE TYPE='text/css'>
  #scroll {
    position: relative;
    left: -5000;
    color: red;
  }
</STYLE>
<SCRIPT LANGUAGE='JavaScript'>
 function scroll(on) {

   var sc = document.all.scroll;
   if (-5000==sc.style.pixelLeft) {
     return;
   } else if (on == false) {
     sc.style.pixelLeft = -5000;
   } else {
     sc.style.pixelLeft -= 10;
     if (sc.style.pixelLeft<=0) {
        sc.style.pixelLeft = document.body.offsetWidth;
     }
     setTimeout("scroll(true)",50);
   }
 }

 function clicked() {
    var lb = document.all.lunchbutton;
    if (lb.value == "Go Out To Lunch") {
      lb.value = "Come Back From Lunch";
      document.all.scroll.style.pixelLeft = document.body.offsetWidth;
      document.all.scroll.innerText = document.all.lunchmessage.value;
      scroll(true);
    } else {
      lb.value = "Go Out To Lunch";
      scroll(false);
    }
 }
</SCRIPT>
</HEAD>
<BODY>
<CENTER>
```

```
<FORM ID="lunchform">
Message: <INPUT ID="lunchmessage" VALUE="I'm out to lunch. Go away!">
<P>
<INPUT TYPE="button" ID="lunchbutton" VALUE="Go Out To Lunch"
onClick="clicked()">
</FORM>
</CENTER>
<HR>
<!-- This is the area in which we will scroll our text. -->
<H1 ID=scroll>Sample Text</H1>
</BODY>
</HTML>
```

Step 4: Keeping State

As your application goes through its paces, it's important for it to be able to keep track of various pieces of information. Any variables that must be used throughout many functions can be stored as global JavaScript variables. For example, in the following block:

```
<SCRIPT LANGUAGE="JavaScript">
var global = 25;
function a() {
  global = 50;
}
function b() {
  writeln(global);
}
</SCRIPT>
```

If you call function b(), at first it prints out 25. But if you call function a() before calling b(), then the value of global is 50.

Global variables don't always save the day, however. What about when the browser is closed or a new Web page is accessed? Any JavaScript variables are gone with the wind.

For example, once you type your name into a field, you should never have to type it in again. Or suppose your application has lots of options, enabling you to custom-craft your application environment. Once you've set the preferences exactly the way you like, you should never have to set them again. It would be a pain in the neck if your settings were lost every time you closed the application.

Traditional applications have no problem keeping state. They just write your preferences to your hard disk or to a special database called the Windows registry or resource fork and simply load up the preferences each time you restart the application. Web applications, though, generally cannot access the hard drive or registry due to security constraints.

So are Web applications stateless? Hardly. There's a special technique that provides a bit of client-side persistence called *cookies*. Think of them as special hidden cookie jars, kept on the client, in which the client or even the server can drop a bit of important information. These cookies can then be retrieved by both the client and the server any time the same application is run again.

Cookies are used for all sorts of applications. Whenever you go to a Web site and it remembers your name or password, it is probably using cookies. More importantly, if you buy some items at an online store and it remembers what you have in your shopping cart even as you browse from page to page, and even from session to session, this is likely being done with cookies.

Why Cookies Work

Suppose a portal site visited by millions of different users wants to keep track of each user's preferences—the stocks they want quotes for, the type of news items they want to read, the cities they want weather forecasts for. The server needs to know these preferences to assemble a good-looking Web page.

Theoretically the portal could have the user log in each time he or she visits. This is a bit of pain, though, and doesn't provide the "quick-surf" feel that most portals desire.

Even if you got past the log in problem, you'd need a place to store preference information. Preferences could be saved right on the server, but that would create an enormous database that would take lots of time and computing power to search and deliver up.

How much sleeker and faster it is to keep preferences on the machine that set them: the client. This also makes the preferences a snap to change, and nothing needs to be sent or written to the server.

The specifics of how to set and read cookies on the client and server can be found in Chapter 13, "User-Configurable Interfaces."

Passing Cookies Between Pages

If you want to share information between two separate Web pages or applications, there are three common techniques to choose from. Two involve cookies, and one involves frames:

- ◆ If Application A sets a cookie, you can call Application B to replace the Application A document and the cookie remains intact. You can change the contents of a Web page on the fly like this using the `document.location` object:

```
document.location.href = "applicationB.html";
```

◆ If only two applications need to communicate with each other, you can have Application A assign the cookie explicitly to Application B's domain. Instead of setting the path to "/", set it to the location of Application B:

```
document.cookie = 'COOLNAME=George Washington; path=
"applicationB.html"; expires=Monday, 31-Dec-01 11:11:11 GMT'
```

Application B is now able to read the cookie as usual.

◆ Another way of transferring information between two separate Web pages doesn't involve cookies at all. Instead, you must create a frameset that holds both Application A and Application B. You can then keep the global JavaScript variables in the top frameset itself. This makes it easy to share the variable. You can even load new applications into the frames and the variables will continue to hold their values. For example:

```
<HTML>
<SCRIPT LANGUAGE="JavaScript">
<!--
var GlobalVar;
// -->
</SCRIPT>
<FRAMESET COLS="50%,50%">
<FRAME NAME="top" SRC="applicationA.htm">
<FRAME NAME="bottom" SRC="applicationB.htm">
</FRAMESET>
</HTML>
```

The variable could then be set or read from either application using:

```
document.top.GlobalVar
```

Step 5: Communicate

Although the bulk of a Web application should reside on the client, the server cannot be forgotten. After all, we're living in an internetworked world and might as well take advantage of it. Other than delivering the initial application, the server is used for all sorts of things:

◆ Retrieving data from a huge database. For example, if you want to search a huge bookstore it wouldn't make sense to put the entire bookstore's inventory on the client computer. Instead, the user could issue search parameters and then relevant titles could be sent along.

◆ Storing important data. When the user saves a document that he created in your application, you may very well want to save it on a server. He can then load up the document directly from the server at any later point.

◆ Sending data in that the creator of the application must know about. For example, you might input your shipping address. This could then be sent, once, to the server. If you then ordered a product, the server would know what address to send the order to.

◆ Sending in information that requires secure validation, such as credit card numbers or passwords.

◆ Storing any major information that doesn't fit in cookies.

The tricky part of all this data transfer is that we don't want to squash our application and open up a new Web page every time the server communicates with the client. In Chapter 6, "Client-Side Scripting: Verbs," you saw how every HTTP server request issues forth a response that, in essence, loads a new Web page. This is bad! This tosses away all the variables, scripts, and markup that you have previously processed. In some cases, tons of information is lost and much time is needed to reconstruct the application's state.

Luckily, there are a few techniques that enable the client to communicate with the server and avoid the reloading of a new Web page. One technique involves a messy hack, and the other involves a technology that isn't really supported yet. Welcome to life on the bleeding edge. . . .

Transmitting Cookies Between Frames

A tricky way of transmitting cookies is done by creating an invisible frame. A document can be created that has two frames — a main, large area of the screen and then a tiny, nearly invisible 1-pixel sliver at the bottom:

```
<FRAMESET="*,1">
  <FRAME NAME="main" SRC="main.html">
  <FRAME NAME="sliver" SRC="cookieset.html">
</FRAMESET>
```

The Web application interface with all its bells and whistles can appear in the big frame. The little frame is only to be used as a sort of way station for cookies.

SENDING DATA TO THE SERVER

Cookies can be sent to the server by setting them in the sliver frame and then making a request for the same page. For example, you could set a cookie with the name "COOLNAME" and the value "George Washington":

```
document.cookie = 'COOLNAME=George Washington; path=cookieset.html;
expires=Monday, 31-Dec-01 11:11:11 GMT'
```

The sliver frame can then issue a standard HTTP request for the cookieset.html page. This automatically sends along the cookies.

The server must have a CGI script, servlet, or API smart enough to read in these cookie values and interpret them. It can then send back its response.

GETTING DATA FROM THE SERVER

If the server needs to communicate back, it can send back a new cookie using the response packet. Or it could just send back an empty response packet to close the connection. In either case, the trick here is not to send the response to the entire Web page, but to target the response to the sliver frame.

Targeting is done using the optional HTTP header called Window-Target. Here's an example of the output the server (via a CGI script or server module) might send back:

```
Content-type: text/html
Set-Cookie: NAME=Example; path=/; EXPIRES=Monday, 31-Dec-01 11:11:11
GMT
Window-Target: sliver
```

The Next Generation Way: HTTP 204

A much more elegant way of dealing with data transfer is a little-known HTTP response code known as 204 No Content, or the *no-op* response. This response, if handled correctly, does not refresh the document view.

Recall that the usual response to a request is 200 OK. The 200 OK response is equivalent to the Web server telling the client, "Here's the response with the new Web page for you to display." The 204 No Content response, on the other hand, enables the server to say, "I got what you sent. Thanks much. Carry on doing what you were doing, good sir."

This enables you to submit data using a form or JavaScript without losing the client's state. This means your Web application can, unblinkingly, talk to the server and vice versa.

If there's some sort of error, the server does not send back 204; it sends back 404 Not Found, or some other error response. These error responses cause the application to refresh its display and all the state to be lost. But this is probably an okay behavior. After all, there's an error!

Very cool stuff, isn't it?

The good news is that the current crop of 4.0 level browsers support the 204 No Content response. This means your client application can send as much information as it wants to the server.

The bad news is that none of the current browsers support cookies when set using the 204 No Content response, even though it is in the official HTTP 1.1 specification. This makes it impossible for the server to send any information back to the client without resetting the state. However, there is some buzz claiming that when Netscape Navigator 5.0 comes out, it might support the full 204 response correctly, including cookies, which would finally enable Web applications to have full-fledged data transfer.

HTTP 204 is discussed in length in Chapter 11, "The Hidden Feedback Form."

Breaking the Application into Components

You did it! You created a complete dynamic HTML application. You've used nouns, verbs, adjectives, and adverbs to create a full-fledged paragraph.

But let's back up a step. After all, a paragraph is composed of sentences. The sentences in the Out To Lunch application might be something like:

◆ Handling a button press

◆ Changing the button's label on the fly

◆ Changing the contents of a heading

◆ Scrolling text across the screen

Most of these sentences are pretty simple and routine. Button presses, changing labels, and changing text is handled by one simple line of JavaScript. The most complex behavior is scrolling text across the screen.

The scrolling routine took a bit of work to implement. What if you wanted to use the same behavior on *all* your Web pages? Would you need to cut and paste the same JavaScript throughout your entire site? Wouldn't it be a waste of space? Wouldn't it be a pain setting the right IDs and other variables? What if other developers wanted to use your scrolling script sentence? Wouldn't it be a pain for them to reconstruct all the script? Wouldn't it be nice if you could separate the scrolling script into a simple component that you and others could just drop into your pages with one simple command?

Components are RAD

The capability to separate dynamic HTML sentences into components is clearly very desirable. Chapter 3, "Principles and Lessons Learned," discussed rapid application development (RAD) and the many advantages of reusability and encapsulation:

◆ Components save space. Lots of space, in some cases. Components enable resources to be *centralized*. Most applications are built up with components that are useful in other applications, too. Imagine a special animating dialog box. Or a dynamic HTML form that accepts credit card numbers and does some basic validation. Or a nifty expand-and-contract tree menu. Or a navigation bar with cool pop-up 3D buttons. These are all components that could be found on dozens, if not all of the pages on a site. Surely it's a waste to hand-copy the markup, scripts, and styles – the sentences – to every page in which they're needed.

♦ Easier maintenance. If one of your components has a bug, or you want to add a new feature, just change one file. The results are automatically inserted into any pages that use the component.

♦ Better performance. Most components are cached on the client's computer, the way Web page images are. This means that a component does not need to be reloaded within the same application's Web pages or for commonly used applications.

♦ Easier development. Suppose a developer wanted to copy a useful behavior that had not been made into a component. The poor developer would need to find the original source markup and figure out which code and styles are relevant. The code would then need to be inserted into the new page and hooked up using any special events. Finally, everything would have to be tested to be sure variable names aren't overlapping, events aren't interrupting each other, and so on. Even if the JavaScript and styles are in separate *js* and *css* files, moving code between pages requires lots of testing and finessing.

With components, a developer only needs to drop the object into her page as an object and then set a few parameters to make it work. No further coding is necessary.

Just as style sheets enable developers to create one template that cascades throughout hundreds of pages, dynamic HTML *reusable components* enable various behaviors and graphic elements to be stored in one place and used anywhere.

Components make for a much more efficient way of creating a Web application. Components enable artsy designers to create style sheets for the application and geeky programmers to create separate reusable script components. HTML wizards can then create the skeleton markup of the app, putting the design and programming elements together quite easily.

Three new technologies enable for script components:

♦ Scriptlets

♦ Action sheets

♦ DHTML behaviors

Each of these technologies, however, is proprietary or still in beta form. As such we discuss them briefly, just to whet your palate.

Scriptlets

Scriptlets are supported by Internet Explorer 4.0. Navigator does not support them. Scriptlets are essentially special files that contain JavaScript routines that can easily be dropped anywhere in a document.

 On Windows, scriptlet components can be used not only in Internet Explorer but also within any Win32 application that supports COM objects. Most Windows applications written in Visual Basic or MFC have this support built-in.

USING FROM HTML

You can pop a scriptlet into an HTML page using the `<OBJECT>` tag and setting the DATA attribute to the name of the scriptlet.

You can optionally drop some text between the `<OBJECT>` and `</OBJECT>` tags which appears in browsers that don't support scriptlets.

For example:

```
<OBJECT DATA="scroll.html" TYPE="text/x-scriptlet" WIDTH=300
HEIGHT=100>
   This browser does not support scriptlets!
</OBJECT>
```

WRITING A SCRIPTLET

Scriptlets are stored as standard HTML files. They look like a standard collection of styles and scripts, with a few special additions.

Above all else, the scriptlet files contain the code and styles of the behavior you wish to encapsulate as a component. For example, if you were to make a scriptlet that scrolled text across the screen you would drop all the styles and relevant JavaScript functions into an empty HTML file.

A scriptlet, like any JavaScript object, has *public properties* and *public methods* that can be read or set. The fact that they are public means that you can access or call them from your application's own JavaScript.

You can make any scriptlet variable a public property and you can make any function a public method. In general, though, you only want to publicize the stuff you think the outside world definitely needs to alter in order to change the behavior of your scriptlet.

For example, Listing 8-4 has a basic constructor that sets up two public properties (`text` and `from`) and one method (`start()`).

Listing 8-4: A sample scriptlet

```
<HTML ID=html>
<HEAD>
<TITLE>Scroll Scriptlet</TITLE>
<SCRIPT LANGUAGE="JavaScript">
var public_description = new public_description_nt;
function public_description_nt()
{
    this.put_text = put_text;
    this.get_text = get_text;
    this.get_from = get_from;
    this.put_from = put_from;
    this.start = _start;
}
```

The scriptlet could then go on with the actual `start()` function, as well as functions to get and put the value of the public variables.

Scriptlets are being all but phased out to make way for Microsoft's new encapsulation technology — DHTML behaviors.

Action Sheets

Netscape has proposed a standard for components known as Cascading Action Sheets—in other words, style sheets that have actions built in. Currently Netscape browsers do not support action sheets, although Netscape Navigator 5.0 very well might.

An action sheet can be inserted into the heading area of an HTML or XML document using the `<LINK>` tag:

```
<LINK REL="ActionSheet" TYPE="text/cas" HREF="hover.act">
```

The action sheet idea enables you to create actions using a format similar to styles. The first part of the action sheet is the *selector*—any class, ID, or element tag. The selector can have a *domain,* enabling you to apply styles only to specific HTML or XML tags or attributes. The selector is followed by a *declaration* within curly brackets. This declaration contains an *action domain* (the event to trigger the action) and an *action definition* (the script to be performed).

This sounds a whole lot more complicated than it is. If you are already familiar with CSS, then just think of Cascading Action Sheets as a combination of CSS selectors and client-side scripts within the same sheet. For example, you could make the text within any hyperlink turn yellow when the mouse touches it by using:

```
A *[HREF] {onMouseOver: "this.style.fontColor = 'yellow'";}
```

You can find the W3 action sheets note at:
`http://www.w3.org/TR/NOTE-AS.`

DHTML Behaviors

Dynamic HTML behaviors is a technology created by Microsoft that currently works in the Internet Explorer 5.0 browser. Behaviors combine the best ideas of action sheets and scriptlets to provide components that are easy to develop, easy to share, and easy to use.

In a nut shell, behaviors treat scripts as a type of style. These scripts can then be specifically applied to any element, class, or ID that CSS styles can be applied to.

The format for behaviors written about here is current as of Internet Explorer 5.0 beta 2. There should not be any major changes, but it is possible that certain methods and methodologies will change. Consult the Microsoft Web site for the latest references.

USING FROM HTML Behaviors are dropped into an HTML document as a special type of style that has the `url` property. The `url` points to a separate behavior `htc` file:

```
<STYLE>
.scroll { behavior: url(scroll.htc); }
</STYLE>
```

The attributes for a behavior are set right in the tag using the behavior. For example, to make an area scroll just create a division that is in the `scroll` class:

```
<DIV class = scroll direction = "left" speed = 20>Scroll Me!</DIV>
```

Like any style, the style can also be created as a linked style sheet or as an inline style:

```
<DIV style = "behavior: url(scroll.hrc)" direction = "left" speed =
20></DIV>
```

Even better, behaviors can even be customized to a custom XML tag. For example, the scroll behavior could be programmed to work with a new <SCROLLME> tag. Because everything about a behavior is entirely HTML based, graphic designers who shudder at the thought of using or even seeing any JavaScript can still happily drop complex behaviors into their pages by using these specially created tags:

```
<MYDOC:SCROLLME direction = "left" speed = 20>
Scroll Me!
</MYDOC:SCROLLME>
```

USING FROM JAVASCRIPT   A behavior can also be loaded on the fly and applied to any element. Behavior becomes just another style property.

For example, to begin scrolling any of the elements in the "scrollable" class:

```
scrollable.style.behavior = "url(scrollme.htc)";
```

CREATING DHTML BEHAVIORS

A behavior is stored as an HTML component file, with the .htc suffix. The htc file is written in XML, which means you have to be careful to make sure the file is valid XML.

To create a behavior, just paste the JavaScript or VBScript code and place it in a separate file. You then need to add the public properties, event catchers, and other methods that can be set or called from any tag that implements the behavior's style.

For instance, to add a property named direction to your behavior you would use:

```
<PROPERTY NAME="direction" />
```

The behavior script could then use the data within the direction variable to achieve various results.

Methods are created similarly. For instance, if you wanted to create a method called stop() you could use:

```
<METHOD NAME="stop" />
```

You don't need to define all the functions in your DHTML behavior file as public methods, only the ones that reference window (the browser) or ones that you want the application developer to be able to call via JavaScript.

Any event from the application can be captured by the behavior and used to trigger a piece of script. Catch events using the XML tag <ATTACH EVENT=theevent HANDLER=thehandler />. Your behavior then captures theevent and runs a function named thehandler.

In addition to the standard JavaScript events, DHTML behaviors can be smart enough to fire off their own custom-made events. These events can then be caught by the object that uses the behavior.

Choosing the Best Method

If you want to develop dynamic HTML components today, which method should you use? Scriptlets have basically been superceded by DHTML behaviors. Action sheets are currently only a dream, a specification. Behaviors support many features that action sheets do not, such as a complete event model, the capability be used in any tag, public methods and properties, and better extensibility. But behaviors are a Microsoft-only technology.

So while we'll have to wait and see what component technologies Netscape Navigator 5.0 supports, it's fair to say that DHTML behaviors — or something very similar — will be the way components will eventually be used. Hopefully, Netscape and Microsoft will agree on a standard that will make everyone happy.

For now, however, separating the JavaScript from a document into .js files is a relatively simple way to author, maintain, and pass around the program that harnesses the objects and styles that make your application zoom.

Part III of this book shows you ways to create dynamic HTML components using separate js files that work in all 4.0 browsers.

Rethinking the Interface

By keeping the style, scripting code, and document objects separate, it is now thousands of times easier to achieve our interface objectives:

- ◆ Uncluttered interfaces with precise elements that perform specific functions. With visibility and positioning, the important aspects of an interface can be prominent when needed and can be hidden away when not really part of the current context. If you are in the middle of spell-checking a document, you only care about the spelling and grammar commands. Special menus can be redrawn and dialog boxes reconfigured to account for this. When you go back into editing mode, the entire menu format likely changes. This is complex to design, but ends up making the user's experience much, much easier. Dynamic HTML makes all this complexity of interface design possible and even somewhat systematic to manage.

- ◆ An interface that focuses on and works with the user. Interface items can be linked to each other so that the entire look and feel of an application can change depending on choices a user makes. The capability to easily animate interface elements is an additional perk. Having a special menu slide in or zoom up is not just a pretty special effect — it reminds the user that the menu is there and needs to be clicked.

◆ An interface that the user can customize to his wiles. Dynamic HTML components make it easy to change the entire color scheme of an application. Or even to drag a toolbar from the top of the screen and place it at the bottom.

◆ More constraints can be implemented. Buttons that aren't currently valid can be grayed out. And all sorts of other safety nets can be implemented. After all, with DHTML, you thoroughly control the interface. The interface can nudge the user toward key tasks by using various animations, style changes, sounds, or other subtle pointers. Remember – the goal here is to make the user forget that the interface exists.

◆ Navigation made easy. Traditional Web sites are all about navigation between various pages. Web applications need to help the user navigate between functions. This can be done using special windows, frames, dialog boxes, or any other metaphor that can be thought up. Dynamic HTML makes it possible.

◆ Designed for error. Context-sensitive dialog boxes can clearly explain mistakes. More serious errors can be caught and handled elegantly.

◆ Help the user out. Better context-sensitive help systems can be implemented, guiding the user through every step of the application.

Another key point to remember is that interface design works hand in hand with software design. The model for building dynamic HTML applications has to do with the objects that are on the screen. As such, the way an application looks is inextricably tied to the way an application runs. Dynamic HTML forces you to design and redesign intuitive interfaces. Once you achieve an interface that works, you have an application that works. It's just a matter of stringing things together.

Summary

◆ Web applications take the interface concepts of traditional applications and package them as HTML for easy delivery.

◆ To build a Web application you should start with the interface elements.

◆ These elements can then be harnessed. Your JavaScript commands should either do various things to the interface elements, or should be triggered by events that happen to the interface elements.

◆ CSS can then be used to add precision and style to the interface elements in your application. Exact positioning is also important for achieving a final look.

◆ Different variables can be kept persistent by dropping them into cookies. This enables various applications to communicate with each other.

◆ Communication with the server is possible by using forms or cookies to send data down the line. Data can be sent up from the server to your application using cookies as well. There are special ways to ensure that your application's screen does not refresh when the server sends new data or lets you know that it received the data that you sent.

◆ Components are an important step in encapsulating the dynamic HTML behavior scripts, enabling them to be used by millions of developers across millions of different pages. Components are also much easier for nonprogrammers to work with, often acting just like another HTML tag.

◆ For the first time in history, important interface design imperatives can be applied to the Web.

At last we have finished our tour of nouns, verbs, adjectives, adverbs, sentences, and paragraphs. We have a full-fledged language on our hands. Now let's start talking!

Once you've got great sentences and paragraphs, you can assemble them to craft anything at all—opinionated essays, entertaining stories, or essential news. Of course, crafting a good story from a mishmash of paragraphs is an art form in itself, fraught with its own rules and grammar.

So let's move on to Part III, where we'll use our dynamic language of nouns, verbs, and adjectives to create full-featured applications that work today across all major browsers.

Part III

Examples of Good HCI with Dynamic HTML

IN THIS PART:

Here is where we take the gloves off, bend the browsers' conflicting object models to our will, and work around the widely disparate levels of support for DHTML's component technologies. Using techniques common to object-oriented programming and modular program design, we create a cross-browser and cross-platform wrapper object Application Program Interface. With this API, we construct a small sample application and then add to it using modular components that provide interface functionality or help you debug your application across browser platforms. In the end, you'll have a fully functional example of a cross-platform application, and a working knowledge of the cross-browser API.

Chapter 9

Implementing Effective User Interfaces with DHTML

IN THIS CHAPTER

- ◆ What makes a complete dynamic HTML application

- ◆ Why can't you just learn DHTML itself?

- ◆ How to tackle incompatibilities using abstraction

- ◆ Where to apply branching, design strategies, modularity

- ◆ How to use and extend the `xplatform_wrapper` library

NOW THAT WE'VE GIVEN YOU some background on interface theory and the technologies that make up dynamic HTML, it's time to lay the groundwork for our sample application. In this chapter, we cover the keys to any successful dynamic HTML application and the ways you can achieve independence from cross-browser and cross-platform incompatibilities. Finally, we talk about the object wrapper library upon which we build our sample application, why it's a good idea, and how it can be extended to work around bugs we haven't yet encountered.

Three Key (and Complementary) Perspectives

Any systematic approach to the development of dynamic HTML applications must consider three complementary perspectives throughout the entire life cycle of the application. These approaches involve interface design, rapid application development, and the usability of your application. The approach outlined below is designed to enable everyone involved in the design and planning, development, and ongoing maintenance of the application to contribute to the best of their ability. Rather than focusing on the code, the interface, the end user, or the project management aspects of building and maintaining your application to the detriment of the others, you should take all of these perspectives into account. In doing so, you end up with the best of all worlds.

Interface Design and Architecture

The first of these perspectives concentrates on the context in which your application's functionality is exposed to the user. This context must be understood both in terms of each interface element's relationship to the functionality it exposes, and in terms of the relationship between the interface as a whole and the overarching system context in which it is used.

We've already discussed the importance of proper interface design techniques from the standpoints of iconography, menu systems, and functional decomposition; now let's take a more holistic view. We start with the internal consistency of the interface itself, then move on to the manner in which the interface relates to the external system environment. Finally, we recapitulate some of the ways that both may be achieved.

ACHIEVING INTERNAL INTERFACE DESIGN CONSISTENCY

A badly designed interface stands out like a sore thumb. Its elements aren't placed properly, don't look the same, and don't reflect any guiding principles. If the interface looks ugly on its face, it may suggest that its designers didn't communicate well or perhaps followed a set of inconsistent guidelines.

A properly designed interface, on the other hand, tends to feel intuitive, may be easily learned where intuition fails, and expresses intelligent and consistent relationships between similar types of elements used to provide similar functionality. If an interface *seems* inconsistently put together, it probably was.

PROVIDING INTERFACE CONSISTENCY WITHIN
THE LARGER CONTEXT

Your interface may be in perfect harmony with itself, but if it doesn't leverage existing interface conventions on the system where it is used, you cause the user no end of frustration as they switch from your application to others on the same system.

Most systems have well-documented standards for user interface consistency. Find them, follow them if possible, and ensure that your users don't have to switch context every time they switch applications. This is especially challenging with dynamic HTML, because a fundamental assumption is that the end product may (and very likely will) be used cross-platform. In this case, simply try to make sure that your choices don't go against the grain of any particular system's conventions.

USING PROPER ICONOGRAPHY, TEXT LABELS,
AND TASK DECOMPOSITION

As discussed in detail in the first section of the book, iconography and its text-based counterpart are extremely important to an interface's clarity and ease of use. Using appropriate icons but poorly worded menus or labels can cause confusion.

Additionally, tasks must be broken down on natural boundaries. For example, providing one interface option that enables the user to name the document, then another option to actually save the document under that name is bound to be irritating and confusing. Try to observe users in the field, and find out how they most often combine tasks. Provide aggregate tasks that enable the user to perform all of these things at once.

By the same token, grouping too many tasks together under one interface element, or grouping unrelated tasks on the same menu will certainly upset your users. Appropriate task decomposition should reflect the user's expectations, not the programmer's. Test your assumptions whenever possible, and retest your solutions whenever you change any part of the interface.

Rapid Application Development and Prototyping

Rapid application development, or *RAD,* as it is known, is a popular software development strategy in these fast-paced times. Whereas traditional software project methodologies were known for their slow-paced, thorough, and monolithic approach with a final release of the product after years of development, RAD reflects the modular nature of modern software. By developing and releasing parts of an application or application suite as they become ready, the user (or client) is exposed to a series of opportunities for feedback and iterative development.

MANAGING THE DEVELOPMENT OF YOUR APPLICATION

It's no secret that any large project involving more than a few programmers, designers, or usability experts must also have a project manager, a development cycle, and a delivery schedule. The modular approach, however, along with an iterative release cycle, can both complicate and simplify the process. Things are complicated because the individual components must all go through what amounts to a miniature development cycle. However, depending on the project and the initial complexity of the components themselves, the size of the final application, and so forth, the development of individual components may be much easier than trying to develop an integrated whole.

Depending on your design and architecture, forcing the various pieces to be ready for client exposure can have a radical effect on the way that they are built. Programmers and interface specialists must work together on every phase of the project so individual screens may be readied for release. The entire team must be kept closely in the loop to ensure that feedback centering not only on the look and feel of the application's interface, but also affecting its underlying functionality is dealt with in the appropriate manner.

A team working together in this manner is bound to have a better sense of one another's contributions and be more willing to respond to issues that lie outside their immediate area of expertise. This can have enormous impact on a project manager's ability to manage his or her teams, especially in those environments where hierarchies, rather than flat organizational structures, are the rule.

Empowering your team to work together is one of the goals of rapid application development, but bridging the cultures can be a challenge.

USING RAPID APPLICATION DEVELOPMENT METHODOLOGIES

By now you're probably sick of reading the word *modular* every couple of paragraphs, but it is one of the keys to successful RAD projects. Ensuring that the design of every component in your system relies as little as possible on the other components makes it much easier to release them separately for feedback and iterative development.

The system architect must also be sure to always keep in mind the final integration of the system's components, so the final product is internally consistent and works well as a whole. There are entire books devoted to the study of RAD methodologies; some geared toward the project manager, others toward members of the team. Read them and abide by their advice.

PROTOTYPING YOUR WAY TO A BETTER APPLICATION

A common complaint found on both sides of software development boils down to communication. The client sets requirements that are then interpreted by the project manager and sent along to the programmer and interface designer. The users (usually a different group than those actually setting requirements) have their own ideas about what the application should do, and before long, you have an explosion just waiting to happen. Disappointed users start pointing fingers at developers, developers defend their implementation as the only logical way to interpret the requirements given by the project manager, and the client is ultimately forced to review the previous documentation to ensure that their requirements were clear.

One way to make sure that requirements have been gathered – and communicated – properly is to release prototypes demonstrating that the requirements have been understood and implemented accordingly. Sign-off during each phase of the project, even before development begins, can help nip problems in the bud, but visuals can often reveal ambiguities in the verbal or written requirements in ways that no other method can.

In traditional software development, it is easier to distinguish between a prototype and the final product, as they are often developed in different languages and environments, and even different platforms. When your development environment of choice is dynamic HTML, however, the line between a fully functional prototype and the real deliverable can be very thin, indeed. Some designers, and even programmers, deliver mockups of the interface as static graphics. This is intended to keep the focus of feedback on the interface, not on the functionality, which might not be fully implemented (or tested) in the prototype.

The bottom line is to know the users to whom you are demonstrating the prototype, and craft the prototype appropriately. Some folks are just incapable of understanding that a bug in a prototype is tracked down before the final product is released. Others happily and patiently watch your application crash and spit demonic error messages, knowing that they shouldn't expect more from an early release.

A well-presented prototype can reveal miscommunications, or even provide early opportunities to modify requirements before too much development time has been invested. In addition, visual presentation of ideas that had been communicated verbally can reveal mistakes or poor assumptions in the original requirements themselves. Release prototypes early and often, and carefully document the responses so that you can work them into the final product.

Usability and Accessibility

When the application has been built and the initial interfaces developed, and there is enough functionality present that the software may be given a live demonstration, it is important to make sure that it is usable. Nothing tests an interface like throwing it in front of its intended users. No amount of forethought and prototyping can accurately predict how someone who uses your application for hours at a time, every day, becomes accustomed to your application after the first few weeks or months.

MAKING SURE YOUR INTERFACES ARE USABLE

The best way to determine if your interfaces are usable is to sit down with the end users and watch them try to use your application. Again, there are numerous books, Web sites, articles, scholarly papers, and so forth that discuss usability testing. Seek some of them out and apply their lessons and approaches to your own usability tests.

The benefits of good up-front usability testing are well documented, resulting in less waste, higher productivity, and happier users.

MAKING SURE YOUR APPLICATION IS ACCESSIBLE

Usability over the long term must consider alternative methods by which those with different preferences or abilities may access any one bit of functionality. Where possible, provide keyboard shortcuts for all functionality provided via the mouse. Make sure that you supplement any reliance on color to distinguish interface elements with other, equivalent methods. Don't expect your users to have 20/20 vision, excellent hearing, or even access to a keyboard.

Of course, you must balance accessibility against the cost of providing numerous and redundant methods of using your application, but don't just write off accessibility as something directed at disabled users. You may find that even power users are frustrated by your decision to limit access to certain interface elements to those with mice, or your elaborate use of sound to signify important system events may be lost on those without sound cards installed (or properly configured).

TESTING YOUR ASSUMPTIONS WITH USERS

Nobody can tell you if you've succeeded better than the users themselves. After watching them interact with the interface on their own, ask them to perform specific tasks and note their responses as well as their actions. Don't coach the users; instead, watch as they try to understand the relationships between the components of your application. You can fix some things quite easily in the interface itself, and still others make excellent targets for training.

Watching a user perform tasks that don't make any sense to them, or that are unrelated to the way that they eventually use your application is ultimately damaging to the success of the application, so be sure to test your tests as well.

We've reviewed some of the keys to any successful software development project. Now it's time to dive into some of the problems you are likely to encounter along the way as you begin working with dynamic HTML.

The Problem with Cross-Browser DHTML

In a perfect world, all software runs as intended on all platforms, presents intuitive or easily learned interfaces to well-trained users, and has a long, happy, useful lifecycle. This is not a perfect world, however. Politics, poor design choices, the realities inherent in the insane pace of product development, market pressures, and competitive enhancements all contribute to incompatibilities between platforms, browsers, and implementations. Standards are followed poorly or not at all, or change during development, resulting in wildly different implementations of what is ostensibly the same standard.

Much of the difficulty in developing for our target platforms rests in compatibility issues resulting from the need for legacy support of models that predate standards or reflect competitive pressures to innovate. Unfortunately, despite ongoing efforts to bring browser vendors to support existing standards, the situation is unlikely to change any time soon. Some progress has been made, but much remains to be done.

In the following sections, we review some of the history behind the existing compatibility issues, explain why they exist, and suggest intelligent workarounds.

Incompatible Object Models

The incompatibility of the basic object models found in the existing 4.0 browsers is one of the core issues confronting any developer attempting to build dynamic HTML applications. The reasons for these incompatibilities are legion. Some have to do with innovation, such as Netscape Navigator's Layers, but others have to do with the time frames in which the standards were developed, or when the browsers themselves were released.

NETSCAPE'S DOCUMENT OBJECT MODEL

Netscape Navigator was one of the first browsers to implement HTML forms, and was responsible for developing many of the core features found in browsers today. There are many aspects to the object model found in both major browsers that date back to the early days of the Web. The necessity of supporting legacy documents has limited the degree to which a clean break with the past can be made. Navigator was also the first browser to expose the document's object model at all through the use of JavaScript, so much of what you see in both browsers today can be traced back to those early implementations.

The major difference between the Netscape object model and that found in Microsoft Internet Explorer is Navigator's use of Layers. Limited support for Cascading Style Sheets in the 4.0 generation and the need to provide positionable elements introduces its own weird incompatibility issues as well. The source of much frustration among developers attempting to venture into cross-browser dynamic HTML applications, Layers reproduce the entire document hierarchy within each layer. For example, to access an image that is found inside a layer, the developer must reference the entire hierarchy:

```
document.layers[0].document.images[0].src = "some.gif";
```

This is in stark contrast to the flat model supported by Internet Explorer, where you can reference all images in the document via the `document.images` collection.

Another source of contention is Navigator's use of CSS absolute positioning to provide a sort of backward compatibility for positionable elements. When CSS absolute positioning is applied to a `DIV` element, that element is treated as though it is part of the `document.layers` collection, necessitating the awkward hierarchical reference shown previously.

```
<DIV ID="example"
     STYLE="position: absolute; top:0; left: 0;">
content<BR>
<IMG NAME="theimage" SRC="some.gif">
</DIV>
```

The image element is now only accessible via the `document.layers` array as shown below:

```
myImageSrc = document.layers["example"].document.images[0].src;
```

Similar problems exist for form objects as well.

```
<DIV ID="example"
     STYLE="position: absolute; top:0; left: 0;">
<FORM NAME="test">
<INPUT NAME="myinput" TYPE="TEXT" VALUE="try to access me!">
</FORM>
</DIV>
```

An example of the JavaScript required to access the text input's value is as follows:

```
myVal = document.layers["example"].document.test.myinput.value;
```

As you have no doubt discerned by now, this makes for some very long lines of code. It is possible, through the appropriate use of references, to shorten this somewhat, especially where the form is used repeatedly:

```
myForm = document.layers["example"].document.test;
myVal = myForm.myinput.value;
```

This is still not satisfactory, however, as Internet Explorer doesn't support the document.layers array, so any code you write in this fashion is necessarily bound to the Netscape browser.

 Fortunately, the next generation Netscape browser will likely provide support for W3C standards, as discussed in previous chapters and later in this chapter. For now, we restrict our focus to the 4.0 generation in recognition of the longevity of that browser's installed base.

In the following sections, we show how you can turn some of these liabilities to your advantage. The problem remains, however, that to reconcile the fundamental differences between the browsers you are forced to change your approach to how applications are constructed, manipulated, and used.

MICROSOFT INTERNET EXPLORER/DOM

Microsoft dramatically redesigned Internet Explorer between the 3.0 and 4.0 generations. In 3.0 and its dot versions, JavaScript support for features such as the document.images array varied greatly. This is manifested in the groans of many a Web developer trying to implement simple image swapping when the mouse moved over and then out of the area taken up by an image, among other things.

Between versions, Microsoft worked extensively with the W3C, as did representatives from many other companies including Netscape, to develop what has become known as the Document Object Model. The DOM, discussed in great detail in Chapter 5, "The Document Object Model: Nouns," essentially exposes every element's properties to JavaScript (or Jscript, or VBScript, as the case may be). Many elements are both readable and writable, and their properties, contents, and styles may be modified on the fly. This presents a great opportunity to those developers lucky enough to develop applications to be used only in Internet Explorer, but is a source of immense difficulty to those required to port applications to Netscape Navigator as well.

THE W3C DOM LEVEL 0 AND HTML

One of the key features of the W3C DOM is its definition of a generic API for the manipulation of any document, not just HTML. The generic nature of the DOM is intended to provide support for XML documents, but allowances are made for the current HTML definition as well, and a set of methods is defined specifically for manipulating HTML documents.

Unfortunately for the cross-browser developer targeting the 4.0 browser generation, the W3C DOM is unimplemented by Netscape's browser, so we don't spend
much time on it in this book. Our hope is that the next generation of browsers provides a solid implementation of the DOM so that the workarounds described in this
chapter are only a bridge to a bright, DOM-compliant future. Many of these
approaches, however, apply to any cross-browser application.

Design Your Application, Then Fit It to DHTML

"Design first, make it work on the Web later" is the battle cry of many a print
designer trapped within the confines of 72dpi images and the 216-color Web
palette. While we don't debate the soundness of that advice for Web design, we do
take it as a starting point for the following discussion. The wisdom of that approach
is simple and accurate: Don't allow your understanding of the limitations of the
medium to limit what you try to do.

The trick is not to get too bogged down in worrying about what is possible. The
various native capabilities of the browsers may not translate well across platform
and browser, but dynamic HTML does provide a remarkably flexible environment
for creative workarounds. In the following chapters, you see this in depth as we
begin to build our sample application.

Before we get into the discussions of specific workarounds, let's talk about some
basic design and development strategies for dealing with incompatible interfaces,
object models, and varying levels of support for modularity.

Comparing Design Strategies

Because of the inherent differences between the various browsers, it is vital that
you approach the design of your application from a neutral standpoint, not bound
to one implementation or the other. You must focus on basic concepts affecting *all*
software design, not just dynamic HTML applications.

In order to make the best use of what are likely to be extremely short development time frames, let's review some of the cardinal strategies of software design,
and discuss the dangers and strong points of each as specifically applied to the
development of dynamic HTML applications.

We can't stress enough how important it is to understand the concepts of
abstraction, *modularity*, and *encapsulation*. Everything we do in subsequent chapters depends on the proper application of these key terms.

Abstraction is simply the process of removing from your conception of a thing
or action all characteristics that are not essential to a proper understanding of that
thing or action. In other words, it involves ignoring the specifics for the sake of a
simpler conception of the general aspects.

For example, it is unimportant at a certain stage of design how an object is created or referenced. It is only important to know that objects can be created, and that references to them may be made. Knowing that a specific form object is instantiated using the HTML <FORM> element, that it belongs to the document.forms array, and that its name is "testForm" is not important to an overall understanding of any form object's capabilities.

We use abstraction throughout the process of designing our cross-browser applications as a way to keep from getting bogged down in the specific details of any given implementation.

Modularity is a design technique that suggests that related functions and variables be grouped accordingly, such as in separate source files, in order to maximize their reuse. A key characteristic of modular programming involves the reduction of the module's external dependencies. Modularity relies upon abstraction to a large extent to ensure that any given module is as generic as possible.

Encapsulation is the process of wrapping an object such that the object and its properties are only accessible via the methods explicitly defined for that purpose.

In object-oriented programming languages such as C++ and Java, encapsulation also refers to the manner in which methods and data appropriate for each object are part of the object itself. In JavaScript, this is manifested both through the use of references to document objects and arbitrary objects created for the sole purpose of storing data. We use the first kind of object extensively throughout our development process to hide implementation-specific details from the application-level programmer. We also use the second kind of objects, but in a more limited sense.

It is worth mentioning that a key feature of encapsulation, for devotees of object-oriented programming, is the ability to enforce *data hiding*, or to protect objects from having their internal mechanisms and properties revealed except by way of the methods provided. Because you are going to be using a somewhat ad hoc approach to data hiding, and because JavaScript doesn't really enable you to forbid access to exposed properties and functions, you have to rely on the programmer's self-discipline.

Of course, making it easier for programmers to accomplish their goals is the best way to keep them from trying to do things the hard way. However, it's worth reiterating that encapsulation as a design tactic can only succeed in the long run if such discipline is followed.

Before we go any further, it is worth mentioning that the concepts and methodologies discussed in this section are merely intended to provide developers with a vocabulary and set of strategies for talking about what they already do when designing a system. You should understand the key points, but if it seems a bit abstract now, don't worry — you are still able to develop DHTML applications using the modules discussed in the following chapters, even if you don't quite grasp the concepts involved. It might be worth reading this section again after you've seen some of the concepts illustrated in the next few chapters.

HIGH-LEVEL (ARCHITECTURAL) DESIGN

The first design approach we cover, high-level or architectural design, involves a great deal of abstraction, often to the point of ignoring everything but the core actions associated with, and relationships between, objects in a system. The idea is to discover what objects are necessary, what their key functions and methods should be, and how they should interact. The product of such a design process is an architecture that describes these core objects and their interactions.

Later in the process, once these key objects have been defined, it is necessary to implement them. By restricting the designer to an extremely high-level view of the system, it is hoped that the distractions of implementation-specific details do not interfere with the proper design of the system's architecture.

FOCUSING ON THE INTERACTION OF COMPONENTS Because at this level the designer does not care how the components are implemented, the focus shifts to their interaction as discrete objects with certain behaviors. Relationships between objects, clearly specified methods by which they communicate, and their publicly available properties are all dealt with at this level of abstraction.

Not knowing how any given object implements the functionality assigned to it only serves to enforce the encapsulation of that object. Ideally, it becomes unimportant how an object implements any given functionality, as long as it does and provides known ways of accessing that functionality. This sort of design is appropriate for large systems, especially those that require multiple programmers to implement. The self-discipline discussed above is enforced by the simple fact that a given programmer may not know how any other given object actually does its stuff. Knowing how a function accomplishes its tasks is as unimportant to the programmer *using* that function as knowing what kind of coffee the function's developer drank while coding it, or whether they listened to Radiohead, Chopin, Fugazi, or Drive Like Jehu during the debugging process.

This sort of design is best suited for those development environments that can actually enforce encapsulation, such as by way of a compiler. JavaScript makes it difficult for such encapsulation to be reliably maintained. The lack of scoping mechanisms, such as being able to define a namespace for a particular module other than by the use of simple prefixes, limits developers' ability to protect their code's internals, as does the inescapable fact that the code is visible to anyone with a text editor. The interrelatedness of HTML, style sheets, and JavaScript also serves to break down the encapsulation of components designed in this manner.

IMPLEMENTING MODULAR COMPONENTS One way to fight the challenges dynamic HTML poses to encapsulation is to create modular components in separate source files. In other words, stick all your JavaScript into .js files with well-chosen names that represent the module of which they are a part. Similarly, you should also place CSS files in their own .css files, also named appropriately to indicate their belonging to a given module. The protection provided by such mechanisms is meager, but giving each module its own space tends to encourage the developer to stick to generic implementations as much as possible.

Scoping Mechanisms and Namespaces

Scoping refers to the way that variables and functions have different lifetimes and access rules based on where they are defined in a script. A variable defined outside of a function is considered to have *global scope*, and may be accessed by any JavaScript object or function within the current execution context (for example, a browser window). A variable defined inside a function, or *local* variable, is only accessible from within that function, while the function is being called. As soon as the function is done executing, the variable no longer exists. (It's worth noting that JavaScript doesn't support *block scope*, in which variables defined within a block such as a for loop are only accessible from within that block.) It is possible to declare a variable named my_var globally, and to use a variable by the same name within a function, as long as that variable is also declared within the function. The second instance overrides the first, but only within the context of that function.

Namespaces, on the other hand, are used in some programming languages to provide ways of explicitly defining global variables and functions as being part of a specific package or module. That way, a variable named my_var but declared in module the_mod would be referred to from other modules as the_mod:my_var or by some other mechanism, and would not override a global variable of the same name in a different module. One way to fake this using JavaScript is to simply use prefixes for your function and variable names, such as the_mod_my_var or the_mod$my_var, both of which are legal identifiers in JavaScript 1.1 and up. The decision is up to you and your choice of stylistic conventions.

What all this means is that you have to take extra care when choosing your variable and function names in JavaScript, and be mindful of the conventions used by other developers (or in other components, whether concurrently developed or already existing). Otherwise, you could end up with flaky behavior as your variables and functions clobber those used by other parts of your application.

When properly implemented, modular JavaScript components may be reused very easily, and any necessary workarounds may be relegated to the application's main source code rather than corrupting the modules themselves. Alternately, it may make sense for some workarounds to be implemented in the modules so as to avoid corrupting the application. It all depends on the nature of the workaround in question.

LOW-LEVEL (ALGORITHMIC) DESIGN

On the opposite end of the continuum from high-level design, which ignores the specific implementation details, is low-level design. Low-level design focuses entirely on the specific implementation details, such as internal data structures, private or unpublished methods, and utility functions.

The intent of low-level design is to make the best use of programmers whose interest in systems tends more toward the nitty-gritty details. Some folks just don't like the head-in-the-clouds approach required by high-level design, and it is to these people that we owe whatever speed and efficiency our actual implementations may have.

FOCUSING ON SPEED AND EFFICIENCY One drawback to high-level design is also its greatest strength: It ignores implementation details in favor of manageable decomposition and systems architecture. The problem here is that no system is perfect, and there is often a disconnect between the high-level plan and the gruesome reality of the existing means by which it may be implemented. In such cases, it is necessary to make up for these disconnects by squeezing as much speed and efficiency out of the code as possible.

Speed is obvious, and usually involves profiling, algorithmic analysis, and other mechanisms to make sure that the application doesn't put the user to sleep. How this is done in the context of JavaScript, with its lack of a native profiling capability, is left as an exercise for the reader. Careful analysis of the algorithms used can often result in speed improvements as wasteful code is tuned to maximize its efficient use of system resources such as memory or CPU cycles.

CHOOSING APPROPRIATE DATA STRUCTURES One key element in the internal implementation of high-level components is the use of appropriate data structures. Memory is getting cheaper every day, but that doesn't always mean that average users' desktop workstations are up to par with the developer's environment. What runs perfectly well on a Pentium II with 128MB of RAM may bring the average 486 to its knees, and similarly so for Power Macintoshes versus 68K-based machines.

Unfortunately, there isn't much you can do to get snapshots of a given object or function's memory usage. You need to be as careful as possible when you initialize your objects and local variables not to use up every last bit of available memory, even if you can rely on JavaScript's internal garbage collection to clean up after you.

High-level and low-level design strategies tend to emphasize opposite aspects of a system's components. One focuses on how objects and their external relationships are determined, while the other tries to deal with everything the first one ignores, significantly focusing on the objects' internals. A similar, but slightly different, approach involves the question of when to integrate disparate components into a holistic application, using a sliding scale of granularity rather than an internal/external split.

TOP-DOWN DESIGN

Top-down design generally involves the gradual definition of the details of an application's components. Starting with vaguely defined high-level components, or even less granular subsystems, each component is fleshed out in greater and greater detail, moving into specifics only at the very end of the development cycle.

PROS In well-understood environments, top-down design can be the most efficient way to make use of programmers' time, enabling individual programmers to focus on varying levels of the abstraction of a system without having to constantly jump back and forth between levels. Many programmers work this way anyway, so it seems natural to begin the practice at the system level and work down from there.

Top-down design is also efficient when a system is likely to change substantially due to a lack of solid requirements, as it doesn't waste lots of time on implementation specifics while the system's functionality is still being defined.

CONS Top-down design is especially vulnerable to the well-known 80/20 rule, which states that the development of 80 percent of any system is accomplished in 20 percent of the time, whereas the other 20 percent takes 80 percent of the time allotted. Too much time spent in the high-level planning stage can severely limit the amount of time available to finish the implementation.

It can be difficult to know when a system's top-level design is complete and that it is therefore safe to begin implementation of the low-level details. Some churn is inevitable, especially when requirements are constantly changing, and if low-level implementation begins too early, much time can be lost.

BOTTOM-UP DESIGN

Bottom-up design takes the opposite approach, focusing heavily on the development of components and subcomponents at the expense of an overarching plan for final integration. This approach is best for applications that need to accomplish well-known tasks, but for which there is little sense of the sum total of the tasks that must be implemented.

PROS Bottom-up design makes efficient use of programmers' time when a system is still being defined, in that work can begin immediately on those portions that are known to be necessary for the final application.

CONS As with any situation involving poorly determined requirements, the developer may waste some time developing components that are not included in the final application.

It is possible to design components that do not function well together at final integration time. Dynamic HTML applications are especially vulnerable due to the high degree of interreliance of HTML, style sheets, and JavaScripts.

AN ITERATIVE SOLUTION

The preceding examples of design strategies have been somewhat theoretical in their distinctions. Most real software development projects use a combination of the approaches outlined above, usually in an iterative cycle moving from high- to low-level design, and vacillating between top-down and bottom-up approaches. The best approach always lies somewhere in between.

For dynamic HTML projects, due to the large degree of interreliance between the different technologies used as well as the difficulty of enforcing encapsulation of components, a top-down approach may best serve to maximize the efficient use of programmers' time. This approach also tends to minimize the amount of redesign and recoding required at integration time. The demands of rapid application development and prototyping, however, tend to frustrate attempts to work gradually toward a total and final integration of components.

In the final analysis, it all boils down to the size and complexity of the project in question, as well as the nature and preferred working style of the developers and designers involved. The fact that most dynamic HTML applications require that the interface be developed at the same time as the scripting tends to minimize the separation between those portions that must be released as prototypes and the underlying functionality accomplished by way of scripting.

Modularity, Modularity, Modularity

Perhaps the best thing we have going for us as developers of dynamic HTML applications is the ability to include code modules into our application by way of external references. This enables modules to be developed and tested independently of the application, which is no small feat given the relationships between style sheets, scripts, and HTML. It also enables code to be included in both components developed expressly for the purpose of testing and in the final application.

This encourages true modularity of design, as hidden dependencies are more easily discovered when the module is tested in a variety of contexts. It then becomes a project management task to keep track of the relationships between your JavaScript module, any style sheets and HTML on which it may rely, and any configuration variables needed by the including application.

Good, clear, accurate documentation can be a project's saving grace. Use the Web to document your module, its exposed methods, any dependencies it has on other modules, and what sort of HTML and style sheet support is required. In addition, if the module may be extended or configured using externally defined global variables, list them and what effect they have on the module's behavior. If the module must be initialized in order to be used, provide documentation on how and when initialization must take place.

CODE REUSE IS A GOOD THING

As any veteran programmer will tell you, code reuse is vital as it saves time and effort as well as promotes the use of more thoroughly debugged components. The development of a few good generic modules containing commonly needed functions ensures that less time is spent debugging the same things over and over. In addition, reusable code enables developers to focus on what is unique about an application, rather than worrying about whether or not a new approach to an old problem is appropriate.

The other benefit to code reuse is that it tends to enable the sort of rapid application development that is becoming commonplace as time frames and schedules are compressed. Project managers can spec out entire applications using existing modules, leaving only the overarching application and interface logic to be implemented.

Macromedia's Dreamweaver application takes this concept to heart with its behaviors, which are basically common routines that may be applied by the developer in new contexts. Other applications are also beginning to support the reuse of code, though some of the more recently announced mechanisms, such as Microsoft's behaviors or Netscape's action sheets, extend existing HTML standards rather than working within them.

FOCUSING ON HOOKS

A *hook* is a software construct that enables subsequent developers to manipulate basic assumptions about how a chunk of code should work. For example, if you have a function that returns a date string, being able to specify the format for the string is a simple sort of hook. Being able to specify the starting date, or even the calendar to use, such as a choice between Roman, Hebrew, Muslim, and Mayan calendars, is even more useful as it enables the basic functionality to be applied to numerous other contexts. A more powerful hook would provide the definition of another function entirely, to be called in the place of the default behavior.

In JavaScript, because there is no granular way to restrict the scope of variables, all variables declared outside a function definition become global. In essence, these variables may be used as hooks by your main application logic, especially if they modify the behavior of the function or module itself.

Another way to look at hooks from the standpoint of dynamic HTML (or any event-driven GUI system, for that matter) is to take event handlers as a certain type of hook. The application can assign certain event handling routines to manage user input, overriding any default behavior. For instance, assigning an onClick handler to a link that calls a JavaScript confirm() pop-up box is a way of making sure that the user really wants to follow the link before handling the event.

Providing hooks — whether via the appropriate use of variables or overriding default behavior using functions — is the best way to make sure that your module has the maximum possible reuse. The difference between good modules and great ones is the extent to which they enable the developer to override and extend default behavior.

ALLOWING CONFIGURABLE AND EXTENSIBLE MODULES

Having said all that, how does a developer tasked with producing a module go about providing extensibility and configurability? The trick is knowing when your module makes assumptions about default behaviors, properties, and intended usage. Rather than hard-coding these default properties, define them using variables. This enables anyone using your code to define these properties themselves, before calling your routines.

Adding tests to check the calling context of a function can also be a good way to enable the most flexible and widespread possible usage. For example, a function that may be called from an event handler or from within another function needs to be able to tell how it was called. In this example, the calling parameters themselves may vary, due to the default browser behavior of passing a reference to the event object as the only parameter. Such a function should check to see whether the arguments array contains more than one value, doing the right thing in either case.

Here's a function drawn from the Dynamic Menu module to be discussed in Chapter 14, "Dynamic Menus." It may be called from an event handler, in the case of an `onmouseover`, or by another function. In the first case, the first argument is a reference to the `event` object, and the second argument is empty, and so defaults to the special JavaScript reference `this`. In the second case, the second argument should be a reference to an object.

```
function menu_item_hilight(e,i) {
  i = i || this;
  var the_item = menu_item[i.id];
  the_item.set_bg_color( menu_hilight_color );
}
```

Notice as well that the color used to set the menu highlight is not hard-coded, but provided as a global variable, so the developer (or even the user) can set the color to their heart's content.

Another way to help provide configurability involves the use of initialization functions, where the application-level developer can use whatever namespace they wish to define a set of data, and then pass that data to your function. For example, Chapter 15, "Help," makes use of the following initialization function:

```
function help_init(defs, type) {
  // actual function body not shown
}
```

The argument `defs` is an array of help topics and associated information, defined as appropriate by the application programmer. The function doesn't assume the use of certain variable names, such as `help_definitions[]` or `restrictively_named_array[]`. The application-level developer can name his or her own help definitions in a manner appropriate to the application itself, such as `my_help_defs[]` or `applicationname_help_defs[]`. The use of the `type` variable also enables the application developer to use the same initialization function for different purposes. In this case, the choice is between tool tips and a pop-up help window with a topic browser.

An even more extensible model might provide a function reference to be passed to the initialization, perhaps as an optional third parameter, to be called on completion of the function or even in place of the default initialization routines. When called upon completion, such a function is known as a *callback*, and is a commonly used mechanism for tying interfaces to back-end code. It's up to your judgment as a developer when to allow such massively extensible code and when to restrict the downstream developer to using code you provide.

The bottom line is to enable any characteristic of a function that is not intrinsic to the proper behavior of the function to be configurable by the developer or end user. The best modules don't assume anything but the bare bones.

PROVIDING INTEROPERABILITY

Part of being a good citizen in the world of reusable, modular code is making sure that your code doesn't override or interfere with code outside of the module. This can be thought of as the flip side of configurability. Instead of maximizing the extent to which your code can be customized or enhanced by subsequent developers, you're minimizing the extent to which your code places demands on the surrounding context.

What this means in practice is that your code can be mixed in with other modules and the main application logic without interfering with or overriding higher-level behavior. There are many approaches to managing this kind of design, but they can be summarized as follows:

◆ Use carefully chosen global variable and function names. If your module provides doohickeys, or ways of manipulating doohickeys, it might make sense to prefix your variable names with `doohickey`. This reduces the chance that your chosen namespace interferes with top-level application logic, or with other modules.

◆ Enable downstream developers to supply their own variable names for configuration data that can be passed as a reference, especially when the size of the data set is flexible, such as in the help example mentioned previously. This gives them the flexibility to work within their own application's namespace.

◆ Don't be greedy with your event grabbing routines. Localize any event handler assignments, or store the previously defined event handler, restoring it on successful completion of your routine.

◆ Don't force the initialization of your module if it is not absolutely necessary to the proper functioning of the including application. Always enable the downstream developer to choose if and when to initialize your module.

◆ Don't use global variables when local variables will do. This decreases the chance of your clobbering application logic or the namespace of other modules.

You have probably noticed by now that namespace issues top the list of things to watch out for when it comes to providing interoperable code. What you may not have noticed is that namespace issues apply equally to JavaScript, HTML, and CSS. Though a CSS class name is unlikely to interfere with a JavaScript function, if your module depends on a class having a certain name and you haven't taken steps to also manage the namespace of your style sheet, you could cause problems for the application developer. Similarly, when you name HTML elements (such as those used for placeholders for objects dynamically created and positioned by your module), you should take namespace issues into account.

MAINTAINING ENCAPSULATION

Now that we've dealt extensively with the flip side of configurability, it's time to talk about the flip side of extensibility. As we discussed above, encapsulation is the manner in which you protect other code (and other developers) from making assumptions about how to call your module that are not explicitly specified in your public methods.

You can only do so much to enforce encapsulation, unfortunately. Any programmer can look at your code and find out exactly how it works, and then use that knowledge to use your functions in ways that limit your ability to extend your own module, or change the way it internally accomplishes its tasks.

In the end, it boils down to discipline on the developer's part and your support of those efforts at discipline by proper documentation of your exposed methods. Documentation is necessary so the developers who use your module don't need to peek at your module's internals to figure out how it works. Project managers must deal with these issues as well, and make sure that everything is handled as needed to enforce both the interoperability and encapsulation of modules used by your application.

Now that we've discussed some of the best development practices to use for your project, let's dive into the mind-numbing complexity involved in building cross-browser and cross-platform dynamic HTML applications.

Cross-Browser and Cross-Platform Design Strategies

On the face of it, it would seem that the fundamental incompatibilities between the object models used by the major browsers rule out any sane cross-browser development. If you've been paying attention, however, you may have begun to see how we plan to deal with these issues. Before we show you how to build applications that function effectively across browsers, let's discuss several strategies for handling cross-browser differences and talk about some of their advantages and disadvantages.

Incompatibility, Branching, Browser-Sniffing, and You

The most common mechanism for implementing quick workarounds, the branch, is quite simple. If you know that a given browser supports something that you want to use, and another doesn't, you check to see which browser you're using and execute the appropriate code. In practice, however, this quickly leads to obscenely unreadable code and support nightmares straight out of H. P. Lovecraft.

The general approach goes something like this. First, set aside a flag or two (as many as you need) that you can use to signify the browser that requires the workaround. Test the JavaScript `navigator` property against known user agents, and set the appropriate flag to `true` based on the browser you're using. Then, when the time comes to apply the workaround, simply test for the value of the flag and apply the appropriate code in each case. For example, the following code lets you know whether you're dealing with Internet Explorer or Netscape Navigator:

```
var ie = false;
if( navigator.userAgent.indexOf("MSIE") != -1 ) {
  ie =  true;
} else {
  ie = false;
}
```

The problem here is that there are far too many features, browser versions, and incompatibilities to keep track of. There are browser-sniffing scripts out on the Web whose length far exceeds that of the average image swapping script. A far saner approach involves testing for the availability of the feature you really want to use, such as the following image swapping test. First, the code checks for the availability of the `document.images` array, without which you are unable to set the `src` property of the image you want to swap.

```
function swap_on(image) {
  if( document.images ) {
    // do the swap
  } else {
    // do nothing, or just set window.status
  }
}
```

Of course, the presence of the `document.images` array doesn't guarantee that all features associated with it work as you want them to, so you may have to introduce further branching to keep things functioning smoothly.

```
function swap_on(image) {
  if( document.images ) {
    if( navigator.appVersion.indexOf("4.0") != -1) {
      // do something appropriate for the 4.0 browsers
    } else {
      // do something less exciting ;-)
    }
  } // ...
}
```

To make matters worse, some features are only available on certain platforms, or have bugs that require weird workarounds. The following code only executes on

Windows, in the 4.0 generation of Microsoft's Internet Explorer, if Java is enabled, and if the user's environment currently supports French. It's somewhat contrived, of course, but we've seen even more complex nested if tests in production code.

```
function swap_on(image) {
  if( document.images ) {
    if( navigator.appVersion.indexOf("4.0") != -1) {
      // do something appropriate for the 4.0 browsers
      if( navigator.userAgent.indexOf("Windows") != -1) {
        if( navigator.javaEnabled ) {
          if( navigator.language == "fr") {
            // qu'etait-ce nous allaient-il faire?
          }
        }
      }
    } else {
      // do something less exciting ;-)
    }
  } // ...
}
```

As you can see, this approach quickly descends into the realm of the ludicrous, to say nothing of it being difficult to maintain. As an added bonus, it doesn't work in the forthcoming 5.0 generation of browsers, even if the required features are all supported. Steve learned this the hard way, when all of the image swapping on his personal home page broke when the 4.0 versions came out.

So how does a developer deal with the nightmare? Let's go through some of the steps we've already outlined, discussing each in detail, then summarize everything and delve into a much saner approach.

KEEPING TRACK OF COMPATIBILITY ISSUES

First of all, it is important to know what features your application needs in order to operate correctly. The easiest way to find out is to write quick test scripts and run them through each browser and platform you need to support. (This assumes you've done some basic research into what each browser *claims* to support, so you can weed out the obvious limitations before you even start coding.) As you test, keep track of which versions have bugs and other issues that you may need to work around.

How you keep track of these bugs is a matter of personal preference. We've found that attempts to track whether specific browsers and versions support a given feature using a spreadsheet or other tabular method quickly degenerate into madness. This is partly due to the sheer number of features to test for, but also because of the difficulty of actually determining the following things with any degree of accuracy over time:

- ◆ Browser vendor (IE 3.0 was quick to claim it was Mozilla compatible, for example)

- ◆ Browser version (the modular nature of IE makes it difficult to tell what versions of the necessary scripting engines are installed, for example)

- ◆ Platform (this one is easier, but still not quite granular enough for some tasks)

- ◆ Whether a given feature is available read/write, or just read-only

- ◆ Interdependencies between specific features (CSS is plagued with this problem)

- ◆ Environment (such as screen size and color depth)

There are services and Web sites that provide detailed information regarding the degree to which a given browser version is derived from another, or what features it supports, but these are subject to some of the same difficulties discussed previously. In general, the best tack to take when dealing with issues of support is to stick to the high ground and only use those features that are well-supported in all browsers of a given generation. We discuss this in more detail in the following sections.

BRANCHING INSIDE FUNCTIONS FOR QUICK WORKAROUNDS

When you know without a doubt that a certain feature is unavailable on a certain platform or in a specific browser, and the workaround is simple to implement without introducing the massive complexity we saw above, you may use branching to ensure that the code does the right thing. The first image swapping example above is a great illustration of this sort of code.

Burying the branch inside a function can be an effective means of reducing complexity for commonly called-upon tasks. The rule is simple, and applies to all development: Don't repeat the same code over and over again — stick it into a function and call the function instead. This makes it easier to track down all occurrences of a given problem and fix them once, as you know the problem only occurs within the one function. Using the same code (or slightly different code) repeatedly throughout your application is a recipe for disaster.

In any case, this sort of quick test should only be used for small incompatibilities, or those that don't require much recoding to support the workarounds.

BRANCHING AT PAGE LEVEL FOR MAJOR INCOMPATIBILITIES

When the incompatibilities go far and above the usual minor annoyances, it may be useful to provide two different versions of your code and use a page-level branch. This may involve using `document.write` statements, which build the appropriate page on the fly, or simply calling different initialization routines depending upon the browser being used.

The problem with this approach is that the user ends up downloading far more code than is actually executed on their system. For medium-sized and larger applications, this can be prohibitive, to say nothing of annoying to your users.

BROWSER-SNIFFING FOR SPEED

A final strategy involves the use of *browser-sniffing* or *browser-sensing* techniques. That way, when users with an offending browser visit your site, you can redirect them to the page containing the appropriate implementation without them having to download all of the code for each workaround. There are many mechanisms for doing this, available as JavaScripts, CGI programs, and other types of server-specific functionality.

The problem with this approach is that you end up maintaining two or more separate versions of your code, which in the case of the example application we build in the following chapters can be daunting, if not simply too expensive. For small workarounds, however, or for relatively limited applications, such as those involving a single page and a few functions, this may be a satisfactory approach to take.

ADVANTAGES AND DISADVANTAGES OF
THE VARIOUS APPROACHES

It may be clear from the preceding paragraphs that there are some advantages and serious disadvantages associated with each strategy. After weighing them all and comparing and contrasting technical issues with the project management investment and associated costs, we think you'll agree that a different approach is called for. Bear in mind that everything we've said so far regarding the importance of modularity, encapsulation, and the ability to make leaps of abstraction – they become more important as we continue on.

First, application developers (as opposed to Web developers simply charged with enlivening static content) need a solid platform to build their applications on. Any application of significant complexity, before all the cross-browser workarounds are figured in, becomes a maintenance nightmare even on a single platform or target browser.

The costs of producing an application are far outweighed by those required to provide ongoing support and enhancements. The requirements of a fast-paced marketplace or an aggressive schedule for an internal project should not mean that the resulting application becomes impossible to maintain. Such are the challenges of rapid application development: balancing time to implementation with the costs of maintenance.

The more workarounds that are built in at the application level, the harder the code becomes to maintain effectively. This technical difficulty easily turns into a management difficulty, especially for those apps expected to evolve constantly to support more and more features. If workarounds are not well documented, or code is written in a cryptic fashion, developer turnover also presents a problem as new hands start to rework existing code.

Don't forget that there is still enough cachet and hype surrounding the use of the Web to encourage many users to upgrade their browser whenever a new version becomes available. The use of version-specific features may present problems when users upgrade, as support for proprietary features is often excluded from new versions due to political reasons or even praiseworthy efforts to achieve some level of standards support. Even in intranet environments or in large corporations, the control exerted over basic application configuration becomes more and more tenuous the closer you get to the Web.

Time frames are often compressed for enhancements to existing applications, even if those applications must be heavily reworked to support the new requirements. Executive-level management doesn't want to hear about incompatibilities between dot versions of their pet project's target platform. They want results, and are more concerned with the bottom line than with technical issues. This is exacerbated by the rosy-lensed marketing that bombards them day in and day out. No amount of pleading overcomes the messages they are being fed by vendors concerned with market share or pushing e-commerce solutions and messaging platforms.

We don't want to paint too bleak a picture, though. There are solutions. They may not be the ones most immediately evident to inexperienced developers, however. So let's start to outline the approach we take in the construction and deployment of our basic cross-browser library.

Starting with the Lowest Common Denominator

Throw everything you know about the IE object model out the window for now. Stick to the simplest of Cascading Style Sheets properties, and don't forget to polish up your JavaScript skills. We gave the earlier warnings about understanding abstraction and encapsulation in earnest. We don't use too many specifics from either browser's implementation of the core standards much, either. (Well, technically we do, but for the most part they are hidden from the average application developer.)

USING A SUBSET OF DOM, CSS, AND EVENT MODELS

Because the W3C DOM is not supported in both major browsers, you can't use much of it at the application level. The legacy DOM is supported, but the problems with Layers and CSS-P/DIVs in Netscape Navigator make it difficult to rely on. We show you how to use the reliably implemented stuff while avoiding the more esoteric.

CSS is not fully supported by the 4.0 browsers, either. In order to keep from making yourself crazy, stick to the simple CSS stuff that is already available via HTML equivalents, or that reflects some proprietary extension or other:

- ◆ Font color, size, weight, and family

- ◆ Object color and size

- ◆ Object z-index and visibility

- ◆ Object positioning

Exciting and wonderful things like margins, borders, padding, and the like are better set using HTML attributes, as they are not reliable across platforms. The really esoteric stuff like indentation, first-letter, floating typography, and so on, is either unimplemented or is implemented so poorly as to make it utterly laughable.

CSS support in the major browsers is coming, but it will be a while before you can use it as a matter of course for cross-platform development.

As we discuss in more detail below, the event models provided are completely incompatible across browsers from different vendors. Netscape Navigator expects the developer to specify which events to grab for which elements. Internet Explorer lets events bubble up from the target object all the way to the top-level window object. You still need to specify event handlers, but you don't need to also specify which events to grab — they are all handled by default, even if that means the browser does nothing with them. We don't really resolve these basic event incompatibilities, but we show you how to work around them for now.

It may be best to think about what we're doing as creating solid, if not very flashy, building blocks that we create even more useful things from later. For now, though, things are so weird that we have to focus on the blocks before we can make any headway against specific compatibility issues.

WHERE COMPATIBILITY ISN'T POSSIBLE, FAKE IT

When a useful feature is available in one browser but not available in another, the first impulse is to give up. Don't give in so easily, though — if it is important enough to your application, there may be other mechanisms by which you can implement the same functionality.

For example, it is possible to dynamically alter the text or markup of a DIV object in Internet Explorer. You can't do that in Netscape Navigator, but it is possible to dynamically alter the contents of a Layer object. So, to avoid confusion, just create a wrapper routine that enables you to replace the contents of a layer object and call that routine when the time comes. The routine's internals are then tasked with carrying out the right thing using as many branches or if tests as necessary (or whatever ugly tricks you can come up with), but the application-level programmer isn't burdened by grotesque code.

Think of the entire third part of this book and all the code in it as a series of exercises in localizing ugly workarounds. Rather than subjecting the application developer to introducing ugly code into their pristine and logical structures just for the sake of cross-browser compatibility, you hide the ugliness away under a stable and consistent API layer.

If you think about it, you're doing the same thing for your code that the interface designer is doing for her interface. The user shouldn't have to think about the details of your implementation, but rather about the task at hand.

You may find yourself slightly dismayed by the amount of work you have to do in order to emulate existing functionality on an unsupported platform. Once you get used to it, however, it's amazing how powerful grassroots interface design using DHTML primitives can really be. Of course, some effects are only available on one platform, no matter what kind of primitives you implement on the other browser. Dynamically specified cursors, for example, are a feature of CSS level 2 that only IE 4.0 and above supports. So what do you do when you want to add value to your application, but can't do it equitably across platform?

Enhancing Functionality Afterwards

When should you use browser- and platform-specific code to enhance an application? There are many answers, all dependent on your environment, your project manager, and the time available. The dogmatic cross-browser purist answer is "Never!", but there really isn't any good reason not to enhance an interface when the functionality is available. To do otherwise would cheat your users both coming and going.

The caveat, of course, is that you should wait until the application is near completion so as not to disrupt the development of core cross-browser functionality. That way, the app's baseline functionality is present and tested, and you have a solid foundation on which to enhance your application for specific browsers or platforms.

When adding enhancements, you should be careful when checking if the feature is present. Check for the feature itself where possible. If you can't just test for the presence of an array, as we did in the image swapping example, then be sure not to rely too much on browser versions. If you have to use version information, then be sure not to lock out newer versions by simply testing for equality with a current version number. Test for that version or greater.

ADDING BROWSER-SPECIFIC ENHANCEMENTS

Most of the features you want to add as enhancements are likely to be browser-specific. The vendors usually introduce proprietary enhancements and then do their best to implement them across platform. When this is the case, you should check for the browser name or version, and, if present, call the function that implements the enhancement.

Make sure not to put too much interface responsibility in the hands of browser-specific enhancements, especially if you want to live a long and healthy life. Enhancements of this sort (for example, the use of specialized cursors) should be restricted to nonessential activities or provide extra information to the user in addition to the existing feedback mechanisms. Adding special functionality on one browser but not the other invites technical support difficulties and frustrates your users.

ADDING PLATFORM-SPECIFIC ENHANCEMENTS

Some functionality is bound to the platform itself, such as ActiveX on Win32 systems, or most plug-ins, which aren't usually available on UNIX. The vast majority of the platform-specific issues that you confront, however, are minor workarounds for bugs in JavaScript and CSS. These issues are best dealt with at the library level or below.

For example, let's say you find that Netscape browsers on the Macintosh have a problem in the way they report the width of an object. If you know the difference between what is reported and what should be reported, and the difference is constant, you can modify the library function responsible for reading an object's width. The new function would take into account the existence of the bug, and perform the appropriate workaround on that platform.

We talk about how best to manage these sorts of workarounds in the following sections. You should understand, however, that application programmers should not have to worry about these issues, as the API they use should hide such implementation-specific details. It is up to the maintainer of the cross-platform library to ensure that they get the correct value when they call the method.

Custom Solutions

When all else fails, and you can't fake compatibility, you need to develop custom solutions for those browsers and platforms that don't support what you need. This should be the last resort, after you've done everything to try to provide a compatible solution for the application developer.

Do not undertake this step lightly. Consider that such a custom solution may not be reusable, may require additional support and development time, and may be forever bound to the browser for which it is developed. You should always try to provide browser-neutral, nonplatform-specific code. Otherwise, you may end up reimplementing everything when your target platform changes.

The xplatform Library

By now you should be more than ready to start asking the question, "But how can I provide a browser- and platform-independent dynamic HTML implementation?" The ideal answer would be, "No problem! Just use dynamic HTML right out of the proverbial box!" Of course, in the real world, as you've already seen, this is far from the truth. You have to deal with and work around major incompatibilities. The high-end capabilities of both browsers must be made subservient to a lowest common denominator. Developers must work toward providing interface primitives, rather than using the native capabilities of any browser.

It would be great if there were a library that successfully implemented these interface primitives, hid incompatibilities, and provided a stable development platform for the application developer. Unfortunately, there isn't one.

 In the preceding sections, we've tried to maintain a distinction between the terms *browser* and *platform*. The first refers to a specific vendor's software (such as Microsoft Internet Explorer 4.0) and the second refers to the operating system distribution (such as Windows 98). In the subsequent discussion, we use the term *platform* to refer to the combination of browser and operating system. In the end, we use it to refer to the stable baseline library that hides all platform-specific details from the application developer. The goal is to eventually stop concerning ourselves with which browser or OS we're dealing with, other than to make sure we're targeting a specific generation and above.

You Need to Roll Your Own

Actually, there are many cross-browser workarounds, and even complete libraries available that make it possible to write or port applications across platforms. The authors of these libraries use many different strategies, and all succeed to some extent or another. By all means, do your own research into the libraries available on the Web and pick the one best suited for your needs. There are libraries that claim to make it possible to write applications for Navigator using Internet Explorer syntax, for IE using Navigator syntax, and for both using a mixture of the capabilities of each. There are significant advantages to using each library appropriate to different contexts.

In the end, it doesn't matter one way or the other which library you use, as long as you take away an understanding of how they are all designed and constructed. We feel that our library is useful, and hope to prove this to you through the next few chapters as we use our library and several modules to build a fully functional application. Let's talk about some of the assumptions we made during the design of our library, and shed some light on why we did things the way we did.

A FEW DESIDERATA

We've always considered programming to be a sort of art – a realm where design decisions had an enormous impact on the elegance and sensibility of the result. Comparisons to poetry aren't far off the mark, as all code has a certain voice, a style, that reflects the mindset of its creator. Work with enough programmers and you gradually get to know their voice, and through their voice, the way their mind works.

Some people will tell you that the constraints placed on a programmer by the requirements of the application or system under development are so restrictive as to make self-expression impossible. They will say that code cannot be considered poetry because there is no opportunity for personal expression. In some languages, this may be true. In many, however, there is more than enough room for self-expression of a sort.

Of course, project managers must be vigilant, making sure that the code comprising an application isn't too personal, too particular to the programmer who wrote it. Otherwise, long-term support becomes a problem. But there is always room for arbitrary decisions, and we figure it is best to talk about some of the decisions we made while designing the library so as to help you understand our process. We also hope to make sure that you don't waste much time wondering why we did things the way we did. So without further ado, here is our wish list and some design criteria for the library.

A SINGLE API FOR ACCESS TO OBJECTS AND THEIR PROPERTIES   When we started working with dynamic HTML, it quickly became apparent that although you could do powerful things with either major implementation, nothing worked across browsers. The examples we saw online that claimed to be cross-browser compatible were a mishmash of nested code – usually two complete versions of an application held together with one all-encompassing `if/else` block. Most made use of `document.write()` and other mechanisms to further complicate matters, or had strangely named custom routines that were only appropriate to the application using them.

Rather than try to explain the exceptions and one-time workarounds, we quickly decided that what was needed was a stable, if custom, baseline API that application developers could code to. Code reuse and clarity of application-level code took precedence over concerns for speed, efficiency, or memory usage, though we look at ways to streamline the final application a bit later.

Ultimately, we decided that the best approach was to provide access to objects (forms, images, and positionable elements, as well as other properties) via a set of object wrappers and associated methods. The resulting core API exposes the most commonly needed properties without requiring the application developer to test for browser versions.

For example, instead of having to write code that looks like this:

```
if((document.someObject.style.visibility == "show") ||
  (document.layers["someObject"].visibility == "show")) {
  if(ie){
    // hide the object
    document.someObject.style.visibility = "hidden";
  } else {
    // it's Netscape
    document.layers["someObject"].visibility = "hide";
  }
} else {
 if(ie){
    // show the object
    document.someObject.style.visibility = "visible";
  } else {
    // it's Netscape
    document.layers["someObject"].visibility = "show";
  }
}
```

We thought it would be better to be able to write code that looks like this:

```
var theObject = object_name[current];
if( theObject ) {
  if( theObject.is_visible() ) {
    theObject.conceal();
  } else {
    theObject.reveal();
  }
}
```

Which would you rather maintain? How about over the lifetime of an application that does a lot of hiding and showing of objects? Which one makes more sense when you read it quickly? We think that the more compact version, once you become accustomed to the methods, is much easier to code and maintain.

MOVING WORKAROUNDS BELOW THE API   One very important side effect of hiding properties and implementation-specific methods behind a consistent API is that workarounds for bugs in specific browsers and platforms may be fixed *once*, in the function assigned as a method. This alone saves enormous amounts of coding and makes your applications more stable. Application developers no longer need to hunt down every place they tickle a bug on a given browser in order to add a workaround.

The workaround can be safely added to the method's implementation, making it possible to truly fix bugs as soon as they are discovered. With the rate that new browsers, betas, and patches are being released, each with their own quirks, wouldn't it be better to be able to review your library for bugs rather than having to review all of your applications?

HIDING IMPLEMENTATION-SPECIFIC DETAILS   The third thing we wanted the library to do was hide implementation-specific details from the developer. This was a tougher decision, because we hope that one day the W3C DOM is the standard platform for browser-based development, and it seemed to deny the average developer a chance to get more familiar with the DOM.

Unfortunately, the DOM, despite being a W3C Recommendation, is not properly implemented across the 4.0 browsers, and level 2 is, in fact, still under development. Rather than shoot for a falsely implemented DOM level 0 with unpredictable results, we made the decision to simplify the work required to perform common tasks, such as reading certain properties, moving objects, replacing their contents, or showing/hiding objects.

Purists complain that the library is corrupt because it makes things easier for the casual application developer and hides the true nature of the underlying code. We respond by saying that good programmers do this anyway, and that we haven't closed off access to the code itself, so nothing prevents an interested developer from figuring out how we did what we did. This book, especially the discussions found here and in the next few chapters, serves as proof that we aren't out to prevent anyone from learning about the DOM or specific implementations.

When the browser vendors provide stable platforms for browser-neutral development, we expect to continue using similar approaches to minimize development time and the cost of ongoing maintenance.

SOME INFLUENCES

The creative process we discussed earlier involves a slew of influences from other languages and environments. These influences are revealed in variable and function names, formatting style, design strategies, and in other, less obvious ways. Here are a few of ours, in an attempt to rationalize what are inherently aesthetic decisions on our part.

PERL ASSOCIATIVE ARRAYS   One of the most common languages on the Internet, Perl is used extensively for CGI programming and other Web-related programming and systems administration tasks. Associative arrays, a key feature of Perl, cited by JavaScript's creator as an influence on the language itself, enable the programmer to store and access elements by way of text strings rather than numeric indices. In dynamic HTML, where most, if not all, of the coding you do involves some reference to HTML objects that have been given names for clarity, associative arrays make such access much easier.

```
# begin horribly contrived Perl example
$day{'wed'} = "Wednesday, market day";
$day{'thu'} = "Thursday, the day of Thor";
print STDOUT "What is today? (wed|thu) ";
chomp($today = <STDIN>);
print STDOUT "Today is $day{$today}!\n";
```

Because JavaScript supports associative arrays natively, it seemed only natural to use them as often as possible to provide access to our wrapper objects. There is an interesting and useful side effect to using associative arrays, however.

THE DOM'S FLAT ACCESS OBJECT MODEL   One of the first things you notice about the object model used by Internet Explorer is that it provides access to everything in the document by way of a few collections, or arrays organized by type. You can see all of the elements in a document by looping over the document.all array, all of the images by way of document.images, and so on. It's very handy.

Netscape Navigator, for various reasons, treats all layer objects as containing new documents with their own hierarchies of elements. As a result, you need to remain constantly aware of whether the object you want to access is referenced by way of the root window or by way of some subordinate layer or other. The situation gets even more confusing when layers themselves contain layers.

Without debating the merits of either approach, we find it easier to write clean code using the flat model. This may be a result of our experience with Perl's associative arrays, or it may simply reflect our love of clean, short code. In any case, one of the key characteristics of our model is the way it enables access to any wrapped object by way of a single, associative, identifier. The IE-specific object reference document.myObject   and   the   Netscape-specific   document.layers["myObject"] becomes object_name["myObject"] under our library, regardless of target platform.

The same is true for forms and images, which are nested relative to layers in Netscape Navigator but not in IE and the W3C DOM.

OBJECT-ORIENTED ANALYSIS AND DESIGN   People have been writing modular code since FORTRAN introduced the idea of functions and subprograms. We were first exposed to the use of encapsulation and abstraction in programming through an introduction to object-oriented analysis and design. Although we make no claims to having produced a model worthy of the praise of Booch, Rumbaugh, or Jacobson, we should acknowledge the influence of their ideas on our approach to managing the complexity of dynamic HTML.

The Strategy

This book is about building user interfaces, not manipulating nodes in HTML or XML document element hierarchies. Therefore, our library and the approach you see in the coming chapters is geared toward the creation, manipulation, and dynamic management of interface primitives. Rather than using the native object models of the various browsers to produce dynamic HTML documents, we are really using them to create the building blocks of dynamic GUI-driven applications. This is an important distinction.

Although we anxiously await the day when XML and the DOM enable us to create truly dynamic documents tailored by the user's preferences and styles into uniquely experienced hypertext or data-driven hierarchies, the current browsers are far from realizing that dream. Rather than try to pretend that they have, we decided that it would be far better to show you how to build real, cross-browser applications with intelligent client-side logic and relatively configurable GUIs.

In order to achieve these GUIs, we've stripped away a lot of the capabilities of both browsers to arrive at a lowest common denominator set of primitives. It is from these primitives that we expect you to build your own applications, hopefully using our library and modules to minimize development time, concentrate maintenance and workarounds into the library rather than the applications themselves, and provide a stepping stone toward the construction of your own libraries.

A Few Words About Objects

As we saw in Chapter 5, "The Document Object Model: Nouns," document objects are simply reflections of HTML elements in JavaScript or some other scripting system. They have properties and can be operated on via native methods or custom JavaScript functions. However, it is also possible to create objects whose sole purpose is to wrap these document objects. These *object wrappers*, as they are called, can be used to provide quick access to the objects themselves while hiding implementation-specific detail from the application developer.

In addition, methods may be defined that provide access to the objects' properties in a platform-independent manner. These methods may be written in many ways, may themselves contain internal branches and browser-specific workarounds, or may be designed with a specific browser in mind and assigned at object creation time to maximize run-time efficiency.

These wrapper objects are the secret to implementing our cross-browser strategy. There are some downsides to this extensive use of objects, however.

MEMORY INTENSIVE OBJECTS

Objects tend to be memory intensive. The more layer, form, and image objects in your application, the more memory is required to store them all. In addition, the mechanisms available for manually deleting objects once their usefulness has passed are unreliable. All this adds up to long-term difficulty for the end user if their system is underpowered.

JAVASCRIPT REFERENCES AND WEAK TYPING

Objects in JavaScript, especially wrapper objects, make extensive use of references in order to manage the assignment of methods, new object names, and so forth. The upside to this is that object wrappers don't take up as much space as they would if they were pure copies.

The downside is that there is no way to enforce encapsulation on our object wrappers. Developers are free to manipulate the core objects we've wrapped, without using the methods we've provided. This isn't very important when it comes to the objects themselves, but it can have drastic effects on properties created or modified by our object's methods. This is especially important when we have created our own global variables in order to store certain cross-browser properties, such as the height or width of the root window. It is inadvisable to simply rely on custom global variables, as the values they may have been initialized with may be changed by undisciplined access to other objects.

We cannot claim to have ruled out entirely the possibility that, even with the use of our wrappers, developers manipulating other objects may have an effect on related objects and their properties. Be careful!

SPEED AND PERFORMANCE

The area in which the most noticeable impact occurs is that of speed. Applications making use of a great deal of branching, wrapper objects, and other generic code tend to be slower than applications written with the native object models of each browser and target platform. However, we feel that as with all software development, the compromise of rapid development cycles, long-term maintenance, and uncluttered code versus a slight speed hit for the user is a worthwhile tradeoff.

If your application absolutely must be implemented using the most efficient code, and you can justify the development time or specify the target platform, by all means avoid this library and the modules built on top of it like the plague. If you're like the rest of us and you can't control your target platform or justify long-term development, read on.

A Few Words About Events

There is one more thing we should cover before we get into the actual implementation of our library. The event models of the two major browsers are like night and day. In fact, you could say with very little sarcasm that they are exactly opposite one another. To complicate matters, there is just enough difference between the way that events are handled – even when you take away the question of how they bubble – that some applications require careful rethinking of the manner in which handlers are assigned.

Fortunately, once these differences are addressed, events are an extremely powerful way to manage user input and interaction. They form the topmost layer of the dynamic face our application presents to the user.

OH, BOY, DO WE HAVE A FEW WORDS ABOUT EVENTS

During the course of our initial attempts at a cross-browser API, we considered a generic event wrapper extremely important for the success of our design. We saw the use (at the application level) of Netscapisms such as `document.captureEvents()` as the ugly thorn in the side of what was shaping up to be a fairly clean API.

As time went on, however, we found that with the use of certain generic property names and some minor shuffling of assigned event handlers, events weren't all that difficult to deal with. Sure, we had browserisms in our application's nice clean code, but they tended to stay out of the way for the most part. And there were other browserisms that snuck in as well, so they weren't the last thing to track down and kill.

Keyboard event handling was a pain, but could be addressed as well as could be expected with a standardized set of event object wrapper properties representing the key code and modifiers pressed. This is what gave us the clue to our eventual compromise.

In the end, we decided that to try to provide generic wrapper functions for assigning and managing events and event handlers was sort of futile, especially given the diametrically opposed nature of the models we were dealing with. You may disagree. Let's quickly review the event models of each major browser, and discuss our final compromise.

THE NETSCAPE MODEL

Netscape Navigator is standoffish with regard to events. If you don't tell it you want to deal with them, it ignores all user interaction other than that built into the browser, such as clicking hypertext links. When you do want it to handle events, however, you have to specify which object, window, or element should grab and process events. You also need to specify which events you want handled through the use of the appropriate `onEventType` handler in HTML elements, or by way of calls to `captureEvents()` and `releaseEvents()`.

Keyboard input, as well as the peculiar syntax for specifying which events should be captured, is based on the model used by Java. Modifier keys are detected through the use of a bitwise-OR operator (|), and syntax differs widely from that used by Explorer.

One other important thing to understand about Netscape's event model is the way it differs most from Internet Explorer. Events are sent first to the window, then to the document, and down through the hierarchy from generic to specific, until a layer or other object is finally encountered that knows how to deal with the event.

THE MICROSOFT MODEL

Microsoft's model, on the other hand, features the exact opposite event propagation scheme. In the Microsoft model, events "bubble" from the target element up through the document hierarchy (as defined by the DOM) until two things happen:

◆ The event encounters an element that has been declared as a handler for that type of event.

◆ The event bubbling is canceled.

This makes for some interesting effects. The most obvious is that event bubbling must be canceled once the application has properly dealt with the event.

What isn't so obvious is that the event object doesn't always look like you would expect if you were used to the Netscape model. An event may have a target that represents the element over which it was first fired, or that is assumed to be the default element that should handle the event. If you aren't familiar with the document hierarchy (as opposed to the object hierarchy) this can get very confusing indeed.

Keyboard input in Explorer is handled in similar fashion to that used by Navigator. The integer key code is returned for the key that was pressed, but, oddly, IE fully supports Unicode, whereas Navigator currently only supports ASCII. Fortunately, they are the same for the first 128 characters. Explorer differs from Navigator in that modifiers are discovered by way of testing individual properties of the event object, rather than using bitwise-OR.

Fortunately, we don't make much use of event propagation in our application. If you do, you may need to reexamine the nature of bubbling and the properties of the `window.event` object in the two browsers.

OUR COMPROMISE

We finally decided that the different directions traveled by events in the two browsers simply weren't all that important to most of the scenarios we could consider. It's rare that any given element has multiple event handlers defined at once, either by way of multiple event handler assignments at different levels of the document hierarchy, by way of embedded HTML event handlers, or both.

If you have two elements or more in a single hierarchy that are set up to handle the same event types, you've got a bigger problem with your application's design than could be addressed by a generic wrapper. If you absolutely need things to be set up that way, there are mechanisms (such as `routeEvent()` in Navigator, or manual event firing in both browsers, as well as the `cancelBubble` property in Explorer) that may be used to construct elaborate event handling schemes not well served by generic wrappers.

Instead of hiding the event handler assignment behind a wrapper method, we chose to provide a generic set of properties for the event object to minimize the aggravation of trying to remember whether Navigator uses `target` or `srcElement`, or which browser uses the `page*` properties and which the `client*` properties.

We're ready to dive into the wrappers themselves. Let's examine a few representative examples of methods and object initialization routines.

Browser-Neutral Wrapper Objects

We provide methods for wrapping three types of interface objects:

◆ Positionable document objects (named DIVs and layers)

◆ Form objects (the input types, option lists, and check boxes/radio buttons)

◆ Image objects

These methods provide easy access to all positionable objects via associative array references in the flat method used by the DOM and Internet Explorer. This is designed to eliminate the need to keep track of the hierarchical relationships between layer objects and their associated documents and the objects that they contain in Netscape Navigator.

We also provide a method for wrapping event objects, in order to provide a consistent means of obtaining keyboard input (key codes and modifiers) and other event properties.

INITIALIZING THE WRAPPERS

On application startup, which for the most part coincides with the loading of the document containing the JavaScript, style sheets, and HTML markup, the object wrappers are initialized by way of a call to the create_base_objects() function. This function loops over all named DIV elements, which must use CSS absolute positioning in order to be recognized by Netscape as part of the document.layers array. This call to create_base_objects() results in references to all named DIV objects. Here is the relevant code from the create_base_objects() function:

```
var object_name = new Array();
function create_base_objects() {
  if( document.all ) {
    objects = document.all.tags("DIV");
  } else {
    objects = document.layers;
  }

  for( i = 0; i < objects.length; i++ ) {
    current_name = objects[i].id;
    object_name[current_name] = new base_object(objects[i]);
  }
}
```

The `object_name[]` array is declared outside of the function in order to ensure that its members are available to all other functions. Note that for Internet Explorer, the `document.all.tags` collection is used, but the `document.layers` array is used in Netscape Navigator. The other thing worth noting is that the really exciting stuff happens as a result of the call to `base_object()`. There are several ways that `base_object()` may be constructed, depending on your requirements and preferences. The version shown below simply assigns methods to the current object regardless of the browser being used. These methods themselves contain branching code to determine the current browser being used and return (or set) the appropriate property value as a result.

For brevity, we only show the assignments for the first few methods.

```
function base_object( object ) {
  if( object.style ) {
    this.css1 = object;
  } else {
    this.style = object;
  }
  object_count++;
  this.name = object.id;

  // handle visibility
  this.conceal    = conceal;
  this.reveal     = reveal;
  this.is_visible = is_visible;

  // handle positioning variables
  this.left      = get_left;
  this.get_left  = get_left;
  this.set_left  = set_left;
  this.top       = get_top;
  this.get_top   = get_top;
  this.set_top   = set_top;

  // other assignments...
}
```

You should notice a few things right away. First of all, the object being passed is either a reference to a DIV from the `document.all.tags` array (in Explorer), or a reference to an element of the `document.layers` array (in Navigator). We check for the `.style` array, and assign the object a temporary placeholder name for use by the methods themselves.

You should also notice that we assign the function `get_left()` to both the `left()` and `get_left()` methods of the object. This enables us to use either method to access the appropriate property. In other words, the same functions may be assigned to object methods as many times as necessary to suit your development environment, taste, company coding style, and so forth.

This way, any object may be accessed, regardless of its place in the Netscape Navigator hierarchy, through a reference to the `object_name[]` array, using the name given the object in the ID attribute in the HTML markup. Following is a DIV element with the ID exampleDiv:

```
<DIV ID="exampleDiv">
... contents ...
</DIV>
```

From within your application, the preceding example may be referenced as:

```
object_name["exampleDiv"]
```

You *must* specify that the DIV is positioned absolutely using a CSS style sheet. This may be done using an ID reference, as in the following example:

```
<HEAD>
<STYLE TYPE="text/css">
#exampleDiv {
  position: absolute;
  top: 0;
  left: 0;
}
</STYLE>
</HEAD>
<DIV ID="exampleDiv">
... contents ...
</DIV>
```

Alternately, you may use the CLASS mechanism to define a single set of styles to be used across several different DIV elements, like so:

```
<HEAD>
<STYLE TYPE="text/css">
.exampleStyle {
  position: absolute;
  top: 0;
  left: 0;
  width: 400;
  height: 200;
}
</STYLE>
</HEAD>
```

```
<DIV ID="exampleDiv" CLASS="exampleStyle">
... contents ...
</DIV>
<DIV ID="otherExampleDiv" CLASS="exampleStyle">
... contents ...
</DIV>
```

If you use the second example, you may also wish to define one of the elements as visible and the others as hidden to prevent overlap and unwanted display of multiple elements in the same space. The net effect of reusing styles in this manner is twofold. First, you save some download time, as the style sheet definitions are smaller. Second, you can quickly modify the definition of the area occupied by multiple elements through editing the style sheet.

In essence, you are defining a standard area to be occupied by common interface elements, such as dialog boxes, forms that are to be displayed in the same area of your application's screen, and other interface characteristics.

 Although it is necessary to define certain positioning characteristics, such as top and left, and width and height, in order to ensure that the elements are accessible via the `document.layers` array in Navigator, this doesn't imply that the settings you define in the style sheet are fixed. On the contrary, the developer can subsequently redefine the placement and size of any such object, as well as other characteristics, using the methods provided.

So now you know how to create referenceable objects and position them accordingly in the space your application occupies. Let's turn our attention to the generic methods we use to read and set their properties.

METHODS FOR LAYER OBJECTS

The objects we refer to as *layers* are not necessarily Netscape Navigator LAYER objects, although they are available via the `document.layers` array in that browser. It may be useful to think of them either as interface primitives or as containers for other interface elements, depending on how you intend to use them. The following chapters provide plenty of examples of both.

For now, let's focus on the methods we provide in order to enable developers to read and set their associated properties.

READING THE OBJECT'S PROPERTIES   Due to the different manners in which the major browsers expose their objects' style properties to JavaScript, we supplement the properties themselves with methods that may be used to read the properties in a platform-independent fashion. For example, to obtain the top and left settings for a layer object named `tim`, you might use the following code:

```
var my_top = 0;
var my_left = 0;
my_top = object_name["tim"].get_top();
my_left = object_name["tim"].get_left();
```

 An important thing to note about this use of methods as opposed to accessing the native properties directly is that the temporary variables *are not references to the properties themselves.* What this means is that although you can count on the values returned from the method being accurate at the time you call the method, you cannot subsequently assign values to these variables and expect them to affect the object's position. If a developer (or the user) manipulates the object in question in any way between the time the values are obtained and the time they are used, they cannot be relied upon with any degree of accuracy. Moral: Always grab the latest values by way of the methods when you intend to use them.

For the sake of illustration, let's look at the actual function code for the get_left() method shown previously.

```
function get_left() {
  if( this.css1 ) {
    if( this.css1.style.pixelLeft ) {
      var l = this.css1.style.pixelLeft;
    } else if( this.css1.style.clientLeft ) {
      var l = this.css1.style.clientLeft;
    } else if( this.css1.style.posLeft ) {
      var l = this.css1.style.posLeft;
    } else {
      var l = 0;
    }
  } else {
    if( this.style.left ) {
      var l = this.style.left;
    } else {
      var l = 0;
    }
  }
  return l;
}
```

The first branch is used if the object is being called from within Internet Explorer, using an arbitrarily named variable assigned during the call to `base_object()`. We start with the most likely property, `pixelLeft`, and keep trying values until we reach one that is set, returning zero if none are found. If our application is being run from Netscape Navigator, on the other hand, there is only one property to check for. You could also look for clipping properties, but we provide other methods that specifically check those properties, so we don't do it here.

You may wish to experiment with the order in which these variables are tried, or change the library to return a different value (such as -1) if the expected properties are not set. In our experience with the sample application discussed in the following chapters, however, if the object itself exists, at least one of the properties is set to the appropriate value.

 We list the internal implementation of the `get_top()` function for demonstration purposes only. Further testing and workarounds for platform- or browser-specific bugs may alter the nature of these functions. Relying on the internals as shown here is not advised.

SETTING THE OBJECT'S PROPERTIES   The corollary to the warning about always grabbing the most current values of whatever property settings you wish to use is that you should always use the object wrapper methods to set those properties as well. To set the position of an object, you would use something like the following code:

```
var new_top = 100;
var new_left = 100;
object_name["tim"].set_top(new_top);
object_name["tim"].set_left(new_left);
```

For the sake of illustration, here's the code for `set_top()` from the library:

```
function set_top(t) {
  if( this.css1 ) {
    this.css1.style.pixelTop = t;
  } else {
    this.style.top = t;
  }
}
```

Again, we check for Internet Explorer, then Netscape Navigator, setting the appropriate property in either case. Because the function is called as a method, the special variable `this` always represents the object by which the method was accessed. The use of the `css1` placeholder is arbitrary, and should be considered private data. If we released the wrapper library to the Internet, and changed the placeholder variable to `mangrove` after this book went to press, you have no reason to complain should you use the latest library but attempt to access the `css1` variable directly.

Also, bear in mind that we're providing these examples for the sake of illustrating one of several ways to construct the functions. It is just as feasible, and may be recommended under certain circumstances, to assign browser-specific functions that do not contain branching at all, or if so, only to work around bugs in specific versions or on certain platforms. In addition, you may wish to test for Navigator first, then Explorer, depending upon your target audience and platform. It's relatively easy to reorder the library code to meet your specific needs. See the Web site for different versions of the wrapper library optimized for specific browsers, environments, or platforms.

MANIPULATING LAYER OBJECTS IN OTHER WAYS   Both browsers provide native methods for manipulating objects, such as the `MoveBy()` or `MoveTo()` methods in Netscape Navigator, or the `scrollIntoView()` method in Internet Explorer. For the sake of duplicating some of these methods for enhanced cross-browser ease of use, we also provide several methods that accomplish the same thing.

We also provide several methods that enable the object in question to be shown or hidden, that manipulate its z-index, or that set some of its styles (such as background color, text color, and various clipping regions). See the chapters that follow for examples.

METHODS FOR FORM AND IMAGE OBJECTS

Because form and image objects in Netscape Navigator may be relative to a layer, we provide methods that enable flat access to all forms and images in a document by way of associative arrays. The call to `create_base_objects()`, modified to show the appropriate calls to the initialization functions for form and image objects, is as follows.

```
var form_name = new Array();
var form_count = 0;
var image_name = new Array();
var image_count = 0;
var object_name = new Array();

function create_base_objects() {
  if( document.all ) {
    objects = document.all.tags("DIV");
```

```
  } else {
    objects = document.layers;
  }

  for( i = 0; i < objects.length; i++ ) {
    current_name = objects[i].id;
    object_name[ current_name ] = new base_object( objects[i] );
    if( navigator.appName == "Netscape" ) {
      create_image_objects(objects[i].document);
      create_form_objects(objects[i].document);
    }
  }
  if( navigator.appName != "Netscape" ) {
    create_image_objects(document);
    create_form_objects(document);
  }
}
```

Notice that just as with the `object_name[]` array, the `form_name[]` and `image_name[]` arrays are declared outside the call to `create_base_objects()`, and for the same reason. The appropriate test is performed to ensure that the form and image wrappers are only created once for Internet Explorer, but `create_image_objects()` and `create_form_objects()` are called for each member of the `document.layers` array for Navigator.

Again, for the sake of illustration only, here is the code for `create_image_objects()`:

```
function create_image_objects(d) {
  var i = d.images;
  var n = i.length;
  for( var x = 0; x < n; x++ ) {
    current_name = i[x].name;

    if( current_name == "" ) {
      current_name = "image" + image_count;
      image_count++;
    }

    if( ! image_name[current_name] ) {
      image_name[current_name] = new image_object(i[x]);
    }
  }
}
```

The document object d is passed either as the full document (in Internet Explorer) or as the current document contained within each layer object (in Netscape Navigator). We then loop over the `document.images` array, creating handy wrappers to the images based on their name as determined by the `NAME` attribute in HTML. For illustration's sake, here is the markup for a sample `IMG`:

```
<IMG NAME="sample" SRC="sample.gif" HEIGHT=20 WIDTH=20>
```

This image is subsequently available via JavaScript as:

```
image_name["sample"]
```

You must be careful when marking up your document not to give images or forms duplicate names. If the image markup does not contain a name, then a name is constructed from the `image_count` variable and may be accessed that way:

```
image_name["image1"]
```

It is highly recommended that you supply your own names, however, as otherwise you must keep track of the order in which your images occur in the markup. As this order could feasibly change during the course of development, causing the usual frustrating search through the markup, the latter approach is discouraged.

READING IMAGE OBJECT PROPERTIES   Reading image object properties is performed similarly to reading layer objects. For example, to get the URL of a given image named `sample`, you would call the following method:

```
var my_img_src = "";
my_img_src = image_name["sample"].get_src();
```

Methods are provided for accessing all the usual image properties, including the image's URL, x and y coordinates on the page, height and width, name, and so forth.

SETTING IMAGE OBJECT PROPERTIES   Just as you would expect, you may set an image property through the use of methods as well. To set the `src` property of an image named `banner` to `alt_banner.gif`, you would call the following method:

```
var new_src = "alt_banner.gif";
image_name["banner"].set_src(new_src);
```

Due to the nature of the current generation of browsers, however, this is the only property that may be set reliably.

READING FORM OBJECT PROPERTIES   Forms are perhaps one of the most powerful mechanisms available to any Web developer, enabling data entry and display of arbitrary data generated on the fly, regardless of browser. The code for `create_form_objects()` is identical in nature to that used to create image object wrappers above.

The methods associated with forms themselves are somewhat limited, compared to those for manipulating their elements. However, it is possible to read the method, encoding type, action, and even target from a form object. For the sake of example, following is some code that demonstrates how to read all of the properties of a form object:

```
var my_form_method = "";
var my_form_action = "";
var my_form_enctype = "";
var my_form_target = "";
my_form_method  = form_name["sample"].get_method();
my_form_action  = form_name["sample"].get_action();
my_form_enctype = form_name["sample"].get_enctype();
my_form_target  = form_name["sample"].get_target();
```

For examples of how to dynamically generate, read, set, and manipulate form input elements, see the following chapters.

SETTING FORM OBJECT PROPERTIES   Setting the properties of form objects is as easy as you would expect. Methods are provided for each property. Each method takes an argument that is used to set the appropriate property of the object. Here's a sample:

```
var my_form_method = "POST";
var my_form_action = "http://example.com/cgi-bin/blah.cgi";
var my_form_enctype = "text/plain";
var my_form_target = "myWindow";
form_name["sample"].set_method(my_form_method);
form_name["sample"].set_action(my_form_action);
form_name["sample"].set_enctype(my_form_enctype);
form_name["sample"].set_target(my_form_target);
```

METHODS FOR EVENT OBJECTS
Because event properties are, for the most part, read-only, we don't provide methods for setting event properties. A noteworthy side effect of this is that developers still need to explicitly set the `cancelBubble` property of the `window.event` object when using Internet Explorer.

The "Object Wrapper Quick Reference" discusses the generic event properties associated with the event object wrapper returned by a call to wrap_event(), which, unlike many of the methods discussed above, is just a regular function. To illustrate the use of the wrap_event() function in an application context, see the following code snippet:

```
function drag(e) {
  if( selected ) {
    var new_x, new_y;

    e = wrap_event(e);
    new_x = e.page_x - drag_x;
    new_y = e.page_y - drag_y;

    // place the selected object
    selected.place(new_x,new_y);

    // offset the shadow to create the illusion of height
    var new_shadow_x = new_x + moving_shadow_height;
    var new_shadow_y = new_y + moving_shadow_height;
    selected_shadow.place(new_shadow_x,new_shadow_y);
  }
}
```

The drag() function shown above is assigned as an event handler, and so its only argument is a reference to an event object, e. The event object is passed to wrap_event(), which returns a wrapped object with generic properties to make it easy to access the relevant event properties without application-level branching. The variables drag_x and drag_y represent the movement of the mouse, and the properties e.page_x and e.page_y represent the initial starting point of the object so that the object being dragged may be placed appropriately using global variables defined elsewhere in the application. The object references selected and selected_shadow are defined in another event handler. See the next chapter for details.

Providing Neutral Access to Properties and Methods

In addition to the methods discussed above, several other methods and functions enable the application developer to set styles (such as visibility, colors, and font styles), place objects on the screen, and update the contents of a given layer object. As you would expect by now, these functions and methods are provided to enable the application developer to use generic mechanisms rather than browser-specific ones.

We only discuss a few relevant examples in the following sections, leaving the appropriate demonstrations to the following chapters. You can find a full listing of the available methods and functions for layer objects in the "Object Wrapper Quick Reference" at the back of this book.

SETTING AND READING LAYER OBJECT STYLES

Showing and hiding objects are two of the most common operations an application developer performs. This is accomplished by way of the CSS style property visibility, which is exposed in different ways (and for a different set of objects) by the major browsers. In order to hide the gory details of managing visibility from the application developer, we provide the following methods:

```
object_name["example"].conceal(); // hides the object
object_name["example"].reveal();  // shows the object
```

In addition, a method is provided that may be used to test an object's visibility before attempting to hide or show it. The is_visible() method returns a Boolean value (either true or false) depending on the current setting of the visibility style property of the object. For example, to check for an object's visibility before hiding it, and reveal it if it is already hidden, use something like the following code:

```
if( object_name["example"].is_visible() ) {
  object_name["example"].conceal();
} else {
  object_name["example"].reveal();
}
```

Of course, visibility is only one aspect of the styles that may be associated with an object. Objects may also have a background and foreground color, clipping regions, and other style information associated with them. Due to the limitations in the current generation of the Netscape browser, other CSS properties such as font information, margins, padding, and border may not work reliably and usually do not reflect dynamic updates of this type. So we only provide cross-browser methods for modifying the color and clipping region properties.

To read or set an object's background or foreground color, use the following methods. This example swaps the background and foreground colors of one object with those of another.

```
var my_first_bg_color = "";
var my_first_fg_color = "";
var my_second_bg_color = "";
var my_second_fg_color = "";

my_first_fg_color  = object_name["first"].color();
my_first_bg_color  = object_name["first"].bg_color();
my_second_fg_color = object_name["second"].color();
my_second_bg_color = object_name["second"].bg_color();

object_name["second"].set_color(my_first_bg_color);
```

```
object_name["second"].set_bg_color(my_first_bg_color);
object_name["first"].set_color(my_second_bg_color);
object_name["first"].set_bg_color(my_second_bg_color);
```

Navigator doesn't support much in the way of dynamic updates to color properties to arbitrary elements. However, our experience with the sample application suggests that if an element is hidden before style properties are modified, then shown again once the changes have been made, the changes take effect as desired. This doesn't necessarily give you the kind of powerful dynamic updates enabled by Internet Explorer, but it can be useful in a pinch.

One other useful mechanism available across browsers (although not in a compatible manner) is the dynamic modification of clipping properties. A *clipping region* is a rectangular subset of the area occupied by an object. If you want to gradually hide or display an object, or show only a portion of the object, you modify the clipping region so that only the desired area is displayed.

We provide several mechanisms for setting clipping region properties. Developers can set and read each property individually, set the values of the four corners of the clipping region at once, and use dynamic mechanisms for animated *slides* and *wipes*. The dynamic methods are discussed in detail in Chapter 16, "Timers and Other Fun Stuff."

To inset an object's clipping region by 10 pixels on each side, use code such as the following, which demonstrates the use of both methods for obtaining individual properties and setting an entire region at once:

```
var my_top, my_left, my_right, my_bottom;
var ex = object_name["example"];

// get each property and subtract/add 10 from each
// as appropriate, then use to set new clipping region
my_top = ex.clipper_top() + 10;
my_left = ex.clipper_left() + 10;
my_right = ex.clipper_right() - 10;
my_bottom = ex.clipper_bottom() - 10;

// now use modified values to inset clipping region
ex.clipper(my_top, my_left, my_bottom, my_right);
```

You could also use the individual methods for setting each corner's value.

Internet Explorer 4.0 for the Macintosh doesn't support clipping regions at all. While this may change with subsequent releases of the browser, it would be unwise to count on clipping regions behaving properly or being present at all if your target platform requirements include IE on the Macintosh.

We were alternately lulled by the ease with which Internet Explorer enables you to set all four corners at once and frustrated by the way it deviated from a function format by forcing you to assign a string to the `style.clip` property. It just seemed wrong, so we provide the function format, which works in Navigator as well, despite the fact that Navigator doesn't natively provide a similar function. This is a matter of taste on our part, as the mechanism supported by IE is actually the one standardized by the W3C CSS1 Recommendation.

UPDATING LAYER OBJECT CONTENTS

We'd be very happy indeed if Netscape Navigator supported the `innerText` and `innerHTML` properties provided by the DOM and implemented in Internet Explorer. Unfortunately, Navigator's support for dynamic updating of document and element contents is severely limited in the 4.0 generation. To help work around this limitation, we provide a few generic functions that allow for the replacement of object contents. The solution isn't complete, though; there is no reliable way to read the previous contents of a given object and manipulate them, as you can with IE. In our sample application, we wrote entire functions that knew how to regenerate the markup for objects as necessary.

To replace the entire contents of an existing layer object, use code such as this:

```
var markup = '<b>new stuff!</b>';
object_name["thelayer"].replace(markup);
```

There isn't any limit to how much markup you can pass to the `replace()` method, so feel free to build elaborate documents and then stick them into existing layer objects.

PLACING LAYER OBJECTS

Sometimes it just isn't enough to move an object by setting individual properties. You want to be able to specify a position, either absolute or relative, where the object should be placed. To place an object absolutely, using the cross-browser library, simply call the `place()` method:

```
var new_x = 100;
var new_y = 200;
object_name["thingie"].place(new_x,new_y);
```

In order to move an object relative to its current position, you can use the `shove()` method:

```
var delta_x = 20;
var delta_y = 10;
object_name["thingie"].shove(delta_x,delta_y);
```

Feel free to use negative values as well:

```
var delta_x = -20;
var delta_y = -10;
object_name["thingie"].shove(delta_x,delta_y);
```

Being able to place and shove objects is useful, but you may find it even more useful to set their position based on the position of other objects. The abut() and overlay() methods enable you to do exactly that, using compass points, alignment, and offsets to specify exactly how your object should be placed. To abut an object named "utah" to the north of another object named "arizona," aligning the two by the right side with a 2-pixel border, you would use something like this:

```
var ut = object_name["utah"];
var az = object_name["arizona"];
ut.abut(az,"N","RIGHT",2);
```

To overlay an object atop another, you follow a similar syntax. For example, to place a stamp 10 pixels from each side of the top right-hand corner of an envelope, you might call overlay() with the following arguments:

```
var stamp = object_name["stamp"];
var envelope = object_name["envelope"];
stamp.overlay(envelope,"NE","TOP",10);
```

These methods are discussed in greater detail in the "Object Wrapper Quick Reference," as well as demonstrated in subsequent chapters.

Providing Information About the Environment

At times it is appropriate to tailor your application to a given platform's peculiarities of color, screen size, and so forth. We've provided for this eventuality as well, through the use of the get_screen_props() function. You should call this function just before trying to use any of the variables it defines to make sure that the information is accurate. The function defines properties of the xp_screen object, but also returns a reference to that object if you want to give it your own name.

```
var my_screen_props;
my_screen_props = get_screen_props();
```

SCREEN DIMENSIONS

Screens may have two kinds of height and width: *raw* dimensions, which describe the full area of the client's monitor; and *available* dimensions, which simply describe the area available to the browser. The second set of values factors in the system taskbar and menu bar on various operating systems. Unfortunately, the calculation isn't always performed correctly, so we wrap the values and build in the appropriate tests so you don't have to. To get the raw and available height and width, you could use code like this:

```
var my_h, my_w, my_ah, my_aw;
get_screen_props();
my_h = xp_screen.height;
my_w = xp_screen.width;
my_ah = xp_screen.aheight;
my_aw = xp_screen.awidth;
```

SCREEN DEPTH

Color depth may be used, for example, to adjust the color maps used in an onscreen color picker. To find out what color depth is supported by the current environment, you should read the following variables:

◆ `xp_screen.color_depth` — Set to the bits per pixel of the current display.

◆ `xp_screen.depth` — Similar to the previous setting, but may be influenced by a custom color palette. Compare to `color_depth` to ensure that your images are buffered to the same palette as used to display them.

We do not provide any mechanism for setting these properties, but if you're concerned about buffering and display of images in higher-end environments, you may want to take a closer look at these properties.

Well, that's it! We hope you take the time to review the more detailed information in the "Object Wrapper Quick Reference." Even more importantly, we hope that the example provided by this admittedly somewhat limited library spurs you on to create even more powerful cross-browser libraries of your own. In the following chapters, you see the library put to use, and you get a chance to see how easy it is to build entire applications that work across browsers without coding in lots of browser-specific workarounds.

Expectations Management

We end this chapter with a warning of sorts. As with any cutting- or bleeding-edge technology, dynamic HTML is unreliable, unstable, untrustworthy, not suitable for powering nuclear plants or providing traffic control information, and generally fails when you least want it to for no good reason. Anything we tell you in the subsequent chapters, as well as anything we've said previously, may be a lie. If you build applications with this library, they probably won't work. If you build your own library, it won't work either. Applications you code that pass all of your tests with flying colors, are popular with users when you show off interface prototypes, and generally do everything you want them to, suddenly stop working when the next security patch is released for your target platform for no reason at all.

No, of course things aren't that bad. But it is important that you practice a bit of reasoned "expectations management" – a humorous term employed quite often by consultants and project managers. The term reflects the need to temper your enthusiasm for a given technology (or time frame, or design, and so on) in the face of the reality of unforeseen setbacks, changing requirements, and the other factors that affect the quality and schedule of any software development project.

We set out to prove that you could build useful and powerful applications using dynamic HTML. For the most part, we feel we have succeeded, although there are certainly areas for improvement. The bottom line is that dynamic HTML is an exciting new technology with enormous potential, but if you fall in love with it, it will likely crush your tender soul with its black heart and leave you for dead on the roadside – bleeding, defeated, and crying out for mercy.

Summary

In this chapter, you learned some important strategies for implementing complete applications using dynamic HTML. We covered the cross-platform library in some detail, and discussed individual methods we use in a real application in the following chapters. Some other things you learned include:

◆ Why abstraction is a powerful tool for managing complexity

◆ How encapsulation can be applied in the design of useful libraries

◆ Why JavaScript is a poor language for trying to enforce encapsulation

◆ What branching is, how and where to use it, and why it belongs hidden behind an API layer

◆ What methods and properties are provided by the cross-platform library we use for the next few chapters

◆ How to extend and optimize the cross-platform library for your own purposes

In the next chapter, our sample application takes form and we have some fun at the expense of people who use too many buzzwords.

Chapter 10

Executive Dynamic Poetry

IN THIS CHAPTER

- ◆ Getting started
- ◆ Using DHTML for positioning
- ◆ Defining the general layout
- ◆ Creating dynamic word magnets
- ◆ Enabling click and drag
- ◆ Showing/hiding your application's screens and dialog boxes
- ◆ Rounding out the user experience
- ◆ Identifying gotchas

NOW THAT WE'VE SPENT the last several hundred pages tantalizing you with the prospect of a day when you, too, are able to create applications of your very own, it's time to strut our stuff a little. Unless you're the type that never reads ahead in books like these, you know by now that the application we have in mind is a dynamic HTML version of the popular magnetic poetry refrigerator magnet game. In case your friends aren't all unemployed liberal arts graduates, and you've never actually enjoyed its guilty pleasures, we give you a rundown in the next section.

Understanding Magnetic Poetry

Essentially, magnetic poetry is a collection of a couple hundred little magnets with words on the front that stick to your refrigerator or filing cabinet. Using the words provided, it is up to you to arrange any masterpieces of poesy you happen to find into crude, repetitive phrases, that, depending on how much you're enjoying the party, may or may not also denigrate the party's hosts. It is *imperative* that you leave suggestive and tasteless phrases if the host's parents are going to be visiting from out of town within the next few days, so that they can be suitably shocked and appalled at the moral vacuum in which their Theodore has fallen. It is then up to Theo to blame it on the plumber, or, if he's lucky, on the cats.

The problem with magnetic poetry is that, until recently, there just weren't that many really good words to use in your quest to upset your friends' parents. There were a few blanks you were encouraged to write your own words on, but that lacks the joy of discovering the astounding combinations you can make with the words provided. And besides, it looks tacky when some of your art is screenprinted consistently in black 12-point Helvetica Bold on white, and some is handwritten in smeared blue ballpoint. The other problem is that there is no way to save your favorite works before the big party, when they will be mocked, trivialized, and mined for words that work well in conjunction with "iniquity" and "gin blossom." Now, some may argue that it is their short-lived nature, the fragile beauty of a flower before a storm, that makes refrigerator magnetic poetry so much fun. These deluded folks might object to a version of magnetic poetry that enables the addition of arbitrary words and the saving and sharing of phrases from the nonmagnetized safety and comfort of your own computer.

But we've got a book to write here, and if we get bogged down in metaphysical, ethical, and moral discussions we'll never get to show off this cross-browser object model we've slaved over for the past few weeks. So here we go.

We've decided to throw in a little twist, though — we're sure you've heard of Buzzword Bingo, the game played by bored members of middle management during long, tedious meetings. Basically, it involves the typical bingo setup, a checkerboard populated by certain numbers, only in this case the numbers are buzzwords they can expect to hear during the course of the meeting. As the buzzwords are uttered, the player marks them off their board until someone gets a row of matches, either horizontally or vertically. It was recently revealed that there is even a version of the game for the Palm OS. So we're going to borrow the idea for the wordlist from Buzzword Bingo for our foray into Executive Dynamic Poetry. You, too, will be able to create vacuous, meaningless phrases with an emphasis on sounding important and all-knowing! For now, though, let's start with some basics.

Beginning the DHTML Application

Building a DHTML application is just like building a regular Web site; there are numerous ways that the content, markup, client-side scripting, back-end CGI programs, and so forth interact with and depend on each other. In order to make this as smooth a process as possible, it is necessary to outline what components are necessary and determine the order in which they should be implemented. Following the nouns/verbs/adjectives model we discussed in Chapters 5 through 8, let's break out the components first.

Nouns

The "nouns" that are needed to play the game, both specific (the playing field) and general (the wordlist), are as follows. These are implemented using normal HTML and dynamic HTML, and are associated with certain actions (the verbs) and styled and/or positioned using CSS and CSS-P (the adjectives).

- The playing field
- The words themselves
- A menu palette and menu items
- The forms ("add a word," "delete a word," "save a phrase," "view a phrase," "delete a phrase")
- The instructions screen
- Any user preferences (such as favorite wordlists, menu state, and so on)

Verbs

The game requires the following "verbs," or actions, that are implemented using JavaScript and HTML event handlers, and, in some cases, cookies. Technically speaking, the "verbs" listed below are actually more like verb phrases, which take an object. The important thing to remember is that the actions you define always act on the objects in your application, the application itself, or the network. The closer you get to defining pure verbs (those that don't include their object in their definition), the better off you are from the standpoint of what's known as *decomposition*, or the art of properly breaking down the components of your application during the design phase.

- Add a word
- Delete a word
- Save a phrase
- View a phrase
- Delete a phrase
- Quit playing
- A routine to display/hide the various forms
- Other utility functions, such as drag-and-drop, shift-select (for selecting a phrase to save), and preferences

Adjectives

The game requires the following "adjectives," or styles, that are implemented using CSS and CSS-P, and that apply to the nouns listed previously:

◆ Positioning for the playing field itself

◆ Styles and positioning for the various words

◆ Styles and positioning for the various forms

◆ Styles and positioning for the menu palette

In this early phase of the application's development, it is easy to map the nouns to HTML and DHTML constructs, such as plain old markup inside DIV tags. It is also easy to point to the style sheets and say, "These are the adjectives," just as it is easy to say, "The verbs are all just JavaScript functions." As we delve deeper into the application, however, it becomes clear that the somewhat natural lines we have drawn blur quickly. But for now, it is easier to start with the simplistic one-on-one mappings we have drawn.

 Because the first part of this exercise involves marking out the boundaries of our application's playing field, we start by defining the layers (understood in the cross-browser sense of "DHTML objects that accept styles and act as containers for other markup") and the styles that position them. Now might be a good time to review Chapter 7, "Cascading Style Sheets: Adjectives and Adverbs," as much of this section uses CSS for positioning.

Defining the General Layout

The first thing we should do is figure out the layout and dimensions of the game's playing field, where all the words live. In order to make the game accessible to our target audience, middle management with laptop computers, we should define everything in terms of a screen size of roughly 600 × 400. The main playing field is smaller than this, of course, because we have to leave room for the game's title, menu palette, forms area, and status bar. For this example, we use absolute styles. Other applications with a much broader appeal might need to be more flexible to fit not only laptops, but also smaller screens with a different aspect ratio or larger browser windows on platforms like the Macintosh or UNIX where users rarely maximize their application windows.

The main playing area uses absolute CSS to define a container approximately 640 pixels wide by 480 pixels tall, with adjustments to allow for the vagaries of the images used by the menu palette and various other components. We've decided that the area occupied by the word playing field is reused by both the instructions page and feedback form, so we've made the style sheet entry affect a class of DIV. We're using the *dot* convention, where the name of the element is immediately followed by a period and then the name by which the style sheet is accessed from the elements. We had originally set this container up to use the ID attribute and style sheet naming convention, but as we got further along we realized that there were several uses for it, so we made it use a CLASS. The style sheet specifies that the styles it contains should be interpreted in terms of absolute positioning, and gives the top and left coordinates in terms of pixels, the default. It is also possible to use the .px suffix to make the units more specific, but it is not necessary. We also specify a text indent of 30 pixels, using explicit pixel units because it is easy to get confused between pixels and the other text units, such as picas or points. Here's the code for the main playing area:

```
div.main {
    position: absolute;
    top: 30;
    left: 118;
    width: 483;
    height: 390;
    text-indent: 30px;
}
```

The DIV element for the playing field references the style sheet listing above through the use of the CLASS attribute, specifying the name main. Remember that class and ID names cannot contain spaces, underscores, or dashes, which makes things a bit less readable. A conscientious effort to name your style sheets using single words or common, unmistakable abbreviations pays off in the long run.

Also be aware that the DIV element doesn't accept a NAME attribute according to the HTML 4.0 DTD. Use ID instead of NAME for DIV elements. Interestingly enough, both Internet Explorer and Navigator support the NAME attribute, but because this is nonstandard behavior, you should not rely upon it.

Because the DIV in question merely acts as a playing field for the placement of words, it is empty of other markup.

You might want to include a header or other text in your application to label the container better. The mainlayer DIV, shown in the following code, originally used a STYLE attribute to indicate that it should be visible when the application starts up, but we moved it out into a separate style sheet instead.

```
<!-- the main playing field. -->
<div id=mainlayer class=main>

</div>
```

   Notice the name we have given the layer is also devoid of underscores, spaces, or dashes. Underscores are allowed in object names, but for reasons that become clear later in the chapter we have chosen not to use them.

   The form background container is probably the most commonly used container area in this application. It specifies the area to be occupied by all of our forms. This suggests that it should also use the CLASS attribute and style sheet naming format, rather than ID, which is more appropriate for single containers:

```
div.formbg {
    position: absolute;
    top: 280;
    left: 120;
    width: 480;
    height: 140;
}
```

   The form background container references the style sheet by way of the CLASS attribute. Because we use the single style sheet for several different forms, we only list one, the "save a phrase" form, as an example. This form is invisible on startup, and is only revealed when the user selects the "save phrase" menu item. It is also worth mentioning that this form, unlike the menu items, uses an <H1> header, whose style definition may be seen in the file poetry.css, which incorporates all of the styles we use for the application. We usually try to separate the standard attributes, such as ID, CLASS, and so forth, from those that specify scripting language event handlers by starting a new line for each event handler before closing the start tag. We're a little weird, in that we usually line up the first attribute or event handler with the beginning of the first attribute or event handler on the previous line, which makes for some interesting (and sometimes sort of irritating) formatting. But hey, it works for us. We find that it is easier to keep track of what element the attribute belongs to if it is aligned with the other attributes within that element's start tag. For an example, see Listing 10-4.

Examining Noun-Adjective-Verb

We discuss the forms and their associated actions in greater detail later on in this chapter, but because this is the first example of a fully integrated noun-adjective-verb we've run across, let's talk about it a little. Notice that the form as defined, shown in Listing 10-1, does not allow for a full submission, trapping the `onSubmit` event (triggered when the user presses Enter, for example), and returning false. This prevents the form from being submitted. A more robust application would also call the appropriate JavaScript routine before returning false, thereby enabling users to use the keyboard, rather than forcing them to use the mouse.

The `onClick` event handler calls a JavaScript routine, passing the name of the form that called it as an argument to the function, to make it easier to access the value of the form's only input. This also demonstrates good software practice, in that the JavaScript routine doesn't need to know anything more than a property of the object passed to it, rather than building the name of the form directly into the routine itself. We could also have passed the value of the input itself, which only really makes sense when there are relatively few inputs. However, we want to be able to extend the form and its corresponding function if necessary by adding other inputs. This makes it easier to change the names of your forms, say, when you're writing the documentation (or a book) and realize that the form has a silly name. Of course, this also makes it easier to internationalize the code, giving the form a French or German name (just to pick a more dignified reason why you'd want to do this).

When passing form references to a JavaScript function, it is also possible to pass the identifier `this.form` rather than explicitly passing the form by name. You may also pass the identifier `this` from the event handler for any given form input to refer to the input itself. It's a matter of taste and readability on the developer's part. On the JavaScript side of things, all you see is a reference that has been named in the formal parameters to the function, so it doesn't matter which method you use.

Listing 10-1: The markup for the "save a phrase" form

```
<!-- save a phrase. -->
<div id=savephraselayer class=formbg
     style="visibility: hidden;">
<h1>save a phrase</h1>
<form name="save_phrase_form"
      onSubmit="return false;">
give your phrase a name:<br>
<input type=text name=phrase size=30>
<input type=button value="save"
       onClick="save_phrase_check(save_phrase_form);">
</form>
</div>
```

The "save a phrase" form, shown in Figure 10-1, occupies the lower right and central area of the game's main window.

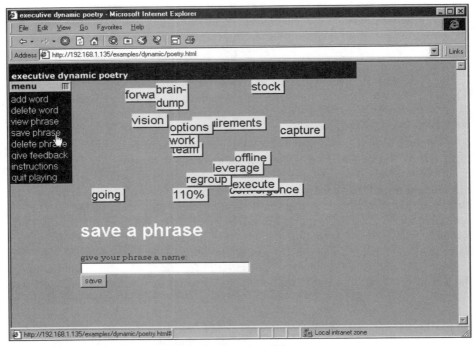

Figure 10-1: Saving a phrase using the "save a phrase" form

Exploring the Menu Palette

The menu palette is perhaps the most important interface element from the user's perspective, because it contains the menu items that enable the user to perform advanced tasks such as adding or deleting words, or manipulating phrases. It also gives the user a way to ask for help or give feedback on the game itself. The style sheet for the menu palette is still fairly simple, but the markup for the various menu items and title bar is a bit more involved, so we discuss it in detail. In Chapter 14, "Dynamic Menus," we replace this menu palette with dynamic menus more reminiscent of those found in traditional GUI applications. For now, we use the menu palette as a way to quickly access the application's functionality.

On startup, the menu palette and all of its items are found in the same place, on the left side of the screen. We've defined style sheets for each menu item, the menu header or title bar, and the menu palette container itself.

The following style sheet defines the DIV that contains both the menu header and the other menu items. We have used absolute positioning again, specifying the top left-hand corner as well as the menu width, but in the interest of flexibility we have not specified a height, preferring to let the menu palette grow with its contents.

```
#menu {
    position: absolute;
    top: 30;
    left: 0;
    width: 107;
}
```

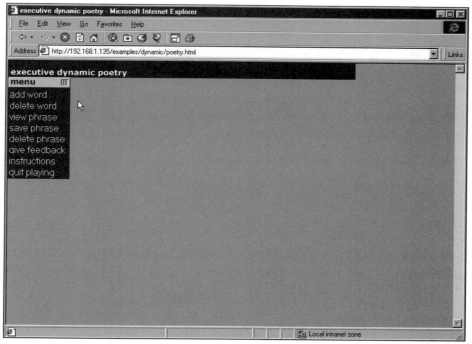

Figure 10-2: The menu palette in its nonminimized state

The menu header is interesting because it has two positions (see Listing 10-2). The first position, defined relative to the menu container itself, is to be displayed horizontally, with the individual menu items stacked beneath it. Note that CSS absolute positioning values, when applied to an object contained by another, are relative to the container, not to the root window. The second, hidden on startup, is for minimizing the menu bar as a whole, including the menu items beneath the header. When minimized, the menu bar is aligned vertically against the left side of the screen, using a different image to convey its minimized state. The Minimize/Maximize icon, shown in Figure 10-2 in its nonminimized state, changes to reflect the different actions that may be taken depending on the state of the menu bar itself. The icon is on the right-hand side of the menu's title bar. It looks like a little box with two vertical lines in it, meant to suggest the position that the menu's title bar end ups in if the user clicks the button. When minimized, the icon suggests the menu's title bar is restored to a horizontal position. Like many nonpictorial icons, it tries to provide a very simple symbolic representation that is easily learned and that the user may quickly link to its function.

Listing 10-2: The menu header style sheet, both states

```
#menuhead {
    position: absolute;
    top: 0;
    left: 0;
    width: 107;
}

#menuminimized {
    position: absolute;
    top: 0;
    left: 0;
    width: 20;
    visibility: hidden;
}
```

The image we've created for the menu bar measures 107 pixels by 20 pixels. In the interest of not defining any more than we have to, we've only specified the width for each style sheet. Later on, we may find that it makes more sense from a JavaScript perspective to define both the width and the height in the style sheet to enable easier access to their respective values, but for now we leave them the way they are. Note that the values for top and left are relative to their container, not to the root window. This can be confusing to first-time style sheet authors, because the relative keyword would seem to make more sense in this context.

ASSOCIATING EVENT HANDLERS WITH THE MENU HEADER
In order to associate event handlers with the menu header later on, we've wrapped the image with an anchor whose HREF attribute is set to "#." This defeats the browser's urge to reload the page or try loading another page, and is overridden by an onClick event handler, shown in the following listing. The menu bar is discussed in greater detail in Chapter 14, "Dynamic Menus." We have stuck with the tried-and-true border=0 here as well, although CSS provides a way to specify that the anchor's border be invisible. We've found that support for this feature of CSS is spotty at best.

```
<div id=menuhead>
<a href="#" onClick='toggle_menu();'>
<img src="/images/menu.gif"
```

```
     width=107 height=20 border=0></a>
</div>
```

BUILDING OTHER MENU COMPONENTS

The rest of the menu components, the items, each have a style sheet associated with them as well. We don't describe each in detail, but you can see them all in Listing 10-3. Notice that they are all defined relative to the top-left area of their container (menulayer) and are intended to be tall enough to accommodate the menu text each contains, although this isn't the safest bet, depending on the platform in question.

Listing 10-3: Style sheets for the menu items themselves

```
#menuaddword {
    position: absolute;
    top: 20;
    left: 0;
    width: 107;
    background-color: black;
}


#menudeleteword {
    position: absolute;
    top: 40;
    left: 0;
    width: 107;
    background-color: black;
}


#menuviewphrase {
    position: absolute;
    top: 60;
    left: 0;
    width: 107;
    background-color: black;
}


#menusavephrase {
    position: absolute;
    top: 80;
    left: 0;
    width: 107;
    background-color: black;
}
```

```
#menudeletephrase {
    position: absolute;
    top: 100;
    left: 0;
    width: 107;
    background-color: black;
}

#menugivefeedback {
    position: absolute;
    top: 120;
    left: 0;
    width: 107;
    background-color: black;
}

#menuinstructions {
    position: absolute;
    top: 140;
    left: 0;
    width: 107;
    background-color: black;
}

#menuquitplaying {
    position: absolute;
    top: 160;
    left: 0;
    width: 107;
    background-color: black;
}
```

The style sheet for each menu item is the same, making use of the CLASS style to specify a white, 12-point, sans serif font for the menu item text. We had originally specified that the font also be bold, but differences between the various browsers' rendering of 12-point fonts – even on the same platform – made it necessary to readjust the default weight. Note the comments (similar to those used by the C programming language) in the following code:

```
.menuitem {
    background-color: black;
    color: white;
    font-family: Sans-serif;
    font-size: 12pt;
```

```
/*      font-weight: bold; */
}
```

We have specified that the menu items' background color be black, although due to a difference in the way that Netscape Navigator and Microsoft Internet Explorer renders background colors on text objects, we've had to supply a workaround as well. IE treats a DIV as a sort of full-width container by default, so in IE the black background extends all the way to the right side of the browser unless the CSS width and height properties are set. In Navigator, however, the background color for the DIV is only used with respect to the text in the DIV. To make up for these bugs, we've added table markup, which Navigator does use, and explicitly set the width of the table so that IE restricts the size of the DIV. There are other ways of dealing with the problem, involving explicitly setting the clipping area in Navigator, or explicitly setting the height and width CSS attributes for the DIV, but this method works in both browsers.

Because these are ID styles, intended to position unique objects, we created a special CLASS style sheet as a workaround:

```
.bgcolorworkaround {
    background-color: black;
}
```

The HTML code for the workaround is shown in Listing 10-4, using the "add word" menu item as an example. Essentially, all we're doing here is using a single cell table as yet another container for the link, in addition to the DIV and SPAN elements. The TABLE is the only cross-browser and cross-platform workaround for bugs in Navigator's handling of the background color style attribute.

To be fair, we could have just used bgcolor="black" here and saved a few keystrokes, but it just goes to show the interchangeable nature of DHTML. The same could be said of the width, height, cellpadding, and cellspacing attributes as well, which would make a better excuse to just move their values out into the style sheet and refer to them via the CLASS attribute.

Listing 10-4: Sample markup for a menu item that hides/shows a form

```
<div id=menuaddword>
<table cellpadding=2 cellspacing=0
       width=107 height=20
       class=bgcolorworkaround>
<tr><td>
<a href="#"
   onClick='toggle_form("addwordlayer");'>
<span class=menuitem>
add word</span></a>
</td></tr></table>
</div>
```

The "add word," "save phrase," "give feedback," and "instructions" menu items all use one form or another of a relatively simple JavaScript function. The function simply hides the current contents of a given area and displays the appropriate form or, as in the case of the instructions, another container. The first two call `toggle_form()`, a generic DIV-swapping function, and the latter call more specialized functions that check the state of both the other form and the words as well, hiding them if shown and revealing them if hidden. The specialized functions also check to see if they are being called back-to-back, in which case the words should not necessarily be revealed, as this would just get in the way of the other layer.

TOGGLE_FORM()

The first of these JavaScript functions, and the first we discuss, is called `toggle_form()`, the listing for which may be seen in Listing 10-5. A fairly simple function, it checks to see if the object whose name is passed as the sole argument is visible, and if so, conceals that object while revealing a blank layer. If not, it reveals that object, hiding the blank layer and setting a global variable to track state. This could have been made a bit simpler if we hadn't used a blank layer. However, the instructions and feedback form screens actually use more than just the top half of the screen, so we need to be able to track the state of the forms area from other functions as well. Another way to handle this would have been to simply use a Boolean (a variable that may be either true or false) to track whether the forms area was displaying a form at all. The function does illustrate the way you might go about working with several screens occupying the same space, however. In the specialized version of this function for the instructions layer, we actually have a three-way set of values for forms that occupy either one or two areas onscreen. Because the word magnets should never be placed within the forms area, there is no need to check for their presence. Of course, the user can drag them anywhere they want, but in the interest of keeping things simple we do not check.

Listing 10-5: The toggle_form JavaScript function

```
var visible_form_screen = "blanklayer";
// toggle the form screens
function toggle_form(screen) {
  if( object_name[screen].is_visible() == true ) {
    object_name[screen].conceal();
    object_name["blanklayer"].reveal();
    visible_form_screen = "blanklayer";
  } else {
    object_name[visible_form_screen].conceal();
    object_name[screen].reveal();
    visible_form_screen = screen;
  }
}
```

The other menu items are a bit more complex in that they must first check the state of the application and generate forms on the fly. We don't get into the guts of saving phrases just yet, as that involves the use of cookies, but we do talk about the functions that populate the "delete word" form on the fly, based on up-to-the-minute client state, and shown in Figure 10-3. Bear with us if you're wondering where all these words we're supposed to be making into poetry are coming from — it's coming up very soon.

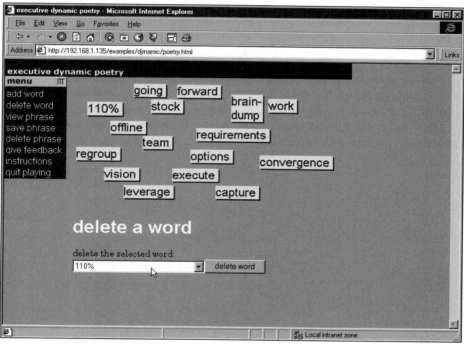

Figure 10-3: Revealing the "delete word" form

The "delete word" form found in the original HTML document is merely a placeholder, and is in fact never used. Whenever the user invokes the "delete word" menu item, the prep_delete_word_form() function, shown in Listing 10-6, dynamically builds a list of the words currently in play and uses that list to populate a drop-down list box. This form, in turn, calls another function that takes the selected word and removes it from play. The list box uses a fixed-length string of underscores to try and regulate the horizontal size of the list box itself, but this is ultimately somewhat futile because the application doesn't actually check for the length of words as they are initialized and/or added to play. (Yet another exercise left to the reader.)

Listing 10-6: The prep_delete_word_form() JavaScript function

```
function prep_delete_word_form( ) {
  var dwl = "deletewordlayer"; // shorthand
  // create a new form and select
  var new_form = '<h1>delete a word</h1>'
    + '<form name="delete_word_form"'
    + ' onSubmit="return false;">'
    + 'delete the selected word:<br>'
    + '<select name="words">';

  // get the current wordlist
  for( i = 0; i < words.length; i++ ) {
    if( words[i] ) {
      new_form += '<option value="'
        + words[i].name + '">'
        + words[i].word + '</option>';
    }
  }

  new_form += '<option>'
    + '_____'
    + '</option>'
    + '</select>'
    + '<input type=button value="delete word"'
    + ' onClick="delete_word(delete_word_form);">'
    + '</form>';

  // print the form and other stuff to
  // deletewordlayer

  object_name[dwl].replace(new_form, dwl);

  // and finally, reveal the form
  toggle_form(dwl);
}
```

The way the application works now, there is a simple array of words called, appropriately enough, words[], whose members are set to either true or false depending on whether the word is in or out of play. Each member of the array also has a property containing the name of the object representing it onscreen and another property containing the word itself. By looping through this array, and testing for the value of each member, the wordlist may be constructed in the order in which words were added, as you can see in Figure 10-4. Another approach would be to use a linked list and delete words from the array altogether, rather than setting the member's value to false. In memory-scarce environments, this may be preferable to the brute-force method used here.

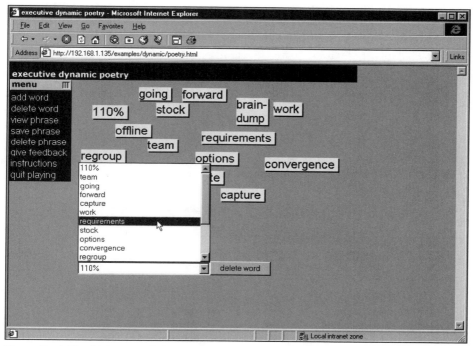

Figure 10–4: The "delete word" form, showing the list of all current words

Once the form has been constructed, it is then written to the placeholder container and revealed. Once revealed, the form enables the user to study all the words in the game and delete them one at a time. The user makes a selection and clicks the button, which sends an `onClick` event to the form, calling the function that actually deletes the words from the list. Note that once again the application is trapping the `submit` event, which might accidentally be invoked otherwise. In this case, there's not so much to worry about, because `SELECT` doesn't enable the user to just hit return or use other shortcuts to submit the form.

TIP It is a good habit to always know what events might be invoked, whether on purpose or accidentally, from your application, so you can be prepared to deal with them if they occur.

The user may also hide the form without taking any action at all, either by selecting another menu item or by selecting the "delete word" menu item again. Due to the confusion that might result from overloading the same menu item label with two different functions, we extend this function in Chapter 14, "Dynamic Menus." When we're done, the menu item label also changes to reflect the current state of the forms area and acts to remind the user of what they most recently set out to do. The form is also hidden following a successful deletion, so as not to confuse the user with a now out-of-date list of words. To delete another word, the user must choose the item explicitly from the menu, which just starts the whole process over again.

The instructions layer, shown in Listing 10-7, is probably the simplest bit of markup in the whole application next to the blank layer; it contains (or should contain) a set of instructions for use. Invoked from the menu using the `toggle_instructions()` function, it also contains a link ("return to the game") that returns the game to whatever state it was in before the user clicked the menu item. Because it calls the same function as the menu item, the user may also click the menu item again. We talk about this sort of state-management and user feedback in greater detail in Chapter 14, "Dynamic Menus." The instructions layer uses the same styles that are used by the feedback form, discussed in more detail in Chapter 11, "The Hidden Feedback Form."

Listing 10-7: Instructions layer markup

```
<div id=instructionslayer
     class=main>
<h1>instructions</h1>
instructions will go here.
<p>
<a href="#"
   onClick="toggle_instructions();">
return to the game</a>
</div>
```

The `toggle_instructions()` function is similar to the more generic `toggle_form()`, and is in fact based on it, but because the instructions layer occupies the same space the word magnets do, we check their state, hiding them and revealing them as necessary. The function, shown in Listing 10-8, simply checks to see if the instructions layer is visible, and if so, hides it while showing the main layer. A better design for this application might use JavaScript's object prototyping functionality to provide a common set of methods and properties for a `toggle()` function, subclassing from it to create specific classes for each form.

Listing 10-8: The toggle_instructions() JavaScript function

```
function toggle_instructions () {
  var il = "instructionslayer";
  var ml = "mainlayer";
```

```
if( visible_main_screen != il ) {
  // show the instructions screen
  object_name[visible_main_screen].conceal();
  if( words_are_visible ) {
    toggle_words();
  }
  object_name[ il ].set_z_index(frontmost);
  object_name[ il ].reveal();
  visible_main_screen = il;
} else {
  // hide the instructions screen
  object_name[visible_main_screen].conceal();
  if( ! words_are_visible ) {
    toggle_words();
  }
  object_name[ ml ].set_z_index(frontmost);
  object_name[ ml ].reveal();
  visible_main_screen = ml;
}
}
```

The `toggle_instructions()` function could have been written to also check whether the feedback form was visible before the instructions layer was shown, enabling the user to toggle back and forth between them rather than having to go back to the main playing area first, but that would require keeping a record of the most recently displayed alternate layers as well as the word magnets' state. For the best, most bulletproof application, we recommend this approach.

The feedback form, discussed in Chapter 11, is relatively complex. Its role as a feedback mechanism puts it in a different category of user interface object, rather than a simple task-oriented component. Feedback mechanisms in general are discussed in Chapter 12, "Other Kinds of Feedback."

Creating Dynamic Word Magnets

No magnetic poetry application would be complete without a few magnets. Originally, we had hoped to be able to construct a magnet, complete with its "shadow," using nothing more than Cascading Style Sheets. However, support for style elements such as `border` is extremely poor across the 4.0 generation of browsers, so we had to resort to a kludgy method. Basically, what we do here is define a style for magnets and another for their shadows, and reference that style sheet via the `CLASS` attribute. The word magnet and shadow are layers, and use z-index to keep the physics straight. When the words are initialized, their magnets' z-index is incremented by one more than the shadow, so the shadow always has a lower z-index than its magnet, but never interferes with that of any other magnet/shadow pair. For the user, the magnet appears as a black word on a white background, representing the magnet to which the word is affixed. When the user "lifts" the word with the mouse, the shadow's color changes and its positioning offset is modified to make the word look as though it is hovering above the playing surface. Incidentally, to overcome a bug in the way that Navigator sets the size of a DIV object based on the size of the text it contains, the shadow contains the same text as is found in the word magnet DIV. This ensures that the shadow is the same size as the magnet. The magnet's appearance is determined by the style sheets shown in Listing 10-9.

Listing 10-9: The style sheets for magnet and shadow

```
.magnet {
    font-size: 16pt;
/*    font-weight: bold; */
    font-family: Sans-Serif;
}

.shadow {
    font-size: 16pt;
/*    font-weight: bold; */
    font-family: Sans-Serif;
}
```

The original style sheets created for the application during testing used individual style sheet entries to describe the positioning and z-index of each magnet. The limitations of this approach, shown in Listing 10-10, quickly reared their ugly heads.

Listing 10-10: An example of the original magnet style sheet

```
#word0 {
    position: absolute;
    top: 50;
    left: 220;
    z-index: 1;
}

#shadow0 {
    position: absolute;
    top: 52;
    left: 222;
    z-index: 0;
}
```

We then moved the CSS-P style information into the DIVs themselves, which made things a bit easier to deal with. Listing 10-11 illustrates this method.

Listing 10-11: The original, static, magnet DIVs

```
<div id="word0"
     class=magnet
     style="visibility: hidden; top: 50;">
   </div>

<div id="shadow0"
     class=shadow
     style="visibility: hidden; top: 52;">
   </div>
```

Eventually, after running into problems with hard-coded limits on the number of words the application would enable the user to enter, we moved the creation of the magnets into a JavaScript function, create_word_divs(), shown in Listing 10-12. When the page loads, this function is invoked after everything else on the page, but before the onLoad event handler fires. This way, an arbitrary number of magnets can be generated at load time with the appropriate styles, automatically calculated z-index, and appropriately staggered positioning. The magnets are empty, and are used by other functions that populate them with arbitrary words. This method has its drawbacks, as the user still encounters a hard-coded limit (max_words) for the number of words they can use, but relieves the programmer the burden of maintaining accurate, lengthy style sheets and HTML markup. Chapter 13, "User-Configurable Interfaces," discusses how this may be used to enable the user to specify how many words they want to use when they first load the application.

Listing 10-12: The create_word_divs() JavaScript function

```
function create_word_divs( n ) {
  var word_label = "";
  var shadow_label = "";
  max_words = n + 20;
  var new_w, new_s;
  var w_t, s_t;
  var w_l, s_l;
  var w_z, s_z;
  var new_stuff = "";

  for( var i = 0; i <= max_words; i++ ) {
    word_label = "word" + i;
    shadow_label = "shadow" + i;
    w_t = 50 + i;   s_t = 52 + i;
    w_l = 220 + i; s_l = 222 + i;
```

```
w_z = i * 2; s_z = w_z + 1;

// style those words...
var w_style = ' style="visibility: hidden;' +
              ' position: absolute;' +
  ' top: ' + w_t +
  '; left: ' + w_l +
  '; z-index: ' + w_z +
  ';"';

// and shadows...
var s_style = ' style="visibility: hidden;' +
              ' position: absolute;' +
  ' top: ' + s_t +
  '; left: ' + s_l +
  '; z-index: ' + s_z +
  ';"';

new_w = '<div id="' + word_label + '" ';
new_w += 'class=magnet ' + w_style + '> </div>';
new_stuff += new_w;

new_s = '<div id="' + shadow_label + '" ';
new_s += 'class=shadow ' + s_style + '> </div>';
new_stuff += new_s;
  }

document.open("text/html");
document.writeln( new_stuff );
document.close();
}
```

It's worth mentioning that Netscape Navigator seems to dislike it when you perform multiple `document.write()` statements before the page has finished loading. For this reason, we append all of the markup for our new layers to two variables, and then write them to the document all at once. Bear in mind, also, that `document.write()` must be performed carefully with respect to the rest of the document, or you replace the current document's contents with the output of your `document.write()` statement. The last things in our HTML file are the call to `create_word_divs()` and the call to `create_base_objects()`. The call to `create_word_divs()` must be inside its own set of `SCRIPT` tags as well, or it can cause problems.

```
<script language="JavaScript">
create_word_divs( wordlist.length );
```

```
</script>
<script language="JavaScript">
create_base_objects();
</script>
</body>
</html>
```

You can find the complete code, markup, and style sheets for this sample application on the support Web site for the book. The files are broken out by chapter, as well as being provided in their finished glory, so you can either follow along with the book as we add features to the application, or just gaze in astonishment at the full-featured application as a whole.

The URL for the support Web site is:

`http://www.dhtml-guis.com`

There is also a support mailing list for the cross-browser object wrappers, more documentation, and updates, errata, and various fixes on the site. Please take the time to visit the site and tell us how you are using the wrappers or the various modules discussed in the following chapters.

The application creates the DIVs for the magnets on the fly, then runs the application's initialization function, which contains a call to create_base_objects(). This ensures that the new DIVs are present to the browser before the cross-platform wrapper builds its objects from the current list of layers. You can see the cross-platform wrapper object for the instructions and other layers referenced by name in Listing 10-8, for example.

A routine that would recognize new objects created after load time would have to be able to reference the internal names for those objects, such as _js_layer_n on Navigator, for example. Because the application as it stands is capable of producing words in sufficient number to bring our systems to a halt, we didn't code the more dynamic routines. Yet another exercise left to the reader.

Enabling Click and Drag

Having the words, even complete with funky shadows, is not enough, however. The true magnetic poetry aficionado demands the illusion of full-blown interactivity. Before we delve into the details of the click-and-drag routines, a few words should be said about events. So far, we've been relying on the fact that the internal object models of both major browsers are relatively similar, despite having widely varying names and methods for manipulating objects. Perhaps the biggest difference between Microsoft and Netscape's dynamic HTML environments is in the way they handle events. Microsoft uses an *event bubbling* model, where the event is propagated automatically up the object hierarchy until bubbling is canceled by the routine that handles it. Netscape, however, uses a much different model, where the events handled by an object must be explicitly declared, and the specific events captured by the handling routine.

Fortunately, the two major browsers both recognize event handlers defined in the object's HTML markup. In the case of the menu items and header, we use event handlers to call the appropriate routines. For the click-and-drag routines, however, we resort to yet another method, declaring the event handler for each type of event and using a series of tests to determine which object the event should reference. This is overkill, especially in Internet Explorer, because the event is already aware of the object that received it. It also causes some interesting problems when trying to figure out which word in a series of overlapping objects is being referenced. The following code uses a somewhat primitive method to determine the target word, but in later chapters we refine this model a bit. For now, pay attention to the way that the application initializes event capturing in Netscape Navigator, and the way event handlers are assigned to various objects in both browsers.

When the application loads, a routine is run that initializes the cross-platform object array, performs a number of other startup functions, and finally sets the event capturing for Netscape Navigator. Technically, as pointed out in earlier chapters, we have tried to avoid mentioning specific browsers, checking instead for the availability of certain methods. If a method is available, we use it. If not, we keep going through a series of tests to determine the best way to obtain the desired functionality. The following function, shown in Listing 10-13, tests to see if the Navigator-specific function `captureEvents()` is available, and if so, sets the appropriate event capturing. It then sets the event handlers that are used by both browsers.

 Remember, if you're going to set an event handler from within JavaScript (as opposed to from an HTML tag), use the all-lowercase version of the event handler's name. Some folks are in the habit of using staggered capitals in their HTML event handlers so they stand out better. This doesn't fly in JavaScript, however.

Listing 10-13: Cross-browser event handling setup

```
function set_netscape_events() {
  if( document.captureEvents ) {
    document.captureEvents(Event.MOUSEDOWN |
                           Event.MOUSEMOVE);
  }
  document.onmousedown = bobble;
  document.onmousemove = drag;
}
```

The idea is that the user should click the word they want to lift and move, drag it to its new position, and click again to release it. The event handler associated with `mousedown` events, `bobble()`, shown in Listing 10-14, is in charge of determining if the word is already being dragged, and calling the appropriate routine. The global variable `selected` is set when the user is dragging the word. If the user is not already dragging the word, and the Shift key is down, the word is highlighted and added to an array that temporarily stores the list of words that compose the current phrase or poem. If the word is already highlighted, it removes the word from the current phrase and also removes the highlighting. The playing field with no words selected is illustrated in Figure 10-5.

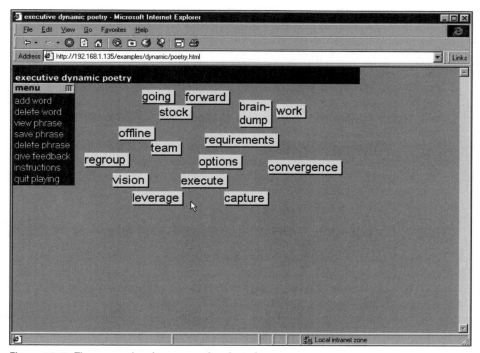

Figure 10-5: The game, showing no words selected

Listing 10-14: The bobble() JavaScript event handler

```
function bobble(e) {
  if( window.event ) {
    e = window.event;
  }

  if( selected ) {
    drop(e);
  } else {
```

```
    // was shift key down? if so, don't pick it up,
    // just add it to the phrase array. if it's
    // already part of the phrase array, remove it.
    if( window.event ) {
      // handle IE
      if( e.shiftKey ) {
         phrasify(e);
      } else {
         pickup(e);
      }
    } else {
      if( e.modifiers & Event.SHIFT_MASK ) {
         phrasify(e);
      } else {
         pickup(e);
      }
    }
  }
}
```

The `bobble()` routine is the linchpin of the click-and-drag library, performing all of the required tests for high-level dispatching of events directed at draggable objects, but it doesn't do most of the work. Three things can happen if a word is clicked:

◆ The word is picked up

◆ The word is dropped

◆ The word is added to or removed from a phrase

The first of these possibilities is handled by the `pickup()` routine, shown in Listing 10-15.

Listing 10-15: Picking up a magnet

```
function pickup(e) {
  if( window.event ) {
    e = window.event;
  }
  get_selected(e);

  if( selected ) {
    if( e.pageX ) {
      drag_x = e.pageX - selected.left();
      drag_y = e.pageY - selected.top();
    } else {
      drag_x = e.offsetX - document.body.scrollLeft;
```

```
        drag_y = e.offsetY - document.body.scrollTop;
    }
  }
}
```

The event is sent to a routine, get_selected(), that figures out which word is being selected. If there is actually something being selected, the routine then assigns the value of the selected object to the global variable selected. This test is necessary because the event capture model applies to the whole document at this point. The bobble() function is called every time the user clicks an object that doesn't have its own mouse click event handler. There are better ways to do this. One way involves defining onClick or onMouseDown event handlers for each word object, which works across browsers. Another method involves performing extensive checking on the target of the event itself, but the drawback to this method is that it only works reliably on objects of a certain type, such as document, image, or link. We look at other ways to handle this problem when we discuss the menu in Chapter 14, "Dynamic Menus."

If the get_selected() routine finds that a word is selected, the shadow's color is set, and the appropriate offsets are modified, giving the magnet the illusion of being lifted slightly off the playing surface while being dragged. The effect is illustrated in Figure 10-6. This code could all be included in the pickup() routine, and in fact, the inverse is included in the drop() routine.

If there is a selected object, it is time to figure out how far to drag the word. This check could in fact be done in the drag() routine, but it would entail performing incremental checks to see where the mouse was when the last mouseMove event was received, rather than moving the word relative to the initial mouseDown event. Ideally, the test for e.pageX should be done deep in the cross-browser library, and the event should itself should be wrapped appropriately, but as wrapping every event has extremely adverse effects on the performance of the application it should be done selectively by the event handlers themselves. The alternative is to wrap every event as part of the application's initialization process, assigning the event wrapper itself as an event handler for all events. For reasons of complexity, this is not the way the cross-browser library works, although such an approach is possible.

If the user clicks a word that is already selected, it is dropped. The shadow's colors, along with any offsets that have been set to give the illusion of being raised above the surface, return to normal. The z-indexes of both the selected word and its shadow return to their previous values. The drop() function is illustrated in Listing 10-16. The global variables shadow_height and moving_shadow_height may be set in one place, at the beginning of the module, enabling a configurable experience.

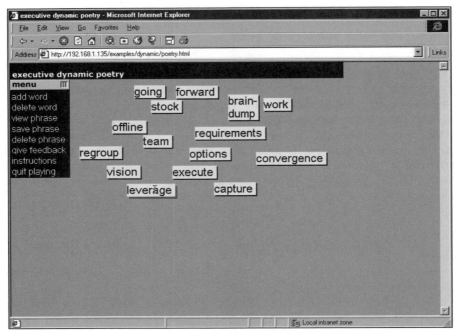

Figure 10-6: The word "leverage," selected and ready to drag

Listing 10-16: The drop() function

```
function drop(e) {
  selected_shadow.set_z_index( old_shadow_z_index );
  selected_shadow.set_bg_color( shadow_bg_color );
  selected_shadow.set_color( shadow_bg_color );

  // now set shadow properly
  var shadow_difference = moving_shadow_height -
    shadow_height;
  var shadow_x = selected_shadow.left() -
    shadow_difference;
  var shadow_y = selected_shadow.top() -
    shadow_difference;
  selected.place( shadow_x, shadow_y );

  selected.set_z_index( old_z_index );
  selected = null;
}
```

Additionally, the user may wish to select a phrase, a word at a time, and save it for later or to share with others over the network. Rather arbitrarily, we use the shift key to signal that this sort of phrase selection is underway. Because a user may wish to highlight words first, then maneuver them into position, the pickup and drop routines don't affect the highlight at all. The routine called by bobble() if the Shift key is held down is named phrasify(), and is shown in Listing 10-17.

Listing 10-17: The phrasify() routine, for shift-selection of words to add to a phrase

```
function phrasify(e) {
  if( window.event ) {
    e = window.event;
  }
  get_selected(e);

  if( selected ) {
    if( phrase_words[selected_word] ) {
      // word is already part of the phrase array,
      // so remove from phrase array and reset colors
      phrase_words[selected_word] = null;
      selected.set_bg_color("#eeeeee");
      words_in_phrase--;
    } else {
      // add to phrase array
      phrase_words[selected_word] = new Object();
      phrase_words[selected_word].name = selected_name;
      phrase[words_in_phrase] = selected_word;
      selected.set_bg_color("gray");
      words_in_phrase++;
    }
  }
  bobble(e);
}
```

The first thing phrasify() does is determine if the user has clicked inside a word. This test could be performed by bobble(), but because bobble() is called by phrasify() when the highlight is toggled, the test has been moved inside. Otherwise, we would run into difficulties and there would be no way to deselect a word once selected. If the user does click a word, the word is checked to see if it is already part of the phrase_words[] array, and if so, it is removed and the highlight is toggled. If the word is not already part of the current phrase, it is added and the word highlighted. A selected phrase, "going forward," with the word "forward" being dragged, is illustrated in Figure 10-7. You have to look closely — the only way to tell which word is being dragged is by the shadow's color and the difference in its offset.

The phrase_words[] array also stores the name of the object, though it does not store its position, saving that for when the phrase is actually saved. Initially, the x and y coordinates of each word were stored at the time they were selected, but that made it possible for the user to select a phrase and then rearrange it before it was actually stored. This caused all sorts of problems when the user went to restore the phrase, as some of the words' positions were incorrectly stored.

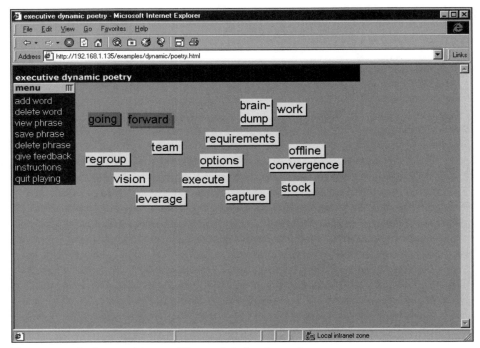

Figure 10-7: A phrase, with one of its words being dragged

In Chapter 13, "User-Configurable Interfaces," we discuss ways of customizing the application. For now, we just tantalize you with one last startup activity, the substitution of different wordlists for the game itself. Although we enjoy the executive wordlist, and can literally spend hours creating important-sounding phrases that happen to also be completely devoid of any meaning whatsoever, others may find that they wish to extend the game with their own, slightly less exciting wordlists. The example below, shown in Listing 10-18, and illustrated in Figure 10-8, uses an alternate wordlist, specified in the HTML markup as an included JavaScript file.

Listing 10-18: An included JavaScript file containing a wordlist array

```
// wordlist for Dynamic Poetry
var wordlist = new Array();
wordlist[0] = "two";
wordlist[1] = "all";
wordlist[2] = "beef";
```

```
wordlist[3] = "patties";
wordlist[4] = "special";
wordlist[5] = "sauce";
wordlist[6] = "lettuce";
wordlist[7] = "cheese";
wordlist[8] = "pickles";
wordlist[9] = "onions";
wordlist[10] = "on";
wordlist[11] = "a";
wordlist[12] = "sesame";
wordlist[13] = "seed";
wordlist[14] = "bun";
```

At game startup time, this file is included via an HTML SCRIPT element, and the last script that is called before the onLoad event handler is fired automatically generates the DIVs for each word in the wordlist. The function, create_word_divs(), shown in Listing 10-19, doesn't actually insert the words themselves. This happens after the cross-browser objects have been created by dynamically replacing the contents of each new magnet DIV with the word and style information.

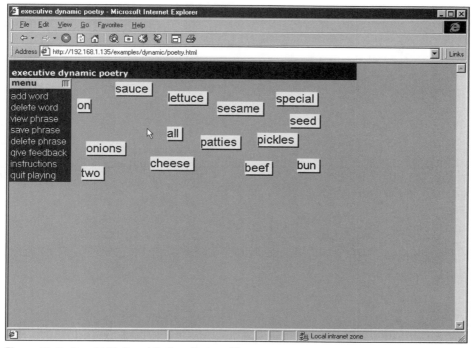

Figure 10-8: Ronald McDonald's favorite wordlist

Showing/Hiding Your Application's Screens and Dialog Boxes

Now that we have defined the general style and position for our application's components and shown how some of them are created and manipulated, it's time to dig further into the functionality each has and illustrate the ways in which the style definitions we've supplied are used by each interface element.

Adding a Word

To save redundancy and memory, we enable the user to define their own words and add them to the wordlist after startup, although there is still a hard-coded limit on the number of words that he or she may add. If you refer back to Listing 10-12, you see that this is currently set to 20 words over the length of the wordlist[] array. When the "add word" menu item is clicked, it traps the onClick event and calls toggle_form() with the name of the "add a word" form, as shown in Listing 10-19.

Listing 10-19: The "add a word" form

```
<div id=addwordlayer class=formbg>
<h1>add a word</h1>
<form name="add_word_form"
     onSubmit="return false;">
add the following word:<br>
<input type=text name=word size=20>
<input type=button value="add word"
     onClick="new_word_from_form(add_word_form);">
</form>
</div>
```

The form, illustrated in Figure 10-9, features a text input and a button. When clicked, the button traps the onClick event and calls the new_word_from_form() function, shown in the following code:

```
function new_word_from_form(f) {
  word = f.word.value; // get word from form
  new_word(word);
  f.word.value = "";
}
```

The new_word_from_form() function is merely a wrapper for the more useful new_word() function, shown in Listing 10-20. The wrapper function grabs the value of the form input named word and passes it straight through to new_word().

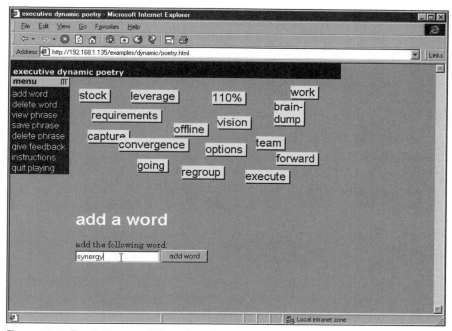

Figure 10-9: The "add a word" form in action

Listing 10-20: The new_word() JavaScript function

```
function new_word(the_word) {
  var word = the_word;
  var label;
  var shadow_label;
  var word_div;
  var shadow_div;
  var styleinfo = "position: absolute; top: 0; left: 0; " +
    "height: 20; width: 50;";

  if( word_counter == max_words ) {
    alert("Sorry, you're only allowed " + max_words +
        " words, and you've already used them all!");
    return false;
  }

  label = 'word' + word_counter;
  shadow_label = 'shadow' + word_counter;
  var shadow_z = (word_counter * 2);
  var word_z = shadow_z + 1;
```

```
word_div = '<span class=magnet> '
  + word + ' </span>';
shadow_div = '<span class=shadow> '
  + word + ' </span>';

if( object_name[label] ) {
  object_name[label].replace(word_div, label);
} else {
  new_layer( label, styleinfo, word_div );
  object_name[label].conceal();
}

if( object_name[shadow_label] ) {
  object_name[shadow_label].replace(shadow_div, shadow_label);
} else {
  new_layer( shadow_label, styleinfo, shadow_div );
  object_name[shadow_label].conceal();
}

// set z index so shadow is below word, not above ;)
object_name[label].set_z_index( word_z );
object_name[shadow_label].set_z_index( shadow_z );

stylize_word( label );
stylize_shadow( shadow_label );

// we want to place these randomly
var x_seed = Math.random();
var y_seed = Math.random();

place_new_word( label, x_seed, y_seed );
place_new_word( shadow_label, x_seed, y_seed );

// add to arrays
object_name[label].name = label;
object_name[label].word = word;

words[word_counter] = new wordify(label, word);
word_counter++;

// show the word and its shadow
object_name[shadow_label].reveal();
object_name[label].reveal();
```

```
    return label;
}
```

The new_word() function is where things get really fun. After checking to see if the user has exceeded their limit for new words, and warning them if they have, the function creates the markup required for insertion into the existing DIVs. If the attempt to replace the contents of an existing word fails due to the nonexistence of the magnet DIV, the routine new_layer() is called, passing the string to use as a label for the new object, default style information, and the HTML the layer should contain. new-layer is part of the cross-browser wrappers, and simply hides the specific details of layer creation from the application developer. The new_layer() function returns a label that may be used to refer to the new layer object.

After the DIV has been prepared with its new contents, it is styled and placed randomly within the main playing field. For the sake of easy reference to both the magnet's label and the word it contains, the name and word properties of the object are set appropriately. The word is added to the words[] array, so we can keep track of them all for the delete_word() function, and the global variable word_counter is incremented. See? Isn't this fun?

Saving a Phrase

After you've labored hard to create your masterpiece, it seems a shame to let it go. The great thing about this application is that you no longer have to. After the user selects a set of words, using the shift-select method outlined in Listing 10-14, they can select the "save phrase" menu item, that, as expected, shows the "save a phrase" form. This form calls the JavaScript function save_phrase_check(), which checks to see if the user has in fact selected a set of words. If not, the function complains and does not let the user save the nonexistent phrase. Otherwise, the function then calls save_phrase(), shown in Listing 10-21, which does the dirty work of writing the phrase to a couple of cookies — one that stores the master list of saved phrases, and another that stores the phrase's words and their positions. We don't got into the mechanics of cookies here, as we're saving that for Chapter 13, "User-Configurable Interfaces."

Listing 10-21: The save_phrase_check() JavaScript function

```
function save_phrase_check(f) {
  if( words_in_phrase == 1 ) {
    alert("You must select more than one word!");
    return false;
  } else if( words_in_phrase == 0 ) {
    alert("You must select words to save as a phrase!");
    return false;
  } else {
```

```
        save_phrase(f);
        return true;
    }
}
```

The `save_phrase()` function, illustrated in Listing 10-22, is really fun. After grabbing the name to use when storing the phrase from the form's text input, it gradually builds a string out of each word, its position onscreen, and a delimiter, and then stores that string in a cookie. Having stored the phrase, it then adds the phrase's name to the master list of all locally stored phrases. When you then go to the "view a phrase" and "delete a phrase" forms, we use these cookies to restore old phrases and to build the list of phrases to delete. At the end of the game, when the user selects "quit playing," these cookies may be sent on to the server and stored alongside the user's e-mail address or other contact information. In this way, others can visit the server and see a list of all publicly available poems and view others' work (see Figure 10-10).

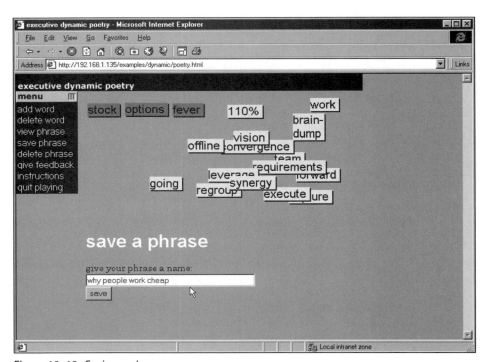

Figure 10-10: Saving a phrase

Oh, and one more thing—the function also then deselects the selected phrase and hides the form. In Chapter 13, "User-Configurable Interfaces," we discuss how to enable the user to customize their own experience, either by asking them if that's what they want to happen and storing their preference, or by simply remembering what they did the last time.

Listing 10-22: The save_phrase() JavaScript function

```
function save_phrase(f) {
  var phrase_name = f.phrase.value;
  var phrase_cookie_string = "";
  var str;

  // loop through the phrase array
  for( i = 0; i < phrase.length; i++ ) {
    var the_word = phrase[i];
    var the_name = phrase_words[the_word].name;

    if( phrase_words[the_word] ) {
      phrase_words[the_word].x =
        object_name[the_name].left();
      phrase_words[the_word].y =
        object_name[the_name].top();
      str = the_word + ","
        + phrase_words[the_word].x + ","
        + phrase_words[the_word].y + "|";
      phrase_cookie_string += str;
      var n = phrase_words[the_word].name;
      object_name[n].set_bg_color("#eeeeee");
      phrase_words[the_word] = null;
      words_in_phrase--;
    }
  }
  var expires = new Date();
  var today = new Date();
  expires.setTime( today.getTime() +
              (1000*60*60*24*365) );
  // set a cookie with the phrase value
  set_cookie( phrase_name,
            phrase_cookie_string,
            expires );

  // and store a handle to cookie so we can find it later
```

```
var all = get_cookie( "all_phrases" );
if( all ) {
  if( all.indexOf(',') > 0 ) {
    all += phrase_name + ",";
  }
} else {
  all = phrase_name + ",";
}

set_cookie( "all_phrases", all );

// clear form
f.phrase.value = "";
toggle_form("blanklayer");
return true;
}
```

Viewing a Saved Phrase

Now that we've seen how to create words, move them around, select them and save the selected group as a phrase, we're scraping the bottom of the barrel for new things to talk about. The "view a phrase" form is dynamically generated using the function shown in Listing 10-23 from the values of the various cookies, unless there are no cookies (and hence no stored poems), and enables the user to select a phrase to view. When selected, the application grabs the appropriate cookie and restores its contents to the screen. Voila!

Listing 10-23: The prep_view_phrase_form() JavaScript function

```
function prep_view_phrase_form() {
  var vfl = "view_phrase_layer"; // shorthand
  // get the current phrase list
  var all_cookies = document.cookie;
  if( all_cookies == "" ) {
    alert("there are no phrases defined!");
    return false;
  }

  var all = get_cookie( "all_phrases" );
```

```
  if( all ) {
    var all_phrases = new Array();
    all_phrases = all.split(',');

    var new_form = '<h1>view a phrase</h1>'
      + '<form name="view_phrase_form"'
      + ' onSubmit="return false;">'
      + 'view the following phrase:<br>'
      + '<select name="phrases">';

    for( i = 0; i < all_phrases.length; i++ ) {
      if( all_phrases[i] ) {
        new_form += '<option value="'
          + all_phrases[i] + '">'
          + all_phrases[i] + '</option>';
      }
    }

    new_form += '<option>'
      + '_____'
      + '</option>'
      + '</select>'
      + '<input type=button value="view"'
      + ' onClick="view_phrase(view_phrase_form);">'
      + '</form>';

    // print the form to viewphraselayer
    object_name[ vfl ].replace(new_form, vfl);

    // reveal the form
    toggle_form( vfl );
  } else {
    alert("sorry, there are no phrases defined!");
  }
  return true;
}
```

If the user selects one of the stored phrases, as in Figure 10-11, magic happens. Well, not exactly magic, but lots of JavaScript and dynamic HTML and cookies and styling happens, anyway.

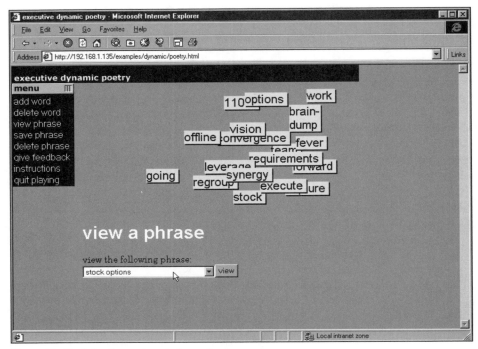

Figure 10-11: Selecting a stored phrase to view

In Listing 10-24, you see the function called by the "view a phrase" form that grabs the cookie named by the selected form option, grabs its words out of the cookie, parses their positions, and then displays them on the screen.

Listing 10-24: The view_phrase() JavaScript function

```
function view_phrase(f) {
  var phrase = f.phrases.options;
  var to_view = f.phrases.options.selectedIndex;
  var p = phrase[to_view].value;

  // get the top, left, and word combos
  // for each word in phrase
  var the_phrase = get_cookie(p);
  if( the_phrase ) {
    // should look like 'word,x,y|word2,x,y|'
    var the_words = the_phrase.split('|');
    var the_pieces = new Array();
    var label, shadow_label;
    for( var i = 0; i < the_words.length - 1; i++ ) {
```

```
      the_pieces = the_words[i].split(',');
      w = the_pieces[0]; // w is the word
      l = the_pieces[1]; // l is the left
      t = the_pieces[2]; // t is the top
      label = new_word(w);
      shadow_label = get_shadow(label);
      s_t = parseInt(t + 2); //shadow_height;
      s_l = parseInt(l + 2); //shadow_height;
      object_name[label].place(l,t);
      object_name[shadow_label].place(s_l, s_t);
    }
  } else {
    alert("sorry, there is a problem with
          the stored phrase!");
  }
  return true;
}
```

Deleting a Saved Phrase

Deleting a saved phrase is just like deleting a word, only with cookies. Listing 10-25 tells all. You can see what this looks like, including the cookie that is set, in Figure 10-12. The delete_phrase() function sets the cookies so that the phrase is removed from the master phrase list and deletes the cookie that stores the phrase's words and positions. You can see from the security pop-up box that the cookie named all_phrases has been set to null; the data section of the cookie is empty.

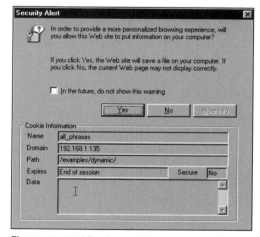

Figure 10-12: Viewing cookie contents in Internet Explorer

Listing 10-25: Preparing the "delete a phrase" form

```
function prep_delete_phrase_form() {
  var dpl = "deletephraselayer";
  // get the current phrase list
  var all_cookies = document.cookie;
  if( all_cookies == "" ) {
    alert("no cookies!");
    return false;
  }

  var all = get_cookie( "all_phrases" );

  if( all ) {
    var all_phrases = new Array();
    all_phrases = all.split(',');

    var new_form = '<h1>delete a phrase</h1>'
      + '<form name="delete_phrase_form"'
      + ' onSubmit="return false;">'
      + 'delete the following phrase:<br>'
      + '<select name="phrases">';

    for( i = 0; i < all_phrases.length; i++ ) {
      if( all_phrases[i] ) {
        new_form += '<option value="'
          + all_phrases[i] + '">'
            + all_phrases[i] + '</option>';
      }
    }

    new_form += '<option>'
      + '_____'
      + '</option>'
      + '</select>'
      + '<input type=button value="delete"'
      + ' onClick="delete_phrase(delete_phrase_form);">'
      + '</form>';

    // print the form to deletephraselayer
    object_name[ dpl ].replace( new_form, dpl );

    // reveal the form
    toggle_form( dpl );
  } else {
    alert("sorry, there are no phrases defined.");
```

```
    }
    return true;
}
```

Rounding out the User Experience

By now, we're sure you're itching to move on to the customization and interface development chapters to come. We just want to add a few words here, though, about what happens when the user decides they've had enough. There are three ways to deal with the saved phrases, if there are any: one, forget them; two, send them on to the server without asking; and three, ask the user what they want to do. Of these, we prefer the third. Besides, it might just improve our wordlist.

Because the phrases are stored as cookies, when the browser asks for another page (or CGI script) from the server where the application came from in the first place, it sends them along with the HTTP request. A CGI script can easily grab them along with any other data that you might want, such as an e-mail address, their browser version, and so on, and store that information on the server. Enterprising people might want to harvest those phrases for great words and word combinations, statistics, or even just get the e-mail address of the next Basho or Rimbaud.

Gotchas

During the course of the development of this chapter, we ran across several annoying things to look out for—bugs that were hard to track down, cross-browser incompatibilities, and fumble-finger typos that caused huge problems. Here are just some of the things you should be aware of as you build your applications:

◆ Netscape Navigator and Internet Explorer differ in their methods for handling background colors of DIV elements, especially when the element contains text. Navigator only uses the background color for the area occupied by the text. If you want a DIV that contains text to use a specific background color, you need to use inelegant workarounds, such as table markup.

◆ In Internet Explorer, a DIV object without explicit CSS height and width properties is assumed to be as wide as the browser window itself. To prevent this you must explicitly set the height and width properties.

◆ onMouseOver only works for HTML markup. In JavaScript, assign event handlers to onmouseover instead, using the lowercase form to refer to the handler. (The same is true for all event handlers in JavaScript.)

◆ Navigator doesn't deal well with too many `document.write()` statements in a row while the document is still loading, and crashes on Macintosh and Windows unless you are very careful. We work around this in `create_word_divs()` by simply saving up the text to be written to the document and writing it all at once.

◆ Cross-browser font specs can be a major pain, even on the same platform. Using generic font specifiers (such as `Sans-Serif`) should be a last resort, as each browser is free to choose the font to use, and they may not always choose the same font.

◆ `relative` positioning doesn't mean "relative to the container." Use `absolute` when positioning elements relative to their parent element.

◆ Wherever possible, use `CLASS` for formatting styles and `ID` for positioning, unless the area is shared by many objects, in which case use `CLASS` as well.

◆ Specify units in style sheets where a suitable default cannot be inferred, or where the unit you're using is different from the default.

◆ After you've used the style sheet for testing dynamically created elements, it may make sense to move the positioning specifications into the markup instead. Keep the formatting specifications in the style sheets, and reference them using `CLASS`. Navigator 4.0 may have trouble with inline styles in nested `DIV` elements, though, so be cautious.

Summary

In this chapter, you saw several examples of positioning using Cascading Style Sheets, some basic JavaScript functions for showing and hiding various elements, and lots of fun code that dynamically produces elements and parts of elements on the fly. From our inauspicious beginnings with the nouns, verbs, and adjectives, we proceeded to blur the lines between them a bit, eventually producing nouns from our own verbs, and then changing the modifiers we use to give them style. This chapter covered how to:

◆ Identify the nouns, verbs, and adjectives (or objects, functions, and styles) in your application

◆ Use style sheets for positioning objects

◆ Use style sheets to specify fonts, colors, and other formatting effects

◆ Use event handlers in a cross-browser fashion

◆ Create usable, bulletproof interface elements and associate actions with them

- Use cookies and other state-maintenance mechanisms

- Dynamically construct and modify forms and other objects

- Manage the entire user experience provided by your application

In the next chapter, you will learn advanced techniques for providing status feedback, reporting errors, and debugging.

Chapter 11

The Hidden Feedback Form

IN THIS CHAPTER

◆ Using the Tab Widget module

◆ Intelligent client-side forms processing

◆ Using forms split across several DIV objects

◆ More on showing and hiding layers

◆ Using DHTML as the interface to a client/server application

◆ The HTTP "No Content" response

IN THE LAST CHAPTER, we introduced you in a roundabout way to the cross-browser object wrapper library as we put it to use in a basic application. In this chapter and those that follow, we extend the application through the use of several independent JavaScript modules. In an ideal world, the modules would have been designed so that you could simply plug them into your application without any modifications to your markup or other code. But for now, we forsake such lofty ambitions, using the modules for the sake of illustration. When you build your own applications, however, you may find them useful as starting points for your own modules, and, with luck, you may even find that the ideal of perfect "plug and play" has been achieved.

This chapter discusses the use of one independent module, the *Tab Widget module*, and applies it to a custom, multiple-part feedback form. You will get a taste of what is involved in integrating a module into a small sample application, and then later we integrate the whole thing into the Dynamic Poetry application itself. Along the way, you will become familiar with more aspects of the cross-browser object wrapper library and its uses, and hopefully have fun tickling bugs in the various browsers.

What the Heck Is a Widget?

A *widget* (pronounced WIH-jit), in the generic sense, is anything whose name you've forgotten. In programming, however, it refers to a class of interface elements used to provide access to specific application functionality. Menus, icons, buttons, windows, scrollbars, and so forth, are all widgets; and most, if not all, GUI toolkits provide standard sets of widgets for use by programmers. Technically, the term *widget* also refers to the code that implements a given interface element. We use both senses more or less interchangeably. The key is to remember that the thing you can see is a widget, and that its functionality and appearance are provided by the code.

Generally speaking, an important characteristic of widgets is that they are written in such a way as to be highly flexible, enabling the application programmer to associate certain behaviors with the interface element, or use it to display arbitrary information without having to reimplement the whole thing from scratch. In more advanced programming environments, widgets are often provided as classes that may be subclassed from. These subclasses override common, but generic, functionality in order to implement customized requirements. Java and C++ are two languages that provide this capability, and even lowly JavaScript has certain object-oriented features that provide such high-level program design, although we don't use them here.

One type of widget, the *tabbed interface,* or *tab widget,* is popular among GUI programmers for its capability to conserve precious screen real estate while providing quick and easy access to several different portions of a dialog box or screen. You can see tab widgets in use in Windows 95, for example, in the Display Properties dialog box seen in Figure 11-1.

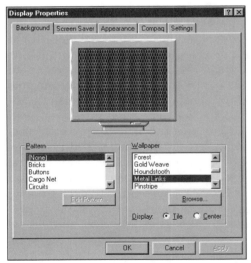

Figure 11-1: The Windows 95 Display Properties dialog box, demonstrating the tab widget

Using one dialog box, the tab widget offers the user several different options for configuring the basic screen and window properties, such as color schemes, background image, screen saver, and so forth. By clicking each tab, the user can focus his attention on a complete set of properties and settings without the overhead involved in opening and closing several dialog boxes. It also enables the user to quickly switch back and forth between screens, which is especially useful in cases where the items in the various screens are related in function. From this, you can draw several conclusions. In general, tab widgets:

◆ Help conserve screen real estate

◆ Serve to connect related screens in a dialog box

◆ Provide alternate navigation between screens

◆ Can provide much-needed context to sequential interface components

In the example code that follows, we use a simple JavaScript Tab Widget module to do all of these things in the context of a multiple-screen feedback form. Rather than building a long, scrolling list of questions and feedback opportunities, we use the tab widget to keep the user in the same window, revealing and concealing the various subcomponents of the feedback form as they are needed. This is just one of many uses for the tab widget, however; several others are highlighted as we progress through the application's development.

Working with the Tab Widget Module

As mentioned previously, no widget worthy of the name would dare show its face without making it easy for the programmer to customize its appearance and behavior. In that mindset, the tab widget JavaScript module presented here provides extensive customization. Because we're working with the capabilities provided by a baseline lowest common denominator between the two major browsers, the custom properties are fairly limited compared to the whole range of possibilities in either browser, but we've covered the basics. The following default values are provided for the colors and related presentation properties:

```
var tab_color = "#333333";
var tab_selected_color = "#000000";
var tab_bgcolor = "#cccccc";
var tab_selected_bgcolor = "#ffffff";
var tab_z_index = 1000;
var tab_gutter = 3;
```

In our sample application, we use the defaults provided. When we integrate the feedback form into the Dynamic Poetry application, however, we modify these to suit the new environment by setting them in the markup following our inclusion of the module. By default, we see that there are color values for both text color and background color for selected and nonselected tabs. In general, it is wise to use muted colors for nonselected tabs to imply that they are in the "background," and to use brighter colors for the selected tab to imply that it is in the "foreground." More advanced widget sets also provide other mechanisms to support this illusion, but for now our focus is on the basics.

The tab_z_index global variable is chosen more or less arbitrarily, and should be adjusted to suit the application at hand. The tab_gutter global variable is used to specify how far apart from one another the tabs should be displayed. Two other global variables expose specific aspects of the module; namely, tab_widget_version and tab_widget_module_initialized. The first uses a header from the version control system we're using, and simply provides access to the specific revision of the module for quality assurance and debugging purposes. The second may be used by the application to ensure that any code that relies on the Tab Widget module is not executed unless the module has been initialized properly.

```
var tab_widget_version = "$Revision: 1.3 $";
var tab_widget_module_initialized = false;
```

In order to provide a list of labels and the associated behaviors for each tab, the tab_widget_defs array is initialized in the module. This array contains items for each tab that define the label for the tab as well as the JavaScript function to be placed into an onClick handler when the tab is created. This function is called whenever the user clicks the tab label. The tab_selected variable is used to track which tab is currently displayed as "selected," using the array index value. The tab array contains references to the tab objects themselves, once they are initialized. Finally, the tab_count variable is simply provided as a shorter alternative to the tab_widget_defs.length property.

```
var tab_widget_defs = new Array();
var tab_selected = 0;
var tab = new Array();
var tab_count = 0;
```

The tab_widget_init() JavaScript function, shown in Listing 11-1, assumes that the cross-browser object wrapper has been initialized, and that a DIV object named tabwidget has been created from markup in your HTML:

```
<div id="tabwidget">
<table width=483><tr><td> </td></tr></table>
</div>
```

Nothing too complicated, eh? The CSS style sheet we use is pretty simple as well. The tabwidget object serves to act as a placeholder for the subsequent positioning of the dynamically created tab objects, and helps define their width.

```
#tabwidget {
  position: absolute;
  visibility: hidden;
  top: 30;
  left: 118;
  width: 483;
  height: 15;
}
```

Anyway, back to the initialization function. Once we've obtained a reference to the `tabwidget` placeholder object, we get its width and use that to calculate the width of each tab. We divide the total length of the placeholder object by the number of tabs (as obtained from the `tab_widget_defs.length` variable, because we haven't yet set `tab_count`), and then subtract the tab gutter from the result. Given our example, the width of a single tab is approximately 158 pixels (483/3 - 3). This gives us a fairly wide area to work with, but we have to be careful not to use labels that are too long for the tab. Testing across platforms is fairly useful here.

We subsequently use the height of the placeholder object to calculate the height of each tab. Although the browsers usually override this setting, it's useful to have when creating the tab objects themselves. For each of the tabs defined in the `tab_widget_defs` array, we then create a tab object for each, passing the definition, name, width, and height, along with a Boolean variable to determine whether the tab thus created should be of a "selected" type or not. This last variable determines which of the color variables defined previously should be used to set the tab's foreground and background colors. The nonselected tabs are given the names `tab0,tab1,tab2...` as required, and the selected tabs are named `tab0s,tab1s,tab2s. . . .`

Once the first tabs are created, we position them using the cross-browser method `overlay()`, which takes three arguments. The first is a reference to the object that is to be overlaid by the calling object, in this case, the `tabwidget` placeholder. The second is a compass point, here `NW` for "northwest," in the top-left corner. The third argument is the offset, or `tab_gutter`, which positions the calling object slightly to the right of the placeholder's top-left corner. Once the object has been properly positioned, we set its z-index appropriately, with the selected object one higher than the nonselected object. We conceal all of the tab objects. We also set the variable `tab_selected`, which is used when we toggle the tabs, to determine which tab should be hidden and which should be displayed.

Positioning the other tab objects is done relative to the last tab, using the cross-browser wrapper method `abut()`, which accepts a similar set of arguments to that expected by `overlay()`. First, the `last_tab` object reference is passed, letting `abut()` know relative to which object the caller should be positioned. Second, the compass point `E` is passed, specifying that the caller should be placed to the right of the last tab. The third argument is the alignment, in this case `TOP`, which forces the caller object to be aligned with the top, rather than the bottom, of the previous object. Finally, the `tab_gutter` variable determines the offset.

When we've created all of the tabs, positioned them relative to the placeholder and to one another, and counted them up using the `tab_counter` variable, we're all ready to go, so we set the `tab_widget_module_initialized` variable to `true` and return.

Listing 11-1: The tab_widget_init() JavaScript function

```
function tab_widget_init() {
  var obj = object_name["tabwidget"];
  var w = parseInt( obj.get_width() / tab_widget_defs.length);
  w -= tab_gutter;
  var h = parseInt( obj.get_height() );
  var last_tab;
  var tab_def, tabname, tabname_s;
  for( var x = 0; x < tab_widget_defs.length; x++ ) {
    tab_def = tab_widget_defs[x];
    tabname = "tab" + x;
    tab_widget_create_tab( tab_def, tabname, w, h, false );
    tabname_s = "tab" + x + "s"; // selected
    tab_widget_create_tab( tab_def, tabname_s, w, h, true );

    if( x == 0 ) {
      // first time through, we overlay oriented to NW corner
      tab[tabname].overlay(obj,"NW", tab_gutter);
      tab[tabname].set_z_index(tab_z_index);
      tab[tabname].conceal();
      tab[tabname_s].overlay(obj, "NW", tab_gutter);
      tab[tabname_s].set_z_index(tab_z_index + 1);
      tab_selected = x;
    } else {
      // we abut it to the E side of the previous tab
      tab[tabname].abut(last_tab, "E", "TOP", tab_gutter);
      tab[tabname].set_z_index(tab_z_index);
      tab[tabname_s].abut(last_tab, "E", "TOP", tab_gutter);
      tab[tabname_s].set_z_index(tab_z_index + 1);
      tab[tabname_s].conceal();
    }
    last_tab = tab[tabname];
    tab_count++;
  }
  tab_widget_module_initialized = true;
}
```

Okay, now that you've seen how the module determines how many tabs to create, where to put them, and so forth, it would probably help to have an example of what sort of tab definitions you can provide for the tabs you create. In our example, we use the following code to include the `tab_widget.js` JavaScript file in our application, and define the labels and their handlers:

```
<script language="JavaScript"
        src="/JavaScript/tab_widget.js"></script>
<script language="JavaScript">
tab_widget_defs[0] = 'What you liked|feedback_show(0)';
tab_widget_defs[1] = 'What you disliked|feedback_show(1)';
tab_widget_defs[2] = 'Who you are|feedback_show(2)';
</script>
```

Because we're defining items in the `tab_widget_defs[]` array, which is declared in the `tab_widget.js` file, we need to make sure that our definitions follow the inclusion of the module. The same caveat applies to overriding color settings as well, although we don't do that here either.

The definitions are composed of a string containing the label for the tab, a pipe ("|"), and the actual JavaScript function that is used as the `onClick` handler for the tab when it is created. Be careful not to use the pipe character in the labels for your tabs or in the handler, or else you might get unexpected (and usually nonfunctional) results. A possible area for future extension of the Tab Widget module would be to enable the programmer to customize this delimiter using a global variable. In any case, this is how it works now, so let's look at the function used to create the tabs themselves, `tab_widget_create_tab()`, shown in Listing 11-2.

As you may recall from Listing 11-1, the tab definitions themselves are passed directly to the `tab_widget_create_tab()` function, along with the name of the tab, its height and width, and a Boolean value representing whether the tab to be created is selected or not. The function begins by splitting the tab definition up into its label and handler. If the tab to be created is a selected tab, the `tab_selected_*` color variables are used; otherwise, the default nonselected values are used. In addition, the label is bolded for selected tabs, to further reinforce the illusion of the tab's prominence in the foreground.

Listing 11-2: The tab_widget_create_tab() JavaScript function

```
function tab_widget_create_tab(def, name, w, h, selected) {
  var defs = new Array();
  defs = def.split("|");
  var label = defs[0];
  var handler = defs[1];

  if( selected == true ) {
    var color = tab_selected_color;
    var bgcolor = tab_selected_bgcolor;
    label = "<b>" + label + "</b>";
  } else {
```

```
    var color = tab_color;
    var bgcolor = tab_bgcolor;
}

var the_tab = '<table border=0 cellpadding=4 cellspacing=0 '
  'width=' + w + '><tr><td bgcolor=' + bgcolor +
  ' align=center valign=middle nowrap>' +
  '<a href="#"' + ' onClick=\'' + handler + ';\'>' +
  label + '</a>' +
  '</td></tr></table>';

var the_div = '<div id="'+name+'" style="position: absolute;'
  ' overflow: none; ' +
  ' top: 0; left: 0; ' +
  ' width: ' + w + '; height: ' + h + '; ' +
  ' color: ' + color + ';' +
  ' background-color: ' + bgcolor + ';' +
  '">' +
  the_tab +
  '</div>';

// create the object as appropriate
if( document.all ) {
  document.open("text/html");
  document.write( the_div );
  document.close();
  var all_divs = document.all.tags("DIV");
  var new_layer = all_divs[all_divs.length - 1];
} else {
  var new_layer = new Layer(1);
  new_layer.document.open("text/html");
  new_layer.document.write( the_tab );
  new_layer.document.close();
}
tab[name] = new base_object( new_layer );
tab[name].conceal();
}
```

The function then creates the markup for the tab itself, using a table to set the colors and extent of each tab to ensure that the background color fills the entire tab. (See the "Gotchas" section in Chapter 10, "Executive Dynamic Poetry," for the reason why.) The anchor surrounding the label uses the `handler` variable to set the `onClick` event handler that is executed when the user clicks the tab's label. The new `DIV` object is also created, using inline CSS styles to set the width and height for the tab, along with its colors. The table markup for the tab is then enclosed in the `DIV` tags.

In a rare display of browser-specific code, which really should be buried in the cross-browser library, the function then checks for the existence of the `document.all` collection signifying Internet Explorer, and if it is found, writes the entire `DIV` to the document. This makes it the last `DIV` in the `document.all.tags("DIV")` collection, which we use to get a reference to the object. A potentially unpleasant side effect of this method, and one reason why we included it here instead of sticking it into the library, is that it requires the `tab_widget_init()` function to be called before the document has finished loading in Internet Explorer. In Navigator, naturally, there is a different potentially unpleasant side effect; namely, that creating a new layer (using the `Layer()` core JavaScript function) must be performed *after* the document has finished loading. When we get to the markup for our sample application we talk about one way to handle this situation.

The Tab Widget module has a few other functions, `tab_widget_toggle()`, `tab_widget_show()` and `tab_widget_hide()`, shown in Listing 11-3. The first enables the application to switch back and forth between tabs, displaying the selected tab and concealing the nonselected tab as appropriate to represent the current state. In the sample application, the handler we've defined for the tab should call this function before continuing on. The `tab_widget_toggle()` function takes one argument: the array index of the tab to toggle. Given that, it constructs references to both the selected and nonselected tab objects and does its thing. The `tab_widget_hide()` function takes no arguments, relying instead on the `tab_count` variable to loop over all of the tabs, hiding them all in turn. It is then necessary to provide an additional function that restores the tabs' visibility, following the pattern set in `tab_widget_hide()`. This is what `tab_widget_show()` does, along with making sure that the selected tab is displayed.

Listing 11-3: The tab_widget_toggle(), show(), and hide() JavaScript functions

```
function tab_widget_toggle(t) {
  var s = "tab" + t + "s";
  var u = "tab" + t;
  tab[u].conceal();
  tab[s].reveal();
  s = "tab" + tab_selected + "s";
  u = "tab" + tab_selected;
  tab[s].conceal();
  tab[u].reveal();
  tab_selected = t;
}

function tab_widget_hide() {
  var s, u;
  for( var x = 0; x < tab_count; x++ ) {
    s = "tab" + x + "s";
    u = "tab" + x;
```

```
      tab[s].conceal();
      tab[u].conceal();
    }
  }
}

function tab_widget_show() {
  var s, u;
  for( var x = 0; x < tab_count; x++ ) {
    u = "tab" + x;
    s = "tab" + x + "s";
    if( x == tab_selected ) {
      tab[s].reveal();
    } else {
      tab[u].reveal();
    }
  }
}
```

Okay, now that we've covered the magic behind the Tab Widget module, it's time to move on to the application at hand: the multiple-screen feedback form.

The Dynamic Multiple-Screen Feedback Form

An ordinary, non-DHTML feedback form usually consists of either one long form on a page, or multiple forms produced by a CGI script that generates them on the fly based on previous user input. The CGI script is responsible for formatting the response and either mailing it to the final recipient of the input, or perhaps processing it and placing its results into a database or flat file. In the interest of sticking to our client-side directive, our feedback form consists of multiple screens, and is processed entirely on the client side before final submission to a server-side script for storage and/or further processing. For the sake of our example, we assume that the CGI script is quite simple, perhaps mailing its input directly as received or storing it in a flat file on the server. What this means is that what would have traditionally been the responsibility of the CGI script is now the responsibility of the client-side application. This also entails a good deal more complex processing code on the client, including the use of multiple forms (because you can't split a single form across several DIV objects). Finally, we use a *metaform* to gather all the data from the other form components and arrange it in a manner that reduces the load and processing requirements of the server-side script. This metaform is then used to submit the final data, giving users an opportunity to modify their input one last time before submission.

An Overview of the Multiple-Screen Feedback Form

First things first. The feedback form consists of three separate form components, one per tab, the first of which is shown (along with the initialized tab widget) in Figure 11-2. The forms are simple in order to demonstrate how to read values from the different input types. The first form element is a pull-down menu containing several choices of application features that the respondent may have liked the best. The second is a group of check boxes that enable the user to check some of the other features they may have enjoyed, and the third is a more flexible text area so users can give arbitrary feedback. Finally, the last form component is a group of radio buttons that enable users to signify if they simply do not want to answer the preceding group of questions.

From an interface design perspective, the last group is a sort of forcing function that overrides the form processor's intention to force the user to answer each of the form components. In keeping with the fact that this last component is considered somewhat rude, we ignore the radio group if the "false" button is not selected. A more preferable solution would be to add event handlers to each of the other components that automatically set the radio button to "false" if the user provides any input whatsoever.

The tab widget is shown with the first tab displayed using the selected style (in reality, this is a tab object by itself), as opposed to using two different states of the same object, which would necessitate constantly writing and rewriting the object's contents. Either method is acceptable, but the best solution would be to use dynamic CSS settings to simply modify the characteristics of the object's contents if both browsers simply supported the dynamic updating of styles in this way. However, this isn't necessarily the case, so we've chosen to use the ugly hack presented here. Anyone writing a tab widget for future versions of the browsers should take this dynamic updating into account and use it if supported.

In addition to the tabs for navigation, a button at the bottom of the screen enables users to move to the next screen. This is another example of a sort of forcing mechanism in that it has the following characteristics:

◆ It is presented at the bottom, so it is suited to the natural flow of the user's focus as they fill out the form.

◆ It limits navigation options to the next screen only, rather than providing all navigation options at once as the tabs do.

◆ It suggests (through the use of the ">" symbol) a directionality to the experience, reinforcing the directionality of the tabs.

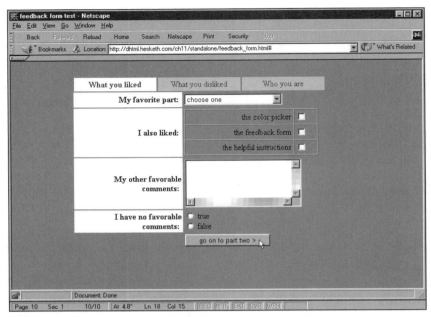

Figure 11-2: The first screen of the feedback form, showing the tabs

A "Wizardized" Tab Interface

It is important to realize that we are mixing two GUI models here: that of the *wizard*, a goal-oriented, directional, controlled experience; and that of the task-oriented multiple tab interface. The "next" and "previous" buttons are more appropriate for a wizard, whereas the tabs are really more appropriate for a loosely-related collection of independent screens. Think about the contrast between the typical software installation program that leads you inexorably through a series of steps including acceptance of a license agreement, selection of options, and finally choosing where to install; and the typical preferences dialog box, with its color preferences on one screen, and other options on another. The first interface is a wizard, the second is more loosely bound. Our example feedback form unpardonably demonstrates both styles of interface at the same time, so be sure to choose one or the other when designing your own interfaces.

That said, plenty of traditional software programs also mix the tabbed interface with a more rigid serial flow, such as MacInTax from Intuit. MacInTax enables the user to fill out a series of forms either sequentially or by randomly hopping around between them via a tabbed interface. Recall the discussion of goal-oriented versus task-oriented interfaces in Chapter 3, "Principles and Lessons Learned," where we warned that no interface is fully one or the other. Our demonstration feedback form is no exception to that statement.

In the second form screen, illustrated in Figure 11-3, we have the inverse of the previous screen. All of the same elements are present, with the addition of another navigational button at the bottom, this time pointing back to the previous screen. The contents of this form, however, are geared toward gathering negative feedback.

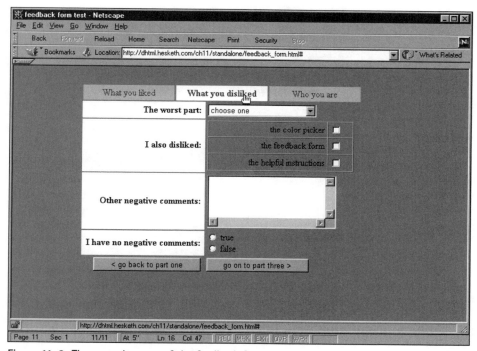

Figure 11-3: The second screen of the feedback form

In the third and final form screen, illustrated in Figure 11-4, we have a wrap up, where the user is requested to enter her name and e-mail address. In contrast to the previous screens, where the radio group forcing function enabled the user to skip the form component altogether, this screen requires that both name and e-mail address be entered, validating the address and producing pop-up alert windows when the inputs are not filled in on submission of the form, or when the e-mail address is considered invalid. The appropriate tab has been selected, and the previous tab deselected. A navigation button, just as in the previous screen, enables the user to go back to the previous screen. The forward navigation button of the previous screen has been replaced with a button that submits the form when clicked. In reality, the button processes the various form components and creates yet another form containing a TEXTAREA element populated with the results of the preprocessing, as well as a button that actually submits the metaform.

Please note that the e-mail address validation function is woefully insufficient for any real application, and is provided for demonstration purposes only.

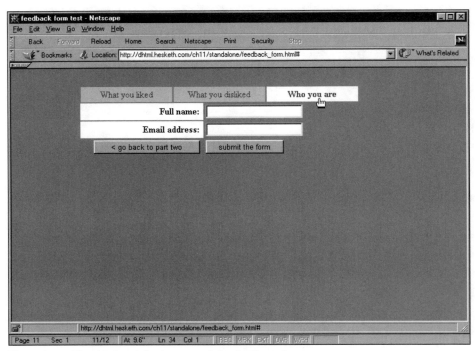

Figure 11–4: The third and final screen of the feedback form

In addition to requiring the user to enter both their name and e-mail address, the presubmission validation check requires the user to fill out at least one of the previous forms, because without any feedback at all the submission is pretty pointless. It might be a good idea (and positive reinforcement) to send the user to the positive feedback form, using the appropriate function to set the tabs and display the first form screen. Such manipulation is generally frowned upon as assuming too much about the user, however, as well as limiting their input by forcing a change in setting, and could potentially confuse or annoy the user. Therefore, we've left such annoyances out of the example. A less irritating example of such automatic interaction would be to set the browser's focus on the appropriate input on the last form. If the user did not fill out the name field, the focus could be shifted to that field after the alert window is dismissed. In more robust and demanding applications, the user could be alerted with a confirm window asking him if he wanted to fill in the name input field, and the entire submission would be canceled if the user answered negatively.

Assuming everything has gone well, the form preprocessor gets the various input from the three form components, and uses it to construct a new form (illustrated in Figure 11-5) that is actually submitted to the server when the user clicks the button at the bottom of the screen.

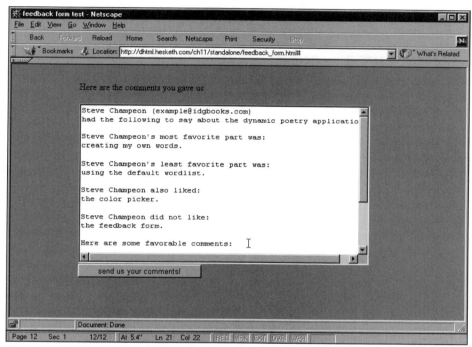

Figure 11-5: The final metaform, ready to submit

This multiple-screen feedback form, while far from being a technological marvel or work of demographics-gathering genius, involves some considerably more complex client-side processing than your average form. Let's turn our attention to the markup and code that makes it all work.

Dissecting the Multiple-Screen Feedback Form

First of all, because the individual form components, shown in Listing 11-4, are concealed and revealed at the user's request, they must be created using individual DIV objects. Named `feedbackform0`, `feedbackform1`, and `feedbackform2` — to make it easier to toggle them along with their respective tabs also named using zero-index offsets — the form DIVs contain tables that help set apart the individual input components from their labels and from each other. The check box group, for example, is marked up using a nested table whose border is set to one to further signify that the elements belong together. Another approach might be to use the

CAPTION as a label for the group, but differences in the way that Navigator and Internet Explorer render the CAPTION make this a shaky proposition at best. Traditional GUI toolkits nest the label for a check box group within the border, creating a much more salient association between the group and its label.

 JavaScript arrays, like arrays in most programming languages, begin with the index "zero" and proceed through to the end, where the index of the last member of the array is one less than the array's total length. Get used to this idiom, as it crops up often.

Listing 11-4: The HTML markup for the various form components

```
<div id="feedbackform0" class="feedback">
<form name="fbone">
<input name=strictvalidate type=hidden value="true">
<table border=0 cellpadding=2 cellspacing=2 width=100%>
<tr>
  <th align=right valign=middle width=33%>
  My favorite part:
  </th>

  <td align=left valign=middle>
  <select name="favoritepart">
    <option value="">choose one
    <option>creating my own words
    <option>using the default wordlist
    <option>reading the works of others
  </select>
  </td>
</tr>

<tr>
  <th align=right valign=middle>
  I also liked:
  </th>

  <td align=left valign=middle>
    <table cellpadding=4 cellspacing=0 border=1 width=60%>
    <tr>
      <td align=right>the color picker</td>
      <td align=left
      ><input type="checkbox"
              name="colorpicker"
```

```
                    value="the color picker"
        ></td>
      </tr>

      <tr>
        <td align=right>the feedback form</td>
        <td align=left
        ><input type="checkbox"
                name="feedback"
                value="the feedback form"
        ></td>
      </tr>

      <tr>
        <td align=right>the helpful instructions</td>
        <td align=left
        ><input type="checkbox"
                name="instructions"
                value="the helpful instructions"
        ></td>
      </tr>
      </table>
    </td>
</tr>

<tr>
  <th align=right valign=middle>
  My other favorable comments:
  </th>

  <td align=left valign=top>
  <textarea name="goodcomments"
            rows=4 cols=25></textarea>
  </td>
</tr>

<tr>
  <th align=right valign=middle>
  I have no favorable comments:
  </th>

  <td align=left valign=top>
  <input name="nocomment" value="true" type=radio> true<br>
  <input name="nocomment" value="false" type=radio> false<br>
  </td>
```

```
</tr>

<tr>
  <td> </td>

  <td align=left valign=top>
  <input type="button" value="go on to part two >"
         onClick='feedback_show(1);'>
  </td>
</tr>
</table>
</form>
</div>

<div id="feedbackform1" class="feedback">
<form name="fbtwo">
<input name=strictvalidate type=hidden value="true">
<table border=0 cellpadding=2 cellspacing=2 width=100%>
<tr>
  <th align=right valign=middle width=33%>
  The worst part:
  </th>

  <td align=left valign=middle>
  <select name="worstpart">
    <option value="">choose one
    <option>creating my own words
    <option>using the default wordlist
    <option>reading the works of others
  </select>
  </td>
</tr>

<tr>
  <th align=right valign=middle>
  I also disliked:
  </th>

  <td align=left valign=middle>
    <table cellpadding=4 cellspacing=0 border=1 width=60%>
    <tr>
      <td align=right>the color picker</td>
      <td align=left
      ><input type="checkbox"
              name="colorpicker"
```

```
            value="the color picker"
      ></td>
    </tr>

    <tr>
      <td align=right>the feedback form</td>
      <td align=left
      ><input type="checkbox"
              name="feedback"
              value="the feedback form"
      ></td>
    </tr>

    <tr>
      <td align=right>the helpful instructions</td>
      <td align=left
      ><input type="checkbox"
              name="instructions"
              value="the helpful instructions"
      ></td>
    </tr>
    </table>
  </td>
</tr>

<tr>
  <th align=right valign=middle>
  Other negative comments:
  </th>

  <td align=left valign=top>
  <textarea name="negativecomments"
            rows=4 cols=25></textarea>
  </td>
</tr>

<tr>
  <th align=right valign=middle>
  I have no negative comments:
  </th>

  <td align=left valign=top>
  <input name="nocomment" value="true" type=radio> true<br>
  <input name="nocomment" value="false" type=radio> false<br>
  </td>
```

```
    </tr>

    <tr>
      <td align=right valign=top>
      <input type="button" value="< go back to part one"
             onClick='feedback_show(0);'>
      </td>

      <td align=left valign=top>
      <input type="button" value="go on to part three >"
             onClick='feedback_show(2);'>
      </td>
    </tr>
    </table>
    </form>
    </div>

    <div id="feedbackform2" class="feedback">
    <form name="fbthree">
    <input name=strictvalidate type=hidden value="true">
    <table border=0 cellpadding=2 cellspacing=2 width=100%>
    <tr>
      <th align=right valign=middle width=33%>
      Full name:
      </th>

      <td align=left valign=middle>
      <input name="fullname" type=text size=20>
      </td>
    </tr>

    <tr>
      <th align=right valign=middle>
      Email address:
      </th>

      <td align=left valign=top>
      <input name="email" type=text size=20>
      </td>
    </tr>

    <tr>
      <td align=right valign=top>
      <input type="button" value="< go back to part two"
             onClick='feedback_show(1);'>
```

```
  </td>

  <td align=left valign=top>
  <input type="button" value="submit the form"
         onClick='feedback_validate();'>
  </td>
</tr>
</table>

</form>
</div>
```

The markup makes use of CSS style sheets, shown in Listing 11-5, to set the foreground and background colors, font choices, positioning, and other characteristics of the forms. Because the forms occupy the same position, the `.feedback` style is referenced using the CLASS attribute rather than ID. For the sake of easily integrating the whole shebang into the Dynamic Poetry application, we've taken the liberty of using CSS positioning values appropriate to the form's final home in the application. Eventually, we stick this style sheet into its own file and include it using a `<LINK>` element. The feedbacksummary style specifier is used by the final metaform, while the tabwidget style specifier, as we've already seen, is used as a placeholder to position the tabs. Therefore, they both use the visibility: hidden; specification. The feedbacksummary DIV is displayed after the user has submitted the form for initial processing.

Listing 11-5: The style sheet for the feedback form

```
<style type="text/css">
BODY {
  font-family: arial,helvetica,sans-serif;
  font-size: 12pt;
}
TH {
  background-color: white;
}
.feedback {
  position: absolute;
  color: #000000;
  background-color: #999999;
  top: 60;
  left: 118;
  width: 483;
  height: 360;
  visibility: hidden;
}
```

```
#tabwidget {
  position: absolute;
  visibility: hidden;
  top: 30;
  left: 118;
  width: 483;
  height: 15;
}
#feedbacksummary {
  position: absolute;
  visibility: hidden;
  color: #000000;
  background-color: #999999;
  top: 30;
  left: 118;
  width: 483;
}
</style>
```

The navigational buttons shown at the bottom of each form call the function feedback_show(), shown in Listing 11-6, with an array index argument. Note that this is the same function that we used as a handler when we initialized the tabs, but the individual forms only supply button-based navigation between the previous and next forms, as appropriate. The global variable feedback_form_current_screen is set after toggling the tabs and then the form screens. Notice that a property of a variable from feedback_form array is referenced to provide the name of each screen; the one currently visible as well as the one we want to show next.

Listing 11-6: The feedback_show() JavaScript function

```
function feedback_show(screen) {
  var form_screen = feedback_form[screen].name;
  var current = feedback_form[feedback_form_current_screen].name;
  tab_widget_toggle(screen);
  if( object_name[current] ) {
    object_name[current].conceal();
  }
  object_name[form_screen].reveal();
  feedback_form_current_screen = screen;
}
```

The feedback form itself is initialized by way of the appropriately named function feedback_form_init(), shown in Listing 11-7. There's nothing magical going on here. The loop sets object properties for the form components that are referenced later on via members of the feedback_form[] array, and then conceals each component. Finally, a reference to the summary screen is appended to the array. This way, the number of form components can easily be changed without having to specify each form by name, and the name of the final form can quickly be deduced from the array.

Listing 11-7: The feedback-form_init() JavaScript function

```
var feedback_form = new Array(3);
function feedback_form_init() {
  var n = "";
  var last = feedback_form.length;
  for( var x = 0; x < last; x++ ) {
    n = "feedbackform" + x;
    feedback_form[x] = new Object();
    feedback_form[x].name = n;
    feedback_form[x].completed = false;
    object_name[n].conceal();
  }
  feedback_form[last] = new Object();
  feedback_form[last].name = "feedbacksummary";
}
```

In order to provide global access to the variables used by the validation routines, they are declared as global variables at the beginning of the JavaScript file, as shown in Listing 11-8. The feedback_form[x].completed property for each member is used to track which parts of the form have been completed, and is initialized to false. The remaining variables are used to store the processed values of the various form components, based on user input. Finally, the feedback_action variable is simply provided for convenience should the developer find a need to change it. One possible option for the action would be to use a mailto: handler, rather than a server-side CGI script, because the metaform data is already suitably formatted for sticking into an e-mail message. In this instance, however, the form's encoding type would need to be set using a cross-browser wrapper method to ensure the correct transmission of the data.

Listing 11-8: Global variables used by the Feedback Form module

```
var feedback_form_visible = false;
var feedback_form_current_screen = 0;

var fb_favepart = "";
var fb_liked = "";
var fb_goodcomments = "";
var fb_worstpart = "";
var fb_hated = "";
```

```
var fb_negativecomments = "";
var fb_email, fb_name;
var feedback_action = 'http://dhtml-guis.com' +
  '/cgi-bin/nph-feedback.cgi';
```

Now that we have all the pieces of the various forms and the utility routines that help expose it to the application, we need to look at how the form components are validated, as well as how the summary and metaform are generated based on the user's input.

Validating the Feedback Form

The task of validating the feedback form is fairly complex, due to the need to not only validate individual forms, but also check to see if the others have been completed as well. To ease the pain of this validation process, and to ensure that it is only fully undertaken when required — such as on the user's first attempt to submit, or when the user has not set the radio buttons that override the requirement that a given form be filled out — several global variables have been created. We have already seen the first set, the `completed` property assigned to members of the `feedback_form` array, in Listing 11-8. The second set is derived from the forms themselves, rather than as the result of the validation process.

The form property `fb1.nocomment[0].checked`, shown in Listing 11-9, makes use of shorthand references to the cross-browser form objects `form_name["fbone"]`, and so on. The property is interesting because it checks the array formed by the `nocomment` radio button group. A radio group consists of a set of radio button elements that have the same name but different values, representing the fact that radio groups are best used in situations where their values are exclusive of one another, such as in the Boolean choice `true/false`. Both cannot be checked, unlike values represented by check boxes such as `fb1.colorpicker` or `fb1.instructions` in which all or none may be checked without compromising the usefulness of the data. The validation function first checks the state of the radio buttons on the first and second forms, only performing validation on the form in question if the radio button signifying that the user wants to ignore the form is not selected. Otherwise the form is skipped, and the `completed` property is set to `false`.

It's worth pointing out that the routines that check for the presence of name and e-mail also refresh the form screen to make sure that the third and final screen is displayed. Presently, such a refresh is redundant as there is no way to submit the form as a whole except from the final form, which must already be displayed. Code like this may be considered protection against potential further modification, where a submit button might be added to the other forms, for example, and where such checking would become necessary. As mentioned previously, a more appropriate response might be to set the focus to the offending input and save the user the trouble.

Listing 11-9: Validating the feedback forms and preparing to summarize the data

```
function feedback_validate() {
  var fb1 = form_name["fbone"];
  var fb2 = form_name["fbtwo"];
  var fb3 = form_name["fbthree"];

  // check each form field
  // first, check forms one and two for 'no comment' radios
  if( ! fb1.nocomment[0].checked ) {
    // if comments, validate individual form fields
    var fave = fb1.favoritepart;

    fb_favepart = get_selected_option(fave);
    if( fb1.colorpicker.checked ) {
      fb_liked += fb1.colorpicker.value;
    }
    if( fb1.instructions.checked ) {
      fb_liked += fb1.instructions.value;
    }
    if( fb1.feedback.checked ) {
      fb_liked += fb1.feedback.value;
    }

    if( fb1.goodcomments.value.length > 0 ) {
      fb_goodcomments += fb1.goodcomments.value;
    }

    // be strict?
    if( fb1.strictvalidate.value == "true" ) {
      if(( fb_favepart.length > 0 ) &&
         ( fb_liked.length > 0 ) &&
         ( fb_goodcomments.length > 0 )) {
        // everything was filled out
        feedback_form[0].completed = true;
      } else {
        feedback_form[0].completed = false;
      }
    } else {
      // assume everything required has been completed
      feedback_form[0].completed = true;
    }
  } else {
    // assume everything's been completed
    feedback_form[0].completed = true;
```

```
    }

    if( ! fb2.nocomment[0].checked ) {
      // if comments, validate individual form fields
      var worst = fb2.worstpart;
      fb_worstpart = get_selected_option(worst);
      if( fb2.colorpicker.checked ) {
        fb_hated += fb2.colorpicker.value;
      }
      if( fb2.instructions.checked ) {
        fb_hated += fb2.instructions.value;
      }
      if( fb2.feedback.checked ) {
        fb_hated += fb2.feedback.value;
      }

      if( fb2.negativecomments.value.length > 0 ) {
        fb_negativecomments += fb2.negativecomments.value;
      }

      // be strict?
      if( fb2.strictvalidate.value == "true" ) {
        if(( fb_worstpart.length > 0 ) &&
          ( fb_hated.length > 0 ) &&
          ( fb_negativecomments.length > 0 )) {
          // everything was filled out
          feedback_form[1].completed = true;
        } else {
          feedback_form[1].completed = false;
        }
      } else {
        // assume everything required was completed
        feedback_form[1].completed = true;
      }
    } else {
      // assume everything required was completed
      feedback_form[1].completed = true;
    }

    // require name and email address
    fb_name = fb3.fullname.value;
    if( fb_name.length == 0 ) {
      alert("Please enter your name!");
      feedback_show(2);
```

```
    return false;
  }

fb_email = fb3.email.value;
if( ! feedback_is_email(fb_email) ) {
  alert("Please enter a valid email address!");
  feedback_show(2);
  return false;
}

// check to make sure that there were some comments, anyway...
if( feedback_form[0].completed ||
    feedback_form[1].completed ) {
  feedback_display_summary();
} else {
  // ask for more comments?
  alert("Please fill out at least one of the\n" +
        "of the forms. Is that so much to ask?");
  return false;
}
}
```

The hidden form input strictvalidate forces the validation routine to ensure that the user has filled out something for each input, which it checks by testing the length of the variables used to store the data. If they have zero length, the variable used to store whether the form in question has been completed is set to false. If the strictvalidate field is set to false, however, or if it is not present, the user is allowed to skip certain fields.

The next-to-last form validation step checks to see if the user has supplied both a name and e-mail address, complaining if not, and refusing submission of the form as a whole until the inputs are both filled out correctly. The feedback_is_email() function does some perfunctory (and admittedly rather pathetic) checking to make sure that the e-mail address is valid, returning an appropriate Boolean value to signal success or failure. A more robust validation function might check against a complete list of known top-level domains. The function as is merely checks to see that:

◆ There is an at sign ("@") in the address.

◆ There is at least one dot (".") in the address.

◆ A dot follows the at sign (but not immediately after, nor at the very end).

◆ The address is at least five characters long (a@i.am, for example).

Provided that both name and e-mail have been filled out properly, the validation routine then checks to see if at least one form has been filled out (in accordance with the `strictvalidate` variable mentioned previously). If so, the function calls `feedback_display_summary()`, which does the work of formatting the input data for potential modification and final submission by the user. Failing the test for completeness produces an alert asking the user to at least fill out one form if she's going to go through the trouble of submitting the whole thing.

Listing 11-10: Validating an e-mail address with feedback_is_email()

```
function feedback_is_email(address) {
if(( address.indexOf("@") > 0 ) &&
   ( address.indexOf(".") > 0 ) &&
   ( address.lastIndexOf(".") > (address.indexOf("@") + 1)) &&
   ( address.lastIndexOf(".") != (address.length -1)) &&
   ( address.length > 5 )) {
   return true; // it's an address
  } else {
   return false;
  }
}
```

Okay, so now we've gone through all the required validation steps and the user has passed with flying colors, supplying ample criticism or praise for all our hard work. Now it's time to pass the information along to its final recipient.

Creating the Summary and Metaform

The function `feedback_display_summary()` simply grabs the values we've already prepared in the preceding validation steps and formats them for presentation to the user via a TEXTAREA. The form it creates calls `feedback_action`, which we discussed previously (and is defined in Listing 11-8), with the `onSubmit` handler set to call `feedback_submit()`, shown in Listing 11-12. The form thus created is written to the `feedbacksummary` object, replacing the existing contents and then displaying the result.

Listing 11-11: Preparing the final summary with feedback_display_summary()

```
function feedback_display_summary() {
  var summary = fb_name + " (" + fb_email + ")\n" +
    "had the following to say about the dynamic " +
    "poetry application:\n\n" +
    fb_name + "'s most favorite part was:\n" +
    fb_favepart + ".\n\n" +
    fb_name + "'s least favorite part was:\n" +
    fb_worstpart + ".\n\n" +
```

```
    fb_name + " also liked:\n" +
    fb_liked + ".\n\n" +
    fb_name + " did not like:\n" +
    fb_hated + ".\n\n" +
    "Here are some favorable comments:\n" +
    fb_goodcomments + "\n\n" +
    "Here are some negative comments:\n" +
    fb_negativecomments + "\n\n";

  var summary_form = "Here are the comments you gave us:<br>" +
    "<form action=\"" + feedback_action +
    "\" method=POST onSubmit='feedback_submit();'>" +
    "<textarea name=summary cols=60 rows=16>" +
    summary +
    "</textarea><br>" +
    "<input type=submit value=\"send us your comments!\">" +
    "</form>";

  // write the form to the summary layer
  var s = object_name["feedbacksummary"];
  s.replace(summary_form);
  // display the summary layer
  var current = "feedbackform" + feedback_form_current_screen;
  object_name[current].conceal();
  tab_widget_hide();
  s.reveal();
}
```

Although in the standalone example this function simply returns `true`, enabling the form to be submitted, we add other function calls to the routine when it comes time to integrate the feedback form into the Dynamic Poetry application. For example, the feedback form should hide itself and toggle the display back to whatever screen was previously visible before the user chose to give their feedback.

Listing 11-12: A very simplistic feedback_submit() function

```
function feedback_submit() {
  return true;
}
```

We're almost done on the client side; we just have to wait for the server to process the submission. Because we're using a CGI script to manage and store the already-formatted user data, let's take a brief time-out from client-side issues and talk about the network.

The Back-End CGI Script

At the beginning of the chapter, we discussed the use of CGI scripts for processing form data. In the early days of the Web, such CGI scripts were fairly simple and often written in a hundred lines of C or Perl, or even using shell scripts. Forms were simple, the requirements were limited, and you couldn't set the browser's background color, either. Those were the days. Soon, the browsers' forms capabilities were expanded beyond measure, the demands placed on CGI scripts became immense, and the need to provide global access to the simplistic applications they implemented, regardless of the capabilities of the browser, placed incredible demands on the CGI programmer. We have had to write CGI scripts whose length approached several thousand lines of Perl, for example. A far cry from the halcyon days of the Web's youth.

One hopeful characteristic of client-side tools built with DHTML is the promise of simplifying the server-side processing of complex applications. This feedback form is just an example. If the validation and so forth had not been done on the client, the CGI script would be responsible for decoding the input, testing all of the various values, and — horror upon horrors — perhaps even generating the form anew with the appropriate inputs prepopulated and input fields highlighted where the user had neglected to fill them out. As the client-side capabilities require more and more complex templates and markup, the task becomes daunting. This complexity is reduced somewhat through the intelligent use of client-side processing.

Dealing with Unpredictable and Insecure Form Input

This is not a book on CGI, or else we'd spend a great deal of time on this topic just to hammer home the fact that client-side processing is a good thing. Security issues abound in the world of CGI, such as those that arise when a poorly coded CGI script is passed an e-mail address of ill intent, or when a buffer overflow is found in a standard CGI program distributed with Web servers. This was the case with the highly publicized hole in `phf`, a sample program intended to demonstrate the use of CGI itself that was a standard part of the NCSA and later the Apache Web server distributions. The problem was so severe and so potentially damaging that the Apache group set up a Web server solely for the purpose of logging attempts made by crackers to exploit the hole. The Apache Web server distribution still includes a CGI script intended to log such abuses, named `phf_abuse_log.cgi`.

Of course, one could argue that buggy client-side implementations could produce security risks just as horrible as complex server-side programs, and there's something to be said for that. Whatever your stance on the best way to solve security problems, it is good to be aware of the existence of potential security holes, their damaging effects, and how they can be prevented.

Flexible Form Input Parsing

One useful approach to dealing with the increasing complexity of hypertext forms is the generic forms processor, which uses hidden inputs to specify metainformation about the form itself, how its fields should be handled, what types they expect, whether they are required, and so forth. This is an excellent way to deal with multiple, relatively simple (but arbitrary) forms using the same generic CGI script. Forms with multiple possible output paths, however, such as shopping carts or surveys whose question sets depend on the answers to previous questions during a given session, require much more complex logic. Generic forms processors break down at this point, and other approaches are needed.

Suffice it to say that server-side processing is no panacea for complex forms. The simpler the server side is kept, the more secure the server, the less load is required to process form input, and the lower the cost to maintain such scripts and server modules. Let's look at a somewhat contrived, but possibly quite useful, mechanism for dealing with the submission of forms by dynamic HTML applications.

Using HTTP's 204 Response to Indicate Success

With the current implementation of forms in browsers, it is assumed that the browser's display is refreshed by any form submission. In the world of large (and state-driven) DHTML applications, however, this represents a huge problem. There may be several times during a given session when the user needs to submit little pieces of data to the server, and if the act of submitting a form disrupts the client, you have to start over each time. Not the best way to approach client-side applications, in our opinion. Fortunately, there is a way around this problem.

Background: 204 Is the No-Content HTTP Response

When the browser contacts the server, it does so using a TCP socket (the low-level protocol) over which they communicate, using HTTP (Hypertext Transfer Protocol, the higher-level protocol in this case). HTTP uses response codes, such as the dreaded 404 Not Found, to signify the result of a request. Ordinary CGI scripts generally return a 200 OK response, followed by a lengthy set of MIME type information and other headers, and eventually the document itself. In HTTP 1.1, several documents may be sent during the same session using the Keep-Alive header. In any case, it is the 200 OK response, and others like it, that cause the browser to refresh its display. We won't discuss the numerous response codes and their intended meanings, or the reaction induced in the browser.

One response, however, is of a type commonly referred to as a *no-op*, short for *no operation* – the 204 No Content response. In reaction to this header, the browser does nothing at all. For our purposes, this is perfect. We use this response in a reversal of the traditional CGI paradigm, where a successful response is indicated by a change in the browser's display. Instead of indicating success this way, however, the 204 No Content response can be used to indicate success *by not changing the browser's display*. The error condition is more likely to require a change in the display, as it represents a potential loss of data, for example, whereas success could be noted and ignored by the client-side app.

Why You Would Want to Use It

The HTTP 1.1 specification says that the 204 No Content response should be processed for headers, such as cookies, that could be used to pass small bits of information (otherwise known as *semaphores*) back and forth between the browser and server without disrupting the page view. As client-side apps get more complex, and the need increases for more common data transfer, a way to maintain state between the client-side app and the server could be very useful. Unfortunately, the current browsers do not read cookies sent back in 204 responses. Hopefully, the next crop of browsers will. In any case, we use one-way client-to-server information transfer to enable the users of our application to submit feedback many times in a single session, save their favorite phrases to the server where they may be shared with other users, and more. You may want to ask your Webmaster or systems administrator about the 204 response if you don't deal with the server side of things.

For now, however, let's set aside the 204 No Content response and leave the world of CGI altogether, using the example of a forms handler, which works independently of the Web server.

The mailto: Forms Handler – Avoiding CGI

There may be instances where you don't have access to CGI on your server, or where such access is overkill for the minor application you have, such as submitting a name or e-mail address for addition to a manually maintained mailing list, or some other tiny thing. Maybe you just like to get e-mail. Whatever your reasons, the mailto: forms handler can be useful.

How to Use mailto: as a Forms Handler

Ordinarily, when specifying the action of a form, you specify a URL to the CGI application or server module that processes the form submission. In that case, you need to specify the method by which the form should be submitted, but that's all – the data transfer format and related mechanisms are all prescribed by the Common Gateway

Interface itself. With the `mailto:` handler, however, you have a couple of options. Because the submission is to be sent via a mail server, rather than via CGI, you need to set the encoding type (using the `ENCTYPE` attribute to the `FORM` tag) appropriately. The usual encoding for CGI applications is called `application/x-www-form-urlencoded`, which implies the substitution of plus characters for spaces, hexadecimal encoding of nonalphanumeric ASCII characters, and other obstacles to readability. With `mailto:` in supporting browsers, however, you can set the `ENCTYPE` to several different types, including `text/plain`. It's still pretty ugly, but it might just beat having to write a CGI script. So, for example, if you wanted to use the `mailto:` handler for the feedback form, you might specify the `FORM` start tag like so:

```
<FORM ACTION="mailto:example@hesketh.com"
      ENCTYPE="text/plain">
```

The resulting submission looks something like Listing 11-13.

Listing 11-13: A sample mailto: form handler message from Netscape Communicator

```
Date: Thu, 17 Sep 1998 05:15:42 -0400
From: Steven Champeon <example@hesketh.com>
To: example@hesketh.com
Subject: Form posted from Mozilla

summary=Steve (example@hesketh.com)
had the following to say about the dynamic poetry application:

Steve's most favorite part was:
creating my own words.

Steve's least favorite part was:
reading the works of others.

Steve also liked:
the color picker.

Steve did not like:
the feedback form.

Here are some favorable comments:
great color picker.

Here are some negative comments:
the feedback form could use some work.
It didn't like my favorite email address, for example.
```

Note that the first message body line begins with `summary=`. This is the name of the TEXTAREA tag containing the summary information. Everything else is the contents of the TEXTAREA itself. Pretty simple, eh?

Unfortunately, the mailto: handler isn't supported in all browsers, and doesn't work well for complex data transfer. It simply doesn't work at all in the "stand-alone" Netscape Navigator, for example; although the warning dialog box pops up and the form appears to have been submitted, nothing happens, as there is no way to specify the SMTP server to use when actually sending the message.

Now, having run through a few options for how to deal with your form input and outlined a future strategy for reasonably intelligent client-server interaction using HTTP 1.1 and cookies, it's time to integrate the feedback form into the Dynamic Poetry application.

Integrating the Feedback Form into the Application

Because we took such liberties with the positioning and naming of the DIVs for the feedback form, integrating it into the Dynamic Poetry application is a piece of cake. All we need to do is stick the style sheet definitions into a file that we call feedback.css for simplicity's sake, and include it in the application like so:

```
<link rel="STYLESHEET" type="text/css"
    href="/css/feedback.css" title="feedback form">
```

Then, we just paste the HTML markup for the various DIV objects into the file poetry.html along with the appropriate SCRIPT tags to include the files tab_widget.js and feedback_form.js, and make a few minor modifications to the order in which the application is initialized. For one thing, as we mentioned previously, the tab widget objects need to be written to the application using document.write(), so we include calls to the functions tab_widget_init() and tab_widget_hide() in an embedded SCRIPT element right before the end of the document. This is only required by Internet Explorer, though, so we test for the browser after calling the create_base_objects() and feedback_form_init() functions:

```
<script language="JavaScript">
create_base_objects();
feedback_form_init();
if( navigator.appName != "Netscape" ) {
  tab_widget_init();
  tab_widget_hide();
}
fully_loaded = true;
</script>
```

For Netscape, we need to be sure that the document is loaded before we use the `Layer()` call to create the tab objects, so we put a similar test in the `executive_poetry_init()` function, which is called by the `onLoad` handler for the document:

```
function executive_poetry_init() {
  // moved to HTML
  //  create_base_objects();
  if(navigator.appName == "Netscape" ) {
    tab_widget_init();
    tab_widget_hide();
  }
  init_words();
  shadow_set_events(); // was set_netscape_events();
}
```

We have also renamed `set_netscape_events()` for purposes that becomes clear in Chapter 13, "User-Configurable Interfaces," where we set other event handlers for the Color Picker module.

Now all that remains to be done is to modify the feedback form submission function so that it toggles the playing field after submitting the form. The function that performs the toggling is discussed next, and here's the call to it in a modified `feedback_submit()`:

```
function feedback_submit() {
  // toggle the entire feedback form and submit
  toggle_feedback();
  return true;
}
```

Showing and Hiding the Form Layer Itself

The feedback form by itself is pretty useless, so it makes sense to include it in the application as a user option. In order to do this properly, however, we need to define a function that toggles the feedback form, define a menu item, and associate the function with the item. The `toggle_feedback()` function, shown in Listing 11-14, uses the variable `feedback_form_visible` to check whether the form needs to be hidden or shown, and calls the appropriate functions in either case. First of all, when hiding the form, the functions `feedback_form_hide()` and `tab_widget_hide()` are called, and the words are toggled if they are not visible (they shouldn't be, but we may have entered the form from the instructions screen or some other application state). The form screen last shown, or the first screen if this is our first time through, is hidden, and the `mainlayer` object is also revealed. Finally, the `visible_main_screen` variable is set so we can keep track of what layers are visible.

Listing 11-14: The toggle_feedback() JavaScript function

```
function toggle_feedback() {
  var ml = "mainlayer";
  var fb = "feedbackform" + feedback_form_current_screen;
  if( feedback_form_visible ) {
    feedback_form_hide();
    tab_widget_hide();
    if( ! words_are_visible ) {
      toggle_words();
    }
    object_name[visible_form_screen].reveal();
    object_name[ ml ].reveal();
    visible_main_screen = ml;
  } else {
    object_name[visible_main_screen].conceal();
    if( words_are_visible ) {
      toggle_words();
    }
    toggle_form("blanklayer");
    tab_widget_show();
    feedback_show(feedback_form_current_screen);
    visible_main_screen = fb;
    feedback_form_visible = true;
    tab["tab0s"].reveal();
  }
}
```

If the form is being shown, on the other hand, we do basically the opposite. We hide the currently displayed layer and the words; set the blanklayer object so as to hide any of our auxiliary forms, such as savephraselayer, that might be displayed at the time; and then show both the form itself and the tab widget. We set visible_main_screen and feedback_form_visible appropriately, and then explicitly set the first tab to "selected." And that's it. As we add more functionality to the Dynamic Poetry application, we do some more robust stuff, such as tracking visible and hidden form layers. For now, however, this is sufficient.

To ensure that our users have access to the form when they need it, we check that the toggle_feedback() function is set as the handler in the appropriate menu item, and off we go into testing mode.

Testing Your Form with the Application

The first thing we need to test is if the form is actually shown when the menu item is clicked. As we can see in Figure 11-6, this works just fine. We also need to test if selecting the menu item again hides the form as it should, and that it restores the playing field to its previous state. Figure 11-7 illustrates the application after returning the feedback form to its hidden state.

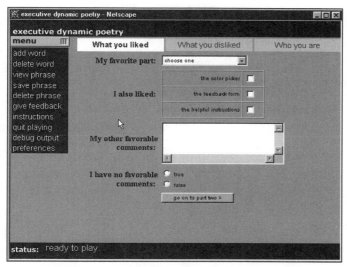

Figure 11-6: The feedback form integrated into the Dynamic Poetry application

Now that we've seen that the toggle_feedback() function is working from the menu item, it is time to check the form itself for proper functionality.

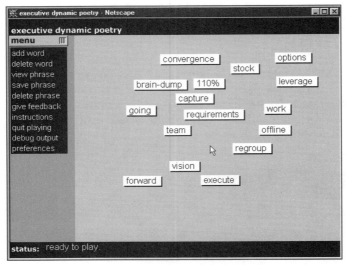

Figure 11-7: The Dynamic Poetry application with the feedback form hidden

Testing Various Branches

Because we've made it possible for the user to forgo filling out one or the other of the initial form screens, we need to check whether the form reacts appropriately when one or both of the screens is incomplete. Figure 11-8 illustrates the form's reaction when both screens are left incomplete, asking the user to go back and fill out at least one.

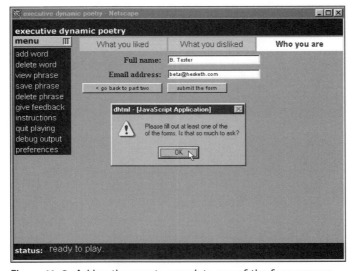

Figure 11-8: Asking the user to complete one of the form screens

In addition to the one-or-the-other rule, we insist that the user supply both their name and e-mail address so we can harass them for being so critical, thank them for the kind words, or follow up on problem reports. If the name field is left blank, the user can expect to see the alert illustrated in Figure 11-9.

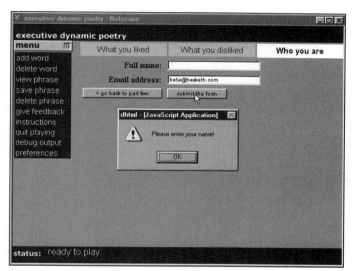

Figure 11-9: Making sure that the user supplies their name and e-mail address

Once the user has successfully completed the form, or at least to our satisfaction, it is submitted and the summary is displayed for the user to add to or change if they so desire. Figure 11-10 shows the results of a successful first-phase submission.

Once the form is finally submitted, the `toggle_feedback()` function is called again, and the user is returned to the playing field. Later, we may wish to provide further feedback to the user indicating that the form has been submitted. That's the subject of the next chapter, however.

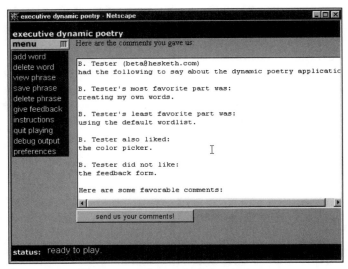

Figure 11-10: The summary form submission text area

Testing Form Validation

One of the areas in which this form is incredibly weak is in its validation of user input. We've already heavily disclaimed the further use of the e-mail address validation function, for example. What's worse, the summary quite happily includes headers for sections that the user did not fill out at all. A more robust validation routine, which must be custom written for whatever form you intend to include, would check for the existence of each piece of form data and format the summary appropriately, only including the pieces that the user filled out.

Testing Metaform Rollup

Testing the summary of form information entails a tedious process of filling out one field or selecting each check box or pull-down menu item at a time, and then attempting to submit the form for summary. Fortunately, the code as written enables the user (or beta tester) to hide the feedback summary and restore the initial screen with its previous settings intact. The beta tester can then make a small change and resummarize the form. Once testing has been completed, and all of the summaries have been approved, it might make sense to add a navigational element to enable users to jog back and forth between the summary form and the previous form screens; although to be fair, the summary does enable the user to edit their responses prior to submission. Tailor your form to your audience and application.

Testing Both Form Actions

Beyond testing the form summary and validation, the only thing that remains to be done is to actually submit the form, either using a CGI application (returning the appropriate 204 No Content response), or the mailto: handler. As mentioned earlier, the mailto: handler is not supported on all platforms, so it may be wise to include some logic that checks for the platforms on which it is not supported and substitutes the CGI in the event of a nonsupported browser. Writing and testing CGI applications to deal with the submission is beyond the scope of this book, but you should play around with the best formatting and data presentation for your purposes.

Gotchas

There are a few gotchas in this chapter, most notably the issue surrounding where to write the tab widget objects to the document during initialization. Here are a few others:

◆ Watch out for interference between style sheet definitions and form elements. In the first version of the feedback form during development, the TD styles used by the form caused some problems with the display of the TEXTAREA.

◆ Remember that radio button elements, when grouped, create an array, not just a single variable. You need to check for the checked property for each element in the array.

◆ Using forcing functions (such as the radio buttons in the examples in this chapter) can be annoying to the user. A better option might be to differentiate such functions from the form itself and present them as an alternative with appropriate styling and instructional text.

◆ Using a tab widget for a goal-oriented interface, as we did in our examples, might be confusing for users accustomed to a tab representing alternatives, rather than a handy mechanism for jumping around between tasks in a workflow. Consider the user's reaction to your choice of interface paradigms.

◆ Make it easy for the user to do what you require. If you're going to complain about missing fields in the input, consider setting the document focus to the field the user needs to fill out. Be careful about switching screens when doing this, though. Sudden changes, especially if they don't provide a quick way back to the last form, can be very annoying and disorienting to the user, who may just give up and hide the form again without bothering to feed back to you how annoying it was.

Summary

In this chapter, you learned how to deal with forms in a DHTML application, including how to validate, summarize, and submit forms using several different screens and types of form elements. You also learned how to:

◆ Make use of the tab widget to provide sequentially-oriented navigation for a goal-based interface: the feedback form

◆ Include the tab widget in your application and configure the labels and handlers for your tabs

◆ Use the HTTP 204 No Content response to keep your page display from getting refreshed unnecessarily

◆ Argue for the use of intelligent client-side processing to simplify or even eliminate back-end server processing requirements against the heathen who irrationally insist that server-side apps are just going to get more and more complex and there's nothing we can do to stop it

On that note, let's move along to the next chapter, where you will learn about some other, more indirect forms of feedback, including debugging information, error reports, and status feedback to the user.

Chapter 12

Other Kinds of Feedback

IN THIS CHAPTER

♦ Compensate for routines that do not otherwise provide useful feedback

♦ Provide a user-level view of the application's current status

♦ Provide the developer with useful debugging output

♦ Provide a way for the developer to obtain useful information when an error occurs

♦ Demonstrate the use of independent code modules in other applications

IN THE LAST CHAPTER, we used a simple feedback form to enable users to tell the developer and support staff in charge of maintaining the application exactly how they feel about it. Such a feedback form assumes that users provide feedback of a more high-level nature, such as comments about the usability of the interface or the appropriateness of the word list. However, not every application always works as intended, especially when it is built with "bleeding-edge" technology. In this chapter, we discuss a few other feedback mechanisms that:

Some Principles of User Feedback

Feedback is a key characteristic of the user interface. Essentially, an interface provides both input and output. Feedback makes up a large portion of the application's output, keeping the user informed at every moment about what is happening inside the bowels of the software. In order for any application to provide meaningful feedback, the developer and interface designer must first determine what information the application is already providing by the nature of the interface itself. The lighter shadow beneath a lifted magnet and the dark color assumed by a selected word are examples of this straightforward feedback. The user is aware at all times of the state of the application. We talk more about this sort of direct feedback throughout our discussion of the sample application, but now it is time to take a gander at feedback mechanisms that provide glimpses into what would otherwise be an unknown state – that of the application's internals, the latest completed action, and the reason why an error occurred. The last of these also provides valuable feedback to the developers; feedback whose absence often results in hefty tech support costs as the user and tech support personnel play an expensive game of tennis trying to figure out what went wrong.

In the early days of JavaScript, image rollovers were all the rage, along with goofy scrolling messages that flickered and whizzed by in the window status bar. The apex of such interface tricks came when some wizard figured out how to "drop" a letter at a time, from the right side of the status bar to the left, gradually building a message and capturing the user's attention. Unfortunately, there was no way to turn off such annoying displays of virtuosity. It didn't matter that you'd already read the message being displayed; it just kept on cycling through, distracting your attention from the business at hand on the page itself. This demonstrates several important principles both in terms of user interface design in general, and the appropriate choice of feedback specifically:

◆ Feedback should be provided in an accurate and timely manner.

◆ Feedback should not be misleading or incorrect.

◆ Feedback should be evident without being obtrusive.

◆ Feedback should not be redundant.

◆ Feedback is not a toy.

The first of these principles, providing accurate and timely feedback, is perhaps the most difficult of all to implement due to differences in the way that the various browsers deal with timing and other issues. The bottom line is that you need to be careful when choosing what feedback to provide, at the risk of providing feedback that does not appear at the right time or that does not appear at all. The second principle is the inverse of the first, but deserves to be stated because it drives decisions you make in the process of choosing when and where to provide feedback.

The third principle, that feedback should be evident without being obtrusive, is very important due to the potential for distraction from poorly implemented feedback. Balancing the need to provide feedback with the requirement not to distract the user can be extremely difficult. Fortunately, you may make compromises in which generic messages are printed to an area of the screen set aside for just that purpose. This enables the user to glance at that area to check the status of the application without being disrupted by attention-grabbing alert dialog boxes, whose use is best limited to those times when a disruption is necessary.

Along the same lines, redundant feedback, where the user is notified of the same event more than once, can be a problem as well. If feedback cannot be counted upon to provide new information, the user quickly learns to ignore it. Bear in mind, however, that providing feedback on the same event or internal state to two different outlets — say, to the application's status bar and the debugging console — is not redundant as long as the user is not expected to view both simultaneously. In addition, having two or more outlets for feedback can be especially useful if the feedback is tailored to the expectations of the audience. Whereas the user might not care about the names of function calls, their arguments, and other internal status information, preferring instead to deal with high-level messages, the debugging console is extremely useful to the developer. Printing a great deal of information to the debugging console might bore, threaten, confuse, or overwhelm the average user; it helps to better place certain events in their appropriate context with regard to the overall program flow.

Lastly, and we shouldn't even have to say this at all, feedback is not a toy. Just because you have figured out how to create an animated pop-up window that lets the latest status message flutter by from a different side every time while changing the message's text colors all within a five-frame frameset populated by "kewl" background color animations, does not in fact suggest that this should be your application's default feedback mechanism. In the example application, which is a game, feedback mechanisms are given an appropriate role and no more. Exercise responsible feedback.

The code modules illustrated in this chapter deal with a range of feedback mechanisms from the basic status bar, whose contents are directed at the user, to the debugging console, whose messages are intended for the developer. We show you how to incorporate these functions into your application. In addition, the handy combination of a JavaScript error dialog box and a feedback form providing useful information to the developer blends the user feedback function illustrated in the last chapter with the more indirect feedback mechanisms illustrated in this chapter.

Our Very Own Status Bar

The first of the three feedback modules discussed in this chapter, the *Status Bar module*, is the only one whose feedback is directed solely at the user. The model is simple, but there is a certain risk of redundancy here. After all, most applications nowadays come with their own status bar, don't they? The problem is that many people have become accustomed, for good or ill, to ignoring everything outside the browser's root window (the space occupied by the Web pages as the user surfs). Controlling the visibility of the browser's status bar is beyond the control of the average JavaScript programmer, who must use signed scripts to show and hide the status bar in the default window. This solution, like the `window.statusbar.visibility` property that controls it, is unfortunately only available in Netscape Navigator 4.0 as of this writing.

A cross-browser solution, like many of those introduced in this book, is to create your own window without the default status bar, and use CSS positioning and dynamic object updates to make your own status bar whose style, position, and visibility you can control. In addition to those listed previously, other benefits include the following:

◆ Full control over font style

◆ Full control over visibility and positioning

◆ No contention between internal browser messages and your own status

◆ Full control over the look and feel of the status bar

◆ Consistent presentation of status information

◆ Cross-platform and cross-browser

The Status Bar module is really very simple, but integrating it into your application is more complex, as you must make decisions as to when your application should provide feedback and when it should stay quiet. In the following section, we add the Status Bar module to the Dynamic Poetry application, demonstrating how simple the code is while discussing the more esoteric decisions that must be made regarding exactly when and how to use it.

Including the Status Bar Module

The Status Bar module is a separate JavaScript file, and like the other generic modules we've seen in previous chapters, it may be included via the <SCRIPT SRC> mechanism. All of the other customization we perform takes place as additions to the existing code or markup in JavaScript, CSS, or HTML. The status bar SCRIPT element must be included after the xplatform_wrapper.js file, but before the other code, such as executive_poetry.js and the other modules. Actually, you may include the Status Bar module anywhere relative to the other modules as long as they do not use the status bar themselves.

```
<script src="/javascript/status_bar.js"></script>
```

Defining the Status Bar Layer

The second thing that must be defined in order to add the status bar to an application is the layer to which the status messages are written. For the Dynamic Poetry application, we have decided to put the status bar at the bottom of the application window in front of a black background featuring the label "status:". The messages themselves are written in front of the bar and offset enough so that the messages do not overwrite the label itself. This requires two DIVs, one for the background and one for the status layer itself, as illustrated in Listing 12-1. Note that the graphic containing the status background is 30 pixels by 600 pixels – we get to the offset when we define the fonts and positioning using CSS.

Listing 12-1: The status background and status layer DIVs

```
<div id=statusbg
     class=statusbg>
<img src="/images/status.gif"
     height=30 width=600>
</div>
```

```
<div id=statuslayer class=statusbg>

<h1>status</h1>
</div>
```

The CSS style definitions for the status background are simple, as illustrated in Listing 12-2. Basically, all this style sheet does is place the graphic using CSS absolute positioning. Listing 12-3, however, not only uses positioning but also defines the default fonts, colors, and so forth.

Listing 12-2: The style sheet for the status background

```
div.statusbg {
  position: absolute;
  top: 420;
  left: 0;
  width: 600;
  height: 30;
}
```

Messages are displayed (unless otherwise defined by the code calling the status_write() function) using a 13-point sans serif font, white on the black background, aligned vertically within the layer, and offset by 65 pixels to compensate for the label. You may modify these settings, of course, without modifying the Status Bar module itself.

Listing 12-3: The style sheet for the status layer

```
.status {
  color: white;
  font-family: Arial, Espy, Verdana, Helvetica, Geneva, Sans-Serif;
  font-size: 13pt;
  text-indent: 65px;
  vertical-align: middle;
}
```

There is a problem at this point in the integration, however. If the application is displayed within the main browser window, the application's status bar competes with the browser's status bar, which is something we don't want to cause. You can see this effect in Figure 12-1. Our solution is to launch the game in its own browser window, which is created without the default browser status bar. This also enables precise definition of the space occupied by the game, constraining it to the exact size of the application's layers. The code for the launch page, shown in Listing 12-4, uses a call to window.open to create the window that houses the game from now on. The anchor traps onClick and calls the launch() function, creating the window if it doesn't exist. Note that the JavaScript for the launch() function is simply embedded in the HTML markup, rather than being included separately.

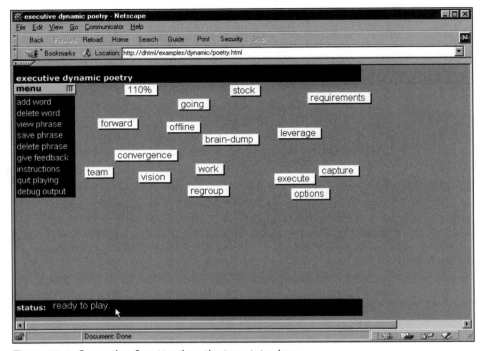

Figure 12-1: Competing for attention: the two status bars

If you decide to reuse such code, it might be worth the time it would take to make the function generic to enable you to pass a features list or other variables to the function itself. Note also that the first line in the script assigns the name `main` to the window that currently contains the launch page to enable the application to refer to the default browser window, which is nameless unless otherwise explicitly named. We also checked for the `window.opener` property and set it if was not already defined. We find it is clearer and less error-prone to assemble the arguments for a new window separate from the call to `window.open` for a couple of reasons. First, if the arguments have been defined in a single place and assigned to a variable, the definition for that window type may be reused in other parts of your application. Second, if each argument property is on its own line, it makes it easier to comment on changes to the individual property values if and when they are made.

Listing 12-4: The Dynamic Poetry launch page

```
<html>
<head><title> launch page for dynamic poetry </title>
<script language="JavaScript">
<!--// hide me
// make up for initial nameless window
window.name = "main";
```

```
function launch () {
  var root = "/examples/dynamic/";
  var args = "width=600," +
             "height=450," +
             "toolbar=0," +
             "menubar=0," +
             "scrollbars=0," +
             "resizable=1," +
             "status=0," +
             "location=0," +
             "directories=0," +
             "copyhistory=0";

  new_win = window.open( root + "/poetry.html",
                         "poetrygame",
                         args );

  if( ! window.opener ) {
    window.opener = this.window;
  }
}


//-->
</script>
</head>
<body>
<a href="#" onClick="launch();">start playing</a>
</body>
</html>
```

The new window, shown in Figure 12-2, gives us a much tighter playground, fitting the boundaries we've defined and no more. At this point, however, there are no status messages, as we have not yet added the appropriate statements to the JavaScript. A word of caution here: When first running through your code looking for appropriate places to add status messages, it is easy to overcompensate for the previous lack of feedback. A better strategy is to play with the application for a while, making note of where users might benefit from some feedback and where they might be distracted by too much. Then, and only then, should you go into the code itself. Because of the static nature of the paper this book is printed on, this step is somewhat difficult to portray. However, in the next section we outline a few obvious places where feedback makes sense and discuss the process by which we determined its importance.

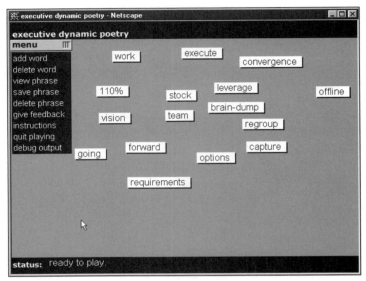

Figure 12-2: Exerting tighter control over our environment: the pop-up window

Integrating the Status Bar into the Application

The Dynamic Poetry application makes literally dozens of different tasks and functions available to the user. So which of these should provide feedback via the status bar? The user can choose from a number of different menu items, each with its own associated task. Every form containing a pull-down menu has a number of options that the user can make. The user can manipulate the magnets herself using the mouse, and select them for inclusion in a saved phrase. So which of these functions requires feedback?

The answer may surprise you. Almost none of the tasks mentioned previously require any status bar feedback at all, because they provide their own feedback in the form of changing position, color, and other state change mechanisms. The user does require status feedback, however, when the tasks alone do not produce their own. A good example of this is the "view phrase" menu item. When the user selects the "view phrase" task, the application first checks to see if there are any saved phrases. If there are saved phrases, the application uses the names of those phrases to dynamically construct a form with a pull-down menu containing the choice or choices available to the user. If there are no saved phrases, and therefore no choices, the form is not built and the pull-down menu is not displayed. But how does the user know that the form has not been displayed due to a lack of saved phrases? Aha! That is what status bar feedback is for; it makes up for an otherwise uninformative function.

The Status Bar module, as mentioned previously, is ludicrously simple. It only has two functions of any real value. The first, `status_write()`, is illustrated in Listing 12-5. It takes a single message as an argument, which is wrapped in a P element. The P element uses the `status` style sheet defined in Listing 12-3. For special cases, such as those where the developer wishes to provide more emphasis, the message itself may also be wrapped in SPAN markup defining extra style information, such as a different, more alarming color, italics, or even the dreaded BLINK tag or text decoration — whichever approach the application calls for. The example we discussed previously, where the user is informed of the reason why the "view phrase" form has not been displayed, is shown in Figure 12-3. Note that the status bar layer is hidden before its contents are changed, and then displayed again. This is to prevent flicker and weird overwriting effects as the content of the layer is changed.

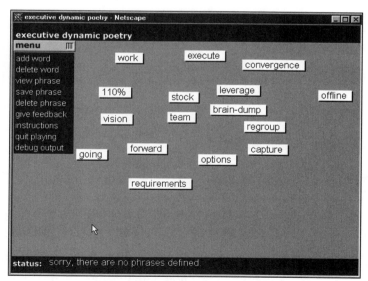

Figure 12-3: Making up for silent failures with status feedback

Listing 12-5: The status_write() function

```
var default_status = "";
var current_status;
var sl = "statuslayer"; // shorthand

function status_write( message ) {
  current_status = message;
  var markup = '<p class="status">' +
               message + '</p>';

  var status_bar = object_name[ sl ];
  status_bar.conceal();
  status_bar.replace( markup, sl );
  status_bar.reveal();
}
```

The second useful function in the Status Bar module is the one that clears the status bar. Those who have used the window.status method of writing to the browser's status bar may note the similarities to JavaScript's window.status and window.defaultStatus properties. The status_clear() function, illustrated in Listing 12-6, is even simpler than status_write(), taking no arguments at all and simply clearing the status message.

Listing 12-6: The status_clear() function

```
function status_clear() {
  current_status = "";

  var status_bar = object_name[ sl ];
  status_bar.conceal();
  status_bar.replace( "", sl );
  status_bar.reveal();
}
```

Because the code is so simple, and because there are actually several places in the Dynamic Poetry application that need to provide feedback otherwise absent from the existing code, we don't show you all of them here. But we do show the code from the piece of executive_poetry.js that uses both functions, namely the init_words() function. We've modified init_words(), illustrated in Listing 12-7, to inform the user of the application's progress in creating and placing the word magnets found in the word list. This use of the Status Bar module borders on the redundant, as it should be evident to the user when the various magnets appear on the playing field that they are being placed, as seen in Figure 12-4.

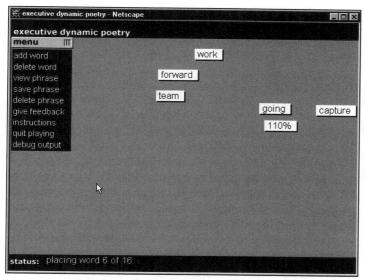

Figure 12-4: Displaying redundant (and useless) status feedback

Listing 12-7: The init_words() function, complete with status reports

```
function init_words() {
  for( i = 0; i <= wordlist.length; i++ ) {
    var word_label = 'word' + i;
    var shadow_label = 'shadow' + i;

    if( i < wordlist.length ) {
      new_word(wordlist[i]);
    }

    if( i < word_counter ) {
      object_name[word_label].reveal();
      object_name[shadow_label].reveal();
      status_write("placing \"" +
        object_name[word_label].word + "\"...");
    } else {
      object_name[word_label].conceal();
      object_name[shadow_label].conceal();
    }
  }

  frontmost = object_name[word_label].z_index();
  status_clear();
}
```

It might make more sense to display a count of the words remaining, so the user can estimate how long it will be until the game is ready to play. This small change is illustrated in Listing 12-8 and displayed in Figure 12-5.

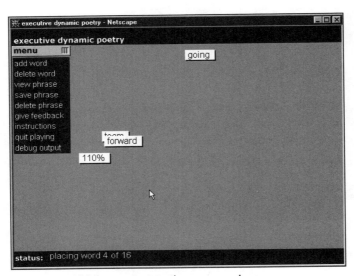

Figure 12-5: Adding context to the user experience

Note that we've added one to the index variable i so as to avoid the issue of array indices beginning with zero in JavaScript. The variable wordlist_length is fine, however, as it is not an array offset, but a true count of the number of words to initialize. The application also notifies the user when the game is ready to play, using a call to status_write(), as shown in Figure 12-6.

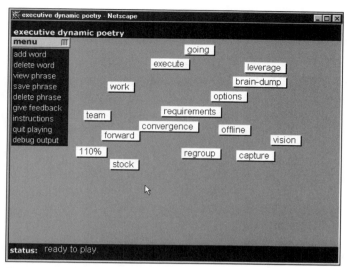

Figure 12-6: We're ready to play

Listing 12-8: An even more helpful form of feedback

```
//status_write("placing \"" +
//        object_name[word_label].word + "\"...");
status_write("placing word " + (i + 1) +
            " of " + wordlist.length );
```

Some other places in the application where feedback is required due to a lack of other informative manipulation of the interface, or as supplementary information upon completion of a task, include the following:

◆ When a word has been added or deleted

◆ When a phrase has been restored, saved or deleted

◆ When the application encounters a condition that prevents an action from being successfully completed

◆ When a condition exists that has no corresponding interface feature that might signal the internal state of the application

Notice that the descriptions of conditions where status reports may be required got more and more general. It is good practice to start with the areas of your application that definitely require feedback to be given to the user to prevent confusion, and proceed until you've started having doubts about the appropriateness of more feedback. Odds are that you've reached a point where the feedback you are considering is spurious and unnecessary. At that point, it is time to consider if the feedback you want to provide comes more as a result of your efforts to debug the application, rather than out of an attempt to inform the user. Debugging information is invaluable, as we discuss soon, but most users are only confused by such output and don't have any interest in seeing it. We also show you where the user *does* need to see such output, in a last-ditch, compromise use of debugging information in the case of an irrecoverable error. But first, let's walk through the status bar test plan and make sure that everything is working properly.

Testing Your Status Bar with the Application

Fortunately, the simplicity of the Status Bar module is a boon to testing. It should be as easy as delineating the places where your application should give feedback (which you should have anyway from the previous section) and following a set procedure to see if the appropriate message is being printed to the status bar. There are some things to look out for while you're testing, however:

◆ Timing of the appearance of status messages on different browsers and platforms

◆ Accurate and correct positioning and styles rendering (specifically font sizes) that differ widely even with CSS

◆ Appropriateness of "borderline redundant" feedback

◆ Phrasing, conciseness, and brevity of the messages themselves

If you have the budget or time (or willing family members) to do user testing, by all means do it. They tell you things you never wanted to hear about your application that are, of course, exactly the sorts of things you need to hear.

Providing Debug Information (for Those Who Want It)

Giving your users feedback at the appropriate times is essential, especially when the application has been completely developed, debugged, tested, and released. But what about the stomach-churning interim when the application is still in the early stages of development? As a developer, there are times when you need to know what's going on even when such information is likely to confuse and annoy your users. The previous section was devoted to defining the appropriate feedback for your users. This section deals with providing feedback on the application's internals, the guts of the code, which users hopefully never see.

Although there are now professional-quality debuggers available for certain platforms, the majority of them only deal with JavaScript itself. Because dynamic HTML applications use JavaScript to define the verbs in your application, this is quite helpful. There is other information that you'd like to be able to see, however; information that may exist in the form of CSS values (the adjectives), or the properties of HTML objects (the nouns). We use JavaScript for the Debug module because it enables you to access the information that you, as a developer, need. The trick now is to figure out just exactly what information you require, and determine the best way to provide access to that information during development and testing.

Java Console, Debug Layer, or window.status?

Because the major browsers differ so widely in their support for the various output mechanisms there are to choose from, we must provide several different methods for accessing that output. In Netscape Navigator, the browser provides access to the Java Console, perhaps the easiest output mechanism to implement. Essentially, we just print our debug information to the Java Console, and that's it. However, Microsoft's Internet Explorer does not expose the Java Console, so the solution is not cross-browser compatible. Because it is so easy to implement, however, we provide it as a default and disable it if the browser does not support it.

Another mechanism for providing debug output is to use a layer and write our debug output to a text area in that layer. This mechanism is supported across browser platforms, albeit somewhat shakily, and enables us to provide a simple yet powerful way to duplicate the functionality built into the Java Console. We may then hide or show that layer as required. The last-ditch effort, and likely the least useful of the bunch, is to use the `window.status` property to report debug information.

In this section, we show you how to implement each of these solutions, and we discuss their inherent flaws and strengths. After implementing the various methods and choosing which of them is appropriate for the specific situation, we show you how to choose between them at runtime and provide fallback methods for those browsers that do not support the first choice. We then discuss some strategies for determining when and how to give useful debug feedback.

The Debug Module

Using the Debug module is extremely easy, because all the hard stuff is built into the module itself. The developer only needs to choose a default output mechanism, lightly sprinkle their code with debug() statements, and watch the information stream forth. Because this book is supposed to be about interface design as opposed to low-level rapid application development, we don't go into tedious detail about the actual mechanisms at work, but there is a lot to cover with regard to integrating the Debug module into your application. Without further ado, let's dive right into integration itself.

Just as with the Status Bar module, the Debug module is an independent JavaScript file. This makes it easier to include the module in your HTML without having to copy and paste, or worse, rewrite it every time. Remember: "Code reuse is a good thing." The markup by which you include the file into your application is illustrated in Listing 12-9. It's remarkably similar to that used by the Status Bar module and other modules, but with the added bonus of a few extra variables. It would be nice if you could include a file, and then use the space between the beginning and ending SCRIPT tags to assign values to flags and other variables, but this is not the case. So we set the "on/off switch" for the module using the Boolean debug_flag, and choose our default output mechanism; in this case, the Java Console. We include the Debug module immediately after the cross-browser wrappers, so we can debug the following modules as well.

Listing 12-9: Including the Debug module in your application

```
<script src="/javascript/debug.js"></script>
<script language="JavaScript">
debug_flag = true;
debug_to = "java_console";
// debug_to = "layer";
// debug_to = "winstatus";
</script>
```

Now that the module has been included, let's look at how and when it should be initialized.

Initializing the Debug Module

In order to ensure that the appropriate mechanisms are in place before the Debug module starts reporting on the state of your application's innards, we provide a debug_init() function, illustrated in Listing 12-10. This function should be called right after the call to create_base_objects(), which initializes the cross-browser object wrappers. The code first checks to see which output mechanism has been defined as a default. It then tries to prepare the appropriate output target, whether it is a pop-up window, a layer, or the Java Console. Note that the flag debug_ready is either set to true by the debug_init() function, or set to false by the debug_disable() function, as shown in Listing 12-11. Either way, the function always returns a value, so your application can check for the success or failure of the initialization.

Listing 12-10: The debug_init() JavaScript function

```
function debug_init() {
  if( debug_to == "layer" ) {
    debug_ready = debug_layer_init();
  } else if( debug_to == "java_console" ) {
    debug_ready = debug_console_init();
  } else if( debug_to == "winstatus" ) {
    debug_ready = true;
  }

  if( debug_ready ) {
    debug("initialization complete.");
  }
  return debug_ready;
}
```

In the version of the code shown in Listing 12-10 there is no fallback logic, although it would be easy enough to add, essentially checking the default first and then trying the mechanisms in order of likelihood that they are supported by the browser. The debug_disable() function, illustrated in Listing 12-11, displays an alert to the user that consists of a brief message explaining that debugging has been disabled due to lack of support for that particular output method, with the extra information passed as an argument displayed at the bottom of the dialog box. The debug_disable() function also sets the appropriate flags, in this case debug_flag and debug_ready, to prevent any more attempts at debugging. This effectively stops the debugger cold.

Listing 12-11: The debug_disable() JavaScript function

```
function debug_disable( addtl_info ) {
  var msg = "This application is not properly\n";
  msg += "configured to use, or does not support,\n";
  msg += "the specified output setting for the\n";
  msg += "debug module.\n";
  msg += "\nDebugging has been disabled.\n\n";
  msg += "Please contact the program\'s author.\n";
  msg += "\nAdditional info:\n\n";
  msg += addtl_info;

  alert( msg );
  debug_flag = false; // keep this from popping up again
  debug_ready = false;
  return true;
}
```

For each of the several available mechanisms the Debug module provides, there are certain specific initialization procedures that are covered in the appropriate section. The basic idea, however, is simple: Check for the existence of the output target (or some other indicator of its likelihood) and make sure that it is ready to receive debugging output. The debug() function itself (illustrated at the end of this section in its entirety in Listing 12-13) checks for the readiness of the target, but should not have to check all the minutiae every time. Such checking slows down the processing of the application immensely. The caveat here is that when debugging your application using this module, be careful not to affect the environment such that the output target goes away, or else you may need to reload the application from scratch. There are ways around this problem, but the tradeoff between performance and absolutely bulletproof debugging is significant enough in this case that we assume you know what you're doing.

Writing to the Java Console

As we said earlier, writing to the Java Console is so simple that it is an absolute shame that Microsoft doesn't support it in their browser. Essentially, the debug() function calls the Java function java.lang.System.out.println() that — if Java is enabled, but regardless of whether or not the Console is visible — is then written directly to the Console, followed by a new line. A proverbial piece of cake. In fact, the code is literally only one line long, as you can see. No post-processing of the message is required, nor do you need to perform any elaborate checks each time the debug() function is called. (Can you tell we really like this method of providing debug information?) Figure 12-7 shows the output.

```
if( debug_to == "java_console" ) {
    java.lang.System.out.println( message_buffer );
}
```

If you're in a hurry, and don't want to bother with the rest of the Debug module, you can always use the following code for a quick-and-dirty debug(). Then, just call debug() with the string you want to print to the console. Not as elegant as the module, in that it only prints what you tell it to and doesn't provide any other information, but useful in a pinch. Note that this method only works if you're using Netscape Navigator as your test bed browser, but you should have already figured that out.

```
var debug = java.lang.System.out.println;
debug("Heh. Debugging to the Java Console is *easy*!");
```

Okay, we've crowed aplenty about the virtues of the Java Console. Next on our list of possible output mechanisms is the debug layer.

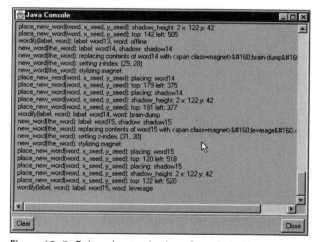

Figure 12-7: Debugging to the Java Console in Netscape Navigator

Writing to the Debug Layer

The debug layer is just another layer, initialized very simply by checking to see if the debug layer wrapper object exists, as seen in Listing 12-12. If not, the initialization routine fails, calls the debug_disable() function previously discussed, and returns false, so the debug_init() routine knows whether it succeeded or not.

Listing 12-12: The debug_layer_init() JavaScript function

```
var dl = "debuglayer";
function debug_layer_init() {
  if( object_name[ dl ] ) {
    return true;
  } else {
    debug_disable("Cannot initialize debug layer!");
    return false;
  }
}
```

 On the Macintosh, Netscape Navigator sometimes fails to initialize the object wrappers before proceeding on to other operations. As a result, it may be worthwhile to use a timer when checking to see if an object exists. See Chapter 16, "Timers and Other Fun Stuff" for more details on JavaScript timers and examples for their use.

Once the debug layer has been initialized, the debug() function uses it as its target, based on the debug_to variable. Because the Java Console debugging method is so simple, we didn't go into detail as to how it works, so let's examine that now. The debug() function always checks to see whether the debug_flag Boolean variable is still set to true in case an abnormal condition was encountered elsewhere and the flag was set to false. This disables debugging altogether after notifying the user with an informative alert, as shown in Figure 12-8.

Figure 12-8: Disabling debugging and notifying the user

If the flag is set to enable debugging, the next step is to gather some information about the function that called it using the `caller` property. This property is set automatically every time a function is called by another function, using the calling function's name. If the function is called from the root, such as is the case when calling from inside a `<SCRIPT>` element, the `caller` property is not set, so we allow for that in the code. Next, we check to make sure that the debugger has been initialized, using the `debug_ready` variable discussed previously. If the debugger is not ready, we hold on to the message until such a time as the debugger *is* ready, storing its value in the `message_buffer_all` variable. This buffer can get pretty big if you've encountered an abnormal condition, and slow your application down enormously; yet another reason why you want to restrict the use of the Debug module to those cases where you're prepared to deal with its vagaries.

The `debug()` function then checks to see where its output should go. If you're printing to the Java Console, as you saw previously, you print your message and return.

Listing 12-13: The debug() JavaScript function

```
function debug( m ) {
  if( debug_flag ) {
    if( debug.caller ) {
      var calling_function = debug.caller.toString();
      var i = calling_function.indexOf(")") + 1;
      function_name = calling_function.substring(9, i);
    } else {
      function_name = "called from root";
    }

    // if we're ready to print messages, clear buffer
    // else store the message for when we are ready...
    if( debug_ready == true ) {
      message_buffer = function_name + ": " + m;
    } else {
      message_buffer += function_name + ": " + m;
      message_buffer_all += message_buffer;
      return false;
    }

    // java console
    if( debug_to == "java_console" ) {
      if( message_buffer_all.length > 0 ) {
        java.lang.System.out.println( message_buffer_all );
        message_buffer_all = "";
      } else {
        java.lang.System.out.println( message_buffer );
      }
```

```
      // debug layer
      } else if( debug_to == "layer" ) {
        if( object_name[ dl ] != null ) {
        // print msg to debug layer
        dlth = form_name["debuglayer"].elements[0];

        old_debug_info = dlth.value;
        if( message_buffer_all.length > 0) {
          debug_info = old_debug_info + '\n' +
                       message_buffer_all;
          message_buffer_all = "";
        } else {
          debug_info = old_debug_info + '\n' + message_buffer;
        }
        dlth.value = debug_info;
        } else {
        debug_disable();
        }

    // debug to window.status
    } else if( debug_to == "winstatus" ) {
      debug_ready = true;
      window.status = message_buffer;

    } else {
      debug_disable();
    }
  }
  return true;
}
```

If you're printing to the debug layer, however, you should perform some perfunctory checks of the readiness of the layer before printing, get a handle to the
text area, and grab its current value. This value is attached to the front of the message, and then printed to the text area again. If Netscape Navigator supported the
innerHTML and insertAdjacentHTML functionality provided by Internet Explorer,
this would be a good deal easier.

In order to make up for the possibility that the message buffer has been written
to before we were ready to handle it, the function also checks to see if the length of
message_buffer_all is greater than zero, and if so, writes it to the debug layer.
When it is done, it zeroes out the buffer so it doesn't happen again. If the layer
wasn't ready, we assume that it won't ever be, and call disable_debug().

Writing to the window.status Line

The most pathetic of all of our debugging methods, the `window.status` line is really just a nod to the fact that it is supported across browsers, and not much more. Because the length of the `window.status` area is so limited, to say nothing of the fact that it may only contain one line of text, we don't expect to use this except for the most limited of debugging information. The `debug()` routine just dumps its text to the status line and exits. Bear in mind, also, that this method is useless in the example application if the status line is hidden, as it is in the pop-up version of the game. Yet another strike against the `window.status` method.

Defining the Debug Layer

There is not much to the debug layer—just a form with a `<TEXTAREA>` inside and buttons to clear the output and toggle visibility of the layer itself. Listing 12-14 illustrates the HTML required. The `<TEXTAREA>`, named `output`, is located directly above two buttons to resemble the Java Console (refer to Figure 12-7) as much as possible. The effect could probably be heightened through the use of tables as aids to formatting if the enterprising reader wishes to emulate the Java Console window even more closely.

Listing 12-14: Defining the debug layer HTML markup

```
<!-- debug output -->
<div id=debuglayer class=main>

<h1>debug output</h1>
<form name="debugging">
<textarea name="output" rows=15 cols=30>
debugging output:
</textarea><br>
<input type=button onClick='toggle_debug();' value="close">
<input type=button onClick='debugging.output.value="";'
value="clear">
</form>
</div>
```

Showing/Hiding the Debug Layer

The first button calls the function `toggle_debug_layer()` from the `executive_poetry.js` file, which simply hides all the words in the playing field and then shows the debug layer. That function is illustrated in Listing 12-15. This method of showing and hiding layers should be familiar to you from the earlier chapters. The second button simply sets the value of the `<TEXTAREA>` to nothing, effectively clearing the screen of debugging output.

Listing 12-15: Showing and hiding the debug layer with the toggle_debug_layer() JavaScript function

```
function toggle_debug_layer() {
  var dbl = "debuglayer"; // shorthand
  var ml = "mainlayer";
  var bl = "blanklayer";
  if( visible_main_screen != dbl ) {
    debug("showing the debug output screen");
    object_name[visible_main_screen].conceal();
    // if words are visible, hide them
    if( words_are_visible ) {
      toggle_words();
    }
    toggle_form( bl );
    object_name[ dbl ].set_z_index(frontmost);
    object_name[ dbl ].reveal();
    visible_main_screen = dbl;
  } else {
    debug("hiding the debug screen");
    object_name[visible_main_screen].conceal();
    // if words are hidden, show them
    if( ! words_are_visible ) {
      toggle_words();
    }
    object_name[visible_form_screen].reveal();
    object_name[ ml ].set_z_index(frontmost);
    object_name[ ml ].reveal();
    visible_main_screen = ml;
  }
}
```

Figure 12-9 shows the debug layer in Netscape Navigator, and Figure 12-10 shows it in Internet Explorer. Note that you can clearly discern the program flow from the output visible in the form. Another advantage to using the text area as an output target is that the entire set of debugging information may be copied and pasted into another application, such as a text editor, and saved for posterity (and for nerve-wracking analysis).

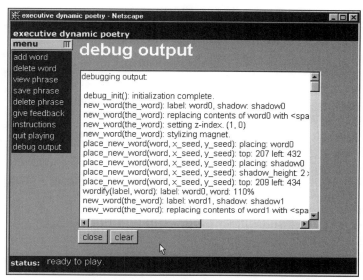

Figure 12-9: The debug layer in Netscape Navigator

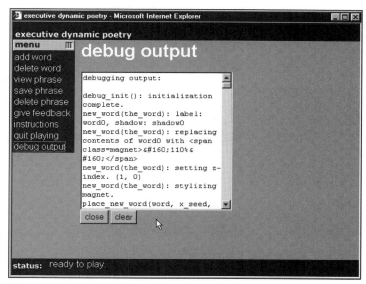

Figure 12-10: The debug layer in Internet Explorer

In the next section, you will learn about the ways in which debugging output can be structured to provide the most useful information without obscuring the true program flow with useless ephemera.

Integrating the Debug Module into the Application

Okay, so now you know how the module works, but how do you know when to use it? Some debugging is obvious—you should debug the parts of the application that simply aren't working, getting more and more detailed as you try harder and harder to understand why things aren't working. Other debugging information should be provided simply for the sake of placing the more specific debugging details in context. There are no hard and fast rules for how to provide debugging output. Oddly enough, it's one of the things many programmers spend most of their time doing, yet it is often neglected in computer science programs on the assumption that the programmer just figures out how. In fact, debugging has historically been treated as a design problem. Got bugs? Redesign your application. There's some sense in this, as many serious bugs result from a major error in the initial design, but this attitude really has more to do with the fact that computer time was once much more expensive than pad-and-pencil time. Obviously, this is no longer the case—unless you think better at a whiteboard than at a keyboard.

One common approach to debugging assumes that you have two applications, the first containing all the debugging code for testing, and the other not. By the time the application is considered fully debugged, such code may be removed or commented out, leaving functional code stripped of the debugging infrastructure.

We are operating on the following assumptions:

1. You don't have time to redesign or rewrite your application.

2. You want to provide contextual information for more specific debugging.

3. You will eventually strip your debugging code from the application.

This section discusses how to provide the debugging information you need when you need it without inundating yourself (and your testers) with streams of unnecessary information.

Determining When and Where to Provide Debug Information

Any application, whether it is a C program consisting of millions of lines of code or a simple collection of small JavaScripts, has an order in which its functions and subroutines are executed. This order may vary with user input, as in the event-driven model we're using, or it may be predictable and repetitive. In larger applications, you find both types of "program flow." Each type needs to be debugged in its own way. The predictable flow may be debugged without much context, as you already know the flow. The unpredictable, event-driven portions of your application, however, may need a great deal of contextual information in addition to the values of the variables you may need to test.

In general, initialization routines and other predictable components do not require much in the way of context. You can simply provide debug() statements when they are entered and perhaps when they are exited. In many cases, it may be sufficient to note when they have been successfully completed, using a set of conditionals that test for such completion.

The successful execution of the event-driven portions of your application may depend heavily on the initial conditions of the application when those routines are entered, and may also make use of a great many limited-scope variables. These initial conditions, especially where they affect the result of these routines, should be output via debug() statements to ensure that your efforts at debugging do not assume false conditions. By the same token, if your event-driven routines also affect other global variables, the values of those variables should also be output. The trick is knowing which variables are global and which are specific to the routine at hand. Because you are dealing with DHTML, many of the properties that concern you have visual correspondence to the elements of your interface. Nonetheless, you should test such values, as their visual representation may be misleading.

During the course of writing the code discussed in Chapter 10, "Executive Dynamic Poetry," we found a bug in the code responsible for restoring saved phrases. For whatever reason, the code was correctly placing the magnet, but incorrectly calculating the coordinates for its shadow. At first, we assumed because there was no JavaScript error alert, and the magnet was visible and in the correct place, that perhaps the shadow was directly below the magnet and the shadow's offset was being set to the same value as the magnet. The shadow's z-order was correct, and we assumed that the problem was with the variables used to set the shadow's offset, not code that calculated the shadow's offset during placement. If we had written the Debug module first, we'd have been able to tell quickly which was the case.

First, we'd have output the values of all relevant variables when the function was entered. Then, if that didn't reveal an obvious scoping problem or other mistake (such as a typo), we would have gone into the routine that calculated the values used to place the shadow, and output all of those variables at that point. We would have first cast a wide net to find out as much as we could about the environment at the time that the problem occurred, and then narrowed the scope of our inquiry using an iterative process of analyzing the code, coming up with hypotheses for what was wrong, adding debug() statements as appropriate for each hypothesis, and analyzing the debugging output. Depending on whether the output confirmed or denied a hypothesis, we would then either remove those statements we felt added nothing to the inquiry, or drill down and add more and more to see in much greater detail what was going on.

Eventually, the errant function was discovered (when we noticed that the scrollbars were getting longer in Internet Explorer, suggesting that the shadow's values were too large, not the same as the magnet), and the problem was fixed. It would have been a lot more methodical to use the Debug module, though. For the sake of illustration, we show the bug and its solution; only this go-round, we take the time to debug the application properly.

Testing Debug with the Application

You've already seen how to include the Debug module in the application in Listing 12-9. We then looked at how to initialize the module, placing a call to debug_init() in the executive_poetry_init() function, right after the call to initialize_base_objects(). Now, let's take a look at the bug in the executive_poetry.js module, using the Debug module to track down the error.

When a phrase is saved, the *x* and *y* coordinates of each word are stored in a cookie. When the phrase is restored, the cookie is analyzed in order to get those values that are then used to position each word. The positions of the shadows are derived from these values, using the shadow_height variable to determine the proper offset. In the original code, however, the position of the shadow was calculated as follows. First, the values for the stored phrase were obtained from the cookie and placed in the variable the_phrase. The position values for each word were then obtained by splitting the string on the comma, giving us the word w, its top (or t) position, and its left (or l) position. Second, the shadow's placement was calculated by adding the appropriate offset and storing the result in the variables s_t and s_l.

Unfortunately, the function treated the addition of "2" to the word's top and left coordinates as a string concatenation that had the effect of multiplying the value by ten and then adding two. Instead of 102 (the result of 100 + 2), the result was 1002, a string concatenation that was then turned into an integer value via the parseInt() function. The original magnet value was not affected, as it was automatically treated as an integer when passed to the place() function.

Voila — a bug. Difficult to track down, as there was little difference between the values used by the function that placed the magnet versus those it should have used to place its shadow.

Listing 12-16: The view_phrase() JavaScript function, complete with a bug

```
function view_phrase(f) {
  var phrase = f.phrases.options;
  var to_view = f.phrases.options.selectedIndex;
  var p = phrase[to_view].value;

  // get the top, left, and word combos for each word in phrase
  var the_phrase = get_cookie(p);
  if( the_phrase ) {
    // should look like 'word,x,y|word2,x,y|'
    var the_words = the_phrase.split('|');
    var the_pieces = new Array();
    var label, shadow_label;
    for( var i = 0; i < the_words.length - 1; i++ ) {
      the_pieces = the_words[i].split(',');
      w = the_pieces[0]; // w is the word
```

```
      l = the_pieces[1]; // l is the left
      t = the_pieces[2]; // t is the top
      label = new_word(w);
      shadow_label = get_shadow(label);
      s_t = parseInt(t + 2); //shadow_height;
      s_l = parseInt(l + 2); //shadow_height;
      object_name[label].place(l,t);
      object_name[shadow_label].place(s_l, s_t);
    }
  }
  return true;
}
```

This snippet is from an earlier revision of the code, before we started using the shadow_height variable. Instead, we were simply using the value "2," which made things even harder to spot, because we assumed the "2" would be interpreted as an integer, rather than wondering if the bug involved an automatic conversion to a string value. Of course, that was the problem, but we did not know that then. The bug was even harder to spot until we substituted the shadow_height variable, and even tried explicitly converting the value to an integer using parseInt (shadow_height).

First, we need to contextualize the debug output by making a note of which phrase is being viewed:

```
function view_phrase(f) {
  var phrase = f.phrases.options;
  var to_view = f.phrases.options.selectedIndex;
  var p = phrase[to_view].value;

  debug("viewing phrase: " + p);
```

Then, we need to determine the value of the shadow top and left values. In this case, we're lucky — we have a good idea of where to look because the application has shown us exactly what the problem is. In other circumstances, we would insert debug() statements after every statement that contained (or changed the value of) a variable, until something funky showed up in the output. In such a case, the number of debug() statements would rival the number of statements in the original function.

```
    for( var i = 0; i < the_words.length - 1; i++ ) {
      the_pieces = the_words[i].split(',');
      w = the_pieces[0]; // w is the word
      l = the_pieces[1]; // l is the left
      t = the_pieces[2]; // t is the top
      label = new_word(w);
```

```
    shadow_label = get_shadow(label);
    s_t = parseInt(t + 2); //shadow_height;
    s_l = parseInt(l + 2); //shadow_height;
    debug("placing magnet: (" + l + "," + t + ")");
    object_name[label].place(l,t);
    debug("placing shadow: (" + s_l + "," + s_t + ")");
    object_name[shadow_label].place(s_l, s_t);
}
```

When we run the application and select, save, and restore the phrase, we get the following debug output, most of which is from other functions called by the one we're dealing with here. We've only shown the output for the first word to be restored, as it clearly shows the bug. We can see that the view_phrase() function was called to restore the phrase bug_demo. That function, in turn, called the new_word() and place_new_word() functions, from which we see that the application is replacing the contents of an empty magnet with the first word from the stored phrase, setting its z-index, and placing it and its shadow correctly — albeit randomly — on the playing field with the offsets correctly set. Then, when the word is placed according to the stored settings we got from the cookie, we see the bug. The values have been concatenated, rather than added, resulting in the error.

```
view_phrase(f): viewing phrase: bug_demo
new_word(the_word): label: word16, shadow: shadow16
new_word(the_word): replacing contents of word16 with <span
  class=magnet> regroup </span>
new_word(the_word): setting z-index. (33, 32)
new_word(the_word): stylizing magnet.
place_new_word(word, x_seed, y_seed): placing: word16
place_new_word(word, x_seed, y_seed): top: 40 left: 382
place_new_word(word, x_seed, y_seed): placing: shadow16
place_new_word(word, x_seed, y_seed): shadow_height: 2 x: 122 y: 42
place_new_word(word, x_seed, y_seed): top: 42 left: 384
wordify(label, word): label: word16, word: regroup
view_phrase(f): placing magnet: (138,51)
view_phrase(f): placing shadow: (1382,512)
```

Note that despite the fact that there were only three debug statements in the view_phrase() function, we got a whole slew of output, most of it from other functions. Some of this output was useful for determining where the bug *wasn't* — namely, the place_new_word() function — and some was only useful for determining the general program flow. The former, where we eliminated a possible source of the bug, is just as useful as the output that showed beyond a shadow of a doubt (pardon the pun) that the bug was in the view_phrase() function itself.

We can't emphasize enough how important it is to remember that your debug statements are viewed in the context of, and provide the context for, many other statements. This output may or may not contribute to your overall understanding of the program flow or the current environment, but they almost always distract you from the information that helps you find the bug in question. Always keep this in mind when deciding where to put your debug() statements. Ask yourself the following questions about the debugging output:

◆ Does it help to clarify the current program environment?

◆ Does it help to make the program flow more explicit?

◆ Does it reveal where the bugs are, as well as where they are not?

◆ Does it display the appropriate values for the appropriate variables?

The Debug module takes care of part of the last problem by printing the correct name of the current function so you don't have to, but it still enables you to print a value with the wrong label or put the debug statement just before the value changes. Always check the placement of your statements to ensure that you can clearly read the debug output even without the accompanying source code. This is less of an issue for JavaScript, as there is no compiled version, but because it is possible to include modules — making it hard for someone to view their source with just a browser — you must be careful to provide all the information a tester needs to make an educated guess about the cause of the bug. In any case, always double-check your debug statements to make sure your label accurately reflects the name of the variable whose value follows it. Otherwise, you're even worse off than when you had no debug output at all.

One way to ensure the accuracy of debugging output or user feedback, especially in the context of an error message or bug report, is to have your application generate that output itself. That way, you can be relatively sure that you've gathered the information you need, not just what the user considered important or worth reporting. As anyone who has done technical support for novice users can tell you, it is unwise to assume *anything* about the user's environment or abilities. Tales abound in the world of tech support of users who thought that the mouse was a foot pedal, or that the CD-ROM tray was a cup holder. Don't put yourself in the position of providing novice PC training or having to walk someone through an arcane process of gathering debugging information. Gather it yourself, using the module described in the next section.

The Automated Bug Report Form

Try as you might, you can't always expect your code to work correctly in the field. There are simply too many variables – platforms, browser versions, operating system patches, display issues, font incompatibilities, and so forth. No matter how diverse your testing environment may be, there's always someone with a different environment who ends up stumbling across an unforeseen error. The best thing you can hope for is an accurate description of the error, the user's environment, and the information necessary to properly contextualize and possibly reproduce the error.

The window.onerror Event Handler

Fortunately, JavaScript provides an event handler for dealing with errors. In fact, it is invoked automatically by the browser if an error occurs. The `window.onerror` handler, if left to its own devices, pops up the browser's standard error dialog box, with the following arguments:

- The standard error message for the error that occurred

- The URL of the document in which the error occurred

- The line number of the script in which the error occurred

Unfortunately, the usefulness of these standard dialog boxes varies widely across browser platforms. Internet Explorer, for example, does not tell you which script an error occurred in, only its line number. If, as in the sample application, you're including multiple JavaScript files, the error message does not distinguish between them. The dialog box is also useless if the user doesn't know enough to copy down the information the dialog box presents. As any developer will tell you, a bug report that starts with the phrase "I didn't write down the error, but . . ." is worse than useless, because the developer is left banging her head against the walls of her cubicle, cursing the user base. Ideally, you want to relieve the user of any responsibility for providing information.

What is the best way to do this, you ask? Like any other event handler in JavaScript, you may define your own routine to be called when there is an error. Your routine should gather as much information as possible about the user's environment, provide a place for the user to give any extra feedback, and then let the user submit the entire bug report using a CGI script or `mailto:` handler to gather the reports and redirect them appropriately.

The first few lines in the script define the height and width of the window to open, as well as the URL to be used by the action of the bug report form. Of course, you need to update these to reflect the appropriate URL for your own CGI script.

```
var action = 'http://www.dhtml-guis.com/cgi-bin/bug_reporter';
var wh = 500;
var ww = 600;
```

```
// declare ourselves the error handler for this window
window.onerror = generate_bug_report_form;
```

generate_bug_report_form

Our automatic bug report form should contain as much information as possible. We start with the basic information provided, useless though it may be on some platforms, and add everything we can. The generate_bug_report_form() function, shown in Listing 12-17, starts out by informing the user that there has been an error. To make sure that the user doesn't change the basic information, we include it as hidden inputs in the form. We then supply the user with a text area where they can add their own comments. Additionally, we use two other functions to generate a list of all available information about the browser and a stack trace, which shows the function calls and their arguments leading up to the error. Finally, it opens up a new window containing the form, just as the user is accustomed to seeing from the standard browser error handler.

Listing 12-17: An automatic bug report: the generate_bug_report_form() function

```
function generate_bug_report_form( m, url, line ) {
    // build the form
    var f = "<form action=" + action + " method=POST>\n";
    f += "<h1>Ooops!</h1>\n";
    f += "There was an error in the JavaScript on this page.\n";
    f += "Please help us out by submitting this form, with any\n";
    f += "other comments you wish to add.\n<p>\n";
    f += "<input type=hidden name=url value='" + url + "'>\n";
    f += "<input type=hidden name=line value='" + line + "'>\n";
    f += "<textarea name=message rows=20 cols=60 wrap=hard>\n";
    f += print_line("=",60) + '\n';
    f += "Error message:";
    f += m + " at line " + line + " on " + url;
    f += print_line("-",60) + '\n';
    f += "Please add any further comments below:\n\n\n";
    f += print_line("=",60) + '\n';
    f += "Stack Trace:";
    f += print_line("-",60) + '\n';
    f += stack_trace();
    f += print_line("-",60) + '\n';
    f += "Browser Info:";
    f += print_line("-",60) + '\n';
    f += browser_info();
    f += "</textarea>\n";
    f += "<input type=submit value='submit bug report'>\n";
    f += "</form>\n";
```

```
// open a window containing the form
var args = "width=" + ww + "," +
  "height=" + wh + "," +
  "toolbar=0," +
  "location=0," +
  "directories=0," +
  "status=0," +
  "menubar=0," +
  "scrollbars=1," +
  "resizable=1," +
  "copyhistory=0";

var bug_report = window.open("", "bug_report", args);
bug_report.document.open();
bug_report.document.write( f );
bug_report.document.close();

// return true if we're happy with how this was handled
// this also suppresses the standard error dialog.
return true;
}
```

The form as shown doesn't enable the user to choose whether or not to continue on with the application, although it is possible (if not very useful) to do so. The function assigned to the `window.onerror` handler returns `true` if the error handler has successfully handled the error, `false` if otherwise. If the function returns `false`, the browser's standard error dialog box is also displayed, which in this case could be confusing to the user – especially because the dialog box does not wait until the form is submitted before jumping in the way. It might be possible to assign a different handler, say, a function called when the form is submitted, to `window.onerror`, thereby handling the entire process of error reporting. This is left as an exercise for the reader.

The form should gather as much information about the user's browser as possible, and could even reproduce the entire set of values for every variable in the application if it were considered important. For the sake of this demonstration, however, we just gather the basic information. It would take far too long, and wouldn't necessarily be useful, to print everything about the current state of the browser. For example, do we really care about the position and contents of every magnet on the playing field? Decisions like this are best made by the developer, or by technical support staff. You may find that they are important, though, so it's possibility is worth pointing out.

The stack trace, however, is usually quite important to the developer, providing details about the exact situation that caused the error. What is a *stack trace*? In traditional programming, the stack trace is a printout of the functions and their arguments that were called leading up to a specific point in the execution of an application. These arguments are usually placed in a portion of memory known as the *stack*, because things tend to get stacked up there as functions nest and call each other, and get popped off as those functions return. (There's also an obscure relationship between the terminology of the "stack" and those spring-loaded wells containing cafeteria trays, but we won't go into that here.) In our version, shown in Listing 12-18, we "walk the stack" and return a string containing the list of functions and their prototypes.

Listing 12-18: Walking the stack with the stack_trace() function

```
function stack_trace() {
  var trace = "";
  if( ! arguments.caller ) {
    return "stack trace failed; caller unimplemented.";
  } else {
    var tray = arguments.caller;
    var name, args, len;

    for( ; tray != null; tray = tray.caller ) {
      if( ! tray.callee ) {
        return "stack trace failed; callee unimplemented.";
      } else {
        name = func_name( tray.callee );

        if( name != "called from root" ) {
          trace += name + "\n";
          args = tray.caller.arguments;
          if( ! args ) {
            return "stack trace failed; args unimplemented.";
          }
          len = tray.caller.arguments.length;
          trace += " args: ";
          for( var e = 0; e < len; e++) {
            trace += args[e];
            if ( e < (len - 1) ) {
              trace += ",";
            }
          }
          trace += "\n\n";
        } else {
          trace += name + "\n";
        }
      }
```

```
      if( tray.caller == tray ) {
        break;  // work around bug in NS4
      }
    }
  }
}
return trace;
}
```

The stack_trace() function uses a couple of tricks to produce not only a list of the functions that led up to the error, but their arguments as well. First, we grab the name of the function, using the function_name() function. You may want to play around with this function, the code for which is shown in Listing 12-19, as you may notice that the caller object not only contains the name and prototype string, but the entire function's contents. With a little creative commenting and substring grabbing, it should be possible to provide even more debugging information if you want. For example, it should be possible to find the name of the current file by using a commenting convention that specifies the name of the file. But that's too much fun for this chapter. Notice that we check to see if the caller is equivalent to the current function as well, which works around a bug in Netscape Communicator where tray.caller does not return null as it should when it reaches the top of the calling chain.

Listing 12-19: Naming the function with the function_name() function

```
function function_name(f) {
  if( f.caller ) {
    var c = f.caller.toString();
    var i = c.indexOf(")") + 1;
    var n = c.substring(10,i);
  } else {
    var n = "called from root";
  }
  return n;
}
```

Next, stack_trace() loops through the arguments array for each caller, walking up the calling chain until we've reached the root, printing the function name, the function prototype, and the actual arguments with which the function was called. Finally, in Listing 12-20, we see the function that gathers information about the browser, browser_info(). On Internet Explorer 4.0, some information may not be present. You may wish to customize browser_info() to gather specific information depending on the browser, but that quickly becomes a support headache if you get too specific.

Listing 12-20: Gathering information about the browser: browser_info()

```
function browser_info() {
  var n = navigator; // shorthand
  var s = get_screen_props();
  var b = "";

  // get info about the browser version
  b += "name: " + n.appName + "\n";
  b += "version: " + n.appVersion + "\n";
  b += "codename: " + n.appCodeName + "\n";
  b += "user agent: " + n.userAgent + "\n";
  b += "\n\n";

  // get info about the OS and environment
  b += "operating system and environment:\n";
  if( n.platform ) {
    b += "platform: " + n.platform + "\n";
  }
  if( n.javaEnabled() ) {
    b += "java: " + n.javaEnabled() + "\n";
  }
  if( n.taintEnabled() ) {
    b += "tainting: " + n.taintEnabled() + "\n";
  }
  b += "\n\n";

  // get info about the screen
  b += "screen info:\n";
  b += "height: " + s.height + "\n";
  b += "width:  " + s.width + "\n";
  b += "color depth: " + s.color_depth + "\n";
  b += "depth:  " + s.depth + "\n";
  b += "\n\n";

  // get plugins info
  if( n.plugins ) {
    b += "plugins:\n";
    for( i = 0; i < n.plugins.length; i++ ) {
      b += "name: " + n.plugins[i].name + "\n";
      b += "description:\n" + n.plugins[1].description + "\n";
      b += "filename: " + n.plugins[i].filename + "\n\n";
    }
    b += "\n\n";
  }
```

```
// get mime types info
if( n.mimeTypes ) {
  b += "mime types:\n";
  for( i = 0; i < n.mimeTypes.length; i++ ) {
    b += "type: " + n.mimeTypes[i].type + "\n";
    b += "description:\n" + n.mimeTypes[i].description + "\n";
    b += "suffixes: " + n.mimeTypes[i].suffixes + "\n\n";
  }
  b += "\n\n";
}
return b;
}
```

On the Server Side: The CGI Application

Because your form does not care what language is used to write the remote CGI application, we don't bother to illustrate one here. Suffice it to say that the more information your form can supply, the better off you are on the remote end. You can discard detail as needed later, but it's difficult to track someone down by way of his IP address and get him to reproduce the error. You can also write your application so that it scans for interesting bugs based on the contents of the error output.

Or, Just Use a mailto:

Barring the use of a CGI script, you can always use the simpler (and uglier) `mailto:` as the action to your form, which then sends the output to a specified e-mail address. Remember to use an appropriate `ENCTYPE` specifier in the form as well, so you don't just get a stream of URL-encoded gibberish. A good value is `text/plain`, although some browsers also support other formats and perform interesting processing on them. Other allowable values for `ENCTYPE` include `application/x-www-form-urlencoded` (the default), and `multipart/form-data`.

The standalone Navigator doesn't provide built-in mail services, so if you specify a `mailto:` as an action for a form it fails silently in the Navigator standalone, unless there is a `mailto:` handler defined.

Integrating the Bug Report Form into the Application

Like the rest of our modules (is this really a surprise by now?) we include the Error module into our application using the following HTML markup:

```
<script src="/javascript/error.js"></script>
```

Testing the Bug Report Form

In the example HTML file shown in Listing 12-21, the function `one()` is called with arguments that are then passed on through the chain and printed in the stack trace, shown in Listing 12-22.

Listing 12-21: Causing an error on purpose: cause_nested_error.html

```html
<html>
<head>
<title> bug report test </title>
<script src="/javascript/xplatform_wrapper.js"></script>
<script src="/javascript/error.js"></script>
</head>

<script language="JavaScript">
function one(a,b,c) {
  two(a,b,c,1,2,3);
}

function two(a,b,c,x,y,z) {
  three(x,y,z,a,b,c);
}

function three(a,b,c,d,e,f) {
  if( true ) {
    window.onerror();
  }
}
</script>
<body>
<script language="JavaScript">
one("A", "B", "C");
</script>
</body>
</html>
```

Because the `window.onerror()` call is made without arguments, the error message, line number, and URL are undefined. This is the only way we could deliberately cause an error that would walk the stack, rather than just complaining about an error in the definition of the function itself, which wasn't as cool, um, we mean, demonstrative.

Listing 12-22: Causing a stack trace using error.js

```
================================================================
Error message:undefined at line undefined on undefined
_____
Please add any further comments below:



================================================================
Stack Trace:
_____
three(a, b, c, d, e, f)
 args: 1,2,3,A,B,C

two(a, b, c, x, y, z)
 args: A,B,C,1,2,3

one(a, b, c)
 args: A,B,C

called from root
```

 The stack trace demonstrated in Listing 12-21 and Listing 12-22 does not work on the Macintosh or Windows in either Internet Explorer or Netscape Navigator. Instead, a short explanation is printed to the bug report, noting the feature that made it impossible to perform a full stack trace. It does work on Solaris in Netscape Navigator, however. Use the stack trace at your own discretion — you may find that the next generation of browsers actually supports the arguments array properly.

Dynamic Updating

In the original plan for this chapter, we had intended to provide a pop-up window containing a layer just like the debug layer previously discussed. However, the current implementations of the browsers did not provide seamless treatment of dynamically updated layers in pop-up windows. We found that the pop-up window, when it worked at all, would generally just produce a never-ending update loop, never refreshing completely to enable the output to be viewed.

Gotchas

The gotchas for this section are pretty unexciting. The browsers either supported what we tried to do, or they didn't. In some cases, we provided workarounds. In others, we simply gave up on what we were trying to do.

◆ The Java Console is only supported by Netscape Navigator.

◆ The `<TEXTAREA>` element is treated differently in Internet Explorer and Navigator, making it difficult to specify an appropriate width for the element.

◆ Most of the browser information we print to the bug report form is supported by Navigator only.

◆ The stack trace function is only supported on Solaris.

◆ The debug layer doesn't seem to be supported in Netscape Navigator on the Macintosh. This is probably because the object isn't initialized by the time we go looking for it. A timer could possibly provide a workaround.

◆ Specifying a `mailto:` as an action only works if the browser supports `mailto:` or has a handler defined. Navigator standalone doesn't support `mailto:` as the action on a form by default.

Summary

This chapter covered several mechanisms for providing different forms of feedback, each appropriate to its unique situation, whether it is user-level information about the application's current status, developer-oriented information about the application's gory internal workings, or a combination of the two.

It also covered some strategies for how to best structure your debugging output to provide the best mix of program flow and context on the one hand, and variable-specific output on the other.

This chapter also covered how to:

◆ Include the Status Bar, Error Dialog Box, and Debug modules in your own application

◆ Compensate for quiet routines, providing the user with helpful status information

◆ Balance useful redundancy with overwhelming and confusing status reporting

◆ Produce useful debugging output for the developer

◆ Produce an error dialog box using built-in JavaScript functions

◆ Gather error output, including a stack trace and other environmental information

In the next chapter, you will learn how to enable users to configure their own interface according to their own whims and fancies. You will also learn how to store those preferences using persistent-state client-side cookies and how to structure your applications so that such preferences are taken into account during the application's startup and initialization procedures.

Chapter 13

User-Configurable Interfaces

IN THIS CHAPTER

- ◆ The Cookie Handler module

- ◆ The Preferences module

- ◆ The color picker and custom color picker

- ◆ Updating application settings

- ◆ Integrating the Preferences module into the application

- ◆ Testing the Preferences module

- ◆ Gotchas (things to look out for)

THIS CHAPTER COVERS an important aspect of designing user interfaces – namely, enabling the user to configure his or her own environment by choosing colors and other settings, and ensuring that when he or she returns to the application those settings are used. User preferences should always be used wherever possible, to help reduce the user's alienation and provide customization of experience. Changing an application's color schemes and related settings is a popular user pastime, so we discuss how to provide a color picker in the sample application. Because this is a book on dynamic HTML, and because there are few other client-side methods for storing user preferences, we also talk about the structure and uses of client-side persistent cookies. So, without further ado, let's dive right in.

The Cookie Handler Module

One of the mechanisms we've been using all along to store little bits of data, the Cookie Handler module, forms the core of our dynamic HTML Preferences module and the modules that make use of it. A *client-side persistent cookie*, or just *cookie* for short, is a small chunk of information stored on the client, usually by a Web server, but often by way of JavaScript. The nomenclature is derived from the early days of computing, when it was often used to refer to a special, small access token, usually encrypted, whose possession provided some form of access to computing resources. Cookies like the ones we are using, however, are much simpler in form, are unencrypted, and are merely used to store a small string of data on the client where they may be passed back to a Web server when the user returns to the site or domain that delivered them. Because we're using JavaScript to set our cookies, rather than relying on the server to send a special request header, we don't go into the details of the HTTP headers that set and retrieve cookies. Suffice it to say that there are a few limitations to the size and number of cookies, their visibility to any given Web server, and their lifetime. For example, the cookie specification requires that a Web browser only retain 300 cookies total, and of those only 20 may be delivered by a Web server (or set by JavaScripts delivered by the server) in a given domain. The cookies may not exceed 4K in length, including their name and value. We discuss the implications of these restrictions later in the chapter, but for now it is sufficient to realize that there are limits.

The Structure of a Cookie

A cookie is really nothing more than a named piece of information with a few qualifying attributes that determine its scope, its lifetime, and other characteristics related to how it may be passed around from the browser to the server, and vice versa. If you're using Netscape Navigator, you can open the cookies file (named cookies.txt in your Navigator user profile directory on Windows, or MagicCookie in the Navigator Preferences folderon the Macintosh) and examine its contents in a text editor. You should find something like this:

```
www.dhtml-guis.com   FALSE  /examples/dynamic    FALSE  936201582
   dynamic_poetry.pref_magnet_color  %23663366
```

The first field is the server name or domain that the cookie was sent from (or that served the HTML file containing JavaScript that set the cookie). The second field is set to TRUE if the cookie was set by a Web server using the HTTP header Set-Cookie; or to FALSE if the cookie was set by another mechanism, such as via JavaScript. The next field is the path variable, in this case, /examples/dynamic, meaning that the cookie is only returned to the originating server during requests for URLs containing that string. The fourth field signifies if the cookie is secure, which really just means that it should not be sent back via an insecure connection, but must use SSL or some other encrypted channel. The fifth field is just a big number representing the expiration date and time of the cookie in seconds since January 1, 1970, GMT. Finally, we get to the meat of the cookie, the name and value pair.

You learn more about the structure of the name and value in the following example, as this is one of the cookies the color picker sets in order to store the user's color choices, but it's worth mentioning that the value has been escaped using the JavaScript escape() function. If you've done any CGI programming, you should recognize the encoding. Basically, escape() takes its input, encodes any special characters using a method known as *URLencoding*, where the hexadecimal equivalent of the character's ASCII code is used to replace the character, preceded by a percent sign. So, %23 becomes the ASCII character 35, which just happens to be "#". The entire string is returned encoded, and may be unencoded using the `unescape()` JavaScript function. Fortunately, this is all taken care of by the cookie handler library, so you never have to see it again. It's helpful to be able to decipher what other folks are sticking in your cookies file in any case, though most cookies are often just arbitrary values used as keys to server-side processing. One popular use of cookies is to track visitors across sites for more informative log file analysis.

The format of the string used to set a cookie is as follows:

```
name=value; expires=date; path=path; domain=domain; secure
```

The string, once constructed, is simply assigned to the `document.cookie` property in JavaScript like so:

```
document.cookie = 'hey=ho; ' +
                  'expires=Friday, 31-Dec-1999 23:59:00 GMT;' +
                  'path=/; ' +
                  'domain=.example.com;';
```

The previous statement leaves a cookie named `hey` with the value `ho`, on the user's client until a minute before the year 2000. Whee! Now let's look at what that means.

NAME

The name field is used to store the name of the cookie, by which its value is retrieved. The name string may not contain any semicolons, commas, or white space. It is unique and does not happily coexist with another cookie of the same name from the same domain. If a cookie is set with the same name as an existing cookie, the existing cookie is replaced. So be careful! The name field is required in order to set a cookie.

VALUE

The value of the cookie is also required, and, like the name, may not contain semicolons, commas, or white space. As we have seen previously, though, encoding is often used to overcome this restriction (in fact, we do this later). The name and value taken together may not be larger than 4K, though it is generally recommended that you keep your cookies under 2K in size for backward compatibility with older browsers. Of course, for our purposes, the 4K limit is fine.

EXPIRES

The expiration, as we saw previously, is stored on the client in UNIX `time_t` format, namely, a big number representing the number of seconds since January 1, 1970. However, we use a standard JavaScript `Date()` to actually set the cookie's expiration date. It doesn't matter to us, in any case. The only fields that are exposed to reading via JavaScript are the `name` and `value` fields. The `expires` field and several others may only be written to, but not read from, in the interest of security. If you don't set the field, most browsers hold onto the cookie until the end of the user's session, which ends when they close the application. Some browsers, including Lynx, delete all cookies, regardless of their expiration date, at the end of the session.

PATH

The `path` field is set automatically by the browser based on where the cookie came from, which is determined by the URL of the resource that set it. This is true regardless of whether the cookie was set via JavaScript or the HTTP `Set-Cookie:` header. The net effect of this behavior is reflected in the scope given to the cookie by the browser. If the path is set to "/", for example, the cookie is sent back to the server (using the HTTP `Cookie` header) along with any request for any URL on that server. Or, as we show later, to any host in the same domain.

DOMAIN

The browser automatically sets the `domain` field to the domain of the host that set the cookie (or delivered the JavaScript that set the cookie, as you'd expect by now). Domain names must contain at least two periods to avoid sharing potentially sensitive information with the entire `.com` top-level domain, for example. If explicitly set to a hostname, cookies are only be sent back to the host in that domain. Subdomain values (such as `.in.hesketh.com` and `.out.hesketh.com`) are acceptable as well, and further restrict the cookie's scope.

SECURE

The `secure` keyword is useful for ensuring that the cookie is only sent back to a server over an encrypted connection. It has no bearing on the way the cookie is stored on the client. If the keyword is not present, the cookie is assumed to be insecure.

Armed with these pieces, you are now prepared to dive headlong into the world of preparing and setting your own cookies using the Cookie Handler module. The first thing we go over is how to create your own default expiration string.

Expiration

In a perfect world, dynamic HTML application developers would face a serene, unencumbered clime, where users trusted developers and where cookies were seen as the mostly harmless tool they are. However, due to rumors, misinformation, and a lack of perspective on the part of many in the popular media, as well as fear of potential abuses by some Web sites and software manufacturers, cookies generally have a lifetime of the span between reboots on most machines. Software that removes cookies, increasingly configurable browsers, and other tools have limited the usefulness of well-intended mechanisms. The upshot is that the user has more control over their environment, but the developer who relies on properly used cookies is left with very little in the way of state-management mechanisms. For the remainder of the chapter and book, we assume that the user has been well-versed in the pros and cons of cookies and has done whatever configuration is necessary on the client end to enable us to set cookies in the interest of an enhanced user experience. Don't expect this kind of courtesy or consistency in the real world, however.

Having said all that, it is time to roll out the expiration() JavaScript function, shown in Listing 13-1, that quite simply accepts a number, gets today's date, and returns a GMT-formatted date that many days into the future. It is possible to set expiration dates at a much finer granularity if your application requires it (down to the second, in fact), but for now we just worry about one day at a time.

Listing 13-1: The expiration() JavaScript function

```
function expiration(days) {
  var expires = new Date();
  var today = new Date();
  expires.setTime( today.getTime() +
    (1000*60*60*24*parseInt(days)) );
  return expires;
}
```

Fortunately, you don't even need to worry about the expiration date for the color picker and other preferences-oriented applications, as this function is buried in the Cookie Handler module, which is called from the Preferences module itself. But should you want to set and/or read your own cookies, this is how it is done.

Setting Cookies

Setting a cookie is as easy as pie. The JavaScript function call set_cookie(), the definition for which is shown in Listing 13-2, is invoked with three arguments. The first is the name, the second is the value, and the third is an expiration date such as that returned by the expiration() function defined previously. The set_cookie() function takes care of escaping your value for you, and if the expiration date has not passed, it creates a session cookie that has no expiration date and is deleted when the user ends their browsing session by closing their browser. We provide lots of examples of how this function may be used when we get into the Preferences module if you can be patient for another page or so. Let's first talk about reading cookie values.

Listing 13-2: The set_cookie() JavaScript function

```
function set_cookie( name, value, expire ) {
  document.cookie = name + "=" + escape(value) +
    ((expire == null) ? "" : ("; expires=" +
    expire.toGMTString()));
}
```

Reading Cookies

The only trick to reading a cookie is making sure that you know its name. Because the other properties of the cookie are write-only, and the name is unique whereas the value may not be, it is necessary to have the name of the cookie you want to read. Listing 13-3 shows the get_cookie() function that takes only one argument, the name of the cookie, and returns either a string containing the cookie's value, if any, or the Boolean value false to represent failure. The cookie's value, if found, is unescaped for you. It's up to you to test for the return value of the function to make sure that the cookie you were looking for was found.

Listing 13-3: The get_cookie() JavaScript function

```
function get_cookie( Name ) {
  var search = Name + "=";
  if( document.cookie.length > 0 ) { // if there are any cookies
    offset = document.cookie.indexOf( search );
    if( offset != -1 ) { // if this particular cookie exists
      offset += search.length;
      // set index of beginning of value
      end = document.cookie.indexOf(";", offset);
      // set index of end of cookie value
      if( end == -1 ) {
        end = document.cookie.length;
      }
      return unescape(document.cookie.substring(offset,end));
    }
  } else {
    return false;
  }
}
```

Okay, so now you know how to set a cookie and retrieve it. All that's left to learn is how to delete a cookie once it is no longer needed, and how to figure out which cookies are present and available for reading.

Deleting Cookies

The first of these tasks is quite simple, because a cookie with no expiration date is removed when the browser is closed. Just set the cookie to a null value or with an expiration date in the past.

Getting a List of All Cookies

The second task is a little trickier, but not much. In Listing 13-4, the function `get_all_cookies()` returns a string with the names of all available cookies delimited by commas.

Listing 13-4: The get_all_cookies() JavaScript function

```
var max_cookies = 20; // no more than twenty cookies
var cookie_name = new Array(max_cookies);
function get_all_cookies() {
  var cookie_jar = document.cookie;
  var my_cookies = cookie_jar.split(';');
  var crumbs;

  for( var x = 0; x < my_cookies.length; x++ ) {
    crumbs = my_cookies[x].split('=');
    if( crumbs[0] != "" ) {
      cookie_name[x] = crumbs[0];
    }
  }
  return cookie_name.join(',');
}
```

The string passed as a return value may then be split on the comma character, and the individual elements of the array accessed one at a time. You can also just use the entire string to test for the existence of a cookie you are thinking about setting in order to avoid clobbering the existing cookie.

Now that you're intimately familiar with cookies themselves, it is time to put them aside as we travel further up the chain of abstraction into the land of user preferences.

The Preferences Module

User preferences are often dealt with in terms of a name and value. Although there are undoubtedly more complex preferences and sets of preferences, this method works pretty well, and it is well suited to the cookie-based architecture we're pretty much limited to. Fundamentally, the Preferences module is intended to provide storage of any number of single preferences (up to the 20 per domain limit prescribed by the cookie standard) or groupings of up to six preferences associated by a common name. The latter method is more efficient and less taxing on your already limited resources, but let's start simple.

Saving a Single Preference

All of our examples in this section consist of saving and retrieving a single user preference. The Preferences module is almost as simple as the Cookie Handler module, but there is one small detail that should be taken into account. You may have complete control over your Web server, or even over your entire domain, but find that you want to develop and serve multiple applications down the line, each with their own user preferences. With that in mind, you need to set a global variable that defines the name of the application to which these preferences apply. Otherwise, one application might want to set a preference with the same name as a corresponding preference in another, and your users end up confused and frustrated by the lack of consistency. Because we eventually integrate our color picker example into the Dynamic Poetry application, let's go ahead and define our application name right now. This global variable should be defined within the main JavaScript file or HTML `<SCRIPT>` tag for the application, or in the module responsible for setting the preferences:

```
var app = "dynamic_poetry";
```

With that out of the way, we can start setting user preferences to our heart's content.

The `set_preference()` function, shown in Listing 13-5, accepts three arguments. The first, which we have just defined, is the name of the application that the preferences apply to. The second and third, respectively, are the name of the preference and its value. We've gone ahead and hard-coded a default expiration value of one year into the function, but if your needs differ, feel free to define another global variable in terms of the number of days your preferences should apply and use it instead. The application name is attached to the front of string, `.pref_`, that is parsed out of the preference value by the other functions and serves only to further distinguish your cookie value as a preference setting and not temporary data storage (or other use). Then, the function simply calls `set_cookie()` to save the setting on the user's computer. Because JavaScript doesn't automatically return the value of the last statement in a function as do some other scripting languages (notably Perl), the function doesn't return a value (or, more accurately, it returns the special `undefined` value). For more robust applications, you may wish to enhance this and other similar functions to check for the success of the attempt. However, as there is no way for `set_cookie()` to check for the success of its attempt, you need to follow up with a call to `get_cookie()` and see if the change took effect.

Listing 13-5: The set_preference() JavaScript function

```
// set a single preference value
function set_preference(app, name, value) {
  var pref_name = app + ".pref_" + name;
  var expires = expiration(365); // leave it for a year
```

```
      set_cookie(pref_name, value, expires);
}
```

Setting preferences is just one side of the story, however. To really make use of the Preferences module, you need to be able to read saved settings as well.

Reading a Single Preference

In keeping with the simplicity of the earlier functions, the get_preference() function only accepts two arguments. The first is the name of the application as defined in the global variable app previously. The second is the name of the preference setting you wish to read. The function, shown in Listing 13-6, performs a little more work, however. You may wish to provide a set of default preferences to which the application is initialized on the user's first time through. With this in mind, the get_preference() function first checks to see if a custom preference is available (having the application name as a prefix, followed by the .pref_ prefix discussed previously). If that fails to return a usable value, the function then checks to see if a default preference (signified by the .dpref_ prefix) is available, and if so, it returns that instead. If the default is not present either, the function returns false, so you can finally start checking to see if you should just make something up (or default to preference settings encoded into your application, if you're into that sort of thing).

Listing 13-6: The get_preference() JavaScript function

```
// retrieve a single preference value
function get_preference(app, name) {
  var pref = get_cookie(app + ".pref_" + name);
  if( pref ) {
    return pref;
  } else {
    pref = get_cookie(app + ".dpref_" + name);
    if( pref ) {
      return pref;
    } else {
      return false;
    }
  }
}
```

The flip side to the get_preference() function, then, is the function you call to store the default setting for a given preference. Shown in Listing 13-7, the set_preference_default() function is called exactly as you would call the set_preference() function, with the only difference being that it sets a default preference for use by get_preference(), rather than the more prosaic and ordinary user setting.

Listing 13-7: The set_preference_default() JavaScript function

```
// set a single preference default
function set_preference_default(app, name, value) {
  var pref_name = app + ".dpref_" + name;
  var expires = expiration(365); // leave it for a year
  set_cookie(pref_name, value, expires);
}
```

The limitations put upon the more ambitious dynamic HTML application developer being what they are (20 cookies per server, of a piddly 4,096 bytes each, maximum), it may behoove you to stuff as many of these user preferences as you can into a single cookie. This may also serve as a useful technique for consolidation, in addition to its basic purpose of trying to conserve limited resources. For example, you might want to combine all of your color settings (and perhaps fonts, default images, sounds, and all manner of other nonsense) into groups and make them available as schemes. Or, you might want to enable different users who share a single computer, such as in a lab environment, to save and restore their own environment at will, thus keeping it safe from meddling by others who think that neon green is a good background color. Whatever your reasoning, the task is easily accomplished. Listing 13-8 shows the code necessary to create a string containing multiple preference settings. For the sake of keeping the function prototype short, we've limited the number of settings you can store in a single preference to six, but provided a workaround in the form of the arguments array. When any JavaScript function is called, the arguments array is created to contain the entire argument list. Similar to argc and argv in C, or @_ in Perl, the array may then be iterated over using its length property, with the arguments and their names separated by colons and the results joined by ampersands (encoded by the cookie_handlers function later). The end result that is returned to the caller is a string containing a set of related preference settings. For example, say you were to call the function like so:

```
var my_pref = create_multi_preference(app,"tim", 1,2,3,4,5,6);
```

The variable my_pref would then contain the following string:

```
tim1:1&tim2:2&tim3:3&tim4:4&tim5:5&tim6:6
```

Luckily, this isn't something you ever need to look at, unless you like to dig through your own cookies.txt files.

Listing 13-8: The create_multi_preference() JavaScript function

```
// create a preference string from multiple values (6 max)
// pref string will look like this:
//   name1:v1&name2:v2&name3:v3&name4:v4&name5:v5&name6:v6
function create_multi_preference(app, name,
```

```
                                      v1, v2, v3, v4, v5, v6) {
  var tmp = "";
  for( var x = 2; x < arguments.length; x++ ) {
    tmp += name + (x-1) + ':' + arguments[x] +
      ((x < arguments.length-1) ? "&" : "");
  }
  return tmp;
}
```

Saving Multiple Preferences

The pattern should be pretty obvious to you by now. The function
set_multi_preference(), shown in Listing 13-9, uses the same convention for
setting a multiple preference as that used by both the set_preference() and the
set_preference_default() functions.

Listing 13-9: The set_multi_preference() JavaScript function

```
// set a multiple preference
function set_multi_preference(app, name, value) {
  var pref_name = app + ".mpref_" + name;
  var expires = expiration(365); // leave it for a year
  set_cookie(pref_name, value, expires);
}
```

Reading Multiple Preferences

Okay, we're on a roll now. Why store a collection of preferences into a single cookie
if you can't read them? There's a twist, though, as you can see in Listing 13-10. The
all_mprefs array is used by get_multi_preference() to store the settings. The
variable total_mprefs is used to count the number of preferences, in case you
need to make a comparison against some expected number of settings.

Listing 13-10: The get_multi_preference() JavaScript function

```
var all_mprefs = new Array();
var total_mprefs = 0; // number of multiple prefs set
// retrieve a multiple value preference
function get_multi_preference(app, name) {
  var tmp = get_cookie(app + ".mpref_" + name);
  var mtmp = "";
  var namevals = tmp.split('&');

  for( var x = 0; x < namevals.length; x++ ) {
    mtmp = namevals[x].split(':');
    all_mprefs[total_mprefs] = mtmp[1]; // just grab the value
```

```
    total_mprefs++;
  }
}
```

So, now that we've gone through all those functions, you're probably wondering, "How do I know what these preferences are called?" Well, you'd be right to wonder. And we thought of that. Listing 13-11 shows the list_all_prefs() function, which works in a similar fashion to both the get_multi_preference() function and the related get_all_cookies() function it relies on. The single argument, the application name, is used to find an index into the entire set of cookies that is then used to populate the array all_prefs containing the total_prefs number of distinct preference settings. The calling function can then loop over the array and extract the names of various settings.

Listing 13-11: The list_all_prefs() JavaScript function

```
var all_prefs = new Array();
var total_prefs = 0; // number of preferences set
// get a list of all available preferences for this app
function list_all_prefs(app_name) {
  total_prefs = 0;
  var tmp_prefs = get_all_cookies();
  var tmp_prefs_array = tmp_prefs.split(',');
  for(var x = 0; x < tmp_prefs_array.length; x++) {
    if( tmp_prefs_array[x].indexOf(app_name + ".pref_") >= 0 ) {
      all_prefs[total_prefs] = tmp_prefs_array[x];
      total_prefs++;
    }
  }
  return all_prefs;
}
```

Now you know how to use cookies and save preferences, but how do you know which preferences to make available to the user for customization? That's a tough question, and one that can only truly be answered by the developer, who knows what the application is capable of, and by the interface designer, who knows what the user wants. Collaboration between these two people, between the two sides of your brain, or between two teams (depending on how involved the project is), usually brings up a long list of possible preferences. The trick is to keep things simple for the user to modify while not excluding anything really important to their day-to-day work environment. Some areas that might be good candidates for active customization are as follows:

◆ Color choices and schemes

◆ Keyboard shortcuts (accelerators)

◆ Choice of language or locale

Beyond the user-customizable preferences, however, are myriad application-specific settings that might be best remembered by the application itself without forcing the user to make their preferences known. Examples of these include:

◆ Application state

◆ Autocorrection for commonly made mistakes

◆ Commonly overridden default settings

◆ A list of the last few actions performed

For example, for the Dynamic Poetry application, it might be a good idea to provide a set of color schemes, a few well-chosen wordlists, and a color picker with a way to override the default color settings as user preferences. The application could keep a running record of the most common words that the user added without prompting the user for confirmation. Then, the application could perhaps prompt the user when they go to add a new word, asking if he would like to choose from the common list or if he would rather add a totally new word.

The most important thing is to keep the user satisfied with the performance of the application and comfortable with his environment, and for the application to "learn" and improve in efficiency as the user interacts with it. There is nothing in the world of personal computing more frustrating than a stupid application that asks you over and over again if you meant to do what you just did (were you serious about deleting a file?), or one that constantly prompts you to choose between two options when you have never used the second and (as far as you know, anyway) never want to do so. A well-implemented application memory can overcome some interface design flaws, but if you find yourself implementing a lot of these workarounds, the best thing might just be a redesign of the interface for a future version of the software. In that spirit, let's look at some user input that the Dynamic Poetry application might want to keep around for later use.

Storing User Profile and Preferences

During the course of game play, the Dynamic Poetry application asks the user for a good deal of information. Some of the information is fleeting, such as the next word to add (or delete), and some of it is more persistent, such as saving a list of favorite phrases, and some of it should never change over the life of the application. Following, in reverse order, are some important settings to keep track of:

NAME AND E-MAIL ADDRESS

When the user quits the game by way of the "quit playing" menu item, the application prompts the user, asking if she wishes to post her saved phrases to the Web. If the answer if affirmative, the application then prompts the user for her name and e-mail address to be used to organize her submissions. The application should remember these settings and provide them by default in a dialog box that the user can just confirm if no changes are required, or edit if changes are required. This would make an excellent candidate for a saved user preference, or as part of a multiple-preference profile.

DEFAULT WORDLIST

As the application becomes increasingly sophisticated on the server end, phrases should be analyzed and correlated to provide more robust wordlists. If every phrase saved to the server contains a word that is not in the default wordlist, for example, that word might best be added to the default wordlist. By another token, as unique groups of wordlists are compiled and perhaps geared toward certain specialties – the Shakespearean English magnetic poetry add-on kit, for example – such wordlists could be provided as alternates, and the application could prompt the user to choose between them. Such choices could then be remembered and the user's individual default could be initialized on the next visit.

OTHER SETTINGS

Because the application's interface is really very simple, this doesn't leave much else for the user to customize. One area that seems appealing is the realm of custom colors. So that's what we wrap up the chapter with: a color picker and its associated preference settings.

The Color Picker

Anyone who has worked with Windows 95 at all is familiar with the System Properties dialog box, with its extensive set of user-customizable features. The entire interface is adjustable, from font choices and colors to the relative size of the buttons, scrollbars, and other features. We aren't able to top the Windows color picker, but we make a concerted effort.

The Purpose of the Color Picker

There are several reasons to provide a color picker for the Dynamic Poetry application. First, our early beta testers all complained about the monochromatic nature of the application to the point where we considered adjusting the default colors. In the end we didn't bother because the screenshots for this book are all in black and white anyway. Second, if we had provided a certain set of colors as a default, we would have risked running afoul of some color sensitivity or color blindness issues. Third, a Color Picker module is useful in other contexts, and it seems like a good idea for a book on designing user interfaces to cover areas of interface design beyond the simple HTML form elements, draggable magnets that are unlikely to have any real widespread applicability, and a floating menu palette.

Finally, and perhaps most important, the color picker makes an excellent test bed for several interesting strategies for application development using DHTML. So, without further ado, let's look at the standalone fixed color picker, its underlying structure, and the custom slider bar color picker. We also discuss saving user color choices and dynamically updating an application based on user-provided preferences. Hang on to your hats — this is going to be fun.

The Structure of the Color Picker

The color picker has two parts. The first is a set of standard colors arranged in a table with a pull-down menu containing the interface elements to which the colors should be applied, along with an OK button that saves the preferences set by the user. The second part features a custom color picker that enables the user to choose from among the 216 Web-safe colors and save them as preselected custom colors that may then be applied to the individual interface elements listed in the pull-down menu. Figure 13-1 illustrates the standard color picker, along with the storage area for the preselected custom colors.

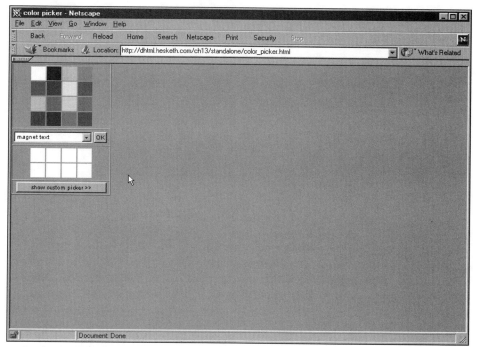

Figure 13-1: The standard color picker

The interface demonstrates several interesting application feedback mechanisms. The first is seen in Figure 13-1, where the currently selected element, the magnet text color, is set to use black, which is in the top row, second from the left. This is shown by the fact that the color square is surrounded by a subtle highlight with a slightly different color square behind it, and outlined with a 1-pixel-wide border. Due to the lack of support for CSS border styles in Netscape Navigator, the effect is achieved instead by placing two layers behind the selected color square, one gray and the other black and slightly larger than the square itself. The user is always kept apprised of the currently selected color, as well as the interface element to which it is applied if they save their changes.

Figure 13-2 illustrates another user feedback mechanism. When the user holds the mouse over any of the standard color choices, the color is highlighted by a white border, using yet another layer whose z-index is set behind the actual colored square itself.

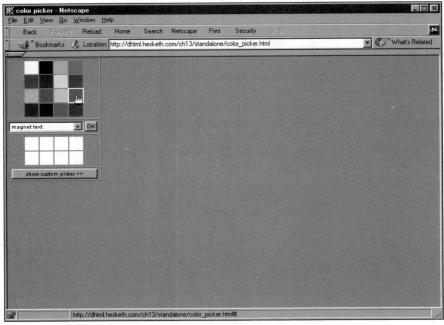

Figure 13-2: Demonstrating feedback with onMouseOver highlighting

In Figure 13-3, you can see the complete list of interface elements that the user may customize listed in the pull-down menu. They include the foreground and background colors for the magnets and their shadows, the selected magnet color, and the playing field itself. Each of these items may be customized by way of the standard color picker or the custom color picker, which may be shown by clicking the button at the bottom of the screen below the preselected custom color squares.

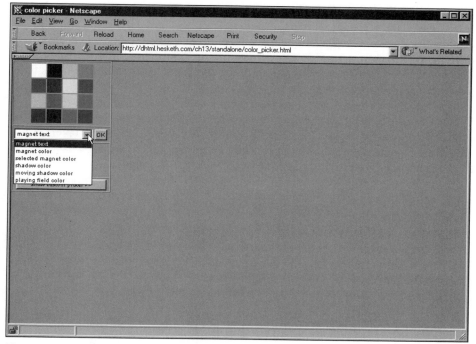

Figure 13-3: Displaying the list of customizable user interface elements

The screen layout is achieved with a combination of HTML DIV elements, Cascading Style Sheets, CSS positioning, and JavaScript, much as the other elements in the application have been constructed. The standard color picker markup, shown in Listing 13-12, contains table cell elements for the colors that each include a named, transparent 1 pixel GIF for better coverage for the anchor (hence the onClick, onMouseOver, and onMouseOut event handlers). The custom color placeholders are also in a table, with named IMG elements. The named IMG elements enable the JavaScript routines to determine where to place the highlight layer, based on the image's x and y offsets.

The entire table is wrapped in a form that also contains the pull-down menu, the OK button, and the button that toggles the custom color picker. The arguments to cp_save_setting() and cp_highlight_on() are used to give the user even more feedback, effectively communicating the color choice and the element name to which it is to be applied, in support of the more visual highlight effect. The transparency of the GIF files enables the table cell background colors to show through, although you need to keep a separate list of those colors for ease of matching the currently highlighted or selected color square to the hexadecimal color value itself.

The pull-down menu contains a list of properties and their plain text equivalents, for reasons that become clear as we examine the associated JavaScript functions.

The custom color layer objects, such as custom0, all follow the same format and so we have not reproduced them all here. They are basically just color squares exactly like the cells of the standard color table or custom color table, only they have the DIV to themselves for ease of positioning, concealing, and revealing them as needed. They use the same highlighting functions and color value save functions the rest of the color table objects do.

The last objects in Listing 13-12, cphilight and cpselected, are used to highlight the currently selected color square and to highlight the square over which the user has moved the mouse. The former simply uses a slightly larger layer with a white table inside, and the latter uses a pair of nested tables to represent a border, the CSS property not currently supported by Netscape Navigator.

Listing 13-12: Laying out the standard color picker with DIV elements and tables

```
<div id="colorpicker">
<form name="colorpicker">
<table width=150 border=1 cellpadding=2 cellspacing=0>
<tr>
<td width=150 align=center valign=center>
  <table width=100 border=0 cellpadding=0 cellspacing=2>
  <tr>
    <td width=25 align=center valign=center
        bgcolor=#FFFFFF
    ><a href="#"
        onClick='cp_save_setting(0);'
        onMouseOver='cp_highlight_on("white", 0);'
        onMouseOut='cp_highlight_off();'
    ><img src="/images/clear.gif"
        name="color0" border=0
        width=25 height=25></a></td>
    ><td width=25 align=center valign=center
        bgcolor=#000000
    ><a href="#"
        onClick='cp_save_setting(1);'
        onMouseOver='cp_highlight_on("black", 1);'
        onMouseOut='cp_highlight_off();'
    ><img src="/images/clear.gif"
        name="color1" border=0
        width=25 height=25></a></td>
    ><td width=25 align=center valign=center
        bgcolor=#CCCCCC
    ><a href="#"
        onClick='cp_save_setting(2);'
        onMouseOver='cp_highlight_on("light gray", 2);'
        onMouseOut='cp_highlight_off();'
    ><img src="/images/clear.gif"
```

```
            name="color2" border=0
            width=25 height=25></a></td>
   ><td width=25 align=center valign=center
       bgcolor=#999999
   ><a href="#"
       onClick='cp_save_setting(3);'
       onMouseOver='cp_highlight_on("dark gray", 3);'
       onMouseOut='cp_highlight_off();'
   ><img src="/images/clear.gif"
         name="color3" border=0
         width=25 height=25></a></td>
</tr>
<tr>
   <td width=25 align=center valign=center
       bgcolor=#FF0000
   ><a href="#"
       onClick='cp_save_setting(4);'
       onMouseOver='cp_highlight_on("bright red", 4);'
       onMouseOut='cp_highlight_off();'
   ><img src="/images/clear.gif"
         name="color4" border=0
         width=25 height=25></a></td>
   <td width=25 align=center valign=center
       bgcolor=#990000
   ><a href="#"
       onClick='cp_save_setting(5);'
       onMouseOver='cp_highlight_on("dark red", 5);'
       onMouseOut='cp_highlight_off();'
   ><img src="/images/clear.gif"
         name="color5" border=0
         width=25 height=25></a></td>
   <td width=25 align=center valign=center
       bgcolor=#FFFF00
   ><a href="#"
       onClick='cp_save_setting(6);'
       onMouseOver='cp_highlight_on("yellow", 6);'
       onMouseOut='cp_highlight_off();'
   ><img src="/images/clear.gif"
         name="color6" border=0
         width=25 height=25></a></td>
   <td width=25 align=center valign=center
       bgcolor=#666600
   ><a href="#"
       onClick='cp_save_setting(7);'
       onMouseOver='cp_highlight_on("olive", 7);'
```

```
              onMouseOut='cp_highlight_off();'
        ><img src="/images/clear.gif"
              name="color7" border=0
              width=25 height=25></a></td>
    </tr>
    <tr>
      <td width=25 align=center valign=center
          bgcolor=#00FF00
      ><a href="#"
          onClick='cp_save_setting(8);'
          onMouseOver='cp_highlight_on("green", 8);'
          onMouseOut='cp_highlight_off();'
      ><img src="/images/clear.gif"
            name="color8" border=0
            width=25 height=25></a></td>
      <td width=25 align=center valign=center
          bgcolor=#009900
      ><a href="#"
          onClick='cp_save_setting(9);'
          onMouseOver='cp_highlight_on("dark green", 9);'
          onMouseOut='cp_highlight_off();'
      ><img src="/images/clear.gif"
            name="color9" border=0
            width=25 height=25></a></td>
      <td width=25 align=center valign=center
          bgcolor=#00FFFF
      ><a href="#"
          onClick='cp_save_setting(10);'
          onMouseOver='cp_highlight_on("cyan", 10);'
          onMouseOut='cp_highlight_off();'
      ><img src="/images/clear.gif"
            name="color10" border=0
            width=25 height=25></a></td>
      <td width=25 align=center valign=center
          bgcolor=#009999
      ><a href="#"
          onClick='cp_save_setting(11);'
          onMouseOver='cp_highlight_on("sea blue", 11);'
          onMouseOut='cp_highlight_off();'
      ><img src="/images/clear.gif"
            name="color11" border=0
            width=25 height=25></a></td>
    </tr>
    <tr>
      <td width=25 align=center valign=center
```

```
              bgcolor=#0000FF
      ><a href="#"
          onClick='cp_save_setting(12);'
          onMouseOver='cp_highlight_on("blue", 12);'
          onMouseOut='cp_highlight_off();'
      ><img src="/images/clear.gif"
            name="color12" border=0
            width=25 height=25></a></td>
      <td width=25 align=center valign=center
          bgcolor=#000099
      ><a href="#"
          onClick='cp_save_setting(13);'
          onMouseOver='cp_highlight_on("dark blue", 13);'
          onMouseOut='cp_highlight_off();'
      ><img src="/images/clear.gif"
            name="color13" border=0
            width=25 height=25></a></td>
      <td width=25 align=center valign=center
          bgcolor=#FF00FF
      ><a href="#"
          onClick='cp_save_setting(14);'
          onMouseOver='cp_highlight_on("magenta", 14);'
          onMouseOut='cp_highlight_off();'
      ><img src="/images/clear.gif"
            name="color14" border=0
            width=25 height=25></a></td>
      <td width=25 align=center valign=center
          bgcolor=#990099
      ><a href="#"
          onClick='cp_save_setting(15);'
          onMouseOver='cp_highlight_on("purple", 15);'
          onMouseOut='cp_highlight_off();'
      ><img src="/images/clear.gif"
            name="color15" border=0
            width=25 height=25></a></td>
    </tr>

    </table>
    </td>
</tr>

<tr>
  <td nowrap>
  <select name="attribute"
          onChange='cp_select_current_color(this.form);'>
```

```
<option value="magnet_color">
  magnet text</option>
<option value="magnet_bg_color">
  magnet color</option>
<option value="selected_magnet_bg_color">
  selected magnet color</option>
<option value="shadow_bg_color">
  shadow color</option>
<option value="moving_shadow_bg_color">
  moving shadow color</option>
<option value="playing_field_bg_color">
  playing field color</option>
</select>
<input type=button name="ok" value="OK"
       onClick='save_preferences(this.form);'>
</td>
</tr>

<!-- custom colors -->

<tr>
<td width=150 align=center valign=center>
  <table width=100 border=0 cellpadding=0 cellspacing=2>
  <tr>
    <td width=25 align=center valign=center
        bgcolor=#FFFFFF
    ><a href="#"
        onClick='cp_save_custom_setting(0);'
        onMouseOver='cp_highlight_custom_on(0);'
        onMouseOut='cp_highlight_off();'
    ><img src="/images/clear.gif"
        name="custom0" border=0
        width=25 height=25></a></td>
    <td width=25 align=center valign=center
        bgcolor=#FFFFFF
    ><a href="#"
        onClick='cp_save_custom_setting(1);'
        onMouseOver='cp_highlight_custom_on(1);'
        onMouseOut='cp_highlight_off();'
    ><img src="/images/clear.gif"
        name="custom1" border=0
        width=25 height=25></a></td>
    <td width=25 align=center valign=center
        bgcolor=#FFFFFF
    ><a href="#"
```

```
        onClick='cp_save_custom_setting(2);'
        onMouseOver='cp_highlight_custom_on(2);'
        onMouseOut='cp_highlight_off();'
  ><img src="/images/clear.gif"
        name="custom2" border=0
        width=25 height=25></a></td>
  <td width=25 align=center valign=center
      bgcolor=#FFFFFF
  ><a href="#"
      onClick='cp_save_custom_setting(3);'
      onMouseOver='cp_highlight_custom_on(3);'
      onMouseOut='cp_highlight_off();'
  ><img src="/images/clear.gif"
        name="custom3" border=0
        width=25 height=25></a></td>
</tr>

<tr>
  <td width=25 align=center valign=center
      bgcolor=#FFFFFF
  ><a href="#"
      onClick='cp_save_custom_setting(4);'
      onMouseOver='cp_highlight_custom_on(4);'
      onMouseOut='cp_highlight_off();'
  ><img src="/images/clear.gif"
        name="custom4" border=0
        width=25 height=25></a></td>
  <td width=25 align=center valign=center
      bgcolor=#FFFFFF
  ><a href="#"
      onClick='cp_save_custom_setting(5);'
      onMouseOver='cp_highlight_custom_on(5);'
      onMouseOut='cp_highlight_off();'
  ><img src="/images/clear.gif"
        name="custom5" border=0
        width=25 height=25></a></td>
  <td width=25 align=center valign=center
      bgcolor=#FFFFFF
  ><a href="#"
      onClick='cp_save_custom_setting(6);'
      onMouseOver='cp_highlight_custom_on(6);'
      onMouseOut='cp_highlight_off();'
  ><img src="/images/clear.gif"
        name="custom6" border=0
        width=25 height=25></a></td>
```

```
          <td width=25 align=center valign=center
              bgcolor=#FFFFFF
          ><a href="#"
              onClick='cp_save_custom_setting(7);'
              onMouseOver='cp_highlight_custom_on(7);'
              onMouseOut='cp_highlight_off();'
          ><img src="/images/clear.gif"
                name="custom7" border=0
                width=25 height=25></a></td>
      </tr>
      </table>
      </td>
  </tr>

  <tr>
    <td nowrap align=right valign=top>
    <input type=button name="custom" value="show custom picker >"
          onClick='cp_toggle_custom_picker();'>
    </td>
  </tr>

  </table>
  </form>
  </div> <!-- end "colorpicker" -->

  <div id="custom0" align=center valign=center>
  <table border=0 cellpadding=0 cellspacing=0>
  <tr>
  <td align=center valign=center>
  <a href="#"
     onClick='cp_save_custom_setting(0);'
     onMouseOver='cp_highlight_custom_on(0);'
     onMouseOut='cp_highlight_off();'
  ><img src="/images/clear.gif"
        border=0 hspace=0 vspace=0
        width=25 height=25></a></td>
  </tr>
  </table>
  </div>

  <!-- custom1, custom2, and so on... through custom7 -->
  <!-- seven more just like the last one :-) -->
```

```
<div id="cphilight" align=center valign=center>
<table border=0 cellpadding=0 cellspacing=0>
<tr>
<td bgcolor=#ffffff align=center valign=center>
<img src="/images/clear.gif"
     border=0 hspace=0 vspace=0
     width=29 height=29></td>
</tr>
</table>
</div>


<div id="cpselected" align=center valign=center>
<table border=0 cellpadding=0 cellspacing=0>
<tr>
  <td bgcolor=#ffcc00 width=29 height=29 align=center valign=center>
  <table border=0 cellpadding=0 cellspacing=0>
  <tr>
    <td bgcolor=#cccccc align=center valign=center>
    <img src="/images/clear.gif"
        border=0 hspace=0 vspace=0
        width=28 height=28></td>
  </tr>
  </table>
  </td>
</tr>
</table>
</div>
```

The positioning of the standard color picker, highlight layer, selected color lay-ers, and so forth, is achieved through CSS positioning using the style sheet in Listing 13-13 and included in the document by way of the following markup:

```
<link rel="stylesheet" type="text/css"
     href="/css/color_picker.css">
```

Because the highlight and custom color layers are hidden until dynamically positioned and displayed by cp_highlight_on(), cp_highlight_custom_on(), cp_save_setting(), cp_save_custom_setting(), and other utility functions, their top and left CSS coordinates are unimportant. What is important is their width and height, which must be set explicitly for Internet Explorer to display them at the proper size.

Listing 13-13: The CSS style sheet for the standard color picker

```
TD {
    font-family: Arial, Helvetica, Sans-Serif;
    font-size: 8pt;
}

#colorpicker {
    position: absolute;
    top: 30;
    left: 118;
    visibility: hidden;
    z-index: 1000;
}

#cphilight {
    position: absolute;
    background-color: white;
    top: 30;
    left: 118;
    height: 29;
    width: 29;
    visibility: hidden;
}

#cpselected {
    position: absolute;
    background-color: orange;
    top: 30;
    left: 118;
    height: 29;
    width: 29;
    visibility: hidden;
}

#custom0 {
    position: absolute;
    top: 0;
    left: 0;
    height: 25;
    width: 25;
    visibility: hidden;
}

/* again, seven more just like the last one */
```

The color picker and custom color picker are initialized by way of a call to the initialization functions shown in Listing 13-14. color_picker_init() figures out its position using the top() and left() methods, and uses the offsets throughout the function to position other elements. It then hides the layers used to display the custom colors, checks the list of attributes using the utility function cp_check_color(), and initializes the selection of the color square corresponding to the currently selected attribute using cp_set_selected(). If the attribute list contains any references to colors whose value is not listed among the standard colors (the cp_colors array), it sets custom color squares to those colors using the utility function custom_add_selected_color(), shown in Listing 13-20, incrementing the last_custom_color variable, and displaying the layer. Finally, the global Boolean variable color_picker_initialized is set to true, and the custom picker initialization is called. The utility functions are shown in Listing 13-15.

Listing 13-14: The color picker initialization functions

```
var app = "dynamic_poetry";
var slider_x = 0;
var slider_y = 0;
var doober, grabbed;
var old_mousedown, old_mousemove, old_mouseup;
var max_left_x = 0;
var max_right_x = 0;
var max_drag_length = 0;
var picker_x_offset = 0;
var picker_y_offset = 0;
var custom_x_offset = 0;
var custom_y_offset = 0;
var red_y_axis = 0;
var green_y_axis = 0;
var blue_y_axis = 0;

var cp_frontmost = 1000;
var new_rgb_seed = 0;
var attribute_settings = new Array();
var cp_colors = new Array(16);
cp_colors[0] = "#FFFFFF";
cp_colors[1] = "#000000";
cp_colors[2] = "#CCCCCC";
cp_colors[3] = "#999999";
cp_colors[4] = "#FF0000";
cp_colors[5] = "#990000";
cp_colors[6] = "#FFFF00";
cp_colors[7] = "#666600";
cp_colors[8] = "#00FF00";
```

```
cp_colors[9] = "#009900";
cp_colors[10] = "#00FFFF";
cp_colors[11] = "#009999";
cp_colors[12] = "#0000FF";
cp_colors[13] = "#000099";
cp_colors[14] = "#FF00FF";
cp_colors[15] = "#990099";
var custom_colors = new Array(8);
for( var c = 0; c < 8; c++ ) {
  custom_colors[c] = "#FFFFFF";
}
var last_custom_color = 0;
var selected_custom_color = 0;
var color_picker_visible = false;
var custom_picker_visible = false;
var color_picker_initialized = false;

// initialize the color picker settings
function color_picker_init() {
  // get our offsets
  picker_x_offset = object_name["colorpicker"].left();
  picker_y_offset = object_name["colorpicker"].top();

  // hide our custom squares
  for( var x = 0; x < 8; x++ ) {
    object_name["custom" + x].conceal();
  }

  var cp = form_name["colorpicker"];
  var the_option, the_var, the_color, the_square;

  // go through the list of attribute options
  for( var o = 0; o < cp.attribute.options.length; o++ ) {
    the_option = cp.attribute.options[o];

    // get the color from the eval()'d name, which should be a
    // variable used in the application itself.
    the_var = the_option.value;
    attribute_settings[o] = eval(the_var);
    the_color = attribute_settings[o];

    the_square = cp_check_color(the_color);

    // if square exists, set it.
```

```
    // if not, create new custom color
    if( the_square == "" ) {
      the_square = custom_add_selected_color(the_color);
    }

    // is the option selected?
    if( the_option.selected ) {
      // select the appropriate color square
      cp_set_selected(the_square);
    }
    the_square = "";
  } // end options list

  color_picker_initialized = true;
  custom_picker_init();
}

// initialize the doobers
function custom_picker_init() {
  // get our offsets
  custom_x_offset = object_name["custompicker"].left();
  custom_y_offset = object_name["custompicker"].top();

  // get the grooves
  var red_groove = image_name["redgroove"];
  var green_groove = image_name["greengroove"];
  var blue_groove = image_name["bluegroove"];

  var red_groove_x = red_groove.get_x();
  var red_groove_y = red_groove.get_y();
  var green_groove_x = green_groove.get_x();
  var green_groove_y = green_groove.get_y();
  var blue_groove_x = blue_groove.get_x();
  var blue_groove_y = blue_groove.get_y();

  // and the doobers
  var rd = object_name["reddoober"];
  var gd = object_name["greendoober"];
  var bd = object_name["bluedoober"];

  // and the doober image
  var doober = image_name["reddoober"];

  var doober_h = doober.get_height();
```

```
var doober_w = doober.get_width();
var doober_w_offset = parseInt(doober_w / 2);
var doober_h_offset = parseInt(doober_h * 1.5);

max_drag_length = red_groove.get_width();
max_drag_length -= doober_w_offset;

// don't use Y layer offsets for doobers in IE (!)
if( navigator.userAgent.indexOf("MSIE") != -1 ) {
  red_y_axis = red_groove_y - doober_h_offset;
  green_y_axis = green_groove_y - doober_h_offset;
  blue_y_axis = blue_groove_y - doober_h_offset;
} else {
  red_y_axis = red_groove_y - doober_h_offset
    + custom_y_offset;
  green_y_axis = green_groove_y - doober_h_offset
    + custom_y_offset;
  blue_y_axis = blue_groove_y - doober_h_offset
    + custom_y_offset;
}

max_left_x = custom_x_offset;
max_right_x = max_left_x + max_drag_length;

rd.set_z_index(cp_frontmost);
gd.set_z_index(cp_frontmost);
bd.set_z_index(cp_frontmost);

rd.set_top( red_y_axis );
gd.set_top( green_y_axis );
bd.set_top( blue_y_axis );

rd.set_left(doober_w_offset + custom_x_offset);
gd.set_left(doober_w_offset + custom_x_offset);
bd.set_left(doober_w_offset + custom_x_offset);

// set currentcustom in the right place
var current = image_name["current"];

var current_x = custom_x_offset + 5;

// don't use Y offsets for currentcustom - only the X offset
if( navigator.userAgent.indexOf("MSIE") != -1 ) {
  var current_y = current.get_y();
```

```
    } else {
      var current_y = current.get_y() + custom_y_offset;
    }


  object_name["currentcustom"].place( current_x, current_y )
  object_name["currentcustom"].set_z_index(cp_frontmost);

    // and finally set the custompicker at front, but only in IE
    // otherwise we lose sight of the doobers (!)
    if( navigator.userAgent.indexOf("MSIE") != -1 ) {
      object_name["custompicker"].set_z_index( cp_frontmost );
    }
}
```

The custom_picker_init() function does a similar set of things, getting the offsets and figuring out the location of other named IMG elements whose sole purpose is to serve as a guide for the placement of the *doobers*, or thumbs, for each color's slider bar. The variables max_left_x, max_right_x and max_drag_length are used by the function custom_picker_place() to set the bounds of the doobers so the user cannot drag them any further than the ends of the slider bars.

We call the thingamabobs *doobers* because it is much shorter than calling them *thingamabobs*. If you come up with a better name for them, please let us know.

Listing 13-15: The utility functions used by the standard color picker

```
// highlight the color currently under the mouse pointer
function cp_highlight_on(color, c) {
  var f = form_name["colorpicker"];
  var a = f.attribute;
  var i = a.selectedIndex;
  var setting = a.options[i].text;

  cp_place_highlight("color" + c);

  window.status = "set " + setting + " to " + color;
}

// remove the highlight
function cp_highlight_off() {
  window.status=defaultStatus;
```

```
    object_name["cphilight"].conceal();
}

// highlight the custom color currently under the mouse pointer
function cp_highlight_custom_on(c) {
  var f = form_name["colorpicker"];
  var a = f.attribute;
  var i = a.selectedIndex;
  var setting = a.options[i].text;

  cp_place_highlight("custom" + c);

  window.status = "set " + setting + " to this custom color";
}

// given the name of an image, center highlight
// div beneath it
function cp_place_highlight(p) {
  var thecolor = image_name[p];
  var thehilight = object_name["cphilight"];
  // don't use offsets in IE
  if( navigator.userAgent.indexOf("MSIE") != -1 ) {
    var x = thecolor.get_x();
    var y = thecolor.get_y();
  } else {
    var x = thecolor.get_x() + picker_x_offset;
    var y = thecolor.get_y() + picker_y_offset;
  }
  thehilight.place( (x-2), (y-2));
  thehilight.set_z_index(1);
  thehilight.reveal();
}

// given the form, select the current attribute's color
function cp_select_current_color(f) {
  var o = f.attribute.options;
  var i = f.attribute.selectedIndex;
  var the_color = attribute_settings[i];
  var the_square = cp_check_color(the_color);
  cp_set_selected(the_square);
}

// given a color, figure out whether it is a standard color,
// a custom color, or needs to be added. returns name of the
```

```
// square containing that color, or the empty string.
function cp_check_color(c) {
  var the_square = "";
  // check for standard colors
  for( var x = 0; x < cp_colors.length; x++ ) {
    if( cp_colors[x] == c ) {
      the_square = "color" + x;
      break;
    }
  }

  // any existing custom colors?
  if( the_square == "" ) {
    for( var cc = 0; cc < custom_colors.length; cc++ ) {
      if( custom_colors[cc] == c ) {
        the_square = "custom" + cc;
        break;
      }
    }
  }
  return the_square;
}


// save the setting based on currently selected option
function cp_save_setting(c) {
  // get selected option
  var f = form_name["colorpicker"];
  var a = f.elements[0];
  var i = a.selectedIndex;
  var setting = a.options[i].text;
  var val = a.options[i].value;
  attribute_settings[i] = cp_colors[c];
  cp_set_selected("color" + c);
  custom_picker_set_color( cp_colors[c] );
  window.status = "saved setting for " + setting + " as " + c;
}


// save the custom setting based on currently selected option
function cp_save_custom_setting(c) {
  // get selected option
  var f = form_name["colorpicker"];
  var a = f.elements[0];
  var i = a.selectedIndex;
  var setting = a.options[i].text;
```

```
   var val = a.options[i].value;
   var color = custom_colors[c];

   if( color != "#FFFFFF" ) {
     attribute_settings[i] = color;
     cp_set_selected("custom" + c);
     custom_picker_set_color( custom_colors[c] );
     window.status = "saved setting for " + setting +
                      " as " + color;
   } else {
     alert("no color defined.");
   }
   if( ! custom_picker_visible ) {
     cp_toggle_custom_picker();
   }
}

function cp_set_selected(c) {
  var thecolor = image_name[c];
  var selected = object_name["cpselected"];
  // don't use offsets in MSIE
  if( navigator.userAgent.indexOf("MSIE") != -1 ) {
    var x = thecolor.get_x();
    var y = thecolor.get_y();
  } else {
    var x = thecolor.get_x() + picker_x_offset;
    var y = thecolor.get_y() + picker_y_offset;
  }
  selected.place( (x - 2), (y - 2));
  selected.set_z_index(2);


  if( c.indexOf("custom") >= 0 ) {
    var custom_square = object_name[c];
    custom_square.place( x, y );
    custom_square.set_z_index(cp_frontmost);
    selected_custom_color = c.charAt(c.length -1);
  }

  if( object_name["colorpicker"].is_visible()) {
    selected.reveal();
    if( custom_square ) {
      custom_square.reveal();
    }
```

```
  }
}
// set a custom color square to a given color
function custom_set_color(position, color) {
  object_name[position].set_bg_color(color);
}
```

All in all, the process is fairly simple – in principle, anyway. The cross-browser
API creates a set of objects for the management, identification, and placement of
the image objects on the page. These objects and their associated methods are used
to obtain the various *x* and *y* coordinates of the images, which enable them to be
used as placeholders and guides for other, more important and visible interface elements. This is necessary due to differences in the way that browsers render form
elements and tables across platforms, modifying the characteristics of the layout in
unpredictable ways.

The standard color picker may be shown or hidden by an enclosing application
by calling cp_toggle_color_picker(), which itself toggles the custom picker. The
standard color picker also contains a button whose onClick event handler calls
cp_toggle_custom_picker(), shown in Listing 13-16, which is responsible for
hiding and revealing the various layers and objects associated with the custom
color picker.

Listing 13-16: Showing and hiding the color pickers

```
function cp_toggle_color_picker() {
  var p = object_name["colorpicker"];
  var s = object_name["cpselected"];
  var h = object_name["cphilight"];
  if( color_picker_visible ) {
    p.conceal();
    s.conceal();
    h.conceal();
    for( var x = 0; x < 8; x++ ) {
      object_name["custom" + x].conceal();
    }
    color_picker_visible = false;

    if( custom_picker_visible ) {
      cp_toggle_custom_picker();
    }
  } else {
    p.reveal();

    for( var x = 0; x < 8; x++ ) {
      object_name["custom" + x].reveal();
```

```
      }
      color_picker_visible = true;
   }
}

function cp_toggle_custom_picker() {
  var s = object_name["custompicker"];
  var r = object_name["reddoober"];
  var g = object_name["greendoober"];
  var b = object_name["bluedoober"];
  var c = object_name["currentcustom"];
  var cp = form_name["colorpicker"];

  if( custom_picker_visible == true ) {
    s.conceal();
    r.conceal();
    g.conceal();
    b.conceal();
    c.conceal();
    cp.custom.value = "show custom picker >";
    custom_picker_visible = false;
  } else {
    s.reveal();
    r.reveal();
    g.reveal();
    b.reveal();
    c.reveal();
    cp.custom.value = "<< hide custom picker";
    custom_picker_visible = true;
  }
}
```

Now that you've digested all of the code for the color picker, it's time to move on to the custom color picker with its delightful intricacies.

The Custom Color Picker

It's relatively easy, once you know how, to provide a simple standard color picker. All you're really doing is some fancy dynamic repositioning of layers (highlights) and relating mouse clicks to the currently selected option in a pull-down menu. But what if the user wants something a little more exciting than the standard 16 colors? Enter the custom color picker. We've limited the custom picker to 216 colors – the Web-safe palette. It could support millions of colors, but most people can't differentiate between a couple of hundred colors, much less sixteen million.

The Purpose of the Custom Color Picker

The custom picker, illustrated in Figure 13-4, enables the user to click and drag the doobers and select one of the six Web-safe color settings for red, green, and blue. The custom color picker automatically updates the text inputs to the right and bottom of the sliders, with the decimal and hexadecimal equivalents of the doobers' positions. The Add New button enables the user to add up to eight new custom colors, regardless of whether one of the custom colors is already selected. The Replace button, just below the Add New button, enables the user to replace the currently selected custom color with the setting currently occupying the custom picker.

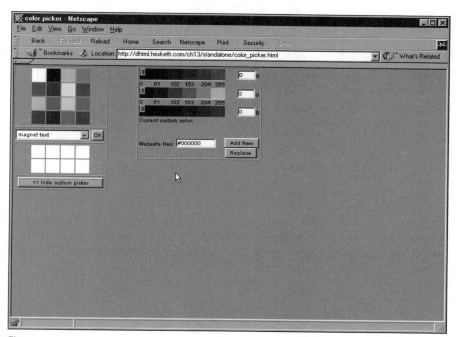

Figure 13-4: Enabling the user to choose their own colors with the custom color picker

In addition, the standard color picker and custom color picker are integrated such that if the user selects one of the standard colors, the custom color picker is set to that color, enabling the user to modify existing colors instead of simply coming up with his or her own. Figure 13-5 illustrates the relationship between the standard and custom color pickers.

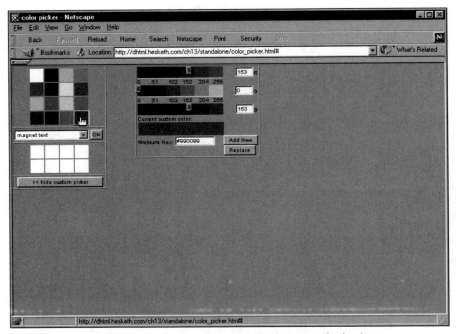

Figure 13-5: Setting the custom color picker by selecting a standard color

The custom color may then be modified and added to the custom color table, as seen in Figure 13-6. The color started out in Figure 13-5 as a nice bright purple, hex value #990099, and the user darkened things up by one step on the blue color bar, and selected the Add New button to propagate the changes to the custom table. Adding the custom color to the table automatically selects it, so the currently selected attribute, "magnet text," is now set to #990066, as illustrated in Figure 13-6. The changes have not yet been made permanent, however; the user must hit the OK button to save the changes as preferences (using the Preferences module and cookies). In Figure 13-7, the red value has been incremented to 255 or FF, and the Replace button selected, replacing the currently selected custom color square with the color from the custom color picker.

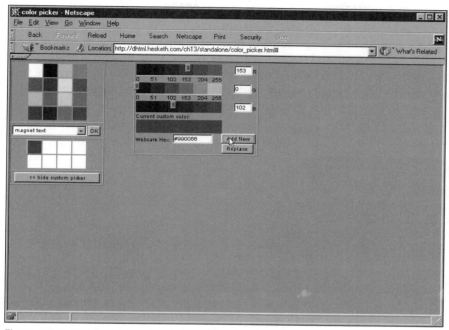

Figure 13-6: Modifying a custom color without saving changes

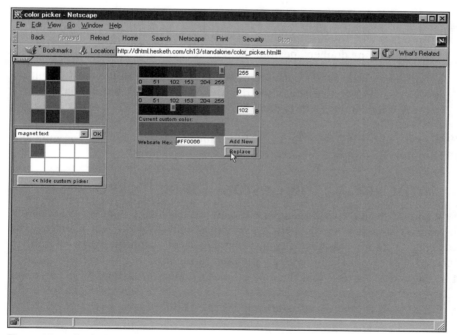

Figure 13-7: Replacing a currently selected custom color using the custom color picker

The custom color table is set to all white squares by default. When the user clicks in one of the white custom squares, the application pops up an alert (that could just as well be a status bar message, come to think of it) that points out that there is no custom color defined for that square, as seen in Figure 13-8. If the notification is to remain an alert, it could probably provide more instruction to the user, say, the first five times they click an empty square, and after that start giving them steadily more and more irritated error messages. But you need to provide something that's appropriate for your audience.

Figure 13-8: Trying to select a custom color that is not yet defined

Other features that might be worth implementing include the following:

◆ Adding onChange handlers to the text input fields so that the color values and doober positions are automatically updated when the text is updated

◆ Adding a test bed area with a sample magnet so the user can try out settings before making them permanent

◆ Adding a way to click the slider bars themselves to increment and decrement the doobers' position (and hence the color value)

◆ Adding a quick-access pull-down menu populated with the most recently selected color choices, enabling the user to easily back out of changes or recover a mistakenly lost color setting

Well, that's about it from a functionality standpoint. Let's dig into the guts and talk about how this thing works.

The Structure of the Custom Color Picker

The custom color picker uses a similar structure to that of the standard color picker, with the exception that the doobers require more sophisticated event handling. The custom color picker assigns the appropriate event handlers after a call to custom_picker_over() is initiated by the user during an onMouseOver event, specified in the anchor surrounding the doober image, shown in Listing 3-21. The event handlers, custom_picker_over(), custom_picker_grab(), custom_picker_drag(), and custom_picker_drop(), are shown in Listing 13-17.

Listing 13-17: The custom color picker event handlers

```
function custom_picker_over(the_doober) {
  var o = document;
  if( o.captureEvents ) {
    o.captureEvents(Event.MOUSEDOWN |
                    Event.MOUSEMOVE |
                    Event.MOUSEUP );
  }

  o.onmousedown = custom_picker_grab;
  o.onmousemove = custom_picker_drag;
  o.onmouseup = custom_picker_drop;

  doober = the_doober;
}

function custom_picker_grab(e) {
  grabbed = object_name[doober];

  if( window.event ) {
    window.event.cancelBubble = true;
  }
}

function custom_picker_drag(e) {
  if( grabbed ) {
    var new_x;

    if( window.event ) {
      e = window.event;
      e.cancelBubble = true;
    }

    if( e.clientX ) {
      new_x = e.clientX - slider_x;
    } else {
      new_x = e.pageX - slider_x;
    }
    custom_picker_place(doober, new_x);
  }
}

function custom_picker_drop() {
  custom_picker_set_rgb(new_rgb_seed);
  grabbed = null;
```

```
if( window.event ) {
  window.event.cancelBubble = true;
}

// restore events

}
```

Basically, the `mouseover` sets things up so that the next `mousedown` event sets the `grabbed` object reference, which the `mousemove` event handler tests the existence of. If it is really an object, it is then manipulated via `custom_picker_place()`. The next `mouseup` event then calls `custom_picker_set_rgb()` with an argument that is seeded by `custom_picker_place()`. It is then up to the module to restore events back to the previous state, as you see when we fully integrate the pickers into the Dynamic Poetry application. The utility functions `custom_picker_set_rgb()` and `custom_picker_place()` are shown in Listing 13-19, along with the rest of the custom color picker utility routines.

The `custom_picker_place()` function is responsible for setting the doobers down within a certain range and generating the seed (the current x position of the doober) to be used in calculating the new color. Each doober has its own horizontal range, along the groove formed by reference to a transparent GIF that spans the table row directly beneath each doober and color prism. These grooves, if you recall, were initialized along with everything else in `custom_picker_init()`, shown in Listing 13-14. The `custom_picker_set_rgb()` function figures out the width of the slider bar in pixels and then divides the seed by the width to get a ratio that may be multiplied by 255 in order to arrive at the new color setting and refresh the values of both the RGB text inputs and the hex input. This refresh is accomplished by way of a call to `custom_picker_calc_hex()`, which, in turn, calls `custom_picker_get_websafe_hex()` on each of the three color values, using the results to build a new string for the hex input. Finally, the background color of the appropriate layer is set to the current custom color.

Note something interesting about `custom_picker_set_rgb()`: Although the slider prism only contains six values, there are five lines between them, representing the transitions from one to the next. Rather than comparing the x coordinate of the given doober with the nice, neat divisions on which the Web-safe color palette is based (0, 51, 102, 153, and so on), the comparison had to be made such that the next value was set as soon as the center of the doober crossed one of the five lines. This comes across as slightly counter-intuitive at first, so we figured we'd mention it. It should certainly go a long way toward helping to explain where a number like "42.5" came from.

Listing 13-18 shows the CSS positioning information for the custom color picker. Notice that everything is invisible at first, and is only shown later when the user has explicitly specified that it be shown.

Listing 13-18: Positioning information for the custom color picker

```
#custompicker {
    position: absolute;
    top: 30;
    left: 343;
    visibility: hidden;
}

#reddoober {
    position: absolute;
    top: 0;
    left: 0;
    width: 10;
    visibility: hidden;
    z-index: 1;
}

#greendoober {
    position: absolute;
    top: 0;
    left: 0;
    width: 10;
    visibility: hidden;
    z-index: 1;
}

#bluedoober {
    position: absolute;
    top: 0;
    left: 0;
    width: 10;
    visibility: hidden;
    z-index: 1;
}

#currentcustom {
    position: absolute;
    top: 30;
    left: 0;
    height: 15;
    width: 29;
    visibility: hidden;
}
```

The other functions should be fairly straightforward; they either manipulate text strings to produce numbers, or manipulate decimal numbers to produce hexadecimal text strings.

Listing 13-19: Utility functions for the custom color picker

```
function custom_picker_place(name, x) {
  var s = object_name[name];

  if( x >= max_right_x ) {
    x = max_right_x;
  } else if( x <= max_left_x ) {
    x = max_left_x;
  }

  var the_y_axis;
  if( name.indexOf("red") >= 0 ) {
    the_y_axis = red_y_axis;
  } else if( name.indexOf("green") >= 0 ) {
    the_y_axis = green_y_axis;
  } else if( name.indexOf("blue") >= 0 ) {
    the_y_axis = blue_y_axis;
  }

  new_rgb_seed = x - max_left_x;

  // place the selected object
  s.place( x, the_y_axis );
}

function custom_picker_set_rgb(x) {
  // given x, which should be 1 <-> slider width, figure
  // out what to set the appropriate r/g/b value to.
  var slider_width = image_name["redgroove"].get_width();
  var v = parseInt((parseInt( x ) / slider_width ) * 255 );
  var s = form_name["customform"];

  // need to compensate for the width of the doober
  // so its appearance on the slider matches what is
  // set on the rgb textbox.
  var doober_width =
      parseInt(object_name[doober].clipper_width());

  v += (doober_width / 2);
```

```
    if(( v >= 0 ) && ( v < 42.5 )) {
      v = 0;
    } else if(( v >= 42.5 ) && ( v < 85 )) {
      v = 51;
    } else if(( v >= 85 ) && ( v < 127.5 )) {
      v = 102;
    } else if(( v >= 127.5 ) && ( v < 170 )) {
      v = 153;
    } else if(( v >= 170 ) && ( v < 212.5 )) {
      v = 204;
    } else {
      v = 255;
    }

    if( doober == "reddoober" ) {
      s.red.value = v;
    } else if( doober == "greendoober" ) {
      s.green.value = v;
    } else if( doober == "bluedoober" ) {
      s.blue.value = v;
    }
    custom_picker_calc_hex();
}

function custom_picker_calc_hex() {
  var s = form_name["customform"];
  var r = s.red.value;
  var g = s.green.value;
  var b = s.blue.value;

  var hex_r = custom_picker_get_websafe_hex(r);
  var hex_g = custom_picker_get_websafe_hex(g);
  var hex_b = custom_picker_get_websafe_hex(b);
  var new_hex = '#' + hex_r + hex_g + hex_b;
  s.hex.value = new_hex;
  object_name["currentcustom"].set_bg_color(new_hex);
}

function custom_picker_get_custom_color() {
  var s = form_name["customform"];
  custom_picker_calc_hex();
  return s.hex.value;
}
```

```
function custom_picker_get_websafe_hex(d) {
  var tmp = parseInt(d);

  if( tmp <= 0 ) hex = '00';
  if(( tmp > 0    ) && ( tmp <= 51  )) hex = '33';
  if(( tmp > 51   ) && ( tmp <= 102 )) hex = '66';
  if(( tmp > 102  ) && ( tmp <= 153 )) hex = '99';
  if(( tmp > 153  ) && ( tmp <= 204 )) hex = 'CC';
  if(( tmp > 204  ) && ( tmp <= 255 )) hex = 'FF';
  if( tmp > 255 ) hex = 'FF';

  return hex;
}


// based on the text box values, set the doobers
// basically the reverse of custom_picker_set_rgb
function custom_picker_set_doobers() {
  var s = form_name["customform"];
  var r = s.red.value;
  var g = s.green.value;
  var b = s.blue.value;
  var rd = object_name["reddoober"];
  var gd = object_name["greendoober"];
  var bd = object_name["bluedoober"];

  var slider_width = image_name["redgroove"].get_width();
  var x = 0;
  // set reddoober
  x = parseInt( (parseInt( r ) / 255) * slider_width);
  x += custom_x_offset;
  rd.place( x, red_y_axis);
  rd.set_z_index( cp_frontmost );
  // set greendoober
  x = parseInt( (parseInt( g ) / 255) * slider_width);
  x += custom_x_offset;
  gd.place( x, green_y_axis);
  gd.set_z_index( cp_frontmost );
  // set bluedoober
  x = parseInt( (parseInt( b ) / 255) * slider_width);
  x += custom_x_offset;
  bd.place( x, blue_y_axis);
  bd.set_z_index( cp_frontmost );}
```

```
// finally, given a color, set the custom picker's rgb vals
function custom_picker_set_color(color) {
  var s = form_name["customform"];
  var c = color.toString();
  var r = c[1] + c[2];
  var g = c[3] + c[4];
  var b = c[5] + c[6];

  // set the textboxes
  s.red.value = cp_hex_to_decimal(r);
  s.green.value = cp_hex_to_decimal(g);
  s.blue.value = cp_hex_to_decimal(b);

  // set the doobers
  custom_picker_set_doobers();

  // set the hex value
  custom_picker_calc_hex();
}

function cp_hex_to_decimal(h) {
  if( h == "00" ) {
    return 0;
  } else if( h == "33" ) {
    return 51;
  } else if( h == "66" ) {
    return 102;
  } else if( h == "99" ) {
    return 153;
  } else if( (h == "CC") || (h == "cc")) {
    return 204;
  } else if( (h == "FF") || (h == "ff")) {
    return 255;
  } else {
    return 0;
  }
  return 0;
}
```

Now that you've seen how the events that produce the values for the inputs representing the custom color value are handled, let's talk a bit about how the custom colors are applied to the custom color table.

Setting Arbitrary Colors Using the Custom Color Picker

The buttons on the custom color picker enable the user to apply the custom colors to the custom color table, and from there, possibly to the attributes in the pull-down menu. When the new color has been created in the custom color picker, its hex value is placed in the hex text input. The two buttons call functions that read that hex value and use it to set the background color of a hidden custom layer object. But the `custom_add_selected_color()` function may be invoked either via the button's `onClick` event handler or by other functions, such as the `color_picker_init()` function, which checks the preference attributes' values and adds new custom colors to the table if their color value is not found in the list of standard colors. Again, we use the `arguments` array, this time not just to check for the number of arguments, but to see if any argument has been passed at all. If not, such as is the case when the function is invoked via the `onClick` event handler, the function `custom_picker_get_custom_color()` then reads that value from the form. The function `custom_picker_get_custom_color()` calls `custom_picker_ calc_hex()` just to make sure that the hex value is up to date. It sounds pretty convoluted, but it's for the best. After the hex value is updated, the function checks to make sure that there is an available custom color square, using the `last_custom_color` global variable, which represents the last custom color square to be used. If there are no more squares, the function throws up an alert and returns false to indicate failure.

Because the `custom_replace_selected_color()` function is always invoked from the button via an `onClick` event handler, there is no need to test for the existence of an argument — it just grabs the hex value from the form, sets the background color of the selected custom color, modifies the color setting in the `custom_colors` array, sets the `attribute_settings` array as appropriate, and selects the custom square.

Listing 13-20: Adding and replacing custom colors dynamically

```
// using last_custom_color, create a new custom color
function custom_add_selected_color(color) {
  if( arguments.length == 0 ) {
    color = custom_picker_get_custom_color();
  }
  if( last_custom_color == 8 ) {
    alert("you have already defined colors for\n" +
          "all of the custom color slots!");
    return false;
  }
  var the_square = "custom" + last_custom_color;
```

```
    object_name[ the_square ].set_bg_color(color);
    custom_colors[last_custom_color] = color;
    custom_set_color( the_square, color );
    last_custom_color++;
    cp_set_selected( the_square );
    return the_square;
}


// get the selected custom color, if any, and replace it
// with the current custom color
function custom_replace_selected_color() {
    var color = custom_picker_get_custom_color();
    object_name["custom"+selected_custom_color].set_bg_color(color);
    custom_colors[selected_custom_color] = color;
    attribute_settings[selected_custom_color] = color;
    cp_set_selected("custom" + selected_custom_color);
}
```

The event handlers we've been talking about, as well as the named images and other markup are shown in Listing 13-21. The prism tables use table cell background colors to represent the transitions between color values. The *groove* graphics are used to help position the doobers and the current custom color layer, and the doobers are all relegated to their own DIV objects as well. The doobers contain anchors with onMouseOver event handlers defined that flip the switch in motion for the rest of the event handling.

Listing 13-21: The HTML markup for the custom color picker

```
<div id="custompicker">
<form name="customform">
<table width=200 border=1 cellpadding=2 cellspacing=0>
<tr>
  <td valign=top>
  <table width=200 cellpadding=0 cellspacing=0 border=0>
  <tr> <!-- red -->
    <td width=26 align=left valign=top bgcolor=#000000>
    <img src="/images/clear.gif"
        width=26 height=10 border=0></td>
    <td width=26 align=left valign=top bgcolor=#330000>
    <img src="/images/clear.gif"
        width=26 height=10 border=0></td>
    <td width=26 align=left valign=top bgcolor=#660000>
    <img src="/images/clear.gif"
        width=26 height=10 border=0></td>
```

```
  <td width=26 align=left valign=top bgcolor=#990000>
  <img src="/images/clear.gif"
      width=26 height=10 border=0></td>
  <td width=26 align=left valign=top bgcolor=#CC0000>
  <img src="/images/clear.gif"
      width=26 height=10 border=0></td>
  <td width=26 align=left valign=top bgcolor=#FF0000>
  <img src="/images/clear.gif"
      width=26 height=10 border=0></td>
  <td width=20 align=right valign=top>
  <input type=text size=3 name=red value=0>R</td>
</tr>

<tr>
  <td colspan=6 align=left bgcolor=#FFFFFF>
  <img name="redgroove" src="/images/clear.gif"
      width=156 height=1></td>
</tr>

<tr>
  <td width=26 align=left valign=top>0</td>
  <td width=26 align=left valign=top>51</td>
  <td width=26 align=center valign=top>102</td>
  <td width=26 align=center valign=top>153</td>
  <td width=26 align=right valign=top>204</td>
  <td width=26 align=right valign=top>255</td>
  <td width=20 align=center valign=top> </td>
</tr>

<tr> <!-- green -->
  <td width=26 align=left valign=top bgcolor=#000000>
  <img src="/images/clear.gif"
      width=26 height=10 border=0></td>
  <td width=26 align=left valign=top bgcolor=#003300>
  <img src="/images/clear.gif"
      width=26 height=10 border=0></td>
  <td width=26 align=left valign=top bgcolor=#006600>
  <img src="/images/clear.gif"
      width=26 height=10 border=0></td>
  <td width=26 align=left valign=top bgcolor=#009900>
  <img src="/images/clear.gif"
      width=26 height=10 border=0></td>
  <td width=26 align=left valign=top bgcolor=#00CC00>
  <img src="/images/clear.gif"
```

```
            width=26 height=10 border=0></td>
   <td width=26 align=left valign=top bgcolor=#00FF00>
   <img src="/images/clear.gif"
        width=26 height=10 border=0></td>
   <td width=20 align=right valign=top>
   <input type=text size=3 name=green value=0>G</td>
</tr>

<tr>
   <td colspan=6 align=left bgcolor=#FFFFFF>
   <img name="greengroove" src="/images/clear.gif"
        width=156 height=1></td>
</tr>

<tr>
   <td width=26 align=left valign=top>0</td>
   <td width=26 align=left valign=top>51</td>
   <td width=26 align=center valign=top>102</td>
   <td width=26 align=center valign=top>153</td>
   <td width=26 align=right valign=top>204</td>
   <td width=26 align=right valign=top>255</td>
   <td width=20 align=center valign=top> </td>
</tr>

<tr> <!-- blue -->
   <td width=26 align=left valign=top bgcolor=#000000>
   <img src="/images/clear.gif"
        width=26 height=10 border=0></td>
   <td width=26 align=left valign=top bgcolor=#000033>
   <img src="/images/clear.gif"
        width=26 height=10 border=0></td>
   <td width=26 align=left valign=top bgcolor=#000066>
   <img src="/images/clear.gif"
        width=26 height=10 border=0></td>
   <td width=26 align=left valign=top bgcolor=#000099>
   <img src="/images/clear.gif"
        width=26 height=10 border=0></td>
   <td width=26 align=left valign=top bgcolor=#0000CC>
   <img src="/images/clear.gif"
        width=26 height=10 border=0></td>
   <td width=26 align=left valign=top bgcolor=#0000FF>
   <img src="/images/clear.gif"
        width=26 height=10 border=0></td>
```

```
   <td width=20 align=right valign=top>
   <input type=text size=3 name=blue value=0>B</td>
 </tr>

 <tr>
   <td colspan=6 align=left>
   <img name="bluegroove" src="/images/clear.gif"
       width=156 height=1></td>
 </tr>

 <tr>
   <td colspan=6 align=left>
   Current custom color:<br>
   <img name="current" src="/images/clear.gif"
       width=156 height=25></td>
 </tr>

 <tr>
   <td colspan=6 align=left valign=top>
   Websafe Hex:
   <input type=text size=8 name=hex value="#000000"></td>
   <td align=center valign=bottom>
   <input type=button name="addnew" value="Add New"
       onClick='custom_add_selected_color();'>
   <input type=button name="replace" value="Replace"
       onClick='custom_replace_selected_color();'>
   </td>
 </tr>
 </table>

 </td>
</tr>

</table>
</form>

</div><!-- end "custompicker" -->

<div id="reddoober" align=center><a href="#"
   onMouseOver='custom_picker_over("reddoober");'
>
<img name="reddoober" src="/images/doober.gif"
     height=15 width=10 border=0></a>
</div>
```

```
<div id="greendoober" align=center>
<a href="#"
   onMouseOver='custom_picker_over("greendoober");'
>
<img name="greendoober" src="/images/doober.gif"
     height=15 width=10 border=0></a>
</div>
<div id="bluedoober" align=center>

<a href="#"
   onMouseOver='custom_picker_over("bluedoober");'
>
<img name="bluedoober" src="/images/doober.gif"
     height=15 width=10 border=0></a>
</div>
<div id="currentcustom" align=center valign=center>
<table border=0 cellpadding=0 cellspacing=0>
<tr>
<td align=center valign=center>
<img src="/images/clear.gif"
     border=0 hspace=0 vspace=0
     width=156 height=25></td>
</tr>
</table>
</div>
```

That pretty much covers it for the color picker, with the exception of perhaps the most important function of all that is called upon to finish the job: cp_save_all_settings(). Without this last function, the foregoing has been just for fun.

Updating Settings

Let's take a deep breath and let it out slowly. Remember why we're here? We're here to set user preferences, thereby giving them an enormous sense of control over their own workaday lives. The function in Listing 13-22 is the keystone, the pinnacle, the apex of what we have set out to do today. It is cp_save_all_settings().

Listing 13-22: Saving user preferences set via the color picker interface

```
function cp_save_all_settings(f) {
  var a = form_name["colorpicker"].attribute.options;
  for( var x = 0; x < attribute_settings.length; x++ ) {
    set_preference(app, a[x].value, attribute_settings[x]);
  }
}
```

The function is really quite simple, as it relies on virtually every other function we've looked at so far to get its data. (Well, actually, it could be invoked immediately after the `color_picker_init()` function, and still do exactly the same thing, but let's play with the idea a bit.) After getting a reference to the color picker form's `attribute` options list, it loops through every option, setting a preference with each option's value as its name and the corresponding value from the `attribute_settings` array, which we modified whenever we selected a different color square. In short, it sets all of the user's preferences, based on a combination of what was there before (if the setting was not changed) and what settings have been changed by way of the color picker.

This is probably the best time to ask if it might be a better idea to use the `set_multi_preference()` function and store all of these values in a single setting. Unfortunately, the function really isn't suited to storing values whose names are variable. It's much better suited to storing sequences of the same property, such as offsets into a list of words, or the like. It might be a good idea to write a function that simply enabled you to call it again and again to iterate over a list of settings, adding each to the cookie. Consider it an exercise.

Dynamically Updating Settings

Now that we have our user preferences stored as cookies, it's time to ask if we should go ahead and update the settings right away so that the changes are immediately reflected in the application. In some cases, yes, this is a good idea, and in fact, we're going to try to do that next. But in others, the settings are such that they cannot be reflected immediately, especially in a consistent manner across platforms. Navigator's document object model doesn't provide the dynamic update of many of the styles and window text reflow that Internet Explorer does with ease. So we leave the question open for now. You may want to ask again when you've got your own application to update.

Updating Settings on Reload

Where it is simply not possible or sensible to update settings immediately, one option is to supply a function in your application that reads the preferences at roughly the same time that other global variables are being set, or just after, so as to override their settings. That way, the settings you chose to expose to the user's customization can be leveraged across the entire session.

Integrating the Preferences Module and Color Picker into the Application

The Dynamic Poetry application is about to get a facelift. You've seen how the color picker can be used to set preferences. You've seen how easy it is to define a list of properties to be used in the pull-down menu, only to have their values updated dynamically, either immediately after setting them or on the next reload. What you haven't seen is an example of such an application. Well, that's what we're about to do, so hang on.

Listing Your Preferences

The first thing we need to do is compile a list of the preferences we want to expose to the user. Fortunately, we've already done it, much like Julia Child and the turkey under the counter. So, let's recap. For now, we're only going to use the color picker to set the following colors in the Dynamic Poetry application:

- `magnet_color`
- `magnet_bg_color`
- `selected_magnet_bg_color`
- `shadow_bg_color`
- `moving_shadow_bg_color`
- `playing_field_bg_color`

These comprise the colors of major importance in the application. There are other preferences we'd eventually like to set, such as name and e-mail address, favorite wordlists, and so forth, but for now let's just stick to colors.

Defining Defaults for Each Preference Setting

Because the colors we chose were already in use by the application, we already have their default values. Rather than redefine them, or remove them and set default preferences for them, we're not taking any chances, leaving everything just the way it is for right now. For your application, you can choose one of three strategies:

1. Use the user's preferences and nothing else (risky if the user turns off cookies, or loses them in an upgrade, or some other catastrophe occurs)

2. Use both the user's preferences and your own defaults, which you set using the Preferences module (less risky, but still reliant on cookies)

3. Use hard-coded defaults, your cookie-based defaults, *and* finally the user's preferences

Of the three, the last is the safest. This should be obvious by now, but if it isn't, just build one application that relies on the end user being able to use cookies. You learn soon enough that redundancy is the best policy when it comes to making assumptions about your users' environment.

In any case, for the Dynamic Poetry application, we be using the following hard-coded defaults, and following that up with the user's preferences:

```
// default colors
var magnet_color = "#000000";
var magnet_bg_color = "#FFFFFF";
var selected_magnet_bg_color = "#999999";
var shadow_color = "#000000";
var shadow_bg_color = "#000000";
var moving_shadow_color = "#999999"; // lighter than default
var moving_shadow_bg_color = moving_shadow_color;
var playing_field_bg_color = "#CCCCCC";
```

It's worth noting that with the current implementation, you must match the case of the colors you supply as defaults with that of the case found in the cp_colors array. Otherwise, your standard colors might be interpreted as custom just because of case-sensitivity issues. Yet another exercise for the reader.

Adding Routines That Implement Preference Settings

Fortunately, if you've defined your attribute settings (the values in the option list) using the actual variable names of the settings you want to change, this part is easy. Using the JavaScript eval() function, you can turn a variable whose contents are the name of another variable into the "l-value," or that part of the statement that receives the assignment for the values you got back from the Preferences module. Listing 13-23 shows how we do it in the Dynamic Poetry application. Notice the workaround for setting the color of the mainlayer DIV. For some reason, on Macintosh browsers especially, the mainlayer object isn't always initialized properly when this routine is called. So we check for it, and if we don't find it, we set a timer that sets the color later. For more information on timers, see Chapter 16, "Timers and Other Fun Stuff."

Listing 13-23: Initializing the list of preference values using init_preferences()

```
// preferences helper routines
var app_preferences = new Array();
function init_preferences() {
    // set the list of preferences to read/set
    app_preferences[0] = "magnet_color";
    app_preferences[1] = "magnet_bg_color";
```

```
  app_preferences[2] = "selected_magnet_bg_color";
  app_preferences[3] = "shadow_bg_color";
  app_preferences[4] = "moving_shadow_bg_color";
  app_preferences[5] = "playing_field_bg_color";

  // then get them and apply them as appropriate
  apply_preferences();
}


// manual right now, but could probably be automated
function apply_preferences() {
  read_preferences();

  // set the colors for all the magnets and shadows
  for( var x = 0; x < words.length; x++ ) {
    if( object_name["word" + x] ) {
      object_name["word" + x].set_color(magnet_color);
      object_name["word" + x].set_bg_color(magnet_bg_color);
      object_name["shadow" + x].set_bg_color(shadow_bg_color);
    }
  }
  // set the playing field color
  // workaround for Macintosh platform
  if( object_name["mainlayer"] ) {
  object_name["mainlayer"].set_bg_color(playing_field_bg_color);
  } else {
    setTimeout('
object_name["mainlayer"].set_bg_color(playing_field_bg_color);',
1000);
  }
}


function read_preferences() {
  var setting_str = "";
  var temp_pref;
  var app_pref;
  for(var x = 0; x < app_preferences.length; x++ ) {
    temp_pref = get_preference(app, app_preferences[x]);
    if( temp_pref ) {
      setting_str = app_preferences[x] + " = \"" +
                    temp_pref + "\"";
      eval( setting_str );
    }
  }
}
```

The `init_preferences()` function is called from the application's root initialization function right after the call to `debug_init()`. This is so everything else, including the rest of the main application and all of the other modules, uses these settings as retrieved from the `apply_preferences()` function.

`apply_preferences()`, in turn, calls `read_preferences()`, as you can see in Listing 13-23. The exciting part is where the `eval()` sets each of the variables named by the `app_preferences` array to its preference value as retrieved from the cookies. After this set of functions runs, your colors are set based on the values in the cookies, if there was a value to override the default setting.

Pretty easy, huh? Okay, now let's just add a few more status messages to the application before we go taking any more screenshots.

Working with the Status Bar Module

You've already seen how to use the Status Bar module to print useful and informative messages to the application-specific status bar in Chapter 12, "Other Kinds of Feedback." Now here's a chance to take what you learned out for a spin. The standard color table already uses mouseovers to pass the color string to the highlight routines, so let's start there. Listing 13-24 shows the resulting code, and Figure 13-9 illustrates the effect.

Listing 13-24: Modifying the highlighting functions using the Status Bar module

```
// highlight the color currently under the mouse pointer
function cp_highlight_on(color, c) {
  var f = form_name["colorpicker"];
  var a = f.attribute;
  var i = a.selectedIndex;
  var setting = a.options[i].text;

  cp_place_highlight("color" + c);

  if( status_write ) {
    status_write( "set " + setting + " to " + color );
  }
}


// remove the highlight
function cp_highlight_off() {
  if( status_clear ) {
    status_clear();
  }
  object_name["cphilight"].conceal();
}
```

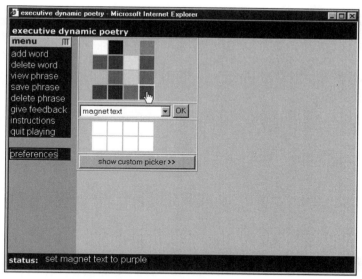

Figure 13-9: Giving the user redundant feedback

Next, let's add status messages to the selection of new colors. Listing 13-25 shows the results, and Figure 13-10 illustrates the feedback mechanism.

Listing 13-25: Adding even more feedback to the application

```
// save the setting based on currently selected option
function cp_save_setting(c) {
  // get selected option
  var f = form_name["colorpicker"];
  var a = f.elements[0];
  var i = a.selectedIndex;
  var setting = a.options[i].text;
  var val = a.options[i].value;
  attribute_settings[i] = cp_colors[c];
  cp_set_selected("color" + c);
  custom_picker_set_color( cp_colors[c] );
  if( status_write ) {
    status_write("saved setting for " + setting +
        " as " + cp_colors[c]);
  }
}
```

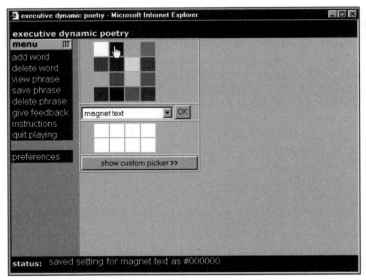

Figure 13-10: Still more status feedback

We don't show you every place we've added status feedback. Suffice it to say that wherever there is a form of visual feedback, such as a highlight or selection, we've added additional text-oriented status feedback.

Adding Preferences Initialization to Application Initialization

We have already discussed to some extent how we added the preferences initialization to the main initialization routine for the application. In Listing 13-26, you can see the entire `executive_poetry_init()` routine, including a twist. In the Shadow Drag module, we had originally called the event capturing routine `set_ netscape_events()`. We've renamed it to `shadow_set_events()` so that it is more specific to the sort of events it is capturing. You can also see that the preferences initialization function is called right after the Debug module's `init` routine is called, so any preferences settings are available to the subsequent modules.

Listing 13-26: Initializing preferences before the rest of the application

```
function executive_poetry_init() {
  debug_init();
  init_preferences();
  init_words();
  menu_debug_init();
```

```
shadow_set_events();  // was set_netscape_events();
status_write("ready to play.");
}
```

In addition to the minor changes to the nomenclature of shadow_drag, we've also defined a menu item (which you can see in the screenshots) that calls a new routine to toggle the color picker. Any future addition to the preferences dialog box should also be added to this routine so that all of the appropriate objects are displayed when users wish to modify their preferences. The style sheet addition is as follows.

```
#menuprefs {
    position: absolute;
    top: 200;
    left: 0;
    width: 107;
    background-color: black;
}
```

This style sheet positions the new menu item DIV just below the debug menu item. The next chapter, "Dynamic Menus," does away with this method of dealing with menus altogether. For now, though, this is the DIV object we've added to the menu:

```
<div id=menuprefs>
<table cellpadding=2 cellspacing=0
        width=107 height=20
        class=bgcolorworkaround>
<tr><td>
<a href="#"
onClick='toggle_color_picker();'>
<span class=menuitem>
preferences</span></a>
</td></tr></table>
</div>
```

The toggle_color_picker() function, as its name suggests, is a simple wrapper function for the existing togglers in the Color Picker module. It only initializes the color picker on the first time through if the color picker has not yet been set up, after which the global variable color_picker_initialized evaluates to true, and the call to the color_picker_init() function is skipped. In addition to the existing togglers, this function also calls the toggle_words() function, so the playing field is cleared away before the preferences screen is displayed.

```
// toggle the color picker
function toggle_color_picker() {
  // initialize the first time through
  if( ! color_picker_initialized ) {
    color_picker_init();
  }
  toggle_words();
  cp_toggle_color_picker();
}
```

That's it! Now all we have to do is test, test, test. For fun, the results of reversing the default colors for the magnets are illustrated in Figure 13-11.

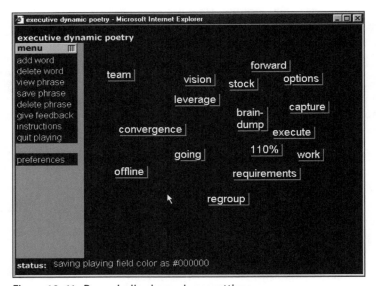

Figure 13-11: Dynamically changed user settings

Testing the Preferences Module

Fortunately, the Preferences module and color picker provide fairly quick and easy testing. If everything works, you should be able to see your color changes the next time around. Also, because the preferences are stored as cookies, you can simply set your browser to notify you before accepting a cookie, and you can examine its contents right then and there to ensure that everything is working the way it should. Figure 13-12 illustrates the Internet Explorer cookies dialog box, storing a new preference. You can see the status message being written to the status bar as well, confirming that the cookie and status message agree.

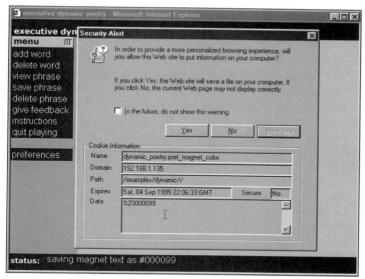

Figure 13-12: Examining cookies in Internet Explorer

The trick to debugging something like this is making sure that you focus on the right level of the process. If the Cookie Handler module is screwing up your cookies, don't spend a lot of time worrying about whether or not you coded the HTML correctly for the pull-down menu. On the other hand, if the cookies, preferences, and status messages all agree on what is being saved, but for some reason your application is not initializing the new settings properly, focus on the application-specific sections of the initialization code.

Testing the Color Picker Itself

First of all, test that the color picker's components are all functioning properly, that the color names match up with their location, that the various layers (cpselected, cphilight, currentcustom, the other custom layer objects, and so on) are displaying correctly, at the correct offsets, and so forth. Check the event handlers to ensure that the appropriate routines are being called, and in the proper order. Verify that custom colors are being added to the custom color array as well as being displayed on the custom color table. Ensure that the Add New and Replace functions are working as they should.

The biggest problem we encountered with the color picker during our own testing was that we had originally developed it using a CSS absolute position of 0,0. When we shifted the app down 30 pixels, we had to track down a lot of flakeys due to assumed zero offsets and so forth. Second in order of irritation during debugging was problems in event handling due to differences in the z-index of the various layers in the new application and that of the color picker. We go into that in more detail in the next section.

Testing Cookie Routines

Because of the relative simplicity of the Cookie Handler module, this one is easy. Set some cookies. Read some cookies. Are they the same? Set a cookie and look at its representation in the `cookies.txt` file or equivalent. Compare and contrast with the version displayed by your browser's confirm dialog box. Set some more cookies. Get a list of all cookies. Are they all there? Set a cookie. Set the same cookie with a different value but the same name. Did it overwrite the old one? Set a cookie with a negative expiration date (in other words, a date that has already passed) and see if it disappears when you restart your browser. See if it disappears right after you set it. (Browser behavior is a bit uneven on this point.) After a while, you not only know more about the internal structure of cookies than you ever wanted to know, but you also have either burned out on cookies entirely and stick to the Preferences module, or you have figured out that you know a better way and have written your own module. Please send a copy to us, if you don't mind.

Testing Using Debug Module

Concerned about the way your application is handling the values of your preferences, say, during initialization? Use the Debug module to print its associated values out to the debugging console (regardless of which one you use) and see what's going wrong. Be careful with the `eval()` statement, as it can give you some strange-looking and unintuitive results. Be sure to test using two different browsers, to isolate any differences in the browser's internal handling of your data. For more information on how to use the Debug module, see the previous chapter, "Other Kinds of Feedback."

A Word about Tab Widgets

We don't use it here, partly due to the fact that this is already a really long chapter, but the preferences dialog box would be an excellent place to use the tab widget. Preferences are often fairly unrelated to one another, but capable of being grouped. For example, the color preferences the user sets here are applied to many different objects within the application. They are grouped together here because the color picker enables us to set their color, and that's it. A dialog box that enables the user to set different preferences settings, such as choosing a default wordlist to start the game up with, or specifying their name and e-mail address for use by the feedback form and in other areas of the application, would be ideal. These dialog boxes could then be hidden, with access to them provided by a tab widget. Look for a full-featured upgrade to the sample application, with enhancements such as this, on the support Web site for the book.

Gotchas

During the course of this chapter, and the corresponding development of the color picker, we tickled more bugs and incompatibilities in the handling of CSS-P, forms, image and other element offsets, event handling, the `eval()` statement, and various other features of dynamic HTML than in any other chapter. Here's a brief summary of some of the things we ran into that you may want to look for as well. We don't claim to have the final word on these, but we will continue to look into the problems we had. If we discover anything new, we will post the explanations on the companion Web site for the book.

♦ For some reason, when we tried to write to `window.status` under Windows 95 in both Internet Explorer and Netscape Navigator 4.0, nothing happened. Even in the standalone color picker test bed we developed before integrating it into the rest of the Dynamic Poetry application this didn't work. Test pages worked fine, but not from within the highlight routines for some reason.

♦ Forms whose elements occupied different z-indexes (where one form and a button were on a layer beneath another form with a different button) didn't work under Internet Explorer, but worked fine under Netscape Navigator. We attribute this to the difference in event handling between IE and Netscape, but whatever it was it seemed to clear up when we set both forms to the same z-index setting.

♦ When we first laid out the tables containing the standard and custom colors in the color picker, we used the entity for a nonbreaking space to flesh out the table cell. Empty table cells do not display their background color. However, when we subsequently added the anchors and event handlers, the single character simply did not provide sufficient coverage for the `onmouseover` event, and two characters screwed up the careful sizing of the table cells. In the end, we settled on a transparent GIF file, in true David Siegel fashion. As white space, we don't like the idea, but as a way to enhance the event handling pleasure of dynamic HTML applications, we could be persuaded.

♦ If the image border CSS properties were supported in both IE and Navigator, we could have done away with the extra layers (`cpselected` and `cphilight`, for example) altogether. Highlighting would have been a simple matter of setting the border color and width.

♦ When reading from an options list, don't forget to read from `value` if you want the actual value of the setting; and from `text` if you want what is being displayed in the pull-down menu itself. Beware of trying to use bare `OPTION` elements, without the accompanying `VALUE`, as the results are less than predictable.

◆ The SRC attribute to the LINK tag is only supported under Navigator. Use HREF. Save yourself hours of frustration, especially if you develop under Navigator to ensure the lowest common denominator, and then copy and paste into other files without checking for Navigator-specific markup.

◆ For some reason, browsers on the Macintosh platform don't always seem to initialize all of the wrapper objects before going on to other code. We had to place a test for the mainlayer object into our preferences initialization to work around this problem. You may find similar behavior in your applications.

◆ Netscape supports the x and y properties of images. In other words, you can read these properties given an image, and find out exactly where on the page it is, similar to the offsetLeft and offsetTop properties of IE. However, IE returns the offset from the next containing object, not relative to the edge of the page. So, you have to walk the hierarchy of containing elements until the offsetParent property is equal to null or undefined, adding the results and returning the sum. Netscape Navigator, however, has no such mechanism for overcoming the fact that its coordinates are always relative to the enclosing layer, at least not if that layer is actually just a DIV positioned with CSS-P. The upshot? No clear cross-platform way to determine the exact location of an image file. Debug until it works, if you're going to use image offsets.

Summary

In this chapter, you learned how to use cookies to store little bits of information on the client computer, and how to abstract that storage into a mechanism for handling the storage of user preferences. Finally, you learned how to use such a mechanism in concert with another module, which enabled you to set user preferences using more advanced DHTML tricks and some goofy workarounds. You also saw yet another example of integrating traditional form elements such as buttons, text fields, and options lists with nontraditional user interface elements such as color pickers and slider bars. This chapter also covered the following:

◆ Understanding the structure and limitations of persistent client-side cookies

◆ Storing and retrieving client-side data using cookies

◆ Using one module as the basis for another, hiding implementation details behind a layer of abstraction

◆ Providing layout-independent centering of layers on top of other elements, such as images, or relative to other elements such as other layers, images, and the document

- Switching back and forth between one set of event handlers and another, and mixing embedded markup event handlers with directly assigned event handlers

- Integrating an independent module/application into another

- Restoring user-configurable application settings on reload

- Dynamically updating application settings using CSS and JavaScript

The next chapter, "Dynamic Menus," discusses how to provide a flexible and configurable mechanism for creating your own menus on the fly and managing menu items and their associated actions.

Chapter 14

Dynamic Menus

IN THIS CHAPTER, you will take another step toward emulating the traditional user interface by learning how to dynamically create menus and expose their items to other functionality within your applications. First, we discuss the mechanisms by which a standalone menu may be dynamically created from a configuration file. Then we integrate the new menu into the Dynamic Poetry application, using it to replace the somewhat limited menu palette you've seen in the previous chapters. Strategies for organizing the functionality you'll want to expose — using the Dynamic Poetry application as an example — are covered. In addition, you will learn how to manage your menu items so as to keep in sync with your application's state. Along the way, we touch on the use of keyboard events, but we really don't dive into that topic until the next chapter. So, without further ado, let's begin.

The Dynamic Menu Module

The Dynamic Menu module is really quite simple, like many of our other examples. Using DHTML objects as primitive screen objects representing the elements of our user interface, we build a functional system and integrate it into the application. However, this module differs from previous modules in that it uses a JavaScript configuration file with a nested structure based on object properties, rather than a simple JavaScript array. It is also the first module we look at that combines the use of both mouse and keyboard event handlers, although we save the gory details of managing keyboard input until the next chapter. Perhaps most importantly, the Dynamic Menu module illustrates certain architectural characteristics of good GUI-based applications. By encapsulating the functionality of your application behind a commonly understood interface component, you not only leverage users' previous familiarity with the interface, but also provide a level of control over the application's functionality that other interface components might lack.

Required HTML Objects

In a perfect world, any GUI toolkit would provide a complete set of API calls that expose functionality to the programmer. Because this is not a perfect world, you have to make do with simple objects, using them as elemental building blocks to create what you need. Building the components of the Dynamic Menu module requires little beyond the module itself, a configuration file, and a placeholder DIV object for the menu bar. If you recall from the previous chapter, placeholder DIV objects enable you to position other objects relative to the placeholder. In effect, this gives you a way to let the browser define the width of the object itself using style sheets and other mechanisms. From there, you can piggyback yourself the rest of the way. In this case, we use a CSS style sheet to define the initial width and height of the menu bar. Such style definitions could be embedded within the place-holder's markup using STYLE attributes or, in some cases, using TABLE markup to set the width using a percentage. For this application, however, style sheets seem like the best way to go. The placeholder in this case is extremely simple:

```
<div id="menubarstub"></div>
```

There is no markup internal to the placeholder, or *stub*, object. It simply uses the CSS property definitions found in the externally referenced style sheet:

```
#menubarstub {
  position: absolute;
  top: 0;
  left: 0;
  width: 600;
  height: 20;
  visibility: visible;
}
```

This style sheet is included in the document via the usual method:

```
<link rel="stylesheet" type="text/css"
    href="/css/dynamic_menu.css">
```

Okay, now that we've defined the area our menu bar occupies using the stub, we can go ahead and create the actual menu bar object, the menu labels, and the menu items themselves. Because our dynamic menus are created on the fly using a configuration file, we need to be careful to perform the initialization *before* the document is fully loaded in Internet Explorer, and *after* the document has fully loaded in Netscape Navigator. We can accomplish the former by way of the following markup, inserted at the very end of the BODY of our document:

```
<script language="JavaScript">
create_base_objects();
if( navigator.appName != "Netscape" ) {
  menu_init(my_menu_defs, my_help_menu_defs);
}
</script>
```

Note that we call our `create_base_objects()` routine before we initialize the new menus, so that both browsers have access to the menu bar stub wrapper object. Navigator does not enable the creation of new Layer objects until the document has fully loaded, so we place our initialization for Navigator into the BODY onLoad handler definition:

```
<body bgcolor="#999999"
      onLoad='if(navigator.appName == "Netscape" )
menu_init(my_menu_defs, my_help_menu_defs);'>
```

We have already called the `create_base_objects()` routine from within the SCRIPT element, so there is no need to call it again here. For the sake of aesthetics, if nothing else, we've also used a BGCOLOR attribute to set the document's background color. As always, this could have been done just as easily inside the CSS style sheet. Enjoy the flexibility of dynamic HTML when you can.

Initializing the Menus

The `menu_init()` function, shown in Listing 14-1, simply collects the various other initialization functions together and calls them in order. First, the menu bar itself is initialized using `menu_init_menubar()`, passing the menu definitions (`menu_defs`) and Help menu definitions (`menu_help_defs`) as arguments. These definitions are set in the configuration file, `dyn_menu_config.js`, which we talk about in more detail later. For now, it is sufficient to recognize that the menu definitions determine the label text and function to be called when the user selects the menu, as well as other information such as keyboard shortcuts.

The definitions for both the regular menus and Help menu must be passed as arguments as they contain each menu's label text, which is used to create the menu label visible on the menu bar. Second, the menu items themselves are initialized using the `menu_init_menu_items()` function, passing just the menu definitions as

an argument. Third, the Help menu is initialized, if needed, using a call to
menu_init_help_menu(), passing just the Help menu definitions as an argument.
The flag menu_help_flag may be defined in the application if you do not want to
use the Help menu. The global variables define default colors, font sizes, and other
style information, as well as flags and version information for the Dynamic Menu
module itself. Note that the variable used to set the z-index of the menu components is defined more or less arbitrarily. When we integrate the module into a real
application, we can define this variable relative to the z-index of our other layers.

Listing 14-1: The menu_init() JavaScript function

```
var menu_version = "$Revision: 1.4 $";
var menu_module_initialized = false;
var menu_bar_initialized = false;
var menu_help_initialized = false;
var menu_items_initialized = false;
var menu_help_flag = true;

var menu_color = "#000000";
var menu_bgcolor = "#FFFFFF";
var menu_hilight_color = "#99FFFF";
var menu_disabled_color = "#CCCCCC";
var menu_font_size = "12pt";
var menu_font_weight = "plain";
var menu_font_family = "Arial,Helvetica,Espy,Geneva,Sans-Serif";
var menu_item_indent = 15;
var menu_z_index = 1000; // arbitrary

var menu = new Array();
var menu_item = new Array();
var menu_active = null;

function menu_init(menu_defs, menu_help_defs) {
  // initialize menubar if needed
  if( ! menu_bar_initialized ) {
    menu_init_menubar(menu_defs);
  }
  // initialize remaining menus
  if( ! menu_items_initialized ) {
    menu_init_menu_items(menu_defs);
  }
  // initialize help menu if needed
  if( menu_help_flag && ( ! menu_help_initialized )) {
    menu_init_help_menu(menu_help_defs);
  }
  menu_module_initialized = true;
}
```

The `menu` array is used to store information about each menu — its label text, items, and style information. The `menu_item` array is used in a similar fashion to store the item label text, alternate label text, keyboard shortcuts, and style information. When everything has been initialized, the `menu_module_initialized` flag is set to `true`.

Initializing the Menu Bar and Menu Labels

The `menu_init_menubar()` function, shown in Listing 14-2, creates the objects for each menu's label and sets up `onClick` event handlers that toggle the menus when the user clicks them. First, the cross-browser wrapper function `set_window_width()` is called to initialize the `winWidth` variable based on the current width of the screen. This variable is then used to stretch the stub object to the current width of the window, and its background color is set, leaving a full-window menu bar. Next, each menu label object is created, using the menu definitions passed as the argument to the function. When the `menu_create_menu()` function, shown in Listing 14-3, is passed a name (the same as the text used for the label) and the markup for the object, it creates an object called `menu[name]`. The first menu label object is overlaid on top of the menu bar in its northwest corner. Subsequent menu label objects are abutted to the previous object, thereby spacing them out a bit and lining them up along the menu bar. The function sets their z-index so they are in front of the menu bar, and their clip height is set to the height of the menu bar itself. The same process is performed for each of the Help menu items if the `menu_help_flag` variable is set to `true`. Finally, the menu bar's height and clipping region is set. This compensates for the possibility that the menu labels are taller than the original menu bar due to the use of larger font sizes, and gives the entire menu bar a consistent appearance.

Listing 14-2: The menu_init_menubar() JavaScript function

```
function menu_init_menubar(menu_defs) {
  // set menubarstub to width of current window
  set_window_width();
  var menubar = object_name["menubarstub"];
  menubar.set_clipper_right( winWidth );
  menubar.set_width( winWidth );
  menubar.set_bg_color( menu_bgcolor );

  var last_label = null;
  for( var x = 0; x < menu_defs.length; x++ ) {
    var label = menu_defs[x].name;
    var m = '<table class="menulabel">';
    m += '<tr>';
    m += '<td>'; // class="menulabel">";
    m += '<a href="#" ';
    m += ' onClick=\'menu_toggle("' + label + '");\'';
    m += '>' + label + '</a>';
```

```
    m += '</td>';
    m += '</tr></table>';
    menu_create_menu(label, m);
    if( x == 0 ) {
      menu[label].overlay(object_name["menubarstub"], "NW", 2);
    } else {
      menu[label].abut(last_label, "E", "TOP", 20);
    }
    last_label = menu[label];
    menu[label].set_z_index(menu_z_index + 1);
    menu[label].set_height( menu[label].clipper_height() );
    menu[label].reveal();
  }

  // use Help menu?
  if( menu_help_flag ) {
    var hlabel = '<table class="menulabelhelp" width=100%>';
    hlabel += '<tr>';
    hlabel += '<td align="right">';
    hlabel += '<a href="#" ';
    hlabel += ' onClick=\'menu_toggle("Help");\'';
    hlabel += '>Help</a>';
    hlabel += '</td>';
    hlabel += '</tr></table>';
    menu_create_menu("Help", hlabel);
    menu["Help"].overlay(object_name["menubarstub"], "NE", 2);
    menu["Help"].set_z_index(menu_z_index + 1);
    menu["Help"].reveal();
  }

  // set the clip on the menubar - on IE, we need to also set
  // the height property or it doesn't quite take...
  var label_bottom = last_label.top() + last_label.height();
  object_name["menubarstub"].set_clipper_bottom( label_bottom );
  object_name["menubarstub"].set_height( label_bottom );
  menu_bar_initialized = true;
}
```

A couple of things are worth noting here. First, we had originally used the CSS classes menulabel and menuhelplabel, shown in Listing 14-4, in both the <TABLE> and <TD> markup for the menu label object. We did this so we could define the general characteristics of all table cells by way of a cascading effect from the <TABLE> element, and then override them in those cells that required it. This makes a lot more sense in the context of the menu items, where there is more than one cell in each table. Unfortunately, the urge to cut and paste led to problems. Internet Explorer doesn't deal well with elements that nest but use the same CSS properties. It did not work at all in Navigator when the styles were only applied to the table cell, so we had to move the CLASS attribute to the TABLE, solving the problem in both browsers. Note that the only significant difference between the two definitions is that the Help menu label is right-aligned, whereas the other uses the browser default, which is left-align.

Second, if the height of the menu bar object is not set explicitly, Internet Explorer uses the height value set in the style sheet rather than the actual clipping region. In other words, the height of an object in IE is not calculated using the clipping region, despite the fact that the visible area of the object has been altered. On the Macintosh, IE does not support clipping at all.

Listing 14-3: The menu_create_menu() JavaScript function

```
function menu_create_menu(name, contents) {
  var new_menu = menu_create(name, contents);
  menu[name] = new base_object( new_menu );
  var real_name = menu[name].name;
  menu[real_name] = menu[name];
  menu[name].items = new Array();
  menu[name].set_color(menu_color);
  menu[name].set_bg_color(menu_bgcolor);
  menu[name].conceal();
}
```

The menu_create_menu() function, like its counterpart menu_create_item(), is basically a wrapper for the menu_create() function, which does the dirty work of actually writing the new DIV or LAYER and returning a reference to the newly created object. The menu_create_menu() function then uses the cross-browser API function base_object() to create the cross-browser wrapper object. We talk more about menu_create() later when we look at the menu_create_item() function.

The variable real_name is used because Netscape Navigator returns a string such as _js_layer_1 when a new Layer object is created, and there is no way to name the Layer at the time it is being created. The use of the real_name variable ensures that the object menu[name] is accessible either by the name we have given it or by the name Navigator gave the layer, in case we need to determine which layer we are dealing with at some later date and we don't have the layer's name handy.

The resulting menu object is then styled and concealed, but not before the array items is created as a place to store a list of the items that the menu contains.

Listing 14-4: The CSS style sheet used to define the regular menu and Help menu labels

```
.menulabel {
  position: absolute;
  top: 0;
  left: 0;
  width: 50;
  height: 20;
  font-family: Arial,Helvetica,Espy,Geneva,Sans-Serif;
  font-weight: bold;
  font-size: 14pt;
}

.menulabelhelp {
  position: absolute;
  top: 0;
  left: 0;
  width: 50;
  height: 20;
  font-family: Arial,Helvetica,Espy,Geneva,Sans-Serif;
  font-weight: bold;
  font-size: 14pt;
  text-align: right;
}
```

The initialized menu bar, as seen in Navigator, is illustrated in Figure 14-1. You can see that the mouse pointer has turned into a hand to signify that the label may be clicked. One feature of CSS2 already implemented in Internet Explorer, but not in Navigator, is the ability to define the icon used to represent the cursor. Because it is not supported across browser platforms, we don't talk about it in this book. If your target audience is using IE, however, you may want to consider using that mechanism where appropriate.

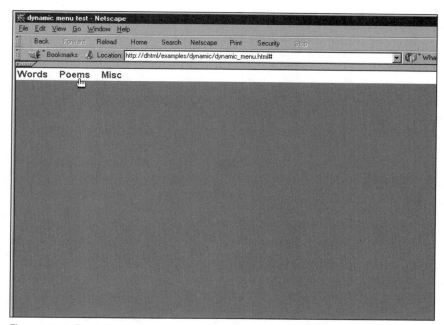

Figure 14-1: The initialized menu bar in Navigator, with three menus and Help menu

Initializing the Menu Items

After the menu labels have been created, it is time to create the items for each menu. This is performed by the `menu_init_menu_items()` JavaScript function shown in Listing 14-5, which basically loops over the set of menu items defined in the configuration file, creates `menu_item` objects, registers each item with its parent menu, and then registers its associated handler and keyboard shortcut, if any. Finally, the items are positioned. The first item in each menu is positioned below the menu label, and subsequent items are positioned below the previous item using the `abut()` method. If any of the items have alternate text, a menu item object is created for that alternate item as well, and it is positioned in the same place as the default item. We also register alternate items' keyboard shortcuts and handlers. The z-index for each item is set, with the alternate menu items set just behind the default menu items.

Listing 14-5: The menu_init_menu_items() JavaScript function

```
function menu_init_menu_items(defs) {
  var name, label, alt_name, last_item, items;
  for( var i = 0; i < defs.length; i++ ) {
    items = defs[i].items;
    label = defs[i].name;
    for( var j = 0; j < items.length; j++ ) {
      name = menu_create_item(items[j]);
      menu_register_item(label, name);
      menu_register_handler(name, items[j].handler);
      menu_register_shortcut(items[j].key, items[j].handler);
      if( j == 0 ) {
        menu_item[name].abut(menu[label], "S", "LEFT", 0);
      } else {
        menu_item[name].abut(last_item, "S", "LEFT", 0);
      }
      menu_item[name].set_z_index(menu_z_index);
      last_item = menu_item[name];
      if( items[j].alt ) {
        alt_name = menu_create_item(items[j], "alt");
        menu_register_item(label, alt_name);
        menu_register_handler(alt_name, items[j].handler);
        menu_register_shortcut(items[j].key, items[j].handler);
        menu_item[alt_name].overlay(last_item, "NW", 0);
        menu_item[alt_name].set_z_index(menu_z_index - 1);
        menu_item[name].toggled = false;
      }
    }
  }
  menu_items_initialized = true;
}
```

The function menu_create_item(), shown in Listing 14-6, is very similar to the menu_create_menu() function, shown in Listing 14-3, but with a few key differences. First of all, it may be called with one or two arguments. The first argument, as with many of the functions we've seen so far, is a reference to the menu definitions provided by the configuration file. The second argument, alt, is a string that is used to differentiate the alternate menu item object from the default menu item object.

The variable alt is initialized to the empty string, if not passed explicitly, to prevent the creation of menus named MyMenuMyItemundefined that would result if alt were not defined. The function menu_item_markup() is called with the name and alt variables as arguments, and it returns the necessary markup for the menu item. The function menu_create() is then called, and returns a reference to the new DIV object or LAYER, which is used to create the cross-browser wrapper object. The rest is pretty much the same as menu_create_menu().

 In this example, we always use the string alt, and in fact make a foolhardy assumption that the string is always the same. In more robust applications, this would have been a global variable to allow for language differences. For example, it is possible that your application may require multilingual support, and the menu definitions in the configuration file may include labels and menu item definitions in those languages. Because the alternate menu item name is pretty well hidden inside the application (a user is unlikely to ask for it by name), this doesn't present much of a problem. In other circumstances, however, it might.

Listing 14-6: The menu_create_item() JavaScript function

```
function menu_create_item(defs, alt) {
  if( ! alt ) alt = "";
  var markup = menu_item_markup(defs, alt);
  var name = defs.menu + defs.label + alt;
  var new_item = menu_create(name, markup);
  menu_item[name] = new base_object( new_item );
  var real_name = menu_item[name].name;
  menu_item[real_name] = menu_item[name];
  menu_item[name].set_color(menu_color);
  menu_item[name].set_bg_color(menu_bgcolor);
  menu_item[name].conceal();
  return name;
}
```

The menu_create() function, shown in Listing 14-7, in a rare show of browser-specific behavior, creates a new DIV if the document.all collection is supported (as with Internet Explorer), and creates a Layer object if not. A more formidable application would also test to see if the document.layers object was supported as well, instead of just making the either/or assumption. Anyway, enough harping on unsound software design strategies. The interesting thing about the IE-specific branch of this function is the way that it writes a new DIV object to the browser, using the document.all.tags("DIV") collection to get a reference to all of the DIV objects, and then grabs the last of those objects and returns. Because the latest DIV object to have been created would have been the one that we just wrote, this returns the appropriate reference.

Listing 14-7: The menu_create() JavaScript function

```
function menu_create(name, contents) {
  if( document.all ) {
    var the_div = '<div id="' + name + '" ' +
      ' class="menucontainer">' + contents + '</div>';
    document.open("text/html");
    document.writeln( the_div );
    document.close();

    var all_divs = document.all.tags("DIV");
    var new_m = all_divs[all_divs.length - 1];
  } else {
    var new_m = new Layer(1);
    new_m.document.open("text/html");
    new_m.document.writeln( contents );
    new_m.document.close();
  }
  return new_m;
}
```

The style sheet used by the menu object is shown here:

```
.menucontainer {
  position: absolute;
  top: 0;
  left: 0;
  width: 50;
  height: 20;
  font-family: Arial,Helvetica,Espy,Geneva,Sans-Serif;
  font-weight: plain;
  font-size: 14pt;
  padding: 0;
}
```

The Netscape Navigator branch of the function doesn't wrap the new object's contents in DIV markup, because we pass the Layer itself to the cross-browser object wrapper function base_object(). Using DIV markup here would only confuse matters.

We isolated the code that produces the markup for menu items into its own function, menu_item_markup(), shown in Listing 14-8. Separating the code like this enables the programmer to keep the higher-level code more legible. All we need to know is that we are dealing with a block of markup—to stick 40 lines of relatively unrelated string handling into the higher-level code makes it difficult to keep straight what the higher-level code is supposed to do.

The original version of this module used a nested approach to the problem of handling menu/menu item collections. The menu initialization function actually created a menu container that itself contained nested DIV objects. However, Navigator appears not to recognize DIV objects correctly when they are children of a LAYER. The approach we used, looping over the entire list of items, creating DIV markup for each, and then writing the entire shooting match to a new LAYER object, failed miserably. For whatever reason, even DIVs positioned using CSS-P were not recognized by their name in Navigator. So we took a somewhat less efficient, but still effective, approach.

The function first figures out what name to give the new DIV object by concatenating the name of the item's menu, its label, and its type (alt, if the item is an alternate). Then, the object's markup is constructed by concatenating strings together. The onMouseOver, onMouseOut, and onMouseUp event handlers are assigned, such that the item is highlighted when the mouse passes over the item, returned to its regular state when the mouse passes out of the item, and the handler registered with the item is called when the user clicks and then releases the mouse button.

Internet Explorer does not capture the onmouseup event when the user lets up on the mouse button outside the menu item, whereas Netscape Navigator does. One method for dealing with this problem is to release the event capture for Event.MOUSEUP when the user mouses outside of the menu item, but this is left as an exercise for the reader.

The table markup contains a cell for the menu item text and another containing a representation of the keyboard shortcut. The entire string is then returned to the calling function.

Listing 14–8: The menu_item_markup() JavaScript function

```
function menu_item_markup(the_item, type) {
  // create and return the menu item markup
  var menu = the_item.menu;
  var name = menu + the_item.label;
  if( type == "alt" ) {
    var text = the_item.alt;
  } else {
    var text = the_item.text;
  }
```

```
    var handler = the_item.handler;
    var key = the_item.key;

    var the_div = '<div id="' + name + type + '"';
    the_div += ' onMouseOver="menu_item_hilight(null,this);"';
    the_div += ' onMouseOut="menu_item_lolight(null,this);"';
    the_div += ' onMouseUp="menu_do_action(null,this);"';
    the_div += ' class="menuitemdiv">';
    the_div += '<table width=150 border=0';
    the_div += ' cellpadding=0 cellspacing=0>';
    the_div += '<tr>';
    the_div += '<td class="menuitem" nowrap>' + text + '</td>';
    the_div += '<td class="menukey">' + key + '</td>';
    the_div += '</tr></table>';
    the_div += '</div>';

    return the_div;
}
```

Notice that in the previous function we have formatted the markup so that individual event handlers and HTML tags are on their own lines, for the most part. This makes it easy to comment out individual handlers during testing without having to ensure that the tags are all properly closed, as the event handler or table cell is the only thing on a given line.

Listing 14-9 shows the style sheets used by the menu_item_markup() function.

Listing 14-9: The CSS style sheets used by menu items

```
.menuitemdiv {
  position: absolute;
  top: 0;
  left: 0;
  width: 50;
  height: 10;
  font-family: Arial,Helvetica,Espy,Geneva,Sans-Serif;
  font-weight: plain;
  font-size: 10pt;
  padding: 0;
}

.menuitem {
  text-align: left;
  font-family: Arial,Helvetica,Espy,Geneva,Sans-Serif;
  font-weight: plain;
  font-size: 12pt;
```

```
    padding: 0;
}

.menukey {
    text-align: right;
    font-family: Arial,Helvetica,Espy,Geneva,Sans-Serif;
    font-weight: plain;
    font-size: 12pt;
    padding: 0;
}
```

Registering the Item

When an item is created from the loop inside menu_init_menu_items(), shown in Listing 14-5, it registers its associated handler and keyboard shortcut with the application, as well as registering itself with its parent menu. This registration is performed by the functions menu_register_item(), menu_register_handler(), and menu_register_shortcut(). The first of these functions, shown in Listing 14-10, simply adds the name of the item to its parent menu object's items array. It then sets the name of the item's menu property to the name of the menu with which it is registered. This enables the menu object to know which items "belong" to it, as well as enabling the menu item itself to determine its parent. This structure more or less duplicates that which would have been provided by nesting the items within a menu container, but virtually, rather than by way of an actual parent/child relationship within the document object model hierarchy.

Listing 14-10: The menu_register_item() JavaScript function

```
function menu_register_item(the_menu, the_item) {
    var len = menu[the_menu].items.length;
    menu[the_menu].items[len] = the_item;
    menu_item[the_item].menu = the_menu;
}
```

The second function, shown in Listing 14-11, is more involved in that it not only registers the handler and keyboard shortcut as properties of the item, but it must also set the event handlers for each event. Bear in mind that the handler being registered is actually a JavaScript function that is called when the user selects the menu item, not a true JavaScript event handler. In any case, if the browser is Navigator (or another browser that supports the document.layers array), the appropriate event capturing methods are set. If the browser is IE, the appropriate event handlers are assigned to the item. All items are considered enabled upon initialization on the assumption that the enclosing application disables them when necessary as part of the regular course of the session. It might be useful, in those cases where the majority of the items are disabled on startup, to provide a Boolean flag that is checked to see whether the items should be enabled by default or not.

Listing 14-11: The menu_register_handler() JavaScript function

```
function menu_register_handler(the_item, handler) {
  var i = menu_item[the_item];
  i.handler = handler;
  i.enabled = true;

  if( document.layers ) {
    if( document.layers[i.name] ) {
      document.layers[i.name].captureEvents(Event.MOUSEUP |
                                            Event.MOUSEOUT |
                                            Event.MOUSEOVER);
      document.layers[i.name].onmouseover = menu_item_hilight;
      document.layers[i.name].onmouseout = menu_item_lolight;
      document.layers[i.name].onmouseup = menu_do_action;
    }
  } else {
    eval("document.all." + the_item +
         ".onmouseover = menu_item_hilight");
    eval("document.all." + the_item +
         ".onmouseout = menu_item_lolight");
    eval("document.all." + the_item +
         ".onmouseup = menu_do_action");
  }
}
```

The `menu_item_hilight()`, `menu_item_lolight()`, and `menu_do_action()` routines are covered later in the chapter. Suffice it to say that for now the item has been properly initialized so that any function, when passed a reference to the item, can determine its handler, keyboard shortcut, and status simply by reading a property of the object.

The issue of keyboard shortcut handling is complex due to the manner in which the different browsers (and the GUI toolkits that they are built with) handle keyboard input. On Windows, the events generated when a key is pressed always pass the value of the key and its modifiers. However, on Solaris, Netscape Navigator does not support keystroke events unless the object to which the event is sent contains an object that supports such events. This makes it difficult to manage keyboard input across platforms. We discuss these issues in depth, as well as the functions required to deal with them, in the next chapter. For now, let's just register the appropriate key as a handler for the item, and figure out how to deal with it later.

The `menu_register_shortcut()` function, shown in Listing 14-12, relies on the `kb_register_shortcut()` function discussed in the next chapter. The configuration file for the menus and their associated items enables the programmer to specify certain modifier keys that should be checked for in the event (pardon the pun) of a keystroke. For this example, we use the plus character (+) to represent Shift, the caret (^) character to represent Ctrl, and the at sign (@) to represent Alt. Shortcuts may be defined in such a way as to require multiple modifier keys in addition to the alphanumeric key that generates the keystroke event. When registering the shortcut, therefore, we test for the presence of each modifier symbol and pass appropriate Boolean values for each modifier, as well as the numeric ASCII value of the key, to the keyboard input registration function. In addition, we pass the handler that should be invoked when the keystroke event is generated, so that the `kb_register_short-cut()` function knows what to do when the appropriate shortcut is invoked.

Listing 14-12: The menu_register_shortcut() JavaScript function

```
function menu_register_shortcut(k, h) {
  // k should be "@+^A" or some combination thereon
  var shift = (k.indexOf("+") != -1) ? true : false;
  var alt = (k.indexOf("@") != -1) ? true : false;
  var control = (k.indexOf("^") != -1) ? true : false;
  var key_chr = k.charCodeAt(k.length -1);
  kb_register_shortcut(key_chr, shift, alt, control, h);
}
```

By now, the entire menu structure and all of its items have been initialized. Figure 14-2 shows the menu bar in Navigator, along with one of the menus revealed via a mouse click.

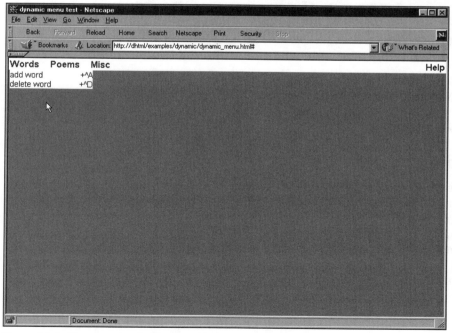

Figure 14-2: The menu bar in Netscape Navigator, with one of its menus revealed

The same thing is shown in Figure 14-3, only in this case we see the Internet Explorer version. Note that the menu labels are much larger and aligned with the bottom of the menu bar, as opposed to their appearance in Navigator.

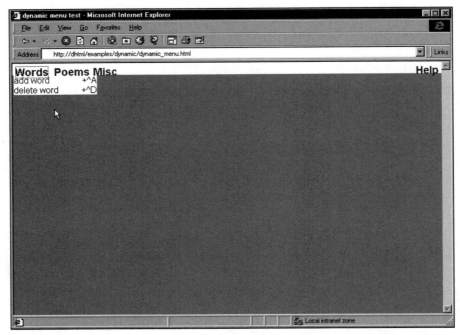

Figure 14-3: The menu bar in Internet Explorer, with one of its menus revealed

Now that the menu bar, menu labels, menu items, and their alternates are all initialized, and their handlers and keyboard shortcuts registered, we're ready to talk about how the module itself works when integrated into the application.

Adding a New Item

One aspect of menus not explicitly covered here is being able to add a new item or menu on the fly during the course of an application session. All of the routines you need to do so are discussed in this chapter, but we have not implemented an API function that specifically enables this kind of thing because the example application does not require it. However, because it is likely that this is required by someone's application, here are the steps you would take to define a new menu and menu items on the fly.

1. Define the menu and menu items, including the menu's name or label, and any handlers and keyboard shortcuts that you would like to associate with the item.

2. Call `menu_create_menu()` with the menu's label and markup.

3. Call the `abut()` method of the new menu object, aligning it with the last menu.

4. Set the menu object's height and z-index appropriately.

5. Call `menu_create_item()` iteratively, passing each item as an argument.

6. Call `menu_register_item()` for each menu item, passing its label and parent menu name.

7. Call `menu_register_handler()` for each item, passing the parent menu name and handler.

8. Call `menu_register_shortcut()` with the key and handler as arguments.

9. Call the `abut()` method of each item, placing it below the previous item.

10. Do the same with each item's alternate, only place the item object beneath the default item and set the alternate item's `toggled` property to `false`.

Inserting a new menu item into an existing menu is a matter of figuring out where you want the new item positioned in the menu, and repositioning each subsequent item relative to the new item. You still need to register all of the items' characteristics (handler, shortcut, parent, and so on) appropriately in addition to creating the menu item object itself. You also need to be careful not to name your items in such a way as to overwrite an existing object.

Collapsing and Expanding Menus

The first few things that you want any application to be able to do with a menu are taken care of by the Dynamic Menu module already. When the user clicks the menu label, the menu is revealed. When the user clicks again, the menu is hidden. Also, if a menu is exposed when a user clicks a different menu, that menu is hidden and the new menu is exposed. This implements an interface characteristic sometimes known as *stickiness*, meaning that a menu stays visible until the user explicitly clicks to hide it or display another. The fact that the menu is toggled by way of a mouse click is a result of the `onClick` event handler defined in `menu_init_menubar()`. The event handler calls the function `menu_toggle()`, shown in Listing 14-13, with the name of the menu label that was clicked.

Listing 14-13: The menu_toggle() JavaScript function

```
function menu_toggle(name) {
  if( menu_active == name ) {
    menu_conceal(name);
  } else {
    menu_reveal(name);
  }
}
```

The function simply checks to see if the menu that was clicked is the active (revealed) menu, and if so, hides it. If not, it reveals the menu. The functions that actually do the showing and hiding are shown in Listing 14-14. The functions are the exact opposite of each other, so we just discuss their general characteristics. First of all, the routines check to see if a menu is currently being displayed. If so, it is either hidden or shown, depending on the purpose of the function. Then, each of the menu's items are shown or hidden. The functions also check the `toggled` property of each item to see if the alternate menu item is supposed to be visible or not. The `menu_active` variable that we saw in the previous function is used to determine if any menus are visible, and is also set appropriately.

Listing 14-14: The menu_reveal() and menu_conceal() JavaScript functions

```
function menu_reveal(name) {
  if( menu_active ) {
    menu_conceal(menu_active);
    menu_active = false;
  }
  // reveal the items
  var items = menu[name].items;
  for( var x = 0; x < items.length; x++ ) {
    var def = items[x];
    var alt = items[x] + "alt";
    if( menu_item[def].toggled ) {
      menu_item[alt].reveal();
    } else {
      menu_item[def].reveal();
    }
  }
  // set menu_active
  menu_active = name;
}

function menu_conceal(name) {
  // conceal the items
  var items = menu[name].items;
```

```
for( var x = 0; x < items.length; x++ ) {
  var def = items[x];
  var alt = items[x] + "alt";
  if( menu_item[def].toggled ) {
    menu_item[alt].conceal();
  } else {
    menu_item[def].conceal();
  }
}
// set menu_active
menu_active = false;
}
```

Color Changes and Other Event-Driven Behavior

The user must be able to tell which menu item they are currently mousing over in order to know when to click or release the mouse to activate the appropriate item. One method, used more or less universally by mainstream windowing environments, is to toggle the menu item from its default color to another. Our Dynamic Menu module approximates this behavior by assigning the functions `menu_item_hilight()` and `menu_item_lolight()` to the `onmouseover` and `onmouseout` event handlers for each item, respectively. These functions are shown in Listing 14-15. The functions may either be called by way of an HTML event handler or as the result of being assigned directly to the event handlers for the object using JavaScript. In the first instance, the first argument is explicitly defined as `null` to override the default behavior of assigned event handlers, which is to pass the event object as the first argument. The second argument is the special JavaScript variable `this`, which represents the object in question. The first function changes the background color of the object to whatever color was defined for the `menu_hilight_color` variable, and the second returns the object to its default background color.

Listing 14-15: The menu_item_hilight() and menu_item_lolight() JavaScript functions

```
function menu_item_hilight(e,i) {
  i = i || this;
  var the_item = menu_item[i.id];
  the_item.set_bg_color( menu_hilight_color );
}

function menu_item_lolight(e,i) {
  i = i || this;
  var the_item = menu_item[i.id];
  the_item.set_bg_color( menu_bgcolor );
}
```

The behavior can be seen in Figure 14-4, where the user has moused over the first menu item and its background color has changed from white to cyan.

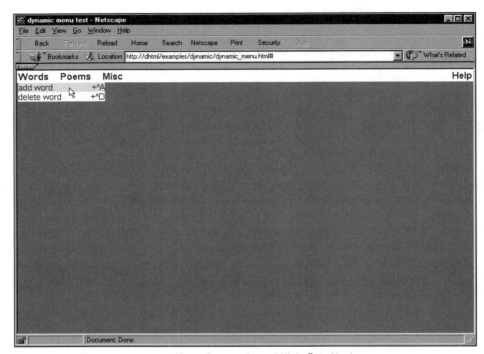

Figure 14–4: The onmouseover effect of menu_item_hilight() in Navigator

State Changes

From time to time, it is necessary for an application to disable a menu item temporarily. Usually, this is shown by graying out the menu item text to suggest that the menu item is not necessarily permanently disabled, but is currently unavailable. Any application using the Dynamic Menu module can disable any menu item by calling the menu_item_disable() method shown in Listing 14-16. This function simply sets the text color for the item to the value of the menu_disabled_color variable and sets the item's enabled property to false.

Listing 14-16: The menu_item_disable() JavaScript function

```
function menu_item_disable() {
  // set text color to "gray"
  this.color = menu_disabled_color;
  // disable action
```

```
    this.enabled = false;
}
```

So what good does it do to go through all of this mess without having the item actually do something when invoked? The onmouseup event handler for every item calls the function menu_do_action(), shown in Listing 14-17. The function first checks to see if the object that called it exists, returns if not, and then grabs a reference to the appropriate menu_item object, using the id attribute of the object that called it. The item is checked to see if it is actually enabled using the enabled property, and if so, it runs the core JavaScript function eval() on the item's handler. A more robust implementation would also check to ensure that the handler was defined, that the handler as defined was actually a JavaScript function available to the current application, and so forth. For the purposes of demonstration, however, the function just produces an alert containing the name of the handler. We remove this alert when we integrate the module into our example application. After invoking the handler, we cancel event bubbling in IE and hide the currently visible menu.

Listing 14-17: The menu_do_action() JavaScript function

```
function menu_do_action(e,i) {
  i = i || this;
  if( !i ) return;
  var the_item = menu_item[i.id];
  if( the_item.enabled ) {
    //eval(the_item.handler + "");
    alert("handler: " + the_item.handler);
  }
  // cancel event bubbling in IE
  if( window.event ) {
    window.event.cancelBubble = true;
  }
  // hide menu
  var the_menu = the_item.menu;
  menu_toggle(the_menu);
}
```

An example of the menu_do_action() function in action may be seen in Figure 14-5. The user has clicked the "delete poem" menu item, and the browser has responded by popping up an alert dialog box containing the name of the handler associated with that item, in this case prep_delete_phrase_form().

Armed with these tools, we're ready to integrate our dynamic menu into the example application.

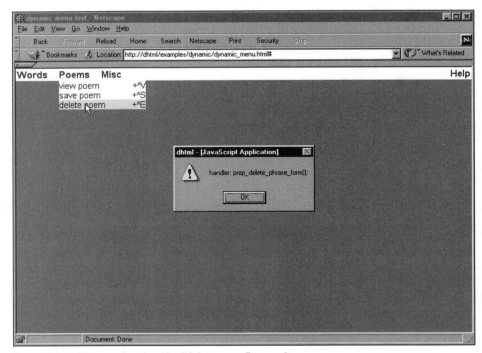

Figure 14-5: The user invokes the "delete poem" menu item

Integrating the Dynamic Menu Module into the Application

Because the whole point behind a menu interface is to provide access to application functionality, the definition of each menu and their items is highly application-dependent. In the example code you've seen previously, we've taken the liberty of assuming that the menu is used in our Dynamic Poetry sample application. Based on the early menu palette interface and the functions it exposed, we've defined our menus around those sets of functionality. Because we are now using drop-down menus to group related functions, however, the organization is a bit different. We've also done a little renaming of the menu items themselves, abandoning the previous term "phrase" for the more user-friendly (and appropriate) "poem." We get into exactly how we define the menus and their associated items in a minute, but first let's look at the positioning of the menu bar and menu items.

Defining Positioning

The menu bar itself is easily defined, as it abuts the top of the window by convention. Some applications may require a more flexible menu bar, such as is found in

Windows 95 and Windows 98, where the user can drag the menu to any of the four sides of the root window, but we do not provide that capability in this module. Refer back to the style sheets listed previously, as they define the positioning for all of our elements. For the most part, however, the Dynamic Menu module takes care of positioning the menu bar, labels, and items by itself. We use CSS-P merely to ensure that the menu objects are accessible via our cross-browser wrapper library.

Defining the List of Menu Items

Perhaps the two most arduous tasks confronting the interface developer when having to deal with menus are the following:

- Figuring out how to label the menus themselves

- Deciding what items go with what menu

Because this can be a somewhat circular process (grouping the menu items by function and then assigning them a menu of their own, or deciding what basic high-level functions are available and then associating each function with the appropriate menu), interface designers tend to hold one of two opinions on the matter. The first is the approach dictated by Apple in their *User Interface Guidelines*, which mandates the use of a few standard menus (such as File, Edit, and the Help or Balloon menus, along with the Finder menu and Apple menu) and a few standard items that should be provided (even if permanently grayed out) such as Edit:Cut:, Edit:Copy, and Edit:Paste. Despite the helpful consistency this sort of fascist approach provides the user, it can also engender a certain foolishness, such as having cut/copy/paste items in an application that does not support any of the associated functionality.

The other commonly used approach involves simply making a concerted effort to follow a few simple guidelines when defining menus, and trying to match the application's intended functionality with the menus as best you can. This is the approach we have taken, because we don't really provide the sort of key functionality discussed by Apple, as such functionality is already provided by the browser. Some of the guidelines that should be followed when defining menus and their items are as follows:

- Keep menu label names short and unambiguous (one word, if possible).

- Keep menu item text short and begin with a key word, such as a verb.

- Order the menus according to how often they are used.

- Don't name a menu item using the same word as the menu label.

- Treat item text as though it were a command to the application.

- Use parallel ordering on menus grouping similar or related functions.

There are other conventions surrounding capitalization, alphabetical ordering, and so forth, but opinions vary on their utility and the scope of their applicability. Some experts recommend alphabetical ordering for long lists of menu items, such as may be found in a cascading menu exposing font options. Others recommend use-based ordering, where the most recently used items are placed toward the top of the menu. However, this dynamic reordering of menu items presents its own problems, among which are a steeper learning curve and user confusion. Introduce such inconsistencies with caution, as they tend to hurt the novice user and prolong the learning process, though they may help the expert or power user.

A couple of features also recommended for menu interfaces that we have not implemented are menu *separators*, to distinguish between subgroups of related menu items, and *cascading submenus*, which save screen and menu real estate by hiding seldom-used choice-based items until they absolutely must be shown. These features are relatively simple to implement using the HTML HR tag for the former, and a nested menu definition structure for the latter. When a menu item with a cascading submenu is moused over, a timeout function could be called that would eventually reveal the submenu (after a short pause), positioned to the right of the selected item. When the user mouses out of the submenu's parent item, the cascading submenu would then be hidden. If the user moused over the submenu, the submenu items' handlers would be invoked as defined by the application developer.

Organizational Strategies and User Feedback

The first of the sample application's menus was pretty obvious – the game deals with words, after all. Hence, we grouped the functions that deal with words, enabling the user to create and delete word magnets under a single menu labeled "Words." Despite the near-universal convention that the left-most menu in any application be named "File," it is completely inappropriate for our application, which uses no files, either "New" or otherwise, does not enable the user to save their work to their local file system, and manages to successfully avoid the use of most, if not all, PC application conventions due to the very nature of Web-borne applications. We expect the traditional File/Edit/Special triumvirate to quickly fall by the wayside as more and more Web-based applications arise. Alan Cooper predicted the demise of the File convention, as described in an earlier chapter, even before the era of network-delivered applications.

When we initially designed the sample application, we took a somewhat typical developer's approach to the problem of naming the elements of the user interface. We figured that because we were dealing with words, a group of words should be referred to as a "phrase." As nearly unanimous user feedback showed us, nobody familiar with the magnetic poetry game knew what we meant by a phrase, preferring the term "poem." Because we saved the task of writing the online documentation and instructions for last, most of our alpha testers didn't have the faintest idea what the menu items meant, and had no recourse but to ask the developer how the darn thing was supposed to work. In the end, we realized the folly of our ways and renamed the menu items to refer to poems, not phrases, and balance and harmony was restored to the user interface. To hammer the point home, we also named the menu item under which the related items are grouped "Poems."

The last specially defined menu presents a certain problem for the serious GUI designer. It is clear that we have lumped together everything that didn't seem appropriate under Words or Poems into a category called "Misc." We can hear the usability experts weeping into their notepads now, but there were good reasons for lumping everything together. Our application is somewhat limited in scope, with only four other functions to provide access to after the main business of adding/deleting/grouping words into poems has been taken care of. The idea of creating a Preferences menu appealed to us initially, but because we have only one set of preferences currently exposed, it seemed a bad idea to create a menu with only one menu item. The same line of reasoning also applies to the "give feedback," "show debugging info," and "quit playing" menu items, each of which are singular and more or less unrelated to the others. The choice of menu label was more or less mandated by the poor availability of better terms to describe a catchall.

We stand confident knowing that we could expose more preferences to the user, such as a choice of wordlist, font face and size, and user profile, and split these functions into a menu of their own. However, this doesn't solve our initial problem of trying to avoid having menus containing but a single menu item. As we split our Misc menu into more full-featured menus, it threatens to leave us with the single-menu-item-per-menu problem all over again.

That's how we decided to organize the sample application. Your application may benefit from other strategies, however.

Other Organizational Strategies

In addition to the problem of figuring out how to organize menus and their items, you have the somewhat more flexible option of not using a menu bar at all, relying on contextual pop-up menus or other mechanisms. Here are some alternatives to the way we did things:

- Use an object-oriented approach, enabling a new menu to be created whenever and wherever the application needs it. This has the unpleasant side effect of making it extremely difficult for the user to predict where and what they find when they access the menu, however.

- Use nested hierarchical menus to conserve screen real estate. This approach is most appropriate when a huge number of options are available to the user that must be organized in a tree-like pattern; for example, country/state or province/city, where the hierarchical menus could be generated on the fly based on the user's previous choices.

- Use contextual pop-up menus, rather than anchoring them to the menu bar. Many Web navigation schemes use this approach, relying on the user's familiarity with certain navigational systems to replace the stability and consistency of the menu bar.

The steps recommended a few paragraphs back in order to allow for hierarchical or cascading submenus would also enable the creation of contextual pop-up menus. Basically, the "menu" is nothing more than a bunch of layers that have been grouped together and anchored to a menu bar. Such a menu is just as easily displayed in the event of a `mousedown` event in a specific area as it is as the result of a mouse click on the menu bar. Anyone wishing to create a contextual or hierarchical pop-up menu would need to:

◆ Provide a routine to stub out or place the menu after creating it

◆ Provide a way to track levels of hierarchical menus as they are shown, hiding them all when the parent menu is concealed

◆ Implement true nesting as opposed to a faked link list

Enough about the way we could have done things. Let's talk about how we chose to implement the menu configuration file, using JavaScript objects to hold our settings and definitions.

The Menu Configuration File, dyn_menu_config.js

The menu and menu item definitions are contained within a separate JavaScript file for the sake of encapsulating all of the application-specific settings into one file, rather than incorporating them into the Dynamic Menu module itself. In order to provide an easily read and understood format for configuring our menus, we chose to make use of a feature of JavaScript 1.2; namely, the use of *object literals*. An object literal is constructed in the following manner. First, the variable is declared as an object. Next, each property the new object is to have is declared within a block, with each property followed by a colon and the value that is to be assigned to the property. Successive properties may be defined, provided that each is followed by a comma. If the last property is followed by a comma, however, an error is generated. You may use comments to describe what each property represents.

```
var my_object = new Object();
my_object = {
  prop_one: "value one",   // double-quoted string
  prop_two: 2,             // numeric value
  prop_three: true,        // Boolean
  prop_four: 'value four'  // single-quoted string
}
```

In our menu configuration file, shown in Listing 14-18, we also make use of nested arrays of objects. The first menu definition, `my_menu_defs[0]`, is assigned a name (`Words`), and a new array is created. Each element in the array is then initialized as an object, and the menu item properties are assigned using the object literal method described previously. For each menu, we define a name. For each menu item in that menu's items array we then define the parent menu; the label to use for the menu item, which is used to name the DIV object; the text and alternate text to use for the item; its handler; and the keyboard shortcut.

Listing 14–18: The dyn_menu_config.js menu configuration file

```
// our menu definitions
var my_menu_defs = new Array();

// "Words" menu
my_menu_defs[0] = new Object();
my_menu_defs[0].name = "Words";
my_menu_defs[0].items = new Array();

my_menu_defs[0].items[0] = new Object();
my_menu_defs[0].items[0] = {
  menu:     "Words",      // menu name
  label:    "add",        // used to name DIV
  text:     "add word",   // menu item text
  handler:  'toggle_form("addwordlayer");', // item handler
  key:      "+^A" // shift-control-A
}

my_menu_defs[0].items[1] = new Object();
my_menu_defs[0].items[1] = {
  menu:     "Words",        // menu name
  label:    "delete",
  text:     "delete word",  // menu item text
  handler:  'prep_delete_word_form();', // handler
  key:      "+^D" // shift-control-D
}

// "Poems" menu
my_menu_defs[1] = new Object();
my_menu_defs[1].name = "Poems";
my_menu_defs[1].items = new Array();

my_menu_defs[1].items[0] = new Object();
my_menu_defs[1].items[0] = {
  menu:     "Poems",      // menu name
  label:    "view",
  text:     "view poem",  // menu item text
  handler:  'prep_view_phrase_form();', // handler for this item
  key:      "+^V" // shift-control-V
}
```

```javascript
my_menu_defs[1].items[1] = new Object();
my_menu_defs[1].items[1] = {
  menu:     "Poems",        // menu name
  label:    "save",
  text:     "save poem",   // menu item text
  handler:  'toggle_form("savephraselayer");', // handler
  key:      "+^S" // shift-control-S
}

my_menu_defs[1].items[2] = new Object();
my_menu_defs[1].items[2] = {
  menu:     "Poems",        // menu name
  label:    "delete",
  text:     "delete poem",  // menu item text
  handler:  'prep_delete_phrase_form();', // item handler
  key:      "+^E" // shift-control-E
}

// "Misc" menu
my_menu_defs[2] = new Object();
my_menu_defs[2].name = "Misc";
my_menu_defs[2].items = new Array();

my_menu_defs[2].items[0] = new Object();
my_menu_defs[2].items[0] = {
  menu:     "Misc",         // menu name
  label:    "feedback",
  text:     "give feedback",  // menu item text
  alt:      "hide feedback",  // menu alt text
  handler:  'toggle_feedback();', // item handler
  key:      "+^F" // shift-control-F
}

my_menu_defs[2].items[1] = new Object();
my_menu_defs[2].items[1] = {
  menu:     "Misc",         // menu name
  label:    "prefs",
  text:     "edit preferences",  // menu item text
  alt:      "hide preferences",  // menu item alt text
  handler:  'toggle_color_picker();', // handler
  key:      "+^P" // shift-control-P
}

my_menu_defs[2].items[2] = new Object();
my_menu_defs[2].items[2] = {
```

```
  menu:      "Misc",         // menu name
  label:     "debug",
  text:      "show debug info",  // menu item text
  alt:       "hide debug info",  // menu item alt text
  handler:   'toggle_debug();', // handler
  key:       "+^G" // shift-control-G
}

my_menu_defs[2].items[3] = new Object();
my_menu_defs[2].items[3] = {
  menu:      "Misc",         // menu name
  label:     "quit",
  text:      "quit",  // menu item text
  handler:   'quit_playing();', // handler
  key:       "+^Q" // shift-control-Q
}


// Additional Help menu items
var my_help_menu_defs = new Array();
my_help_menu_defs[0] = new Object();

my_help_menu_defs[0] = {
  menu:      "Help",
  label:     "instructions",
  text:      "show instructions",
  alt:       "hide instructions",
  handler:   'toggle_instructions();',
  key:       "+^I" // shift-control-I
}
```

Note that the Help menu definition only contains one menu item, despite the fact that the Help menu itself contains three. The other two, Help Contents and About..., are standard Help menu items and are present in every application that chooses to use the Help menu, discussed in detail in the next section. The first of these items presents the user with a list of the available help topics, and the last provides a place for the developers to give general information about the application, such as a list of credits, copyright information, and other fun stuff. This is a great place to stick Easter eggs, those fun little code snippets that developers write to fend off burnout.

We need to do a few things in order for the Dynamic Menu module as defined to be fully integrated into the application. We've already defined the handlers for each menu item, as well as keyboard shortcuts. Now we need to make sure that the handlers work as intended, that any preferences governing the style and presentation of the menu bar and menu items are defined, and so forth.

Exposing Menu States to Preferences

One important thing about enabling users to configure their own interface is making sure that you expose any nonessential preferences they might have, such as colors and font choices used to render the application. Menu and menu item colors are just one of the things that could be exposed via the preferences dialog box. As we saw in Chapter 13, "User-Configurable Interfaces," the color picker dialog box may be populated with JavaScript global variables and their values set via a simple pull-down element. For purposes of demonstration, let's add the menu highlight color variable to the color picker drop-down box so the user can determine which color they should see when they mouse over the menu item.

First, we must add the variables and their text descriptions to the pull-down list in the Dynamic Poetry HTML file:

```
<select name="attribute"
        onChange='cp_select_current_color(this.form);'>
  <option value="magnet_color">
    magnet text</option>
  <option value="magnet_bg_color">
    magnet color</option>
  <option value="selected_magnet_bg_color">
    selected magnet color</option>
  <option value="shadow_bg_color">
    shadow color</option>
  <option value="moving_shadow_bg_color">
    moving shadow color</option>
  <option value="playing_field_bg_color">
    playing field color</option>
  <option value="menu_hilight_color">
    menu highlight color</option>
</select>
```

Next, we add the variable to the list of application preferences we are to check for during the preferences initialization phase. This should probably be done automatically, based simply on the contents of the option list, but for now we do it manually. We add the variable to the init_preferences() routine in the file executive_poetry.js:

```
var app_preferences = new Array();
function init_preferences() {
  // set the list of preferences to read/set
  app_preferences[0] = "magnet_color";
  app_preferences[1] = "magnet_bg_color";
  app_preferences[2] = "selected_magnet_bg_color";
```

```
app_preferences[3] = "shadow_bg_color";
app_preferences[4] = "moving_shadow_bg_color";
app_preferences[5] = "playing_field_bg_color";
// added for ch14.
app_preferences[6] = "menu_hilight_color";

// then get them and apply them as appropriate
apply_preferences();
}
```

From there, everything is taken care of. Now, when the user defines the color to be used for menu item highlighting, it is automatically applied by the application.

Associating Menu Items with Handlers

As we have seen, each menu item has a handler that is then associated with the item's `onmouseup` event handler. The event handler actually assigned to the `onmouseup` is not the handler we've defined, but rather a wrapper that checks first to see if the item is actually enabled before executing the handler we've defined. This is just good programming design, because this enables the enclosing application to disable or enable any menu item as required without having to keep track of each item's handler and state. It's all taken care of for you by the Dynamic Menu module. In the configuration file, you can see that each handler is presented as a JavaScript function call. This function call is actually just a string, but when the handler is evaluated using the JavaScript call `eval()`, it gets executed just as if it were a real function call. There is a slight distinction between a regular string and a function call, but not much. The only difference is that the first may be stored and `eval()`'d at will. This convenience enables us to define our handlers without having to hard-code them into a less flexible arrangement. The function `menu_do_action()` is shown in Listing 14-17.

Defining Alternate Text for State Changes

Some, but not all, of the menu item definitions in our configuration file have alternate text. This is yet another method for dealing with functionality that toggles the state of part of the application. In the definition for the Preferences menu item "give feedback," for example, the alternate is given as "hide feedback." This enables the user to toggle back and forth between the feedback form and the regular playing field at will, without affecting either one's state, and names the menu item more appropriately depending on the context. In order to make this change take place, we add the following line at the very end of the function called by the menu item, `toggle_feedback()`:

```
menu_item_toggle("Miscfeedback");
```

This ensures that the menu item text accurately reflects the state of the application. We do the same thing for all menu items with alternate text. For each function defined as a handler, we add a line with the appropriate menu item object name passed as an argument to the `menu_item_toggle()` function.

Other Required Changes

The Dynamic Poetry application we've seen in previous chapters used the menu palette, complete with its own style sheet and HTML markup. Integrating the dynamic menu into the application requires the removal of the old menu style sheet and replacement with the one we have defined for the dynamic menu. In addition, we add the initialization routines to the appropriate places in the HTML file `poetry.html`, as follows:

```
<script language="JavaScript">
create_base_objects();
feedback_form_init();
if( navigator.appName != "Netscape" ) {
  menu_init(my_menu_defs, my_help_menu_defs);
  tab_widget_init();
  tab_widget_hide();
}
fully_loaded = true;
</script>
```

We also add the `menu_init()` routine to the `executive_poetry_init()` function, as shown below. We juggle things around a bit to make sure that our users' preferences for the menu highlight color are properly applied before the menu is initialized:

```
function executive_poetry_init() {
  debug_init();
  init_preferences();
  if(navigator.appName == "Netscape" ) {
    menu_init(my_menu_defs, my_help_menu_defs);
    tab_widget_init();
    tab_widget_hide();
  }
  init_words();
  error_init();
  shadow_set_events();
  status_write("ready to play.");
}
```

Note also that we have removed the call to `menu_debug_init()`, which served the purpose of figuring out — based on the `debug_flag` variable — whether or not to reveal the debugging menu item in the menu palette. We should probably perform a similar check, however, to figure out whether or not to enable the "show debug info" menu item. If there is no debugging turned on, it might be worth it to simply remove the menu item and shove the rest up, or just disable it by calling `menu_item_disable()`, as shown in Listing 14-16.

We also redefined the playing field area in the main style sheet to take up the entire application area above the space reserved for the various forms, and removed the old title bar, which becomes more or less redundant at this point. The Dynamic Poetry application, complete with menu bar and menus, is illustrated in Figure 14-6.

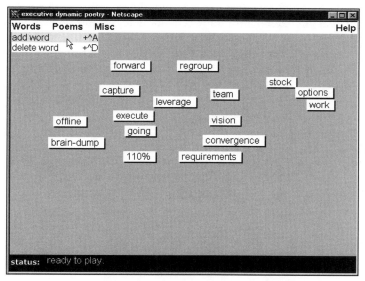

Figure 14-6: The dynamic menu integrated with the Dynamic Poetry application

Testing the Dynamic Menu Module

Testing the Dynamic Menu module is no different than testing any other portion of your application, although the ease with which it provides access to your application's functionality may in itself reveal unexpected bugs in other parts of your application. Here are a few things to look for when you're testing the Dynamic Menu module.

Testing Each Menu Item

Test each menu item and make sure that it:

- ◆ Reacts appropriately to state changes (show/hide the alternate menu item)
- ◆ Reacts appropriately to being disabled ("save phrase," for example)
- ◆ Reacts to both mouse events and keyboard events
- ◆ Invokes the appropriate handler

Make careful notes regarding the success and failure of each item. In some cases, you may also need to prepare the application beforehand to make sure that the appropriate state is being tested. For example, we would like to make sure that the "save poem" menu item is not enabled until there is actually a poem to save. In this case, we would select a few words, then check the menu item to see if it is in fact enabled. Similarly, if there are no saved poems defined, the "view poem" and "delete poem" menu items should be disabled. You may find that entire routines need to be written to make sure that the menu items reflect the actual state of the application.

In any case, here are some more things to look for.

COLOR CHANGES

When the user mouses over and out of an item, the item should change color appropriately. If you have exposed the menu highlight color to the user's preferences, as we have, also check to make sure that the right color is being used.

STATE CHANGES

When those items that toggle some state are selected, they should reflect that in the menu item text.

ACTION HANDLERS AND EVENT HANDLERS

When the user selects the menu item, does it do the right thing? More importantly, does it keep doing the right thing? Sometimes, poor design can result in a function being called once but never called again due to failure to set the right flag variable, for example. In the initial test run of the dynamic menu, we realized we had forgotten to register the action handlers and event handlers for the alternate menu item. The Dynamic Menu module was hiding the right item and revealing the right item, but the alternate had not been sufficiently prepped to actually enable us to toggle back to the initial state.

PREFERENCES

If we use the preferences dialog box to set menu color, menu background color, disabled color, or highlight, are these colors used correctly by the application after saving them out of the preferences dialog box? How about upon reload? Upon a new user session?

Testing Using Debug Module

Testing the module using the Debug module is the same as testing any other module. Simply turn debugging on and add some debugging statements, show the debugging output – only this time, using the debug menu item.

If everything passes, you're ready to go!

Gotchas

There were literally dozens of small problems with the Dynamic Menu module during coding. However, most of them were simply the result of not anticipating the complexity involved in using alternate menu items as described previously. Here are the misery-inducing compatibility issues sent by the Furies to torment us:

◆ Using the same CSS class in TABLE and TD breaks IE 4.0. For some reason, referencing the same CSS CLASS in both a TABLE and TD caused Internet Explorer to throw screaming hysterical fits, where it refused to enable any of the objects so afflicted to be manipulated in any way. This one was really hard to catch, as it was more or less unintentional on our part.

◆ Dealing with clipping and the extent of the menu bar. One of the toughest problems encountered during the coding of this module was trying to get the menu items to align flush with the bottom of the menu bar. Finally, we had to set the height of the menu bar explicitly for IE to recognize it. Otherwise, it preferred to use the height setting in the CSS style sheet once we tried putting it in. Unfortunately, using CSS to define explicit pixel heights of a menu bar affected by font size changes was less than useful.

◆ Dynamic creation of layers. This one we'd seen before. Netscape Navigator doesn't enable the creation of a new Layer object before the HTML page has fully loaded. On the other hand, IE doesn't seem to recognize DIV objects added after the page has loaded, so we needed to put the call to the initialization function inside a browser-sensing code snippet.

◆ Navigator apparently doesn't deal well with nested DIV objects inside a Layer object. When we tried creating nested menus, where the menu acted as an actual container for the menu items themselves, we had persistent problems referencing the DIV objects by name via document.layers. This occurred even though we were using CSS-P absolute positioning, which should have made them show up. Trying to access them via document.layerName.document.layers didn't work either, so we gave up and faked it.

♦ One gotcha we ran into during the first shot at the Dynamic Menu module had to do with events being improperly dealt with twice if the menu item was in the same place as the menu container. Even when they were not nested, if they occupied the same z-index, two events were fired. This made for some interesting viewing, as a `mouseover` event first highlighted and then removed the highlighting from the menu item. Making sure to keep all of your objects on different planes can help here.

Summary

In this chapter, you learned how to:

♦ Create a dynamically configured menu bar and menus

♦ Define a set of menus (or anything else, for that matter) using the object literal notation provided by JavaScript 1.2

♦ Expose application functionality to another module, and vice versa, through the use of action handlers and the `eval()` JavaScript statement, and carefully encapsulated methods such as `menu_do_action()` or `menu_item_disable()`

♦ Place objects dynamically using the `abut()` and `overlay()` methods, just as in the previous chapter

♦ Set clipping regions and object properties using the methods provided by the cross-browser library

♦ Handle mouse events to create sophisticated user interface effects like menu item state changes and highlights

♦ Register characteristics of an object with a controlling mechanism to provide for ease of management and state control

♦ React to early alpha testing feedback before it's too late for your application's interface

In the next chapter, we go into more detail about keyboard input handling and how to provide help to your users without using a paper manual.

Chapter 15

Help

IN THIS CHAPTER

◆ Principles of online help systems

◆ Limitations of DHTML-based help systems

◆ Structuring navigation systems for online help

◆ How to provide context-sensitive help

◆ Coping with keyboard input and shortcuts

◆ More on how to position elements based on mouse events

IN THE LAST CHAPTER, we added menu functionality to our application. In this chapter, we go a step further and add a complete (if somewhat underpowered) online help system, including context-sensitive help "tips" and a full suite of documentation. You will learn the rationale behind what we implemented, and (more importantly) what we couldn't implement due to rather severe limitations placed on us by the current state of the browsers. You will also learn how to implement keyboard shortcuts (also known as *accelerators,* in case that's ever a Jeopardy question) in the last chapter, and hear some griping about why keyboard input across platforms is unpredictable, unreliable, and sometimes simply unavailable in certain contexts. Despite the shortcomings of current DHTML implementations, we managed to accomplish quite a bit, though not as much as we wanted. Read on to find out more. . . .

Principles of Online Help Systems

Many authors of help systems forget that online help isn't just an electronic version of the documentation. Online help serves many purposes in several different contexts, and differs from traditional documentation in that help is usually consulted in order to remind the user of something he or she already knows. While many software manuals take a tutorial approach, others take a more reference-oriented approach, but it is important not to forget that it is almost always a bad idea to consider help systems and paper manuals as equivalent. Their manner of presentation, indexing, and the context in which they are usually accessed can differ widely. In fact, that's often the whole point.

In addition, authoring procedures for documentation versus those followed for online help may be different and require specialized tools. Back in the days when Steven was writing help files for a cross-platform application that had to run on both Sun Solaris and Microsoft Windows, he eventually had to resort to hacking the RTF files by hand to ensure consistent results. Fortunately, things have gotten much better for traditional help authoring. Unfortunately, such tools are not always available for the Web. In all cases, however, a few rules of thumb should be followed regardless of the tools you use and the target platforms you intend to support.

Provide Task-Oriented Information

Help systems are usually consulted while the user is actively trying to accomplish something. Help files that get right to the point and inform users how to accomplish their tasks tend to be more useful than those that overburden the user with background information unnecessary for completing the task. Not that there is anything wrong with goal-oriented information, such as tutorials or other overview materials, but if you do not provide information that directly assists the user in the completion of tasks, your help system quickly falls into disuse. For more on the distinction between task-oriented and goal-oriented interfaces, see Chapter 3, "Principles and Lessons Learned."

Don't Assume the User Is Dumb

Many authors of online help systems make the mistake of assuming that users are dumb just because they have to check the help file. This is a fallacy. People who are really dumb don't use the help file, preferring instead to go find a human being who can explain the system to them in simple terminology. You are more likely to find savvy users consulting help or the paper manual, and more often than not, they tend to know roughly what they are looking for. Don't insult their intelligence by providing extremely simplistic explanations of the obvious. Focus on the key characteristics and functions, but without necessarily dumbing the explanations down. Remember, if your help system is too hard for the user to understand, they may very well look elsewhere in the help file for a simpler explanation, but if they are insulted upon first look, they are more likely to write off the usefulness of the help system in general.

Provide Redundancy Where Appropriate

Help systems, like the Web itself, are usually delivered as hypertext, because of the relationships between the various parts of an application. There is no reason not to provide redundant information, wherever appropriate, and there are many reasons why it is in fact a better strategy. For one thing, it is difficult to know in advance what context the user finds themselves in when they need more information. Providing information that applies to many different components in the help system for each component ensures that the user can find it when they need it. Their mental model of the system may be different, or their nomenclature may disagree with the author's. Redundancy may be provided through the use of multiple keywords for the same topic, for example, in those systems that support keyword searches. In our help system, we provide redundancy by dealing with the same information in multiple contexts: the first is a linear and hierarchical presentation; the second is a context-sensitive pop-up window that doesn't need to provide all the context of the linear version because the context is already present to the user.

Let Users Decide When They are Done

Help, like any other form of reference material, should remain open until the person consulting it has had a chance to see if they understand what they have just learned. Would you use a dictionary that put itself back on the shelf after every lookup? Your users won't, either. Help pop-up windows should stay displayed until the user decides (by closing the window, or clicking a close box of some sort) that they are finished with the help file.

Goals, Operators, Methods, and Selection Rules

One popular model for designing online help systems recommends the use of four principles, outlined below:

- ◆ **Goals** – Focus on the tasks that the users of the system are expected to perform and the procedures they should follow in order to accomplish them.

- ◆ **Operators** – Provide information on the exact actions the user should take, including keyboard shortcuts, menu items, or other interface components.

- ◆ **Methods** – Provide demonstrations, procedures, and step-by-step explanations when applicable.

- ◆ **Selection rules** – When multiple procedures exist, or different interface elements provide the same or similar functionality, help users choose the appropriate method.

As with anything that consumes much human energy, there are literally hundreds, if not thousands, of books and essays on online help systems, from the anecdotal to the systematic, from the early days of computing to the recent past. What matters is that your users are happy and productive, so count on them to give you feedback and make the product or application better. Nonetheless, your help system should observe several fundamental characteristics if possible.

Availability

Help should always be available to the user in one form or another. If possible, provide several ways to access it; for example, from a Help menu, via keyboard shortcuts, and/or as a clickable icon with pop-up information. Using help should not lock the user out of any other part of the system, nor should any part of the system forbid access to help. Even modal dialog boxes should enable the user to consult the help system before making a decision.

Context-Sensitivity

Help should be context-sensitive, not only in terms of how it is accessed, but also in terms of the way it is written. Lengthy, detailed, and generic discussions of functionality can be overwhelming and redundant in the wrong context. Provide quick reminders appropriate to the context, rather than full-blown documentation.

Searchability

Help, like all other online documentation, should be indexed and searchable. Great care must be taken, however, when indexing help documentation, to provide a high level of redundancy and to ensure that the keywords match the interface as well as the problem domain in which your application is used.

Consistency

Help systems used to be the only hypertextual component of an application, though of course the Web has changed all that. In any case, help systems tend to be radically different from the rest of your application by their very nature. Don't add to the complexity by providing the system with an interface that is even more inconsistent in the context of the larger application. In addition to the requirement of consistency with the application, many help systems are used from all applications in a given operating system environment. Where possible, try to use globally available mechanisms to provide help, rather than trying to roll your own every time.

Hierarchical Organization

Most applications tend to be constructed such that there is a generic/specific relationship between the functionality provided and the interface components that implement that functionality. Help systems should duplicate this relationship wherever possible so that the user can first locate the class of tasks they want to perform, and then drill down to the specific procedures or operations required to carry out the task. Hierarchy is a great way to differentiate between goal-oriented and task-oriented discussions as well. Just because many help systems are hypertextual in nature does not mean that they do not benefit from a bit of good old hierarchical organization.

Okay, now that we've discussed the desiderata for any good help system in some detail, it's time to talk about the rather paltry subset of those features we can actually provide using the current DHTML implementations.

Limitations of Dynamic HTML– Based Help Environments

When we first started planning the book and sample application, we made a concerted effort to include a help system in the list of features. We based our core feature set and interface on that found in Microsoft Windows Help, because it is perhaps the best, most full-featured and consistent implementation available, and also because it is familiar to a wide range of computer users. Windows Help includes a standard authoring environment (or several), searchability based on indexed keywords, a hierarchical view of covered topics using a tree widget, and other features. We also planned to use the Tab Widget module discussed in Chapter 11, "The Hidden Feedback Form," to maximize the available real estate in our implementation, much like the one found in the Help Topics: Windows Help dialog box, shown in Figure 15-1.

Figure 15-1: The Help Topics: Windows Help dialog box

Unfortunately, what we planned to do and what we found was actually possible were extremely different. As a result, the following DHTML help system discussed is somewhat less than optimal. Until such a time as DHTML help authoring tools become widely available, however, you may find that some of the features we provide are useful.

Combo Box-Based Keyword Search

The first thing we tried to do was provide a Combo Box module that would take a list of keywords and stick them into a SELECT form element, enabling the user to type into a text field above the list. When the user typed a word or part of a word that matched one of the words in the list, the module should have selected that word and placed it into the user's text field, scrolling the list so that the selected word was visible. Unfortunately, although there is a way to set the selectedIndex of an options list using JavaScript, there is no way at present to force the selected item to scroll into view once it has been selected. We tried several approaches, including giving the window focus to the selected option, but nothing worked. Perhaps the next generation of browsers will provide the feature. We could place the matched keyword into the combo box, however, as seen in Figure 15-2.

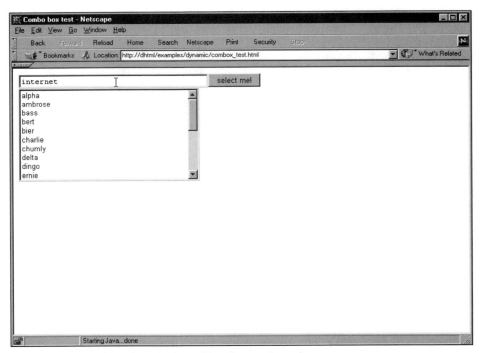

Figure 15-2: Our aborted combo box widget keyword search

One possible route for future development would be to reveal a smaller list and cycle the visible options such that those that matched the user's input were visible, but we decided against that approach for our purposes here. The argument was that the interface thus provided was too similar to existing systems on its face, but functioned differently. You may find that such an approach is better than nothing, though. Watch the book's support Web site for possible future developments in this area.

Hierarchical Topic Contents (Tree Widget)

We also developed a Tree Widget module for this chapter for use in a hierarchical table of contents for help topics. Unfortunately, there were several problems with using a DHTML-based tree widget, especially within a pop-up window. As the tree is expanded and collapsed, there is no way (except through the use of signed scripts) to dynamically adjust the size of the pop-up window to make room for the new content. Because our tree widget was based on the `overlay()` and `abut()` cross-browser API methods, each branch in the tree was a layer. When the tree expanded, its components went beyond the bounds of the window, but the window did not recognize this as it does with traditional tree widgets by supplying a scroll-bar. While we could have scrolled the tree to ensure that the most recently selected item was in view, again, we found that mimicking existing functionality while not actually providing it in full would be frustrating for the user.

Of course, it would be possible to simply regenerate the HTML for the tree every time its state changed, but in our experience such an approach just causes a lot of flicker and is just as irritating to the user. Well, it is to us, anyway. What you don't see in Figure 15-3 is that the tree widget's last node contains children that extend offscreen. You don't see a scrollbar, either. Until certain features of CSS, such as the `overflow` property, are fully supported across browsers and platforms, we recommend that you don't use layer objects whose size may change drastically.

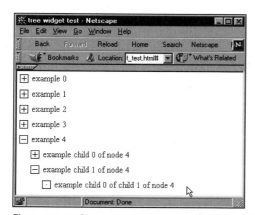

Figure 15-3: Our tree widget–based hierarchical topic display

One other problem that we ran into, which we discuss in more detail at the end of the chapter, was that a convention exists in many PC application and operating system environments such that the F1 function key corresponds directly to the system or application's help facility, launching the Help window or dialog boxes when pressed. However, the only keyboard combinations reliably available across platform are straight alphabetical characters and a couple of modifiers. So we couldn't provide the F1 keyboard shortcut, either. Oh, well.

In our opinion, it may just be easier to write the Help separately and point to it via plain old HTML. Tools exist to ease the authoring process, provide exporting to HTML, and so forth. Leave it to the people who write the browsers and the books to play on the bleeding edge, and stick to things that you know work, especially for something as important as help facilities.

Structuring Navigational Systems for Online Help

Help systems, by necessity, must mirror the functionality of the applications they describe. Within that restriction, however, many alternatives are available for structuring the presentation of and navigation between various elements, and how to relate those to components within the application itself. Here are a few guidelines to follow when designing the navigation structure of your help facility:

◆ Reflect hierarchical structure

◆ Provide task-oriented summaries as well as brief overviews

◆ Provide targeted entry into the system based on context

Whatever tools you provide for navigating within your help facility, it is important to remember that the user can easily get disassociated from the place the help topic describes, especially if the help system does not automatically refresh to follow the user as they interact with the application. Some help systems, such as Apple's Guide, provide animated demonstrations and actually walk the user through the process they describe. In any case, it is best to provide a way to enter the help system from a specific point in the application, and find the help topic or a brief reminder in the form of a pop-up tip relevant to the user's context.

Providing Context-Sensitive Help

Several available methods provide context-sensitive entry into a help system. Some examples are tool tips and Balloon Help. Some are mouse-driven, such as the facility in Windows that enables users to select the element with the mouse and reveal a context-sensitive pop-up window containing more information about the element that was clicked. Others are keyboard-driven, such as the use of the F1 key, which in some systems determines which help topic to reveal based on the interface element that has the focus when the shortcut is pressed.

Tool Tips

Made popular by the Windows programming environment, *tool tips* are time-sensitive pop-up windows that remind the user of the purpose of interface elements or their equivalent keyboard shortcuts. When the user's mouse lingers too long over a given interface element, the element is obscured by the tool tip reminder until the mouse is moved again.

Balloon Help

Apple's Balloon Help, introduced with Macintosh System 7, enables programmers to define help topics that would be revealed if Balloon Help was active, containing helpful reminders of interface functionality or, in some cases, Easter eggs. A favorite example of a Balloon Help Easter egg is included in MacsBug, the system-level debugger extension. When Balloon Help was activated and the user moused over the extension's icon, MacsBug revealed a balloon that said, "This file provides programmers with information proving that it really was a hardware problem." (MacsBug enables programmers to interface directly with the hardware, revealing information about the program counter, the current state of the CPU registers, and so on.)

Other Examples

Other examples of context-sensitive help abound, from specialized help messages in applications to such oddities as the Microsoft Office Assistant, which featured an array of characters from a talking, winking paperclip to Shakespeare or a wise Siamese cat that "watched" the user's interactions with the application, popping up every now and again to suggest that they use more appropriate grammar or use a helpful wizard to simplify the task of writing a memo. The Office Assistant was almost universally hated among developers and power users, despite some popularity among Office users. As of this writing, support for the development kit that made the cute little bugger work was officially killed by Microsoft in a ceremony at a developer's conference. There was some discussion on various mailing lists and forums of ways in which the Office Assistant could better serve the various tastes of a wider range of users, but most of this discussion was either obscene or merely intended to be humorous, so we leave the topic for now.

The Help Module

At this point, you're probably wondering what we were actually able to accomplish, given the severe limits placed on what we could do by the current dynamic HTML implementations. Fortunately, it wasn't a total loss. We were able to provide a navigable, task-oriented suite of help documents using DHTML as opposed to more traditional HTML, as well as context-sensitive tips that function as quick reminders to the user. We had to abandon our plans for a fully functional tree widget, or visual hierarchy of help topics, as well as the searchable keyword index, but some help in the right places is better than no help at all.

Pop-up Help Window

Following the principle of redundancy and varying degrees of detail in different presentations of online documentation and support, we chose to focus on two primary methods of delivering help. The first, illustrated in Figure 15-4, is a pop-up window containing several help topics, organized such that the user can quickly scan through summaries of the entire application's functionality.

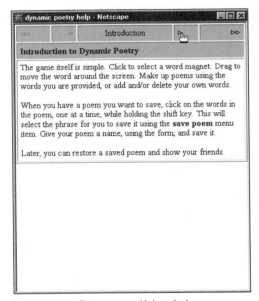

Figure 15-4: The pop-up Help window

The navigation scheme is designed to enable topic- or subject-level browsing, and provides a constant reminder of the user's context within the help system by placing the subject title in the navigation bar (see Figure 15-5). The single arrow in either direction enables single-topic navigation, whereas the double arrow icon represents the subject-level navigation. If no further help is available in either direction, the icons are grayed out. The topic title and help information is provided in the lower half of the window, using table cell background colors to differentiate between the text and navigation as well as context within the system. When the user is done, they may close the window using the window's close box.

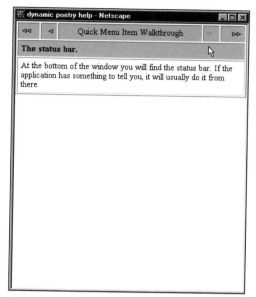

Figure 15-5: The pop-up Help window with partially disabled navigation

The interface would greatly benefit from a few improvements, such as a built-in, brief introduction to the navigation scheme of the Help window itself, a hierarchical display of topics, and perhaps a summary of the next and previous topics so the user didn't have to go on a goose chase for the topic or subject they were looking for. The bottom line, unfortunately, is that our DHTML pop-up Help window, though it uses some interesting DHTML tricks and strategies, is probably not robust enough for deployment in a real production environment. If you need to provide extensive online help documentation, we recommend that you provide it using standard HTML. Perhaps as the browsers improve and support more powerful features of the various Web standards, this judgment will no longer be applicable. For now, however, let's stick to the basics.

Context-Sensitive Tips

In addition to the pop-up window, we provide short summaries describing the immediate application context and its functionality. These summaries are made available as *tips*, or little boxes that are displayed when the user clicks a question mark icon, and follow a similar convention to that used in the more detailed help. The topic's title is presented in bold with the tip text below. The icon in the top-right corner follows a convention for the close box, which conceals the tip when clicked. If the short summary is not sufficient to explain the purpose of the user interface component or assembly, the link at bottom right may be followed, launching the pop-up window help system (see Figure 15-6).

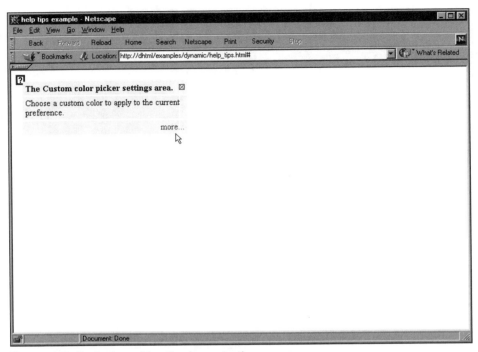

Figure 15-6: Context-sensitive tips demonstration

We didn't go so far as to provide complete context-sensitivity in the way that the pop-up window is launched from the tips, which is a deficiency in the current module. Such functionality, launching the pop-up Help window to the appropriate topic, could be added fairly easily using session cookies and an appropriate initialization routine in the pop-up window. In short, the window could be launched and a cookie set containing the topic it should display. On initialization, the pop-up window could check for the presence of the cookie, and, if found, could reveal the appropriate topic.

An interesting question arises here, though. Should the help system immediately delete the cookie, thereby forgetting the user's last help topic on the next launch, or should it only do so if the user browses the rest of the help documents? The advantage to remembering the user's last help topic is that the pop-up window is always initialized to the same screen on launch; however, this may be confusing to the user if they launch the pop-up Help window from the Help menu, rather than from the context-sensitive help tip. In addition, there is no way to tell if the system is being used by the same user, so it might be best to start fresh with a new Help window every time, or provide a configurable option as a preference, so systems administrators at university computer labs could configure their publicly available applications differently than for a single-user desktop.

Standalone Examples of DHTML Help

Before we go whole hog into integrating the help system into our sample application, let's look at the mechanisms by which the two different types of help are initialized and activated. Following our trend away from the noun-verb-adjective model of building DHTML applications, the Help module is generated almost entirely from JavaScript, including the Help configuration file, which is in JavaScript rather than HTML for reasons that quickly become clear.

It is important to make sure that the context-sensitive help we provide via tips is related to the more detailed information presented in the pop-up Help window. For this reason, among others, we chose to provide tips as an adjunct to the more detailed help. Some of the topics covered in the pop-up window do not lend themselves well to the quick reminder format, whereas others are well suited to the task. Where we found a direct or nearly direct correspondence between a detailed explanation and a quick reminder, we tried to find a suitable place to embed a tip within the application itself. The tip, in turn, contains a reference to the more detailed explanation, making it possible to jump from the immediate context of using the application to the more generic discussion of the feature or function.

The complete example is shown in Listing 15-1. We include the CSS style sheet and JavaScript modules in the usual fashion, and perform the typical test before dynamically adding content to the document. Because the help_init() function creates new layer objects, we need to write DIVs to the document before it has finished loading in Internet Explorer, or after if we're using Netscape Navigator. The example tip happens to discuss the custom colors area of the color picker. When the user clicks the question mark icon, the tip is displayed. The user then has the choice of either hiding the tip by clicking the close box, or launching the pop-up window from the link at the bottom of the tip.

Listing 15-1: The HTML markup for the standalone tip example

```
<html>
<head>
 <title>help tips example</title>
<link rel="stylesheet" type="text/css"
      href="/css/help.css">
<script language="JavaScript"
        src="/javascript/xplatform_wrapper.js"></script>
<script language="JavaScript" src="/javascript/help.js"></script>
<script language="JavaScript"
        src="/javascript/help_config.js"></script>
</head>
<body onLoad='if(navigator.appName == "Netscape") {
help_init(my_help, "tips");}'>
<a href="#" onClick='help_tip_reveal(event, "cpcustomarea");'>
<img src="/images/help_border12x14.gif"></a>
<script language="JavaScript">
```

```
create_base_objects();
if( navigator.appName != "Netscape" ) {
  help_init(my_help, "tips");
}
</script>
</body>
</html>
```

Because we are initializing the tips and not the full pop-up window, we pass the help definitions along with the argument `tips` to the `help_init()` function. This way, only those elements of the help file that are needed within this context are created.

One problem with the tips is a result of the way form elements are handled in Navigator. No matter what the z-index of the layer containing a form element, it is always displayed atop other layers as long as that layer is visible. We had to be very careful to position the help tips in places where such bleed-through did not interfere with the tip itself. We weren't always successful, as can be seen in Figure 15-7.

The pop-up Help window, shown in Listing 15-2, uses a similar initialization procedure, only instead of `tips`, we pass the keyword `popup` to the `help_init()` function along with our help definitions. Because the help topics are all constructed on the fly based on what is found in the help configuration file, and because the `help_init()` function displays the first topic on startup, there is no need for further markup inside the HTML file to help position the topics or provide access to navigation, show/hide, and so on.

Listing 15-2: The HTML markup for the pop-up Help window example

```
<html>
<head>
 <title>dynamic poetry help</title>
<link rel="stylesheet" type="text/css"
      href="/css/help.css">
<script language="JavaScript"
        src="/javascript/xplatform_wrapper.js"></script>
<script language="JavaScript" src="/javascript/help.js"></script>
<script language="JavaScript"
        src="/javascript/help_config.js"></script>
</head>
<body onLoad='if(navigator.appName == "Netscape") {
help_init(my_help, "popup");}'>
<script language="JavaScript">
create_base_objects();
if( navigator.appName != "Netscape" ) {
  help_init(my_help, "popup");
}
</script>
```

```
</body>
</html>
```

   Because the whole help interface is created on the fly, this code listing doesn't tell you much about how it all happens. So let's take a look at the JavaScript routines used to initialize and create the pop-up Help window and tips.

Creating the Help Components

The various components of the help system are created on the fly from the help file definitions, but either the tips or full topics are actually created depending on the context, not both. We saw in the markup how this is triggered by the arguments tips or popup to the call to help_init(), shown in Listing 15-3. For each topic category defined in the help configuration file, we loop over its topics and create either topic objects or tips, depending on the type and whether or not a tip exists for the topic. Some topics do not have a tip, as it is not appropriate within the context. Topics are referenced by way of a descriptor such as 1t7, which stands for "subject one, topic seven." Tips, on the other hand, because of their relationship to icons embedded in the markup, are referred to by a tipref, which is defined in the help configuration file for each tip. The variables prevsubj, nextsubj, prevtopic, and nexttopic are used by later routines to determine how to generate the markup for navigation. The help_subject[] array, as we see shortly, is used to store the title of the current subject.

Listing 15-3: The help_init() JavaScript function

```
function help_init(defs, type) {
  var topics, prevsubj, nextsubj, prevtopic, nexttopic;

  for(var subj = 0; subj < defs.length; subj++ ) {
    if( ! defs[subj] ) break;
    if( defs[subj].topics ) {
      topics = defs[subj].topics;
      help_subject[subj] = defs[subj].title;
      for( var topic = 0; topic < topics.length; topic++ ) {
        if( ! topics[topic] ) break;
        // are we in the popup window? if so, create topics
        if( type == "popup" ) {
          if( defs[subj-1] ) {
            prevsubj = (subj - 1) + 't0';
          } else {
            prevsubj = null;
          }
          if( defs[subj+1] ) {
            nextsubj = (subj + 1) + 't0';
          } else {
```

```
        nextsubj = null;
      }
      if( topics[topic-1] ) {
        prevtopic = subj + 't' + (topic - 1);
      } else {
        prevtopic = null;
      }
      if( topics[topic+1] ) {
        nexttopic = subj + 't' + (topic + 1);
      } else {
        nexttopic = null;
      }
      help_add_topic(subj, topic,
                        topics[topic].title,
                        topics[topic].text,
                        prevsubj, nextsubj,
                        prevtopic, nexttopic);
    } else {
      // create tip if appropriate
      if( topics[topic].tip ) {
        help_add_tip(topics[topic].tipref,
                        topics[topic].title,
                        topics[topic].tip);
      }
    }
  }
 }
 }
 }
 if( type == "popup" ) {
  help_topic_reveal("0t0");
 }
}
```

Topics are created by way of a call to `help_add_topic()`, shown in Listing 15-4, while the tips are created by a similar call to `help_add_tip()`, shown in Listing 15-5. Finally, if we are initializing the Help pop-up window, the first topic is revealed.

The function `help_add_topic()` gathers together all of the function calls necessary to:

◆ Create the appropriate markup for each topic

◆ Create a `DIV` object or Layer containing that markup

◆ Create a wrapper object for the new native object

One noteworthy aspect of the function is that it gives the help topic its real name, which is the same as the earlier identifier but prefaced by `helptopic` to avoid any namespace conflicts with the rest of the application it might be embedded in. Of course, because this is usually launched into its own window, and therefore its own namespace, this is overkill, but it's easier to build in overkill at the beginning than add it later.

Listing 15-4: The help_add_topic() JavaScript function

```
function help_add_topic(subj, topic, title, text,
                        prevsubj, nextsubj,
                        prevtopic, nexttopic) {
   var topic_name = "helptopic" + subj + 't' + topic;
   var topicmarkup = help_topic_markup(title, text, subj,
                                       prevsubj, nextsubj,
                                       prevtopic, nexttopic);
   var newtopic = help_create(topic_name, topicmarkup);
   help_topic[topic_name] = new base_object(newtopic);
}
```

The `help_add_tip()` function is extremely similar to the previous function, except that it doesn't need quite so many pass-through arguments because of the lack of a navigational requirement. The string `helptip` is appended to the real name, this time to avoid likely namespace conflicts. In the end, we have wrapper objects for `help_topic` and `help_tip`, which may be accessed the same as any of our other wrapped layer objects.

Listing 15-5: The help_add_tip() JavaScript function

```
function help_add_tip(name, title, text) {
   var tip_name = "helptip" + name;
   var tipmarkup = help_tip_markup(name, title, text);
   var newtip = help_create(tip_name, tipmarkup);
   help_tip[tip_name] = new base_object(newtip);
}
```

The markup for the tips themselves is generated by the `help_tip_markup()` function, shown in Listing 15-6. The title is wrapped in bold tags, the right corner is occupied by a close box that hides the tip when clicked by the user, the text is placed below in a separate cell, and the bottom row is occupied by a link to launch the Help pop-up window. Even though the `help_init()` routine doesn't check for context sensitivity, we pass a reference for the sake of future support.

Listing 15-6: The help_tip_markup() JavaScript function

```
function help_tip_markup(name, title, text) {
   var tm = '<table class="helptip" cellpadding=4 ';
   tm += 'cellspacing=0>';
   tm += '<tr>';
```

```
tm += '<td nowrap>';
tm += '<b>' + title + '</b>';
tm += '</td><td>';
tm += '<a href="#" onClick=\'help_tip_conceal("';
tm += name + '");\'>';
tm += '<img src="' + help_icon_close + '" border=0></a>';
tm += '</td></tr>';
tm += '<tr>';
tm += '<td colspan=2>';
tm += text;
tm += '</td></tr>';
tm += '<tr>';
tm += '<td colspan=2 align=right>';
tm += '<a href="#" onClick=\'help_pop_launch("';
tm += name + '");\'>more...</a>';
tm += '</td></tr></table>';

return tm;
}
```

The CSS style sheets referred to in the previous and next functions are as follows:

```
.helptopic {
  color: #000000;
  background-color: #CCCCCC;
}

.helptip {
  color: #000000;
  background-color: #FFFFCC;
  width: 150;
}

.helpcontainer {
  color: #000000;
  position: absolute;
  top: 0;
  left: 0;
  visibility: hidden;
}
```

The `help_topic_markup()` function, shown in Listing 15-7, is a bit more complex than the one that creates the tip. Because each topic object contains its own navigation, we do a lot of testing to see if references to the next and previous subjects, and next and previous topics, actually exist (if not, they are `null`) and build our navigation that way. If there is no appropriate topic to link to, the "disabled" graphic is substituted in for the "enabled" graphic, and no anchor is added.

Listing 15-7: The help_topic_markup() JavaScript function

```
function help_topic_markup(title, text, subj,
                           prevsubj, nextsubj,
                           prevtopic, nexttopic) {
  var tm = '<table class="helptopic" border=1 ';
  tm += 'cellpadding=5 width=400>';
  tm += '<tr>';
  tm += '<td align=left>';
  if( prevsubj ) {
    tm += '<a href="#" onClick=\'help_topic_reveal("';
    tm += prevsubj + '");\'>';
    tm += '<img src="' + help_icon_leftleft + '" border=0></a>';
  } else {
    tm += '<img src="' + help_icon_leftleft_disabled + '">';
  }
  tm += '</td><td align=right>';
  if( prevtopic ) {
    tm += '<a href="#" onClick=\'help_topic_reveal("';
    tm += prevtopic + '");\'>';
    tm += '<img src="' + help_icon_left + '" border=0></a>';
  } else {
    tm += '<img src="' + help_icon_left_disabled + '">';
  }
  tm += '</td><td align=center nowrap>';
  tm += help_subject[subj] + '</td>';
  tm += '<td align=left>'
  if( nexttopic ) {
    tm += '<a href="#" onClick=\'help_topic_reveal("';
    tm += nexttopic + '");\'>';
    tm += '<img src="' + help_icon_right + '" border=0></a>';
  } else {
    tm += '<img src="' + help_icon_right_disabled + '">';
  }
  tm += '<td align=right>';
  if( nextsubj ) {
    tm += '<a href="#" onClick=\'help_topic_reveal("';
    tm += nextsubj + '");\'>';
    tm += '<img src="' + help_icon_rightright + '" border=0></a>';
  } else {
    tm += '<img src="' + help_icon_rightright_disabled + '">';
  }
```

```
tm += '</td></tr>';
tm += '<tr><td colspan=5><b>' + title + '</b></td></tr>';
tm += '<tr><td colspan=5 bgcolor="' + help_bgcolor + '">';
tm += text + '</td></tr></table>';

return tm;
}
```

Each topic header consists of the navigation and the title of the current subject. The title of each topic is written below the header in its own cell. Finally, the text for the topic itself is included in the markup and returned.

Both functions call the `help_create()` function, shown in Listing 15-8, which is almost identical to those we've seen in other modules. The function takes two arguments: the name of the object to create and the contents to write to it. It returns a reference to the newly created object, either a `DIV` object in IE or a Layer reference in Navigator.

Listing 15-8: The help_create() JavaScript function

```
function help_create(name, contents) {
  if( document.all ) {
    var the_div = '<div id="' + name + '" ' +
      'class="helpcontainer">' + contents + '</div>';
    document.open("text/html");
    document.writeln( the_div );
    document.close();

    var all_divs = document.all.tags("DIV");
    var new_h = all_divs[all_divs.length - 1];
  } else {
    var new_h = new Layer(1);
    new_h.document.open("text/html");
    new_h.document.writeln( contents );
    new_h.document.close();
  }
  return new_h;
}
```

Now that our system is fully initialized, let's turn our attention to the functions that are called during its lifetime to hide, show, launch, and otherwise manage the help objects.

Managing the Help Components

The JavaScript just doesn't want to end. In Listing 15-9, we see the `help_pop_launch()` function, which opens a new window based on the arguments and then returns `false` so that the call may be embedded in an anchor. We also cancel the event bubbling in Internet Explorer, which should be overkill, but better safe than sorry.

Listing 15-9: The help_pop_launch() JavaScript function

```
function help_pop_launch(topic) {
  var args = "width=400," +
             "height=480," +
             "toolbar=0," +
             "menubar=0," +
             "scrollbars=1," +
             "resizable=1," +
             "status=0," +
             "location=0," +
             "directories=0," +
             "copyhistory=0";

  window.open( help_popup_url, "helppop", args );

  if( window.event ) {
    window.event.cancelBubble = true; // for IE
  }
  return false;
}
```

Once the window has been opened, if you recall, the initialization routine is called and the first help topic is displayed. The embedded `onClick` handlers in the navigation enable the user to go forward one topic, backward one topic, or jump either way to the first topic in each subject. This is accomplished by way of a call to the functions in Listing 15-10 and Listing 15-11. The first of these, `help_topic_reveal()`, hides any other visible topic and then reveals the new topic whose identifier was passed as an argument. Finally, it sets the global variable `help_topic_visible` to the name of the visible topic itself.

Listing 15-10: The help_topic_reveal() JavaScript function

```
function help_topic_reveal(topic) {
  var the_topic = "helptopic" + topic;
  if( help_topic_visible ) {
    help_topic[help_topic_visible].conceal();
  }
  help_topic[the_topic].reveal();
  help_topic_visible = the_topic;
}
```

The function that reveals the tip is paired up with a similar function that conceals it. Listing 15-11 contains `help_tip_reveal()`, which figures out where to place the tip based on the event information from the mouse click that called it. The first argument is the `event` keyword, used by the browsers to inform the function that if an event is passed, it should be the first argument. When we are done, we set the z-index to ensure that the tip is not obscured by other layers, but it is worth mentioning again that form elements in Netscape Navigator always show through layers, regardless of the z-index of any other layers.

We use `e.page_x` and `e.page_y` because the `click` information is relative to the current layer, not the entire page, and we want to be able to overlay the tip on top of the Help icon image. The call to the `overlay()` wrapper method is commented out due to a similar problem — the `image_name` properties used by the `overlay()` function are relative to the current layer, not the window itself. Something to look out for if you want to overlay something atop an image using our library.

Listing 15-11: The help_tip_reveal() JavaScript function

```
function help_tip_reveal(event, tipref) {
  var the_tip = "helptip" + tipref;
  var e = wrap_event(event);
  help_tip[the_tip].place(e.page_x, e.page_y);
  //help_tip[the_tip].overlay(image_name[the_tip], "NW", 0);
  help_tip[the_tip].set_z_index(help_tip_z_index);
  help_tip[the_tip].reveal();
}
```

The purpose of the `help_tip_conceal()` function, shown in Listing 15-12, is to make up for the namespace issues and continue with the convention of passing just the tip reference, rather than the whole name of the tip object. Otherwise, we'd just call `help_tip[tipref].conceal()` and be done with it.

Listing 15-12: The help_tip_conceal() JavaScript function

```
function help_tip_conceal(tipref) {
  var the_tip = "helptip" + tipref;
  help_tip[the_tip].conceal();
}
```

Well, that's it for the Help module. Next, let's take a look at the configuration file as we prepare to integrate the Help into our sample application.

Defining Your Help File

The help configuration file is constructed in much the same way as the dynamic menu configuration file was in the last chapter. Using JavaScript object literals, we build the documentation and supporting information into a set of JavaScript objects. The first of these is shown here, in Listing 15-13. First, we create the `my_help` array to contain the objects and their children. Next, we initialize the first element of the array as an object, set the title, and add a new array to contain topics. Each topic then sets properties for the following bits of data:

◆ The title of the topic

◆ A brief summary for use in a hierarchical view

◆ The full text of the topic

◆ A shorter, more context-sensitive tip

◆ A reference to the tip to be used in calls to `help_tip_reveal()`

◆ A set of keywords that help to uniquely identify the topic

In a more highly developed help system, the keywords and summaries would be used to help users find what they are looking for without having to read the entire topic. In our example help system, of course, we don't use either, but our intent is to demonstrate what any full-featured help file needs in order to be used to its best potential.

Listing 15-13: A couple of snippets from help_config.js

```
var my_help = new Array();

// Help topics
my_help[0] = new Object();
my_help[0].title = 'Introduction';
my_help[0].topics = new Array();

my_help[0].topics[0] = new Object();
my_help[0].topics[0] = {
  title: 'Introduction to Dynamic Poetry',
  summary: 'A brief overview of the dynamic poetry game.',
  text: '' +
  'The game itself is simple. Click to select a word magnet. ' +
  'Drag to move the word around the screen. Make up poems ' +
  'using the words you are provided, or add and/or delete ' +
  'your own words.<p>When you have a poem you want to save, ' +
  'click on the words in the poem, one at a time, while ' +
  'holding the shift key. This will select the phrase for ' +
  'you to save it using the <b>save poem</b> menu item. Give ' +
  'your poem a name, using the form, and save it.<p>Later, ' +
  'you can restore a saved poem and show your friends.',
  keywords: 'introduction|overview'
}
```

```
my_help[1] = new Object();
my_help[1].title = 'Quick Menu Item Walkthrough';
my_help[1].topics = new Array();

my_help[1].topics[0] = new Object();
my_help[1].topics[0] = {
  title: 'Adding a New Word',
  summary: 'How to add a new word to the game.',
  text: '' +
  'Select the <b>add word</b> menu item from the ' +
  '<b>Words</b> menu. This will bring up a form ' +
  'field at the bottom of the game\'s playing field. ' +
  'Just type your word there and click ' +
  'the button to add the word to the game.',
  tip: 'Type the word you would like to add into the field ' +
  'and click the button to add the word to the game.',
  tipref: 'addword',
  keywords: 'add word'
}
```

Integrating the Help Module into the Application

Now that we've defined the help file format, if not actually shown you its entire contents, it's time to begin integrating the Help module into the sample application. We follow the same conventions for including the Help module and help configuration file into the HTML file for the application as we've been doing all along. We then define the appropriate places to stick tip icons, and include those in the file. Because we've already shown you the help definitions for the "add word" component, let's look at the markup for that form, shown in Listing 15-14. Following the form elements, due to the problem with Netscape Navigator's forms ignoring z-index, we add an anchor-wrapped IMG tag, set to reveal the addword tip when the user clicks the icon. The anchor must be inside the form element or else the icon is displayed below the form – definitely not what we want, as the form is already at the bottom of the screen.

Listing 15-14: Example markup for the "add word" tip

```
<div id=addwordlayer class=formbg>
<h1>add a word</h1>
<form name="add_word_form" onSubmit="return false;">
add the following word:<br>
<input type=text name=word size=20>
```

```
<input type=button value="add word"
 onClick="new_word_from_form(add_word_form);">
<a href="#" onClick='help_tip_reveal(event, "addword");'>
<img src="/images/help_border12x14.gif" border=0></a>
</form>
</div>
```

We sprinkle these icons throughout the markup (and, where the form contents are dynamically generated, such as with `prep_word_delete_form()`, we add the icon markup to those as well). The only thing remaining for us to do is add the function definitions for the Help menu. The first default function, `help_show_contents()`, would be a great place to put any code we wanted to use for prepopulating the pop-up Help window with a particular topic, perhaps using cookies to pass the topic name as a parameter. This function can go in the application's code itself, or in the Help module itself. We've chosen to do the latter, but if your application requires special treatment, such as that discussed previously, it might make sense to stick it in the Help module instead.

```
function help_show_contents() {
  help_pop_launch();
}
```

Of course, hindsight is 20/20. In reality, we probably could have just named the pop-up window function `help_show_contents()` and saved ourselves some hassle. The About box is the place where programmers go to brag about themselves, plant Easter eggs, and generally fight burnout. The last item in the standard dynamic menu help calls the `help_about()` handler, so for completeness (and so you go visit the code on the support Web site for the book to see what wild and crazy things we build into the About box), here is the code that implements that function:

```
function help_about() {
  if( object_name["aboutbox"] ) {
    object_name["aboutbox"].set_z_index(10000);
    object_name["aboutbox"].reveal();
  }
}
```

The markup for the About box is what you might expect in any boring About box: a table set to obscure the entire screen, the name of the application and various copyright statements, a hint as to who is to blame, and so on. The button merely closes the About box by concealing the object.

```
<div id="aboutbox">
<table width=600 height=450 border=0 cellpadding=10 cellspacing=0>
<tr>
```

```
<td align=center valign=middle bgcolor=#000000>
<h1>Dynamic Poetry</h1>
<h1><i>(c) 1998 by Steven Champeon</i></h1>
<p>
<form>
<input type="button" value="return to game"
       onClick='object_name["aboutbox"].conceal();'>
</form>
</td>
</tr>
</table>
</div>
```

The last thing we need to do is add the calls to `help_init()` to the `executive_poetry_init()` routine (for Netscape Navigator) and the final SCRIPT tag in the HTML markup (for Internet Explorer), and we're ready to test. You can see the sample application, complete with the Help pop-up window and a tip, in Figure 15-7.

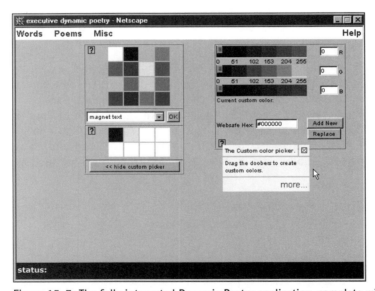

Figure 15-7: The fully integrated Dynamic Poetry application, complete with Help

Testing Your Help

Testing the Help is relatively easy, because it is broken up into two different phases. The first, obviously, is the pop-up window, which is easily walked through and compared to the contents and organization of the help configuration file. Make sure the topic subject is correct, that every topic is available by way of the navigation, and that all of the links point to the proper places. They should, if the configuration file was properly written, because they are all automatically generated. When we first tested the pop-up window, however, we discovered a few fumble-finger issues in the configuration file that we never would have noticed without fully testing the resulting pop-up window.

Secondly, when you are done testing the topics, visit every tip in the application and make sure that they:

◆ Aren't obscured by form elements

◆ Reveal the appropriate tip when the user clicks the icon

◆ Close when the user clicks the close box

◆ Are legible

Single out any problems and revisit the help configuration file or HTML markup to correct them. If you're using JavaScript to generate any of the markup for the tip icons, make sure that those scripts are functioning properly as well.

Keyboard Shortcuts

Given the way that we had to pull back from our original intentions for the Help module, we almost hate to talk about keyboard shortcuts, as support for keyboard events is notoriously spotty. However, the Keyboard module we use works in both browsers on Windows and the Macintosh, so all the nasty stuff we're going to say about the (usually very stable) Solaris version of Netscape Navigator will probably be ignored. The good news is that keyboard shortcuts are possible across platforms. The bad news is that we're limited to alphabetic characters, and the only sure combination that doesn't conflict with other keyboard shortcuts in the browsers themselves is to use Shift, Ctrl, and a letter. Function keys are not yet supported by the browsers, nor are arrows or many other relatively standard keys.

Centrally Managing Keyboard Shortcuts

The trick to managing keyboard shortcuts, as we saw by way of oblique reference in the last chapter, is to register all shortcuts with a central repository that can handle the actions they've been assigned. Then, set up event capture for keyboard events for the entire window. If the key combination doesn't kick off an action, it is routed to the element to which it was originally intended.

Recall the last chapter, where we defined keyboard shortcuts for the various menu items. Each was registered by the Dynamic Menu module, and the application was responsible for making sure that event handling was set up and so forth. The Keyboard module, the next module we discuss, provides mechanisms by which registration, event handling, and action handling may be performed without having to write custom keyboard event handling code for every application you develop.

The Keyboard Module

The purpose of the Keyboard module is to manage keyboard shortcuts, from registration through setting up event handling and performing the actions associated with the shortcuts themselves. We start on page load by creating the array where the shortcut information is stored, shown in Listing 15-15. Because we can only use the letters of the alphabet, we create an array of length 27. We could have used 26, as there are obviously only that many letters in the alphabet, but we decided that people are accustomed to thinking of "a" as letter number one, so to accommodate that expectation, the first element in the array (zero) remains unused. Each element is then initialized as an object, and properties for each modifier and the handler are set to `false`, to ensure that no phantom behaviors creep in.

Listing 15-15: The Keyboard module initialization

```
var kb_shortcuts = new Array(27);
// pre-initialize shortcuts array with nulls
for(var x = 0; x < kb_shortcuts.length; x++ ) {
  kb_shortcuts[x] = new Object();
  kb_shortcuts[x] = {
    shift:    false,
    alt:      false,
    control:  false,
    handler:  false
  }
}
```

We saw the `kb_register_shortcut()` function in Chapter 14, "Dynamic Menus," but didn't talk about it much. Well, now we can—it is shown in Listing 15-16. Recall that we pass the key, Boolean values representing the modifiers, and the JavaScript function to act as a handler for the shortcut. The key is passed to a function that normalizes it to a value between 1 and 27, based on the alphabet, and that shortcut element in the `kb_shortcuts` array is assigned the values appropriately.

Listing 15-16: The kb_register_shortcut() JavaScript function

```
function kb_register_shortcut(key, shift, alt, control, handler) {
  var the_key = kb_normalize_key(key);
  var kbs = kb_shortcuts[the_key];
  if( shift )   { kbs.shift = true; }
  if( alt )     { kbs.alt = true; }
  if( control ) { kbs.control = true; }
```

```
  kbs.handler = handler;
  return true;
}
```

The `kb_normalize_key()` function, shown in Listing 15-17, is simple. It takes a number and checks to make sure it falls within a certain range (based on the ASCII values of the alphabetical characters) and normalizes it to a value representing its place within the alphabet, with 1 representing "a," 2 representing "b," and so on. This value is used to index into the array of shortcuts when assigning the handler and other information, as seen previously. More robust versions of the two functions would handle error conditions, such as those that occur when the key is out of range, returning -1 for failure, but that is left as an exercise for the reader.

Listing 15-17: The kb_normalize_key() JavaScript function

```
function kb_normalize_key(k) {
  if((( k > 122 ) && ( k < 65 )) ||
     (( k > 90 ) && ( k < 97))) {
    return -1;
  } else { // normalize to lowercase
    if(( k <= 90 ) && ( k >= 65 )) {
      k -= 64;
    } else if(( k >= 97 ) && ( k <= 122 )) {
      k -= 96;
    }
    return k;
  }
}
```

After the keyboard shortcut has been registered, we need to make sure that the application captures the input, otherwise we have accomplished nothing. Because some browsers generate keyboard events for key down when modifier keys are pressed, we use the key up event handler to associate with our action handler. Listing 15-18 shows the details, which should be familiar by now. The Netscape Navigator event capture stuff is set up at the document level, and the `kb_do_shortcut()` handler is assigned to the `onkeyup` event handler.

Listing 15-18: The kb_set_event_handlers() JavaScript function

```
function kb_set_event_handlers() {
  if( document.captureEvents ) {
    document.captureEvents( Event.KEYUP );
  }
  document.onkeyup = kb_do_shortcut;
}
```

Now we're all set to use our keyboard shortcuts. The keyup event is generated when we let go of our keys, not when we press them, and the key's ASCII value is passed as part of the event structure to the kb_do_shortcut() function, shown in Listing 15-19. First, we wrap the event so we have access to the cross-browser properties, and then pass the key's value to kb_normalize_key(), which returns the index into the kb_shortcuts array. If no shortcut is defined for that particular combination of keys and modifiers, the function returns without invoking the handler, routing the event if necessary for Navigator. The rest of the function is necessary in order to test for the presence of modifier keys and compare the final combination of modifiers and the alphabetic character to that defined in the shortcut.

Listing 15-19: The kb_do_shortcut() JavaScript function

```
function kb_do_shortcut(e) {
  // get our cross-browser event vals
  evt = wrap_event(e);
  var the_key = kb_normalize_key(evt.key);
  if( the_key == 0 ) { return false; }

  var shortcut = kb_shortcuts[the_key];
  // if there is no shortcut defined, bail
  if( ! shortcut.handler ) {
    if( routeEvent ) {
      routeEvent(e);
    } else {
      return true;
    }
  }
  var do_it = false;

  // which modifier keys does the shortcut want?
  // is shift required?
  if( shortcut.shift ) {
    // was shift pressed?
    if( evt.shift ) {
      do_it = true;
    } else {
      do_it = false;
    }
  }
  // is alt required?
  if( shortcut.alt ) {
    // was it pressed?
    if( evt.alt ) {
      do_it = true;
    } else {
```

```
      do_it = false;
    }
  }
  // is control key required?
  if( shortcut.control ) {
    // was it pressed?
    if( evt.control ) {
      do_it = true;
    } else {
      do_it = false;
    }
  }

  // if all required keys were pressed,
  // eval the handler if there's one set.
  if( do_it && shortcut.handler ) {
    eval( shortcut.handler );
    // and handle bubbling in IE
    if( window.event ) {
      window.event.cancelBubble = true;
    }
  }
  return true;
}
```

If the handler is defined, and the modifiers test was passed with no problems, the handler is invoked by way of an `eval()` JavaScript call. Event bubbling in Internet Explorer is canceled, just to be sure, and we're done.

It is worth noting that the way the Keyboard module is defined, it is impossible to assign different shortcuts to the same alpha character but with different modifiers defined. This is less important a limitation than it would seem, as Ctrl and Shift seem to be the only two modifier keys that are consistently captured across platforms. Sun uses the Meta key, Apple Macintoshes use the Command and Option keys, and Windows uses the Alt key. We won't go into why it is unlikely that you'll see arrow key handling in place across platforms any time soon.

Gotchas

More gotchas than you can shake a stick at:

◆ We've already gone into great detail discussing problems with DHTML's help-ready capabilities, such as lack of support for the conventional F1 key, so don't expect to use anything but straight alphabetic characters for keyboard input.

◆ There seems to be no easy way to build a useful combo box. The options list `selectedIndex` may be modified, but it doesn't scroll the selected setting into view if hidden.

◆ There also seems to be no good way to provide an interactive, visual hierarchy of help topics, because you cannot control whether the browser displays a scrollbar just because you've extended a layer beyond the edge of the screen. In future generations of browsers, support for the `overflow` properties of CSS will make this possible. To be fair, we should mention that Internet Explorer enables you to set `overflow` to `scroll`, which does what we want, but the same is not true of Navigator.

◆ Support for keyboard events across platforms is spotty. On Solaris, keyboard events don't seem to be supported by Navigator unless a form element is present. We decided that to include a form element on every layer that expected keyboard input would complicate matters enormously, especially given the way that form elements are difficult, if not impossible, to hide beneath other layers in Navigator.

◆ No matter what you do, form elements always shine through.

◆ The values returned by the image wrapper `height()` and `width()` methods are relative to the enclosing layer, not the root browser window. This is only a problem when trying to `overlay()` an object atop an image that is inside a layer object, but it's still a problem. It's a difficult decision — should the image wrapper methods be fixed, or the `overlay()` function be extended to deal with layers? Let us know what you think by visiting the support Web site for the book.

Not a bad rollup, all told. We managed to implement keyboard shortcuts, if somewhat limited by the letters in the alphabet, and we also managed to provide a navigable help system complete with context-sensitive tips, with suggestions as to how to enable the pop-up window for more targeted context sensitivity. Now all you have to do is avoid trying to cover up a form element with a floating layer in Netscape Navigator, and you're all set to build your own full-featured applications.

Summary

In this chapter, you learned:

◆ Important principles and guidelines to follow when designing online help systems

◆ Why DHTML is currently not the best choice for implementing full-blown help systems, and that you would probably be better off using traditional HTML in this case

- How to structure your help system's navigation

- How to present your help to maximize benefit to the user in a variety of contexts

- How to capture and centrally manage keyboard input

- How to use mouse events to position elements, as we do with the help tips

In the next chapter, we take a look at some more nifty extensions to the basic cross-browser API in order to build a really kicking About box, schedule JavaScript actions for delayed or regular execution, gradually show or hide objects using clipping regions, and generally fuss about a bit as we clean up loose ends.

Chapter 16

Timers and Other Fun Stuff

IN THIS CHAPTER

◆ Using `setTimeout()` to provide delayed, one-time behaviors

◆ Using `setInterval()` to provide regular, repeated behaviors

◆ Creating independent, self-terminating loops

◆ Using the cross-browser object wrappers to manage clipping regions and move objects around

◆ Adding animated footnotes to the sample application

◆ Jazzing up your About box and other minor tweaks

IN THE LAST CHAPTER, we assisted the user by building an online help system. In this chapter, we pause to have a little fun with animated objects, discussing ways in which core JavaScript can make it possible to delay the execution of a statement or provide repetitive, looping execution of a statement complete with self-terminating loops. Along the way, we add some brief instructions for those who can't be bothered to read the Help, along with animated footnotes that expand upon the limited explanations found in the instructions. We wrap up our sample application by tweaking a few things to round out the user experience.

An Overview/Review of JavaScript Timers

JavaScript provides a couple of different ways to create *timers*, routines that continually check for the truth of a condition and execute statements independently of other code that may be running at the same time. The first method, the core JavaScript routine `setTimeout()`, simply checks to see if the appropriate amount of time has elapsed before executing the statement. The second, `setInterval()`, provides a way to execute a statement (or group of statements) repeatedly until the timer is cleared. Let's look a little closer.

Delaying an Action with setTimeout()

JavaScript provides the setTimeout() function so that developers can set a function, statement, or set of statements to be executed after a certain amount of time has elapsed. The other benefit to setTimeout() is that other code can be running independently of the delayed function. In other programming languages, this independent subprocess is called a *thread*, or a lightweight process that runs separately from other program flow. The common JavaScript terminology refers to these processes as *timers*, however, and that is the term we use here.

The setTimeout() function takes up to three arguments, but we only concern ourselves with two: the JavaScript statement to execute, and the delay before execution specified in milliseconds. The function returns a unique integer value identifier that should be saved as a global variable so that the timer may be killed before the statement is executed. For example, note the following call to setTimeout(), which is assumed to have been called outside any functions:

```
var global_id = setTimeout('alert("executing statement!");', 1000);
```

The identifier global_id is then used, as we show later, to clear the timer. The second example declares a global variable outside the function call, and uses it to store the identifier for later use. You might also declare an array to store multiple timer ids, and increment a counter variable to ensure that the global_id variable is not overwritten by consecutive and overlapping calls to the function. In fact, we do this in both the wipe() and slide() functions discussed later in the chapter.

```
var global_id = 0;
function example_timer(expr, delay) {
  global_id = setTimeout(expr, delay);
}
```

Note that although the setTimeout() function accepts up to three arguments, Navigator and Internet Explorer differ in their treatment of the third argument. Netscape's browser enables you to specify a string containing parameters to be used as arguments to a function call passed as the first argument. Internet Explorer, on the other hand, uses the third parameter to specify which scripting engine should be used to execute the first argument. Because Navigator does not support VBScript, and because IE wouldn't deal well with a list of arguments where it expects to find a language specifier, we don't use the third argument at all.

Killing a Timer with clearTimeout()

Sometimes, you may want to set a timer but clear it before it actually executes its statement. This is why we save the identifier — to pass it as the sole argument to the clearTimeout() JavaScript function, as follows:

```
clearTimeout(global_id);
```

The timer associated with the identifier `global_id` is killed as a result of this function call. For debugging purposes, you may want to wrap `clearTimeout()` in a function that prints a debugging message if it is called successfully. Unfortunately, there is no way to test if the timer has been killed, as `clearTimeout()` does not return a value. You just have to take it on faith that the timer is dead.

Setting Up a Timed Loop with setInterval()

The `setInterval()` JavaScript function is similar to the `setTimeout()` function, except that the function/statement/statements that are passed as its first argument are executed repeatedly every time the delay specified as its second argument elapses. For example, if you wanted to check to see if an image has been loaded, and keep checking until it has, you could set a timer to test the image's `readyState` property in Internet Explorer, or its `complete` property in Navigator. Alternately, if you're using the cross-browser library, you could call the `is_loaded()` method, as follows:

```
var expr = 'if( myimage.is_loaded() ) { my_function(); }';
var global_interval_id = setInterval(expr, 1000);
```

The problem with this approach is that unless you clear the interval timer after the test is successful, the timer repeatedly executes the function `my_function()` every second until the browser crashes or your user bails out in mortal fear that they have broken something. A better way to handle this is illustrated in the next section.

Note that like `setTimeout()`, the `setInterval()` function also allows a third variable, which is identical in use (and divergence between the way the two major browsers use it) to that mentioned in relation to `setTimeout()`.

Killing a Timed Loop with clearInterval()

Sometimes, it is necessary to kill an interval timer, perhaps as soon as some internal condition has been met or if conditions elsewhere in the browser require it. For example, let's say that the situation we described requires that the function `my_function()` only be called once when the image has been loaded. In that case, we would use the following code to kill the interval timer when the condition has been met:

```
var expr = 'if( myimage.is_loaded() ) { my_function();' +
  clearInterval(global_interval_id); }';
var global_interval_id = setInterval(expr, 1000);
```

Because the variable `global_interval_id` is a global, it may be used to construct the expression that is evaluated when the condition has been met. The variable contains the interval's unique identifier, and when the condition proves true, the statement is evaluated, calling `my_function()` and then killing the interval timer. Again, there is no way to check if the interval timer has been successfully cleared, but we haven't had any trouble with it not working.

Gradually Revealing or Concealing Objects

Although traditional interface design tends to prefer relatively static interface elements, it has become fashionable to make things whiz around the browser screen, and you may even find that whizzing objects are required by your application. If you do, let us know, and we will put your example next to the sole example of an appropriate use of the <BLINK> tag.

Windows 98, for example, has added to its vast arsenal of flashy interface functionality by making pop-up windows quickly reveal themselves, starting in one corner of the pop-up window and growing to the full size. We remain unconvinced that this extra flash is useful, but we are willing to listen to arguments.

In any case, before we get into the gory details of showing you how to provide moving interface elements, or interface elements that gradually reveal or conceal themselves, we must cover the concepts behind clipping regions. Why? Because all of our examples use timers to dynamically alter the visible area of objects, and to do that you need to use clipping regions.

Using Clipping Regions

A *clipping region* is an area of an object, distinct from the object's actual dimensions, that defines the portion of the area that should be revealed. Clipping regions are defined differently in the two browsers, naturally, so we've taken care to hide the differences behind a set of wrapper methods. The key to understanding clipping regions is that they are (at least for now, anyway) strictly rectangular, but are described differently than you may be used to. Whereas we are accustomed to thinking of rectangles as boxes with a top, left, width, and height, the clipping region is defined in terms of top, left, bottom and right. This is because the area described by the clipping region is distinct from the size of the object it reveals or conceals. Rather, it is described in terms of the region itself, which has a starting top and left coordinate and a corresponding corner. There is nothing at all that requires that a clipping region actually reveal any part of the object, and the top and bottom may in fact overlap. The same is true for the left and right values.

The cross-browser wrappers provide methods for manipulating layer objects' clipping areas as a whole, as well as manipulating individual parameters. Listing 16-1 illustrates the clipper() method, called on an object like so:

```
object_name["myobject"].clipper(top,left,bottom,right);
```

The call above (assuming that top and the other variables have been defined) sets the clipping region of the object. Because Navigator and Internet Explorer differ in their implementation of clipping regions, we have to test for the appropriate method. IE follows the CSS Recommendation, and therefore expects the clip property to be set using a string containing pixel values for each corner of the region. These values must be in the following form for IE to set the clip appropriately:

```
rect(0px 0px 100px 100px)
```

This approach probably enables IE's developers to implement nonrectangular clipping regions in a future version of the browser, using different strings such as circle(center radius).

Internet Explorer for Macintosh 4.01 does not support clipping regions at all. You may read the values of the clipping region's properties, but modifying them has no effect whatsoever on the object in question. If your application requires clipping regions, you may need to convince your Macintosh users to stick to Netscape Navigator.

In Navigator, however, the clip property has several children, representing the four arguments (top, left, bottom, and right) so we set them individually if we're using Navigator.

Listing 16-1: The cross-browser clipper() method

```
function clipper(top, left, bottom, right) {
  if( this.css1 ) {
    var rect_str = "rect("+top+"px "+right+
      "px "+bottom+"px "+left+"px)";
    this.css1.style.clip = rect_str;
  } else {
    this.style.clip.left = left;
    this.style.clip.right = right;
    this.style.clip.top = top;
    this.style.clip.bottom = bottom;
  }
}
```

The cross-browser wrapper library also provides several methods for reading individual clip properties. For the sake of brevity, we only illustrate one, clipper_right(), in Listing 16-2. In IE, we grab the style.clip property and parse it into its constituent parts, returning the one we want. If the clip is not present, we return zero. In Navigator, because the individual properties are already broken out, we simply return the appropriate value. The other methods work in a similar manner.

Note that we've added some code dealing with three potentially troublesome cases. In the first, the value returned for the clipping rectangle is not four pixel values, but the keyword `auto`, so we have to test for that and return zero. In the second, we work around a bug in Internet Explorer for the Macintosh, where the string is actually returned as `rect(0px 0px) 0px 0px`, obviously not what we want. The third and final case addresses the instance where the value returned doesn't contain the `px` unit specifiers, but does contain a value worth parsing into an integer. Looks like a lot of work, eh? The really annoying thing is that IE for the Macintosh simply doesn't recognize modifications made to clipping regions at all. The only reason we're even showing you this function is to demonstrate the sort of platform-specific workarounds that we've conveniently buried in the cross-platform wrapper library. Well, it's not the only reason. The other reason is to hammer home the point that even extensive workarounds cannot address every instance of a poorly supported or buggy piece of functionality. Sometimes, you aren't able to do everything that you want.

Listing 16-2: The clipper_right() JavaScript function

```
function clipper_right() {
  if( this.css1 ) {
    if( this.css1.style.clip ) {
      var the_clip = this.css1.style.clip;
      // the_clip should be rect(0px 0px 0px 0px) or auto
      if( the_clip == "auto" ) {
        return this.width();
      } else {
        var paren = the_clip.indexOf(')');
        if( paren != the_clip.length ) { //
          // it probably looks like rect(0px 0px) 0px 0px
          var coords = the_clip.substring(5);
          // coords should look like 0px 0px) 0px 0px
        } else {
          var the_len = the_clip.length - 1;
          var coords = the_clip.substring(5, the_len);
          // coords should look like 0px 0px 0px 0px
        }
        var rect = coords.split(" ");
        // this should give us:
        //   rect[0]: top in 'n' pixels
        //   rect[1]: right in 'n' pixels
        //   rect[2]: bottom in 'n' pixels
        //   rect[3]: left in 'n' pixels
        var r = rect[1].split("p"); // 'n', 'x'
        if( r.length > 1 ) {
```

```
            return parseInt(r[0]);
        } else {
            return parseInt(r);
        }
      }
  } else {
    return this.style.clip.right;
  }
}
```

In addition to the methods that enable you to read individual clip properties easily, there are also methods provided for setting the clipping region without having to know all four values of the region. We show `set_clipper_right()` as an example, in Listing 16-3. The methods are similar, however. When the method is called, it in turn calls the methods that read the missing properties, and finally calls the `clipper()` method to set the region using the new values.

Listing 16-3: The set_clipper_right() JavaScript function

```
function set_clipper_right(r) {
  var t = this.clipper_top();
  var b = this.clipper_bottom();
  var l = this.clipper_left();
  this.clipper(t,l,b,r);
}
```

Now that we've covered the basics of clipping regions, let's put them to use with the `wipe()` function, described in detail in the next section.

Wiping an Object Off the Screen with wipe()

You may, after reviewing this section, decide that `wipe()` is the ugliest function that you've ever seen. With the exception of some of the BASIC code we wrote when we were just getting started with programming, you may be right. For the sake of argument, however, we ask that you reserve judgement until later in the chapter, when you've seen how easy it makes the process of gradually revealing or concealing objects.

The `wipe()` function uses global variables, actually members of arrays, to store the intermediate values of the various clipping region settings. Because the `setInterval()` function is evaluated outside of the function that calls it, the variables must be globally defined. Otherwise, you throw up repeated errors every time the specified delay passes, which can be quite rapid indeed depending on the delay you've specified. The `wipe()` function basically constructs a set of statements based on the direction in which the object is to be revealed or concealed. The statements include a test for the completion of the operation, based on comparisons between the current coordinates of the clipping region and those that we determine to be the final coordinates of the operation itself. Listing 16-4 illustrates the `wipe()` function, including a few global arrays that are initialized when the page is loaded by the browser.

We use funny-looking variables such as `_winterval[0]` because it is traditional for global variables used by the system to begin with an underscore or pair of underscores. Recall the use by Navigator of `_js_layer0` for its internal naming convention for layers. We define arrays for the top, left, bottom, and right values for the final clipping region for each object on which we call the `wipe()` function. The `_winterval` array is used to store the unique interval identifier associated with each call to `setInterval()`, and the `_wcount` variable is used to provide a unique identifier for the current operation, for later use by the `clearInterval()` function. The `wipe()` function is called as follows, with the name of the object on which to operate, the direction in terms of a compass point, an offset in pixels, the delay time in milliseconds, and whether to reveal or conceal the object. The object is revealed if `reverse` is true, in increments of `offset` pixels, every `time` milliseconds, from the direction specified. If `reverse` is false, the object is hidden, starting from the direction passed as the second argument.

```
wipe(name, "NW", 10, 100, false);
```

This conceals the object in increments of 10 pixels every tenth of a second, starting with the northwest corner. For the sake of making this a bit clearer, let's take a look at the test and other variables set by the call above:

```
//////////    NORTHWEST   //////////
    if( reverse ) {
      top = 'parseInt(_wb['+_wcount+']-='+offset+')';
      left = 'parseInt(_wr['+_wcount+']-='+offset+')';
      last_top = 'parseInt(_wb['+_wcount+']-='+y_remainder+')';
      last_left = 'parseInt(_wr['+_wcount+']-='+x_remainder+')';
    } else {
      top = 'parseInt(_wt['+_wcount+']+='+offset+')';
      left = 'parseInt(_wl['+_wcount+']+='+offset+')';
      last_top = 'parseInt(_wt['+_wcount+']+='+y_remainder+')';
      last_left = 'parseInt(_wl['+_wcount+']+='+x_remainder+')';
    }
    test = '(_wb['+_wcount+'] > _wt['+_wcount+']) || ' +
    '(_wr['+_wcount+'] > _wl['+_wcount+']))';
```

If `reverse` is true, the `top` variable is set to contain a statement that decrements the member of the `_wb` array referred to by `_wcount`, but because it is possible that `_wcount` could be incremented by a separate call to `wipe()`, we must treat it as a literal, outside of the string, when setting `top`. Similarly, we decrement the appropriate member of the `_wr` array in the statement assigned to `left`. In order that the function knows when it is to stop decrementing the values mentioned, we also calculate the `last_top` and `last_left` variables, which are eventually assigned to the appropriate _w variable. The x_remainder and y_remainder variables are arrived at by finding the modulus of the total distance that must be covered and the offset that is to be used. This enables the function to run just up until the point that it would exceed the parameters of the required clipping region, and no more. The remainders are then used once the timer has been cleared to finish the job started by the timer itself.

These variables are then tested in the statement defined for test, which in this case checks to see that the bottom is still greater than the top, and that the right-side clipping value is still greater than the left. If reverse is not true, the top and left variables are set in the opposite fashion. In essence, we are creating a loop that contains a test for its own completion.

Listing 16-4: The wipe() JavaScript function

```
var _wt = new Array();
var _wl = new Array();
var _wb = new Array();
var _wr = new Array();
var _winterval = new Array();
var _wcount = 0;
function wipe(obj, direction, offset, time, reverse) {
  _wcount++;
  var o = object_name[obj];
  var width = o.get_width();
  var height = o.get_height();
  var test = "";
  var top = 0;
  var bottom = height;
  var left = 0;
  var right = width;
  var expr = "";
  var last_top = top;
  var last_bottom = bottom;
  var last_left = left;
  var last_right = right;
  var x_remainder = width % offset;
  var y_remainder = height % offset;

  _wt[_wcount] = top;
  _wl[_wcount] = left;
  _wb[_wcount] = bottom;
  _wr[_wcount] = right;

  if( direction == "N" ) {
  //////////    NORTH    //////////
    if( reverse ) {
```

```
      top = 'parseInt(_wb['+_wcount+']-='+offset+')';
      last_top = 'parseInt(_wb['+_wcount+']-='+y_remainder+')';
    } else {
      top = 'parseInt(_wt['+_wcount+']+='+offset+')';
      last_top = 'parseInt(_wt['+_wcount+']+='+y_remainder+')';
    }
    test = '_wb['+_wcount+'] > _wt['+_wcount+']';
  } else if( direction == "NW" ) {
  //////////   NORTHWEST   //////////
    if( reverse ) {
      top = 'parseInt(_wb['+_wcount+']-='+offset+')';
      left = 'parseInt(_wr['+_wcount+']-='+offset+')';
      last_top = 'parseInt(_wb['+_wcount+']-='+y_remainder+')';
      last_left = 'parseInt(_wr['+_wcount+']-='+x_remainder+')';
    } else {
      top = 'parseInt(_wt['+_wcount+']+='+offset+')';
      left = 'parseInt(_wl['+_wcount+']+='+offset+')';
      last_top = 'parseInt(_wt['+_wcount+']+='+y_remainder+')';
      last_left = 'parseInt(_wl['+_wcount+']+='+x_remainder+')';
    }
    test = '(_wb['+_wcount+'] > _wt['+_wcount+']) || ' +
      '(_wr['+_wcount+'] > _wl['+_wcount+'])';
  } else if( direction == "W" ) {
  //////////     WEST     //////////
    if( reverse ) {
      left = 'parseInt(_wr['+_wcount+']-='+offset+')';
      last_left = 'parseInt(_wr['+_wcount+']-='+x_remainder+')';
    } else {
      left = 'parseInt(_wl['+_wcount+']+='+offset+')';
      last_left= 'parseInt(_wl['+_wcount+']+='+x_remainder+')';
    }
    test = '_wr['+_wcount+'] > _wl['+_wcount+']';
  } else if( direction == "SW" ) {
  //////////   SOUTHWEST   //////////
    if( reverse ) {
      left = 'parseInt(_wr['+_wcount+']-='+offset+')';
      bottom = 'parseInt(_wt['+_wcount+']+='+offset+')';
      last_left = 'parseInt(_wr['+_wcount+']-='+x_remainder+')';
      last_bottom='parseInt(_wt['+_wcount+']+='+y_remainder+')';
    } else {
      left = 'parseInt(_wl['+_wcount+']+='+offset+')';
      bottom = 'parseInt(_wb['+_wcount+']-='+offset+')';
      last_left = 'parseInt(_wl['+_wcount+']+='+x_remainder+')';
      last_left = 'parseInt(_wb['+_wcount+']-='+y_remainder+')';
    }
```

```
      test = '(_wb['+_wcount+'] > _wt['+_wcount+']) || ' +
        '(_wr['+_wcount+'] > _wl['+_wcount+'])';
} else if( direction == "S" ) {
  //////////    SOUTH    //////////
  if( reverse ) {
    bottom = 'parseInt(_wt['+_wcount+']+='+offset+')';
    last_bottom='parseInt(_wt['+_wcount+']+='+y_remainder+')';
  } else {
    bottom = 'parseInt(_wb['+_wcount+']-='+offset+')';
    last_bottom='parseInt(_wb['+_wcount+']-='+y_remainder+')';
  }
  test = '_wb['+_wcount+'] > _wt['+_wcount+']';
} else if( direction == "SE" ) {
  //////////    SOUTHEAST    //////////
  if( reverse ) {
    bottom = 'parseInt(_wt['+_wcount+']+='+offset+')';
    right = 'parseInt(_wl['+_wcount+']+='+offset+')';
    last_bottom='parseInt(_wt['+_wcount+']+='+y_remainder+')';
    last_right='parseInt(_wl['+_wcount+']+='+x_remainder+')';
  } else {
    bottom = 'parseInt(_wb['+_wcount+']-='+offset+')';
    right = 'parseInt(_wr['+_wcount+']-='+offset+')';
    last_bottom='parseInt(_wb['+_wcount+']-='+y_remainder+')';
    last_right='parseInt(_wr['+_wcount+']-='+x_remainder+')';
  }
  test = '(_wb['+_wcount+'] > _wt['+_wcount+']) || ' +
    '(_wr['+_wcount+'] > _wl['+_wcount+'])';
} else if( direction == "E" ) {
  //////////    EAST    //////////
  if( reverse ) {
    right = 'parseInt(_wl['+_wcount+']+='+offset+')';
    last_right='parseInt(_wl['+_wcount+']+='+x_remainder+')';
  } else {
    right = 'parseInt(_wr['+_wcount+']-='+offset+')';
    last_right='parseInt(_wr['+_wcount+']-='+x_remainder+')';
  }
  test = '_wr['+_wcount+'] > _wl['+_wcount+']';
} else if( direction == "NE" ) {
  //////////    NORTHEAST    //////////
  if( reverse ) {
    top = 'parseInt(_wb['+_wcount+']-='+offset+')';
    right = 'parseInt(_wl['+_wcount+']+='+offset+')';
    last_top = 'parseInt(_wb['+_wcount+']-='+y_remainder+')';
    last_right='parseInt(_wl['+_wcount+']+='+x_remainder+')';
  } else {
```

```
        top = 'parseInt(_wt['+_wcount+']+='+offset+')';
        right = 'parseInt(_wr['+_wcount+']-='+offset+')';
        last_top = 'parseInt(_wt['+_wcount+']+='+y_remainder+')';
        last_right='parseInt(_wr['+_wcount+']-='+x_remainder+')';
    }
    test = '(_wb['+_wcount+'] > _wt['+_wcount+']) || ' +
        '(_wr['+_wcount+'] > _wl['+_wcount+'])';
  }

  expr = 'if( '+test+') {';
  expr += 'object_name["'+obj+'"].clipper(';
  expr += top+','+left+','+bottom+','+right+');'; // phew!
  expr += '} else {';
  expr += 'clearInterval(_winterval['+_wcount+']);';
  if(( x_remainder != 0 ) || ( y_remainder != 0 )) {
    expr += 'object_name["'+obj+'"].clipper(';
    expr += last_top+','+last_left+','+last_bottom+
            ','+last_right+');';
  }
  expr += '};';
  _winterval[_wcount] = setInterval(expr, time);
  return _winterval[_wcount];
}
```

As you can see in Listing 16-4, the very last part of the function uses the values set dependent upon the `direction` argument to construct the compound statement, including the test for near-completion, as well as the statements required to bring the operation to its final completion after the timer has been cleared. The compound statement is then passed to `setInterval()`, and the current member of the globally accessible array `_winterval` is assigned the unique identifier associated with the timer.

We recommend that you visit the support Web site for this book so you can download the files in the example application and see the latest updates to (and bug reports filed against) the cross-platform library. And you don't have to type in ugly code like that shown in Listing 16-4, either. We've already done it for you.

Isn't this fun? Finally, the unique identifier is returned so that the timer may be cleared by another function before it reaches completion and does so on its own. As you can see in the sample application, we have need to clear the timer on occasion before it clears itself.

Unwiping an Object Back into View

Revealing an object, as opposed to concealing it, is just as easy. For example, the call we used previously would be made as follows in order to slowly reveal the object instead of concealing it:

```
wipe(name, "NW", 10, 100, true);
```

You may find it easier to provide a function with a more memorable name, such as unwipe(), that passes the appropriate Boolean value as the final argument to the function.

Now that you know how to gradually hide and reveal an object, it's time to talk about a similar operation: moving objects around on the screen.

Gradually Moving Objects around the Screen

In our sample application, as well as elsewhere in our experience as users of traditional user interfaces, we have usually been in control of the motion of our interface elements. The components usually react to user input of some sort or another, such as keyboard input, mouse events, or even voice. Those of us accustomed to multimedia or gaming are perhaps more forgiving of things moving without our direct manipulation, but it can be quite annoying to a user who doesn't expect it.

When Is Animation Just Annoying?

Most of the time. In fact, outside of the realm of gaming, where the context of a game of Tetris or other action-oriented interface prepares the user for unsolicited action, there are very few instances where animation is acceptable. Because it is entirely possible that you have a legitimate use for a moving object, though, we show you how to make use of the function provided.

When Is Animation Acceptable?

One case where animation of an interface object is acceptable outside of the realm of gaming is when you have limited screen real estate and it is considered best to enable the user to hide or reveal a portion of the interface at will. The component that is then hidden may make use of motion to signal its changing status to the user. Even this use of motion is a stretch, however, as the user is expected to hide and show the interface element at will. This lends a direct relationship between the component's visibility and the user's actions.

Suffice it to say that motion is a highly effective and powerful interface tool, and therefore should be used sparingly to avoid alienating the user.

Moving an Object Around with slide()

The `slide()` function is similar to `wipe()`, but a lot simpler, because only the object's position needs to be modified, rather than the various corners of a clipping region. However, it, too, has its idiosyncrasies, and is worth looking at a piece at a time. To start with, because only the `top` and `left` properties of the object are modified, corresponding to the *x* and *y* coordinates of the object's position, we have defined far fewer globally accessible arrays. We have defined an array for storing the unique interval identifier as a global variable for keeping track of the current index into those arrays.

The `slide()` function, illustrated in Listing 16-5, may be called with the name of an object, the direction in which to move, the distance to move the object, the time to delay between steps, and the increment to use for each step. As with `wipe()`, all eight of the compass points may be passed as a direction. The function differs from `wipe()`, however, in that instead of passing the increment to use for each step, the total distance that the object needs to move is passed as the third argument. The delay in milliseconds to pause between executions of the interval is passed as the fourth argument. An optional increment is the fifth argument. If the increment is *not* passed, the increment defaults to one.

Why didn't we just make `slide()` and `wipe()` methods of the object wrappers? The problem is that the special `this` keyword doesn't mean anything outside of the function in which it is called. Most of the other methods in the cross-platform library are simply functions that have been assigned to the object wrappers, using the `this` keyword. The expression passed to `setInterval()`, however, is always executed outside of the function. It would be possible, but sort of weird, to use the `this` keyword to derive the values required to construct the expressions. The other reason we didn't make these functions part of the standard set of wrapper methods is because we wanted to limit the use of the functions to special cases, and defining them as methods by default seemed memory-intensive and wasteful.

We use global arrays to hold our final position values so that the test can be performed outside of the calling function. Again, as with `wipe()`, the modulus of the total distance and the increment is taken and a final shove is constructed to finish the last leg of the move. Because the final position is known at the beginning, however, and because we always move our objects at either 90- or 45-degree angles, we can calculate the final shove quite easily, making the final movement consistent regardless of the direction of the move. We do check for both x and y however, just in case. A future version of this function might be written to allow for arbitrary x and y offsets, rather than a single compass point.

The `if/else` conditionals are much more compact, as we only need to determine the value of the operation to be applied to the `top` and `left` coordinates. If we are moving north, for example, the *x* coordinate remains the same, while subtracting from the *y* coordinate.

Listing 16-5: The slide() JavaScript function

```
var _sx = new Array();
var _sy = new Array();
var _sinterval = new Array();
var _scount = 0;
function slide(obj, direction, fpos, time, inc) {
  _scount++;
  var finalpos = parseInt(fpos);
  var o = object_name[obj];
  if( inc == null ) {
    var increment = 1; // default
  } else {
    var increment = parseInt(inc);
  }
  var x, y;

  // calculate movement by direction
  if( direction == "N" ) {
    //////////    NORTH   //////////
    x = 0;
    y = -1;
  } else if( direction == "NW" ) {
    //////////   NORTHWEST //////////
    x = -1;
    y = -1;
  } else if( direction == "W" ) {
    //////////    WEST    //////////
    x = -1;
    y = 0;
  } else if( direction == "SW" ) {
    //////////   SOUTHWEST  //////////
    x = -1;
    y = 1;
  } else if( direction == "S" ) {
    //////////    SOUTH    //////////
    x = 0;
    y = 1;
  } else if( direction == "SE" ) {
    //////////   SOUTHEAST  //////////
    x = 1;
    y = 1;
  } else if( direction == "E" ) {
    //////////    EAST    //////////
    x = 1;
    y = 0;
```

```
} else if( direction == "NE" ) {
////////// NORTHEAST //////////
 x = 1;
 y = -1;
}

// now, can we reach the final position by steps of 'inc'?
// or do we have to use a modulus?
var x_distance = parseInt(finalpos * x);
var y_distance = parseInt(finalpos * y);
var extra_expr = "";
var x_remainder = x_distance % increment;
var y_remainder = y_distance % increment;

if( x_remainder != 0 ) {
  extra_expr = 'object_name["'+obj+
               '"].shove('+x_remainder+',0);';
}
if( y_remainder != 0 ) {
  extra_expr += 'object_name["'+obj+
               '"].shove(0,'+y_remainder+');';
}
// calculate final x and y positions
_sx[_scount] = parseInt(o.left() + x_distance - x_remainder);
_sy[_scount] = parseInt(o.top() + y_distance - y_remainder);

// calculate increment
x = parseInt(x * increment);
y = parseInt(y * increment);

// now build the expression - we need to use globals b/c it
// will continue to be run outside the function. if there was
// a remainder, add the final expr to finish the move.
var expr = 'if(( object_name["'+obj+'"].left() != ' +
  _sx[_scount] + ') || ' +
  '( object_name["'+obj+'"].top() != ' +
  _sy[_scount] + ')) {' +
  ' object_name["'+obj+'"].shove('+x+','+y+');' +
  '} else {' +
  ' clearInterval(_sinterval['+_scount+']);' +
  extra_expr +
  '};';

_sinterval[_scount] = setInterval(expr, time);
return _sinterval[_scount];
}
```

As in `wipe()`, we construct an extra expression to be called after the timer is cleared to complete the movement of the object, and allow for inexact offsets.

The expression itself is simply a test to see if the current position of the object matches the expected final position, minus any remainder. Rather than checking to see if the current location is greater or less than the expected location, we check for inequality before proceeding. We do this because the final position has already been calculated, taking into account any remainders. The value stored in _wx and _wy is not the final position, but rather the final position attainable in steps of `increment`. The `extra_expr` statement finishes the job if necessary due to remainders.

Again, as we did in the `wipe()` function, we return the interval identifier so that the calling function may clear the interval if required before the move has been completed.

Testing the Timers

Testing the timers is easy, if you have the right tools. The test suite for the cross-browser object wrappers contains a control panel for testing the `wipe()` and `slide()` functions. The JavaScript calls don't make much sense without the markup for the control panel, but Listing 16-6 provides a sample:

Listing 16-6: Testing the wipe() and slide() functions

```
function test_wipe(f) {
  var o = get_selected_option(f.obj);
  var direction = get_selected_option(f.direction);
  var offset = parseInt(f.offset.value);
  var step = parseInt(f.step.value);
  var reverse = (f.reverse.checked ? true : false);
  wipe(o,direction,offset,step,reverse);
}

function test_slide(f) {
  var o = get_selected_option(f.obj);
  var direction = get_selected_option(f.direction);
  var finalpos = parseInt(f.offset.value);
  var time = parseInt(f.step.value);
  var increment = parseInt(f.increment.value);
  slide(o,direction,finalpos,time,increment);
}
```

For more information about the test suite, shown in Figure 16-1, please visit the book's support Web site. The test suite will be updated as required by changes to the cross-browser wrappers.

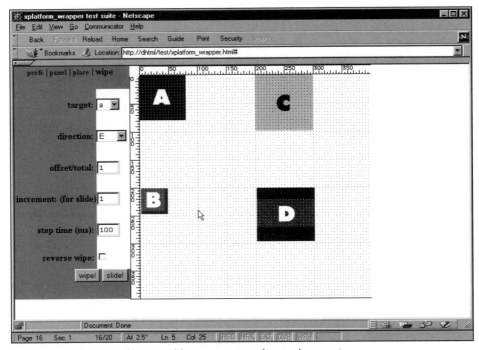

Figure 16-1: The cross-browser object wrapper testing environment

Testing wipe()

Testing the functions is quite straightforward. Simply test from each direction, on several different objects, to make sure that the clipping functions work for your target platform and on the type of object you intend to use.

Test on platforms other than the one or two you intend to target – you may find small timing discrepancies between one platform and another, especially when you take into consideration different hardware and CPU configurations. If you also take into account different display settings, such as 8-bit versus 24-bit screen depths, you may find major differences in the speed of your animations. If you use the screen environment object provided by the cross-platform library, you can determine the values for these settings. Then, depending on what you find, you could either notify the user with a JavaScript alert(), asking them to change their settings for performance reasons, or – on those platforms that support it – modify the display's bit depth accordingly.

Here are some particular things to look out for:

◆ Speed differences

◆ Timer not dying properly when cleared

◆ Interference between two calls of `wipe()` on the same object

◆ Display settings that might interfere with smoothness or speed of animation

The speed issue can be addressed by modifying the delay you specify in the function call. Bear in mind that the milliseconds delay is not a hard and fast timing issue, but the elapsed time between calls to the expression, which may take some time to run. Although we did not run across any browser that failed to clear the interval properly when required, beta versions of the various browsers may very well run into problems. If you intend to support or are required to support any 4.0 browser or above, you may need to check every version you can find on every platform that is appropriate.

Interference between calls to `wipe()` may indicate that your global array values are not being initialized or set properly. You notice this when the object starts oscillating between revealing and hiding itself, for example, or if the object seems to be flickering wildly. How do we know this, you ask? Remember that we tested earlier versions of the function you now see.

Test the function with the opposite value for `reverse` as well, looking for the same things.

Testing slide()

Test `slide()` from each direction, on different objects. In addition, test on different platforms, bearing in mind that Internet Explorer 4.01 on the Macintosh platform does not support clipping regions at all.

Things to look out for:

◆ Speed, premature timer death, or nonstopping timer

◆ Interference

As with the testing regimen recommended for `wipe()`, you may need to check the function on a wide range of hardware and browser platforms and versions, or those that you are required to support.

Testing with Various Delays

Speed of execution and delay time are related, and may differ widely from one platform to the next. A more efficient JavaScript interpreter, faster CPU, or even the current and peak load on the system being tested can all have an effect on the timing of intervals as well as on the expressions' execution. To be on the safe side, test *everywhere*, simulating load where required.

Integrating the Timers into the Sample Application

To demonstrate the timer functions, we chose to use an instructions layer with hidden animated footnotes. Although it is an interesting effect and saves on screen real estate while at the same time providing a way for quick instructions to be delivered to those who want them, and more detailed information to those who want that, the example is a bit contrived. We would not recommend using smart-aleck footnotes in your application, unless your users get a kick out of being guinea pigs for interface experiments.

Instructions with a Bit of Extra Information

While looking for a demonstrable example of the `slide()` function, we settled on a way to provide extra introductory information about our game to those who want it, while keeping the screen clutter-free for those who aren't interested. The quick instructions and embedded links to the animated footnotes are illustrated in Listing 16-7. We use a comfortably binary pair of mouse events, `onMouseOver` and `onMouseOut`, to activate and deactivate the animated footnotes. When the user places the mouse over the link, the footnote appears at the bottom of the screen and moves until it is roughly flush with the top of the status bar. Figure 16-2 shows the instructions screen with the embedded links to the animated footnotes.

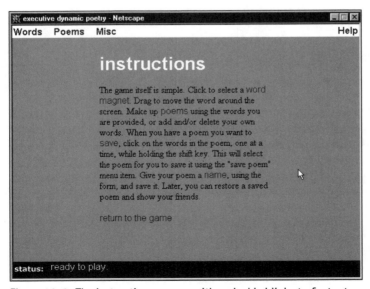

Figure 16-2: The instructions screen, with embedded links to footnotes

Listing 16-7: The new and improved instructions screen

```
<div id=instructionslayer>
<h1>instructions</h1>
The game itself is simple. Click to select a
<a href="#"
onMouseOver='show_footnote(1);'
onMouseOut='hide_footnote(1);'
>word magnet</a>.
Drag to move the word around the screen. Make up
<a href="#"
onMouseOver='show_footnote(2);'
onMouseOut='hide_footnote(2);'
>poems</a> using the words you are provided, or add
and/or delete your own words. When you have a poem
you want to
<a href="#"
onMouseOver='show_footnote(3);'
onMouseOut='hide_footnote(3);'
>save</a>, click on the words in the poem,
one at a time, while holding the shift key. This will
select the poem for you to save it using the "save
poem" menu item. Give your poem a
<a href="#"
onMouseOver='show_footnote(4);'
onMouseOut='hide_footnote(4);'
>name</a>, using the
form, and save it. Later, you can restore a saved
poem and show your friends.
<p>
<a href="#" onClick="toggle_instructions();">
return to the game</a>
</div>
```

Animated Footnotes

The event handlers call the `show_footnote()` and `hide_footnote()` JavaScript functions, illustrated in Listing 16-8. The functions themselves, as promised earlier, are quite simple. We declare a global variable for the footnote interval `id`, rather than an array, because the mouse events are very unlikely to occur independently of one another unless the user reloads the page in the browser, which effectively clears all intervals. We pass the number of the footnote to animate, from which we build the reference to the object. We grab the height of the footnote so we know how far beyond the status bar we should go, set the z-index so the object is visible, and slide the footnote object north, as shown in Figure 16-3. The user has moused over the last link in the instructions, revealing the fourth, ever-so-helpful and encouraging footnote.

Listing 16-8: The hide_footnote() and show_footnote() JavaScript functions

```
var footnote_interval_id = 0;
function show_footnote(f) {
  var note = "footnote" + f;
  var h = object_name[note].height();
  object_name[note].set_z_index(frontmost);
  object_name[note].reveal();
  footnote_interval_id = slide(note, "N", h, 100, 5);
}

function hide_footnote(f) {
  var note = "footnote" + f;
  clearInterval(footnote_interval_id);
  object_name[note].place(footnote_x, footnote_y);
  object_name[note].set_z_index(0);
  object_name[note].conceal();
}
```

The corresponding function first clears the interval timer, using the global variable set in the previous call, and returns the footnote to invisible obscurity in its original location (set by the footnote_x and footnote_y variables elsewhere in the Dynamic Poetry application). We do not return the footnote to its hiding place by way of another call to slide() for two reasons. One, we considered it best to get the footnote out of the way quickly. Two, we did not want to risk bobbling the footnote back and forth between hidden and shown if the user was just wildly moving the mouse around the screen.

Another approach, as we have mentioned and in fact demonstrated in the wipe() function itself, would be to use an array to store each footnote's unique interval id reference, and a value we could check to see if the footnote is being moved to avoid interference.

About Box Animations

As mentioned in the last chapter, About boxes are a place where programmers often blow off steam and hide Easter eggs or provide acknowledgments that would put Sally Field to shame.

In our About box, which is revealed using the function help_about() (seen in Listing 16-9), we just animate the layer into view. To avoid flicker, we set the reveal() function call up on a delay. This guarantees that the layer is mostly hidden before it is revealed, avoiding the flicker. We don't care about catching the identifier from the one-time timer because we are unlikely to want to stop the layer from being revealed.

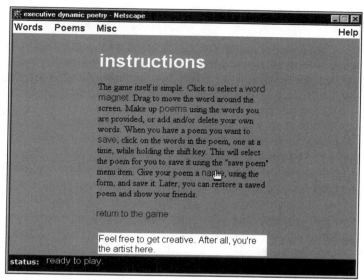

Figure 16-3: The footnote revealed

Listing 16-9: The new, improved help_about() JavaScript function

```
function help_about() {
  // show the about screen!
  if( object_name["aboutbox"] ) {
    object_name["aboutbox"].set_z_index(10000);
    var delayed_reveal = 'object_name["aboutbox"].reveal();';
    wipe("aboutbox", "SE", 10, 50, true);
    setTimeout(delayed_reveal, 50);
  }
}
```

Check the Web site for more exciting uses of bandwidth and processor cycles.

Optimizing Your Application for Final Delivery

You can take a few steps to reduce the time required for app bootup time, usually determined by available bandwidth and likelihood of congestion. If your application starts to execute any of its code before the entire application has downloaded to the browser, your users may get weird errors because of the lag time between the download of the original HTML markup and the externally referenced CSS style sheet of JavaScript modules.

In order to avoid such tragedies, we recommend that you take the following steps to create a network-deliverable release of your product.

Do *not* perform the following steps on your only copy of the code for your application. We *strongly* recommend the use of source and revision control systems when doing development work, but even then the release should be a copy of your original source, not the source itself. The best option is to write a Perl script or use some other automated method of performing the following steps on every release.

First, in order to reduce the amount of time required for file transfer, take the following steps on a copy of the source prepared especially for release:

◆ Remove comments and unneeded white space from code.

◆ Write a quick code optimizer/obfuscator (look for 'function blah(' and 'var blah' and keep a list of all function names in the file, then loop back through and give them shorter names).

Second, you need to reduce the number of errors likely to occur due to an externally referenced file's failure to download:

◆ Include the external JavaScript files directly in your markup.

◆ Include externally referenced style sheets directly in your markup.

Third, and perhaps most important of all, have someone perform a code review on your application. Numerous books provide useful management frameworks for such activities, some of the best of which we have listed in the bibliography. Looking back over our sample application, we have found numerous instances where functions (especially those that create new layers) could have been generalized and called from a single set of utility functions, rather than being redefined for each module. And that's just the first thing that pops into mind. Code reviews are your friends. Friends don't let friends code without the occasional code review.

Anyway, enough about optimization. Let's talk about a few of the things that tripped us up while working with the timing functions and our own functions that used them.

Gotchas

Fortunately, there were very few gotchas this time around, limited mostly to those issues already discussed in detail previously. For the sake of being complete, however, here's a rundown:

◆ In our original implementation of the `wipe()` and `slide()` functions, we attempted to simplify the expression we passed to `setInterval()` by calculating an appropriate delay based on the total distance an object should be wiped or slid, which then killed the timer. Differences in timing across browser and platform made this an abject failure, however, as some timers died too soon and others died too late. Hence, the test for correct positioning in each evaluation.

◆ Clipping regions are not supported at all by Internet Explorer 4.01 for the Macintosh.

◆ The speed with which an object moves or is hidden/shown is highly dependent on how many other intervals or functions are running at the same time.

◆ Speed is also highly dependent on platform, CPU clock speed, and other factors that determine the overall performance of the system. Test your delays across a wide range of target platforms and tune accordingly.

◆ The funniest problem occurred when we first built the test expressions for `slide()`, and implemented them improperly. The object we had intended to move 100 pixels marched straight off the page and, as far as we know, never stopped.

Summary

Well, we've reached the end of our discussion of Dynamic Poetry. What began as a simple illustration of cross-platform drag-and-drop took form over the last six chapters and finally blossomed into the fully featured application. It's easy to forget that we accomplished everything through the use of HTML, JavaScript, and Cascading Style Sheets, especially when you consider the broad range of functionality, the cross-platform nature, and sheer *fun* we had. One of the comments we got from a beta tester sums it up best. He had written several lengthy paragraphs in an e-mail message, complaining about things in the application that didn't work, when he stopped and wrote, "Heh. I just realized this is a *Web* page. And here I am critiquing it like it was a real application. Wow."

Hopefully, we've managed to elicit the same response from you. Even if we haven't, you did learn all kinds of neat stuff about:

◆ Using `setInterval()` to provide regular, repeated behaviors

◆ Using `setTimeout()` to provide delayed, one-time behaviors

◆ Creating independent, self-terminating loops

◆ Using the cross-browser object wrappers to manage clipping regions

◆ Using the cross-browser object wrappers to move objects around

◆ Adding animated footnotes to the sample application

◆ Jazzing up the About box and other minor tweaks

The next few sections of the book have been provided so that you might review the library and how it is used, study the things that tripped us up while we were building the application and testing the modules, and generally become better informed about how DHTML is destined to change the way that we think about (and interact with) the Web.

Object Wrapper Quick Reference

The cross-platform object wrapper API is provided for demonstration purposes only. The following documentation is accurate as of the time of this writing, and represents a relatively simple subset of the functionality available in the 4.0 generation of browsers supporting a JavaScript-accessible document object model.

The library is a set of JavaScript functions, variables, objects, and methods intended to provide a stable and consistent foundation for developers of dynamic HTML applications. The API encapsulates various incompatibilities, inconsistencies, and other charming brokenness beneath a consistent and easily learned set of objects and methods, enabling the developer to use the exposed API to build applications from DHTML interface primitives, while enabling the maintainer of the underlying API code to provide workarounds for platform-specific or browser-specific problems.

This approach makes the best use of the skill sets of both low-level detail freaks on the one hand and high-level functionality-focused interface designers and application developers on the other. Rather than everyone spending time tracking down bugs and adding workarounds that obscure the clarity of the application-level code and do not provide any reusable benefit to subsequent efforts, appropriate attention is given to both problems separately.

Because the API itself is supposed to hide the low-level implementation details from the application developer, we do not provide the entire source listing for the library here. What we *do* provide, however, is a summary and quick reference for each global variable, object array, object method, and utility function provided by the library. Functions and methods also provide descriptions of allowable argument values for each, the action they perform, and their return values where applicable.

Using the xplatform_wrapper

The cross-platform wrapper API is provided as a single JavaScript source file, `xplatform_wrapper.js`. The file may either be included into HTML markup directly, or by way of the `SCRIPT` element, as follows:

```
<script language="Javascript"
       src="xplatform_wrapper.js"></script>
```

Adjust the path as necessary for your installation. The `xplatform_wrapper.js` file should be included in your HTML document before any other JavaScript code or external source file references. Styles do not interfere with the inclusion of the wrapper, however, so place them wherever you like in the HTML document.

Be sure to check the book's support Web site for updates, corrections, and enhancements, as well as different versions of the library optimized for specific environments. In addition, utilities that perform optimization on your final application are also provided.

```
http://www.dhtml-guis.com
```

Global Variables

The library defines a few global variables and object arrays used to provide the wrapper object references to the underlying native browser objects. The following table defines these global variables and object arrays and their purpose. Not all variables or arrays are populated until their initialization functions, described further below, have been called.

GLOBAL VARIABLES

Identifier	Type	Purpose
object_name	Object array	Provide wrapper objects for positioned layers
object_count	Integer	Track number of layer objects
fully_loaded	Boolean	Set when document is fully loaded, used to check if document is actually fully loaded or not
winHeight	Integer	Provide access to window height after resize
winWidth	Integer	Provide access to window width after resize
form_name	Object array	Provide wrapper objects for forms
form_count	Integer	Track number of form objects
image_name	Object array	Provide wrapper objects for images
image_count	Integer	Track number of image objects
mouse_x	Integer	Track mouse x coordinate on page
mouse_y	Integer	Track mouse y coordinate on page
xp_screen	Object array	Provide access to screen properties

Initialization Routines

The variables and object arrays listed above are only populated with the correct values when their associated initialization routines are called from your application. The following table lists all of the initialization functions, along with the variables and object arrays that they initialize. Certain of these functions must be called from a specific context in your application, whereas others may be called whenever the variables or arrays they populate are needed. These contexts are listed where appropriate.

INITIALIZATION ROUTINES

Function Name	Objects Created, Updated or Returned	Initialization Context
set_window_width()	winHeight, winWidth	Whenever the window is resized; may be assigned to the onresize event handler
create_base_objects()	object_name[], image_name[], form_name[], object_count, image_count, form_count	Call from body.onload or from a SCRIPT block placed at end of document
track_mouse()	mouse_x, mouse_y	Whenever mouse movement must be tracked; may be assigned to the onmousemove event handler
wrap_event()	Returns event wrapper object reference	Whenever cross-browser event properties are needed; may be assigned to any event handler, though may be *extremely* inefficient for constantly generated events, such as onmousemove
get_screen_props()	Updates xp_screen array, returns object reference	Whenever screen properties are needed

Layer Objects and Single-Property Methods

The cross-platform layer wrapper objects are references to the native objects created by using CSS-P absolute positioning with HTML DIV elements. These objects use methods to provide read and write access to the native objects' style properties. The canonical form for referring to these objects individually is as follows, where "div_id" is the name assigned to the DIV element using the ID attribute:

```
// get a specific object property
var property = object_name["div_id"].read_method();
// set a specific object property
object_name["div_id"].set_method(new_value);
```

References may also be created, and the same methods used with them, to produce shorter or more significant and readable code:

```
// get object reference
var ref = object_name["div_id"];
// get a specific object property
var property = ref.read_method();
// set a specific object property
ref.set_method(new_value);
```

In addition, each object has a property, the name property, by which the name of an unknown object can be determined. The first example below is somewhat contrived, as the_name should be equivalent to the value of some_unknown_variable. The second example is more likely, as there are many instances in which an object reference is given without knowing the name of the object to which it refers.

```
// get name of an object given unknown variable
var the_name = object_name[some_unknown_variable].name;
// get name of an object given only an object reference
var the_name = object_ref.name;
```

Individual object wrappers may be created as well, by passing a reference to the native object to the base_object() function. A reference to the newly created wrapper object is returned. Note that the object_count variable is incremented by base_object(), not by create_base_objects(), so it continues to accurately reflect the number of object wrappers even when individual wrapper objects are created in this manner.

```
// create an object wrapper using a native object reference
var my_wrapper_object = new Array(); // initialize array
var my_wrapper_object["the_name"] = new base_object(ref);
```

The following table lists the methods associated with each wrapper object, along with their valid arguments and return values or results where appropriate.

LAYER OBJECTS AND SINGLE-PROPERTY METHODS

Method Name	Valid Arguments	Return Values/Results
`conceal()`	None	Hides the object
`reveal()`	None	Shows the object
`is_visible()`	None	Returns Boolean `true` or `false` depending on whether object is visible or hidden
`z_index()`, `get_z_index()`	None	Returns positive integer `z_index` value
`set_z_index()`	New object `z_index` property	None
`left()`, `get_left()`	None	Returns integer value of `left`
`set_left()`	New object `left` property	None
`top()`, `get_top()`	None	Returns integer value of `top`
`set_top()`	New object `top` property	None
`height()`, `get_height()`	None	Returns integer value of object height
`set_height()`	New object `height` property	None
`width()`, `get_width()`	None	Returns integer value of object width
`set_width()`	New object `width` property	None
`bg_color()`	None	Returns object background color
`set_bg_color()`	New object background color	None

Continued

LAYER OBJECTS AND SINGLE-PROPERTY METHODS *(Continued)*

Method Name	Valid Arguments	Return Values/Results
color()	None	Returns object foreground color
set_color()	New object foreground color	None
bg_image()	None	Returns object background image URL
set_bg_image()	New object background image URL	None
clipper_right()	None	Returns clip region right integer value
clipper_left()	None	Returns clip region left integer value
clipper_top()	None	Returns clip region top integer value
clipper_bottom()	None	Returns clip region bottom integer value
clipper_width()	None	Returns clip region width as integer value
clipper_height()	None	Returns clip region height as integer value
set_clipper_right()	New clip region right value	None
set_clipper_left()	New clip region left value	None
set_clipper_top()	New clip region top value	None
set_clipper_bottom()	New clip region bottom value	None

Clipping regions do not work in Internet Explorer 4.01 for the Macintosh. The clip properties may be read, but they always return either zero (top and left), the object width (right, width), or object height (bottom, height). Setting the clip properties has no effect.

Layer Object Composite Methods

Some object methods do not merely read or set a single object style property, but modify several at once, allowing for the dynamic positioning of an object, either absolutely or relative to the current location. Another method, `replace()`, enables the replacement of an object's entire contents.

LAYER OBJECT COMPOSITE METHODS

Method Name	Valid Arguments
`clipper()`	`top`: integer value `left`: integer value `bottom`: integer value `right`: integer value
`place()`	`x`: absolute integer value `y`: absolute integer value
`shove()`	`x`: relative integer value `y`: relative integer value
`abut()`	`o`: an object reference relative to which the calling object aligns `compass`: one of (N|NE|E|SE|S|SW|W|NW) — compass point align: one of (RIGHT|LEFT|TOP|CENTER|BOTTOM) offset: integer value
`overlay()`	`o`: an object reference relative to which the calling object overlays `orientation`: one of (NE|SE|SW|NW) — compass point offset: integer value
`replace()`	`str`: the HTML markup or text with which to replace current object contents

For more information and detailed examples of the `abut()` and `overlay()` methods, see Chapter 14, "Dynamic Menus," and Chapter 11, "The Hidden Feedback Form." For detailed examples of the `clipper()`, `replace()`, `place()`, and `shove()` methods, see Chapter 16, "Timers and Other Fun Stuff," and Chapter 10, "Executive Dynamic Poetry."

Form Objects and Methods

The cross-platform form wrapper objects are references to the native objects created through the use of HTML FORM elements. Each form's elements (text fields, buttons, option lists, and so on) may be referenced by way of these wrapper objects. The form objects themselves have properties that may be read or set using the methods provided. A utility function is also provided for quickly reading the value of a currently selected option in an option list formed by the SELECT and OPTION elements in the HTML FORM.

```
// get a form's action
var my_action = form_name["the_form"].get_action();
// set a form's method
form_name["the_form"].set_method("POST");
```

In addition, individual form object wrappers may be created by passing a document reference to the create_form_objects() function, in which case wrapper objects are created for all of the named forms within the document. If a single form object wrapper is needed, the native form object reference may be passed to the form_object() function. A reference to the newly created wrapper object is returned. Note that the form_count variable is incremented by the form_object() function, so the variable always reflects the number of form wrapper objects even when created individually.

```
// create wrappers for all forms in the document
var d = document;
create_form_objects(d);
// create a single form wrapper object
var my_forms = new Array(); // initialize array
var my_forms["the_name"] =  new form_object(form_ref);
```

The following table lists these methods, along with their arguments and return values where appropriate.

FORM OBJECTS AND METHODS

Method Name	Valid Argument	Return Value
get_action()	None	The form action, if any
set_action()	URL of new form action	None
get_method()	None	The form method, if any

Method Name	Valid Argument	Return Value
set_method()	New form method	None
get_enctype()	None	The form encoding type, if any
set_enctype()	New form encoding type	None
get_target()	None	The form's target, if any
set_target()	New form target	None

Image Objects and Methods

The cross-platform image wrapper objects are references to the native image objects created through the use of HTML IMG elements. The image wrapper objects have associated methods that may be used to read and set the properties of the native image objects. All images within a document may be wrapped by passing a document reference to the create_image_objects() function.

```
// get an image's SRC URL
var my_url = image_name["the_image"].get_src();
// set an image's SRC URL
var new_src = "http://dhtml-guis.com/images/a.gif";
image_name["the_image"].set_src(new_src);
```

In addition, individual image wrapper objects may be created by passing a single native image object reference to the image_object() function. A reference to the new image wrapper object is returned. Note that the image_count variable is incremented by the image_object() function, so the variable always reflects the number of image wrapper objects even when created individually.

```
// create wrappers for all images in a document
var d = document;
create_image_objects(d);
// create a single image wrapper
var my_imgs = new Array(); // initialize array
var my_imgs["the_image"] = new image_object(img_ref);
```

The following table lists the methods associated with the image wrapper objects. Note that only a few properties may actually be set by the developer. Several of the methods are only supported by Internet Explorer 4.0, not Netscape Navigator 4.0.

IMAGE OBJECTS AND METHODS

Method Name	Valid Argument	Return Value
get_name()	None	The image name
get_height()	None	Integer value of image height
get_width()	None	Integer value of image width
get_x()	None	Integer value of image x position on page
get_y()	None	Integer value of image y position on page
get_left()	None	Integer value of image x position on page
get_top()	None	Integer value of image y position on page
get_src()	None	Image URL
set_src()	URL value of new image src	None
get_align()	None	String representing how image is aligned relative to surrounding context (IE 4.0)
get_alt()	None	String representing current alt text assigned to image (IE 4.0)
get_border()	None	Integer value of image border thickness
get_hspace()	None	Integer value of image HSPACE attribute
get_vspace()	None	Integer value of image VSPACE attribute
is_loaded()	None	Boolean value representing whether image is fully loaded in memory
is_map()	None	Boolean value representing whether image is being used as an image map (IE 4.0)
use_map()	None	URL representing the map used

Event Object Wrapper Properties

In order to provide a consistent application-level set of event properties and avoid unnecessary branching, we enable the developer to wrap any event object. The object returned by the wrap_event() function contains generic properties representing the native properties supported by both browsers. These properties of the event wrapper object may then be used in the same manner as the native properties for comparisons, to determine keyboard input, the location of mouse clicks, and so forth. Note that the properties here are read-only, and changing their values does not affect the native event properties they are derived from.

```
// sample event handler function to demonstrate wrap_event()
body.onclick = example;
function example(e) {
  var evt = wrap_event(e);
  alert('you clicked on ('+evt.click_x+','+evt.click_y+')');
}
```

Note that you have to cancel event bubbling using a test for the presence of `window.event`; there is no mechanism provided that does this for you.

EVENT OBJECT WRAPPER PROPERTIES

Event Property	Possible Values	Description
click_x	Integer	x and y coordinates of click relative to top-left corner of current document or frame area
click_y	Integer	
relative_x	Integer	x and y coordinates of click relative to top-left corner of current layer object
relative_y	Integer	
screen_x	Integer	x and y coordinates of click relative to top-left corner of the screen
screen_y	Integer	
page_x	Integer	x and y coordinates of click relative to top-left corner of current document.
page_y	Integer	
source	Object ID	The object ID of the element over which the event was fired
shift	Boolean	The Shift key was pressed
alt	Boolean	The Alt key was pressed
control	Boolean	The Ctrl key was pressed
key	Integer	The ASCII or Unicode value of the key pressed

Continued

EVENT OBJECT WRAPPER PROPERTIES *(Continued)*

Event Property	Possible Values	Description
type	Event type	Type of event fired — may be any allowable event handler, with the "on" removed from the name (for example, "click" or "move")
already	Boolean	This event has already been wrapped (to save time during nested event handling functions that might need to access the event properties)

Environment Object and Properties

The `xp_screen` object may be obtained by calling `get_screen_props()`. Alternately, you may assign a new reference to the object, which is also returned from `get_screen_props()`.

```
// get xp_screen, check for height
get_screen_props();
if( xp_screen.height > 480 ) {
  // do something large
}
// get xp_screen, assign own object reference
the_display = get_screen_props();
if( the_display.height > 480 ) {
  // do something large
}
```

The cross-platform properties and their descriptions are as follows.

ENVIRONMENT OBJECT AND PROPERTIES

Property Name	Description
color_depth	Number of bits per pixel on current display
depth	Number of bits per pixel on current display
height	Raw height of current display in pixels
width	Raw width of current display in pixels

Property Name	Description
aheight	Adjusted height of current display in pixels, not counting system menu and task bars
awidth	Adjusted width of current display in pixels, not counting system menu and task bars

Miscellaneous Utility Routines

Following are a couple of utility routines we found useful during the development of the sample application that we figured we'd throw in for the heck of it: get_selected_option() and get_integer().

The function get_selected_option() makes it easy to grab the currently selected option in an options list. We think it makes your code cleaner as well, which is why we use it. Call with the SELECT object as the only argument. Returns either the currently selected option's value, as specified by the VALUE attribute to OPTION, or the text contained within the OPTION element.

```
function get_selected_option(s) {
  if( s.options[s.selectedIndex].value != "" ) {
    return s.options[s.selectedIndex].value;
  } else if( s.options[s.selectedIndex].text != "" ) {
    return s.options[s.selectedIndex].text;
  } else {
    return "";
  }
}
```

The function get_integer() was a hack we came up with to see why we were getting random errors in the sample application. During the initialization process, the word magnets are placed randomly around the playing field. Occasionally, but not always, we would get an error while the magnets were being placed, saying that "such-and-such was NaN." We discovered that the native JavaScript parseInt() function barfs when it is passed a string representing a number between zero and one because the first digit is not a number; it is a period. When this happens, the parseInt() function returns the special value NaN that is then passed around to the other code in your application. Eventually, something throws up an error, but by then you are far from the function that actually produced the erroneous value, and it can be hard to backtrack. This is a workaround that saves you from the dreaded random NaN.

```
function get_integer(x) {
  var test = parseInt(x);
  if(isNaN(test)) {
    test = Math.floor(parseFloat(x));
  }
  return test;
}
```

Appendix A

Gotchas

Dynamic HTML Gotchas

Developing an application using DHTML can present special challenges. Developing a cross-platform application, designed to work in both major browsers and across the various platforms they support, can be a nightmare. We've already shown you, in vivid detail, many unexpected incompatibilities, bugs, and unintended interactions among the technologies that compose DHTML. In some cases, you hide the incompatibilities behind the tidy abstractions provided by the cross-platform API. At other times, you supply workarounds specific to one browser or the other, introducing all sorts of ugly branching and browser-sniffing into a clean application layer. In a few places, you simply admit defeat in the face of a platform that does not support the feature you need.

Most important in all these cases, however, is to know the causes behind the unexpected behavior and to design with full awareness of the limits of the technologies you are using. Therefore, we assembled this chapter with the following in mind:

◆ To inform developers of things to watch out for during design, coding, and testing

◆ To provide a quick reference to all the problems we encountered during the development of the sample application

◆ To draw attention to common errors in the implementations of a given technology and, where applicable, their effects on the other technologies

◆ To help ensure you don't waste precious development time looking in the wrong place for a tenacious bug

We did *not* write this chapter with the intent of cataloging every bug or incompatibility in the major browsers. Such a task would be Herculean in nature and useful only as an illustrative or historical exercise, as undoubtedly many of the old bugs would be fixed by the time this book is published and new bugs introduced. Nor do we claim to understand every reason why these issues kept cropping up. Sometimes the problem is a clear and unmistakable lack of support for a specific feature. The vast majority of the cases listed in this appendix, however, seem to be minor bugs in a given implementation, interactions between poorly implemented features, or deficiencies of specific platforms and/or operating systems. Where possible, we have tried to break the list down into three major sections:

◆ Common mistakes

◆ Incompatibilities

◆ Bugs or lack of support

Each section is presented with HTML issues first, followed by style sheet issues, and ending with JavaScript issues. Finally, we make special reference to those problems that we believe are the result of a specific interaction between one or more of these technologies. Of course, taken from a certain perspective, all these problems are the result of the interaction among and codependent nature of HTML/DOM, CSS, and JavaScript, but some of these problems are more difficult to track down due to the high degree of interrelatedness.

Before we jump into the ugly details, we want to remind you that the intent of this entire book and the code we discuss within its chapters is to provide Web developers and interface designers with the basic tools necessary to build cross-browser and cross-platform DHTML applications now. It is our sincere and desperate hope that future browser versions will provide much more robust, cross-platform, and standards-compliant implementation of DHTML. The early betas of the latest browsers look promising, and they represent great strides toward a fully featured common foundation for application developers. For now, we make do with what we have and fight back against incompatibilities using strategies known to have been successful in other arenas. Fighting back requires an understanding of the shortcomings, and it is for this reason we present the following.

Common Mistakes

DHTML applications are no different than traditional Web sites in many ways. They still consist of HTML markup, style sheets, and JavaScript; they are still delivered by Web servers; and they are still subject to the same pitfalls that confront traditional site designers. We don't list all the possible problems that developers of DHTML applications may run into, as you should be accustomed to many of them already. The ones we mention here are commonly overlooked by developers, who often mistakenly assume that JavaScript (or HTML or CSS) used in a DHTML application is somehow different from that used in a traditional Web site.

In a perfect world, we would all write valid markup, use standard scripting languages, and follow the DOM and CSS specifications to the letter. It's never too late to start, and with help from browser vendors, perhaps our perfect code will attain the promise of actually being capable of running perfectly in all browsers. Until then, it's test, test, and test again.

Following are a few things we ran into during testing that baffled and frustrated us.

Common Mistakes with HTML Markup

Any developer who has been working with HTML for longer than a couple of years has a small subset of the DTD – a set of preferences and associations between elements and their attributes – permanently engraved on his or her brain. When new elements are introduced or old attributes standardized across other elements, it often takes awhile for the changes to sink in. In many cases, the same is true of the browsers, which lag behind, by months or even years, the standards set by the W3C.

The problem is especially acute with regard to deprecated attributes or elements, which continue to be supported by the browsers – and therefore continue to be used by developers who may be unaware of their deprecated status. Validation is just one answer to the problem, and it will often point out issues that you don't know exist, even before they become problems (such as those that may arise with a new release of a browser, for example).

The weakness of validation as a strategy results from the rarity of validators that can test not only HTML markup, but also CSS and JavaScript, pointing out problems in the relationships between the three technologies. And few, if any, can provide the real-world feedback gained simply by testing the application in a target browser.

Here are a few of the mistakes we made during the development of the sample application and, where appropriate, some suggested workarounds or solutions.

MISTAKEN USE OF ONE ELEMENT'S ATTRIBUTE IN ANOTHER

We've been marking up SGML documents since before the Web and HTML existed. Back in those days, we used visual editors that wouldn't let users insert markup where it wasn't allowed by the DTD. The first iterations of the WYSIWYG editors for HTML were either awful or slow to adapt to the evolution of HTML from a purely structural language into the weird hybrid that it has become. As a result, many Web developers insist on using text editors to mark up their HTML, just as many of us use text editors for programming in other languages. The power and flexibility of a text editor brings with it the risk that you will use the wrong element or attribute or otherwise introduce bizarre errors that are hard to find and even harder to understand without validators.

SRC VERSUS HREF IN THE SCRIPT ELEMENT   We see this problem all the time on mailing lists and in our own projects. The SCRIPT element uses SRC, not HREF, to include external files. We find that it helps to remember that you're including JavaScript *source* code here.

HREF VERSUS SRC IN THE LINK ELEMENT   Introduced a long time ago but rarely implemented or used until now, the LINK element uses the HREF attribute to specify external CSS files to include in the document. Netscape added the SRC attribute in an attempt to maintain consistency across other similar elements, such as IMG, APPLET, and SCRIPT. Naturally, SRC isn't supported by Internet Explorer. HREF seems to work just fine in both browsers, though. We remember this one by imagining LINK as part of the original HTML DTD, back before the IMG element (and the SRC attribute) even existed. It's not quite true, but it helps us remember the difference.

NAME VERSUS ID IN MOST ELEMENTS   An interesting characteristic of the recent HTML DTDs is the way they have moved closer and closer to traditional SGML practice through the use of attributes such as ID. This is done in part for planned versions of HTML described as XML document types, rather than loose SGML-esque guesstimates at the actual behavior of browsers and authors' common usage. The upshot for those of us who have been using HTML for years is that we have to keep reminding ourselves not to use NAME when we mean ID. Maybe an acronym would help — NAME: *N*ot *A*vailable for *M*any *E*lements. Beware that IE and Navigator both support NAME inside the DIV element, and even reflect its value in the .name property. So even if you make a mistake, it may be hard to catch. Oddly enough, this is one case where the browsers support *more* than we want them to!

IMPROPERLY NESTED TAGS

During the course of development, hasty cut-and-paste operations, inattentiveness, and other factors often result in tags that are improperly nested. Check to ensure your tags are all properly nested, as failure to do so can lead to quirky or unpredictable behavior (especially across browsers, as their forgivingness of such often varies markedly). Validation of your HTML can be useful in tracking these problems down, but you may run into trouble when using JavaScript to write markup to the document, which is not usually treated by validators. One approach to this problem involves the use of the JavaScript alert() to display debugging information about the markup you are printing to the document. If the markup is wrong when displayed in an alert, it is probably wrong when being written to the document as well.

IMPROPERLY CLOSED CONTAINERS

Forgetting to properly close containers, such as tables, is a common mistake for all Web site developers, but especially for those using template-driven publishing systems or CGI applications to insert markup into documents. As we often find ourselves writing markup to a document using the JavaScript document.write() function, it is useful to verify that the markup is correct through the alert() debugging method described in the previous section. This is one reason why we often build strings a piece at a time using local variables and then finally write those strings to the document, rather than call document.write() repeatedly for every single step in an extended write operation.

Common Mistakes with Cascading Style Sheets

CSS represents the triumph of compromise between the folks who want to use HTML for pixel-perfect, font-perfect layout on the one hand, and the SGML purists on the other, who prefer to separate a document's structure from its presentation. They don't always work the way you want them to, though. Sometimes, even when they do what you want, the browser manages to throw you a curve ball. Here are a few problems we encountered with the use of CSS that you are likely to encounter as well.

TYPOGRAPHICAL ERRORS IN SELECTORS

As you know, styles are either associated with elements globally, for all elements of a given type, or individually, using the CLASS or ID attribute of those elements. You must be careful to spell the CSS selectors exactly the same as those used in the CLASS or ID attributes. The browsers will not complain if your styles are not actually applied to the elements in your document, and you may see random behavior as a result. This is especially true if you are using position: absolute to create a layer object, for example, as your JavaScript will not work as expected. Using the search and replace functionality of your text editor can be useful to ensure your selectors match the attributes of the elements to which they are supposed to apply.

MISSING SEMICOLONS IN VALUES

When creating a style sheet definition containing one value, it is permissible to leave off the final semicolon. Unfortunately, this often results in silent errors when the definition is extended to contain more than one value, as the definition is no longer valid without the semicolon to separate the two or more values.

FORGETTING TO INCLUDE EXTERNAL STYLE SHEET

It may sound stupid, but we've run into problems by simply forgetting to include an external style sheet. Save yourself some time, and check to make sure the style sheet has been included before immediately assuming that the problem is with your JavaScript or HTML markup.

USING EQUALS SIGN INSTEAD OF COLON

One of the more common mistakes that we see on mailing lists involves the syntax of CSS. You must use a colon to separate the CSS property from its value. We've seen everything from semicolons to equals signs used in place of the colon in style sheets; this type of mistake inevitably leads to frustration as the developer overlooks the obvious and dives into fruitless attempts to modify the property name, the values used, and so forth, when simply changing the character back to a colon would solve the problem.

Common Mistakes with JavaScript

Many developers mistakenly assume that because JavaScript is used in the context of Web pages, it is not really a programming language. On the contrary, it is a complex and powerful language in its own right, plaguing developers with all the problems inherent in the use of any programming language. Many of the following mistakes will be familiar to you already, especially if you have worked with Perl or C or another traditional programming language, but they are just as serious when they arise in JavaScript.

TYPOGRAPHICAL ERRORS IN OBJECT REFERENCES

We ran into this problem repeatedly while developing our sample application. We would define a positionable layer object, using CSS absolute positioning and the HTML `DIV` element, give it a name, check to make sure we had matched the CSS selector with the `DIV ID` or `CLASS` attribute, and then misspell the reference in the `object_name` array. Similarly, typographical errors in function calls are equally common and equally annoying. Programmers who are used to the excellent warning or error messages provided by the Perl interpreter and Java bytecode compiler will be distraught to find that nothing similar exists for JavaScript, so be on guard for typos.

FORGETTING TO INCLUDE EXTERNAL SCRIPT

As we noted previously with CSS, a common source of errors is the result of simply forgetting to include the external script file during testing. Because this exclusion is often first noticed during testing (as functions are called for which there is no definition, due to the missing script), the problem can be confused with typographical errors or other misleading assumptions. Always check to ensure you have included all the scripts whose functions and variables you intend to use before you check for typos or go down other time-wasting debugging paths.

ARRAY OFFSETS BEGIN AT ZERO

Most, if not all, programming languages that use arrays also treat the first element in an array as element zero, and JavaScript is no exception to this rule. Like other programming languages, JavaScript contains idioms that must simply be learned, used, and recognized when scanning through code looking for bugs. This can be especially confusing, as the way that an array is declared often distracts programmers from remembering the zero rule. For example, an array declared as `my_array = new Array(20)` has the first element `my_array[0]` and the last element `my_array[19]`. So it is something worth looking out for.

DOM DIFFERENCES

The major browsers generally feature minor incompatibilities, but the document object models used in each browser are fundamentally incompatible for the most part. This is a direct result of Netscape's introduction of layers and the fact that the W3C DOM spec excludes layers entirely. Without rehashing the various political reasons for the differences, however, it is clear that these fundamental incompatibilities in the object models make for some annoying mistakes and frustrating debugging sessions. Internet Explorer's support for so many different ways of accessing objects combined with the limitations of Navigator's model inevitably leads to code that works in Internet Explorer but not in Navigator, despite being perfectly appropriate according to the DOM. We provide one way to work around some of these incompatibilities with our cross-browser object wrappers, but it also helps to write your code for Navigator and then port it to Internet Explorer to reduce the risk of using Explorer-specific idioms. At any rate, you should be aware of the possibility of writing such Explorer-specific code and of its effect on an ostensibly cross-browser application.

PARENTHESES REQUIRED FOR METHOD CALLS

One problem that seemed to crop up with alarming persistence during the development of our sample application had to do with the use of wrapper methods. There are two main types of methods in our library: those that simply perform an action on their object and those that return a value. An example of the first is `object_name["sample"].conceal()`, which hides the object. An example of the second is `var ex = object_name["sample"].top()`, which returns the pixel value corresponding to the top of the object, assigning that value to the variable.

In either case, it is required that the method be invoked using the parentheses so that the function is actually executed, rather than simply being assigned *as the function itself*. In the second example, if the function is executed properly, it will return an integer value. If not, the variable `ex` is assigned the actual function, rather than its result. We use this distinction when assigning event handlers, as mentioned earlier in the book. Because JavaScript is not strongly typed, a variable may be executed as a function! If we were to assign the preceding function to `ex` and then call `ex()`, it would return the integer value we expect to get from `object_name["sample"].top()`. This is obviously not what we want.

Missing parentheses in function calls can be extremely difficult to spot, as the function assignment returns a true value in some browser implementations. This is especially true when calling functions that return Boolean values inside `if()` tests, such as we often do with the `is_visible()` method. If possible, use an editor with syntax highlighting that is capable of distinguishing between variables, functions, and function calls.

MISSING SEMICOLONS

We're usually big fans of using optional features in languages, especially in situations where the optional feature becomes required under certain circumstances. In C, this means that we use braces to surround our blocks, even when a "block" contains only a single statement. In JavaScript, this extends to the use of semicolons as statement terminators, which are optional *as long as the statement ends with a linefeed*. We've seen too many cases where an additional statement is added, and then the linefeed is removed for one reason or another, and the missing semicolon causes an error. In our case, we found a couple of bugs when we first ran our optimizer program on the source for our sample application. By stripping white space (which includes linefeeds) from our JavaScripts, we unintentionally caused several errors due to missing semicolons. Do the right thing. Use semicolons even though you don't have to.

VARIABLE SCOPING PROBLEMS

As discussed at some length in Chapter 16, JavaScript has simple rules for determining a variable's scope. If the variable is declared outside a function, it is global and therefore accessible for both reading and modification by other functions and statements anywhere in the current document window. If it is declared inside a function, it only exists within that function, and then only for the duration of the current call to the function. In other words, it is recreated anew each time the function is called, and destroyed each time the function exits.

This characteristic of JavaScript scoping has several interesting – and sometimes maddening – side-effects. First of all, you must be careful to always declare new variables using the var keyword. This keyword is often left out by developers, as it seems that several browsers instantiate a new variable even if the var keyword is missing, if the variable identifier has not already been declared elsewhere. Second, you must be very careful to use unique names for your variables and functions; otherwise, you risk accidentally changing a global value from within a function or redefining a previously existing function, neither of which produce JavaScript error alerts. Third, you must be equally careful not to declare local variables when you want their values to be globally accessible, such as in the example in Chapter 16, where it was necessary to define global variables to ensure their accessibility to the functions invoked by timers.

SETTING STYLE PROPERTIES FROM JAVASCRIPT

This may turn out to be a real bug or the result of late-night caffeine deprivation. In any case, several times during the course of developing our sample application, it seemed as though setting style properties on objects that had not had those styles explicitly declared via CSS had no effect on the object's display. In other words, if we gave an object certain CSS styles, and then attempted to modify those settings using their corresponding JavaScript properties, the modifications would take effect. However, if we tried to set style properties that had not been explicitly declared in CSS, the modifications to the JavaScript properties would not take effect. Adding explicit CSS properties seemed to make the difference.

EXTERNAL FILE LOADING SYNCHRONIZATION ISSUES

Depending on the speed and reliability of the network connection, especially over a slow dial-up connection, externally referenced files (such as style sheets and JavaScripts) did not always fully load before the onload event was fired, resulting in some strange errors. This can be worked around in a couple of ways. The first involves checking to make sure that all external files have loaded, or at least that the functions you wish to call upon initialization have loaded. This makes for some ugly code, however. The second, and more attractive, option, especially for final deliverables, simply involves not using externally referenced files. Check the book's support Web site for updated versions of a Perl script that you can run to optimize your applications by including external files in your HTML document, stripping comments and white space, and so forth.

Incompatibilities on Parade

One of the most irritating things about the differences between the two major browsers is the way they introduce unnecessary inconsistencies – whether they are related to HTML element or attribute names, JavaScript properties, or varying support for a CSS property that is fully supported as an HTML attribute. Many of these incompatibilities are the result of competition in the marketplace or other factors, but knowing this is of no comfort to developers. As it is impossible to develop on two platforms simultaneously, we inevitably found ourselves trying to track down little bugs that didn't exist in the browser used for testing during development but appeared in the others during post-development testing.

The goal of the cross-platform wrappers is to hide browser incompatibilities behind a consistent and abstract API layer. However, depending on your application and its requirements, you may wish (or need) to work around some of these things at the application level. Here are a few of the things we stumbled across.

Incompatibilities with the Handling of HTML Markup

Obviously, there are many differences between the way that one browser and another parses, displays, and exposes the objects in an HTML document. We will restrict the following discussion to some of the more pertinent problems from the standpoint of DHTML applications.

DISPLAY ISSUES WITH FORM ELEMENTS AND LAYERS

Visible form elements always shine through other layers on Navigator, even when those layers are defined with higher z-indexes. The only workaround is to hide the layer containing the form element if you want to avoid the conflict.

TEXTAREA TREATED DIFFERENTLY UNDER IE AND NAVIGATOR

Form elements on different platforms have always been susceptible to issues arising from the size of fonts used in the element. Different browsers on different platforms also use different native widget sets, making it difficult to accurately predict how wide a given form element will be, for example, with pixel-perfect accuracy. This is especially true when CSS has been used to define the font face in a TEXTAREA element. Navigator will often ignore the ROWS and COLS attributes, resulting in an extra row and cutting the columns too short.

NESTING ISSUES WITH THE DIV ELEMENT IN NAVIGATOR

An interesting side effect of Netscape's effort to provide CSS-P functionality is that DIV elements that use CSS absolute positioning cannot be nested. You will also run into problems if you try to nest DIVs inside LAYERs. You can, however, nest LAYERs inside other LAYERs.

Incompatibilities with the Handling of Cascading Style Sheets

Style sheets are a boon. Unfortunately, they are an extremely inconsistent boon, often poorly implemented in the current browsers. We hope that the next releases of the browsers provide full support for CSS1 at the minimum, and for many of the features of CSS2. In the meantime, for those of us who are going to be building

DHTML applications for the 4.0 generation of browsers for the next couple of years, here are just a few of the more glaring problems with CSS we ran across.

FONT PROBLEMS

Even when you use CSS to specify a font or series of font choices, the different browsers don't always use the same font on the same platform. The results can be minor or major, depending on the fonts specified and the uses to which they are put.

CSS LEADING IN FONT SPECIFIERS MESSES UP TABLES USED FOR LAYOUT   When using tables to provide backwardly compatible image layout, be careful not to define a default CSS font style for table cells. Regardless of whether or not there is text in the cells used to contain images, the styles will be applied to those cells as well. When the whole point behind using tables in the first place is to fit images closely together without any gaps, misplaced or ill-defined leading can throw your layout off badly.

SPECIFIC AND GENERIC FONT FAMILY CHOICES MUST BE DEFINED CAREFULLY
Although the generic font family specifier is intended as a last resort, it may end up being used unless you are careful about how you specify the more specific font family names. In addition, the order in which you define specific font family names has an effect on which font is chosen by the browser. If you're aiming for font compatibility across platforms, you may want to define the more platform-specific fonts first so that other common fonts aren't used. It is recommended that you specify Macintosh-specific fonts before PC-specific fonts to make sure the preferred choice of Mac font is used even if cross-platform fonts are available.

TEXTAREA BUG   See the `TEXTAREA` bug mentioned previously.

COLOR PROBLEMS

During the course of developing our sample application, we discovered that the only truly reliable way to specify colors in CSS in the current browsers was to use the traditional `#RRGGBB` method, representing the hexadecimal values for red, green, and blue, respectively. Even this method is buggy in Internet Explorer 3.0 for the Macintosh, but we don't suppose that will affect your DHTML application design decisions much. The other mechanism, using the name of the color as defined in the CSS specification, seems to be fully supported but leaves you with few choices.

POSITIONING AND SIZING PROBLEMS

Absolute positioning would be a lifesaver if it worked correctly. Unfortunately, due to minor differences between the major browsers, it is often a source of major headaches.

POSITIONING WITHOUT HEIGHT AND WIDTH IN IE   If you specify a `DIV` element using absolute positioning, but don't also explicitly provide height and width properties, the `DIV` will stretch the width of the browser and only be as tall as its contents. If the element doesn't contain any text or images, it will not be displayed at all. This can be a problem when you are using the DIV as a way to provide an object with a specific color, such as we do with the word magnets in the sample application.

ABSOLUTE POSITIONING OF DIV IN NAVIGATOR CREATES A LAYER   When you specify absolute positioning for a DIV element in Navigator, the object is then part of the document.layers array of the enclosing document, which may not be what you want. We use this effect extensively to provide positionable cross-browser objects, but it can be a surprise if you aren't expecting it.

OTHER CSS FEATURES

Many other features of CSS2 are partially supported in the current browsers, despite a lack of full support for CSS1.

BOX PROPERTIES   CSS features such as borders, padding, margins, and so forth are not fully supported under Navigator 4.0, with borders being the least supported. Specific properties (such as margin-top) tend to be better supported than the short-hand properties (such as margin) but are not completely supported in any case. For example, the border-bottom property is extremely buggy in Navigator.

OVERFLOW PROPERTIES   The overflow property is a feature of CSS2 that enables the author or developer to specify what the browser should do in the case of content overflowing the boundaries of its enclosing box. Internet Explorer supports the scroll property, which would have made it possible for us to provide the hierarchical tree widget discussed in Chapter 15 if only it were supported by Navigator.

VISIBILITY   There are several ways to specify visibility in Navigator, only a few of which are actually standard CSS. This ordinarily wouldn't be a problem, as you would just need to restrict yourself to the standard values supported by both browsers; however, it is possible that the JavaScript value returned by a hidden element's .visibility property is nonstandard, so you need to check for the illegal values.

Whereas CSS defines hidden, inherit, and visible, Navigator may also return show and hide as values for these properties. This is worth knowing, even though we provide a low-level check for this in the cross-platform wrapper API and make it available via the is_visible() method, as well as ensuring that only the appropriate standard values are used inside the reveal() and conceal() methods.

OTHER PROBLEMS   Internet Explorer doesn't deal well with nested elements (such as a TD inside a TR) when both elements have been assigned styles using the CLASS selector.

Incompatibilities with the Behavior of JavaScript

JavaScript is fairly complex as a language, but when you start exposing document object properties and styles, the inconsistencies start multiplying like rabbits. Consider that we had problems with the browsers when they just rendered HTML, and now we have a language that enables us to script the entire browser, dynamically modify the document, create new windows, manipulate object styles, and so forth. All of this behavior is dependent upon the proper interaction between HTML markup, the particular document object model exposed to JavaScript, and your CSS definitions. Given all these interdependencies, you'll begin to see why things are so complex.

SCREEN UPDATE ISSUES

Internet Explorer is much more robust in how it manages dynamic screen updates, such as automatically reflowing text when the document is modified. This has to do, in large part, with the age of the browsers' codebase. Navigator is much older (in Internet years, anyway) than Explorer, so it has to make do with a somewhat overextended rendering engine. The new version of this rendering engine, currently known as Gecko, is a complete redesign and fixes many of the flaws in the 4.0 version, but as of this writing it is only available in beta, and only on the Windows platform at that. The result, for those of us targeting the 4.0 browser generation, is that dynamic screen updates are much less robust in Navigator, although modifications to document objects often display correctly when the object is hidden and then redisplayed. This is especially true of Layer objects. It's something to look out for, in any case, as it may require application-level logic to ensure that your changes are reflected accurately.

FORM ISSUES

Forms, which were among the earliest objects to enable client-side access from scripting languages, are complex. As a result, there are many holes and annoying inconsistencies in how they may be accessed, modified, and so on. In addition, because form elements, such as the option list, may contain both a visible representation and a hidden value, you must take care to read the value you really want. For option elements, this means the difference between `options[x].text`, the text visible to the user, and `options[x].value`, the option's hidden value. To make matters more confusing, if there is no `value` defined, the value of `text` is returned. This can be both a blessing and a curse. You just need to make sure you know what value you want and ask for it explicitly.

There is currently no cross-platform way to scroll a selected option into view. We ran into this problem while coding a combo box for an early version of our help system, and eventually gave up on a solution. It is very likely possible to cheat and to use two arrays, one holding the complete list of values and another displaying the visible options, modifying the visible list based on user interaction, but the limited support in Navigator for dynamic display updates of form elements makes this workaround unattractive and unreliable.

Another form issue has to do with the way that radio buttons are accessed. If a radio button group contains several radio buttons, each radio button is represented in JavaScript as an object in an array, and each object has its own properties. Be sure to check the group and loop over each object in the array, if initialized, examining each object for the desired properties. Otherwise, you will get an error, as the properties you're looking for will not exist as part of the array, but rather as part of each element in the array. This can be extremely frustrating for a developer who writes code for a single radio button, only to find that additional buttons are added later to create a group. Naturally, this requires the developer to rewrite the portion of the code that used to be able to access each property directly from the single radio button.

OBJECT INITIALIZATION PROBLEMS

On some platforms, especially the Macintosh, we found that the wrapper objects weren't fully initialized before other methods were called. The net result for the sample application was a seemingly random error when the preferences initialization tried to set the color of the `mainlayer` object, using the wrapper methods, before the object was fully initialized. Depending on your application's requirements, the order in which certain methods are called, and so forth, this may necessitate the use of a timer, which checks for the existence of the wrapper object in question before trying to call its methods. This workaround solved our specific problem, which had to do with setting the background color of the playing field, but you may find it crops up again in strange places. So be on the lookout.

EVENT PROBLEMS

We've already discussed the biggest problem with events — namely, the way they must either be captured explicitly (in Navigator) or dealt with as they bubble through the document hierarchy (in Internet Explorer). This fundamental incompatibility may be dealt with fairly easily, however, by carefully designing your event handlers. We didn't expect the other problems we encountered, which had to do with other characteristics of the document, including z-index and visibility of specific objects.

When dealing with forms, for example, event handling was screwy when the form elements in question were children of objects having different z-indexes. In other words, when one form was contained within an object having one z-index, and another form was contained within another object having a different z-index, the "lower" of the two often ignored clicks and other events. The workaround is simple: Merely ensure that all active forms are in objects having the same z-index.

Another problem with events and z-indexes has to do with different `DIV` objects occupying the same area of the screen but set to different z-indexes, as was the case with our menu items. The assumption on our part was that the "higher" of the two would obscure the "lower," and it did as far as we could see; however, unless the object below the visible menu item also had its `visibility` property set to `hidden`, it still processed events. This led to some interesting and puzzling behavior, especially with regard to `mouseover` and `mouseout` events. The object lesson here, if you'll pardon the pun, is to make sure that you only reveal those objects if you want them to receive and handle events.

DYNAMICALLY ADDING LAYER OBJECTS

Due to the relatively poor support for the DOM in current browsers along with other minor inconveniences, we used the tried and true methods for adding new objects to our document in the sample application. Rather than using the `createElement()` DOM method, we used `document.write()` in Internet Explorer and `Layer()` in

Netscape Navigator to create new document objects. Because it was easier to simply create a string containing the markup to be written to the document, rather than to fuss with the extended process of creating a new `DIV` object, setting each appropriate style property, and then setting the contents of the new element, that's what we did in Internet Explorer. In Netscape Navigator, we did roughly the same thing using Navigator's native (and proprietary) layers. Unfortunately, this introduced still other hassles to what should have been a relatively painless process.

Writing new content to a document in Explorer must be accomplished before the document has finished loading. In order to accomplish this, we needed to include an inline script at the end of our HTML document, along with a browser test so that it was only executed in Internet Explorer. Similarly, Navigator doesn't allow the creation of new layer objects until after a document has completely loaded, so we needed to call those functions using the `onLoad` event handler for the `BODY` element if the browser being used was Navigator.

OFFSET PROPERTIES – FROM HELL?

We found that when trying to determine the x and y offsets for image objects, the values returned were relative to the enclosing object in Internet Explorer; this made it necessary to check for that browser and walk our way up the object hierarchy, adding each object's offsets to determine the true offset values for the object in question. With Navigator, we faced similar problems in some circumstances as a result of offsets being reported relative to their enclosing layer object. These problems were more easily worked around in Navigator, due to the reliability of page-relative offset values, but we still had some minor issues to deal with.

TIMER DELAY PROBLEMS

You can't calculate a delay for a timer based on how long you think it will execute, because different hardware, software, and platforms execute things at different speeds. Instead, you must provide a test for completion of the activity performed by the timer based on globally accessible values. Using values internal to the function or statements called by the timer doesn't work, as they are initialized each time the function is called, due to JavaScript's function-level variable scoping rules.

KEYBOARD INPUT PROBLEMS

Keyboard events are not fully or properly supported on all platforms. In addition, some platforms do not allow for keyboard input without certain elements (such as form inputs) present, such as Navigator for Solaris, and the same is presumed to be true for Navigator on other UNIX platforms, due to limitations of the Motif widget set.

Not all keyboard characters, such as function keys, are supported. If that wasn't enough, you must also take care that your choices for keyboard accelerators do not conflict with the default shortcuts for the browser itself, such as Alt and Ctrl combinations in Windows. We found that Shift-Ctrl-character combinations were least likely to conflict with any of the defaults, so that's what we used. This limits even more the number of available shortcuts you can define, so depending on the requirements of your applications, you may wish to use less potentially conflicting accelerators.

INFORMATION ABOUT BROWSER ENVIRONMENT

One of the most important things about a detailed bug report is that it must describe not only the problem, but also the environment in which the problem occurred. Due to differences in the various browsers, this information may be easy or difficult to obtain. Navigator, for example, provides information about all installed plug-ins, supported MIME types, and whether or not the user has enabled Java. Internet Explorer, on the other hand, provides only a limited subset of this information and uses a different syntax. To make matters worse, Explorer only provides access to this limited subset on Windows-based machines, not on the Macintosh.

Bugs and Other Heartbreakers

Bugs and the complete lack of support for certain features on specific platforms can ruin your whole day, to say nothing of the work required to get around them if possible. The following list enumerates several issues that we simply couldn't work around using the cross-platform library.

HTML Bugs and Unsupported Features

Fortunately, we found that for our purposes the major browsers support basic HTML well enough to accomplish what we wanted. Unfortunately, this doesn't take into account many of the features of HTML 4.0, which are far too numerous to outline here. See Appendix B, "Tools and Resources," for pointers to online HTML reference sites and discussions of support for various HTML elements and attributes.

CSS Bugs and Unsupported Features

The level of support for CSS1 is still too poor in Netscape Navigator 4.0 to be of much use, and to outline all the deficiencies in the 4.0 generation would take more room than we have here. See Appendix B, "Tools and Resources," for pointers to more up-to-date sites and excellent comparisons between the browsers, showing what each supports and how well. The only good thing that can be said of CSS support in Navigator is that it is at least consistently poor across all platforms.

We did run into one glaring problem, however: Clipping regions are not supported at all under IE for Macintosh, whether defined in CSS or dynamically from JavaScript.

JavaScript Bugs and Unsupported Features

One happy surprise in our travails was the relative solidity of JavaScript across platforms in Navigator, which should not be much of a surprise – Netscape invented JavaScript, after all. The few major problems we did encounter had more to do with features that were missing from one browser or the other, rather than cross-platform issues.

SUPPORT FOR ARGUMENTS ARRAY AND CALLER

The stack trace function we saw in Chapter 12 relies on the existence of the `arguments` array and the `caller` and `callee` variables, which do not seem to be fully supported on any platform but Netscape Navigator for Solaris.

IE DOESN'T SUPPORT WRITING TO THE JAVA CONSOLE

Debugging information is hard to come by in IE, in general. To make matters worse, you can't simply write a quick debug message to the Java console, as you can in Netscape Navigator.

MAILTO: NOT SUPPORTED UNDER NAVIGATOR STANDALONE

When Netscape provided a slimmed-down version of the full browser installation, it answered the prayers of many a developer. Finally, you could install a browser and not the newsreader and mail tool, useful in situations in which your users already had corporate standard mail applications and you wanted to avoid having to support multiple mail applications. Unfortunately, the necessary software surgery was performed rather haphazardly, and if a form or anchor uses the `mailto:` method, Navigator doesn't even throw up an error message, instead failing silently. We know of no workaround for this problem at present, so you may wish to avoid the use of the `mailto:` method in important portions of your applications and documents. If you know your audience is not using the Navigator standalone, however, this shouldn't present a problem.

Interaction Gotchas and How to Avoid Them

Interaction between the various technologies is perhaps the root of the most frustrating problems we encountered, and will likely be the cause of similar heartache as you create DHTML applications of your own. Rather than outline specific problems we ran into, which are unlikely to help you much, we instead discuss several rules of thumb that you may find useful in debugging your applications. Be sure to review and understand the problems previously discussed, however, as many of them are the result of exactly the sort of interaction problems we're trying to avoid.

Keep Your Markup, Code, and Styles Simple

A variation on the old KISS rule (Keep It Simple, Stupid), this is perhaps one of the most important strategies you can adopt. It is the rationale underlying our cross-browser object wrapper library, and it will make things much easier for you during the development, testing, debugging, and maintenance of your applications. If you can come up with ways to simplify your application, implement them. The rewards will be innumerable, and not just because elegance in programming is its own reward.

Name Selectors, Objects, Variables and Functions Sensibly

Although we doubt that any DHTML application will ever be included in the annals of great literature, the more direct and descriptive your choice of names for the various components of your application, the easier it will be to understand, debug, and extend that application. Remember that a `DIV` should be named the same as the unique selector you define in order to contain its styles. If you use `CLASS` to apply a generic style to a number of different `DIV`s, name the style selector based on its intended use, perhaps using adjective forms such as `indentedpara` for an indented paragraph text style. If your JavaScript functions are given active names, perhaps based on verb forms, such as `initialize()`, or combinations of verbs and nouns, such as `delete_word()`, you will find it easier to relate them to their use. Similarly, JavaScript variables and HTML objects such as layers should be named using noun forms.

Design Using an Integrated Component Infrastructure

Rather than trying to split the responsibility for style sheets, JavaScripts, and HTML layout among several different developers, assign individual components of your application to individual members of your team. Barring that, for smaller projects with only one or two developers, ensure that you build each component in as modular a fashion as possible, taking into account all aspects of the component at once. Then, when a solid foundation has been established, designers may tweak the values of style properties as long as the required properties themselves remain defined, and the JavaScripts may be extended as long as the HTML markup remains in sync with the objects your scripts expect to find reflected in the JavaScript.

Separate Structure from Presentation Wherever Possible

Because of the common need during development to refine an application's appearance without changing its functionality, you should try wherever possible to isolate functionality (such as that defined in JavaScript) from presentation (such as that found in CSS or HTML). This enables the interface designer to focus on the appearance of the application, while encouraging the JavaScript programmer to provide modular components and hooks that the designer can use to further tweak the presentation.

Isolate Dependencies between Technologies

If your JavaScript module expects to find an HTML document layer object of a certain name but is failing to do so, check the HTML and then the CSS before trying to modify your script. Similarly, if that object is found but the style property you wish to modify doesn't seem to be working, check the style sheet to ensure the property has been defined, and then check the HTML to ensure the style has been properly applied to the object. You may wish to move such properties into the JavaScript itself for dynamically generated objects, or you may find that proper discipline allows you to externalize and apply styles from style sheet definitions. Your mileage may vary, depending on your team and your own experience.

Have Faith in Your Code

Many of the worst programming we have seen, whether it is our own or the work of others, results from second-guessing the original assumptions that were used during the design phase. It is common for novices, as well as seasoned programmers, to try to stretch existing code to work around flaws in the original design. Unfortunately, this often results in failure, as the programmer realizes too late that his or her original design was simply insufficient for the requirements. Because of the investment in time and effort that finished code represents, and because of the great degree to which DHTML applications are reliant on technologies of very different constitutions working together, it is highly preferable that you check whether an apparent flaw in the design of your JavaScript is just a problem with the CSS or HTML markup *before* you begin to modify the errant functions. Once the problem has been isolated and the other technologies have been cleared of blame, consider whether or not to redesign or modify your function. You may find that the entire component — including the HTML objects, styles, and functions — needs to be redesigned to meet the new (or newly discovered) requirements.

We hope that these rules of thumb are helpful to you in your quest to design robust and useful DHTML applications, and that they help you to avoid or lessen the impact of the inevitable interaction problems you will encounter.

Appendix B

Tools and Resources

Tools and Resources

Here are a few of the sites we consider to be authoritative, useful, and/or well maintained. They all feature reference materials, tutorials, articles, demonstration code, and the like. You can find this list (and more) on the support Web site for this book, which Steven maintains in his voluminous spare time. Please visit the site for updates, code listings, bug information, new versions of the sample application, and other information useful to DHTML developers.

```
http://www.dhtml-guis.com
```

The rest of these sites are *not* maintained by Steven, so please take the listing below as a snapshot, and only send us mail if the links listed below change and the support site hasn't been updated to reflect the change.

Interface Theory and Usability

The Nielsen-Norman Group
```
http://www.nngroup.com
```

Jakob Nielsen's useit.com
```
http://www.useit.com
```

Keith Instone's Usable Web
```
http://www.usableweb.com
```

Dynamic HTML

Netscape's DevEdge Online Dynamic HTML Site
```
http://developer.netscape.com/tech/dynhtml/index.html
```

Microsoft's Site Builder Network (SBN) Workshop DHTML, HTML & CSS Home
```
http://www.microsoft.com/workshop/author/default.asp
```

Macromedia's DHTML Zone
```
http://www.dhtmlzone.com/index.html
```

Macromedia's DHTML Zone Resources
http://www.dhtmlzone.com/resources/

Inside DHTML
http://www.insidedhtml.com

Webmonkey
http://www.webmonkey.com

Shelley Powers' Site
http://www.yasd.com

Danny Goodman's Site
http://www.dannyg.com

Cross-browser Dynamic HTML
http://members.xoom.com/tfriesen/dhtml/index.html

The Dynamic Duo: Cross-Browser DHTML
http://www.dansteinman.com/dynduo/

DOM

Document Object Model (DOM) Level 1 Specification
http://www.w3.org/TR/REC-DOM-Level-1/

Document Object Model (DOM)
http://www.w3.org/DOM/

Document Object Model (DOM) Activity
http://www.w3.org/DOM/Activity

Latest DOM working draft
http://www.w3.org/TR/WD-DOM/

CSS

World Wide Web Consortium's CSS Resources
http://www.w3.org/Style/CSS/

Latest CSS Specification: Level 1
http://www.w3.org/TR/REC-CSS1

Latest CSS Specification: Level 2
http://www.w3.org/TR/REC-CSS2

JavaScript

ECMAScript Specification
http://www.ecma.ch/stand/ECMA-262.htm

Netscape's JavaScript Documentation
http://developer.netscape.com/tech/javascript/index.html

Microsoft's JavaScript Documentation
http://msdn.microsoft.com/scripting/jscript/default.htm

HTML and HTTP

World Wide Web Consortium's HTML Resources
http://www.w3.org/MarkUp/

Latest HTML 4.0 Specification
http://www.w3.org/TR/REC-html40/

Microsoft's HTML Resources
http://www.microsoft.com/workshop/author/html/beghtml.asp

Netscape's HTML and Web Design
http://www.hotwired.com/webmonkey/partners/ns/

Uniform Resource Locator RFC
http://www.w3.org/Addressing/rfc1738.txt

W3C Protocols Site
http://www.w3.org/Protocols/

XML

Extensible Markup Language (W3C)
http://www.w3.org/XML/

W3C XML 1.0 Recommendation
http://www.w3.org/TR/1998/REC-xml-19980210

XML.com
http://www.xml.com

XML FAQ
http://www.ucc.ie/xml/

James Clark's XML Resources
http://www.jclark.com/xml/

Tim Bray's XML Resources
http://www.textuality.com/xml/

Microsoft's XML Resources
http://www.microsoft.com/xml/default.asp

Netscape's XML and Metadata Pages
http://developer.netscape.com/tech/metadata/index.html

Robin Cover's XML/SGML Resources
http://www.oasis-open.org/cover/xml.html

XSL

World Wide Web Consortium's XSL Resources
http://www.w3.org/Style/XSL/

Latest XSL Specification
http://www.w3.org/TR/WD-xsl

Style Sheet Resources
http://www.finetuning.com/xsl.html

Microsoft

Home Page
http://www.microsoft.com/

Netscape

Home Page
http://www.netscape.com/

The Mozilla Project
http://www.mozilla.org/

Other Sites

Igneus
http://www.igneus.com

Panic Software, Inc.
http://www.panic.com

The Web Standards Project
http://www.webstandards.org

Kvetch!
http://www.kvetch.com

Project Cool Developer Zone
http://www.projectcool.com/developer/

Sun's Java Servlets
http://jserv.javasoft.com/products/java-server/servlets/

Server-Side Includes Tutorial at NCSA
http://hoohoo.ncsa.uiuc.edu/docs/tutorials/includes.html

Apache's XSSI documentation
http://www.apache.org/docs/mod/mod_include.html

Microsoft's ASP Overview
http://www.microsoft.com/workshop/server/asp/ASPover.asp

Glossary

abstraction A conceptual representation of a thing or process apart from its actual concrete existence; or the process of arriving at such a representation. In software design, the ability to separate the functional characteristics of a system from their underlying or possible implementations so as to minimize dependence on the requirements or constraints of a given environment.

accelerator See *keyboard shortcut.*

affordance A term referring to the properties of an object that "afford" some action. In a general sense, an affordance implies a relationship between an object and an actor that describes ways in which the actor might use the object. In interface design, the term is often used to represent the perceived properties of an object: a dial affords turning, a button affords pushing, and so on. Many other affordances may exist, but interface design is primarily concerned with those that are evident to the user and supported within the context of an interface. There is a strong relationship between perceived affordances and interface conventions, as an element may afford several kinds of actions but only have one or two meaningful affordances. Tapping into these meaningful perceived affordances by way of consistency and convention in an interface is a primary goal of interface design.

annotation A note or other comment added to a document for the purposes of providing added information or explanation. A handy feature included in the early versions of NCSA Mosaic, but eventually left out of later versions, that enabled the user to keep a set of notes related to given Web pages.

API Application program interface. APIs are used to provide developers with a set of public functions that expose certain library functionality without having to document or expose the entire library's internals. A form of information hiding.

application Software applications are simply programs or systems that are written to perform a certain task. They apply technology to a specific purpose. The term is usually used in contrast to *component* or *applet*, which denote a very limited mini-application designed for a very specific purpose that may be used as part of a larger application or system.

argument A value passed to a function or other routine for use within that routine. Arguments enable a function to be written generically in order to implement a procedure that may be carried out using different values depending on what arguments are passed to it.

array   A group of similar objects, usually (but not necessarily) of the same data type, that may be accessed individually by some method referring to the object's place within the group. Objects in JavaScript arrays may be accessed by way of their numerical position, or *index*, through a process known as *subscripting*, or by a string reference to the object. `my_array[0]` is the first element in the array `my_array`. Arrays are great for operations that require a sequential loop, for example, accessing every element in an array in order. See *associative array*.

associative array   An array indexed by string reference. For example, `my_assoc_array['this_item']` is one element in the associative array `my_assoc_array`. Associative arrays provide immediate access to an object without having to loop over every element, and perform tests on each one until you find the desired object. See *array*.

back end   A back-end system does not interact directly with a user, but usually supports front-end interfaces by providing some service or set of services. In DHTML, the back end is usually a Web server, as browser-based applications are limited in their capability to interact with the local operating system to store data or access other services.

background process   In multitasking environments, a process that runs independently of the processes currently in control of the system console or GUI. A JavaScript timer is an example of a background process, in that it continues to run even as the user interacts with the interface.

bandwidth   An oft-abused technical term from the field of signal processing that refers to the relationship between the highest and lowest frequencies used by an analog signal. The "width" of the "band" is described in terms of the difference between the two. In digital communications, bandwidth is usually described in bits per second (*bps*) or some multiple therein, such as *Kbps* for thousands of bits per second. In common usage, bandwidth refers to the amount of data that can be transmitted over a channel in a given time period, and so has a direct bearing on the size of the object being transmitted. The smaller the object, the less bandwidth is required to transmit it; for the user, often on a channel having a fixed transfer rate, this translates into the amount of time it takes for a file to download.

BASIC   Beginner's All-purpose Symbolic Instruction Code. A programming language popular for its relative simplicity and ease of learning. BASIC is often taught as a first programming language for novices, but is also used extensively in environments where novices may want to script application behaviors. Visual Basic and VBScript are two variants of the original BASIC, which was written in 1963 at Dartmouth College by John Kemeny and Thomas Kurtz.

bitmap   A common, nonscalable format used to store image data having a fixed aspect ratio. Bitmaps are essentially nothing more than descriptions of the color and position of every pixel in an image, although various mechanisms are used to compress this representation for transmission or storage. GIF and BMP are two popular bitmap file formats.

Boolean   Usually refers to a system of logic developed by English mathematician George Boole in which objects may have only true or false values, and that provides for a set of operations that may be performed on collections of such values. In JavaScript, Boolean variables may only be true or false.

bottom-up   A software design methodology that begins by specifying the individual components of a system and then proceeds to integrate them into a larger whole. Excellent for situations when the data formats and algorithms are well known but their eventual use has yet to be determined or may change. The Preferences module is an example of bottom-up design, as it began with JavaScript cookies, then provided a set of functions to manage the setting of generic preferences, and was finally integrated into the larger application and used to store object color settings.

breadth   A general term used to describe something's width, as opposed to its depth. In software design, the breadth of a system refers to how many features it has, while the depth refers to the degree of functionality and flexibility provided by each feature. See also *depth*.

browser   A generic term for file viewer that has more recently become almost exclusively associated with Web clients. A browser enables the user to view, read, hear, and navigate between files delivered by Web servers. Netscape Navigator and Microsoft Internet Explorer are browsers, as are Mosaic, Opera, Lynx, and Arena, among others.

browser-sniffing   The process of determining what browser a user is running in order to tailor the page returned by a server, execute the appropriate code for a given environment, or redirect the browser to a more suitable URL. Server-side solutions often use the `HTTP_USER_AGENT` environment variable under CGI, which simply reflects the HTTP `User-agent:` header. Client-side solutions make use of the `navigator` object and its associated properties.

button   An interface element that resembles a push button. Also refers to an HTML form input that is usually rendered as a push button.

cable modem   A communications device similar to a network card that allows for roughly 1.5Mbps of incoming Internet bandwidth, using cable television lines to carry the data.

Cascading Style Sheets   CSS is the set of proposed and recommended standards for associating style information with HTML document elements. See Chapter 7, "Cascading Style Sheets: Adjectives and Adverbs."

CBT   Computer-based training.

CGI   The Common Gateway Interface, a popular API used by Web developers to communicate with non-Web applications by way of the Web server. Defines a set of environment variables that provide access to HTTP session information, such as the remote IP address or the visitor's browser version.

check box   An interface element that enables the user to select or deselect an option. May be used in HTML forms to provide multiple selections from a group of options, contrasted with *radio buttons*, which are often used to restrict a choice to one of a set of choices.

CLI   Command-line interface. The typical CLI uses a text-based interface that enables the user to specify commands by name, specify options for their execution, and redirect their output to files, the console, or other programs. The UNIX shells and MS-DOS are examples of CLIs. See also *switch*.

click   The result of the user pressing down on the mouse button. May generate a `click` event that may then be handled by an application. Often associated with links, image maps, buttons, check boxes, radio buttons, and other interface elements.

click-and-drag   The action resulting from a combination of a down click, or `mousedown` event, and subsequent mouse movement, usually resulting in an object being moved along with the cursor or mouse pointer until the user releases the mouse button, generating a `mouseup` event. In the meantime, the application may track mouse movement by way of the `mousemove` events thus generated. May also involve other events or event properties, enabling the target object to process information received from the source object, such as a URL.

client   A software program, usually on the user's local machine but not always (see *X Window System*), that requests services from a *server*. Most clients are responsible for providing the user interface to an application and managing the user's input and the application's responses to such input. One half of a *client-server* architecture. For example, Web browsers are clients, as are e-mail applications, many data entry systems, file transfer programs, and so forth. Compare to *terminal*. See also *client-side, client-server, server-side,* and *server*.

client-server   A popular computing architecture that separates responsibility for the user interface and display, entry, and local processing of data from the storage and/or other services related to data.

client-side   Code that runs on the client as opposed to the server. JavaScript is an example of a client-side technology that has migrated to the server. See also *server-side*.

command-line interface   See *CLI*.

Common Gateway Interface   See *CGI*.

component   A discrete and separable part of a software application, usually providing a certain limited type of functionality that may be reused elsewhere. One definition refers to software and hardware systems as being composed of components that are themselves composed of modules. From the standpoint of the interface, a component is a recognizable interface element combined with the functionality it provides.

consistency   The degree of harmony observed between the constituent parts of a whole, contributing to the overall perception of quality of the whole. Associated with the use of standard conventions for interface elements, layout, labeling, and other issues related to an application's presentation and behavior.

constant   A fundamental object in a programming language whose value never changes and may be provided by the language or environment itself. See also *variable*.

context   The conditions in which the user interacts with a software application. Includes the entire operating system environment, the interface conventions used by other applications on the same and other computers, and the conventions used by the current application. May be limited to the current application for the sake of comparing individual dialog boxes or interface elements for consistency.

contextual pop-up menu   A pop-up menu whose contents change depending upon when and where it is invoked by the user. Usually not part of a system menu bar, most contextual pop-up menus appear wherever the user clicks with a mouse, often as the result of an alternate button or a mousedown followed by a delay during which time the menu appears.

convention   An established usage or a correspondence between usage and representation. In the world of software applications and user interfaces, often applied to a relationship between a user activity and the application's expected response.

cookie   Client-side persistent cookies are small pieces of data delivered by a Web server and stored on a Web client's local computer. See Chapter 13, "User-Configurable Interfaces," for more information than you probably want to know about cookies.

correspondence   A similarity between one thing and another, or one thing and a collection. The degree to which they are similar. Often used to refer to the way that an onscreen representation of a real-world object resembles that object.

CPU   Central processing unit. The computer's tiny brain, containing logic circuits, as distinct from memory or input/output. Also known as a *microprocessor*.

cross-browser   Not limited to a single browser implementation. Implies that the object in question is available for users or developers on all browsers, or all browsers supporting a specific core feature set or from a single generation. See also *cross-platform*.

cross-platform   Not bound to a single platform. Implies universality, although by simple definition may only mean that the object (or property, function, feature, or application) may work on one vendor's browser on two different platforms. See also *cross-browser*.

CSS   See *Cascading Style Sheets*.

debug   To remove flaws from a computer program, asymptotically approaching zero. Or, to quote a famous programmer, "There is always one more bug."

depth   The complement to breadth in software design, depth refers to the degree to which a given set of functionality is implemented. May also refer to the extent of abstraction used in a given implementation, or how close the implementation is to the lowest-level underlying programming interface. For example, the color picker uses the Preferences module, that uses the cookie handler functions, that use the JavaScript API for setting and reading cookie values, that uses the functionality provided by the browser, that in turn uses the functionality provided by the under-lying OS to write the cookie to the computer's disk. This module could be said to have a lot of depth. See *breadth*.

desktop metaphor   A common computer interface metaphor in which the background of the user's screen is said to represent the top of their desk. Made famous by the Apple Macintosh.

DHTML   See *dynamic HTML*.

dialog box   An interface element that groups related items together (for example, a preferences dialog box), presents the user with a notice (for example, an alert dialog box), a choice (for example, a confirmation dialog box), or other options. May come in either *modal* or *modeless* types: the first prohibits any other interaction until the user has addressed the dialog box; the second permits free access to other windows, and so on.

direct manipulation   The characteristic by which objects in the real world (such as a mouse) correspond to objects on a computer screen, enabling the user to perform actions on the real object and have some corresponding action result on the screen. Some characteristics of environments providing direct manipulation are constant visibility of objects, reversibility of actions, and the gradual display of the results of incremental actions.

display   The computer monitor or screen.

domain   A set of related concepts or objects, grouped according to some scheme. Internet domains are groups of addresses, constructed hierarchically according to geography or other characteristic, such as the set of all commercial domains (the .com top-level domain). The second level identifies a subset of that group, for which there are Domain Name System records, and within which unique host addresses may be identified. Cookies use the domain as a way to restrict their visibility from other, unrelated clients, and the browser only sends back a cookie to servers within the domain as defined.

drag-and-drop   A mechanism whereby the user clicks an object and changes its position on the screen, usually accompanied by some response from the target object, over which the selected object is "dragged" and finally "dropped" when the user releases the mouse button.

dynamic HTML   The functionality provided by Cascading Style Sheets, JavaScript, and the HTML and XML Document Object Model taken as a whole. See also *JavaScript, CSS.*

element   A single document object, indicated in HTML by the presence of a start tag and often optional end tag as well as various element attributes, and often enclosed content. Elements are reflected in JavaScript by way of the Document Object Model, and may be associated with Cascading Style Sheet definitions.

em   A unit of measure equivalent to the width of a capital *M* in the current or specified font.

en   A unit of measure equivalent to the width of a capital *N* in the current or specified font.

environment variable   A value made available to a program by its environment, such as the shell that spawned it, in UNIX, or via the use of a global mechanism for setting and reading these values. Web servers often provide session information to CGI scripts via environment variables. See *CGI.*

escape   To remove "dangerous" characters from a string by replacing them with encoded strings to prevent their wrongful interpretation by an intermediate environment. In JavaScript, Perl, and the UNIX shell, you escape a character by immediately preceding it with a backslash (\). In URLs, characters are escaped by replacing them with an encoded hexadecimal equivalent of the form "%xx," where "xx" is the hex value of the character's value in the ASCII character set. See *URLencoding*.

event   An object created in response to user input of a certain type, such as clicking the mouse button or entering a character from the keyboard.

event-driven   A quality of software that is constructed to react to user input, rather than to follow a predetermined and unalterable set of procedures. Events are used to signal to the program that the user has interacted with the system. See *event*.

ex   x-height, the height of the letter *x* in the current or specified font.

extranet   An application of Internet protocols and services that links businesses to their clients or suppliers, or other businesses. Usually not public or publicly accessible, but protected by passwords or other mechanisms. Generally, a Web site with a business-to-business purpose. See *intranet*.

fantods   A state of irritability or tension. An emotional outburst.

feedback   In interface design, the quality of the interface that represents accurate and timely reporting of status information regarding an action initiated by the user.

file   A discrete collection of data available to users of a system and capable of being manipulated as a single object. Files may be used to store documents, raw data, or other related information, and must be given unique names within the context of the file system on which they are stored.

FTP   File Transfer Protocol. An Internet protocol used to transfer files from one computer to another.

gateway   A point of contact between two separate systems, usually involving some form of translation between the two. A gateway program, in the context of a Web server, provides access to the resources of one system through the Web server interface.

global   A variable whose value is available to the entire program. In JavaScript, globals are declared outside of function bodies and have the same value no matter where they are accessed in the context of the rest of the browser session.

GMT   Greenwich mean time.

goal   The end result of a directed effort. See *goal-oriented*.

goal-oriented   A type of interface. Goal-oriented interfaces have a clearly defined end and usually include well-defined and restricted methods or rules by which that end may be reached.

Gopher   An Internet protocol and information storage and retrieval mechanism involving the use of hierarchically organized file and directory structures. Distinct from the Web, which uses hypertext principles for organization and features access to multimedia file types, Gopher resources are restricted to hierarchical access of text files (with some exceptions).

granularity   A measure of how modular a system is, based on the level that its components have been broken down into small, flexible, and customizable modules. The more granular a system's components, the easier it is to customize the system as a whole.

grayed out   A common term for the disabled functionality of an interface element, so-called due to the practice of making the element less distinct through the use of masking, resulting in a gray appearance.

GUI   Graphical user interface.

HDTV   High-definition television.

help   Also known as *online help*. A form of electronic documentation readily available to the user of a system, directed at assisting the user in remembering what to do. Distinct from traditional documentation in that it is usually not expected to train the user, but merely remind them of what they should already know.

Help Balloon   A device often used to provide immediate assistance to the user of an application, represented by a balloon containing brief tips and instructions on given interface elements. Introduced by Apple in Macintosh System 7, and now replaced or supplanted by Apple's Guide technology.

hexadecimal   A number system that uses base 16, instead of base 10 (decimal) or base 2 (binary). Represents its values using the alphanumeric characters 0 through 9 and A through F.

hierarchy   A system of classification in which every member of a set is defined in terms of its immediate superior member. Elements in a hierarchical system are usually expressed as a chain of related objects, from most general to most specific. The specific members are said to be included in the more general.

hook   In software, a variable or other feature that allows for later customization or extension by other developers. Usually implies a high degree of flexibility in design.

HTML   Hypertext Markup Language. The *lingua franca* of the Web, HTML is the markup language used by Web authors to provide structural, and more recently, layout and presentation-oriented characteristics to their documents.

HTTP   Hypertext Transfer Protocol. The underlying protocol used by Web browsers and servers to transfer files and other data.

human–computer interaction (HCI)   The study of how people interact with computers, focused on maximizing the ease with which computers may be used and how best to foster accurate mental models of the system through interface design principles and other mechanisms.

hypermedia   The extension of hypertext to include not only textual information but arbitrary file formats such as sound, video, and other types of resources. See *hypertext*.

hypertext   A system of organization in which every individual element in the system may be linked to any other and traversed by users in whatever order they choose; or where arbitrary relationships may be established, such as through the use of links in an HTML document. The term *hypertext* was first coined by Ted Nelson to describe his software system, Xanadu. See *hypermedia*.

icon   In general, icons are images used to represent something else. In interface design, the icon is used to represent an application, capability, or file.

iconography   The set of images or other pictorial representations conventionally associated with a specific subject or within a given environment. The sum of all imagery available for such a purpose. In interface design, iconography refers to those images used on icons within software applications.

identifier   The name given to a function or variable.

identity retrieval   The ability to request and return a resource based on a unique description or name.

idiom   A characteristic of an interface or interface element that enables the user to learn quickly without relying on an overarching metaphor.

image swapping   The common use of JavaScript to manipulate the `document.images` array to display alternating images when the user mouses over or out of an image area.

indirect manipulation   The quality of computer systems that do not provide a way for the user to directly control the objects being acted upon, and must therefore provide their input in mediated form, such as punched cards, a long and complex command line, or other mechanism. Contrast *direct manipulation.*

interactivity   The quality most often associated with the Web as distinct from traditional media, it is the manner in which the user must necessarily take the initiative to respond to the interface in order to continue, and is often invited to provide more information to interact with the system, and so forth.

interface   A user interface is the sum total of the emotional and cultural context in which users interact with a computer, combined with their psychological, rational, and sensory experience of, reaction to, and interaction with the input and output devices that comprise it. It often arises out of many unstated assumptions on the part of the system's designers and programmers that determine its nature, but that remain unstated and must either be learned by or hidden from the user in the form of metaphor, messages and feedback, response time, or training.

Internet   The global network connecting myriad other networks, communicating using TCP/IP and related protocols.

interpreter   A program that translates and executes another program, usually known as a *script.* JavaScript, Perl, and TCL are common examples of languages requiring an interpreter. In the case of JavaScript, the interpreter is a part of the browser, although server-side JavaScript is used as well. See *script.*

intranet   A TCP/IP network inside a company, usually associated with internal Web servers, though intranets can use any other Internet protocol or technology as well. Distinguished from traditional file and print services or proprietary e-mail and bulletin board systems due to its use of open protocols. See *extranet.*

iteration   One cycle of a repetitive sequence of operations or processes.

Java   A programming language and environment created by Sun Microsystems for use in set-top boxes and repurposed for the Internet. Provides a cross-platform, interpreted environment for development of applications or smaller chunks of code known as *applets.* Gaining in popularity for mainstream development as well due to its simplified object-oriented design and ease of use compared to languages like C++.

JavaScript   An interpreted programming language loosely based on Java, with influences from Perl, HyperTalk, and dBASE, among others. It is designed to be used with a Web browser, enabling the browser to expose certain aspects of its functionality while also enabling the contents of the document to be accessed or modified. JavaScript comes in two flavors: server-side (LiveWire) and client-side. See also *dynamic HTML, Java.*

JScript   Microsoft's version of JavaScript, first released with Internet Explorer 3.0.

keyboard shortcut   A keyboard combination used to run a command in an application. Usually redundant with mouse commands in GUI environments, but not always. Also called an *accelerator*.

kiosk   A self-contained terminal used to provide limited public access to information. Usually uses touch screens and graphical displays, though more complex kiosks may also use a keyboard or touch pad for input. In a Web browser, kiosk mode signifies a full screen display featuring limited access to browser functionality.

label   The text used to signify a navigational node on a Web site or serve as the description associated with an interface element.

layout   Manner of presentation, especially for Web pages and printed output.

legacy   A pejorative term applied to old or "inherited" code or other systems, usually those in the process of being replaced or phased out.

life cycle   The length of time between when a system is proposed, designed, and first rolled into production, and its eventual retirement and replacement by other systems. May also be used to refer to just the development process to the exclusion of maintenance, but such poor thinking is usually a sign of even more distorted and dangerous perceptions and should be avoided.

Linux   A freely available UNIX kernel for the Intel x86 and other architectures and associated programs. Often sold in distributions containing many other tools, themselves also consisting of freely available code. An excellent, low-cost upgrade from Windows to a robust, high-quality operating system.

LISP   LISt Processing language, a language developed in the fifties by John McCarthy, with a syntax based on recursive, nested statements and characterized by the heavy use of parentheses (hence the alternate acronymic expansion, "Lots of Irritating Superfluous Parentheses"). Used extensively in Artificial Intelligence research, and the basis for the language Scheme, which was the foundation for DSSSL.

Logo   A high-level programming language developed in the sixties by Seymour Papert and subsequently used in conjunction with children's programming education due to its ease of use. Its graphics programming language is known as "turtle graphics," wherein the cursor is represented by a robotic turtle, and commands are given in terms of driving instructions for the turtle: "go forward five units," "turn left," and so on.

loop   A repetitive programming construct, usually controlled by a self-terminating condition, such as a variable that is incremented every pass through the loop and whose value is tested at the top or bottom.

mainframe   A large computer, also known as "big iron." Originally used to refer to all computers; distinctions were introduced with the birth of the minicomputer and personal computer. Used for large-scale transaction processing and terminal or database management and for other large enterprise applications, especially by the financial industry.

man pages   The online UNIX manual. So-called because the UNIX command for reading the manual is man.

media   Plural of *medium*. A means of conveyance, such as a storage or communications mechanism for data.

MEGO   My eyes glaze over. A common condition among programmers, usually caused by reading marketing materials with low technical information content.

mental model   The conception of a system formed by the user during and as a result of the user's interaction with the system. May or may not accurately reflect the true nature of the system, and may include illogical misconceptions, sequence errors, and other ill-formed ideas. A primary purpose of interface design is to encourage the user to develop a consistent mental model.

menu   A list of actions available to the user grouped together by function and usually activated by the mouse or a keyboard shortcut, and often displayed as a group as the result of user input related to the menu's label.

menu item   A single item on a menu associated with a single application action.

metacharacter   A character used in command-line applications to represent other characters. The asterisk (*), for instance, may be used to represent all characters. Should be avoided when giving names to files, as the characters must be *escaped* to avoid being interpreted by the shell. Also used in regular expressions. See *regular expressions, escape*.

metaphor   A figure of speech involving a word, phrase, or image used in place of another to denote a relationship or similarity between them. In interface design, metaphors tend to be primarily visual and are used to suggest a relationship between the real world and that on the computer screen. Often overused to the detriment of usability and with laughable results, but quite powerful if used carefully, such as the Macintosh *desktop metaphor*. See *desktop metaphor*.

mnemonic   Of or relating to memory. In interface design and programming, often manifested as suggestive keyboard shortcuts or variable names, such as Ctrl+Q for "quit."

modal dialog box   A dialog box that does not allow the user to interact with the application or other applications until it has been dismissed or recognized in some way. Used for important notifications or to gather data required before the application may continue. May be irritating to the user if used indiscriminately. See *dialog box.*

mode   A state into which an application enters under certain conditions, implying alternative modes, such as "command mode" versus "insert mode" for a visual editor.

modem   Short for modulator-demodulator. A device that enables a computer or terminal to communicate with other systems via telephone lines. Converts the digital signals used by the computer into analog signals more suitable for long-distance transmission, and vice versa. Usually required at both ends of a connection.

module   A self-contained software component that may be used by other, larger systems to provide certain functionality. The design principles that encourage modular programming have more recently been encompassed and expanded upon by *object-oriented* analysis, design, and programming.

Mosaic   The first widely distributed graphical Web browser, produced at NCSA (the National Center for Supercomputing Applications at University of Illinois, Urbana-Champlain). Mosaic introduced the Web to a much larger audience, placing a user-friendly interface on the arcane and command-line oriented Internet.

mouseover   The event that is fired when a user moves the mouse over an element. Also used to refer to the resultant effect, such as in *image swapping* constructs. See *image swapping.*

Mozilla   Once a code name for the Netscape Navigator browser. Now representing the open source effort that Netscape launched in early 1998, as well as the browser produced by that effort.

multimedia   The combination of multiple forms of media (such as text, video, images, and sound) in interactive presentations such as those found on CD-ROMs or Web sites.

multitasking   The execution of two or more programs at the same time. Comes in two major forms: *preemptive*, in which the programs being run may be interrupted and their relative execution priorities adjusted as needed; and *cooperative*, in which the program itself is responsible for returning control to other programs as they share execution time. The former is more robust, and found in higher-end environments such as UNIX and Windows NT, as contrasted with the Macintosh OS, which features the latter.

namespace   A mechanism by which identically named identifiers such as variables, functions, or even hostnames or documents may be placed in overarching groups that distinguish between them. The DNS, for example, is just a big distributed hierarchical namespace mechanism. In programming, namespaces are used to create modules and isolate any variables and functions internal to those modules from others. May be informally emulated in JavaScript through the use of prefixes on identifiers. See *identifier.*

natural mapping   A relationship, usually metaphorical, drawn between a graphical presentation on a computer screen, or similar construct, and an object in the real world. Such mappings enable the user to use the representational object much as they would in the real world, or to provide translations of real-world action into similar action onscreen. The mouse makes use of natural mappings when mouse motion corresponds directly to motion of the cursor onscreen.

navigation   The act of accessing pages within a Web site by way of the provided links. Also used to refer to the system by which such access is enabled or encouraged.

NCSA   The National Center for Supercomputing Applications at the University of Illinois at Urbana-Champlain. The birthplace of Mosaic. See *Mosaic.*

node   A single endpoint, such as a hypertext document, in a system of connected objects.

object   A thing, whether an abstract representation or its actual instantiation in a program. Objects can have properties and methods associated with them that provide the manipulation of data, communication with other objects, and so forth. HTML markup is parsed into JavaScript objects that represent the original markup as it has been transformed into an internal set of objects, their relationships, and their visual representation on the screen, if applicable.

object-oriented   An analysis, design, and programming methodology that places emphasis on the construction of programming systems out of objects that contain their own methods for manipulating the data they also contain. These methods are used to hide the data from other objects, which encourages encapsulation and proper modularity of design. JavaScript is said to be an object-oriented language, but is too often used in a purely procedural manner.

operating system (OS)   The portion of a computer that runs all other software, and manages memory, input and output, and scheduling of tasks. Often conflated with the supporting software distributed along with the OS, such as Microsoft has done in claiming that Internet Explorer is part of the operating system in Windows 98.

option list   A list of options presented to the user as a pop-up menu, created in HTML through the use of the SELECT and OPTION elements.

overloading   In interface design, the practice of giving a single interface element type several different possible uses or results, forcing the user to maintain awareness of the context in which the element is to be used. In programming, the practice of giving the same name to many variables or function, and forcing the compiler or interpreter to determine which to use based on context. Should be used cautiously in either case.

parallel   Happening at the same time, as in *parallel processing*. See *serial*.

pc   Pica. A unit of measurement equivalent to ¹/₆ inch, supported by CSS.

Perl   A weird glue language hacked together from the best bits and pieces of a dozen other languages, and then used for systems administration, text processing, reportage, and a good chunk of the CGI scripts on the planet. Perl's associative arrays influenced the design of JavaScript.

pipeline   A series of commands with the output of one forming the input of the next. A common programming practice among UNIX programmers, who can say things like, "Why don't you just cat it through awk then pipe it through sort pipe uniq redirect newfile?" without blinking or smirking, and *mean it*.

platform   Common term for the combination of hardware and operating system environment, often used on the Web to refer to the combination of hardware, OS, and browser. See *cross-platform* and *cross-browser*.

pointer   The cursor.

pop-up menu   Also known as a pull-down menu. A list of options of which only one is displayed until the user selects the menu, after which the entire list is displayed and available for selection.

port   A place or address that enables connections to be made, either hardware (as in *serial port*) or software (as in *port 80*). In software, it represents a logical address, usually associated with a specific service, such as port 80 for HTTP or 23 for Telnet. Also refers to the process or end result of an attempt to reimplement a program on a platform other than that on which it was originally written.

positional retrieval   The practice of retrieving a resource based on the remembered location where it was last stored. Positional retrieval is common under the file system model, where folders and directories act as logical "locations" where files may be stored.

POSIX Portable Operating System Interface for UNIX. A set of standard software and operating system interfaces based on the UNIX system that are designed to bring uniformity to the widely divergent UNIX world. Specifications include not only low-level system calls, but also command-line interfaces, such as switches and arguments for common tools.

preference A configurable setting exposed to the user and applied to the environment whenever it is used, such as choice of colors or other interface features or behaviors.

problem domain The strict definition of the problem to be solved by a program, excluding all irrelevant detail and functionality.

progress indicator An interface element used to show progress of an action that may take some time to complete. May take the form of a dial, a counter, or a rectangular bar whose contents gradually fill or change color as the task is completed.

property A named variable associated with an object, usually also associated with its presentation or behavior in some respect as well. In JavaScript, a property may be arbitrarily created and assigned values, or may be provided by the browser as a reflection of the HTML markup and style information included in the current document.

prototype A demonstration of a piece of software that may be severely limited in terms of its implemented functionality, but that may be used to get feedback from the users of the system under design. Prototyping is considered an important part of rapid application development, and is usually performed iteratively throughout the development process to ensure that the final interface and behavior meet the users' expectations.

pt Point. A physical unit of measurement in typography, equivalent to $1/72$ inch and supported by CSS.

pull-down menu See *pop-up menu, options list.*

px Pixel, short for picture element. A unit of measurement representing the smallest available screen element supported by CSS.

rapid application development (RAD) Rapid application development is a software methodology that promotes the reuse of existing software objects. Characterized by a rapid, prototype-heavy, and iterative development process.

recursion When a program or function calls itself, usually accompanied by a test in order to avoid an infinite loop. This technique can often result in a more elegant program structure. If you have already read this definition, you can stop reading now. See *recursion*.

redundancy The quality of an interface that provides support for multiple, equivalent mechanisms by which user input may be collected or application output presented.

regular expression A pattern specified for matching strings, using a set of well-defined symbols to represent the characters to be matched.

reversibility The capability provided by an application that enables users to reverse their last action or a series of actions. See *undo*.

robust Well-designed and/or implemented, usually in a sense (with operating systems or applications) that suggests that the failure of a single component or system does not result in the failure of the whole.

rollover See *image swapping*.

root metaphor A linguistic structure suggested by George Lakoff and Mark Johnson that is generally derived from our experience of the real world, and that influences language. For example, a root metaphor such as "more is up" is suggested by human experience with piles of physical materials, and is reflected in phrases such as "my income *rose* last year."

scope The range of applicability of a variable's value. JavaScript variables may be defined to have either *global* scope (if they are defined outside of a function, they are accessible from anywhere in the application) or *function-level* scope (if they are defined inside a function, they are only available within that function). Other languages provide for more sophisticated scoping mechanisms, such as block-level scope or namespaces. See also *global*, *constant*, and *variable*.

screen real estate The total screen area available. Many interface improvements have been geared at maximizing the screen real estate available to the primary purpose of the program in question.

screen-scraping The black art of mining terminal data streams for the data they contain, stripping out characters whose only purpose is to position the data characters on the terminal's screen.

screenshot An image captured from the actual computer screen by some mechanism, whether native to the operating system (such as that made available via PrintScrn on DOS and Windows or Shift + ⌘ + 3 under Macintosh) or through the use of other application software. Intended to convey exactly what the user sees or will see.

script   A program whose contents are interpreted by another software program or component, rather than being executed directly by the operating system or processor, such as is the case with compiled code.

scrollbar   An interface element usually consisting of a vertical or horizontal bar on the side of a window and two or more arrows, providing the ability to move the window's contents in one direction or another; and a *thumb* that may be manipulated by the cursor to provide arbitrary movement. A great example of an *idiom* is that scrollbars do not exist in nature, they use an arbitrary convention (scrolling down moves the window contents up), and they are very usable, even by novices.

serial   Occurring in order with one task following the next, as in a series.

server   A computer or program that provides a service and responds to requests from clients. A Web server responds to HTTP requests initiated by a browser, usually for files of many different types. See *client*.

server–side   Happening on the server, as opposed to on the client. See *client-side*.

session   The length of time between when a user launches a browser and the time they close the browser application. Also may be used to apply to the length of time between when a request is sent to a Web server, a response is given, and the connection is closed.

SGML   Standard Generalized Markup Language. ISO Standard 8879:1986. A massive and comprehensive standard for the definition of document markup languages, including HTML. XML is an attempt to simplify SGML while focusing on its most popular and successful features. See *XML*.

shelfware   Software that, once purchased, never leaves the box it came in, but sits on a shelf gathering dust. (The term is already rapidly becoming archaic in this modern day of fully downloadable software.)

shell   In UNIX, the shell is the user interface and command interpreter. Web sites are often built using a shell model, wherein all or a majority of the navigation provided by a site is included with every page.

slider bar   An interface element that enables the user to select a value along a given range.

status bar   Specifically, the browser status bar whose contents are exposed to the JavaScript property `window.status`. In more generic terms, a status bar is simply an area of the application set aside for printing informative but unobtrusive updates on the state of the application.

STDERR   Standard error.

STDIN   Standard input.

STDOUT   Standard output. One of the three standard available mechanisms on UNIX systems for receiving input, printing output, and notifying the user of error conditions. CGI scripts may read from STDIN, print its response to STDOUT, and report any error conditions to STDERR. STDOUT is redirected to the browser, and STDERR is usually redirected to the server's error logs. See *CGI, STDIN, STDERR*.

switch   An argument passed to a command-line program, usually consisting of a dash (-) or double-dash (--) followed by a single letter; a cluster of letters, each representing a different switch; a descriptive word; or a combination of switches and the data passed to them as arguments. May also begin with a forward slash (/), as in MS-DOS. For example, `chmod -R g+w *`. See also *argument, CLI*.

syntax   The structure or grammar of a language, often used in reference to programming and markup languages, as distinct from its meaning, or *semantics*.

tab widget   A type of interface element often portrayed as a set of tabs and used to enable independent access to different screens in a dialog box or other window.

task   The simplest action made possible by an interface.

task-oriented   A type of interface whose elements are geared primarily towards providing immediate access to individual tasks, usually without an overarching or controlling goal or conclusion. See also *goal-oriented*.

terminal   A piece of software or hardware that provides the display of and interaction with applications running on a remote server, such as a mainframe or UNIX workstation, whose interface is entirely dependent on the remote system. The terminal provides display and input but must remain constantly connected to the server by a network or other mechanism in order to be of any use.

thumb   The portion of a scrollbar that, when manipulated by the user, scrolls the page.

toolbar   A group of icons that enable quick visual reference and mouse-based access to common application functionality.

tool tip   A mechanism whereby a user can obtain text reminders of a given interface element's functionality, usually in the form of small floating "kites" or other such representations. Often displayed when the user's mouse pointer hovers over an interface element for a certain period, but may also be shown as the result of a mouse click or other event.

top-down   A software design methodology that starts with or develops a functional description of the system in question, including a high-level decomposition of its constituent parts, before any low-level coding is begun. Generally considered to result in more cohesive systems, but sometimes at the expense of low-level optimization.

transclusion   The inclusion of a resource or part of a resource in another by way of offsets into a file or other mechanisms. One of the fundamental qualities of a classic hypertext system such as Ted Nelson's Xanadu that is mostly missing from the present-day Web. Proposals such as Xlink are intended to provide transclusion and bidirectional linking, among other services, to users of XML documents.

transparency   The quality of an interface or interface components that arises when the user has identified the action they carry out with the interface itself. A goal of all interface design. A nontransparent interface is considered obtrusive and distracting.

undo   The capability whereby a user can reverse an action or series of actions recently performed. Considered an essential part of a forgiving application interface.

UNIX   A robust and elegant multitasking, multiuser operating system environment created by Dennis Ritchie and Ken Thompson at Bell Labs in 1969. Because of a consent agreement that prohibited AT&T from marketing the system, UNIX was more or less given away to universities, where it became a favorite of programmers — some of whom consider it the "One True Operating System," or at least the standard by which all others are measured. Linux, a popular freeware UNIX kernel written by a Finnish student named Linus Torvalds, is often bundled with other freeware implementations of popular UNIX programs. Other versions include Solaris, HP-UX, and AIX. A popular choice of platform for Web servers.

URI   Uniform Resource Identifier. See *URL, URN.*

URL   Uniform Resource Locator. A form of addressing that specifies an Internet resource by way of the protocol used to access it, the server from which it may be accessed, and the path and other information required to uniquely identify the resource on the host system. A type of URI. An example URL: `http://hesketh.com/schampeo/projects/namespace/index.html`.

URLencoding   An encoding scheme used to *escape* certain characters for successful inclusion in URLs. Consists of replacing a given character with a hexadecimal representation based on the character's ASCII value, and including a percent sign followed by the hex value. For example, the tilde (~), having ASCII value 126, becomes `%7E`.

URN   Uniform Resource Name. A more generic form of addressing than URLs, URNs imply that the resource may be available from a number of different sources but be available the same way from any of them. Directory services are a common example. URNs assume that the application using them knows how to find and select from a number of possible sources for the specified resource.

usability   The quality of a software program related to its relative ease of use. Also the study of such characteristics, geared towards discovering and measuring those qualities and documenting and promoting successful techniques and metrics.

USENET   A hierarchical, distributed system for the mass delivery of individual messages related to certain topics, arranged by subject matter into collections known as newsgroups. For example, `comp.lang.perl` is a newsgroup hierarchy devoted to discussions of the computer programming language Perl. Also known as *netnews*.

vaporware   Software or hardware that is announced in order to influence or defer buying decisions, but that may never actually make it to market. Usually refers to software whose actual existence is in doubt, but may also refer to individual features of existing software that have not yet been implemented or implemented so poorly as to be practically absent.

variable   A fundamental object or data type in a programming language that may be given a name and assigned a value. The value may change over the life of the object as a result of manipulation of the environment by the user or the underlying system. See also *constant*.

vector   In the context of graphical file formats, the mathematical expressions that describe curves, lines, and other characteristics in a resolution-independent manner, allowing for scaling and other manipulation. Also refers to the type of file format that uses such mechanisms. See also *bitmap*.

white space   May refer to either the set of characters that includes linefeeds, carriage returns, tabs, and spaces or to the empty space in a visual layout used to offset the other elements on a page or screen.

widget   A generic term for something whose name has been forgotten. In interface design, an interface element, usually discrete, but often a composite of other, more fundamental widgets, that provides a visual mechanism for user interaction with application or operating system functionality. Most GUI development toolkits provide sets of widgets that may be reused as required by an application. Examples include buttons, scrollbars, icons, text input fields, and so forth.

WIMP Windows, icons, menus, and pointers. The interface design paradigm developed at XEROX PARC based on work by Douglas Engelbart at Stanford Research Institute. Made popular by the Apple Macintosh after the initial failure of other systems, such as the XEROX Star, the Canon Cat, and the Apple Lisa. Now implemented on practically every graphical computing platform.

window An area of the screen, usually rectangular, that defines a view of a document or application. Windows are generally capable of being moved, resized, being assigned titles and other characteristics, and closed. Windows may also contain other windows or interface elements.

window manager The subset of a windowing system responsible for keeping track of all application windows and managing user input and display properties of those windows. Often associated with the X Window System, which allows for separation of the window server and window manager, but is not limited to X, as the Windows and Macintosh environments include built-in window managers. Popular X window managers include FVWM, Enlightenment, and the Motif Window Manager.

World Wide Web (WWW) Technically, a subset of Internet services; namely, those that use HTTP. The Web is often confused with the Internet, due to the fact that Web browsers often provide mechanisms for accessing other protocols, such as Gopher or FTP. The sum total of all the content and services provided by all Web servers.

X Window System A distributed, platform-independent, client-server windowing environment developed at MIT and Stanford, X provides a standard mechanism for managing remote applications by way of a GUI. Essentially reverses the traditional client-server relationship in that remote computers are clients to a window server that provides facilities for the display of application GUIs or terminal screens. Perhaps most often found on UNIX systems.

XML The eXstensible Markup Language, a simplified and Web-oriented subset of SGML, intended to restore SGML's formal structure and validation to the Web. Distinct from HTML in that it is extensible; developers can define their own tag sets and structural relationships for document creation and data transfer within specific, well-defined realms.

Bibliography and Suggested Reading

Bradley, Neil. *The Concise SGML Companion.* Reading, MA: Addison-Wesley, 1997.

Brooks, Frederick P. Jr. *The Mythical Man-Month: Essays on Software Engineering.* Anniversary ed. Reading, MA: Addison-Wesley, 1995.

Cooper, Alan. *About Face: The Essentials of User Interface Design.* Foster City, CA: IDG Books Worldwide, 1995.

Csikszentmihalyi, Mihaly. *Flow: The Psychology of Optimal Experience.* New York, NY: Harper-Collins, 1991.

Flanagan, David. *JavaScript: The Definitive Reference.* Cambridge, MA: O'Reilly and Associates, 1997.

Fleming, Jennifer, and Richard Koman, ed. *Web Navigation: Designing the User Experience.* Cambridge, MA: O'Reilly and Associates, 1998.

Galitz, Wilbert O. *The Essential Guide to User Interface Design.* New York, NY: John Wiley and Sons, 1997.

Goodman, Danny. *Dynamic HTML: The Definitive Reference.* 3d ed. Cambridge, MA: O'Reilly and Associates, 1998.

Hafner, Katie, and Matthew Lyon. *Where Wizards Stay Up Late: The Origins of the Internet.* New York, NY: Simon and Schuster, 1996.

Harold, Elliotte Rusty. *XML: Extensible Markup Language.* Foster City, CA: IDG Books Worldwide, 1998.

Heinle, Nick. *Designing with JavaScript.* Cambridge, MA: O'Reilly and Associates, 1997.

Johnson, Steven. *Interface Culture.* San Francisco, CA: Harper, 1997.

Lakoff, George, and Mark Johnson. *Metaphors We Live By.* Chicago, IL: University of Chicago Press, 1980.

Lakoff, George. *Women, Fire, and Dangerous Things: What Categories Reveal About the Mind.* Chicago, IL: University of Chicago Press, 1987.

Landow, George P., ed. *Hyper/Text/Theory.* Baltimore, MD: Johns Hopkins University Press, 1994.

Laurel, Brenda, ed., *The Art of Human-Computer Interface Design.* Reading, MA: Addison-Wesley, 1990.

Laurel, Brenda. *Computers As Theatre.* Reading, MA: Addison-Wesley, 1993.

Levy, Steven. *Insanely Great.* New York, NY: Penguin, 1994.

Lie, Hakon Wium and Bert Bos. *Cascading Style Sheets: Designing for the Web.* Reading, MA: Addison-Wesley, 1997.

Maguire, Steve. *Writing Solid Code.* Redmond, WA: Microsoft Press, 1993.

McCloud, Scott. *Understanding Comics.* San Francisco, CA: Harper, 1994.

685

McConnell, Steve. *Rapid Application Development: Taming Wild Software Schedules*. Redmond, WA: Microsoft Press, 1996.

Mok, Clement. *Designing Business*. Indianapolis, IN: Macmillan Computer Publishing, 1996.

Monmonier, Mark. *How to Lie with Maps*. 2d ed. Chicago, IL: University of Chicago Press, 1996.

Nielsen, Jakob. *Usability Engineering*. AP Professional, 1994.

Nelson, Theodor Holm. *Literary Machines*. Mindful Press, 1981.

Norman, Donald A. *The Design of Everyday Things*. Currency/Doubleday, 1990.

Norman, Donald A. *The Invisible Computer*. Cambridge, MA: The MIT Press, 1998.

Pickover, Clifford A. *Computers, Pattern, Chaos and Beauty*. New York, NY: St. Martin's Press, 1990.

Powers, Shelley. *Dynamic HTML*. Foster City, CA: IDG Books Worldwide, 1998.

Rosenfeld, Louis, and Peter Morville. *Information Architecture for the World Wide Web*. Cambridge, MA: O'Reilly and Associates, 1998.

Sano, Darrell. *Designing Large-Scale Web Sites: A Visual Methodology*. New York, NY: John Wiley and Sons, 1996.

Schneiderman, Ben. *Designing the User Interface*. Reading, MA: Addison-Wesley, 1997.

Siegel, David S. *Creating Killer Web Sites*. 2d ed. Hayden, 1997.

Slater, Robert. *Portraits in Silicon*. Cambridge, MA: The MIT Press, 1987.

St. Laurent, Simon. *Dynamic HTML: A Primer*. New York, NY: MIS:Press, 1997.

St. Laurent, Simon. *Cookies*. New York, NY: McGraw-Hill, 1998.

St. Laurent, Simon. *XML: A Primer*. New York, NY: MIS:Press, 1998.

Stefik, Mark, ed. *Internet Dreams: Archetypes, Myths, and Metaphors*. Cambridge, MA: The MIT Press, 1996.

Tufte, Edward. *Envisioning Information*. Graphics Press, 1990.

Tufte, Edward. *The Visual Display of Quantitative Information*. Graphics Press, 1992.

Tufte, Edward, and Dmitry Krasny (ill.). *Visual Explanations: Images and Quantities, Evidence and Narrative*. Graphics Press, 1997.

Veen, Jeffrey. *Hotwired Style: Principles for Building Smart Web Sites*. San Francisco, CA: Wired Books, 1997.

Wall, Larry, Christiansen, Tom, and Randal L. Schwartz. *Programming Perl*. 2d ed. Cambridge, MA: O'Reilly and Associates, 1996.

Weinman, Lynda. *Designing Web Graphics.2*. New Riders, 1997.

Wurman, Richard Saul, and Peter Bradford, eds. *Information Architects*. Watson-Guptil, 1997.

Index

Continued

Continued

Continued

Continued

Continued

my2cents.idgbooks.com

Register This Book — And Win!

Visit **http://my2cents.idgbooks.com** to register this book and we'll automatically enter you in our fantastic monthly prize giveaway. It's also your opportunity to give us feedback: let us know what you thought of this book and how you would like to see other topics covered.

Discover IDG Books Online!

The IDG Books Online Web site is your online resource for tackling technology — at home and at the office. Frequently updated, the IDG Books Online Web site features exclusive software, insider information, online books, and live events!

10 Productive & Career-Enhancing Things You Can Do at www.idgbooks.com

- Nab source code for your own programming projects.

- Download software.

- Read Web exclusives: special articles and book excerpts by IDG Books Worldwide authors.

- Take advantage of resources to help you advance your career as a Novell or Microsoft professional.

- Buy IDG Books Worldwide titles or find a convenient bookstore that carries them.

- Register your book and win a prize.

- Chat live online with authors.

- Sign up for regular e-mail updates about our latest books.

- Suggest a book you'd like to read or write.

- Give us your 2¢ about our books and about our Web site.

You say you're not on the Web yet? It's easy to get started with IDG Books' *Discover the Internet*, available at local retailers everywhere.